The American Express
International Traveler's Pocket

GERMAN

Dictionary and Phrase Book

The American Express
International Traveler's Pocket
GERMAN
Dictionary and Phrase Book

Simon and Schuster
New York

List of abbreviations

abbrev	–	abbreviation	*num*	– numeral
adj	–	adjective	*pl*	– plural
adv	–	adverb	*pref*	– prefix
art	–	article	*prep*	– preposition
conj	–	conjunction	*pron*	– pronoun
excl	–	exclamation	*vi*	– intransitive verb
f	–	feminine noun	*vr*	– reflexive verb
m	–	masculine noun	*vt*	– transitive verb
n	–	noun	*vt/i*	– transitive/intransitive verb
nt	–	neuter		

The asterisk * denotes an irregular verb, for which the reader is referred
to the list of irregular verbs in the grammar section. The vertical bar
between syllables, e.g. auf|stehen denotes a separable prefix. Help for
this is also found in the grammar section.
Cross-reference letter keys occur in brackets after main section headings.
Phrases are numbered in sequence following each main heading. Phrase
words are cross-referenced in the English-German dictionary section by
letter and number to their relevant phrases.

Collins Publishers

Editor
Lorna Sinclair
with
Nicholas Rollin
Ulrike Seeberger
Valerie McNulty
Anne Findlay
Assistant Editors
Susan Dunsmore
Lesley Robertson
Managing Editor
Richard H. Thomas

Mitchell Beazley Publishers

Editors
James Hughes
Christopher McIntosh
Designer
Philip Lord
Executive Art Director
Douglas Wilson
Production
Julian Deeming

Edited by William Collins Sons & Co Ltd
and by Mitchell Beazley International Ltd
Designed by Mitchell Beazley International Ltd
87-89 Shaftesbury Avenue
London W1V 7AD
© Mitchell Beazley Publishers 1983
© William Collins Sons & Company Ltd 1983

All rights reserved

Published by Simon and Schuster, Inc.
Simon and Schuster Building
Rockefeller Center
1230 Avenue of the Americas
New York, New York 10020

Library of Congress Cataloging in Publication Data
The American Express international traveler's pocket dictionaries and phrase
    books, English/German.
    Includes index.
    1. German language—Dictionaries—English. 2. English
language—Dictionaries—German. 3. German language—Conversation and
phrase books—English. 4. English language—Conversation and phrase
books—German. I. American Express Company. II. Mitchell Beazley Ltd.
PF3640.A43 1984   438.3'421   82-19636
ISBN 0-671-47030-2

No part of this work may be reproduced or utilized in any form by any means,
electronic or mechanical, including photocopying, recording or by any
information storage and retrieval system, without the prior written permission
of the publisher.

Typeset by Coats Dataprint Ltd, Inverness

Printed in Great Britain by William Collins Sons & Co Ltd, Glasgow.

Contents

Pronunciation

English spelling gives only an approximate idea of German sounds, which can be learned only by listening to the Germans themselves. The table below lists close English equivalents to sounds that English-speakers may find particularly difficult.

Many letters are pronounced like their English equivalent, but there are a number of exceptions. These are shown in the table, together with their closest English sounds. The umlaut (¨) alters the sound of vowels, and the two sounds *ö* and *ü* have no real English sound equivalent. The *ur* in *hurt* is nearest to *ö*, except that *r* is silent. To produce this sound, round the lips as for *oo* and try to pronounce the *a* of *gate*. The sound of *ü* is made if you round your lips as for *oo* and try to say *ee*. The letter *e* in German has three sounds. In the table the symbol *è* is chosen to indicate the weak sound it has in English *garden*. For the sound represented by the spelling *ch*, think of trying to say the sound *k* but let the breath escape as in pronouncing *h*. The German *r* is usually pronounced as a short roll of the uvula, similar to the sound made when gargling. But in some parts of Germany it may be rolled, or pronounced with the tongue tip.

There are also some differences in the way the language is written. For instance, all nouns begin with capital letters. And in German there is a letter which doesn't exist in English – the letter ß which is pronounced like the double *s* in *loss* or *mass*.

How to Pronounce German

German spelling	Closest English sound	Shown here by	Example	
a	cat	a (short)	das	*dass*
	or father	ah (long)	haben	**hah**·bèn
ä	met	e	Äpfel	*ep·fèl*
	or gate	ay	Käse	**kay**·zè
au	cow	ow	braun	*brown*
äu	boy	oy	Geräusch	gè·**roysh**
e	met	e	Hotel	hô·**tel**
	or gate	ay	geben	**gay**·bèn
	or garden	è	Woche	*vo·khè*
ei	wine	i . . . e	Wein	*vine*
	goodbye	or -ye	frei	*frye*
		or eye	Eier	**eye**·èr
eu	boy	oy	heute	**hoy**·tè
i	bit	i	bitte	**bi**·tè
	or meet	ee	ihn	*een*
ie	meet	ee	Sie	*zee*
o	note	ô	wo	*vô*
	or thought	o	Woche	**vo**·khè
ö	hurt	ur'	möchte	**mur'kh**·tè
u	hook	oo	Fluß	*floos*
	or food	oo	schuh	*shoo*
ü	see text above	ōō	über	**ōō**·bèr
b	book	b	Bad	*baht*
	or tap	p	Urlaub	**oor**·lowp
ch	loch (Scottish)	kh	Woche	**vo**·khè
d	date	d	die	*dee*
	or cat	t	Bad	*baht*
g	get	g	gehen	**gay**·èn
	or pick	k	Zug	*tsook*
	(rarely) measure	zh	Orange	o·**ran**·zhè
h	hat	h	haben	**hah**·bèn
	or honor	h	gehen	**gay**·èn
j	yes	y	jemand	**yay**·mant
qu	k+v	kv	Qualität	kva·lee·**tet**
s	sat	s or ss	das	*dass*
	or zero	z	Sie	*zee*
sch	sh	sh	Schuhe	**shoo**·è
sp	sh+p	shp	sprechen	**shpre**·khèn

German spelling	Closest English sound	Shown here by	Example	
ß	lo*ss*	*s* or *ss*	Fluß	*floos*
st	*sh*+*t*	*sht*	Stadt	*shtat*
	or la*st*	*st*	nächste	**nekh**·*stè*
th	*t*ime	*t*	Theater	*tay·**ah**·tèr*
v	*f*at	*f*	von	*fon*
w	*v*ine	*v*	Wein	*vine*
z	ca*ts*	*ts*	zu	*tsoo*

*The syllable to be stressed is the one in **heavy type**.*

Introduction

The German language

German is the mother tongue of about 100 million people and is the official language of West and East Germany, Austria and Liechtenstein. It is also one of the official languages of Switzerland and Luxembourg.

Newcomers to German sometimes find it harsh-sounding, but on closer acquaintance it proves to be a language of great beauty, subtlety and resonance, with a rich literary tradition. It is one of the most useful European languages to know, as it is spoken over such a large area.

How the book works

This is a combined phrase-book and dictionary, designed primarily for the needs of the traveler. It enables you to find easily and quickly just the phrase you need, whether you are buying a suit or trying to tell a garage mechanic what is wrong with your car. The German is accompanied in all cases by an instant guide to pronunciation.

Many of the phrases listed consist of a basic group of words which can be linked up with different subsidiary words to produce variations, in the way that a power tool can be fitted with extensions. With phrases of this kind the basic "tool" is shown on one side and the "extension" on the other, with a dash in between; alternative extensions are either indicated by an oblique stroke or shown on the line below. A further stock of extensions is found in the dictionary section at the back of the book, and this serves also as an index to the phrases.

Here is an example. If you look up the word "platform" in the dictionary, you will find "der Bahnsteig" and, at the end of the entry, a cross-reference to Section T (Travel). Here you will see, against the number shown in the cross-reference, the kind of phrase you might need in using this word. With practice, you will soon be able to express yourself with flexibility and confidence, and what you learn can open the door to the whole German language.

Understanding what you hear

This book not only tells you what to say but also helps you to interpret some of the things that will be said to you. For example, the section on "Finding the way" anticipates the sort of directions you may be given. The intonation of German is not markedly different from that of English, and you should be able to tune your ear to it fairly easily. So read, listen, learn and practice. Even a limited competence in German will bring you great satisfaction as you travel. So have a good trip, or, as the Germans say, *gute Reise!*

Basic equipment (B)

Here are some of the words and phrases which make up the basic coinage of German and which it is useful to have in your pocket for a wide variety of situations. You would be well advised to read through this whole section before starting your trip. If you can memorize any of it, so much the better.

Some essentials

Yes
Ja
yah
No
Nein
nine
Please
Bitte
bi·tè
Thank you
Danke
dang·kè

You're welcome
Bitte, gern geschehen
bi·tè, gern gè·shay·èn
No thank you
Nein, danke
nine, dang·kè
You're very kind/I'm very grateful
Das ist sehr freundlich von Ihnen
dass ist zehr froynt·likh fon ee·nèn

Greetings and general exchanges

There are gradations of familiarity in the way Germans address each other. They normally reserve the familiar "du" (you) for close relatives and friends, "Sie" being the usual form which you should use nearly all the time. Surnames are preceded by "Herr" (Mr) and "Frau" (Mrs). Formerly "Fräulein" was used for "Miss", but even an unmarried woman would nowadays tend to be called "Frau" and the word "Fräulein" (without a surname) is reserved for waitresses and telephone operators. A curious feature is that in most parts of the German-speaking world there is no equivalent of "Sir" and "Madam". You either know the person's name or you call them nothing at all. Handshaking is normal when greeting and taking leave and is not restricted to the first meeting.

1 Good morning
 Guten Morgen
 goo·tèn mor·gèn
2 Good day/afternoon
 Guten Tag
 goo·tèn tahk
3 Good evening
 Guten Abend
 goo·tèn ah·bènt
4 Good night
 Gute Nacht
 goo·tè nakht
5 Hello
 (no general equivalent — use any of the above, depending on time of day)
6 Goodbye
 Auf Wiedersehen
 owf vee·dèr·zay·èn
7 Goodbye (*on telephone*)
 Auf Wiederhören
 owf vee·dèr·hur'·rèn
8 How do you do?/I'm very glad to meet you
 Es freut mich sehr, Sie kennenzulernen
 ess froyt mikh zehr zee ke·nèn·tsoo·ler·nèn

9 See you soon
 Bis bald
 biss balt
10 See you later (in the day)
 Bis später
 biss shpay·tèr
11 What's your name?
 Wie heißen Sie?
 vee hye·sèn zee
12 My name is...
 Ich heiße...
 ikh hye·sè...
13 How are you?
 Wie geht es Ihnen?
 vee gayt ess ee·nèn
14 I am very well, thank you
 Sehr gut, danke
 zehr goot, dang·kè
15 I'm sorry
 Es tut mir leid
 ess toot meer lite
16 Excuse me
 Entschuldigung
 ent·shool·di·goong
17 It doesn't matter
 Das macht nichts
 dass makht nikhts

18 **With pleasure**
Mit Vergnügen
mit fer·gnōō·gèn

19 **Just a minute, please**
Ein Augenblick, bitte
ine ow·gèn·blik, bi·tè

20 **What did you say?**
Bitte?
bi·tè

21 **I understand**
Ich verstehe
ikh fer·shtay·è

22 **I don't understand**
Ich verstehe nicht
ikh fer·shtay·è nikht

23 **Do you understand?**
Verstehen Sie?
fer·shtay·èn zee

24 **I don't speak German**
Ich spreche kein Deutsch
ikh shpre·khè kine doytsh

25 **I don't speak German very well**
Ich spreche nicht sehr gut Deutsch
ikh shpre·khè nikht zehr goot doytsh

26 **Please repeat that**
Wiederholen Sie, bitte
vee·dèr·hō·lèn zee bi·tè

27 **Please speak more slowly**
Bitte sprechen Sie etwas langsamer
bi·tè shpre·khèn zee et·vass lang·zah·mèr

28 **Could you please write that down?**
Könnten Sie das bitte aufschreiben?
kur'n·tèn zee dass bi·tè owf·shrye·bèn

29 **Do you speak English?**
Sprechen Sie Englisch?
shpre·khèn zee eng·glish

30 **I'm English**
Ich bin Engländer(in)
ikh bin eng·glen·dèr(·in)

31 **I'm American**
Ich bin Amerikaner(in)
ikh bin a·may·ri·kah·nèr(·in)

32 **I don't mind**
Das ist mir egal
dass ist meer ay·gahl

33 **Agreed**
In Ordnung
in ort·noong

34 **Isn't it? Don't you agree?**
Nicht wahr?
nikht vahr

35 **Do you follow?**
Können Sie mir folgen?
kur'·nèn zee meer fol·gèn

36 **Really?**
Tatsächlich?
taht·zekh·likh

37 **That's true**
Das stimmt
dass shtimt

38 **You are right**
Sie haben recht
zee hah·bèn rekht

Common questions and statements

39 **Is it necessary to do this?**
Muß man das tun?
moos man dass toon

40 **Is there any charge?**
Kostet das etwas?
kos·tèt dass et·vass

41 **Ought I to ...?**
Soll ich ...?
zol ikh ...

42 **Do I have to ...?**
Muß ich ...?
moos ikh ...

43 **Do you have any matches?**
Haben Sie Streichhölzer?
hah·bèn zee shtryekh·hur'l·tsèr

44 **Could you come with me, please?**
Würden Sie bitte mit mir kommen?
vōōr·dèn zee bi·tè mit meer ko·mèn

45 **What's the matter?**
Was ist los?
vass ist lōs

46 **I've made a mistake**
Ich habe mich vertan
ikh hah·bè mikh fer·tahn

47 **I mean that ...**
Ich meine, daß ...
ikh mine·è dass ...

48 **What does that mean?**
Was bedeutet das?
vass bè·doy·tèt dass

49 **What is this/that?**
Was ist das?
vass ist dass

50 **What time is it?**
Wieviel Uhr ist es?
vee·feel oo·èr ist ess

51 **(At) what time?**
Wann?
van

52 **How much?**
Wieviel?
vee·feel

53 **How many?**
Wie viele?
vee fee·lè

54 **How often?**
Wie oft?
vee oft

55 **How long will that take?**
Wie lange dauert es?
vee lang·è dow·èrt ess

56 **Where is ...?**
Wo ist ...?
vō ist ...

57 **Where are ...?**
Wo sind ...?
vō zint ...

58 Here is/are ...
    Hier ist/sind ...
    heer ist/zint ...
59 There is/are ...
    Es gibt ...
    ess gipt ...
60   How do you say ... — in German?
            Wie sagt man ... — auf deutsch?
            vee zahgt man ... — owf doytsh
61   I need — something to drink
            Ich brauche — etwas zu trinken
            ikh brow·khè — et·vass tsoo tring·kèn
62   I want — a cup of coffee
            Ich möchte — eine Tasse Kaffee
            ikh mur'kh·tè — ine·è ta·sè ka·fay
63   I want — to go to Stuttgart
            Ich möchte — nach Stuttgart reisen
            ikh mur'kh·tè — nahkh shtoot·gart rye·zèn
64   I would like — a glass of wine
            Ich hätte gern — ein Glas Wein
            ikh he·tè gern — ine glahs vine
65   May I — borrow your pen?
            Kann ich — mir Ihren Kuli ausleihen?
            kan ikh — meer ee·rèn koo·lee ows·lye·èn
66   Do you mind — if I open the window?
        Haben Sie etwas dagegen — wenn ich das Fenster aufmache?
            hah·bèn zee et·vass
            dah·gay·gèn — ven ikh dass fen·stèr owf·ma·khè
67 Whom should I see about this?
    An wen soll ich mich damit wenden?
    an vayn zoll ikh mikh da·mit ven·dèn

General problems and requests

68 Can you help me, please?
    Können Sie mir bitte helfen?
    kur'·nèn zee meer bi·tè hel·fèn
69 We need someone who can speak English
    Wir brauchen jemanden, der Englisch spricht
    veer brow·khèn yay·man·dèn, der eng·lish shprikht
70 We are in a hurry
    Wir haben es eilig
    veer hah·bèn ess ile·ikh
71 Please repeat that
    Wiederholen Sie bitte
    vee·dèr·hō·lèn zee bi·tè
72 Can you do it for me at once?
    Können Sie es sofort machen?
    kur'·nèn zee ess zō·fort ma·khèn
73 Can you do it for me by Wednesday?
    Können Sie es bis Mittwoch machen?
    kur'·nèn zee ess biss mit·vokh ma·khèn
74   The machine — has broken down
            Die Maschine — ist kaputt
            dee ma·shee·nè — ist ka·poot
75 I have broken the switch/the glass
    Mir ist der Schalter kaputtgegangen/das Glas zerbrochen
    meer ist der shal·tèr ka·poot·gè·gang·èn/dass glahs tser·bro·khèn
76 I have spilled the water/wine
    Ich habe Wasser/Wein verschüttet
    ikh hah·bè va·sèr/vine fer·shōō·tèt
77 I have forgotten my glasses/my key
    Ich habe meine Brille/meinen Schlüssel vergessen
    ikh hah·bè mine·è bri·lè/mine·èn shlōō·sèl fer·ge·sèn
78 I have left my bag in the plane/in the coach
    Ich habe meine Tasche im Flugzeug/im Bus gelassen
    ikh hah·bè mine·è ta·shè im flook·tsoyk/im boos gè·la·sèn
79 I wish to leave a message for Mr Smith
    Ich möchte eine Nachricht für Herrn Smith hinterlassen
    ikh mur'kh·tè ine·è nahkh·rikht fōōr hern Smith hin·tèr·la·sèn

Travel (T)

General

1   I am leaving — tomorrow
                         Ich reise — morgen ab
                         ikh rye·zè — mor·gèn ap
                                  — on Thursday
                                  — am Donnerstag ab
                                  — *am do·nèrs·tahk ap*

2 How long will the train/flight be delayed?
   Wieviel Verspätung hat der Zug/der Flug?
   vee·feel fer·shpay·toong hat der tsook/der flook

3 I have missed my train
   Ich habe meinen Zug verpaßt
   ikh hah·bè mine·èn tsook fer·past

4 I have missed my flight
   Ich habe meinen Flug verpaßt
   ikh hah·bè mine·èn flook fer·past

5   At what time is the next — train?
                         Wann geht der nächste — Zug?
                         van gayt der nekh·stè — tsook
                                  — flight?
                                  — Flug?
                                  — *flook*
                                  — bus?
                                  — Bus?
                                  — *boos*

6 I am a member of the American Express party traveling to
   Düsseldorf
   Ich gehöre zu der American Express Reisegesellschaft nach
   Düsseldorf
   *ikh gè·hur'·rè tsoo der American Express rye·zè·gè·zel·shaft
   nahkh doo·sèl·dorf*

7 My party has left without me
   Meine Gruppe ist ohne mich weggegangen
   mine·è groo·pè ist ō·nè mikh vek·gè·gang·èn

8 I have lost the rest of my party
   Ich kann meine Reisegesellschaft nicht finden
   ikh kan mine·è rye·zè·gè·zel·shaft nikht fin·dèn

9   Where do I change — for Düsseldorf?
                         Von wo aus habe ich
                              Anschluß — nach Düsseldorf?
                         *fon vō ows hah·bè ikh
                              an·shloos — nahkh doo·sèl·dorf*

10   Could you please — keep my seat for me?
                         Könnten Sie bitte — mir einen Platz freihalten?
                         kur'n·tèn zee bi·tè — meer ine·èn plats frye·hal·tèn
                                  — keep an eye on my luggage
                                     for a few moments?
                                  — eine Minute auf mein
                                     Gepäck aufpassen?
                                  — *ine·è mi·noo·tè owf mine
                                     gè·pek owf·pa·sèn*

Arrival and departure

11   Here is — my passport
                         Hier ist — mein Paß
                         heer ist — mine pass
                                  — my driver's license
                                  — mein Führerschein
                                  — *mine foo·rèr·shine*

12 My wife and I are on a joint passport
    Meine Frau und ich haben einen gemeinsamen Paß
    mine·è frow oont ikh hah·bèn ine·èn gè·mine·zah·mèn pass

13 **Our children are on this passport**
Unsere Kinder sind in diesem Paß eingetragen
oon·zě·rě kin·děr zint in dee·zěm pass ine·gě·trah·gěn

14 **I am staying — for two weeks**
Ich bleibe — zwei Wochen
ikh blye·bě — tsvye vo·khěn
— at the hotel
— im Hotel
— *im hō·tel*

15 **I have nothing to declare**
Ich habe nichts zu verzollen
ikh hah·bě nikhts tsoo fer·tso·lěn

16 **I have the usual allowance of cigarettes and liquor**
Ich habe die übliche Menge an zollfreien Tabakwaren und Alkohol
ikh hah·bě dee ōō·bli·khě meng·ě an tsol·frye·ěn ta·bak·vah·rěn oont al·ko·hol

17 **Those are my personal belongings**
Das ist mein Privateigentum
dass ist mine pree·vaht·eye·gěn·toom

18 **I represent Universal Chemicals**
Ich vertrete Universal Chemicals
ikh fer·tray·tě Universal Chemicals

19 **I am looking for the representative of Alpha Engineering**
Ich suche den Vertreter der Firma Alpha Engineering
ikh zoo·khě dayn fer·tray·těr der fir·ma Alpha Engineering

20 **He/she was due to meet me here**
Er/sie wollte sich hier mit mir treffen
er/zee vol·tě zikh heer mit meer tre·fěn

21 **The people I was to meet have not turned up**
Die Leute, mit denen ich mich treffen wollte, sind nicht gekommen
dee loy·tě, mit day·něn ikh mikh tre·fěn vol·tě, zint nikht gě·ko·měn

---

Luggage

22 **Please take these bags — to platform nine**
Bitte bringen Sie diese
bi·tě bring·ěn zee dee·zě Taschen — zum Bahnsteig neun
ta·shěn — tsoom bahn·shtike noyn
— to a taxi
— zu einem Taxi
— *tsoo ine·ěm tak·see*

23 **My luggage — has not arrived**
Mein Gepäck — ist noch nicht angekommen
mine gě·pek — ist nokh nikht an·gě·ko·měn

24 **Where is the luggage from the flight — from London?**
Wo ist das Gepäck vom
Flug — aus London?
vō ist dass gě·pek fom flook — ows lon·don

25 **Is there a baggage checkroom?**
Gibt es hier eine Gepäckaufbewahrung?
gipt ess heer ine·ě gě·pek·owf·bě·vah·roong

26 **Are there any — porters?**
Gibt es hier — Gepäckträger?
gipt ess heer — gě·pek·tray·gěr
— luggage carts?
— Kofferkulis?
— *ko·fěr·koo·leez*

27 **That bag is not mine**
Diese Tasche gehört mir nicht
dee·zě ta·shě gě·hurt meer nikht

28 **Where is my other bag?**
Wo ist meine andere Tasche?
vō ist mine·ě an·dě·rě ta·shě

29 **The contents of that bag are fragile**
In dieser Tasche sind zerbrechliche Gegenstände
in dee·zěr ta·shě zint tser·brekh·li·khě gay·gěn·shten·dě

30 **I wish to have my luggage sent on ahead**
Ich möchte mein Gepäck vorausschicken
ikh **mur'kh**·*te mine gè*·**pek** *för*·**ows**·*shi*·*kèn*

31 **I sent a suitcase in advance. Where do I pick it up?**
Ich habe einen Koffer vorausgeschickt. Wo kann ich ihn abholen?
ikh hah·*bè* **ine**·*èn* **ko**·*fèr för*·**ows**·*gè*·*shikt. vö kan ikh een* **ap**·**hö**·*lèn*

32 **That case is specially insured**
Dieser Koffer ist gesondert versichert
dee·*zèr* **ko**·*fèr ist gè*·**zon**·*dèrt fer*·**zi**·*khèrt*

33 **I wish to leave these bags in the baggage checkroom**
Ich möchte diese Taschen in der Gepäckaufbewahrung lassen
ikh **mur'kh**·*tè* **dee**·*zè* **ta**·*shèn in der gè*·**pek**·*owf*·*bè*·**vah**·*roong* **la**·*sèn*

34   **I shall pick them up — this evening**
Ich hole sie — heute abend wieder ab
ikh **hö**·*lè zee —* **hoy**·*tè* **ah**·*bènt* **vee**·*dèr ap*
        — tomorrow morning
— morgen wieder ab
— mor·*gèn* **vee**·*dèr ap*

35 **How much is it per suitcase?**
Wieviel kostet es pro Koffer?
vee·**feel** **kos**·*tèt ess prö* **ko**·*fèr*

36 **What time do you close?**
Wann machen Sie zu?
van **ma**·*khèn zee tsoo*

Airport and flight inquiries

37   **Where do I get the bus — for the airport?**
Wo fährt der Bus — zum Flughafen ab?
vö fert der boos — *tsoom* **flook**·*hah*·*fèn ap*
        — for the center of town?
— zum Stadtzentrum ab?
— tsoom **shtat**·*tsen*·*troom ap*

38 **I wish to check my luggage to Düsseldorf on the Lufthansa flight**
Ich möchte mein Gepäck für den Lufthansa-Flug nach Düsseldorf aufgeben
ikh **mur'kh**·*tè mine gè*·**pek** *föör dayn* **looft**·*han*·*za*·*flook nakh*
döö·*sèl*·*dorf owf*·**gay**·*bèn*

39 **Where is the departure/arrival board?**
Wo ist die Ankunftstafel/Abflugtafel?
vö ist dee **an**·*koonfts*·*tah*·*fèl/***ap**·*flook*·*tah*·*fèl*

40 **When will the boarding announcement for the flight be made?**
Wann wird der Flug aufgerufen?
van virt der flook **owf**·*gè*·**roo**·*fèn*

41 **Which gate do I go to?**
Zu welchen Ausgang muß ich gehen?
tsoo **vel**·*khèn* **ows**·*gang moos ikh* **gay**·*èn*

42 **Is there a snack bar/duty-free shop in the departure lounge?**
Gibt es in der Abflughalle einen Imbiß/einen Duty-Free-Shop?
gipt ess in der **ap**·*flook*·*ha*·*lè* **ine**·*èn* **im**·*bis/***ine**·*èn* **dyoo**·*ti*·**free**·*shop*

43 **Will a meal be served on the plane?**
Wird während des Fluges Essen serviert?
virt ve·*rènt des* **floo**·*gès e*·*sèn zer*·**veert**

44 **What are weather conditions like for the flight?**
Wie sieht der Flugwetterbericht für unseren Flug aus?
vee zeet der **flook**·*ve*·*tèr*·*bè*·**rikht** *föör* **oon**·*zè*·*rèn flook ows*
(for answers see "The weather" under Making conversation, p.64)

45 **Can I change my seat?**
Könnte ich einen anderen Platz haben?
kur'n·*tè ikh* **ine**·*èn* **an**·*dè*·*rèn plats* **hah**·*bèn*

46   **I should like — to be nearer the front/the window**
Ich würde gern — weiter vorn/näher am Fenster
sitzen
ikh **vöör**·*dè gern —* **vye**·*tèr forn/***ne**·*èr am* **fen**·*stèr*
zit·*sèn*

47 **I suffer from airsickness**
Mir wird beim Fliegen leicht schlecht
meer virt bime **flee**·*gèn lyekht shlekht*

48 I should like to speak to the airport police
   Ich möchte bitte mit der Flughafen-Polizei sprechen
   ikh **mur'kh**·*tè* **bi**·*tè mit der* **flook**·*hah·fèn·pó·lee·*tsye **shpre**·*khèn*
49 I am meeting somebody arriving on a flight from Madrid
   Ich hole einen Passagier von einem Flug aus Madrid ab
   ikh **hó**·*lè* **ine**·*èn pa·sa·*zheer *fon* **ine**·*èm flook ows ma·**drit** ap*
50 At what time do you expect the flight from Madrid to arrive?
   Wann wird der Flug aus Madrid erwartet?
   *van virt der flook ows ma·**drit** er·**var**·tèt*

Trains

The German, Austrian and Swiss railway systems are on the whole well
run and efficient. The trains are fast and reliable and the long-distance
ones very comfortable. Here are some things you will probably need to
say during the course of your journey, and a few pointers to help you
understand the system.

Inquiring

At Frankfurt and Munich there are computerized timetable machines. At
other places you have to rely on printed timetables or ask at the
information office, where you line up in the normal way.

51   Where is — the ticket office/information
                                    office?
                      Wo ist — der Fahrkartenschalter/die
                                    Auskunft?
                      vō ist — *der* **fahr**·*kar·tèn·***shal**·*tèr/dee*
                                    ows·koonft
                              — the timetable board?
                              — der Fahrplan?
                              — *der* **fahr**·*plan*
52 I want to go to Frankfurt tomorrow/next Wednesday
   Ich möchte morgen/nächsten Mittwoch nach Frankfurt reisen
   ikh **mur'kh**·*tè* **mor**·*gèn/***nekh**·*stèn* **mit**·*vokh nahkh* **frank**·*foort*
   rye·*zèn*
53 What are the times of trains between 8 a.m. and noon?
   Wie sind die Abfahrtszeiten zwischen acht Uhr morgens und Mittag?
   vee zint dee **ap**·*fahrts·***tsye**·*tèn* **tsvi**·*shèn akht oo·èr* **mor**·*gèns oont*
   mi·*tahk*
54 Which is the fastest train?
   Welches ist der schnellste Zug?
   vel·*khès ist der* **shnel**·*stè tsook*
55 Could I see a timetable, please?
   Könnte ich bitte den Fahrplan sehen?
   kur'n·*tè ikh* **bi**·*tè dayn* **fahr**·*plan* **zay**·*èn*
56 When does the next/last train to Munich leave?
   Wann fährt der nächste/letzte Zug nach München ab?
   van fert der **nekh**·*stè/***let**·*stè tsook nahkh* **mōōn**·*khèn ap*
57 Is it necessary to change?
   Muß ich umsteigen?
   moos ikh **oom**·*shtye·gèn*
58 What time does the train arrive?
   Wann kommt der Zug an?
   van komt der tsook an

Tickets and reservations

On certain fast inter-city trains an extra charge is imposed. Children
under twelve pay half (in Austria and Switzerland), and
those under four travel free (six in Switzerland, seven in Austria). Trains
have first-class and second-class compartments. Tickets are normally
punched on the train by an inspector and not checked at the gate.
Various types of unlimited-use passes are available for tourists. For
overnight travel you can reserve a sleeper or a couchette, which is a
simple berth with blankets in a compartment shared by several
passengers.

59   A one-way/round-trip ticket
                     to Freiburg — second class/first class
            Einmal einfach/eine
            Rückfahrkarte nach
                     Freiburg — zweiter Klasse/erster Klasse
        ine·mahl ine·fakh/ine·è
            rōōk·fahr·kar·tè nahkh
                     frye·boork — tsvye·tèr kla·sè/er·stèr kla·sè
60   A child's round-trip to Freiburg
        Eine Kinderrückfahrkarte nach Freiburg
        ine·è kin·dèr·rōōk·fahr·kar·tè nahkh frye·boork
61   He is under twelve
        Er ist unter zwölf
        er ist oon·tèr tsvur'lf
62   I would like to book a seat — on the 10:30 to Cologne
        Ich möchte eine Platzkarte — für den Zug um zehn Uhr dreißig
                                        nach Köln
            ikh mur'kh·tè ine·è
                     plats·kar·tè — fōōr dayn tsook oom tsayn oo·èr
                                      drye·sikh nahkh kur'ln
                                   — in a smoking/nonsmoking
                                      compartment
                                   — in einem Raucherabteil/in einem
                                      Nichtraucherabteil
                                   — *in ine·èm row·khèr·ap·tile/in*
                                      ine·èm nikht·row·khèr·ap·tile
63   I would like a seat by the window
        Ich möchte ein Fensterplatz
        ikh mur'kh·tè ine fen·stèr·plats
64   I would like a sleeper/couchette on the 22:00 to Cologne
        Ich möchte einen Schlafwagenplatz/einen Liegewagenplatz für den
            Zug um zweiundzwanzig Uhr nach Köln
        ikh mur'kh·tè ine·èn shlahf·vah·gèn·plats/ine·èn lee·gè·vah·gèn·plats
            fōōr dayn tsook oom tsvye·oont·tsvan·tsikh oo·èr nahkh kur'ln

Station and journey

65   Which platform do I go to for the Hamburg train?
        Von welchem Bahnsteig fährt der Zug nach Hamburg ab?
        fon vel·khèm bahn·shtike fert der tsook nahkh ham·boork ap
66   Is this the right platform for Hamburg?
        Fährt der Zug nach Hamburg von diesem Bahnsteig ab?
        fert der tsook nahkh ham·boork fon dee·zèm bahn·shtike ap
67   Is this the Hamburg train?
        Ist das der Zug nach Hamburg?
        ist dass der tsook nahkh ham·boork
68   Is there a dining car/club car?
        Gibt es einen Speisewagen/einen Büfettwagen?
        gipt ess ine·èn shpye·zè·vah·gèn/ine·èn bōō·fet·vah·gèn
69   When do we get to Munich?
        Wann kommen wir in München an?
        van ko·mèn veer in mōōn·khèn an
70   Do we stop at Stuttgart?
        Halten wir in Stuttgart?
        hal·tèn veer in shtoot·gart
71   Is this a through train?
        Ist das ein durchgehender Zug?
        ist dass ine doorkh·gay·èn·dèr tsook
72   Where do I have to change for Salzburg?
        Wo muß ich nach Salzburg umsteigen?
        vō moos ikh nahkh zalts·boork oom·shtye·gèn
73   Is this seat taken?
        Ist dieser Platz besetzt?
        ist dee·zèr plats bè·zetst
74   This is my seat
        Das ist mein Platz
        dass ist mine plats
75   Can you help me with my bags, please?
        Können Sie mir bitte mit meinem Gepäck helfen?
        kur'·nèn zee meer bi·tè mit mine·èm gè·pek hel·fèn

76 May I open/shut the window?
Kann ich das Fenster aufmachen/zumachen?
kan ikh dass fen·stèr owf·ma·khèn/tsoo·ma·khèn

77 This is a nonsmoking compartment
Dies ist ein Nichtraucherabteil
dees ist ine nikht·row·khèr·ap·tile

78 My wife/husband has my ticket
Meine Frau/mein Mann hat meine Fahrkarte
mine·è frow/mine man hat mine·è fahr·kar·tè

79 Are we in Linz yet?
Sind wir schon in Linz?
zint veer shōn in lints

80 Are we on time?
Ist der Zug pünktlich?
ist der tsook pōōnkt·likh

Buses and subways

Most towns and cities are well-covered by bus or streetcar routes, and some (though none in Switzerland) have subway (U-Bahn) systems. Usually the bus, streetcar and subway tickets are interchangeable. Some cities also have a fast suburban train service.

81 Which streetcar goes to — Schönbrunn?
Welche Straßenbahn fährt nach — Schönbrunn?
vel·khè shtrah·sèn·bahn fert nahkh — shur'n·broon

82 Does this bus go to — Nymphenburg?
Fährt dieser Bus nach — Nymphenburg?
fert dee·zèr boos nahkh — nōōm·fèn·boork

83 Where should I change?
Wo soll ich umsteigen?
vō zol ikh oom·shtye·gèn

84 And then, what number do I take?
Und welche Linie muß ich dann nehmen?
oont vel·khè leen·yè moos ikh dan nay·mèn

85 Should I get out at the next stop for the German Museum?
Muß ich für das Deutsche Museum an der nächsten Haltestelle aussteigen?
moos ikh fōōr dass doy·tshè moo·zay·oom an der nekh·stèn hal·tè·shte·lè ows·shtye·gèn

86 I want to go to the — castle
Ich möchte zum — Schloß
ikh mur'kh·tè tsoom — shlos

87 How many tickets do I need?
Wieviele Fahrkarten brauche ich?
vee·fee·lè fahr·kar·tèn brow·khè ikh

88 A seven-day tourist ticket, please
Eine Touristen-Wochenkarte, bitte
ine·è too·ri·stèn·vo·khèn·kar·tè bi·tè

89 Can you let me off at the right stop?
Sagen Sie mir, wann ich aussteigen muß?
zah·gèn zee meer van ikh ows·shtye·gèn moos

90 How much is the fare to the center of the city?
Was kostet die Fahrt ins Stadtzentrum?
vass kos·tèt dee fahrt ins shtat·tsen·troom

91 How long does it take to get to the opera house?
Wie lange fährt man zur Oper?
vee lang·è fert man tsoor ō·pèr

Taxis

Taxis can be ordered by telephone, picked up at a stand or hailed. The normal tip is 10 percent of the fare (in Basel and Zürich it is included). The easiest way to tell the driver where you are going is just to state your destination and add *bitte* (please). But you might also need some of the following phrases:

92 Can you order me a taxi?
    Können Sie mir ein Taxi rufen?
    *kur'·nèn zee meer ine **tak**·see **roo**·fèn*
93 Where can I get a taxi?
    Wo kann ich ein Taxi bekommen?
    *vō kan ikh ine **tak**·see bè·**ko**·mèn*
94   Take me to — this address, please
    Bitte fahren Sie mich zu — dieser Adresse
    *bi·tè **fah**·rèn zee mikh tsoo — **dee**·zèr a·**dre**·sè*
95   How much is the taxi fare — to/from the airport?
    Wieviel kostet eine Taxifahrt — von hier zum Flughafen/vom
                                      Flughafen hierher?
            *vee·**feel** kos·tèt ine·è*
            ***tak**·see·fahrt — fon heer tsoom **flook**·hah·fèn/fom
                                  flook·hah·fèn heer·**her***
96 Please drive us around the town
    Bitte fahren Sie uns durch die Stadt
    *bi·tè **fah**·rèn zee oons doorkh dee shtat*
97 Would you put the luggage in the trunk?
    Könnten Sie das Gepäck in den Kofferraum legen?
    *kur'n·tèn zee dass gè·**pek** in dayn ko·fèr·rowm **lay**·gèn*
98 I'm in a hurry
    Ich habe es eilig
    *ikh **hah**·bè ess **ile**·ikh*
99 Please wait here for a few minutes
    Bitte warten Sie ein paar Minuten hier
    *bi·tè **var**·tèn zee ine pahr mi·**noo**·tèn heer*
100 Turn right/left please
    Biegen Sie bitte rechts/links ab
    ***bee**·gèn zee **bi**·tè rekhts/links
    ap*
101 Stop here, please
    Bitte halten Sie hier
    *bi·tè **hal**·tèn zee heer*
102 How much is that?
    Wieviel macht das?
    *vee·**feel** makht dass*
103 Keep the change
    Das stimmt so
    dass shtimt zō

Motoring

Although the more crowded towns can be hectic, motoring in the
countries covered by this book is usually a pleasant experience. The
speed limit in built-up areas is 50km/h, except in most of Switzerland
where it is 60km/h. On ordinary country roads the limit is 100km/h, and
on expressways and divided highways it is 130km/h (in Germany this is
only a recommended limit). Cars with house trailers must observe a limit
of 80km/h on all open roads (see Conversion table, p.72).

Renting a car

104 A rental car should be ready for me
    Es müßte ein Mietwagen hier für mich bereitstehen
    *ess **mōos**·tè ine **meet**·vah·gèn heer fōōr mikh bè·**rite**·shtay·èn*
105 I arranged it through the Speed-Link fly-drive service
    Ich habe durch den Speed-Link Fly-Drive Service einen Mietwagen
        gebucht
    *ikh **hah**·bè doorkh dayn Speed-Link Fly-Drive Service ine·èn
    meet·vah·gèn gè·**bookht***
106   I want to rent a car — for driving myself
    /   Ich möchte ein Auto — zum Selbstfahren mieten
        *ikh **mur'kh**·tè ine **ow**·tō — tsoom **zelpst**·fah·rèn **mee**·tèn*
                                 — with a chauffeur
                                 — mit Fahrer mieten
                                 *— mit **fah**·rèr **mee**·tèn*
107   I want it — for five days
        Ich brauche es — für fünf Tage
        *ikh **brow**·khè ess — fōōr fōōnf **tah**·gè*
108 What is the charge — per day/per week?
    Was kostet das — pro Tag/pro Woche?
    *vass **kos**·tèt dass — prō tahk/prō **vo**·khè*

109 Is there a mileage charge?
  Spielen die zurückgelegten Kilometer eine Rolle?
  shpee·lèn dee tsoo·rook·gè·layk·tèn kee·lō·may·tèr ine·è ro·lè

110   Do you have — a car that is larger/cheaper?
          Haben Sie — ein größeres/ein billigeres Auto?
          hah·bèn zee — ine grur'·sè·rès/ine bi·li·gè·rès ow·tō

111   My wife/my husband — will be driving as well
      Meine Frau/mein Mann — wird auch fahren
      mine·è frow/mine man — virt owkh fah·rèn

112 I should like comprehensive insurance
  Ich hätte gern eine Vollkaskoversicherung
  ikh he·tè gern ine·è fol·kas·kō·fer·zi·khè·roong

113 Must I return the car here?
  Muß ich das Auto wieder hierher zurückbringen?
  moos ikh dass ow·tō vee·dèr heer·her tsoo·rook·bring·èn

114 I should like to leave the car in Vienna
  Ich würde das Auto gerne in Wien zurückgeben
  ikh vōōr·dè dass ow·tō ger·nè in veen tsoo·rook·gay·bèn

115 I should like the car delivered to my hotel
  Ich hätte den Wagen gern zu meinem Hotel gebracht
  ikh he·tè dayn vah·gèn gern tsoo mine·èm hō·tel gè·brakht

116 Please show me how to operate the controls
  Könnten Sie mir bitte zeigen, wie alles funktioniert
  kur'n·tèn zee meer bi·tè tsye·gèn vee a·lès foonk·tsee·ō·neert

117 Please explain the car documents
  Bitte erklären Sie mir die Wagenpapiere
  bi·tè er·klay·rèn zee meer dee vah·gèn·pa·pee·rè

Parking

In big towns parking can be a headache. In many areas there are parking
meters; in other zones you can park if you display a special disk
(*Parkscheibe*) which can be obtained from banks, tobacco shops, hotels,
garages, tourist offices or police stations (this varies depending on which
country you are in). If you are lucky there will be a multilevel parking
garage. Otherwise you can settle for a street away from the center.

118 Where can I park?
  Wo kann ich parken? •
  vō kan ikh par·kèn
119 Can I park here?
  Kann ich hier parken?
  kan ikh heer par·kèn
120 Are you leaving?
  Fahren Sie weg?
  fah·rèn zee vek
121 Is there a parking lot nearby?
  Gibt es einen Parkplatz in der Nähe?
  gipt ess ine·èn park·plats in der nay·è
122 What time does the parking lot close?
  Wann macht der Parkplatz zu?
  van makht der park·plats tsoo
123 How much does it cost per hour?
  Wieviel kostet es pro Stunde?
  vee·feel kos·tèt ess prō shtoon·dè
124 How long can I leave the car here?
  Wie lange kann ich hier parken?
  vee lang·è kan ikh heer par·kèn
125 I will only be a few minutes
  Ich bin in ein paar Minuten zurück
  ikh bin in ine pahr mi·noo·tèn tsoo·rook
126 Do I need a parking disk?
  Brauche ich eine Parkscheibe?
  brow·khè ikh ine·è park·shye·bè
127 Where can I get a parking disk?
  Wo kann ich eine Parkscheibe bekommen?
  vō kan ikh ine·è park·shye·bè bè·ko·mèn
128 Do I need parking lights?
  Muß ich das Standlicht anlassen?
  moos ikh dass shtant·likht an·la·sèn

Road conditions

Roads are for the most part well maintained and relatively trouble-free.
There are no tolls except on certain mountain roads in Austria. The
multi-lane expressways are superb, but using minor roads does not
necessarily mean slow going. The main problems you are likely to meet
are peak traffic in summer and heavy snow if you are on a winter sports
trip, in which case studded snowtires or chains may be compulsory.

129 Is there a route that avoids the traffic?
     Gibt es eine Reiseroute, die den Hauptverkehr vermeidet?
     gipt ess ine·è rye·zè·roo·tè dee dayn howpt·fer·kayr fer·mye·dèt
130 Is there a shortcut/detour?
     Gibt es eine Abkürzung/einen Umweg?
     gipt ess ine·è ap·kōōr·tsoong/ine·èn oom·vayk
131 Is the traffic heavy?
     Ist viel Verkehr?
     ist feel fer·kayr
132 What is causing this tie-up?
     Warum ist hier ein Stau?
     va·room ist heer ine shtow
133 When will the road be clear?
     Wann wird die Straße wieder frei?
     van virt dee shtrah·sè vee·dèr frye
134 What is the speed limit?
     Was ist die Höchstgeschwindigkeit?
     vass ist dee hur'khst·gè·shvin·dikh·kite
135 Is there a toll on this highway?
     Ist diese Autobahn gebührenpflichtig?
     ist dee·zè ow·tō·bahn gè·bōō·rèn·pflikh·tikh
136 Is the road to Kitzbühel snowed in?
     Ist die Straße nach Kitzbühel zugeschneit?
     ist dee shtrah·sè nahkh kits·bōō·èl tsoo·gè·shnite
137 Is the pass open?
     Ist der Paß offen?
     ist der pass o·fèn
138 Do I need studded tires/chains?
     Brauche ich Spikes/Schneeketten?
     brow·khè ikh shpikes/shnay·ke·tèn

Road signs

These are nearly always pictorial, but here are a few that you will see in
words.

139	Ausfahrt Exit	143	Polizei Police
140	Autobahn Expressway	144	Stadtmitte Center of town
141	Einbahnstraße One-way street	145	Umleitung Detour
142	Notausfahrt Emergency exit	146	Zoll Customs

Fuel

Gasoline (*Benzin*) comes in two grades: *Normal* (2 star) and the
higher-octane and more expensive *Super* (4 star). Diesel fuel is also used.
See conversion tables (p.72) for fuel quantities and tire pressures.

147   15 liters of — 3 star
              Fünfzehn Liter — Normal
        fōōnf·tsayn lee·tèr — nor·mahl
                             — 4 star
                             — Super
                             — *zoo·pèr*

                    15 liters of — diesel fuel
             Fünfzehn Liter — Diesel
             fōōnf·tsayn lee·ter — dee·zèl

148 ... Marks' worth, please
    Für ... Mark bitte
    fōōr ... mark bi·tè

149 Fill her up, please
    Volltanken, bitte
    fol·tang·kèn bi·tè

150   Check — the oil
             Prüfen Sie — den Ölstand
             prōō·fèn zee — dayn ur'l·shtant
                       — the water
                       — das Kühlwasser
                       — *dass kōōl·va·sèr*
                       — The tire pressure
                       — den Reifendruck
                       — *dayn rye·fèn·drook*

151 The pressure is 1.3
    Der Reifendruck ist eins Komma drei atü
    der rye·fèn·drook ist ines ko·ma drye a·tōō

152 I want some distilled water
    Ich hätte gern destilliertes Wasser
    ikh he·tè gern des·ti·leer·tès va·sèr

153 Could you clean the windshield?
    Könnten Sie die Windschutzscheibe saubermachen?
    kur'n·tèn zee dee vint·shoots·shye·bè zow·bèr·ma·khèn

154 Could you put some water in the windshield washer?
    Könnten Sie die Scheibenwaschanlage auffüllen?
    kur'n·tèn zee dee shye·bèn·vash·an·lah·gè owf·fōō·lèn

155 Can I pay by credit card?
    Kann ich mit Kreditkarte bezahlen?
    kan ikh mit kray·deet·kar·tè bè·tsah·lèn

156 Is there a lavatory/a telephone here?
    Gibt es hier eine Toilette/ein Telefon?
    gipt ess heer ine·è tō·a·le·tè/ine tay·lay·fōn

Breakdowns and repairs

157   My car — has broken down
               Mein Auto — hat eine Panne
             mine ow·tō — hat ine·è pa·nè
                       — will not start
                       — springt nicht an
                       — *shpringt nikht an*

158 There is something wrong with my car
    Mit meinem Auto ist etwas in Ordnung
    mit mine·èm ow·tō ist et·vass nikht in ort·noong

159 I wish to telephone for emergency road service
    Ich möchte den Pannendienst anrufen
    ikh mur'kh·tè dayn pa·nèn·deenst an·roo·fèn

160   Can you — send a mechanic?
             Können Sie — einen Mechaniker schicken?
             kur'·nèn zee — ine·èn me·kha·ni·kèr shi·kèn
                       — send a tow-truck?
                       — einen Abschleppwagen schicken?
                       — *ine·èn ap·shlep·vah·gèn shi·kèn*
                       — take me to the nearest garage?
                       — mich zur nächsten Werkstatt bringen?
                       — *mikh tsoor nekh·stèn verk·shtat bring·èn*
                       — give me a tow?
                       — mich abschleppen?
                       — *mikh ap·shle·pèn*
                       — give me a push?
                       — mich anschieben?
                       — *mikh an·shee·bèn*

Can you — give me a can of gasoline, please?
Können Sie — mir bitte einen Kanister Benzin geben?
kur'·nèn zee — meer bi·tè ine·èn ka·ni·stèr ben·tseen gay·bèn

161 Can you find the trouble?
Können Sie mal nachsehen?
kur'·nèn zee mahl nahkh·zay·èn

162 I have run out of gasoline
Ich habe kein Benzin mehr
ikh hah·bè kine ben·tseen mayr

163 This is broken
Das ist kaputt
dass ist ka·poot

164 It's making a funny noise
Da ist ein merkwürdiges Geräusch
dah ist ine merk·vöör·di·gès gè·roysh

165 The brakes have something wrong with them
Mit den Bremsen ist etwas nicht in Ordnung
mit dayn brem·zèn ist et·vass nikht in ort·noong

166 The windshield wipers — are not working
Die Scheibenwischer — funktionieren nicht
dee shye·bèn·vi·shèr — foonk·tsee·ō·nee·rèn nikht

167 My windshield has shattered
Meine Windschutzscheibe ist gesprungen
mine·è vint·shoots·shye·bè ist gè·shproong·èn

168 I have a flat tire
Ich habe einen Platten
ikh hah·bè ine·èn pla·tèn

169 The battery is dead
Die Batterie ist leer
dee ba·tè·ree ist layr

170 The engine is overheating
Der Motor wird zu heiß
der mō·tor virt tsoo hise

171 There is a leak in the radiator
Der Kühler ist leck
der köö·lèr ist lek

172 I have blown a fuse
Eine Sicherung ist durchgebrannt
ine·è zi·khè·roong ist doorkh·gè·brant

173 There is a bad connection
Da ist irgendwo ein Wackelkontakt
dah ist ir·gènt·vō ine va·kèl·kon·takt

174 I have lost the ignition key
Ich habe den Zündschlüssel verloren
ikh hah·bè dayn tsöönt·shlöö·sèl fer·lō·rèn

175 I need — a new fan belt
Ich brauche — einen neuen Keilriemen
ikh brow·khè — ine·èn noy·èn kile·ree·mèn

176 Can you — replace the exhaust pipe?
Können Sie — den Auspuff auswechseln?
kur'·nèn zee — dayn ows·poof ows·vekh·sèln

177 Is it serious?
Ist es etwas Ernstes?
ist ess et·vass ern·stès

178 How long will it take to repair it?
Wie lange dauert die Reparatur?
vee lang·è dow·èrt dee ray·pa·ra·toor

179 Do you have the parts?
Haben Sie Ersatzteile?
hah·bèn zee er·zats·tile·è

180 Can you repair it for the time being?
Können Sie es provisorisch reparieren?
kur'·nèn zee ess pro·vee·zō·rish ray·pa·ree·rèn

181 Can I have an itemized bill for my insurance company?
Kann ich eine detaillierte Rechnung für meine Versicherung haben?
kan ikh ine·è day·ta·yeer·tè rekh·noong föör mine·è fer·zi·khè·roong hah·bèn

Accidents and the police

The police in the German-speaking countries are vigilant and have the power to impose on-the-spot fines. But they are on the whole well mannered and helpful. If you have dealings with them over an accident or a driving offense, behave in a calm and reasonable manner, and they will do likewise. See also Emergencies and accidents (p.63).

182 I'm very sorry officer
Es tut mir sehr leid
ess toot meer zayr lite

183 I am a foreigner
Ich bin Ausländer
ikh bin ows·len·dèr

184 I did not see the signal
Ich habe das Signal nicht gesehen
ikh hah·bè dass zig·nahl nikht gè·zay·èn

185 I did not know about that regulation
Ich wußte nichts von dieser Verkehrsregel
ikh voos·tè nikhts fon dee·zèr fer·kayrs·ray·gèl

186 I did not understand the sign
Ich wußte nicht, was das Schild bedeutet
ikh voos·tè nikht vass dass shilt bè·doy·tèt

187 Here is my driver's license
Hier ist mein Führerschein
heer ist mine fōō·rèr·shine

188 How much is the fine?
Wie hoch ist das Bußgeld?
vee hōkh ist dass boos·gelt

189 I was driving at 80 km/h (50 mph) (see p.72)
Ich bin mit achtzig Stundenkilometern gefahren
ikh bin mit akh·tsikh shtoon·dèn·kee·lō·may·tèrn gè·fah·rèn

190 He/she was too close
Er/sie ist zu dicht aufgefahren
er/zee ist tsoo dikht owf·ge·fah·rèn

191 I did not see him/her
Ich habe ihn/sie nicht gesehen
ikh hah·bè een/zee nikht gè·zay·èn

192 He was driving too fast
Er ist zu schnell gefahren
er ist tsoo shnel gè·fah·rèn

193 He did not stop
Er hat nicht angehalten
er hat nikht an·gè·hal·tèn

194 He did not yield
Er hat die Vorfahrt mißachtet
er hat dee fōr·fahrt mis·akh·tèt

195 He stopped very suddenly
Er hat plötzlich gebremst
er hat plur·ts·likh gè·bremst

196 He swerved
Er ist ausgeschert
er ist ows·gè·shert

197 The car turned without signaling
Das Auto hat gewendet, ohne Zeichen zu geben
dass ow·tō hat gè·ven·dèt ō·nè tsye·khèn tsoo gay·bèn

198 He ran into me
Er ist mir hineingefahren
er ist meer hin·ine·gè·fah·rèn

199 He passed on a curve
Er hat in einer Kurve überholt
er hat in ine·èr koor·vè ōō·bèr·hōlt

200 His license plate number was...
Seine Autonummer war...
zine·è ow·tō·noo·mèr vahr...

201 The road was wet
Die Straße war naß
dee shtrah·sè vahr nass

202 I skidded
Ich bin ins Schleudern gekommen
ikh bin ins shloy·dern gè·ko·mèn

203 My brakes failed
Meine Bremsen haben versagt
mine·è brem·zèn hah·bèn fer·zahgt

204 I could not stop in time
Ich konnte nicht mehr rechtzeitig anhalten
ikh kon·tè nikht mayr rekht·tsye·tikh an·hal·tèn

205 I have run over a dog/cat
Ich habe einen Hund/eine Katze überfahren
ikh hah·bè ine·èn hoont/ine·è kat·sè ōō·bèr·fah·rèn

206 Do I need to report it?
Muß ich das melden?
moos ikh dass mel·dèn

207 What is your name and address?
Geben Sie mir bitte Ihren Namen und Ihre Adresse
gay·bèn zee meer bi·tè ee·rèn nah·mèn oont ee·rè a·dre·sè

208 What is your insurance company?
Wie heißt Ihre Versicherungsgesellschaft?
vee hyest ee·rè fer·zi·khè·roongs·gè·zel·shaft

209 We should call the police
Wir sollten die Polizei holen
veer zol·tèn dee pō·lee·tsye hō·lèn

210 Will you please be a witness?
Könnten Sie bitte unser Zeuge
sein?
*kur'n·tèn zee bi·tè oon·zèr
tsoy·gè zine*

211 Do you admit responsibility?
Nehmen Sie die Schuld auf
sich?
*nay·mèn zee dee shoolt owf
zikh*

212 Could we settle in cash now?
Könnten wir es mit einer
Barzahlung regeln?
*kur'n·tèn veer ess mit ine·èr
bahr·tsah·loong ray·gèln*

Finding the way   (F)

Questions

The simplest way to get directions is just to say where you want to go and
add "please", as you would with a taxi driver. For example, "Where is
the cathedral?" would be "*Zum Dom, bitte*". Here are some other
phrases that you may need.

1 I have lost my way
Ich habe mich verlaufen
ikh hah·bè mikh fer·low·fèn

2 How do I get to this address?
Können Sie mir sagen, wie ich zu dieser Anschrift komme?
kur'·nèn zee meer zah·gèn vee ikh tsoo dee·zèr an·shrift ko·mè

3 Where is — the station/the castle?
Wo ist — der Bahnhof/das Schloß?
vō ist — der bahn·hof/dass shloss

4 Where are — the toilets?
Wo sind — die Toiletten?
vō zint — dee tō·a·le·tèn

5 I would like to go to the center of town
Ich möchte ins Stadtzentrum
ikh mur'kh·tè ins·shtat·tsen·troom

6 We are looking for — the Tourist Information Office
Wir suchen — das Fremdenverkehrsamt
veer zoo·khèn — dass frem·dèn·fer·kayrs·amt

7 Can you tell me the way to the castle?
Können Sie mir sagen, wie ich zum Schloß komme?
kur'·nèn zee meer zah·gèn vee ikh tsoom shloss ko·mè

8 Can you show me on the map?
Können Sie mir das auf der Karte zeigen?
kur'·nèn zee meer dass owf der kar·tè tsye·gèn

9 Where is the nearest post office?
Wo ist das nächste Postamt?
vō ist dass nekh·stè post·amt

10 Is there — a service station near here?
Gibt es — hier in der Nähe eine Tankstelle?
gipt ess — heer in der nay·è ine·è tank·shte·lè

11 Is this the right way — to the museum?
Ist das der richtige Weg — zum Museum?
ist dass der rikh·ti·gè vayk — tsoom moo·zay·oom

12 Is it far — to the cathedral?
Ist es weit — zum Dom?
ist ess vite — tsoom dōm

13 How far is it — to Vienna?
Wie weit ist es — nach Wien?
vee·vite ist ess — nahkh veen

14 How long does it take to get there?
Wie lange braucht man dahin?
vee lang·è browkht man dah·hin

15 Can one walk there?
Kann man zu Fuß hingehen?
kan man tsoo foos hin·gay·èn

16 Is there a bus that goes there?
Fährt ein Bus dahin?
fert ine boos dah·hin

17 Which road do I take for Salzburg?
Welche Straße muß ich nach Salzburg nehmen?
vel·khè **shtrah·***sè moos ikh nahkh* **zalts·***boork* **nay·***mèn*

18 Do I turn here for Hamburg?
Muß ich hier nach Hamburg abbiegen?
moos ikh heer nahkh **ham·***boork* **ap·***bee·gèn*

19   Which is the best route — to Stuttgart?
       Welches ist die beste
            Strecke — nach Stuttgart?
vel·khès ist dee **bes·***tè* **shtre·***kè* — *nahkh* **shtoot·***gart*

20 Which is the most scenic route?
Welches ist die landschaftlich schönste Strecke?
vel·khès ist dee **lant·***shaft·likh* **shur'n·***stè* **shtre·***kè*

21   How do I get back on to — the Autobahn?
Wie komme ich wieder auf — die Autobahn?
vee ko·mè ikh **vee·***dèr owf* — *dee* **ow·***tō·bahn*

22 Where does this road go to?
Wo führt diese Straße hin?
vō fōōrt **dee·***zè* **shtrah·***sè hin*

23 Will we arrive by this evening?
Sind wir bis heute abend dort?
zint veer bis **hoy·***tè* **ah·***bènt dort*

Answers

These are the key phrases of the answer you will receive when you ask for directions. In this case the German is given first, with the English below.

24   Gehen Sie — geradeaus
            gay·*èn zee* — *gè·***rah·***dè·ows*
            You go — straight ahead
                  — nach rechts
                  — *nahkh rekhts*
                  — right
                  — nach links
                  — *nahkh links*
                  — left
                  — bis zu
                  — *bis tsoo*
                  — as far as

25   Biegen Sie — rechts ab
            bee·*gèn zee* — *rekhts ap*
            Turn — right
                  — links ab
                  — *links ap*
                  — left

26 Gehen Sie immer geradeaus
                weiter — in Richtung
          gay·*èn zee* **i·***mèr*
       *gè·***rah·***dè·ows* **vye·***tèr* — *in* **rikh·***toong*
       Keep going straight ahead — towards
                  — bis
                  — *bis*
                  — until

27   Nehmen Sie — die Straße nach . . .
          nay·*mèn zee* — *dee* **shtrah·***sè nahkh* . . .
          Take — the road for . . .
                  — die erste (Straße) rechts
                  — *dee* **er·***stè* (**shtrah·***sè*) *rekhts*
                  — the first (road) on the right
                  — die zweite (Straße) links
                  — *dee* **tsvye·***tè* (**shtrah·***sè*) *links*
                  — the second (road) on the left

28   Gehen Sie über — die Straße
         gay·*èn zee* **ōō·***bèr* — *dee* **shtrah·***sè*
         Cross — the street

Gehen Sie über — den Bahnübergang
gay·èn zee $\overline{oo}$·*bèr — dayn bahn·*$\overline{oo}$·*bèr·gang*
Cross — the grade crossing
— die Brücke
— *dee bröö·kè*
— the bridge

29 Das ist — ganz in der Nähe
dass ist — gants in der nay·è
It's — not far from here
— an der Kreuzung
— *an der kroy·tsoong*
— at the intersection
— beim Theater
— *bime tay·ah·tèr*
— next to the theatre
— nach der Ampel
— *nahkh der am·pèl*
— after the traffic lights
— der Kirche gegenüber
— *der kir·khè gay·gèn·*$\overline{oo}$·*bèr*
— opposite the church
— da drüben
— *dah dröö·bèn*
— over there
— an der Ecke
— *an der e·kè*
— at the corner

Money   (M)

General

1   How much is that — altogether?
Was kostet das — zusammen?
vass kos·tèt dass — tsoo·za·mèn
2   How much is it — to get in?
Wieviel kostet — der Eintritt?
vee·feel kos·tèt — der ine·trit
— for a child?
— es für ein Kind?
— *ess föör ine kint*
— per person?
— das pro Person?
— *dass prö per·zön*
— per kilo?
— das pro Kilo?
— *dass prö kee·lö*
3 Is there any extra charge?
Gibt es einen Preiszuschlag?
gipt ess ine·èn price·tsoo·shlahk
4 Is the tip/tax included?
Ist Bedienung/Mehrwertsteuer inbegriffen?
ist bè·dee·noong/mayr·vert·shtoy·èr in·bè·gri·fèn
5   Is there a discount for — a group?
Gibt es Ermäßigung für — Gruppen?
gipt ess er·me·si·goong föör — groo·pèn
— students?
— Studenten?
— *shtoo·den·tèn*
— senior citizens?
— Rentner?
— *rent·nèr*
6 How much of a discount can you give me?
Wieviel Ermäßigung geben Sie?
vee·feel er·me·si·goong gay·bèn zee
7 Can you give me a 10 per cent discount?
Können Sie mir 10 Prozent Preisnachlaß geben?
kur'·nèn zee meer tsayn prö·tsent price·nahkh·las gay·bèn

8 Can you give me an estimate of the cost?
   Können Sie mir die Kosten schätzen?
   kur'·nèn zee meer dee **kos**·tèn **shet**·sèn

9 Do I have to pay a deposit?
   Muß ich eine Anzahlung machen?
   moos ikh ine·è **an**·tsah·loong ma·khèn

10 Do I pay in advance or afterwards?
   Zahle ich im voraus oder später?
   tsah·lè ikh im **fōr**·ows ō·dèr **shpay**·tèr

11 Can I pay in installments?
   Kann ich in Raten bezahlen?
   kan ikh in **rah**·tèn bè·**tsah**·lèn

12 Do you accept traveler's checks?
   Nehmen Sie Reiseschecks?
   nay·mèn zee **rye**·zè·sheks

13 I wish to pay by credit card
   Ich möchte mit Kreditkarte bezahlen
   ikh **mur'kh**·tè mit kray·**deet**·kar·tè bè·**tsah**·lèn

14 May I have an itemized bill?
   Kann ich eine ausführliche Rechnung haben?
   kan ikh **ine**·è ows·**fōōr**·li·khè **rekh**·noong **hah**·bèn

15 May I have a receipt?
   Kann ich eine Quittung haben?
   kan ikh **ine**·è **kvi**·toong **hah**·bèn

16 You have given me the wrong change
   Sie haben mir falsch herausgegeben
   zee **hah**·bèn meer falsh he·**rows**·gè·gay·bèn

17 That's too much for me
   Das ist zuviel für mich
   dass ist tsoo·**feel** fōōr mikh

18 I have no money
   Ich habe kein Geld
   ikh **hah**·bè kine gelt

19 I do not have enough money
   Ich habe nicht genug Geld bei mir
   ikh **hah**·bè nikht gè·**nook** gelt bye meer

20 That's all, thank you
   Danke, das war's
   dang·kè dass **vahrs**

21 Can you change a 50-Mark note into 5-Mark pieces?
   Können Sie einen Fünfzigmarkschein in Fünfmarkstücke wechseln?
   kur'·nèn zee **ine**·èn **fōōnf**·tsikh·mark·shine in **fōōnf**·mark·shtōō·kè **vekh**·sèln

22 Can you change a 50-Mark note into 1-Mark pieces?
   Können Sie einen Fünfzigmarkschein in Markstücke wechseln?
   kur'·nèn zee **ine**·èn **fōōnf**·tsikh·mark·shine in **mark**·shtōō·kè **vekh**·sèln

23 Can you give me some small change?
   Können Sie mir Kleingeld geben?
   kur'·nèn zee meer **kline**·gelt gay·bèn

Banks and exchange offices

In Germany banks are usually open from 8:30 to 13:00 and 14:30 to 16:00, staying open until 17:30 on Thursday or Friday (the hours are different for Austria and Switzerland). Most are closed on Saturday and Sunday. You can also change money at large hotels and stores and of course at exchange offices, though the rate there tends to be less favorable. Exchange offices at airports and major railway stations stay open at night and over the weekend. Remember that you need your passport when changing money. Traveler's checks issued by major firms are widely accepted, as are personal checks from Eurocheque banks.

24   Will you — change these traveler's checks?
                 Würden Sie — diese Reiseschecks einlösen?
                 vōōr·dèn zee — dee·zè **rye**·zè·sheks ine·**lur'**·zèn

Will you — change these bills?
Würden Sie — Geld umtauschen?
*vōōr·dèn zee — gelt **oom**·tow·shèn*

25   What is the exchange rate
for — dollars?
Was ist der Kurs für — Dollars?
*vass ist der koors fōōr — **do**·lars*

26   I would like to withdraw 500 Marks
Ich möchte 500 Mark abheben
*ikh **mur'kh**·tè **fōōnf**·hoon·dèrt mark **ap**·hay·bèn*

27   I would like to cash a check with my Eurocheque card
Ich möchte gern einen Eurocheck einlösen
*ikh **mur'kh**·tè gern ine·èn oy·rō·shek ine·lur'·zèn*

28   I would like to obtain a cash advance with my credit card
Ich möchte gern Bargeld auf meine Kreditkarte haben
*ikh **mur'kh**·tè gern **bahr**·gelt owf **mine**·è kray·deet·kar·tè **hah**·bèn*

29   What is your commission?
Wie hoch ist die Bearbeitungsgebühr?
*vee hōkh ist dee bè·**ar**·bite·oongs·gè·**bōōr***

30   Can you contact my bank to arrange for a transfer?
Könnten Sie mit meiner Bank eine Überweisung vereinbaren?
*kur'n·tèn zee mit **mine**·èr bank ine·è ōō·bèr·vye·zoong fer·ine·bah·rèn*

31   I have an account with the Bank of X in London/New York
Ich habe ein Konto bei der X Bank in London/New York
*ikh **hah**·bè ine kon·tō bye der X bank in **Lon**·don/New York*

32   I have made/wish to make an arrangement with this bank
Ich habe mit dieser Bank eine Vereinbarung getroffen/Ich möchte mit dieser Bank eine Vereinbarung treffen
*ikh **hah**·bè mit dee·zèr bank ine·è fer·ine·bah·roong gè·**tro**·fèn/ikh **mur'kh**·tè mit dee·zèr bank ine·è fer·ine·bah·roong **tre**·fèn*

33   I would like to speak to the manager
Ich würde gern mit dem Direktor sprechen
*ikh **vōōr**·dè gern mit daym dee·**rek**·tor shpre·khèn*

Accommodations (A)

Hotel reservations and inquiries

In Germany there are three categories of hotels and boarding houses, as follows: F-hotels and boarding houses providing bed and breakfast; G-inns and boarding houses providing more meals; H-hotels. Each category is classified I, II, or III (simple, good, very good). Austria and Switzerland have a grading system of 1 to 5 stars. The terms *Hotel garni* and *Pension* indicate bed and breakfast only, while a small country inn will tend to be called a *Gasthof* or *Gasthaus*. Most hotels can handle a reservation or inquiry in English, but if you want to take no chances, this section contains some things you might wish to say by letter or telephone, or at the reception desk. Most of the replies will be self-explanatory, but one to be prepared for is "wir sind ausgebucht" (we are full). You should also know the terms *Halbpension* (bed, breakfast and one other meal) and *Vollpension* (full board). Look out for the sign *Zimmer frei* (room free) if you are driving along in search of accommodations. Otherwise the local tourist office (*Verkehrsamt, Verkehrsverband* or *Verkehrsbüro*) will help you.

1   Dear Sir,
Sehr geehrte Damen und Herren!
*zayr gè·**ayr**·tè **dah**·mèn oont he·rèn*

2   I wish to stay in Oberammergau from ... to ... with my wife/family
Ich möchte vom ... bis zum ... mit meiner Frau/Familie Oberammergau besuchen
*ikh **mur'kh**·tè fom ... biss tsoom ... mit **mine**·èr frow/fa·**meel**·yè ō·bèr·**a**·mèr·gow bè·**zoo**·khèn*

3   I wish to stay for three nights
Ich möchte drei Nächte bleiben
*ikh **mur'kh**·tè drye **nekh**·tè **blye**·bèn*

4   Can you provide the following accommodations?
Könnten Sie mir folgende Unterkunft besorgen?
kur'n·tèn zee meer fol·gèn·dè oon·tèr·koonft bè·zor·gèn
    — a single room with toilet and
        shower/bath
    —. ein Einzelzimmer mit WC und
        Dusche/Bad
    — *ine ine·tsèl·tsi·mèr mit vay·tsay*
        oont doo·shè/baht
    — a room with twin beds
    — ein Zimmer mit zwei Einzelbetten
    — *ine tsi·mèr mit tsvye ine·tsèl·be·tèn*
    — a double room — with a bed for a
        child
    — ein Doppelzimmer — mit einem
        Kinderbett
    — *ine do·pèl·tsi·mèr — mit ine·èm*
        kin·dèr·bet
    — a suite with living room, bedroom,
        bath and toilet
    — eine Suite mit Wohnzimmer,
        Schlafzimmer, Bad und WC
    — *ine·è svee·tè mit vōn·tsi·mèr*
        shlahf·tsi·mèr baht oont vay·tsay

5   I should like a room — that is quiet
     Ich hätte gern ein Zimmer — das ruhig liegt
         dass roo·ikh leekt
    — with a view
    — das eine schöne Aussicht hat
    — *dass ine·è shur'·nè ows·zikht hat*
    — on the first floor/second floor
    — im Erdgeschoß/im ersten Stock
    — *im ayrd·gè·shoss/im ayr·stèn shtok*
    — with a TV/radio
    — mit Fernsehen/Radio
    — *mit fern·zay·èn/rah·dee·ō*

6   Please send me a brochure about your hotel
Schicken Sie mir bitte einen Prospekt von Ihrem Hotel
shi·kèn zee meer bi·tè ine·èn pro·spekt fon ee·rèm hō·tel

7   Sincerely yours
Mit freundlichen Grüßen
mit froynt·li·khèn grōō·sèn

8   How much is the room per night?
Wieviel kostet das Zimmer pro Nacht?
vee·feel kos·tèt dass tsi·mèr prō nakht

9   Is breakfast/tax included?
Ist Frühstück/Mehrwertsteuer im Preis inbegriffen?
ist frōō·shtōōk/mayr·vert·shtoy·èr im price in·bè·gri·fèn

10   How much is it — with breakfast?
       Wieviel kostet es — mit Frühstück?
      vee·feel kos·tèt ess — mit frōō·shtōōk
    — with breakfast and evening meal?
    — mit Frühstück und Abendessen?
    — *mit frōō·shtōōk oont ah·bènt·e·sèn*
    — with all meals?
    — Vollpension
    — *fol·pen·zee·ōn*

11   Do you have a swimming pool/sauna?
Haben Sie einen Swimmingpool/eine Sauna?
hah·bèn zee ine·èn svi·ming·pool/ine·è zow·na

12   Can you suggest another hotel that might have a vacancy?
Können Sie mir ein anderes Hotel empfehlen, das vielleicht
noch Zimmer frei hat?
kur'·nèn zee meer ine an·dè·rès hō·tel emp·fay·lèn dass
fee·lyekht nokh tsi·mèr frye hat

Checking in and out

13 I've booked a room in the name of Smith
Ich habe ein Zimmer im Namen Smiths vorbestellt
ikh hah·bè ine tsi·mèr im nah·mèn Smiths fōr·bè·shtelt

14 Can I see the room, please?
Kann ich mich bitte das Zimmer ansehen?
kan ich mikh bi·tè dass tsi·mèr an·zay·èn

15 The room is too — small/noisy
Das Zimmer ist zu — klein/laut
dass tsi·mèr ist tsoo — kline/lowt

16 When will the room be ready?
Wann kann ich das Zimmer belegen?
van kan ikh dass tsi·mèr bè·lay·gèn

17 Where is the bathroom/toilet?
Wo ist das Badezimmer/die Toilette?
vō ist dass bah·dè·tsi·mèr/dee tō·a·le·tè

18 I want to stay an extra night
Ich möchte noch eine Nacht bleiben
ikh mur'kh·tè nokh ine·è nakht blye·bèn

19 We shall be leaving at 9 o'clock tomorrow morning
Wir reisen morgen um neun Uhr ab
veer rye·zèn mor·gèn oom noyn oo·èr ap

20 By what time do we have to vacate the room?
Bis wann müssen wir das Zimmer verlassen haben?
biss van mōō·sèn veer dass tsi·mèr fer·la·sèn hah·bèn

21 I would like the bill, please
Ich hätte gern die Rechnung, bitte
ikh he·tè gern dee rekh·noong bi·tè

22 Can I pay by credit card?
Kann ich mit Kreditkarte bezahlen?
kan ikh mit kray·deet·kar·tè bè·tsah·lèn

23 Do you accept — traveler's checks?
Nehmen Sie — Reiseschecks?
nay·mèn zee — rye·zè·sheks?
— American Express cards/
checks?
— American-Express-Karten/
Schecks?
— *American Express kar·tèn/sheks*

24 Could you have my luggage — brought down/sent on?
Könnten Sie veranlassen, daß
mein Gepäck — heruntergebracht wird/
weitergesandt wird?
*kur'n·tèn zee fer·an·la·sèn
dass mine gè·pek — he·roon·tèr·gè·brakht virt/
vye·tèr·gè·zant virt*

25 Could you have any letters/messages forwarded?
Könnten Sie mir meine Post/Nachrichten für mich nachsenden?
*kur'n·tèn zee meer mine·è post/nahkh·rikh·tèn fōōr mikh
nahkh·zen·dèn*

Service and practical needs

26 What time is — breakfast/lunch
Wann gibt es — Frühstück/Mittagessen?
van gipt ess — frōō·shtōōk/mi·tahk·e·sèn

27 Can we have breakfast in our room, please?
Können Sie uns bitte das Frühstück aufs Zimmer bringen?
kur'·nèn zee oons bi·tè dass frōō·shtōōk owfs tsi·mèr bring·èn

28 Where can I park the car?
Wo kann ich das Auto parken?
vō kan ikh dass ow·tō par·kèn

29 What time does the hotel close?
Wann macht das Hotel abends zu?
van makht dass hō·tel ah·bènts tsoo

30 Is there an elevator?
Gibt es einen Lift?
gipt ess ine·èn lift

31 Can I drink the tap water?
Ist das Leitungswasser Trinkwasser?
ist dass lye·toongs·va·sèr trink·va·sèr

32 Please call me at 8 o'clock
Bitte wecken Sie mich um acht Uhr
bi·tè ve·kèn zee mikh oom akht oo·èr

33 Can I leave these for safe keeping?
Könnten Sie das für mich im Safe aufbewahren?
kur'n·tèn zee dass fōōr mikh im zayf owf·bè·vah·rèn

34 Can I have my things out of the safe?
Kann ich meine Sachen aus dem Safe wiederhaben?
kan ikh mine·è za·khèn ows daym zayf vee·dèr·hah·bèn

35   Can I — make a telephone call from here?
           Kann ich — von hier anrufen?
            kan ikh — fon heer an·roo·fèn
                      — send a telex message from here?
                      — von hier ein Fernschreiben
                          schicken?
                      — *fon heer ine fern·shrye·bèn shi·kèn*

36 Are there any letters/messages for me?
Ist Post für mich da/Haben Sie irgendwelche Nachrichten
für mich?
*ist post fōōr mikh dah/hah·bèn zee ir·gènt·vel·khè
nahkh·rikh·tèn fōōr mikh*

37 I should like a private room — for a conference/cocktail party
Ich hätte gern einen Raum — für eine Besprechung/Cocktail-
Party
*ikh he·tè gern ine·èn rowm — fōōr ine·è bè·shpre·khoong/
kok·tayl·pahr·tee*

38 I am expecting a Herr Bauer
Ich erwarte einen Herrn Bauer
ikh er·var·tè ine·èn hern bow·èr

39 Could you call me when he arrives?
Könnten Sie mir bescheid sagen, wenn er da ist?
kur'n·tèn zee meer bè·shite zah·gèn ven er dah ist

40 Is the voltage 220 or 110?
Ist die Spannung hier zweihundertzwanzig oder
einhundertzehn Volt?
*ist dee shpa·noong heer tsvye·hoon·dèrt·tsvan·tsikh ō·dèr
ine·hoon·dèrt·tsayn volt*

41 Can I have my key?
Kann ich bitte meinen Schlüssel haben?
kan ikh bi·tè mine·èn shlōō·sèl hah·bèn

42 Can I have some soap/some towels?
Kann ich bitte ein Stück Seife/Handtücher haben?
kan ikh bi·tè ine shtōōk zye·fè/hant·tōō·khèr hah·bèn

43 Can I have some note paper/an ashtray?
Kann ich bitte etwas Schreibpapier/einen Aschenbecher haben?
kan ikh bi·tè et·vass shripe·pa·peer/ine·èn a·shèn·be·khèr hah·bèn

44 Can I have another blanket/another pillow?
Kann ich bitte noch eine Decke/noch ein Kissen haben?
kan ikh bi·tè nokh ine·è de·kè/nokh ine ki·sèn hah·bèn

45 Where is the outlet for my electric razor?
Wo ist die Steckdose für den Rasierapparat?
vō ist dee shtek·dō·zè fōōr dayn ra·zeer·a·pa·raht

46 I cannot open the window
Ich bekomme das Fenster nicht auf
ikh bè·ko·mè dass fen·stèr nikht owf

47 The air conditioning/the heating is not working
Die Klimaanlage/die Heizung geht nicht
dee klee·ma·an·lah·gè/dee hye·tsoong gayt nikht

48 I cannot turn the heat off
Ich kann die Heizung nicht abdrehen
ikh kan dee hye·tsoong nikht ap·dray·èn

49 I want to turn the heat up/down
Ich würde gern die Heizung höher/niedriger stellen
*ikh **voor**·dè gern dee **hye**·tsoong hur'·èr/ nee·dri·gèr **shte**·lèn*

50 The lock is broken
Das Schloß ist kaputt
*das shloss ist ka·**poot***

51 There is no hot water
Es gibt kein heißes Wasser
*ess gipt kine **hye**·sès va·sèr*

52 The washbowl is dirty
Das Waschbecken ist schmutzig
*dass **vash**·be·kèn ist **shmoot**·sikh*

53 The plug is broken
Der Stöpsel ist kaputt
*der **stur'p**·sèl ist ka·**poot***

54 There is no toilet paper
Es ist kein Toilettenpapier da
*ess ist kine tō·a·**le**·tèn·pa·**peer** dah*

55 Do you have a laundry room?
Haben Sie eine Wäscherei?
hah**·bèn zee ine·è ve·shè·**rye

56 I want to iron some clothes
Ich möchte ein paar Sachen bügeln
*ikh **mur'kh**·tè ine pahr za·khèn **boo**·gèln*

57 I want some clothes ironed
Könnte ich einige Sachen gebügelt haben?
***kur'n**·tè ikh ine·i·gè za·khèn gè·**boo**·gèlt **hah**·bèn*

58 Thank you, we enjoyed our stay very much
Vielen Dank, es hat uns gut gefallen
***fee**·lèn dank ess hat oons goot gè·**fa**·lèn*

Rented houses

59 We have arranged to rent a house through your agency
Wir hatten durch Ihre Agentur ein Haus gemietet
*veer **ha**·tèn doorkh ee·rè a·gen·**toor** ine hows gè·**mee**·tèt*

60 Here is our reservation
Hier ist unsere Buchung
*heer ist **oon**·zè·rè **boo**·khoong*

61 We need two sets of keys
Wir brauchen zwei Schlüsselsätze
*veer **brow**·khèn tsvye **shloo**·sèl·zet·sè*

62 Will you show us around?
Würden Sie uns herumführen?
***voor**·dèn zee oons he·**room**·foo·rèn*

63 Which is the key for this door?
Welcher Schlüssel ist für diese Tür?
*vel·khèr **shloo**·sèl ist foor dee·zè toor*

64 Is the cost of electricity included in the rental?
Ist der Stromverbrauch im Mietpreis enthalten?
*ist der **shtrōm**·fer·browkh im **meet**·price ent·**hal**·tèn*

65 Where is the main switch for the electricity?
Wo ist der Hauptschalter?
*vō ist der **howpt**·shal·tèr*

66 Where is the main valve for shutting off the water?
Wo ist der Haupthahn für die Wasserversorgung?
*vō ist der **howpt**·hahn foor dee va·sèr·fer·**zor**·goong*

67 Where is the water heater?
Wo ist der Wasserboiler?
vô ist der va·sèr·boy·lèr

68 Please show me how this works
Bitte zeigen Sie mir, wie das funktioniert
***bi**·tè tsye·gèn zee meer vee dass foonk·tsee·ō·neert*

69 How does the heat work?
Wie funktioniert die Heizung?
*vee foonk·tsee·ō·**neert** dee **hye**·tsoong*

70 When does the maid come?
Wann kommt die Putzfrau?
*van komt dee **poots**·frow*

71 Is there any spare bedding?
Gibt es noch Extra-Bettzeug?
*gipt ess nokh **ek**·stra·**bet**·tsoyk*

72 Where can I contact you if there are any problems?
Wo kann ich mich an Sie wenden, wenn es Probleme gibt?
*vô kan ikh mikh an zee ven·dèn ven ess prô·**blay**·mè gipt*

73 The stove does not work
Der Herd funktioniert nicht
*der hert foonk·tsee·ō·**neert** nikht*

74 Where are the trashcans?
Wo sind die Mülltonnen?
*vô zint dee **mōōl**·to·nèn*

75 Is there a spare gas cylinder?
Gibt es einen Reservezylinder?
*gipt ess **ine**·èn ray·**zer**·vè·tsōō·**lin**·dèr*

76 Where can we get logs for the fire?
Wo können wir Brennholz bekommen?
*vō **kur'**·nèn veer **bren**·holts bè·**ko**·mèn*

77 I can't open the windows
Ich bekomme die Fenster nicht auf
*ikh bè·**ko**·mè dee **fen**·stèr nikht owf*

78 We can't get any water
Es kommt kein Wasser
*ess komt kine **va**·sèr*

79 The toilet won't flush
Die Spülung in der Toilette geht nicht
*dee **shpōō**·loong in der tō·a·**le**·tè gayt nikht*

80 The pipe is blocked
Das Abflußrohr ist verstopft
*dass **ap**·floos·rōr ist fer·**shtopft***

81 A fuse has blown
Eine Sicherung ist durchgebrannt
*ine·è **zi**·khè·roong ist **doorkh**·gè·brant*

82 There is a gas leak
Die Gasleitung ist undicht
*dee **gahs**·lye·toong ist **oon**·dikht*

83 I need somebody to fix this
Ich brauche jemanden, der das reparieren kann
*ikh **brow**·khè **yay**·man·dèn der dass ray·pa·**ree**·rèn kan*

Camping

Camping in German-speaking countries is a very sophisticated activity, with campers bringing lots of home comforts with them. There are many official camping sites, many with excellent facilities. If you can't find a site, the local tourist office may be able to help. Never camp without permission in fields or on public land, as penalties are severe.

84 Is there anywhere for us to camp near here?
Können wir irgendwo hier in der Nähe zelten?
***kur'**·nèn veer **ir**·gènt·vō heer in der **nay**·è **tsel**·tèn*

85 Have you got a site for our tent?
Haben Sie einen Platz für unser Zelt?
***hah**·bèn zee **ine**·èn plats fōōr **oon**-zèr tselt*

86 Do you mind if we camp on your land?
Haben Sie etwas dagegen, wenn wir auf Ihrem Grundstück zelten?
***hah**·bèn zee et·vass da·**gay**·gèn ven veer owf **ee**·rèm **groont**·shtōōk **tsel**·tèn*

87 This site is very muddy
Diese Stelle ist sehr matschig
***dee**·zè **shte**·lè ist zehr **mat**·shikh*

88 Could we have a more sheltered site?
Könnten wir eine geschütztere Stelle haben?
***kur'n**·tèn veer **ine**·è gè·**shōōt**·stè·rè **shte**·lè **hah**·bèn*

89 May we put our trailer here?
Können wir unseren Wohnwagen hier hinstellen?
***kur'**·nèn veer **oon**·zè·rèn **vōn**·vah·gèn heer **hin**·shte·lèn*

90 Is there a shop on the site?
Gibt es einen Laden auf dem Campingplatz?
*gipt ess **ine**·èn **lah**·dèn owf daym **kem**·ping·plats*

91 Can I have a shower?
Kann ich duschen?
*kan ikh **doo**·shèn*

92 Where is the drinking water?
Wo gibt es Trinkwasser?
*vō gipt ess **trink**·va·sèr*

93 Where are the toilets and washroom?
Wo sind die Toiletten und der Waschraum?
*vō zint dee tō·a·**le**·tèn oont der **vash**·rowm*

94 Where can we buy ice?
Wo können wir Eis bekommen?
*vō **kur'**·nèn veer ice bè·**ko**·mèn*

95 Where can we wash our dishes/our clothes?
Wo können wir Geschirr spülen/Wäsche waschen?
*vō **kur'**·nèn veer gè·**shir** **spōō**·lèn/**ve**·shè **va**·shèn*

96 Is there another camp site near
here?
Gibt es hier in der Nähe noch
einen anderen
Campingplatz?
*gipt ess heer in der nay·è nokh
ine·èn an·dè·rèn
kem·ping·plats*

97 Are there any washing
machines?
Gibt es Waschmaschinen?
gipt ess vash·ma·shee·nèn

98 We need to buy a new gas
cylinder
Wir brauchen einen neuen
Zylinder Campinggas
*veer brow·khèn ine·èn noy·èn
tsōō·lin·dèr kem·ping·gahs*

99 I would like to move my tent
Ich hätte gern einen anderen
Standplatz
*ikh he·tè gern ine·èn an·dè·rèn
shtant·plats*

Eating out (E)

The German-speaking lands are not as famous for their cuisine as, for
example, France, but food plays an important part in life there, as you
can tell from the abundant portions of everything and the frequency of
meals. And normally quality is commensurate with quantity. You may
wish to treat yourself to some top restaurants, but remember that the
more modest ones are often equally memorable – order a simple meal in
a small country inn, and it will be served with style and care. The
set-price menu (*das Menu* or *das Tagesmenu*) is often good value. The
menu guide will help you decide what to eat. Don't miss the opportunity
to sample local specialties. If you have your family with you, see
Children, p.59.

General

1 Do you know a good restaurant?
Können Sie ein gutes Restaurant empfehlen?
kur'·nèn zee ine goo·tès res·tō·rong emp·fay·lèn

2 Do you know a restaurant specializing in Swiss dishes?
Können Sie ein Restaurant mit Schweizer Spezialitäten empfehlen?
*kur'·nèn zee ine res·tō·rong mit shvye·tsèr
shpe·tsee·a·lee·te·tèn emp·fay·lèn*

3 I would like to reserve a table for two people
Ich möchte einen Tisch für zwei Personen bestellen
ikh mur'kh·tè ine·èn tish fōōr tsvye per·zō·nèn bè·shte·lèn

4 I have reserved a table in the name of . . .
Ich hatte einen Tisch auf den Namen . . . gebucht
ikh ha·tè ine·èn tish owf dayn nah·mèn . . . gè·bookht

5 Do you have a quiet table — by the window/on the terrace?
Haben Sie einen ruhigen
Tisch — am Fenster/auf der Terrasse?
*hah·bèn zee ine·èn roo·ikh·èn
tish — am fen·stèr/owf der te·ra·sè*

6 Is it possible to have a private room?
Können wir ein Zimmer für uns haben?
kur'·nèn veer ine tsi·mèr fōōr oons hah·bèn

7 It is for a business lunch/dinner
Es ist für ein Arbeitsessen
ess ist fōōr ine ar·bites·e·sèn

8 Herr Bauer is expecting me
Herr Bauer erwartet mich
her bow·èr er·var·tèt mikh

9 The menu, please
Die Speisekarte, bitte
dee shpye·zè·kar·tè bi·tè

Menu guide

The area covered by this book encompasses a wide range of food and many regional variations. Here are some of the better-known dishes of Germany, Austria and Switzerland.

Hors d'oeuvres, vegetables and main dishes

Aalsuppe Eel soup

Aal Grün mit Dillsauce Fresh eel with dill sauce

Aufgebackene Spätzli Fried dumplings served with an egg sauce (Switzerland)

Ballen Dish baked with herbs (Switzerland)

Bauernfrühstück Scrambled eggs, bacon, cooked diced potatoes, onions, tomatoes

Bauernschmaus Assortment of roast and smoked pork; sausages, sauerkraut and dumplings (Austria)

Bayerisches Kraut Shredded cabbage cooked with sliced apples, wine and sugar

Biersuppe Beer soup flavored with cinnamon and lemon

Bismarckheringe Herring fillets marinated in a vinegary sauce

Bohnensalat Bean salad

Bohnensuppe Thick brown bean soup with small pieces of smoked bacon (esp. Austria)

Bouillon/Fleischbrühe Clear soup/broth

Brathähnchen Roast chicken

Bratheringe Fresh fried herring marinated in a vinegar, herb and onion dressing

Bratkartoffeln Fried potatoes

Bündnerfleisch Raw beef, smoked and dried, served thinly sliced (Switzerland)

Dampfnudel Yeast dumpling

Deutsche Beefsteaks/ Bouletten/Frikadellen Fried, flat meat balls

Eierkuchen Pancakes

Eisbein Pickled knuckle of pork

Emmentaler Schnitzel Fried veal cutlets with Emmentaler cheese slices fried on each side of the meat (Switzerland)

Erbsenpüree Dried green pea purée

Erdäpfelknödel Potato and semolina dumplings (Austria)

Erdäpfelnudeln Fried, boiled potato balls tossed in fried breadcrumbs (Austria)

Falscher Hase Meat loaf

Fischauflauf Fish pudding (Austria)

Fischsuppe Fish soup

Forelle blau Trout

Forelle Steiermark Small filleted trout, larded with bacon strips, served with a white sauce (Austria)

Gebackenes Goldbarschfilet Fried golden perch fillet in egg and breadcrumbs

Gebratene Ente Roast duck

Gefüllte Kalbsbrust Roast stuffed breast of veal

Gegrillter Lachs Grilled salmon

Gemischter Salat Mixed salad

Gemüseplatte Assorted vegetables

Geräucherter Aal Smoked eel

Geschnetzeltes Kalbfleisch Thinly sliced veal with a thick cream sauce (Switzerland)

Gitziprägel Baked rabbit in batter (Switzerland)

Grießklößchen Semolina dumplings

Grießnockerlnsuppe Beef broth with chives, served with semolina dumplings (Austria)

Grünkernsuppe Green corn and cream soup

Grüner Salat Lettuce with a dressing of vinegar and oil

Güggeli/Mistchratzerli Roast chicken with onions and mushrooms in a white wine sauce (Switzerland)

Gulasch Highly seasoned stew, flavored with paprika

Gurkensalat Cucumber salad

Hühnerfrikassée Chicken fricassée

Hasenpfeffer Jugged hare

Huhn mit Käsesauce Boiled chicken with cheese sauce (Switzerland)

Jägergulasch Venison stew with bacon, ham, juniper berries and sour cream, flavored with paprika (Austria)

Jura Omelette Emmentaler cheese, bacon, tomato, onion and potato omelette (Switzerland)

Kaiserfleisch Boiled, smoked pork (Austria)

Kalbsbraten Roast veal

Kalbsnierenbraten Roast loin of veal including the kidneys

Karpfen in Bier Carp poached in beer, red wine and onion, flavored with bay leaf, lemon peel and peppercorns (Austria)

Kartoffelklöße Potato dumplings

Kartoffelpfluten Potato dumplings served with fried onion rings (Switzerland)

Kartoffelpitte Baked potatoes, dried pears, milk and diced bacon (Switzerland)

Käsefondue Usually made with a mixture of Gruyère and Emmentaler cheese, melted with white wine and Kirsch. Bits of bread are dipped into the hot mixture and eaten straight from the fondue dish (Switzerland)

Käsesalat Cheese salad (Switzerland)

Käsesuppe Cheese soup (Switzerland)

Kasseler Rippenspeer Pickled, smoked saddle of pork

Kloß Dumpling

Knödel Dumpling (Austria)

Kohlroulade Cabbage stuffed with a ground meat mixture and baked in the oven (Austria)

Königsberger Kloß Meatballs, served in a thick white sauce with capers in it

Krautsalat Cabbage salad flavored with caraway seeds

Kümmelbraten Caraway-flavored roast beef (Austria)

Labskaus Traditional sailors' dish consisting of cured pork, herring and potatoes, and highly flavored. Eaten with fried eggs, *Matjesfilets*, and pickled vegetables

Leberkäs Pork liver meat loaf

Leberknödel Liver dumplings

Leberknödelsuppe Beef soup with small liver dumplings (Austria)

Leipziger Allerlei A mixture of green peas, carrots, cauliflower and cabbage

Maluns Sliced and grated potato mixture fried in lard (Switzerland)

Markklößchen Small beef-marrow dumplings

Matjesfilets Soused herring fillets in a thick sauce

Maultasche Small ravioli-like pasta bags filled with a special pork, veal and spinach mixture

Nockerl Small dumplings (Austria)

Nudeln Noodles

Omelette mit Pilzen Mushroom omelette

Ochsenschwanzsuppe Oxtail soup

Paprikahähnchen Chicken stewed with onions and flavored with paprika

Pfannkuchen Pancakes

Pommes frites French fries

Räucherlachs Smoked salmon

Rehrücken Roast saddle of venison

Rinderbraten Roast beef

Rippchen mit Sauerkraut Pickled ribs of pork with sauerkraut

Rollmops Herring fillets marinated in a vinegary liquid and filled with small pieces of onion, gherkins and white peppercorns

Rösti Fried, diced potatoes mixed with small fried bacon cubes (Switzerland)

Rührei Scrambled egg

Salatplatte Selection of salads

Sauerbraten Marinated roast beef

Sauerkraut Shredded, white, salted and fermented cabbage

Schlachtplatte A mixture of cold sausages and meats

Schweinebraten Roast pork

Schweinekotelett Pork chop dipped in egg and breadcrumbs and fried

Semmelknödel Whole roll dumpling (Austria)

Spätzle Home-made noodles served with breadcrumbs and browned butter

Spiegelei Fried egg

Strammer Max Fried egg with raw ham and rye bread

Tiroler Eierspeise Hard-boiled eggs, potatoes, cream, anchovies, topped with breadcrumbs and baked in the oven (Austria)

Topfenknödel Curd cheese dumplings sprinkled with fried breadcrumbs (Austria)

Urner Kraut mit Reis Cooked cabbage strips mixed with cheese and cooked rice, with fried onion

Weckklöße Bread dumplings

Wiener Schnitzel Veal cutlet fried in breadcrumbs

Wiener Fischfilets Fish fillets baked with sour cream, gherkins and capers

Wildgulasch Game stew
Wildbraten Roast venison
Wildsuppe Game soup
Zwiebelsuppe Onion soup

Desserts

Apfelkompott Stewed apple

Apfelrösti Cooked apple slices fried in butter together with bread slices (Switzerland)

Auflauf Soufflé

Eis(creme) Ice cream

Eisbecher Rather like an ice cream soda pop

Kaiserschmarren Chopped-up pancake with raisins, sugar and cinnamon

Palatschinken Pancakes filled with curd cheese mixture, or with apricot jam

Rote Grütze Raspberry, red currant and wine jelly served with fresh cream

Salzburger Nockerl Foamy omelette or soufflé with a very light center and a puffed and golden outside (Austria)

Zwetschkenknödel Boiled plum dumplings fried in breadcrumbs, sprinkled with sugar, and served hot (Austria)

Cheeses

Edamer A German version of the Dutch cheese — mild flavor

Emmentaler Hard cheese produced from whole milk, with fairly large holes (Switzerland)

Limburger Strong cheese flavored with herbs

Liptauer Cream cheese with paprika and herbs (Austria)

Münster Strong cheese with caraway seeds

Quark Curd cheese

Raclette Fried cheese scraped onto a warm plate after having been melted (Switzerland)

Schweizer Käse see Emmentaler

Tilsiter Savory, straw-colored cheese; slightly sour and sharpish taste with a smooth consistency

Topfen Curd cheese (Austria)

Wines

When choosing German wines it helps to know some of the terms used to describe them. The German, Austrian and Swiss wine quality system is based on the amount of natural sugar in the wine. The more sugar, the better the wine. Thus expensive, prestigious wines tend to be sweet. These wines are drunk in Germany on their own. With food, the locals drink ordinary wine (*Tafelwein*) or beer. *Deutscher Tafelwein* is all German, while simple *Tafelwein* can be an international blend. Higher quality wines will be described as *Qualitätswein* or, best of all, *Qualitätswein mit Prädikat*. The words *Kabinett, Spätlese, Auslese* and *Beerenauslese* indicate, in ascending order, better (and usually sweeter) wines. *Trockenbeerenauslese*, the highest level of all, is wine made from grapes that have been left to ripen well after the rest of the harvest so as to give rich, sweet dessert wines. An *Eiswein* is one of the rarest wines of all; the grapes are not gathered until midwinter and give a wine with a honey-sweet, liqueur-like consistency. German wines are usually named after the place where the grapes are grown. Thus a Niersteiner comes from the Nierstein district.

Baden Major medium-quality, good-value wine district

Bernkastel A wine district in the Mosel region

Burgenland A part of Austria that produces good sweet whites and reliable reds

Franken A dry white wine area

Gewürztraminer A full-bodied white wine

Heuriger (Austria) New wine, and the tavern where it is sold and drunk

Johannisberg A wine district in the Rheingau area

Kalterer See A soft red wine from the southern Tyrol in Italy

Kreuznach A wine district in the Nahe region

Liebfraumilch A blended semi-sweet Rhein wine

Müller-Thurgau Grape for white wine

Neuer Wein/Heuriger (Austria) The year's new wine, drunk until the next harvest

Nierstein A Rheinhessen wine district of mixed quality

Oppenheim Above-average Rheinhessen wine district

Riesling Grape that makes the best German white wine

Rüdesheim One of the best Rheingau wine villages

Ruländer A heavy-bodied white wine

Schaumwein Sparkling wine

Sekt Same as Schaumwein but of higher quality

Spätburgunder A full-bodied red wine

Sylvaner Grape for white wine

Weißherbst/Schwarzriesling A rosé

Ordering wine

10 May we see the wine list, please?
Die Weinkarte, bitte
*dee **vine**·kar·tè **bi**·tè*

11 Can you recommend a good local wine?
Können Sie mir einen guten Wein aus dieser Gegend empfehlen?
*kur·nèn zee meer **ine**·èn goo·tèn vine ows dee·zèr gay·gènt emp·**fay**·lèn*

12 Was this a good year?
War das ein gutes Weinjahr?
*vahr dass ine **goo**·tès **vine**·yahr*

13 A bottle/carafe of house wine
Eine Flasche/Karaffe Hauswein
*ine·è **fla**·shè/ka·**ra**·fè hows·vine*

14 Another bottle/half bottle, please
Noch eine Flasche/halbe Flasche, bitte
*nokh ine·è **fla**·shè/hal·bè **fla**·shè **bi**·tè*

15 Would you bring another glass, please?
Würden Sie bitte noch ein Glas bringen?
*vöör·dèn zee **bi**·tè nokh ine glahs **bring**·èn*

16 What liqueurs do you have?
Welche Liköre haben Sie?
*vel·khè lee·**kur'**·rè **hah**·bèn zee*

Ordering the meal and paying

17 Do you have a specialty of the day?
Gibt es ein Tagesmenü?
*gipt ess ine **tah**·gès·mè·nōō*

18 I will take today's specialty — at ... Marks
Ich nehme das Tagesmenü — zu ... Mark
*ikh **nay**·mè dass **tah**·gès·mè·nōō — tsoo... mark*

19 What would you recommend?
Was empfehlen Sie?
*vass emp·**fay**·lèn zee*

20 How is this dish cooked?
Wie wird dieses Gericht zubereitet?
*vee virt dee·zès gè·**rikht** tsoo·bè·rye·tèt*

22 I'll take that
Ich nehme das
*ikh **nay**·mè dass*
23 We will begin with onion soup
Als Vorspeise hätten wir gern Zwiebelsuppe
*als **för**·shpye·zè **he**·tèn veer gern **tsvee**·bèl·zoo·pè*
24 I will have — venison with noodles
Ich hätte gern — Wild mit Nudeln
*ikh **he**·tè gern — vilt mit **noo**·dèln*
25 I like it — very rare
Ich hätte es gern — blutig
*ikh **he**·tè ess gern — **bloo**·tikh*
— rare
— rot
— *röt*
— medium rare
— halbgebraten
— **halp**·gè·brah·tèn
— well done
— durch(gebraten)
— **doorkh**(·gè·brah·tèn)
26 Are vegetables included?
Ist das Gemüse dabei?
*ist dass gè·**möö**·zè da·bye*
27 Is this cheese very strong?
Ist dieser Käse sehr scharf?
*ist **dee**·zèr **ke**·zè zehr sharf*
28 This is not what I ordered
Das habe ich nicht bestellt
*dass **hah**·bè ikh nikht bè·**shtelt**
29 Does the fish (beef etc) come with anything else?
Wird der Fisch (das Rindfleisch etc) mit Beilagen serviert?
*virt der fish (dass **rint**·flyesh etc) mit **bye**·lah·gèn zer·**veert**
30 That is for — me
Das ist für — mich
*dass ist **föör** — mikh*
— him/her
— ihn/sie
— *een/zee*
31 Some more bread/water, please
Könnten wir noch Brot/mehr Wasser haben?
***kur'n**·tèn veer nokh bröt/mehr va·sèr **hah**·bèn*
32 Could I have some butter?
Kann ich bitte Butter haben?
*kan ikh bi·tè **boo**·tèr **hah**·bèn*
33 What is this called?
Wie heißt das?
vee hyest dass
34 This is very salty
Das ist sehr salzig
*dass ist zehr **zal**·tsikh*
35 I wanted cheese
Ich hatte Käse bestellt
*ikh **ha**·tè **ke**·zè bè·**shtelt**
36 Have you forgotten the soup?
Haben Sie die Suppe vergessen?
***hah**·bèn zee dee **zoo**·pè fer·**ge**·sèn*
37 This is cold
Das ist kalt
dass ist kalt
38 This is very good
Es schmeckt sehr gut
ess shmekt zehr goot
39 I'll have a dessert
Ich hätte gern ein Dessert
*ikh **he**·tè gern ine de·**ser***
40 What do you have for dessert?
Welche Nachspeisen haben Sie?
***vel**·khè **nahkh**·shpye·zèn **hah**·bèn zee*

41 What cheeses do you have?
Welche Käse sind auf der Käseplatte?
vel·khè ke·zè zint owf der ke·zè·pla·tè

42 Could I have a salad instead of the cheese course?
Könnte ich statt der Käseplatte einen Salat haben?
kur'n·tè ikh shtat der ke·zè·pla·tè ine·èn za·laht hah·bèn

43   Nothing else, thank you — just coffee
        Danke, sonst nichts — außer Kaffee, bitte
        dang·kè zonst nikhts — ow·sèr ka·fay bi·tè

44 Waiter, could we have the bill, please?
Herr Ober, die Rechnung, bitte
her ō·bèr dee rekh·noong bi·tè

45 We are in a hurry
Wir haben es eilig
veer hah·bèn ess ile·ikh

46 Is the tip included?
Ist Bedienung inbegriffen?
ist bè·dee·noong in·bè·gri·fèn

47 There seems to be a mistake here
Ich glaube, Sie haben sich vertan
ikh glow·bè zee hah·bèn zikh fer·tahn

48 What is this item?
Was ist dieser Posten?
vass ist dee·zèr pos·tèn

49 The meal was excellent
Das Essen war ausgezeichnet
dass e·sèn vahr ows·gè·tsyekh·nèt

Phrases you will hear

50 Für zwei Personen?
fōōr tsvye per·zō·nèn
A table for two?

51 Haben Sie schon bestellt?
hah·bèn zee shōn bè·shtelt
Did you make a reservation?

52 Haben Sie gewählt?
hah·bèn zee gè·vaylt
Are you ready to order?

53 Was hätten Sie gern dazu?
vass he·tèn zee gern da·tsoo
What would you like with it?

54 Und anschließend?
oont an·shlee·sènt
And to follow?

55 Was würden Sie gern trinken?
vass vōōr·dèn zee gern tring·kèn
What would you like to drink?

56 Welche Nachspeise hätten Sie gern?
vel·khè nahkh·shpye·zè he·tèn zee gern
What would you like for dessert?

Cafés and inns

Germans tend not to have separate places for eating and drinking: at a *Wirtshaus* (inn) you can usually have a good meal or a snack, but you can also just sit and have a drink at any time of day. You will be served at your table (stand-up bars are rare) and normally pay when you leave rather than when your order is brought. The same applies, broadly, to Austria and Switzerland.

In all three countries you will also find many types of café, ranging from the kind that sells only tea, coffee and cakes (usually called a *Konditorei*), to those that border on being full-scale restaurants. In most, however, you can get alcohol and at least a snack. The Austrian café (known as a *Kaffeehaus*) is more of an institution than the German variety, and the great cafés of Vienna are legendary.

When you order a drink all you need to do is say "ein/eine . . ., bitte" (a . . ., please). The correct way to address a waiter is "Herr Ober" (*her ō·bèr*), and a waitress is addressed as "Fräulein" (*froy·line*). Here are some of the standard café or *Wirtshaus* orders.

Alcohol

Alcohol is very often ordered in fractions of a liter. Drinks that you might wish to ask for include the following.

57 A glass (⅛ liter) of red wine/white wine
   Ein Glas Rotwein/Weißwein
   ine glahs röt·vine/vice·vine
58 A small carafe (¼ liter) of red wine
   Ein viertel Rotwein
   ine fir·tèl röt·vine
59   A glass (¼ or ½ liter) of
                                    beer — from the barrel
   Ein glas (*or* ein kleines)
                                    Bier — vom Faß
   ine glahs (or ine kline·ès)
                                    beer — fom fass
60 A half-liter/liter (of beer)
   Eine Halbe/ein Liter
   ine·è hal·bè/ine lee·tèr
61 A whiskey/a brandy
   Einen Whisky/einen Cognac
   ine·èn vis·kee/ine·èn kon·yak

   You might also like to try one of the many varieties of Schnaps,
      which include:
   Steinhäger (**shtine**·hay·gèr: juniper brandy)
   Himbeergeist (**him**·bay·èr·gyest: raspberry brandy)
   Kirschwasser (**kirsh**·vas·èr: Kirsch or cherry brandy)
   Kümmel (**kōō**·mèl: caraway liqueur), and
   Doornkaat (**dörn**·kaht: strong juniper gin).

Coffee, tea and chocolate

Coffee is served by the cup or by the pot, and cream (hardly ever
ordinary milk) is usually brought in a separate container. Tea is normally
served with lemon, so if you want milk you have to ask for it.

62 A cup/pot of coffee
   Eine Tasse/Portion Kaffee
   ine·è ta·sè/por·tsee·ōn ka·fay
63 Tea with lemon/milk
   Tee mit Zitrone/Milch
   tay mit tsi·trō·nè/milkh

64 Hot chocolate
   Heiße Schokolade
   hye·sè sho·kō·lah·dè

Soft drinks

Among the most popular of these are apple juice (Apfelsaft **ap**·fèl·zaft)
and grape juice (Traubensaft **trow**·bèn·zaft). Other soft drinks include:

65 Orange juice
   Orangensaft
   o·ran·zhèn·zaft
66 Grapefruit juice
   Grapefruitsaft
   grayp·froot·zaft
67 Pineapple juice
   Ananas-Saft
   a·na·nas·zaft
68 Lemon soda or other
      carbonated fruit drink
   Limonade
   lee·mō·nah·dè

69 Mineral water (carbonated)
   Mineralwasser, weißer Sprudel
   mee·nay·rahl·va·sèr, vice·èr
      shproo·dèl
70 Mineral water (still)
   Mineralwasser ohne
      Kohlensäure
   mee·nay·rahl·va·sèr ō·nè
      kō·lèn·zoy·rè
71 A Coke/Pepsi
   Cola/Pepsi Cola
   kō·la/pep·si kō·la

Cakes and snacks

Here are some of the most popular cakes and savory snacks. As many
have no counterparts in English-speaking countries, the German names
are given first.

72 Belegtes Brot
   bè·layk·tès bröt
   Open sandwich

73 Berliner Pfannkuchen
   ber·lee·nèr pfan·koo·khèn
   Doughnuts with jam

74 Brot und Würstchen
   brōt oont vōorst·khèn
   Bread roll with Frankfurter or
   Vienna sausage

75 Gugelhupf
   goo·gèl·hoopf
   Ring-shaped yeast cake with
   fruit

76 Gulaschsuppe
   goo·lash·zoo·pè
   Goulash soup

77 Käsekuchen
   ke·zè·koo·khèn
   Cheesecake

78 Königinpastete
   kur'·ni·gin·pas·tay·tè
   Chicken vol-au-vent

79 Leberkäse
   lay·bèr·ke·zè
   Meat loaf made with liver

80 Linzertorte
   lin·tsèr·tor·tè
   Almond-flavored pastry with
   jam on top

81 Mohnkuchen
   mōn·koo·khèn
   Poppy seed cake

82 Ochsenschwanzsuppe
   ok·sèn·shvants·zoo·pè
   Oxtail soup

83 Sachertorte
   za·khèr·tor·tè
   Chocolate sponge cake with
   chocolate icing and apricot
   filling

84 Schinkenkäsetoast
   shing·kèn·ke·zè·tōst
   Ham and cheese toasted
   sandwich

85 Schwarzwälder Kirschtorte
   shvarts·vel·dèr kirsh·tor·tè
   Black Forest cherry torte

Leisure (L)

Sightseeing

When you arrive in a town and require some general information about it
you should inquire at the local Tourist Information Office (*Verkehrsamt:*
fer·kayrs·amt), Verkehrsbüro (*fer·kayrs·bōō·rō*) or Verkehrsverband
(*fer·kayrs·fer·bant*). Here are some of the phrases that you might wish to use
there as well as in the street and at museums, churches and other sights.

1 Excuse me, can you tell me, please...?
  Entschuldigen Sie, können Sie mir bitte sagen...?
  ent·shool·di·gèn zee kur'·nèn zee meer bi·tè zah·gèn

2 What are the most important things to see here?
  Was sind die wichtigsten Sehenswürdigkeiten?
  vass zint dee vikh·tikh·stèn zay·èns·vōōr·dikh·kite·èn

3 Where is — the main square?
  Wo ist — der Marktplatz?
  *vō ist — der **markt**·plats*

4 Do you have — a guidebook to the town/area
                (in English)?
  Haben Sie — einen Stadtführer/einen Führer für
              diese Gegend (in englischer
              Sprache)?
  *hah·bèn zee — **ine**·èn shtat·fōō·rèr/ine·èn **fōō**·rèr
               fōōr dee·zè gay·gènt (in
               eng·li·shèr shpra·khè)*
  — a map of the town?
  — einen Stadtplan?
  — *ine·èn shtat·plan*
  — an audio-guide to the museum/
    church?
  — einen Tonbandbegleiter für das
    Museum/für die Kirche?
  — *ine·èn tōn·bant·bè·**glye**·tèr fōōr
    dass moo·**zay**·oom/fōōr dee
    kir·khè*

5 Are there any — local festivals?
  Gibt es irgendwelche — Volksfeste?
  *gipt ess ir·gènt·vel·khè — **folks**·fes·tè*

6 Is there — a guided tour of the town/castle?
  Gibt es — eine Führung durch die Stadt/das
            Schloß?
  *gipt ess — **ine**·è fōō·roong doorkh dee
            shtat/dass shloss*

Is there — a one-day excursion to Cologne?
Gibt es — eine Tagestour nach Köln?
gipt ess — ine·è tah·gès·toor nahkh kur'ln

7 When does the tour begin?
Wann fängt die Führung an?
van fengt dee foō·roong an

8 How long does it last?
Wie lange dauert es?
vee lang·è dow·èrt ess

9 Where is the point of departure?
Von wo geht die Tour?
fon vō gayt dee toor

10 Is there an English-speaking guide?
Ist hier ein Fremdenführer, der englisch spricht?
ist heer ine frem·dèn·foō·rèr der eng·lish shprikht

11 What is this building?
Was für ein Gebäude ist das?
vass foōr ine gè·boy·dè ist dass

12 Can we go in?
Können wir eintreten?
kur'·nèn veer ine·tray·tèn

13 What time does the museum/castle open?
Wann öffnet das Museum/das Schloß?
van ur'f·nèt dass moo·zay·oom/dass shloss

14 What is the admission charge?
Wieviel kostet der Eintritt?
vee·feel kos·tèt der ine·trit

15 Can one go to the top?
Kann man bis nach oben gehen?
kan man biss nahkh ō·bèn gay·èn

16 Is one allowed to take photos with a flash/tripod?
Darf man mit Blitzlicht/Stativ fotografieren?
darf man mit blits·likht/shta·teef fō·tō·gra·fee·rèn

17 Where can one buy postcards/slides?
Wo kann man Postkarten/Farbdias kaufen?
vō kan man post·kar·tèn/farp·dee·as kow·fèn

18 Where can one buy reproductions?
Wo kann man Reproduktionen kaufen?
vō kan man ray·pro·dook·tsee·ō·nèn kow·fèn

Beach, country and sports

19 Is it safe to swim here?
Kann man hier gefahrlos baden?
kan man heer gè·fahr·lōs bah·dèn

20 Is the water warm/cold?
Ist das Wasser warm/kalt?
ist dass va·sèr varm/kalt

21 Can you recommend a quiet beach?
Können Sie mir einen ruhigen Strand empfehlen?
kur'·nèn zee meer ine·èn roo·i·gèn shtrant emp·fay·lèn

22 Where can we change?
Wo können wir uns umziehen?
vō kur'·nèn veer oons oom·tsee·èn

23 Can I rent a sunshade/a deck chair?
Kann ich einen Sonnenschirm/einen Liegestuhl mieten?
kan ikh ine·èn zo·nèn·shirm/ine·èn lee·gè·shtool mee·tèn

24 Can I rent a sailboat?
Kann ich ein Segelboot mieten?
kan ikh ine zay·gèl·bōt mee·tèn

25 Where can I rent a rowboat/a motorboat?
Wo kann ich ein Ruderboot/ein Motorboot mieten?
vō kan ikh ine roo·dèr·bōt/ine mō·tor·bōt mee·tèn

26 Is it possible to go sailing?
Kann man hier segeln?
kan man heer zay·gèln

27 Where can one go water-skiing?
Wo kann man Wasserski fahren?
vō kan man va·sèr·shee fah·rèn

28 What sports can one take part in here?
Welche Sportarten kann man hier betreiben?
vel·khè **shport**·*ar·tèn kan man heer bè·***trye·bèn**

29 Is there a swimming pool?
Gibt es hier ein Freibad?
gipt ess heer ine **frye·baht**

30 Where can I play golf/tennis?
Wo kann ich Golf/Tennis spielen?
vô kan ikh golf/te·nis **shpee·lèn**

31 Is it possible to go riding?
Kann man hier reiten?
kan man heer **rye·tèn**

32 Is it possible to go gliding/hang gliding?
Gibt es hier Möglichkeiten zum Segelfliegen/zum Drachenfliegen?
gipt ess heer **mur'**·*glikh·kite·èn tsoom* **zay**·*gèl·flee·gèn/tsoom*
dra·*khèn·flee·gèn*

33 Can I go fishing?
Kann ich hier angeln gehen?
kan ikh heer **ang**·*èln gay·èn*

34 Can I hire the equipment?
Kann ich die Ausrüstung leihen?
kan ikh dee **ows·rōōs**·*toong lye·èn*

35 Do you know of any interesting walks?
Kennen Sie irgendwelche interessanten Spaziergänge?
ke·*nèn zee* **ir**·*gènt·vel·khè in·tè·re·***san**·*tèn shpa·***tseer**·*geng·è*

36 Do you have a footpath map of the area?
Haben Sie eine Wanderkarte von dieser Gegend?
hah·*bèn zee ine·è* **van·dèr**·*kar·tè fon dee·zèr gay·gènt*

37 What are the conditions like for sailing/skiing?
Wie sind die Bedingungen zum Segeln/zum Skilaufen?
*vee zint dee bè·***ding**·*oong·èn tsoom* **zay**·*gèln/tsoom* **shee·low**·*fèn*

38 Are there any picnic areas near here?
Gibt es in der Gegend Picknickplätze?
gipt ess in der **gay·gènt** *pik·nik·plet·sè*

39 Is there any interesting wildlife in this area?
Gibt es in dieser Gegend interessante Fauna und Flora?
gipt ess in **dee·zèr** *gay·gènt in·tè·re·***san**·*tè fow·na oont* **flô·***ra

40 What is the name of that bird/flower?
Wie heißt dieser Vogel/diese Pflanze?
vee hyest **dee·zèr** **fô**·*gèl/dee·zè pflant·sè*

Entertainment and night life

41 How can I find out about local entertainment?
Wo kann ich Informationen zum lokalen Unterhaltungsprogramm
finden?
*vô kan ikh in·for·ma·tsee·***ō**·*nèn tsoom lô·***kah**·*lèn*
oon·*tèr·hal·toongs·prô·***gram** *fin·dèn*

42	Where can I —	hear jazz/folk music?
	Wo kann ich —	Jazz/Folkmusik hören?
	vô kan ikh —	*jaz/***folk**·*moo·zeek* **hur'**·*rèn*
		— dance?
		— tanzen?
		— **tant**·*sèn*
		— see a floor show?
		— ein Kabarett sehen?
		— *ine ka·ba·***ret** *zay·èn*
43	Are there any —	films in English?
	Gibt es hier —	englische Filme?
	gipt ess heer —	**eng**·*li·shè* **fil**·*mè*
		— good night clubs/discos?
		— gute Nachtklubs/Diskos?
		— **goo**·*tè* **nakht**·*kloobs/***dis**·*kōz*
		— good concerts?
		— gute Konzerte?
		— **goo**·*tè kon·***tser**·*tè*
44	Have you any seats —	for Wednesday evening?
	Haben Sie noch Karten —	für Mittwoch abend?
	hah·*bèn zee nokh* **kar**·*tèn —*	*fōōr* **mit**·*vokh* **ah**·*bènt*

45 I should like to reserve a box
Ich möchte eine Loge buchen
ikh **mur'kh**·*tè ine·è lō·zhè* **boo**·*khèn*

46 I should like to reserve two seats in the balcony/orchestra
Ich möchte zweimal erster Rang/Sperrsitz buchen
ikh **mur'kh**·*tè tsvye·mal er·*stèr *rang/***shper**·*zits* **boo**·*khèn*

47 What is being performed?
Was wird gegeben?
*vass virt gè·***gay**·*bèn*

48 Who is singing/playing?
Wer singt/spielt?
ver zingt/shpeelt

49 How long does the performance last?
Wie lange dauert die Vorstellung?
vee **lang**·*è dow·èrt dee* **fōr**·*shte·loong*

50 Where can one buy a program?
Wo kann ich ein Programm kaufen?
*vō kan ikh ine prō·***gram** *kow·fèn*

51   Is there — an intermission?
                    Gibt es — eine Pause?
                    gipt ess — **ine**·*è* **pow**·*zè*
                    — a snack bar/liquor bar?
                    — einen Imbiß/eine Bar?
                    — **ine**·*èn* **im**·*biss/***ine**·*è bar*

52 When does the performance begin?
Wann fängt die Vorstellung an?
van fengt dee **fōr**·*shte·loong an*

53 How much do the drinks cost?
Wie teuer sind die Getränke?
vee **toy**·*èr zint dee gè·***treng**·*kè*

54 Is there a minimum charge?
Gibt es einen Mindestverzehr?
gipt ess ine·èn **min**·*dèst·fer·tsayr*

55 Is there a cover charge?
Muß man für das Gedeck bezahlen?
*moos man fōōr dass gè·***dek** *bè·***tsah**·*lèn*

Gambling

Without entering into the language of gambling in detail, we include here some of the phrases you might need in a casino. You will need to recognize the phrases "Bitte, machen Sie Ihr Spiel" *bi·tè* **ma**·*khèn zee eer shpeel* ("Place your bets") and "Nichts geht mehr" *nikhts gayt mayr* ("No more bets").

56 What is the minimum/maximum stake?
Was ist der Mindesteinsatz/Höchsteinsatz?
vass ist der **min**·*dèst·ine·zats/***hur'khst**·*ine·zats*

57 Where can I cash my chips?
Wo kann ich meine Jetons einlösen?
vō kan ikh **mine**·*è zhè·***tong** *ine·lur'·zèn*

58 Must one be a member to play here?
Muß man Mitglied sein, um hier spielen zu können?
moos man **mit**·*gleet zine oom heer shpee·lèn tsoo* **kur'**·*nèn*

59 Am I allowed to tip the croupier?
Darf ich dem Croupier ein Trinkgeld geben?
*darf ikh daym kroo·pee·***ay** *ine* **trink**·*gelt gay·bèn*

60 This person is cheating
Diese Person spielt falsch
*dee·zè per·***zōn** *shpeelt falsh*

61 Excuse me, you have picked up my stake/winnings
Verzeihung, Sie haben meinen Einsatz/meinen Gewinn weggenommen
*fer·***tsye**·*oong zee hah·bèn* **mine**·*èn ine·zats/***mine**·*èn gè·***vin** *vek·gè·no·mèn*

62 Where is the cashier's cage?
Wo ist die Kasse, bitte?
vō ist dee **ka**·*sè* **bi**·*tè*

63 Do you have a blackjack table here?
   Haben Sie hier einen Tisch für Siebzehn und Vier?
   *hah·bèn zee heer ine·èn tish fōōr **zeep**·tsayn oont feer*
64 I double (*backgammon*)
   Ich verdopple
   *ikh fer·**do**·plè*
65 May I have my passport back, please?
   Kann ich bitte meinen Paß zurückhaben?
   *kan ikh **bi**·tè **mine**·èn pass tsoo·**rōōk**·**hah**·bèn*

Shopping   (s)

General

1 When do you open?
   Wann machen Sie auf?
   *van **ma**·khèn zee owf*
2 When do you close?
   Wann machen Sie zu?
   *van **ma**·khèn zee tsoo*
3 One of these, please
   Kann ich bitte eins von diesen hier haben?
   *kan ikh **bi**·tè ines fon **dee**·zèn heer **hah**·bèn*
4 Two of those, please
   Zwei von diesen hier, bitte
   *tsvye fon **dee**·zèn heer **bi**·tè*
5 How much does that cost?
   Wieviel kostet das?
   *vee·**feel kos**·tèt dass*
6 I am willing to pay up to ... Marks
   Ich bin bereit bis zu ... Mark zu zahlen
   *ikh bin bè·**rite** biss tsoo ... mark tsoo **tsah**·lèn*
7 I should like to buy some presents
   Ich möchte ein paar Geschenke kaufen
   *ikh **mur'kh**·tè ine pahr gè·**sheng**·kè **kow**·fèn*
8 Do you sell duty-free goods?
   Verkaufen Sie zollfreie Waren?
   *fer·**kow**·fèn zee **tsol**·frye·è **vah**·rèn*
9 Do you sell — sunglasses?
   Verkaufen Sie — Sonnenbrillen?
   *fer·**kow**·fèn zee — **zo**·nèn·bri·lèn*
10 Do you have — any pencils?
   Haben Sie — Bleistifte?
   *hah·bèn zee — **blye**·shtif·tè*
11 I need — some suntan oil
   Ich brauche — Sonnenöl
   *ikh **brow**·khè — **zo**·nèn·ur'l*
12 Where is — the shoe department?
   Wo ist — die Schuhabteilung?
   *vō ist — dee **shoo**·ap·tile·oong*
     — the food department?
     — die Lebensmittelabteilung
     — dee **lay**·bèns·mi·tèl·**ap**·tile·oong*
13 Can I see the hat in the window?
   Kann ich den Hut im Schaufenster sehen?
   *kan ikh dayn hoot im **show**·fen·stèr **zay**·èn*
14 Can I see that hat over there?
   Kann ich den Hut dort sehen?
   *kan ikh dayn hoot dort **zay**·èn*
15 No, the other one
   Nein, den anderen
   *nine dayn **an**·dè·rèn*
16 Have you anything cheaper?
   Haben Sie etwas Billigeres?
   *hah·bèn zee et·vass **bi**·li·gè·rès*
17 Have you anything second-hand?
   Haben Sie irgend etwas gebrauchtes?
   *hah·bèn zee **ir**·gènt et·vass gè·**browkh**·tès*

18 I need a gadget to do this
Ich brauche etwas, um dies zu machen
ikh **brow**·khè *et·vass oom dees tsoo* **ma**·khèn

19 Can you show me how it works?
Können Sie mir zeigen, wie das funktioniert?
kur'·nèn *zee meer* **tsye**·gèn *vee dass foonk·tsee·ō·*neert

20   Have you got — a larger one?
            Haben Sie — einen größeren?
            hah·bèn *zee* — *ine·èn* **grur'**·sè·rèn
                       — a smaller one?
                       — einen kleineren?
                       — *ine·èn* **kline**·èr·èn

21   I'm looking for — a blouse
    Ich hätte gern — eine Bluse
    ikh **he**·tè *gern* — *ine·è* **bloo**·zè

22 I'm just looking
Ich schaue mich nur um
ike **show**·è *mikh noor oom*

23 I like this one
Diese hier gefällt mir
dee·zè *heer gè·*felt *meer*

24 I don't like it
Es gefällt mir nicht
*ess gè·*felt *meer nikht*

25   I'll take — this one
            Ich nehme — diese hier
            ikh **nay**·mè — **dee**·zè *heer*
                     — that one
                     — diese da
                     — **dee**·zè *dah*
                     — the other one
                     — die andere
                     — *dee* **an**·dè·rè

26 Please wrap it
Bitte verpacken Sie es
bi·tè *fer·*pa·kèn *zee ess*

27 There's no need to wrap it, thank you
Danke, Sie brauchen es nicht zu verpacken
dang·kè *zee* **brow**·khèn *ess nikht tsoo fer·*pa·kèn

28 Can I have a plastic bag?
Kann ich eine Plastiktüte haben?
kan ikh ine·è **plas**·tik·tōō·tè **hah**·bèn

29 How much would it cost to send it to England/America?
Was würde es kosten, das nach England/Amerika zu schicken?
vass **vōōr**·dè *ess* **kos**·tèn *dass nahkh* **eng**·gland/a·**may**·ree·ka
    tsoo **shi**·kèn

30 Please send it to this address
Bitte senden Sie es an diese Adresse
bi·tè **zen**·dèn *zee ess an* **dee**·zè *a·*dre·sè

31 Please pack it carefully
Packen Sie es bitte sorgfältig ein
pa·kèn *zee ess* **bi**·tè *zorg·*fel·tikh *ine*

Food and drink

Nearly every town in Germany, Austria and Switzerland has an open-air market with stalls selling a mouth-watering variety of produce. These markets, and the many small family-run food shops, make for more interesting shopping than the big supermarkets, but everywhere in these countries the standard of food is extremely high. In choosing wine you would do well to refer to the wines section under "Eating out" (p.31). Frequently there is a returnable deposit (*Pfand*) on each bottle. A word also about weights. A kilo is just over two pounds, and half a kilo is usually referred to as *ein Pfund* (*ine pfoont*: a pound), while a quarter kilo would be *ein halbes Pfund* (*ine* **hal**·bès *pfoont*: a half pound). For smaller and intermediate weights you would normally ask for X number of grams or possibly slices (*Scheiben*, pronounced: **shye**·bèn).

The Germans and their neighbors place great importance on what they eat and drink, and this makes food shopping in those countries great fun. Be adventurous and try unfamiliar things if you want to get the best out of your stay.

32	Where can I find — a baker/butcher?
	Wo finde ich — eine Bäckerei/eine Fleischerei?
	vō fin·dè ikh — ine·è be·kè·rye/ine·è flye·shè·rye

33 What sort of cheese/butter do you have?
Was für Käse/Butter haben Sie?
vass fōōr ke·zè/boo·tèr hah·bèn zee

34	I would like — a kilo of apples
	Ich hätte gern — ein Kilo Äpfel
	ikh he·tè gern — ine kee·lō ep·fèl
	— half a kilo of tomatoes
	— ein Pfund Tomaten
	— *ine pfoont tō·mah·tèn*
	— a quarter kilo of sugar
	— ein halbes Pfund Zucker
	— *ine hal·bès pfoont tsoo·kèr*
	— 100 grams of ground coffee
	— hundert Gramm gemahlenen Kaffee
	— *hoon·dèrt gram gè·mah·lè·nèn ka·fay*
	— five slices of ham
	— fünf Scheiben Schinken
	— *fōōnf shye·bèn shing·kèn*
	— half a dozen eggs
	— sechs Eier
	— *zeks eye·èr*

35 A package of salt, please
Bitte ein Päckchen Salz
bi·tè ine pek·khèn zalts

36 A can of peas
Eine Dose Erbsen
ine·è dō·zè erp·sèn

37 A liter of milk
Einen Liter Milch
ine·èn lee·tèr milkh

38 A bottle of wine
Eine Flasche Wein
ine·è fla·shè vine

39 Two pork chops
Zwei Schweinekoteletts
tsvye shvine·è·ko·tè·lets

40 A joint of lamb
Eine Lammkeule
ine·è lam·koy·lè

41 I would like enough for two people
Ich hätte gern genug für zwei Leute
ikh he·tè gern gè·nook fōōr tsvye loy·tè

42 Shall I help myself?
Kann ich mich selbst bedienen?
kan ikh mikh zelpst bè·dee·nèn

Pharmacist

In Germany there is a fairly clear distinction between an *Apotheke* (pharmacy), which specializes in medicines, and a *Drogerie* (drug store), which sells such things as toiletries. A chemist will diagnose minor ailments and sell the appropriate medicines. Most pharmacies sell homeopathic as well as allopathic remedies.

43	I want something for — a headache
	Ich hätte gern etwas gegen — Kopfschmerzen
	ikh he·tè gern et·vass gay·gèn — kopf·shmert·sèn
	— insect bites
	— Insektenstiche
	— *in·zek·tèn·shti·khè*
	— chapped skin
	— rissige Haut
	— *ri·si·gè howt*
	— a cold
	— Erkältung
	— *er·kel·toong*

I want something for — a cough
Ich hätte gern etwas gegen — Husten
ikh he·tè gern et·vass
gay·gèn — **hoos**·tèn
— hay fever
— Heuschnupfen
— *hoy·shnoop·fèn*
— a sore throat
— Halsschmerzen
— **hals**·shmert·sèn
— sunburn
— Sonnenbrand
— *zo·nèn·brant*
— a toothache
— Zahnschmerzen
— **tsahn**·shmert·sèn
— an upset stomach
— Magenschmerzen
— **mah**·gèn·shmert·sèn
— insomnia
— Schlaflosigkeit
— **shlahf**·lō·zikh·kite

44 How many do I take?
Wieviele soll ich nehmen?
*vee·**fee**·lè zol ikh **nay**·mèn*

45 How often do I take them?
Wie oft muß ich sie nehmen?
*vee oft moos ikh zee **nay**·mèn*

46 Are they safe for children to take?
Sind sie für Kinder geeignet?
*zint zee fōōr **kin**·dèr gè·**ike**·nèt*

47 Could I see a selection of perfume/toilet water?
Könnten Sie mir eine Auswahl von Parfüms/Eau de Cologne
    zeigen?
kur'n·tèn zee meer ine·è ows·vahl fon par·**fōōms**/ō dè
    kō·**lon**·yè **tsye**·gèn

48 I would like something with a floral scent
Ich hätte gern etwas mit einem blumigen Geruch
*ikh **he**·tè gern et·vass mit ine·èm bloo·mi·gèn gè·**rookh***

49 May I smell/try it please?
Kann ich es bitte riechen/könnte ich es bitte ausprobieren?
*kan ikh ess **bi**·tè ree·khèn/**kur'n**·tè ikh ess **bi**·tè ows·prō·bee·rèn*

Cameras and film

---

50   I need film — for this camera
      Ich brauche einen Film — für diese Kamera
      *ikh **brow**·khè ine·èn film* — *fōōr dee·zè ka·**mè**·ra*
      — for this movie camera
      — für diese Filmkamera
      — *fōōr dee·zè **film**·ka·mè·ra*

51   I want — 35mm black-and-white film
      Ich hätte gern — einen fünfunddreißig Millimeter
                    Schwarz-Weiß-Film
      *ikh **he**·tè gern* — *ine·èn fōōnf·oont·**drye**·sikh*
                    *mi·lee·**may**·tèr **shvarts**·vice·film*
      — fast/slow film
      — einen empfindlichen/
                unempfindlichen Film
      — *ine·èn emp·**fint**·li·khèn/*
           *oon·emp·**fint**·li·khèn film*
      — color-print film
      — einen Farbfilm
      — *ine·èn **farp**·film*
      — color-slide film
      — einen Diafarbfilm
      — *ine·èn **dee**·a·farp·film*

I want — batteries for the flash
Ich hätte gern — Batterien für das Blitzgerät
ikh he·tè gern — ba·tè·ree·èn foor dass blits·gè·ret

52 Can you develop this film, please?
Würden Sie bitte diesen Film entwickeln?
voor·dèn zee bi·tè dee·zèn film ent·vi·kèln

53 I would like two prints of this one
Ich hätte gern zwei Abzüge von diesem Bild
ikh he·tè gern tsvye ap·tsoo·zèn fon dee·zèm bilt

54 When will the photographs be ready?
Wann sind die Bilder fertig?
van zint dee bil·dèr fer·tikh

55 I would like this print enlarged
Ich hätte gern eine Vergrößerung von diesem Bild
ikh he·tè gern ine·è fer·grur'·sè·roong fon dee·zèm bilt

56 There is something wrong with my camera
Mit meiner Kamera stimmt etwas nicht
mit mine·èr ka·mè·ra shtimt et·vass nikht

57 The film is jammed
Der Film klemmt
der film klemt

58 I would like to buy a camera with single lens reflex
Ich möchte gern eine Spiegelreflex-Kamera
ikh mur'kh·tè gern ine·è shpee·gèl·ray·fleks·ka·mè·ra

59 I would like to buy a camera with a built-in light meter
Ich möchte gern eine Kamera mit eingebautem Belichtungsmesser
ikh mur'kh·tè gern ine·è ka·mè·ra mit ine·gè·bow·têm bè·likh·toongs·me·sèr

60 I would like to buy an instant camera
Ich möchte gern eine Sofortbildkamera
ikh mur'kh·tè gern ine·è zō·fort·bilt·ka·mè·ra

61 I need — a flash attachment
Ich brauche — ein Blitzgerät
ikh brow·khè — ine blits·gè·ret

— a close-up/wide-angle lens
— ein Teleobjektiv/ein Weitwinkelobjektiv
— ine tay·lay·op·yek·teef/ine vite·ving·kèl·op·yek·teef

— a camera case
— eine Kameratasche
— ine·è ka·mè·ra·ta·shè

Clothes and shoes

62 I am looking for — a dress
Ich hätte gern — ein Kleid
ikh he·tè gern — ine klite

— a sweater
— einen Pullover
— ine·èn poo·lō·vèr

63 I would like — something informal
Ich möchte — etwas legeres
ikh mur'kh·tè — et·vass lay·zhe·rès

— something for evening wear
— Abendkleidung
— ah·bènt·klye·doong

— something for a cocktail party
— etwas für eine Cocktail-Party
— et·vass foor ine·è kok·tayl·par·tee

64 Can you please show me some sun dresses?
Können Sie mir bitte Sonnenkleider zeigen?
kur'·nèn zee meer bi·tè zo·nèn·klye·dèr tsye·gèn

65 Can you please show me some silk shirts?
Können Sie mir bitte Seidenhemden zeigen?
kur'·nèn zee meer bi·tè zye·dèn·hem·dèn tsye·gèn

66 I would like to have a suit/pair of shoes custommade
Ich hätte gern einen Anzug/ein Paar Schuhe nach Maß
ikh he·tè gern ine·èn an·tsook/ine pahr shoo·è nahkh mahss

67 I would prefer a dark material/natural fiber
Ich würde einen dunklen Stoff/Naturfasern vorziehen
ikh vōōr·dè ine·èn doong·kèln shtof/na·toor·fah·zèrn fōr·tsee·èn

68 I take a continental size 40
Ich habe Größe vierzig
ikh hah·bè grur'·sè fir·tsikh

69 I take a continental shoe size 40
Ich habe Schuhgröße vierzig
ikh hah·bè shoo·grur'·sè fir·tsikh

70 Can you measure me?
Können Sie mir Maß nehmen?
kur'·nèn zee meer mahss nay·mèn

71 Do you have this in blue?
Haben Sie das gleiche in blau?
hah·bèn zee dass glye·khè in blow

72 What is the material?
Was ist das für ein Material?
vass ist dass fōōr ine ma·tay·ree·ahl

73

	I like — this one
	Mir gefällt — dieses
	meer gè·felt — *dee·zès*
	— that one there
	— das da
	— *dass dah*
	— the one in the window
	— das im Schaufenster
	— *dass im show·fen·stèr*

74 May I see it in the daylight?
Kann ich es mal ans Licht halten?
kan ikh ess mal ans likht hal·tèn

75 May I try it on?
Kann ich es anprobieren?
kan ikh ess an·prō·bee·rèn

76 Where are the dressing rooms?
Wo sind die Umkleidekabinen?
vo zint dee oom·klye·dè·ka·bee·nèn

77 I would like a mirror
Ich hätte gern einen Spiegel
ikh he·tè gern ine·èn shpee·gèl

78 I like it
Es gefällt mir
ess gè·felt meer

79 I don't like it
Es gefällt mir nicht
ess gè·felt meer nikht

80 I prefer the blue one
Ich finde das blaue besser
ikh fin·dè dass blow·è be·sèr

81 It does not suit me
Es steht mir nicht
ess shtayt meer nikht

82 It does not fit
Es paßt nicht
ess past nikht

83

	It is too — tight
	Es ist zu — eng
	ess ist tsoo — *eng*
	— small
	— klein
	— *kline*
	— big
	— groß
	— *grōs*

84

	Can you — alter it?
	Können Sie — es ändern?
	kur'·nèn zee — *ess en·dèrn*

	Can you —	take it in?
	Können Sie —	es kleiner machen?
	kur'·nèn zee —	*ess **kline·èr** ma·khèn*
		— let it out?
		— es weiter machen?
		— *ess **vye·tèr** ma·khèn*

85 I'd like one — with a zipper
Ich hätte es gern — mit einem Reißverschluß
*ikh **he·tè** ess gern* — *mit **ine·èm** rice·fer·shloos*
— without a belt
— ohne Gürtel
— *ō·nè **gōōr·tèl***

86 Do you have anything else?
Haben Sie sonst noch etwas?
hah·bèn zee zonst nokh et·vass

87 I'll take it
Ich nehme es
*ikh **nay·mè** ess*

88 Is it washable?
Ist es waschbar?
*ist ess **vash·**bahr*

89 Will it shrink?
Läuft es ein?
loyft ess ine

90 Must it be dry-cleaned?
Muß es chemisch gereinigt
werden?
*moos ess **khay·**mish
gè·**rine·**ikht ver·dèn*

Jewelers, silversmiths and watchmakers

---

91 Have you any antique/modern jewelry?
Haben Sie alten/modernen Schmuck?
*hah·bèn zee **al·**tèn/mo·**der·**nèn shmook*

92 I am a collector of silverware/brooches
Ich sammle Silber/Broschen
*ikh **zam·**lè zil·bèr/**bro·**shèn*

93 Could you show me a selection of your rings/watches?
Könnten Sie mir eine Auswahl Ihrer Ringe/Uhren zeigen?
*kur'n·tèn zee meer ine·è ows·vahl ee·rèr **ring·**è/oo·rèn **tsye·**gèn*

94 What precious stone is this?
Welcher Edelstein ist das?
*vel·khèr **ay·**dèl·shtine ist dass*

95 Is this solid gold/silver?
Ist das massiv Gold/Silber?
*ist dass ma·**seef** golt/**zil·**bèr*

96 Is it gold-/silver-plated?
Ist es vergoldet/versilbert?
*ist ess fer·**gol·**dèt/fer·**zil·**bèrt*

97 Can you repair this watch/necklace?
Können Sie diese Uhr/dieses Halsband reparieren?
*kur'·nèn zee dee·zè oo·èr/dee·zès hals·bant ray·pa·**ree·**rèn*

Books, newspapers, postcards and stationery

Newspapers and postcards can be bought at a newsstand (*Zeitungsstand*
or *Zeitungskiosk*). A bookshop (*Buchhandlung*) and a stationer's
(*Schreibwarengeschäft*) would tend to be separate establishments. Some
major foreign newspapers are available on the larger stands, usually a day
or two late in the smaller towns.

98 Have you any — English/American newspapers?
Haben Sie — englische/amerikanische
Zeitungen?
hah·bèn zee — *eng·gli·shè/a·may·ree·**kah·**ni·shè
tsye·toong·èn*
— postcards?
— Postkarten?
— *post·kar·tèn*

99 I would like — some notepaper
Ich hätte gern — etwas Schreibpapier
*ikh **he·**tè gern* — *et·vass **shripe·**pa·peer*

	I would like — some envelopes
	Ich hätte gern — Briefumschläge
	*ikh **he**·tè gern* — ***breef**·oom·**shlay**·gè*
	— some mailing envelopes
	— gepolsterte Umschläge
	— *gè·**pol**·stèr·tè oom·**shle**·gè*
	— a ballpoint pen
	— einen Kugelschreiber
	— *ine·èn **koo**·gèl·shrye·bèr*
	— a pencil
	— einen Bleistift
	— *ine·èn **blye**·shtift*
100	I need — some airmail stickers/envelopes
	Ich brauche — Luftpostaufkleber/
	Luftpostumschläge
	*ikh **brow**·khè* — ***looft**·post·**owf**·klay·bèr/*
	***looft**·post·**oom**·shlay·gè*
	— some Scotch tape
	— Klebstreifen
	— ***klayp**·shtrye·fèn*
101	Do you sell — English paperbacks?
	Führen Sie — englische Taschenbücher?
	foo·rèn zee — ***eng**·gli·shè **ta**·shèn·boo·khèr*
	— street maps?
	— Stadtpläne?
	— ***shtat**·ple·nè*

102 Have you a postcard of ...
Haben Sie eine Postkarte von ...
*hah·bèn zee ine·è **post**·kar·tè fon ...*

Tobacco shop

You can buy tobacco, cigarettes and cigars either at a tobacco shop (called a *Tabakwarengeschäft* in Germany and Switzerland and a *Tabaktraffik* in Austria) or at most newsdealers and grocers.

103	A pack of ... please — with filter tip
	Eine Schachtel ... bitte — mit Filter
	*ine·è **shakh**·tèl ... **bi**·tè* — *mit **fil**·tèr*
	— without filter
	— ohne Filter
	— *ō·nè **fil**·tèr*

104	Have you got American/ English brands?	108	A cigar
	Führen Sie amerikanische/ englische Zigaretten?		Eine Zigarre
	*foo·rèn zee a·may·ree·**kah**·ni·shè/ eng·gli·shè tsi·ga·**re**·tèn*		*ine·è tsi·**ga**·rè*
		109	A cigarette lighter
			Ein Feuerzeug
			*ine **foy**·èr·tsoyk*
105	A package of pipe tobacco	110	A butane refill
	Ein Päckchen Pfeifentabak		Eine Gaspatrone
	*ine **pek**·khèn **pfye**·fèn·ta·**bak***		*ine·è **gahs**·pa·trō·nè*
106	Some pipe cleaners		
	Ein Päckchen Pfeifenreiniger		
	*ine **pek**·khèn **pfye**·fèn·**rine**·i·gèr*		
107	A box of matches		
	Eine Schachtel Streichhölzer		
	*ine·è **shakh**·tèl **shtryekh**·hur'l·tsèr*		

Presents and souvenirs

111 I am looking for a present for my wife/husband
Ich suche ein Geschenk für meine Frau/meinen Mann
*ikh **zoo**·khè ine gè·**shenk** foor mine·è frow/**mine**·èn man*

112 I would like to pay between 100 and 200 Marks
     Ich würde zwischen 100 and 200 Mark ausgeben
     *ikh voor·dè tsvi·shèn **hoon**·dèrt oont tsvye·hoon·dèrt mark
     ows·gay·bèn*
113 Can you suggest anything?
     Haben Sie einen Vorschlag?
     *hah·bèn zee ine·èn **for**·shlahk*
114 Have you anything suitable for a ten-year-old girl/boy?
     Haben Sie etwas für ein zehnjähriges Mädchen/einen
        zehnjährigen Jungen?
     *hah·bèn zee et·vass foor ine **tsayn**·ye·ri·gès **mayt**·khèn/
     ine·èn **tsayn**·ye·ri·gèn **yoong**·èn*
115 Do you have something made locally?
     Haben Sie etwas, was am Ort hergestellt ist?
     *hah·bèn zee et·vass vass am ort **her**·gè·shtelt ist*
116 Do you have something handmade?
     Haben Sie etwas handgearbeitetes?
     *hah·bèn zee et·vass **hant**·gè·ar·bye·tè·tès*
117 Do you have something unusual?
     Haben Sie etwas ungewöhnliches?
     *hah·bèn zee et·vass **oon**·gè·vur'n·li·khès*

Services and everyday needs (Sn)

Post office

In Germany a post office (*Postamt*) is indicated by a yellow sign with a
black post horn. Mailboxes are similarly marked. Offices are open
Monday to Friday 8:00 to 18:00 and on Saturday from 8:00 to 12:00; but
those in airports and stations have longer hours. Again, different hours
are observed in Austria and Switzerland. In Germany stamps can be
bought only at post offices, but in Austria and Switzerland you can get
them at newsdealers. Mail can be addressed *postlagernd* (general
delivery) (in Switzerland *poste restante*) to any post office.

1   How much is a letter — to Britain?
       Wieviel kostet ein Brief — nach Großbritannien?
       *vee·**feel** kos·tèt ine breef — nahkh grös·bri·**tan**·yèn*
                                     — to the United States?
                                     — in die Vereinigten Staaten?
                                     *— in dee fer·**ine**·ikh·tèn
                                     shtah·tèn*
2   I would like six stamps for
            postcards/letters — to Britain
       Ich hätte gern sechs
            Briefmarken für
            Postkarten/Briefe — nach Großbritannien
       *ikh **he**·tè gern zeks
       breef·mar·kèn foor
       post·kar·tèn/**bree**·fè — nahkh grös·bri·**tan**·yèn*
                                     — to the United States
                                     — in die Vereinigten Staaten
                                     *— in dee fer·**ine**·ikh·tèn shtah·tèn*
3   Six stamps at two Marks, please
       Sechs Briefmarken zu zwei Mark, bitte
       *zeks **breef**·mar·kèn tsoo tsvye mark **bi**·tè*
4   I want to send this parcel/a telegram
       Ich möchte dieses Paket aufgeben/ein Telegramm schicken
       *ikh **mur'kh**·tè dee·zès pa·**kayt** owf·gay·bèn/ine tay·lay·**gram**
       shi·kèn*
5   A telegram form, please
       Ein Telegrammformular, bitte
       *ine tay·lay·**gram**·for·moo·**lar** bi·tè*
6   When will it arrive?
       Wann wird es ankommen?
       *van virt ess **an**·ko·mèn*

7 I want to send this by registered mail
  Ich möchte dies per Einschreiben schicken
  *ikh **mur'kh**·tè dees per ine·shrye·bèn **shi**·kèn*
8 I am expecting a letter general delivery
  Ich erwarte einen postlagernden Brief
  *ikh er·**var**·tè **ine**·èn **post**·lah·gèrn·dèn breef*

Telephoning

The simplest but most expensive way to telephone is from your hotel, but otherwise you will have to use a public telephone, found in post offices and cafés as well as along sidewalks. In telephone booths the coin is inserted before dialing, coins being refunded if you hang up without getting through. The ringing signal is a shrill intermittent tone, while the busy signal is less shrill and more rapid. (For Numbers, see p.67).

Phrases you will use

9 Hello, this is Peter Williams
  Hallo, Peter Williams
  *ha·**lō** Peter Williams*
10 Can I speak to Herr Winkler?
  Kann ich bitte mit Herrn Winkler sprechen?
  *kan ikh **bi**·tè mit hern **ving**·klèr **shpre**·khèn*
11 I would like to make a phone call to Britain/America
  Ich möchte gern nach Großbritannien/den Vereinigten
    Staaten anrufen
  *ikh **mur'kh**·tè gern nahkh grōs·bri·**tan**·yèn/dayn fer·**ine**·ikh·tèn
    shtah·tèn **an**·roo·fèn*
12 The number I want is . . .
  Die Nummer ist . . .
  *dee **noo**·mèr ist . . .*
13 What is the area code for Cologne/Los Angeles?
  Welche Vorwahl hat Köln/Los Angeles?
  *vel·khè **fōr**·vahl hat kur'ln/Los Angeles*
14 Would you write it down for me, please?
  Könnten Sie das bitte für mich aufschreiben?
  *kur'n·tèn zee dass **bi**·tè fōōr mikh **owf**·shrye·bèn*
15 Could you put me through to (international) directory assistance?
  Könnten Sie mir die (internationale) Auskunft geben?
  *kur'n·tèn zee meer dee (in·ter·na·tsee·ō·**nahl**·è) **ows**·koonft
    gay·bèn*
16 May I use the phone, please?
  Kann ich bitte telefonieren?
  *kan ikh **bi**·tè tay·lay·fō·**nee**·rèn*
17 We have been cut off
  Wir sind unterbrochen worden
  *veer zint **oon**·tèr·bro·khèn **vor**·dèn*
18 Is there a cheap rate?
  Gibt es einen verbilligten Tarif?
  *gipt ess **ine**·èn fer·**bi**·likh·tèn ta·**reef***
19 What is the time now in Hong Kong?
  Wie spät ist es zur Zeit in Hong-Kong?
  *vee shpayt ist ess tsoor tsite in **hong**·kong*
20 I cannot get through
  Ich kann diese Nummer nicht erreichen
  *ikh kan **dee**·ze **noo**·mèr nikht er·**rye**·khèn*
21 Can I check this number/code?
  Kann ich diese Telefonnummer/diese Vorwahl nachsehen?
  *kan ikh **dee**·zè tay·lay·**fōn**·noo·mèr/**dee**·zè **fōr**·vahl
    nahkh·zay·èn*
22 Do you have a directory for Bonn?
  Haben Sie ein Telefonbuch von Bonn?
  *hah·bèn zee ine tay·lay·**fōn**·bookh fon bon*

Phrases you will hear

23 Wer ist am Apparat?
ver ist am a·pa·raht
Who is speaking?

24 Ich verbinde Sie mit Herrn Winkler
ikh fer·bin·dè zee mit hern ving·klèr
I am putting you through to Herr Winkler

25 Bleiben Sie am Apparat
blye·bèn zee am a·pa·raht
Hold the line

26 Moment, ich verbinde
mō·ment ikh fer·bin·dè
I am trying to connect you

27 Es ist besetzt
ess ist bè·zetst
The line is busy

28 Versuchen Sie es bitte später noch einmal
fer·zoo·khèn zee ess bi·tè shpay·tèr nokh ine·mahl
Please try later

29 Kein Anschluß unter dieser Nummer
kine an·shloos oon·tèr dee·zèr noo·mèr
This number is out of order

30 Ich kann diese Nummer nicht erreichen
ikh kan dee·zè noo·mèr nikht er·rye·khèn
I cannot reach this number

31 Bitte sprechen Sie
bi·tè shpre·khèn zee
Please go ahead

The hairdresser

32 I'd like to make an appointment
Ich möchte gern einen Termin haben
ikh mur'kh·tè gern ine·èn ter·meen hah·bèn

33 I want a haircut/a blow-dry
Ich möchte mein Haar geschnitten haben/nachgeschnitten haben/gefönt
ikh mur'kh·tè mine hahr gè·shni·tèn hah·bèn/nahkh·gè·shni·tèn hah·bèn/gè·fur'nt

34 I want my hair — fairly short
Ich hätte mein Haar gern — ziemlich kurz geschnitten
ikh he·tè mine hahr gern — *tseem·likh koorts gè·shni·tèn*
— not too short
— *nicht zu kurz geschnitten*
— *nikht tsoo koorts gè·shni·tèn*
— short and curly
— kurz und lockig
— *koorts oont lo·kikh*
— layered
— stufig geschnitten
— *shtoo·fikh gè·shni·tèn*
— in bangs
— mit Pony
— *mit pō·ni*

35 Take more off the front/the back
Bitte vorne/hinten kürzer
bi·tè for·nè/hin·tèn kōōrt·sèr

36 Not too much off the sides/the top
Bitte nicht zu kurz an den Seiten/Bitte oben nicht zu kurz
bi·tè nikht tsoo koorts an dayn zye·tèn/bi·tè ō·bèn nikht tsoo koorts

37 I like a part in the center
Ich hätte gern einen Mittelscheitel
ikh he·tè gern ine·èn mi·tèl·shye·tèl

38 I like a part on the left/right
Ich hätte gern den Scheitel auf der linken/rechten Seite
ikh he·tè gern dayn shye·tèl owf der ling·kèn/rekh·tèn zye·tè

39 I'd like — a perm
Ich hätte gern — eine Dauerwelle
ikh he·tè gern — *ine·è dow·èr·ve·lè*
— a curly perm
— eine krause Dauerwelle
— *ine·è krow·zè dow·èr·ve·lè*
— a shampoo and set
— Waschen und Legen
— *va·shèn oont lay·gèn*

	I'd like	— my hair tinted
	Ich hätte gern	— mein Haar getönt
	ikh he·tè gern	— *mine hahr gè·tur'nt*
		— my hair streaked
		— Strähnen gefärbt
		— *shtray·nèn gè·ferpt*

40 The water is too hot/cold
Das Wasser ist zu heiß/kalt
das va·sèr ist tsoo hice/kalt

41 The dryer is too hot/cold
Die Trockenhaube ist zu heiß/kalt
dee tro·kèn·how·bè ist tsoo hice/kalt

42	I'd like	— a conditioner
	Ich hätte gern	— eine Haarkur
	ikh he·tè gern	— *ine·è hahr·koor*
		— hair spray
		— etwas Haarspray
		— *et·vass hahr·shpray*

43 That's fine, thank you
Das ist schön so. Vielen Dank
dass ist shur'n zō fee·lèn dank

Repairs and technical jobs

The following list tells you how to describe some of the things for which you might need the help of a specialist during your stay (cars are dealt with on p.18, clothes on p.55).

44 Where can I get this repaired?
Wo kann ich das repariert bekommen?
vō kan ikh dass ray·pa·reert bè·ko·mèn

45 I am having trouble with the heating/plumbing
Ich habe Probleme mit der Heizung/mit den Leitungen
ikh hah·bè prō·blay·mè mit der hye·tsoong/mit dayn lye·toong·èn

46 This is broken
Dies ist kaputt
dees ist ka·poot

47 This is not working
Dies funktioniert nicht
dees foonk·tsee·ō·neert nikht

48	This is	— damaged
	Dies ist	— beschädigt
	dees ist	— *bè·shay·dikht*
		— blocked
		— verstopft
		— *fer·shtopft*
		— torn
		— zerrissen
		— *tser·ri·sèn*

49 There is a leak in the pipe/roof
Es ist ein Wasserrohr undicht/ein Leck im Dach
ess ist ine va·sèr·rōr oon·dikht/ine lek im dakh

50 There is a gas leak
Die Gasleitung ist undicht
dee gahs·lye·toong ist oon·dikht

51 Would you have a look at this, please?
Würden Sie sich das bitte anschauen?
vōōr·dèn zee zikh dass bi·tè an·show·èn

52 Can you repair my suitcase?
Können Sie meinen Koffer reparieren?
kur'·nèn zee mine·èn ko·fèr ray·pa·ree·rèn

53 Can you re-heel/re-sole these shoes?
Können Sie neue Absätze auf diese Schuhe machen/Können Sie diese Schuhe sohlen?
kur'·nèn zee noy·è ap·zet·sè owf dee·zè shoo·è ma·khèn/ kur'·nèn zee dee·zè shoo·è zō·lèn

54 Can you get it working again?
Können Sie das wieder zum Laufen bringen?
kur'·nèn zee dass vee·dèr tsoom low·fèn bring·èn

55 Have you got a replacement part?
    Haben Sie ein Ersatzteil?
    hah·bèn zee ine er·**zats**·tile
56 When will it be ready?
    Wann ist es fertig?
    van ist ess **fer**·tikh
57 Can you do it quickly?
    Können Sie es schnell erledigen?
    kur·nèn zee ess shnel er·**lay**·gèn
58 I would like a duplicate of this key
    Könnten Sie mir diesen Schlüssel nachmachen?
    kur'n·tèn zee meer dee·zèn shlōō·sèl **nahkh**·ma·khèn

59   I have — lost my key
                Ich habe — meinen Schlüssel verloren
                ikh **hah**·bè — mine·èn shlōō·sèl fer·**lō**·rèn
                        — locked myself out
                        — mich ausgesperrt
                        — mikh **ows**·gè·shpert

60 Can you open the door?
    Können Sie die Tür aufmachen?
    kur'·nèn zee dee tōōr **owf**·ma·khèn
61 The fuse for the lights has blown
    Die Sicherung ist durchgebrannt
    dee **zi**·khè·roong ist **doorkh**·gè·brant
62 There is a loose connection
    Hier ist ein Wackelkontakt
    heer ist ine **va**·kèl·kon·takt
63 Sometimes it works, sometimes it doesn't
    Manchmal funktioniert es, manchmal nicht
    mankh·mahl foonk·tsee·ō·**neert** ess **mankh**·mahl nikht

Laundry, dry cleaners and clothes-mending

A laundry is called a *Wäscherei*. In Germany and Austria it is usually
combined with a dry cleaner's (*Reinigung* or *chemische Reinigung*), but in
Switzerland the two tend to be separate. Laundries and dry cleaners
normally operate a repair service. Laundromats (*Waschsalons*) are found
in some German towns but are virtually non-existent in Austria and
Switzerland.

64   Will you — clean this skirt?
            Würden Sie bitte — diesen Rock reinigen?
            vōōr·dèn zee **bi**·tè — dee·zèn rok **rine**·i·gèn
                        — press these trousers?
                        — diese Hose bügeln?
                        — dee·zè **hō**·zè **bōō**·gèln
                        — wash and iron these shirts?
                        — diese Hemden waschen und
                            bügeln?
                        — dee·zè **hem**·dèn va·shèn oont
                            bōō·gèln

65 Can you get this stain out?
    Können Sie diesen Fleck entfernen?
    kur'·nèn zee dee·zèn flek ent·**fer**·nèn
66 This stain is grease/ink
    Es ist ein Fettfleck/Tintenfleck
    ess ist ine **fet**·flek/**tin**·tèn·flek
67 This fabric is delicate
    Der Stoff ist sehr empfindlich
    der shtof ist zehr emp·**fint**·likh
68 When will my things be ready?
    Wann sind meine Sachen fertig?
    van zint **mine**·è **za**·khèn **fer**·tikh
69 I need them in a hurry
    Ich brauche sie sehr bald
    ikh **brow**·khè zee zehr balt
70 Is there a laundromat nearby?
    Gibt es hier in der Nähe einen Waschsalon?
    gipt ess heer in der **nay**·è ine·èn vash·za·long

71 Can I have my laundry done?
    Waschen Sie die Wäsche für Ihre Kunden?
    va·shèn zee dee ve·shè fōōr ee·rè koon·dèn
72 Where can I get clothes repaired?
    Wo kann ich Kleider geflickt bekommen?
    vō kan ikh klye·dèr gè·flikt bè·ko·mèn
73 Can you do invisible mending?
    Können Sie kunststopfen?
    kur'·nèn zee koonst·shtop·fèn
74   Could you — sew this button back on?
                            Könnten Sie — diesen Knopf annähen?
                            kur'n·tèn zee — dee·zèn knopf an·nay·èn
                                        — mend this tear?
                                        — diesen Riß reparieren?
                                        — *dee·zèn ris ray·pa·ree·rèn*
                                        — replace this zipper?
                                        — diesen Reißverschluß ersetzen?
                                        — *dee·zèn rice·fer·shloos er·zet·sèn*
                                        — turn up/let down the hem?
                                        — es kürzer/länger machen?
                                        — *ess kōōrt·sèr/leng·èr ma·khèn*

Police and legal matters

75 I wish to call the police
    Ich möchte die Polizei rufen
    ikh mur'kh·tè dee pō·lee·tsye roo·fèn
76 Where is the police station?
    Wo ist das Polizeirevier?
    vo ist dass pō·lee·tsye·ray·veer
77 I should like to report a theft
    Ich möchte einen Diebstahl melden
    ikh mur'kh·tè ine·èn deep·shtahl mel·dèn
78 I should like to report the loss of a camera
    Ich möchte den Verlust einer Kamera melden
    ikh mur'kh·tè dayn fer·loost ine·èr ka·mè·ra mel·dèn
79 Someone has broken into my car/my room
    Jemand hat in mein Auto/mein Zimmer eingebrochen
    yay·mant hat in mine ow·tō/mine tsi·mèr ine·gè·bro·khèn
80 Someone has stolen my wallet
    Mir ist die Brieftasche gestohlen worden
    meer ist dee breef·ta·shè gè·shtō·lèn vor·dèn
81 My insurance company requires me to report it
    Ich muß das wegen meiner Versicherung zur Anzeige bringen
    ikh moos dass vay·gèn mine·èr fer·zi·khè·roong tsoor an·tsye·gè bring·èn
82 I have lost my passport
    Ich habe meinen Paß verloren
    ikh hah·bè mine·èn pass fer·lō·rèn
83 My son is lost
    Mein Sohn ist verlorengegangen
    mine zōn ist fer·lō·rèn·gè·gang·èn
84 I wish to see a lawyer
    Ich möchte mit einem Anwalt sprechen
    ikh mur'kh·tè mit ine·èm an·valt shpre·khèn
85 Where is the British/American Consulate?
    Wo ist das britische/amerikanische Konsulat?
    vō ist dass bri·ti·shè/a·may·ree·kah·ni·shè kon·zoo·laht

Worship

Some parts of the German-speaking world are predominantly Catholic,
others Protestant, but all other main denominations and religions are well
represented, especially in the larger cities.

86   Where is there — a Catholic church?
                            Wo gibt es hier — eine katholische Kirche?
                            vō gipt ess heer — ine·è ka·tō·li·shè kir·khè

Where is there — a Protestant church?
Wo gibt es hier — eine evangelische Kirche?
*võ gipt ess heer — ine·è ay·van·**gay**·li·shè **kir**·khè*
— a Baptist church?
— eine Baptistenkirche?
*— ine·è bap·**tis**·tèn·**kir**·khè*
— a Greek/Russian Orthodox
church?
— eine Griechisch/Russisch
Orthodoxe Kirche?
*— ine·è gree·khish/roo·sish
or·tõ·**dok**·sè kir·khè*
— a synagogue?
— eine Synagoge?
*— ine·è zõõ·na·**gõ**·gè*
— a mosque?
— eine Moschee?
*— ine·è mo·**shay***

87 What time is the service?
Um wieviel Uhr ist der Gottesdienst?
*oom **vee**·feel oo·èr ist der go·tès·deenst*

88 I'd like to see a priest/a minister/a rabbi
Ich möchte mit einem Priester/einem evangelischen Pfarrer/
einem Rabbi sprechen
*ikh **mur'kh**·tè mit ine·èm prees·tèr/ine·èm ay·van·**gay**·li·shèn
pfa·rèr/ine·èm ra·bi shpre·khèn*

89 Is there one who speaks English?
Gibt es einen, der Englisch spricht?
*gipt ess ine·èn der **eng**·glish shprikht*

90 Could you hear my confession in English?
Könnten Sie mir die Beichte in Englisch abnehmen?
***kur'n**·tèn zee meer dee **byekh**·tè in **eng**·glish **ap**·nay·mèn*

Business matters (Bm)

Making appointments (see also Telephoning, p.52)

1 My name is George Baker — of Universal Chemicals
Mein Name ist George
Baker — von der Firma Universal
Chemicals
*mine **nah**·mè ist George
Baker — fon der **fir**·ma Universal Chemicals*

2 Here is my card
Hier ist meine Visitenkarte
*heer ist mine·è vee·**zee**·tèn·**kar**·tè*

3 Could I see/speak to your Managing Director/Buyer?
Kann ich bitte mit Ihrem Direktor/Einkaufschef sprechen?
*kan ikh **bi**·tè mit ee·rèm dee·**rek**·tor/ine·kowfs·shef **shpre**·khèn*

4 He/she is expecting me to telephone
Er/sie erwartet meinen Anruf
*er/zee er·**var**·tèt mine·èn an·roof*

5 Could you put me through to Herr Bauer?
Können Sie mich mit Herrn Bauer verbinden?
***kur'**·nèn zee mikh mit hern **bow**·èr fer·**bin**·dèn*

6 Is Herr Bauer in?
Ist Herr Bauer da?
*ist her **bow**·èr dah*

7 Is his assistant/secretary there?
Ist sein Assistent/seine Sekretärin da?
*ist zine a·sis·**tent**/zine·è zay·kray·**te**·rin dah*

8 When will he/she be back?
Wann wird er/sie zurückkommen?
*van virt er/zee tsoo·**rõõk**·ko·mèn*

9 I would like to make/I have an appointment with Herr Bauer
   Ich würde gern einen Termin mit Herrn Bauer ausmachen/Ich habe
   einen Termin mit Herrn Bauer
   ikh vōōr·dè gern ine·èn ter·meen mit hern bow·èr ows·ma·khèn/
   ikh hah·bè ine·èn ter·meen mit hern bow·èr

10 I am free on Thursday between 9:00 and 11:00
    Ich bin Dienstag zwischen 9 und 11 Uhr frei
    ikh bin deens·tahk tsvi·shèn noyn oont elf oo·èr frye

11 Shall we say 10.00?
    Sagen wir 10 Uhr?
    zah·gèn veer tsayn oo·èr

Miscellaneous

12 I am on a business trip to Germany
    Ich bin geschäftlich in Deutschland
    ikh bin gè·sheft·likh in doytsh·lant

13 I wish to hire a secretary/a typist
    Ich möchte eine Sekretärin/Schreibkraft einstellen
    ikh mur'kh·tè ine·è zay·kray·te·rin/shripe·kraft ine·shte·lèn

14 I wish to hire a conference room
    Ich möchte ein Konferenzzimmer mieten
    ikh mur'kh·tè ine kon·fay·rents·tsi·mèr mee·tèn

15 Where can I do some photocopying?
    Wo kann ich photokopieren?
    vō kan ikh fō·tō·ko·pee·rèn

16 Can I send a telex from here?
    Kann ich von hier ein Fernschreiben schicken?
    kan ikh fon heer ine fern·shrye·bèn shi·kèn

17 My firm specializes in agricultural equipment/illustrated books
    Meine Firma ist auf landwirtschaftliche Geräte/auf Bildbände
       spezialisiert
    mine·è fir·ma ist owf lant·virt·shaft·li·khè gè·re·tè/owf bilt·ben·dè
       shpay·tsee·a·li·zeert

18   I wish — to carry out a market survey
                 Ich möchte — mir einen Überblick über die
                              Marktlage verschaffen
            ikh mur'kh·tè — meer ine·èn ōō·bèr·blik ōō·bèr dee
                              markt·lah·gè fer·sha·fèn
                          — to test the German market for this
                              product
                          — den deutschen Markt für dieses
                              Produkt untersuchen
                          — dayn doyt·shèn markt fōōr dee·zès
                              prō·dookt oon·tèr·zoo·khèn

19 My firm is launching an advertising/sales campaign
    Meine Firma startet einen Werbefeldzug/eine Verkaufskampagne
    mine·è fir·ma shtar·tèt ine·èn ver·bè·felt·tsook/ine·è
       fer·kowfs·kam·pan·yè

20 Have you seen our catalog?
    Haben Sie schon unseren Katalog gesehen?
    hah·bèn zee shōn oon·zè·rèn ka·ta·lōk gè·zay·èn

21 Can I send our sales representative to see you?
    Kann ich Ihnen unseren Vertreter schicken?
    kan ikh ee·nèn oon·zè·rèn fer·tray·tèr shi·kèn

22 I will send you a letter/telex with the details
    Ich schicke Ihnen die genaueren Angaben in einem Brief/
       Fernschreiben
    ikh shi·kè ee·nèn dee gè·now·è·rèn an·gah·bèn in ine·èm
       breef/fern·shrye·bèn

23 Can I see a sample of your product/a selection of your goods?
    Kann ich ein Muster Ihres Produktes/eine Warenauswahl sehen?
    kan ikh ine moos·tèr ee·rès pro·dook·tès/ine·è vah·rèn·ows·vahl
       zay·èn

24 Can I have a copy of this document/brochure?
    Kann ich ein Exemplar dieses Dokuments/dieser Broschüre haben?
    kan ikh ine ek·sem·plahr dee·zès do·koo·ments/dee·zèr
       bro·shōō·rè hah·bèn

25 Can you give me an estimate of the cost?
    Können Sie mir die ungefähren Kosten schätzen?
    kur'·nèn zee meer dee oon·gè·fe·rèn kos·tèn shet·sèn

26 What percentage of the cost is for freight and delivery?
    Wie groß ist der Prozentsatz der Kosten, der durch Transport
    verursacht ist?
    *vee grōs ist der prō·tsent·zats der kos·tèn der doorkh trans·port
    fer·oor·zakht ist*

27 What is the average cost of a pocket calculator?
    Wieviel kostet im Schnitt ein Taschenrechner?
    vee·feel kos·tèt im shnit ine ta·shèn·rekh·nèr

28 What is the wholesale/retail price?
    Wie ist der Großhandelspreis/Einzelhandelspreis?
    vee ist der grōs·han·dèls·price/ine·tsèl·han·dèls·price

29 What is the rate of inflation in Germany?
    Wie hoch ist die Inflationsrate in Deutschland?
    vee hōkh ist dee in·fla·tsee·ōns·rah·tè in doytsh·lant

30 How high are current rates of interest?
    Wie hoch sind zur Zeit die Zinsen?
    vee hōkh zint tsoor tsite dee tsin·zèn

31 How is this project being financed?
    Wie ist dieses Vorhaben finanziert?
    vee ist dee·zès fōr·hah·bèn fee·nan·tseert

32 It's a pleasure to do business with you
    Es ist ein Vergnügen, mit Ihnen geschäftlich zu tun zu haben
    *ess ist ine ferg·nōō·gèn mit ee·nèn gè·sheft·likh tsoo toon tsoo
    hah·bèn*

Children (c)

Traveling abroad with children presents its own special problems. We
have therefore grouped together here certain phrases that parents may
need in a variety of situations.

1   Do you have — a special menu for children?
                    Haben Sie — eine spezielle Speisekarte für
                                      Kinder?
                    *hah·bèn zee — ine·è shpye·tsee·e·lè
                                      shpye·zè·kar·tè fōōr kin·dèr*

                               — half portions for children?
                               — halbe Portionen für Kinder?
                               — *hal·bè por·tsee·ō·nèn fōōr kin·dèr*

2   Can you warm this bottle for me?
    Können Sie diese Flasche für mich aufwärmen?
    kur'·nèn zee dee·zè fla·shè fōōr mikh owf·ver·mèn

3   Have you got a highchair?
    Haben Sie einen Kinderstuhl?
    hah·bèn zee ine·èn kin·dèr·shtool

4   Do you operate a baby-sitting service/a day nursery?
    Haben Sie einen Babysitter-Dienst/eine Kinderkrippe?
    hah·bèn zee ine·èn bay·bee·zi·tèr·deenst/ine·è kin·dèr·kri·pè

5   Do you know anyone who will baby-sit for us?
    Kennen Sie jemanden, der für uns babysitten würde?
    ke·nèn zee yay·man·dèn der fōōr oons bay·bee·zi·tèn vōōr·dè

6   We shall be back at 11
    Wir sind um elf Uhr zurück
    veer zint oom elf oo·èr tsoo·rōōk

7   She goes to bed at 8
    Sie geht um acht Uhr ins Bett
    zee gayt oom akht oo·èr ins bet

8   Are there any organized activities for the children?
    Gibt es irgendwelche Freizeitveranstaltungen für Kinder?
    gipt ess ir·gènt·vel·khè frye·tsite·fer·an·shtal·toong·èn fōōr kin·dèr

9   Is there — a wading pool?
                    Gibt es hier — ein Planschbecken?
                    gipt ess heer — ine plansh·be·kèn

                             — a playground?
                             — einen Spielplatz?
                             — *ine·èn shpeel·plats*

Is there — an amusement park?
Gibt es hier — einen Vergnügungspark?
gipt ess heer — ine·èn fer·gnōō·goongs·park
— a zoo nearby?
— in der Nähe einen Zoo?
— *in der nay·è ine·èn tsō*

10 My son has hurt himself
Mein Sohn hat sich weh getan
mine zōn hat zikh vay gè·tahn

11 My daughter is ill
Meine Tochter ist krank
mine·è tokh·tèr ist krank

12 Have you a crib for our baby?
Haben Sie ein Kinderbett für unser Baby?
hah·bèn zee ine kin·dèr·bet fōōr oon·zèr bay·bee

13 Can my son sleep in our room?
Kann mein Sohn bei uns im Zimmer schlafen?
kan mine zōn bye oons im tsi·mèr shlah·fèn

14 Are there any other children in the hotel?
Sind im Hotel noch mehr Kinder?
zint im hō·tel nokh mehr kin·dèr

15 How old are your children?
Wie alt sind Ihre Kinder?
vee alt zint ee·rè kin·dèr

16 My son is 9 years old
Mein Sohn ist neun Jahre alt
mine zōn ist noyn yah·rè alt

17 My daughter is 15 months
Meine Tochter ist fünfzehn Monate alt
mine·è tokh·tèr ist fōōnf·tsayn mō·nah·tè alt

18 Where can I nurse my baby?
Wo kann ich mein Baby stillen?
vō kan ikh mine bay·bee shti·lèn

19 I need some disposable diapers
Ich brauche ein paar Papierwindeln
ikh brow·khè ine pahr pa·peer·vin·dèln

Illness and disability (I)

The disabled

1 I suffer from a weak heart/asthma
Ich habe ein schwaches Herz/Asthma
ikh hah·bè ine shva·khès herts/ast·ma

2 Do you have — facilities for the disabled?
Haben Sie — Einrichtungen für Behinderte?
hah·bèn zee — ine·rikh·toong·èn fōōr bè·hin·dèr·tè
— a toilet for the disabled?
— eine Behindertentoilette?
— *ine·è bè·hin·dèr·tèn·tō·a·le·tè*

3 Is there a reduced rate for disabled people?
Gibt es eine Ermäßigung für Behinderte?
gipt ess ine·è er·me·si·goong fōōr bè·hin·dèr·tè

4 I am unable to climb stairs
Ich kann keine Treppen steigen
ikh kan kine·è tre·pèn shtye·gèn

5 I am unable to walk very far
Ich kann nicht sehr weit laufen
ikh kan nikht zehr vite low·fèn

6 Can you supply a wheelchair?
Können Sie einen Rollstuhl stellen?
kur'·nèn zee ine·èn rol·shtool shte·lèn

7 Does your elevator accommodate a wheelchair?
Paßt ein Rollstuhl in Ihren Lift?
past ine rol·shtool in ee·rèn lift

Doctors and hospitals

In Germany, Austria and Switzerland, if a visit to a doctor is necessary, you will have to pay on the spot, so proper accident and medical insurance is essential. It is important to make these arrangements with your own insurance company before going abroad, to ensure complete coverage.

Preliminary

8 I need a doctor
   Ich brauche einen Arzt
   *ikh **brow**-khè ine-èn artst*

9 I feel ill
   Ich fühle mich krank
   *ikh **foo**-lè mikh krank*

10 Can I have an appointment with the doctor?
    Kann ich einen Termin beim Arzt haben?
    *kan ikh **ine**-èn ter-**meen** bime artst **hah**-bèn*

11 I would like a general check up
    Ich hätte gern eine allgemeine Untersuchung
    *ikh he-tè gern ine-è **al**-gè-mine-è oon-tèr-**zoo**-khoong*

12 I would like to see a skin specialist/an eye specialist
    Ich würde gern einen Hautarzt/einen Augenarzt sehen
    *ikh **vōōr**-dè gern ine-èn **howt**-artst/ine-èn **ow**-gèn-artst **zay**-èn*

In the event of an accident

13 There has been an accident
    Es ist ein Unfall passiert
    *ess ist ine **oon**-fal pa-**seert***

14 Call an ambulance
    Rufen Sie einen Krankenwagen
    *roo-fèn zee ine-èn **krang**-kèn-vah-gèn*

15 Get a doctor
    Holen Sie einen Arzt
    hō-lèn zee ine-èn artst

16 He is unconscious
    Er ist bewußtlos
    *er ist bè-**voost**-lōs*

17 He is in pain
    Er hat Schmerzen
    *er hat **shmert**-sèn*

18 He/she has been seriously injured
    Er/sie ist schwer verletzt
    *er/zee ist shvayr fer-**letst***

19 I have cut myself
    Ich habe mich geschnitten
    *ikh **hah**-bè mikh gè-**shni**-tèn*

20 He has burned himself
    Er hat sich verbrannt
    *er hat zikh fer-**brant***

21 I have had a fall
    Ich bin hingefallen
    *ikh bin **hin**-gè-fa-lèn*

22 He has been stung
    Er ist gestochen worden
    *er ist gè-**shto**-khèn vor-dèn*

23 She has been bitten
    Sie ist gebissen worden
    *zee ist gè-**bi**-sèn vor-dèn*

24 I have hurt my arm/my leg
    Ich habe mir den Arm/das Bein verletzt
    *ikh **hah**-bè meer dayn arm/dass bine fer-**letst***

25 I have broken my arm
    Ich habe mir den Arm gebrochen
    *ikh **hah**-bè meer dayn arm gè-**bro**-khèn*

26 He has dislocated his shoulder
    Er hat sich die Schulter ausgekugelt
    *er hat zikh dee **shool**-tèr ows-gè-koo-gèlt*

27 She has sprained her ankle
    Sie hat sich den Knöchel verstaucht
    *zee hat zikh dayn **knur'**-khèl fer-**shtowkht***

28 I have pulled this muscle
    Ich habe hier eine Muskelzerrung
    *ikh **hah**-bè heer ine-è **moos**-kèl-tse-roong*

Symptoms, conditions and treatment

29 There is a swelling here
    Hier ist es geschwollen
    *heer ist ess gè-**shvo**-lèn*

30 It is inflamed here
    Hier ist es entzündet
    *heer ist ess ent-**tsōōn**-dèt*

31 I have a pain here
    Ich habe hier Schmerzen
    *ikh **hah**-bè heer **shmert**-sèn*

32 I find it painful to walk/to breathe
Es tut weh beim Laufen/beim Atmen
*ess toot vay bime low·fèn/bime **aht**·mèn*

33   I have — a headache
Ich habe — Kopfschmerzen
*ikh **hah**·bè — **kopf**·shmert·sèn*
         — a sore throat
         — Halsschmerzen
         — **hals**·shmert·sèn
         — a high temperature
         — Temperatur
         — *tem·pè·ra·**toor***

34 I can't sleep
Ich kann nicht schlafen
*ikh kan nikht **shlah**·fèn*

35 I have sunstroke
Ich habe einen Sonnenstich
*ikh **hah**·bè ine·èn
zo·nèn·shtikh*

36 My stomach is upset
Ich habe mir den Magen
verdorben
*ikh **hah**·bè meer dayn **mah**·gèn
fer·**dor**·bèn*

37 I feel nauseated
Mir ist übel
*meer ist **ōō**·bèl*

38 I think I have food poisoning
Ich glaube, ich habe eine
Lebensmittelvergiftung
*ikh **glow**·bè ikh **hah**·bè ine·è
lay·bèns·mi·tèl·fer·**gif**·toong*

39 I have vomited
Ich habe mich übergeben
*ikh **hah**·bè mikh
ōō·bèr·**gay**·bèn*

40 I have diarrhea
Ich habe Durchfall
*ikh **hah**·bè **doorkh**·fal*

41 I am constipated
Ich habe Verstopfung
*ikh **hah**·bè fer·**shtop**·foong*

42 I feel faint
Mir ist schwindelig
*meer ist **shvin**·dè·likh*

43 I am allergic to penicillin/to
cortisone
Ich bin allergisch gegen
Penizillin/Cortison
*ikh bin a·**ler**·gish **gay**·gèn
pe·ni·tsi·**leen**/kor·tee·**zōn***

44 I have high blood pressure
Ich habe zu hohen Blutdruck
*ikh **hah**·bè tsoo **hō**·èn
bloot·drook*

45 I am a diabetic
Ich bin zuckerkrank
*ikh bin **tsoo**·kèr·krank*

46 I am taking these drugs
Ich nehme diese Medikamente
*ikh **nay**·mè dee·zè
may·dee·ka·**men**·tè*

47 Can you give me a German
prescription for them?
Können Sie mir dafür ein
deutsches Rezept geben?
*kur'·nèn zee meer da·**fōōr** ine
doyt·shès ray·**tsept gay**·bèn*

48 I am pregnant
Ich bin schwanger
*ikh bin **shvang**·èr*

49 I am on the pill
Ich nehme die Pille
*ikh **nay**·mè dee **pi**·lè*

50 My blood group is . . .
Ich habe die Blutgruppe . . .
*ikh **hah**·bè dee
bloot·groo·pè . . .*

51 I don't know my blood group
Ich weiß nicht, welche
Blutgruppe ich habe
*ikh vice nikht **vel**·khè
bloot·groo·pè ikh **hah**·bè*

52 Must I stay in bed?
Muß ich im Bett bleiben?
*moos ikh im bet **blye**·bèn*

53 Will I be able to go out
tomorrow?
Darf ich morgen ausgehen?
*darf ikh **mor**·gèn **ows**·gay·èn*

54 Will I have to go to the
hospital?
Muß ich ins Krankenhaus?
*moos ikh ins **krang**·kèn·hows*

56 How do I get reimbursed?
Wie werden mir die Kosten
zurückerstattet?
*vee **ver**·dèn meer dee **kos**·tèn
tsoo·**rōōk**·er·shta·tèt*

Dentists

57 I need to see the dentist
Ich muß zum Zahnarzt
*ikh moos tsoom **tsahn**·artst*

58 I have a toothache
Ich habe Zahnschmerzen
*ikh **hah**·bè **tsahn**·shmert·sèn*

59 It's this one
Es ist dieser Zahn
*ess ist **dee**·zèr tsahn*

60 I've broken a tooth
Mir ist ein Zahn abgebrochen
*meer ist ine tsahn
ap·gè·bro·khèn*

61 The filling has come out
Die Plombe ist herausgefallen
*dee plom·bè ist
he·rows·gè·fa·lèn*

62 Will you have to take it out?
Müssen Sie ihn ziehen?
mōō·sèn zee een tsee·èn

63 Are you going to fill it?
Müssen Sie ihn plombieren?
mōō·sèn zee een plom·bee·rèn

64 That hurts
Das tut weh
dass toot vay

65 Please give me an anesthetic
Bitte geben Sie mir eine
Spritze
*bi·tè gay·bèn zee meer ine·è
shprit·sè*

66 My gums hurt
Mir tut das Zahnfleisch weh
meer toot dass tsahn·flyesh vay

67 My dentures are broken
Mein Gebiß ist kaputt
mine gè·bis ist ka·poot

68 Can you repair them?
Können Sie es reparieren?
kur'·nèn zee ess ray·pa·ree·rèn

Emergencies and accidents (Ea)

Hopefully you will not need the following phrases, but it is better to know them, as they could make a difference in a critical situation.

1 Help!
Hilfe!
hil·fè

2 Stop!
Halt!
halt

3 Stop thief!
Haltet den Dieb!
hal·tèt dayn deep

4 There has been an accident
Es ist ein Unfall passiert
ess ist ine oon·fal pa·seert

5 A fire has broken out
Es brennt
ess brent

6 I have been robbed/attacked
Man hat mich bestohlen/Ich bin überfallen worden
man hat mikh bè·shtō·lèn/ikh bin ōō·bèr·fa·lèn vor·dèn

7 Where is the nearest telephone/hospital?
Wo ist das nächste Telefon/Krankenhaus?
vō ist dass nekh·stè tay·lay·fōn/krang·kèn·hows

8   Call — a doctor
Rufen Sie — einen Arzt
roo·fèn zee — ine·èn artst
          — an ambulance
— einen Krankenwagen
— ine·èn krang·kèn·vah·gèn
          — the police
— die Polizei
— dee pō·lee·tsye
          — the fire department
— die Feuerwehr
— dee foy·èr·vayr

9 This is an emergency
Es ist ein Notfall
ess ist ine nōt·fal

10 It is urgent
Es ist dringend
ess ist dring·ènt

11 Please hurry
Eilen Sie sich bitte!
ile·èn zee zikh bi·tè

12 My address is . . .
Meine Adresse ist . . .
mine·è a·dre·sè ist . . .

Making conversation   (Mc)

Topics

The weather

Germans do not talk about the weather as much as, for example, the Americans and the English do, but there are occasions when you will find the following phrases useful.

1 It's a lovely day
Schönes Wetter heute, nicht (wahr)?
shur'·nès ve·tèr hoy·tè nikht (vahr)

2 It's too hot/cold for me
Es ist mir zu heiß/kalt
ess ist meer tsoo hice/kalt

3 It's raining
Es regnet
ess rayg·nèt

4 It's windy
Es ist windig
ess ist vin·dikh

5 It's snowing
Es schneit
ess shnite

6 It's foggy
Es ist neblig
ess ist nay·blikh

7 Is it going to be a nice day/to rain?
Wird es schön sein/regnen?
virt ess shur'n zine/rayg·nèn

8 What is the temperature?
Wieviel Grad sind es?
vee·feel graht zint ess

9 Is the lake calm?
Ist der See ruhig?
ist der zay roo·ikh

10 Is the water warm?
Ist das Wasser warm?
ist dass va·sèr varm

11 When is high tide?
Wann kommt die Flut?
van komt dee floot

12 It's a clear night
Es ist eine klare Nacht
ess ist ine·è klah·rè nakht

National and regional characteristics

This is an endlessly fruitful source of material for conversation. Here are some of the points that might be raised.

13 My country has a population of...
Mein Land hat ... Einwohner
mine lant hat ... ine·vō·nèr

14 The country has a high/low cost of living
Das Land hat hohe/niedrige Lebenshaltungskosten
dass lant hat hō·è/nee·dri·gè lay·bèns·hal·toongs·kos·tèn

15 The pace of life is fast/slow
Das Leben ist hektisch/geruhsam
dass lay·bèn ist hek·tish/gè·roo·zahm

16 The way of life is — traditional
Der Lebensstil ist — traditionell
der lay·bèns·shteel ist — tra·dee·tsee·ō·nel
— rapidly changing
— raschen Änderungen unterworfen
— *ra·shèn en·dè·roong·èn oon·tèr·vor·fèn*

17 The quality of life/the environment is high/low
Die Lebensqualität/die Qualität der Umwelt ist hoch/niedrig
dee lay·bèns·kva·lee·tet/dee kva·lee·tet der oom·velt ist hōkh/nee·drikh

18 The people are — friendly/hardworking
Die Leute sind — freundlich/fleißig
dee loy·tè zint — froynt·likh/flye·sikh

19 What is the custom in Germany about shaking hands?
Wie hält man es in Deutschland mit dem Händeschütteln?
vee helt man ess in doytsh·lant mit daym hen·dè·shōō·tèln

20 What sports are popular in Austria?
Welche Sportarten sind in Österreich beliebt?
vel·khè shport·ar·tèn zint in ur'·stè·ryekh bè·leept

21 Where did you spend your vacation last year?
Wo haben Sie letztes Jahr Ihre Ferien verbracht?
*vō **hah**·bèn zee let·stès yahr ee·rè **fay**·ri·èn fer·**brakht***

22 Did you like it there?
Hat es Ihnen dort gefallen?
*hat es **ee**·nèn dort gè·**fa**·lèn*

23 What region do you come from?
Aus welcher Gegend kommen Sie?
*ows vel·khèr **gay**·gènt ko·mèn zee*

24 What is the climate like in Bavaria?
Wie ist das Klima in Bayern?
*vee ist dass **klee**·ma in **bye**·èrn*

25 What are the people like?
Wie sind die Leute?
*vee zint dee **loy**·tè*

26 Is the region prosperous?
Ist es eine reiche Gegend?
*ist ess ine·è **rye**·khè **gay**·gènt*

27 Does it remain unspoiled?
Ist es noch relativ unberührt?
*ist ess nokh ray·la·**teef** oon·bè·**rōōrt***

28 Do you know the country around Düsseldorf?
Kennen Sie sich in der Umgegend von Düsseldorf aus?
***ke**·nèn zee zikh in der **oom**·gay·gènt fon **dōō**·sèl·dorf ows*

29 The wine/food in the Mosel region is wonderful
Der Wein/das Essen in der Moselgegend ist wunderbar
*der vine/dass e·sèn in der **mō**·zel·gay·gènt ist **voon**·dèr·bahr*

30 Vienna is a beautiful town
Wien ist eine schöne Stadt
*veen ist **ine**·è **shur**'·nè shtat*

31 Have you ever been to Cologne?
Waren Sie schon einmal in Köln?
***vah**·rèn zee shōn **ine**·mahl in kur'ln*

32 Where is its commercial/administrative center?
Wo sind die Hauptgeschäftsstraßen/Wo ist die Stadtverwaltung?
*vō zint dee **howpt**·gè·shefts·**shtrah**·sèn/vō ist dee **shtat**·fer·val·toong*

Breaking the ice

Here are a few stock questions and answers that tend to be exchanged by people who meet casually (see also Greetings and general exchanges, p.6).

33   Do you mind — if I sit here?
Macht es Ihnen etwas aus — wenn ich mich hier hinsetze?
*makht ess **ee**·nèn et·vass ows — ven ikh mikh heer **hin**·zet·sè*
            — if I smoke?
            — wenn ich rauche?
            — *ven ikh **row**·khè*

34   Can I — offer you a cigarette?
Kann ich — Ihnen eine Zigarette anbieten?
*kan ikh — **ee**·nèn ine·è tsi·ga·**re**·tè **an**·bee·tèn*
            — buy you a drink?
            — Sie zu einem Drink einladen?
            — *zee tsoo **ine**·èm drink **ine**·lah·dèn*

35 May I introduce myself?
Darf ich mich vorstellen?
*darf ikh mikh **fōr**·shte·lèn*

36 Are you German/Austrian/Swiss?
Sind Sie aus Deutschland/Österreich/der Schweiz?
*zint zee ows **doytsh**·lant/**ur**'·stè·ryekh/der shvites*

37 I am American/English
Ich bin aus Amerika/England
*ikh bin ows a·**may**·ri·ka/**eng**·glant*

38 I live in New York/London
Ich wohne in New York/London
*ikh **vō**·nè in New York/London*

39 Is this your first visit to Bonn?
   Sind Sie zum ersten Mal in Bonn?
   zint zee tsoom er·stèn mahl in bon
40 This is my third visit to ...
   Dies ist mein dritter Besuch in ...
   dees ist mine dri·tèr bè·zookh in ...
41 Have you been here long?
   Sind Sie schon lange hier?
   zint zee shōn lang·è heer
42 I've been here two days
   Ich bin zwei Tage hier
   ikh bin tsvye tah·gè heer
43 Are you staying long?
   Bleiben Sie lange?
   blye·bèn zee lang·è
44 I'm staying for two weeks
   Ich bleibe zwei Wochen
   ikh blye·bè tsvye vo·khèn
45 Where are you staying?
   Wo wohnen Sie?
   vō vō·nèn zee
46 I am staying at the hotel Drei Rosen
   Ich wohne im Hotel Drei Rosen
   ikh vō·nè im hō·tel drye rō·zèn
47 What is your job?
   Was machen Sie beruflich?
   vass ma·khèn zee bè·roof·likh

48   I am — a businessman
          Ich bin — Geschäftsmann
         ikh bin — *gè·shefts·man*
                       — a student
                       — Student(in)
                       — *shtoo·dent(·in)*

49 Have you visited England/America?
   Waren Sie schon einmal in England/Amerika?
   vah·rèn zee shōn ine·mahl in eng·glant/a·may·ri·ka

50   What do you think — of the country?
       Was halten Sie — vom Land?
       vass hal·tèn zee — *fom lant*
                       — of the people?
                       — von den Leuten?
                       — *fon dayn loy·tèn*
                       — of the food?
                       — vom Essen?
                       — *fom e·sèn*

51 Are you married?
   Sind Sie verheiratet?
   zint zee fer·hye·rah·tèt
52 Do you have any children?
   Haben Sie Kinder?
   hah·bèn zee kin·dèr

53   Would you like — to go out with me this evening?
       Möchten Sie — heute abend mit mir ausgehen?
       mur'kh·tèn zee — *hoy·tè ah·bènt mit meer*
                         ows·gay·èn
                       — to have lunch/dinner with me?
                       — mit mir mittagessen/zu Abend
                         essen?
                       — *mit meer mi·tahk·e·sèn/tsoo*
                         ah·bènt e·sèn
                       — to go to the movies/theater with
                         me?
                       — mit mir ins Theater/Kino gehen?
                       — *mit meer ins tay·ah·tèr/kee·nō*
                         gay·èn
                       — to show me something of your
                         city?
                       — mir Ihre Stadt zeigen?
                       — *meer ee·rè shtat tsye·gèn*

Reference   (R)

The alphabet

The German alphabet is the same as the English, with the exception of the letters ä, ö and ü (formed by adding an Umlaut to a, o and u) and the combined s and z (written ß and pronounced *es·tset*) which is treated alphabetically as double s. In the following table the names of the letters are given phonetically, and each letter (except for Y) forms the initial of a word printed on the right. This is a standard system for clarification, which might be used, for example, when a word is being spelled out over the telephone.

A	for	Anton	N	for	Nordpol
ah		*an·ton*	*en*		*nort·pōl*
B		Berta	O		Otto
bay		*ber·ta*	*ō*		*o·tō*
C		Caesar	P		Paula
tsay		*tsay·zar*	*pay*		*pow·lah*
D		Dora	Q		Quelle
day		*dō·rah*	*kōō*		*kve·lè*
E		Emil	R		Richard
ay		*ay·meel*	*er*		*rikh·art*
F		Friedrich	S		Siegfried
ef		*freet·rikh*	*es*		*zeek·freet*
G		Gustav	T		Theodor
gay		*goos·tahf*	*tay*		*tay·ō·dor*
H		Heinrich	U		Ulrich
hah		*hine·rikh*	*oo*		*ool·rikh*
I		Ida	V		Victor
ee		*ee·dah*	*fow*		*vik·tor*
J		Julius	W		Wilhelm
yot		*yoo·lee·oos*	*vay*		*vil·helm*
K		Konrad	X		Xanten
kah		*kon·rat*	*iks*		*ksan·tèn*
L		Ludwig	Y		
el		*lood·vikh*	*ōōp·si·lon*		
M		Martin	Z		Zeppelin
em		*mar·tin*	*tset*		*tse·pè·leen*

Numbers

Cardinal Numbers

0 null	10 zehn	20 zwanzig
nool	*tsayn*	*tsvan·tsikh*
1 eins	11 elf	21 einundzwanzig
ines	*elf*	*ine·oont·tsvan·tsikh*
2 zwei	12 zwölf	22 zweiundzwanzig
tsvye	*tsvur'lf*	*tsvye·oont·tsvan·tsikh*
3 drei	13 dreizehn	23 dreiundzwanzig
drye	*drye·tsayn*	*drye·oont·tsvan·tsikh*
4 vier	14 vierzehn	30 dreißig
feer	*fir·tsayn*	*drye·sikh*
5 fünf	15 fünfzehn	40 vierzig
fōōnf	*fōōnf·tsayn*	*fir·tsikh*
6 sechs	16 sechzehn	50 fünfzig
zeks	*zekh·tsayn*	*fōōnf·tsikh*
7 sieben	17 siebzehn	60 sechzig
zee·bèn	*zeep·tsayn*	*zekh·tsikh*
8 acht	18 achtzehn	70 siebzig
akht	*akht·tsayn*	*zeep·tsikh*
9 neun	19 neunzehn	80 achtzig
noyn	*noyn·tsayn*	*akht·tsikh*

90 neunzig	300	2,000
noyn·tsikh	dreihundert	zweitausend
100 hundert	*drye·hoon·dèrt*	*tsvye·tow·zènt*
hoon·dèrt	1,000	1,000,000
110	tausend	eine Million
hundertzehn	*tow·zènt*	*ine·è mi·lee·ōn*
hoon·dèrt·tsayn		
200		
zweihundert		
tsvye·hoon·dèrt		

Ordinal numbers

1st	11th	21st
erste	elfte	einundzwanzigste
er·stè	*elf·tè*	*ine·oont·tsvan·tsikh·stè*
2nd	12th	22nd
zweite	zwölfte	zweiundzwanzigste
tsvye·tè	*tsvur'lf·tè*	*tsvye·oont·tsvan·*
3rd	13th	*tsikh·stè*
dritte	dreizehnte	23rd
dri·tè	*drye·tsayn·tè*	dreiundzwanzigste
4th	14th	*drye·oont·tsvan·*
vierte	vierzehnte	*tsikh·stè*
feer·tè	*fīr·tsayn·tè*	30th
5th	15th	dreißigste
fünfte	fünfzehnte	*drye·sikh·stè*
fōōnf·tè	*fōōnf·tsayn·tè*	40th
6th	16th	vierzigste
sechste	sechzehnte	*fīr·tsikh·stè*
zek·stè	*zekh·tsayn·tè*	50th
7th	17th	fünfzigste
siebte	siebzehnte	*fōōnf·tsikh·stè*
zeep·tè	*zeep·tsayn·tè*	100th
8th	18th	hundertste
achte	achtzehnte	*hoon·dèrt·stè*
akh·tè	*akht·tsayn·tè*	1,000th
9th	19th	tausendste
neunte	neunzehnte	*tow·zènt·stè*
noyn·tè	*noyn·tsayn·tè*	
10th	20th	
zehnte	zwanzigste	
tsayn·tè	*tsvan·tsikh·stè*	

Other numerical terms

a half	10 percent	five times
ein halbes	zehn Prozent	fünf mal
ine hal·bès	*tsayn prō·tsent*	*fōōnf mahl*
a quarter	a dozen	the last (one)
ein Viertel	ein Dutzend	der letzte
ine fīr·tèl	*ine doot·sènt*	*der let·stè*
a third	half a dozen	
ein Drittel	ein halbes Dutzend	
ine dri·tèl	*ine hal·bès doot·sènt*	

Time

In reply to the question "wieviel Uhr ist es?" (*vee·feel oo·èr ist ess*) or "wie spät ist es?" (*vee shpayt ist ess*), both ways of saying "what time is it?", you will hear "es ist" (*ess ist*: it is) followed by the number. If the time is on the hour, say ten o'clock, the answer will be "zehn Uhr" (*tsayn oo·èr*: 10 o'clock). The 24-hour clock is often used. Otherwise, to indicate a.m. you add "vormittags" (*fōr·mi·tahks*: before midday) and for p.m. you add "nachmittags" (*nahkh·mi·tahks*: after midday) or "abends" (*ah·bènts*: in the evening). Noon is "zwölf Uhr mittags" (*tsvur'lf oo·èr mi·tahks*: 12 o'clock midday), and midnight is "zwölf Uhr abends" (*tsvur'lf oo·èr ah·bènts*: 12 o'clock at night). Times in between follow a pattern similar to the English one, with an important exception: "Halb zehn" (half ten) means thirty minutes *to* ten, in other words, half past nine. Here are some examples of times.

9:00 a.m./p.m.	9:30
Neun Uhr vormittags/abends	Halb zehn
noyn oo·èr fōr·mi·tahks/ah·bènts	*halp tsayn*
9:05	9:40
Fünf nach neun	Zwanzig vor zehn
fōōnf nahkh noyn	*tsvan·tsikh fōr tsayn*
9:15	9:45
Viertel nach neun	Viertel vor zehn
fir·tèl nahkh noyn	*fir·tèl fōr tsayn*

The same sequence using the 24-hour clock, and assuming it is p.m., would be:

9:00
Einundzwanzig Uhr
ine·oont·tsvan·tsikh oo·èr
9:05
Fünf nach einundzwanzig
fōōnf nahkh ine·oont·tsvan·tsikh
9:15
Viertel nach einundzwanzig
fir·tèl nahkh ine·oont·tsvan·tsikh
9:30
Halb zweiundzwanzig
halp tsvye·oont·tsvan·tsikh
9:40
Zwanzig vor zweiundzwanzig
tsvan·tsikh fōr tsvye·oont·tsvan·tsikh
9:45
Viertel vor zweiundzwanzig
fir·tèl fōr tsvye·oont·tsvan·tsikh

Here are some other useful phrases connected with time:

tonight	at about 1 o'clock
heute abend	gegen ein Uhr
hoy·tè ah·bènt	*gay·gèn ine oo·èr*
at night	in an hour's time
nachts	in einer Stunde
nakhts	*in ine·èr shtoon·dè*
in the morning	two hours ago
am Morgen	vor zwei Stunden
am mor·gèn	*fōr tsvye shtoon·dèn*
this afternoon	in half an hour
heute nachmittag	in einer halben Stunde
hoy·tè nahkh·mi·tahk	*in ine·èr hal·bèn shtoon·dè*
before midnight	soon
vor Mitternacht	bald
fōr mi·tèr·nakht	*balt*
after 3 o'clock	early
nach drei Uhr	früh
nahkh drye oo·èr	*frōō*
nearly 5 o'clock	late
kurz vor fünf	spät
koorts fōr fōōnf	*shpayt*

The calendar

Sunday	Tuesday	Thursday
Sonntag	Dienstag	Donnerstag
zon·tahk	*deens·tahk*	*do·nèrs·tahk*
Monday	Wednesday	Friday
Montag	Mittwoch	Freitag
mōn·tahk	*mit·vokh*	*frye·tahk*

Saturday	in spring	August
Samstag	im Frühling	August
zams-tahk	*im frōō-ling*	*ow-goost*
on Friday	in summer	September
am Freitag	im Sommer	September
am frye-tahk	*im zo-mèr*	*sep-tem-bèr*
next Tuesday	January	October
nächsten Dienstag	Januar	Oktober
nekh-stèn deens-tahk	*ya-noo-ar*	*ok-tō-bèr*
yesterday	February	November
gestern	Februar	November
ges-tèrn	*fay-broo-ar*	*nō-vem-bèr*
today	March	December
heute	März	Dezember
hoy-tè	*merts*	*day-tsem-bèr*
tomorrow	April	in June
morgen	April	im Juni
mor-gèn	*a-pril*	*im yoo-nee*
spring	May	July 6
Frühling	Mai	der sechste Juli
frōō-ling	*my*	*der zekh-stè yoo-lee*
summer	June	next week
Sommer	Juni	nächste Woche
zo-mèr	*yoo-nee*	*nekh-stè vo-khè*
autumn (fall)	July	last month
Herbst	Juli	letzten Monat
herpst	*yoo-lee*	*let-stèn mō-naht*
winter		
Winter		
vin-tèr		

Public holidays

New Year's Day	January 1
Epiphany	January 6
Good Friday	(not Austria)
Easter Monday	
Labor Day	May 1
Ascension Day	
Whitmonday	
Day of Unity	June 17 (Germany only)
Corpus Christi	
Assumption	August 15 (Austria only)
National Day	October 26 (Austria only)
All Saints' Day	November 1
Repentance Day	November 21 (not Austria or Bavaria)
Feast of the Immaculate Conception	December 8 (Austria only)
Christmas Day	December 25
St Stephen's Day	December 26

Abbreviations

a.M.	am Main (on the Main River)
a.Rh.	am Rhein (on the Rhine River)
BhF	Bahnhof (railway station)
BRD	Bundesrepublik Deutschland (Federal Republic of Germany – West Germany)
bzw	beziehungsweise (and, respectively)
DB	Deutsche Bundesbahn (Federal German Railway)
DDR	Deutsche Demokratische Republik (German Democratic Republic – East Germany)
d.h.	das heißt (i.e. – that is)
Frl.	Fräulein (Miss)
G.	Gasse (lane)
GmbH	Gesellschaft mit beschränkter Haftung (Limited Company)
Hbf.	Hauptbahnhof (main railway station)
Hr.	Herr (Mr)
LKW	Lastkraftwagen (truck)

MEZ	Mitteleuropäische Zeit (Central European Time)
Mio	Million (million)
Mrd.	Milliarde (1000 millions – billion)
n. Chr.	nach Christus (AD)
ÖBB	Österreichische Bundesbahnen (Austrian Federal Railways)
PKW	Personenkraftwagen (automobile)
Pl.	Platz (square)
PS	Pferdestärke (horsepower)
PTT	Post, Telephon, Telegraph (Post, Telephone and Telegraph Office)
SBB	Schweizerische Bundesbahnen (Swiss Federal Railways)
St.	Stock (floor)
Str.	Strasse (street)
TCS	Touring-Club der Schweiz (Swiss Touring Club)
u.s.w.	und so weiter (etc)
v.	von (from)
v. Chr.	vor Christus (BC)
z.B.	zum Beispiel (e.g. – for example)
z.Z.	zur Zeit (at present)

Signs and notices (see also Road signs, p.17)

Achtung	Caution
Aufzug	Elevator
Ausgang	Exit
Auskunft	Information
Äußerlich zu gebrauchen	For external use only
Ausverkauf	Sale
Ausverkauft	Sold out
Besetzt	Occupied
Betreten des Rasens verboten	Keep off the grass
Bitte klingeln	Please ring
Das Sprechen mit dem Fahrer während der Fahrt ist verboten	It is forbidden to speak to the driver while the bus is moving
Drücken	Push
Eingang	Entrance
Eintreten ohne zu klopfen	Enter without knocking
Eintritt frei	No admission charge
Fernsprecher	Telephone
Feuerwehr	Fire Department
Frei	Vacant
Fundbüro	"Lost and Found"
Fundbüro office	"Lost and Found" office
Für Unbefugte verboten	No trespassing
Gefahr	Danger
Geschlossen	Closed
Gift	Poison
Heiß	Hot
Hinten einsteigen	Enter at the rear (on streetcars)
Kalt	Cold
Kasse	Pay here
Kein Durchgang	No outlet
Kein Zutritt	No entrance
Krankenhaus	Hospital
Krankenwagen	Ambulance
Lebensgefahr	Danger of death
Nachmittags geschlossen	Closed in the afternoon
Nicht berühren	Do not touch
Nicht hinauslehnen	Do not lean out
Nichtraucher	No smoking
Notausgang	Emergency Exit
Notbremse	Emergency cord
Nur für Anlieger	Parking for residents
Privatweg	Private road
Radweg	Bicycle path
Rauchen verboten	No smoking
Raucher	Smokers' compartment
Räumungsverkauf	"Going out of Business" sale
Rechts fahren	Keep to the right
Reiseandenken	Souvenirs
Reisebüro	Travel Agency
Schlußverkauf	Sale
Sonderangebot	Special offer
Toilette während des Aufenthalts in Bahnhöfen nicht benutzen	Do not use toilet while train is in station
Trinkwasser	Drinking water
Umleitung	Detour
Unbefugtes Betreten verboten	No trespassing
. . . verboten	. . . forbidden
Vorsicht	Caution
Ziehen	Pull
Zu verkaufen	For sale
Zu vermieten	For rent

Conversion tables

In the tables for weight and length, the central figure may be read as either a metric or a traditional measurement. So to convert from pounds to kilos you look at the figure on the right, and for kilos to pounds you want the figure on the left.

feet		meters	inches		cm	lbs		kg
3.3	1	0.3	0.39	1	2.54	2.2	1	0.45
6.6	2	0.61	0.79	2	5.08	4.4	2	0.91
9.9	3	0.91	1.18	3	7.62	6.6	3	1.4
13.1	4	1.22	1.57	4	10.6	8.8	4	1.8
16.4	5	1.52	1.97	5	12.7	11	5	2.2
19.7	6	1.83	2.36	6	15.2	13.2	6	2.7
23	7	2.13	2.76	7	17.8	15.4	7	3.2
26.2	8	2.44	3.15	8	20.3	17.6	8	3.6
29.5	9	2.74	3.54	9	22.9	19.8	9	4.1
32.9	10	3.05	3.9	10	25.4	22	10	4.5
			4.3	11	27.9			
			4.7	12	30.1			

°C	0	5	10	15	17	20	22	24	26	28	30	35	37	38	40	50	100
°F	32	41	50	59	63	68	72	75	79	82	86	95	98.4	100	104	122	212
Km	10	20	30	40	50	60	70	80	90	100	110	120					
Miles	6.2	12.4	18.6	24.9	31	37.3	43.5	49.7	56	62	68.3	74.6					

Tire pressures

lb/sq in	15	18	20	22	24	26	28	30	33	35
kg/sq cm	1.1	1.3	1.4	1.5	1.7	1.8	2	2.1	2.3	2.5

Fuel

UK gallons	1.1	2.2	3.3	4.4	5.5	6.6	7.7	8.8
liters	5	10	15	20	25	30	35	40
US gallons	1.3	2.6	3.9	5.2	6.5	7.8	9.1	10.4

Basic German Grammar

NOUNS AND ARTICLES

Nouns
All nouns begin with a capital letter in German.

Gender
This is one of the basic differences between German and English. In English, when using the definite article (the), we say 'the fork, the knife, the spoon', but in German it is '*die Gabel*, *das Messer*, *der Löffel*', reflecting the fact that '*Gabel*' is feminine in German, '*Messer*' neuter, and '*Löffel*' masculine. Equally, when using the indefinite article ('a', 'an' in English), it is '*eine Gabel*', but '*ein Messer*' and '*ein Löffel*'. Gender is largely unpredictable, and it simply has to be learned along with each new word you acquire. Nouns referring to female people and animals are, largely, feminine, and for males they are masculine, but even here there are some exceptions, e.g. 'the girl' in German is '*das Mädchen*'.

Cases
As we have seen, the article — either definite (*der*, *die*, *das*) or indefinite (*ein*, *eine*) depends on the gender of the noun. It also depends on how the noun is being used in the sentence. When the noun is the subject of the verb it is in the **nominative** case, and the form of the article is the one shown in the dictionary, e.g.:

the man sings   *der Mann singt*

When the noun is the object of the verb, it is put in the **accusative** case:

I see the man   *ich sehe den Mann*

To show possession, the "man" is in the **genitive** case:

the man's house   *das Haus des Mannes*

And the final 'case' is that which usually corresponds to the English 'to + noun', the *dative* case:

I say to the man   *ich sage dem Mann*

Other articles change according to the same patterns. Words that follow the '*der, die, das*' pattern are *jeder* (each), *dieser* (this), *jener* (that), *mancher* (many) and *welcher* (which). The example of *jeder* is given below.

Words that follow the '*ein, eine*' pattern are *kein* (not a), *mein* (my), *dein* (your — singular), *sein* (his/its), *ihr* (her/its/their), *unser* (our), *euer* (your — plural) and *Ihr* (your — polite form).

Definite Article

	Masculine	Feminine	Neuter	Plural (all genders)
Nominative	der	die	das	die
Accusative	den	die	das	die
Genitive	des	der	des	der
Dative	dem	der	dem	denen

'*der, die, das*' pattern, e.g. *jeder*

	Masculine	Feminine	Neuter	Plural (all genders)
Nominative	jeder	jede	jedes	jede
Accusative	jeden	jede	jedes	jede
Genitive	jedes	jeder	jedes	jeder
Dative	jedem	jeder	jedem	jeden

'*ein, eine*' pattern, e.g. *sein*

	Masculine	Feminine	Neuter	Plural (all genders)
Nominative	sein	seine	sein	seine
Accusative	seinen	seine	sein	seine
Genitive	seines	seiner	seines	seiner
Dative	seinem	seiner	seinem	seinen

Noun Endings

Note that in the second example, above, the word '*Mann*' took an ending in the genitive case. All masculine and neuter singular nouns take '*s*' or '*es*' (if monosyllabic) in this case, e.g. *des Mädchens* (of the girl, the girl's), *des Hauses* (of the house).

In addition, all nouns add '*n*' to the normal plural form in the dative plural, e.g.:

der Mann	*die Männer*	*den Männern*
die Maus	*die Mäuse*	*den Mäusen*
das Buch	*die Bücher*	*den Büchern*

It is a good idea to learn the plural form together with the word and its gender. All nouns are shown with their plural in the German-English side of the dictionary. Usually the plural is formed by adding an ending to the noun, so that '*Frau*' is shown with *-en* placed after it. If you find the symbol ⸚, it means that an Umlaut (two dots) is placed on the last vowel sound of the word, which alters its pronunciation slightly (see Pronunciation Guide, p.4).

ADJECTIVES

Adjective endings

When adjectives are used as the predicate (e.g. 'this house is *old*') the form used is the form found in the dictionary. But when the adjective appears before a noun, an ending usually has to be added to it, depending on the preceding article, i.e. whether it is

a '*der, die, das*' word (see above)   *das alte Haus*   the old house
an '*ein, eine*' word (see above)   *ein neuer Hut*   a new hat
or whether there is no article   *frische Luft*   fresh air

Following '*der, die, das*' words, the adjectival endings are as follows:

	Masculine	Feminine	Neuter	Plural (all genders)
Nominative	-e	-e	-e	-en
Accusative	-en	-e	-e	-en
Genitive	-en	-en	-en	-en
Dative	-en	-en	-en	-en

Following '*ein, eine*' words, the adjective takes these endings:

	Masculine	Feminine	Neuter	Plural (all genders)
Nominative	-er	-e	-es	-en
Accusative	-en	-e	-es	-en
Genitive	-en	-en	-en	-en
Dative	-en	-en	-en	-en

Adjectives before a noun with no article take the following endings:

	Masculine	Feminine	Neuter	Plural (all genders)
Nominative	-er	-e	-es	-e
Accusative	-en	-e	-es	-e
Genitive	-en	-er	-en	-er
Dative	-em	-er	-em	-en

Examples of these endings:

nominative masculine *alter Wein ist gut* old wine is good
accusative feminine *ich mag frische Luft* I like fresh air
genitive masculine *die Vorzüge alten Weines* the advantages of old wine
dative neuter *ich gebe den Vorzug hellem Licht* I prefer bright light

Comparative and superlative

The comparative is formed by adding *-er* to the adjective
The superlative is formed by adding *-st* or *-est* to the adjective, e.g:

billig (cheap)	*billiger* (cheaper)	*billigst* (cheapest)
weit (far)	*weiter* (further)	*weitest* (furthest)

There are a few exceptions to this rule:
a) Adjectives ending in *-el* and *-er* lose the *-e-* in the comparative:

dunkel (dark)	*dunkler* (darker)	*dunkelst* (darkest)
teuer (dear)	*teurer* (dearer)	*teuerst* (dearest)

b) One-syllable adjectives add an Umlaut in the comparative and superlative, where the vowel is 'o', 'a' or 'u', e.g.:

groß (big)	*größer* (bigger)	*größt* (biggest)
hoch (high)	*höher* (higher)	*höchst* (highest)
nah (near)	*näher* (nearer)	*nächst* (nearest)

Note: the comparative and superlative forms also take adjectival endings.
Hence:

der längere Fluß the longer river
ich sage den besten Schülern I say to the best pupils

PREPOSITIONS

These are important in German in that they each govern a case (or cases), which therefore affects the form of the article or adjective before the noun.
1) *Prepositions that take the accusative:*
   bis, durch, für, gegen, ohne, um, wider,
   entlang (always after the noun: '*die Straße/den Bach entlang*')
2) *Prepositions that take the dative:*
   aus, bei, mit, nach, seit, von, zu,
   gegenüber (always after the noun: '*dem Haus/der Kirche gegenüber*')
   entgegen (always after the noun: '*der Sonne/dem Vater entgegen*')
3) *Prepositions that take the genitive:*
   trotz, während, wegen
   You might find that these prepositions — in modern usage — sometimes also take the *dative*.
4) There is a fourth group, including some of the most common prepositions, which, depending on meaning, can take either *accusative* or *dative:*
   an, auf, hinter, in, neben, über, unter, vor, zwischen.
   The rule here is that if the preposition indicates *direction* or *movement*, it is followed by the *accusative*; if it is used to describe a *position* or *state*, it is followed by the *dative*, thus:

ich gehe in die Stadt I go into town
ich bin in der Stadt I am in town

PRONOUNS

Personal pronouns

The following table shows the form of personal pronouns in the nominative, accusative and dative cases:

Nominative		**Accusative**		**Dative**	
ich	I	*mich*	me	*mir*	to me
du	you	*dich*	you	*dir*	to you
er	he/it	*ihn*	him/it	*ihm*	to him/it
sie	she/it	*sie*	her/it	*ihr*	to her/it
es	it/he/she	*es*	it/him/her	*ihm*	to it/him/her
wir	we	*uns*	us	*uns*	to us
ihr	you	*euch*	you	*euch*	to you
sie	they	*sie*	them	*ihnen*	to them
Sie	you	*Sie*	you	*Ihnen*	to you

e.g.: *ich* (**nominative**) *gab es* (**accusative**) *ihm* (**dative**) I gave it to him
wir (**nominative**) *sagten es* (**accusative**) *ihr* (**dative**) we said it to her

Notes

1) As all nouns are either masculine, feminine or neuter in German, and the pronoun reflects the gender of nouns in German, *er* can mean 'he' or 'it', and *sie* and *es* can also refer to feminine and neuter objects as well as to people. Thus a girl is referred to as *es* (it), because it is *das Mädchen*, and a tree is *er* (he), since it is *der Baum*.

2)   You should use the **du** and **ihr** forms only when talking to people you know very well, otherwise you risk causing offense. It is safest to use the third person plural form, which doubles, when spelled with a capital letter, as a polite form to be used for addressing both individuals and groups. However, always address young children and animals as **du/ihr**.

Reflexive pronouns

These are pronouns used with reflexive verbs, shown in the dictionary section with **sich** preceding the infinitive.

	Accusative	*Dative*
ich	mich	mir
du	dich	dir
er/sie/es	sich	sich
wir	uns	uns
ihr	euch	euch
sie	sich	sich
Sie	sich	sich

The reflexive pronoun can be either accusative or dative. When it is accusative, it has the meaning of 'oneself'; when dative, it conveys the idea of 'to oneself' or 'for oneself', e.g. from 'sich waschen':

   *ich wasche **mich** (I wash myself)*
   *ich wasche **mir** die Hände (I wash my hands)*

Interrogative personal pronouns

Case	Pronoun	Example
Nominative	wer (who?)	wer kommt? (who is coming?)
Accusative	wen (whom?)	wen siehst du? (whom do you see?)
Genitive	wessen (whose?)	wessen Buch? (whose book?)
Dative	wem (to whom?)	wem hat er das gesagt? (to whom did he say that?)

The impersonal pronoun

In referring to people in general, the pronoun **man** is used where English often uses 'you', 'one', or 'they':

   they say that . . .   **man sagt, daß** . . .   (= one says that . . .)
   you should always . . .   **man sollte immer** . . .   (= one should always . . .)

ADVERBS

The form of adverbs rarely differs from their corresponding adjectives:
   gut = good/well
   schnell = quick/quickly
Hence, most adjectives shown in the dictionary may also be used as adverbs.

   Other adverbs are not derived from adjectives, and these have to be learned individually, but as they are among the commonest words in the German language, they are very quickly learned, e.g. **sehr** (very), **besonders** (especially).

VERBS

Verb conjugations

The tables below show you how to conjugate both regular (or 'weak') and irregular (or 'strong') verbs. In a separate list of irregular verbs you will find the parts of each verb you will need to help you use the verbs marked with an asterisk in the dictionary section of this book. We only set out the forms of four tenses in this short grammar section, as you will rarely need any tense but the present, imperfect, future or perfect for basic communication.

Tenses

1)   **Present**
(a)   There is no equivalent of the 'progressive' -*ing* form of English (as in: I am read**ing**). This sense of 'being in the process of doing' is rendered by the simple present tense. Hence:
   ich esse = I eat *or* I am eating
(b)   The present tense is not only used to describe events that take place in the present, but also largely replaces the future tense. If there is any other indication in the sentence that the action is in the future — an adverb like **bald** ('soon'), or **morgen** ('tomorrow') — the present is often used instead of the future tense.

2)   **Past**
(a)   Past actions are shown by the perfect or imperfect tense in German. There is no basic difference in meaning between the two tenses as there is in English. Hence:
   ich habe gespielt (perfect tense) can be rendered 'I played' *or* 'I have played'.
(b)   The conjugation pattern for the imperfect tense of both regular (weak) and irregular (strong) verbs is set out in the table below.

   To form the perfect tense the past participle is required. The past participle of regular verbs is formed by the addition of the prefix **ge-** to the infinitive form that you find in the dictionary, and by replacing the final -*en* by -*t* (or -*et* if it already ends in -*d* or -*t*), e.g. *spielen*, *gespielt*; *reden*, *geredet*.

Strong (or irregular) verbs add *ge*- and -*en*, often with a change of vowel. These are all shown in the table of irregular verbs. Verbs which already begin with *ge*-, and those which have a prefix like *be*-, *ent*- etc, do not add *ge*- in the past participle (see also 'separable verbs' below).

To form the perfect tense the past participle is used with the appropriate form of the verb *haben*, e.g.:

    ich habe gespielt   I played *or* I have played
    du hast getan   you did *or* you have done

Some verbs expressing the concepts of 'motion' or 'becoming' require the use of *sein* instead of *haben* in the perfect tense. These are marked with the symbol (*s*) in the table of irregular verbs.

Note: There is a class of verbs which show features of both weak and strong verb conjugations. These 'hybrid' verbs have a vowel change in some tenses, but take the 'weak' endings. There are few of these, but they are among the most common in German, e.g. *bringen* (to bring), *können* (to be able), *kennen* (to know). These are all shown in the irregular verb table, and are recognizable by the ending -*te* shown in the imperfect.

3) *Future*
The future tense is formed by using the appropriate part of the verb *werden* together with the infinitive.

Separable verbs
In German, verbs with a prefix which can exist as a word in its own right, e.g. *auf-stehen* (to stand up), *nach-ahmen* (to imitate) are called 'separable' verbs, since the two elements split apart in the present and imperfect tenses, and the prefix is placed at the end of the sentence:

    Infinitive: *weggehen* (to leave, go away)
    ich gehe morgen früh weg (I'm leaving tomorrow morning)
    er ging am Samstag mittag weg (he left on Saturday at noon)

Such verbs are shown in the dictionary section with a vertical bar between the separable components, e.g. *weg|gehen*.

In the past participle (for the perfect tense), the syllable -*ge*- is placed *between* the two components of the verb, e.g. *weggegangen* (from *weggehen*).

VERB CONJUGATION TABLES

REGULAR (WEAK)		**IRREGULAR**	
Ending -*en*	**Ending -*den*, -*ten***	**HYBRID**	**STRONG**

INFINITIVE

spielen	*reden*	*bringen*	*laufen*

PRESENT

ich	*spiele*	*rede*	*bringe*	*laufe*
du	*spielst*	*redest*	*bringst*	*läufst*
er/sie/es	*spielt*	*redet*	*bringt*	*läuft*
wir	*spielen*	*reden*	*bringen*	*laufen*
ihr	*spielt*	*redet*	*bringt*	*lauft*
sie/Sie	*spielen*	*reden*	*bringen*	*laufen*

IMPERFECT

ich	*spielte*	*redete*	**brachte**	**lief**
du	*spieltest*	*redetest*	**brachtest**	*liefst*
er/sie/es	*spielte*	*redete*	**brachte**	*lief*
wir	*spielten*	*redeten*	**brachten**	*liefen*
ihr	*spieltet*	*redetet*	**brachtet**	*lieft*
sie/Sie	*spielten*	*redeten*	**brachten**	*liefen*

PERFECT (with *haben*)   (with *sein*)

ich	**habe** *gespielt*	*geredet*	*gebracht*	**bin** *gelaufen*
du	**hast** *gespielt*	*geredet*	*gebracht*	**bist** *gelaufen*
er/sie/es	**hat** *gespielt*	*geredet*	*gebracht*	**ist** *gelaufen*
wir	**haben** *gespielt*	*geredet*	*gebracht*	**sind** *gelaufen*
ihr	**habt** *gespielt*	*geredet*	*gebracht*	**seid** *gelaufen*
sie/Sie	**haben** *gespielt*	*geredet*	*gebracht*	**sind** *gelaufen*

FUTURE

ich	**werde** *spielen*	*reden*	*bringen*	*laufen*
du	**wirst** *spielen*	*reden*	*bringen*	*laufen*
er/sie/es	**wird** *spielen*	*reden*	*bringen*	*laufen*
wir	**werden** *spielen*	*reden*	*bringen*	*laufen*
ihr	**werdet** *spielen*	*reden*	*bringen*	*laufen*
sie/Sie	**werden** *spielen*	*reden*	*bringen*	*laufen*

German Irregular Verbs

PATTERNS FOR ALL VERBS MARKED WITH AN ASTERISK IN THE DICTIONARY

If you do not find a verb with a prefix listed here, look under the simple verb form, e.g. for **abbiegen** see **biegen**.

Except for those verbs shown below the main verb table, only the 2nd and 3rd persons are irregular in the present tense, all other persons taking regular endings attached to the stem of the infinitive.

In the imperfect, the 3rd person singular is the root from which all other persons are formed with the appropriate endings shown in the conjugation table above.

In the table, the symbol (*s*) denotes the verb is conjugated with **sein**.

Infinitive	*Present Indicative (2nd, 3rd singular)*	*Imperfect*	*Past Participle*
backen	*bäckst, bäckt*	*backte*	*gebacken*
befehlen	*befiehlst, befiehlt*	*befahl*	*befohlen*
beginnen	*beginnst, beginnt*	*begann*	*begonnen*
beißen	*beißt, beißt*	*biß*	*gebissen*
bergen	*birgst, birgt*	*barg*	*geborgen*
bewegen	*bewegst, bewegt*	*bewog*	*bewogen*
biegen	*biegst, biegt*	*bog*	*gebogen*
bieten	*bietest, bietet*	*bot*	*geboten*
binden	*bindest, bindet*	*band*	*gebunden*
bitten	*bittest, bittet*	*bat*	*gebeten*
blasen	*bläst, bläst*	*blies*	*geblasen*
bleiben (s)	*bleibst, bleibt*	*blieb*	*geblieben*
braten	*brätst, brät*	*briet*	*gebraten*
brechen (s)	*brichst, bricht*	*brach*	*gebrochen*
brennen	*brennst, brennt*	*brannte*	*gebrannt*
bringen	*bringst, bringt*	*brachte*	*gebracht*
denken	*denkst, denkt*	*dachte*	*gedacht*
dringen (s)	*dringst, dringt*	*drang*	*gedrungen*
dürfen	*darfst, darf*	*durfte*	*gedurft*
empfehlen	*empfiehlst, empfiehlt*	*empfahl*	*empfohlen*
erschrecken (s)	*erschrickst, erschrickt*	*erschrak*	*erschrocken*
essen	*ißt, ißt*	*aß*	*gegessen*
fahren (s)	*fährst, fährt*	*fuhr*	*gefahren*
fallen (s)	*fällst, fällt*	*fiel*	*gefallen*
fangen	*fängst, fängt*	*fing*	*gefangen*
finden	*findest, findet*	*fand*	*gefunden*
fliegen (s)	*fliegst, fliegt*	*flog*	*geflogen*
fließen (s)	*fließt, fließt*	*floß*	*geflossen*
fressen	*frißt, frißt*	*fraß*	*gefressen*
frieren	*frierst, friert*	*fror*	*gefroren*
geben	*gibst, gibt*	*gab*	*gegeben*
gehen (s)	*gehst, geht*	*ging*	*gegangen*
gelingen (s)	*—, gelingt*	*gelang*	*gelungen*
gelten	*giltst, gilt*	*galt*	*gegolten*
genießen	*genießt, genießt*	*genoß*	*genossen*
geraten (s)	*gerätst, gerät*	*geriet*	*geraten*
geschehen (s)	*—, geschieht*	*geschah*	*geschehen*
gewinnen	*gewinnst, gewinnt*	*gewann*	*gewonnen*
gießen	*gießt, gießt*	*goß*	*gegossen*
gleichen	*gleichst, gleicht*	*glich*	*geglichen*
gleiten (s)	*gleitest, gleitet*	*glitt*	*geglitten*
graben	*gräbst, gräbt*	*grub*	*gegraben*
greifen	*greifst, greift*	*griff*	*gegriffen*
haben	*hast, hat*	*hatte*	*gehabt*
halten	*hältst, hält*	*hielt*	*gehalten*
hängen	*hängst, hängt*	*hing*	*gehangen*
heben	*hebst, hebt*	*hob*	*gehoben*
heißen	*heißt, heißt*	*hieß*	*geheißen*
helfen	*hilfst, hilft*	*half*	*geholfen*
kennen	*kennst, kennt*	*kannte*	*gekannt*
klingen	*klingst, klingt*	*klang*	*geklungen*
kneifen	*kneifst, kneift*	*kniff*	*gekniffen*
kommen (s)	*kommst, kommt*	*kam*	*gekommen*
können	*kannst, kann*	*konnte*	*gekonnt*
kriechen (s)	*kriechst, kriecht*	*kroch*	*gekrochen*
laden	*lädst, lädt*	*lud*	*geladen*
lassen	*läßt, läßt*	*ließ*	*gelassen*
laufen (s)	*läufst, läuft*	*lief*	*gelaufen*
leiden	*leidest, leidet*	*litt*	*gelitten*
leihen	*leihst, leiht*	*lieh*	*geliehen*
lesen	*liest, liest*	*las*	*gelesen*
liegen (s)	*liegst, liegt*	*lag*	*gelegen*
lügen	*lügst, lügt*	*log*	*gelogen*
mahlen	*mahlst, mahlt*	*mahlte*	*gemahlen*

Infinitive	Present Indicative (2nd, 3rd singular)	Imperfect	Past Participle
meiden	meidest, meidet	mied	gemieden
messen	mißt, mißt	maß	gemessen
mißlingen (s)	—, mißlingt	mißlang	mißlungen
mögen	magst, mag	mochte	gemocht
müssen	mußt, muß	mußte	gemußt
nehmen	nimmst, nimmt	nahm	genommen
nennen	nennst, nennt	nannte	genannt
pfeifen	pfeifst, pfeift	pfiff	gepfiffen
preisen	preist, preist	pries	gepriesen
raten	rätst, rät	riet	geraten
reiben	reibst, reibt	rieb	gerieben
reißen (s)	reißt, reißt	riß	gerissen
reiten (s)	reitest, reitet	ritt	geritten
rennen (s)	rennst, rennt	rannte	gerannt
riechen	riechst, riecht	roch	gerochen
rufen	rufst, ruft	rief	gerufen
salzen	salzt, salzt	salzte	gesalzen
saufen	säufst, säuft	soff	gesoffen
saugen	saugst, saugt	sog	gesogen
schaffen	schaffst, schafft	schuf	geschaffen
scheiden (s)	scheidest, scheidet	schied	geschieden
scheinen	scheinst, scheint	schien	geschienen
schieben	schiebst, schiebt	schob	geschoben
schießen	schießt, schießt	schoß	geschossen
schlafen	schläfst, schläft	schlief	geschlafen
schlagen	schlägst, schlägt	schlug	geschlagen
schließen	schließt, schließt	schloß	geschlossen
schmeißen	schmeißt, schmeißt	schmiß	geschmissen
schmelzen (s)	schmilzt, schmilzt	schmolz	geschmolzen
schneiden	schneidest, schneidet	schnitt	geschnitten
schreiben	schreibst, schreibt	schrieb	geschrieben
schreien	schreist, schreit	schrie	geschrie(e)n
schreiten	schreitest, schreitet	schritt	geschritten
schweigen	schweigst, schweigt	schwieg	geschwiegen
schwellen (s)	schwillst, schwillt	schwoll	geschwollen
schwimmen (s)	schwimmst, schwimmt	schwamm	geschwommen
schwinden (s)	schwindest, schwindet	schwand	geschwunden
schwingen	schwingst, schwingt	schwang	geschwungen
schwören	schwörst, schwört	schwor	geschworen
sehen	siehst, sieht	sah	gesehen
sein (s)	bist, ist	war	gewesen
senden	sendest, sendet	sandte	gesandt
singen	singst, singt	sang	gesungen
sinken (s)	sinkst, sinkt	sank	gesunken
sitzen (s)	sitzt, sitzt	saß	gesessen
sollen	sollst, soll	sollte	gesollt
spinnen	spinnst, spinnt	spann	gesponnen
sprechen	sprichst, spricht	sprach	gesprochen
springen (s)	springst, springt	sprang	gesprungen
stechen	stichst, sticht	stach	gestochen
stecken	steckst, steckt	steckte or stak	gesteckt
stehen	stehst, steht	stand	gestanden
stehlen	stiehlst, stiehlt	stahl	gestohlen
steigen (s)	steigst, steigt	stieg	gestiegen
sterben (s)	stirbst, stirbt	starb	gestorben
stinken	stinkst, stinkt	stank	gestunken
stoßen	stößt, stößt	stieß	gestoßen
streichen	streichst, streicht	strich	gestrichen
streiten (s)	streitest, streitet	stritt	gestritten
tragen	trägst, trägt	trug	getragen
treffen	triffst, trifft	traf	getroffen
treiben (s)	treibst, treibt	trieb	getrieben
treten (s)	trittst, tritt	trat	getreten
trinken	trinkst, trinkt	trank	getrunken
trügen	trügst, trügt	trog	getrogen
tun	tust, tut	tat	getan
verderben	verdirbst, verdirbt	verdarb	verdorben
vergessen	vergißt, vergißt	vergaß	vergessen
verlieren	verlierst, verliert	verlor	verloren
wachsen (s)	wächst, wächst	wuchs	gewachsen
waschen	wäschst, wäscht	wusch	gewaschen
weben	webst, webt	wob	gewoben

Infinitive	*Present Indicative (2nd, 3rd singular)*	*Imperfect*	*Past Participle*
weichen (s)	weichst, weicht	wich	gewichen
weisen	weist, weist	wies	gewiesen
wenden	wendest, wendet	wandte	gewandt
werben	wirbst, wirbt	warb	geworben
werden (s)	wirst, wird	wurde	geworden
werfen	wirfst, wirft	warf	geworfen
wiegen	wiegst, wiegt	wog	gewogen
winden	windest, windet	wand	gewunden
wissen	weißt, weiß	wußte	gewußt
wollen	willst, will	wollte	gewollt
wringen	wringst, wringt	wrang	gewrungen
ziehen	ziehst, zieht	zog	gezogen
zwingen	zwingst, zwingt	zwang	gezwungen

The following verbs show additional irregularities in the present tense only.
(All other tenses, as in the above table.)

sein		*haben*	
ich bin	wir sind	ich habe	wir haben
du bist	ihr seid	du hast	ihr habt
er/sie/es ist	sie/Sie sind	er/sie/es hat	sie/Sie haben

dürfen		*können*	
ich darf	wir dürfen	ich kann	wir können
du darfst	ihr dürft	du kannst	ihr könnt
er/sie/es darf	sie/Sie dürfen	er/sie/es kann	sie/Sie können

mögen		*müssen*	
ich mag	wir mögen	ich muß	wir müssen
du magst	ihr mögt	du mußt	ihr müßt
er/sie/es mag	sie/Sie mögen	er/sie/es muß	sie/Sie müssen

sollen		*wissen*	
ich soll	wir sollen	ich weiß	wir wissen
du sollst	ihr sollt	du weißt	ihr wißt
er/sie/es soll	sie/Sie sollen	er/sie/es weiß	sie/Sie wissen

wollen	
ich will	wir wollen
du willst	ihr wollt
er/sie/es will	sie/Sie wollen

GERMAN SENTENCES

Inversion

German sentences which start with their subject have the same word order as English:

  I saw the children *Ich sah die Kinder*

If the sentence starts with some other word, phrase or clause, the subject and verb of the main clause are inverted:

  Yesterday I saw the children *Gestern sah ich die Kinder*

Infinitives and past participles

These are placed at the end of the clause in which they occur:

  I shall go *Ich werde **gehen***
  I shall go soon *Ich werde bald **gehen***
  I went yesterday *Ich bin gestern **gegangen***

Order of objects

If there is an accusative as well as a dative object in the sentence, the order is 'verb + dative object + accusative object', e.g.

  *Ich gebe **dem Mann** das Buch* I give the book to the man

However, if one of the objects is a pronoun it **precedes** the noun object, e.g.

  *Ich gebe **es** dem Mann* I give it to the man

Where both objects are pronouns the order is usually 'accusative object + dative object', e.g.

  *Ich gebe **es ihm*** I give it to him

GERMAN–ENGLISH DICTIONARY

Aale *ah·lè pl* eels

ab *ap adv* off; **ab und zu** *ap oont tsoo* now and then, now and again □ *prep* from; **ab 8 Uhr** *ap 8 oor* from 8 o'clock

ab|biegen* *ap·bee·gèn vi* turn (*person, car*)

ab|blenden *ap·blen·dèn vt* dim (*headlights*)

Abblendschalter *ap·blent·shal·tèr m* — dimmer

Abend *ah·bènt m* —e evening; **am Abend** *am ah·bènt* in the evening

Abendanzug *ah·bènt·an·tsook m* ⁼e evening dress (*man's*)

Abendbrot *ah·bènt·brōt nt* supper

Abenddämmerung *ah·bènt·de·mè· roong f* dusk

Abendessen *ah·bènt·e·sèn nt* — dinner; supper (*main meal*)

Abendgesellschaft *ah·bènt·gè·zel·shaft f* —en dinner party

Abendkleid *ah·bènt·klite nt* —er evening dress (*woman's*)

Abendschule *ah·bènt·shoo·lè f* —n night school

Abendzeitung *ah·bènt·tsye·toong f* —en evening paper

Abenteuer *ah·bèn·toy·èr nt* — adventure

aber *ah·bèr conj* but

Aberglaube *ah·bèr·glow·bè m* superstition

ab|fahren* *ap·fah·rèn vi* pull out; leave

Abfahrt *ap·fahrt f* —en departure

Abfall *ap·fal m* ⁼e waste (*rubbish*); trash

Abfälle *ap·fe·lè pl* rubbish

Abfalleimer *ap·fal·ime·èr m* — trash can; garbage can

ab|fallen* *ap·fa·lèn vi* shelve (*beach*)

ab|fliegen* *ap·flee·gèn vi* take off (*plane*)

Abflug *ap·flook m* ⁼e takeoff (*of plane*)

Abflughalle *ap·flook·ha·lè f* —n departure lounge

Abflugtafel *ap·flook·tah·fèl m* — departure board

Abfluß *ap·floos m* ⁼e drain

Abflußrohr *ap·floos·rōr nt* —e drainpipe

ab|fragen *ap·frah·gèn vt* retrieve (*data*)

Abführmittel *ap·fōōr·mi·tèl nt* — laxative

Abgase *ap·gah·zè pl* exhaust (*fumes*)

ab|gehen* *ap·gay·èn vi* come off

abgelaufen *ap·gè·low·fèn adj* out-of-date (*passport, ticket*)

abgelegen *ap·gè·lay·gèn adj* private (*secluded*)

abgemacht *ap·gè·makht adj* agreed

abgetragen *ap·gè·trah·gèn adj* worn; worn-out (*object*)

ab|gießen* *ap·gee·sèn vt* drain (*vegetables*)

ab|haken *ap·hah·kèn vt* tick (*mark*)

Abhang *ap·hang m* ⁼e slope

ab|hängen* von *ap·heng·èn fon vt* depend on

abhängig von *ap·heng·ikh fon adj* subject to

ab|heben* *ap·hay·bèn vt* withdraw (*money*)

ab|holen *ap·hō·lèn vt* claim (*lost pro-*

perty, baggage); **ich werde Sie am Bahnhof ab|holen** *ikh ver·dè zee am bahn·hōf ap·hō·lèn* I'll meet you at the station (*go to get*); **einen Freund ab|holen** *ine·èn froynt ap·hō·lèn* to pick up a friend

Abkommen *ap·ko·mèn nt* — agreement

Abkürzung *ap·kōōr·tsoong f* —en shortcut; abbreviation

ab|laden* *ap·lah·dèn vt* unload (*goods*)

ab|lassen* *ap·la·sèn vt* drain (*sump, pool*)

Ablauf *ap·lowf m* ⁼e drainboard

ab|laufen* *ap·low·fèn vi* expire

ab|lehnen *ap·lay·nèn vt* reject; refuse

Ablehnung *ap·lay·noong f* —en refusal

ab|lenken *ap·lenk·èn vt* distract

ab|löschen *ap·lur·shèn vt* blot (*ink*)

Abmachung *ap·makh·oong f* —en understanding; agreement

sich ab|melden *zikh ap·mel·dèn vr* to check out

Abnäher *ap·nay·èr m* — dart (*on clothes*)

ab|nehmen* *ap·nay·mèn vi* reduce (*lose weight*); **das Telefon ab|nehmen** *dass tay·lay·fōn ap·nay·mèn* to answer the phone

ab|nutzen *ap·noot·sèn vt* wear out; **sich ab|nutzen** *zikh ap·noot·sèn* wear (out) (*fabric*)

Abnutzung *ap·noot·soong f* wear and tear

Abonnement *a·bo·nè·mong nt* —s subscription (*to periodical*)

Abonnent *a·bo·nent m* —en subscriber

abonnieren *a·bo·nee·rèn vt* subscribe to (*periodical*)

ab|reisen *ap·rye·zèn vi* depart; set out

abrupt *a·broopt adj* abrupt (*person*)

ab|sagen *ap·zah·gèn vt* cancel

Absatz *ap·zats m* ⁼e heel (*of shoe*); paragraph

ab|schaffen *ap·sha·fèn vt* abolish

ab|schalten *ap·shal·tèn vt* switch off (*engine*); **den Hauptschalter/Haupthahn ab|schalten** *dayn howpt·shal· tèr/howpt·hahn ap·shal·tèn* to turn the electricity/water off at the main

Abscheu *ap·shoy f* disgust

ab|schicken *ap·shi·kèn vt* dispatch

Abschlagszahlung *ap·shlahks·tsah· loong f* —en installment

ab|schleppen *ap·shle·pen vt* tow; **Fahrzeug wird abgeschleppt** *fahr·tsoyk virt ap·gè·shlept* in tow

Abschleppwagen *ap·shlep·vah·gèn m* — tow truck

ab|schließen* *ap·shlee·sèn vt* lock

Abschnitt *ap·shnit m* —e stub (*of check*)

ab|schreiben* *ap·shrye·bèn vt* write off

Abschürfung *ap·shōōr·foong f* —en graze

abseits von *ap·zites fon prep* away from

Absender *ap·zen·dèr m* — sender

Absicht *ap·zikht f* —en aim; intention

absichtlich *ap·zikht·likh adv* on purpose

absolut *ap·zō·loot adj* absolute

Absperrhahn *ap·shper·hahn m* ⁼e stopcock

ab|spülen *ap·shpōō·lèn vi* wash the dishes

ab|stauben *ap·shtow·bèn vt* dust (*furniture*)

ab|stellen *ap·shte·lèn vt* turn off (*water*)

abstrakt *ap·strakt adj* abstract

absurd *ap·zoort adj* absurd

Abszeß *aps·tses m —e* abscess

ab|tauen *ap·tow·èn vt* defrost (*refrigerator*)

Abtei *ap·tye f —en* abbey

Abteil *ap·tile nt —e* compartment (*on train*)

Abteilung *ap·tye·loong f —en* department (*in store*)

abwärts *ap·verts adv* down

abwechselnd *ap·vek·sèlnt adv* in turn

ab|werfen* *ap·ver·fèn vt* throw (*rider*)

ab|werten *ap·ver·tèn vt* devalue (*currency*)

Abwertung *ap·ver·toong f —en* devaluation

abwesend *ap·vay·zènt adj* absent

Abwesenheit *ap·vay·zèn·hite f —en* absence

ab|wischen *ap·vi·shèn vt* wipe (off)

ab|würgen *ap·vöör·gèn vt* stall (*car engine*)

Abzeichen *ap·tsye·khèn nt —* badge (*of cloth*)

ab|ziehen* *ap·tsee·èn vt* deduct; subtract; etwas ab|ziehen* *et·vass ap·tsee·èn* to pull something off

Abzug *ap·tsook m —e* print (*photographic*)

Achse *ak·sè f —n* axle

Achsel *ak·sèl f —n* shoulder; die Achseln zucken *dee ak·sèln tsoo·kèn* to shrug

acht *akht num* eight

achten *akh·tèn vt* respect

achte(r/s) *akh·tè(·tèr/·tès) adj* eighth

Achtung *akh·toong f* respect

achtzehn *akh·tsayn num* eighteen

achtzig *akh·tsikh num* eighty; die achtziger Jahre *dee akh·tsi·gèr yah·rè* the eighties (*decade*)

Acryl- *a·krööl pref* acrylic

ad acta legen *at ak·ta lay·gèn vt* shelve (*project*)

Adapter *a·dap·tèr m —* adapter, adaptor (*electrical*)

addieren *a·dee·rèn vt* add (up)

Addition *a·di·tsee·ōn f* addition

Adler *ahd·lèr m —* eagle

Adlerfarn *ahd·lèr·farn m* bracken

adoptieren *a·dop·tee·rèn vt* adopt (*child*)

Adreßbuch *a·dress·bookh nt —er* directory

adressieren *a·dre·see·rèn vt* address (*letter*)

Adria *a·dree·a f* Adriatic (Sea)

Affe *a·fè m —n* ape; monkey

Afrika *a·fri·ka nt* Africa

afrikanisch *a·fri·kah·nish adj* African

Agent *a·gent m —en* agent

aggressiv *a·gre·seef adj* aggressive

agil *a·geel adj* agile

Ägypten *e·gööp·tèn nt* Egypt

ägyptisch *e·gööp·tish adj* Egyptian

ähneln *ay·nèln vi* resemble; be similar to; er ähnelt seinem Vater *er ay·nèlt zine·èm fah·tèr* he resembles his father

ähnlich *ayn·likh adj* alike; like; similar

Airbus *er·boos m —se* air bus

Akademiker *a·ka·day·mi·kèr m* graduate (*from university*)

Akademikerin *a·ka·day·mi·kè·rin f —nen* graduate (*from university*)

Akkordarbeit *a·kort·ar·bite f* piecework

Akne *ak·nè f —n* acne

Akt *akt m —e* act (*of play*)

Akte *ak·tè f —n* record; file (*dossier*)

Aktenkoffer *ak·tèn·ko·fèr m —* briefcase

Aktenmappe *ak·tèn·ma·pè f —n* portfolio

Aktenschrank *ak·tèn·shrank m —e* filing cabinet

Aktie *ak·tsee·è f —n* share (*finance*); Aktien und Wertpapiere *ak·tsee·èn oont vert·pa·pee·rè* stocks

Aktiengesellschaft *ak·tsee·èn·gè·zel·shaft f —en* joint-stock company

Aktionär *ak·tsee·o·nayr m —e* stockholder

aktiv *ak·teef adj* energetic; active

Aktiva *ak·tee·va pl* assets; die verfügbaren Aktiva *fer·föök·ba·rèn ak·tee·va* liquid assets

Aktivposten *ak·teef·pos·tèn m —* asset (*financial*)

Akzent *ak·tsent m —e* accent

Alarmanlage *a·larm·an·lah·gè f —n* alarm (*apparatus*)

albern *al·bèrn adj* silly

Album *al·boom nt Alben* album

Alge *al·gè f —n* seaweed

Algerien *al·gay·ree·èn nt* Algeria

algerisch *al·gay·rish adj* Algerian

Algier *al·zheer nt* Algiers

Alkohol *al·kō·hol m* liquor; alcohol

alkoholfrei *al·kō·hol·frye adj* soft (*drink*); nonalcoholic

Alkoholiker *al·kō·hō·li·kèr m —* alcoholic

alkoholisch *al·kō·hō·lish adj* alcoholic (*drink*)

Alkoven *al·kō·vèn m —* alcove

Allah *ah·la m* Allah

alle *a·lè pron* all (*plural*); everybody; everyone □ *adj* all (*with plural noun*); alle zwei Tage *a·lè tsvye tah·gè* every other day; alle sechs Tage *a·lè zeks tah·gè* every 6th day; alle Tische *a·lè ti·shè* all the tables; alle Passagiere *a·lè pa·sa·zhee·rè* all passengers

Allee *a·lay f —n* avenue

allein *a·line adj* alone; er hat es allein gemacht *er hat ess a·line gè·makht* he did it on his own

Allergie *a·ler·gee f —n* allergy

allergisch gegen *a·ler·gish gay·gèn adj* allergic to

allerletzte(r/s) *a·lèr·lets·tè(·tèr/·tès) adj* very last

alle(r/s) *a·lè(·lèr/lès) adj* all (*with singular noun*)

alles *a·lès pron* everything; all (*singular*); alles, was Sie brauchen *a·lès vass zee brow·khèn* all you need

allgemein *al·gè·mine adj* general; universal; im allgemeinen *im al·gè·mine·èn* generally; in general

Allgemeinwissen *al·gè·mine·vi·sèn nt* general knowledge

allmählich *al·may·likh adj* gradual □ *adv* gradually

Alpen *al·pèn pl* Alps

Alphabet *al·fa·bayt nt —e* alphabet

alpin *al·peen adj* alpine

Alptraum *alp·trowm m —e* nightmare

als *als conj* than; when (*with past tense*); er ist angekommen, als wir weggingen *er ist an·gè·ko·mèn als veer vek·ging·èn* he arrived as we left; **als ob** *als op* as if, as though; **am Tag, als wir... am tahk als veer** the day when we...

also *al'zō conj* therefore; **also!** *al'zō* well!

alt *alt adj* old; **wie alt sind Sie?** *vee alt zint zee* how old are you?

Altar *al'tahr m* —e altar

altbacken *alt'ba·kèn adj* stale (*bread*)

Alter *al'tèr nt* age (*of person*)

ältere(r/s) *el'tè·rè(·rèr/·rès) adj* older; elder

älteste(r/s) *el·tè·stè(·stèr/·stès) adj* oldest; eldest

altmodisch *alt'mō·dish adj* out of date; old-fashioned

Alufolie *ah·loo·fō·lee·è f* —n foil (*for food*)

Aluminium *a·loo·mee·nee·oom nt* aluminum

Amateur *a·ma·tur m* —e amateur

Ambition *am·bi·tsee·ōn f* —en ambition (*aim*)

Ameise *ah·mye·zè f* —n ant

Amerika *a·may·ri·ka nt* America

Amerikaner *a·may·ri·kah·nèr m* American

Amerikanerin *a·may·ri·kah·nè·rin f* American

amerikanisch *a·may·ri·kah·nish adj* American

Amethyst *a·may·tōòst m* —e amethyst

Ampel *am·pèl f* —n light (*traffic light*); **eine Ampel überfahren** *ine·è am·pèl ōō·bèr·fah·rèn* to go through a red light

Ampere *am·payr nt* — amp

Amsel *am·zèl f* —n blackbird

Amtsdauer *amts·dow·èr f* term of office

Amtszeichen *amts·tsye·khèn nt* — dial tone

amüsieren *a·mōō·zee·rèn vt* amuse; **sich amüsieren** *zikh a·mōō·zee·rèn* to enjoy oneself; **sich gut amüsieren** *zikh goot a·mōō·zee·rèn* to have a good time

an *an prep* at; on; near; **kommen Sie am Freitag** *ko·mèn zee am frye·tahk* come on Friday

Analyse *a·na·lōō·zè f* —n analysis

analysieren *a·na·lōō·zee·rèn vt* analyze

anämisch *a·ne·mish adj* anemic

Ananas *a·na·nas f* —se pineapple

Anbau *an·bow m* —ten extension (*building*)

an|bauen *an·bow·èn vt* cultivate (*crop*)

an|bieten* *an·bee·tèn vt* offer; **sich an|bieten***, *etwas zu tun zikh an·bee·tèn et·vass tsoo toon* to offer to do something

Anblick *an·blik m* —e scene (*sight*)

andauernd *an·dow·èrnt adj* continual

Andenken *an·deng·kèn nt* — souvenir

andere *an·dè·rè adj* other; **das andere Geschlecht** *dass an·dè·rè gè·shlekht* the opposite sex; **ich möchte ein anderes Hemd sehen** *ikh mur'kh·tè ine an·dè·rès hemt zay·èn* I want to see another shirt

ändern *en·dèrn vt* change (*alter*); **sich ändern** *zikh en·dèrn* change

anders *an·dèrs adv* else; **jemand anders** *yay·mant an·dèrs* someone else; **anders als** *an·dèrs als* different from

anderswo *an·dèrs·vō adv* somewhere else

Änderung *en·dè·roong f* —en change

anderweitig *an·dèr·vye·tikh adv* otherwise

an|fahren* *an·fah·rèn vt* hit (*with car*)

Anfall *an·fal m* —e fit (*seizure*)

Anfang *an·fang m* —e start (*beginning*)

an|fangen* *an·fang·èn vt/i* begin; **an|fangen***, einen Sport auszuüben *an·fang·èn ine·èn shport ows·tsoo·ōō·bèn* to take up a sport

Anfänger *an·feng·èr m* — beginner

Anfängerin *an·feng·èr·in f* —nen beginner

an|fordern *an·for·dèrn vt* demand

Anfrage *an·frah·gè f* —n enquiry

sich an|fühlen *zikh an·fōō·lèn vr* feel; **es fühlt sich weich an** *ess fōōlt zikh vyekh an* it feels soft

Angaben *an·gah·bèn pl* directions (*to a place*); **die technischen Angaben** *tekh·ni·shèn an·gah·bèn* specifications

an|geben* *an·gay·bèn vt* give; genau **an|geben*** *gè·now an·gay·bèn* to specify

angeblich *an·gayp·likh adv* supposedly; **er soll angeblich Ingenieur sein** *er zol an·gayp·likh in·zhe·nee·ur zine* he's supposed to be an engineer

Angebot *an·gè·bōt nt* —e offer; **ein Angebot für etwas machen** *ine an·gè·bōt fōōr et·vass ma·khèn* to tender for something; **Angebot und Nachfrage** *an·gè·bōt oont nakh·frah·gè* supply and demand

angeekelt *an·gè·ay·kèlt adj* disgusted

an|gehen* *an·gay·èn vt* tackle (*problem*); **das geht Sie nichts an** *das gayt zee nikhts an* that doesn't concern you; **was dies angeht** *vass dees an·gayt* as for this

an|gehören *an·gè·hur·rèn vi* belong to

Angelegenheit *an·gè·lay·gèn·hite f* —en affair (*matter*)

angelernt *an·gè·lernt adj* semiskilled

Angeln *ang·èln nt* fishing; **angling** □ *vi* **angeln** *ang·èln* fish

Angelrute *ang·èl·roo·tè f* —n fishing rod

angemessen *an·gè·me·sèn adj* suitable (*fitting*)

angenehm *an·gè·naym adj* pleasant

an(geschaltet) *an(·gè·shal·tèt) adj* on (*light, radio*)

angeschwollen *an·gè·shvo·lèn adj* swollen

angespannt *an·gè·shpant adj* tense (*person*)

angestaubt *an·gè·shtowpt adj* shopworn

Angestellte(r) *an·gè·shtel·tè(·tèr) m/f* —n employee

Angler *ang·lèr m* — angler

Angora *ang·gō·ra nt* angora (*fabric*)

an|greifen* *an·grye·fèn vt* tackle (*in sports*)

Angriff *an·grif m* —e raid (*military*); attack

Angst *angst m* —e fear; **Angst haben*** *angst hah·bèn* to be scared; **vor etwas Angst haben*** *fōr et·vass angst hah·bèn* to be afraid of something

ängstlich *engst·likh adj* nervous (*person*)

an|halten* *an·hal·tèn vt/i* stop; **der Wagen hielt an** *der vah·gèn heelt an* the car pulled in

Anhalter *an·hal·tèr m* — hitchhiker; **per Anhalter fahren*** *per an·hal·tèr fah·rèn* to hitchhike; to thumb a ride

Anhalterin *an·hal·tè·rin f* —nen hitchhiker

Anhänger *an·heng·èr m* — trailer (*for goods*)

sich an|häufen *zikh an·hoy·fèn* vr accumulate

sich an|hören *zikh an·hur'·rèn* vr sound; **es hört sich wie ein Auto an** *ess hurt zikh vee ine ow·tō an* it sounds like a car

Anker *ang·kèr m* — anchor

Anklage *an·klah·gè f* —n charge (*accusation*)

an|klagen *an·klah·gèn* vt accuse

Ankleidekabine *an·klye·dè·ka·bee·nè f* —n changing cubicle

an|kommen* *an·ko·mèn* vi arrive; **an|kommen* an/in** *an·ko·mèn an/in* to reach (*arrive at*); **es kommt darauf an** *ess komt da·rowf an* it depends

an|kündigen *an·kōōn·di·gèn* vt announce

Ankunft *an·koonft f* —e arrival

an|kurbeln *an·koor·bèln* vt boost (*sales*)

Anlage *an·lah·gè f* —n enclosure (*in letter*)

Anlagen *an·lah·gèn pl* plant (*equipment*)

an|lassen* *an·la·sèn* vt switch on (*engine*)

Anlasser *an·la·sèr m* — starter (*in car*)

an|laufen* *an·low·fèn* vi open (*play*)

an|legen *an·lay·gèn* vt invest

an|machen *an·ma·khèn* vt toss (*salad*); **das Licht an|machen** *dass likht an·ma·khèn* to put on the light

sich an|melden *zikh an·mel·dèn* vr to check in (*at hotel*)

anmutig *an·moo·tikh* adj graceful

Annahme *an·nah·mè f* —n acceptance

an|nehmen* *an·nay·mèn* vt assume (*suppose*); accept

Annehmlichkeiten *an·naym·likh·kye·tèn pl* amenities

Anorak *a·no·rak m* —s anorak

an|probieren *an·prō·bee·rèn* vt try on (*clothes*)

Anreiz *an·rites m* —e incentive

Anrichte *an·rikh·tè f* —n sideboard

Anruf *an·roof m* —e call (*on phone*)

an|rufen* *an·roo·fèn* vt telephone (*person*)

sich an|sammeln *zikh an·za·mèln* vr accrue

Anschaffung *an·sha·foong f* —en acquisition

Anschauungsmaterial *an·show·oongs·ma·tay·ree·ahl nt* —ien visual aids

an|schießen* *an·shee·sèn* vt shoot (*injure*)

Anschlag *an·shlak m* —e notice (*sign*)

Anschlagbrett *an·shlahk·bret nt* — bulletin board

an|schlagen* *an·shlah·gèn* vt beat; **sich den Kopf an|schlagen*** *zikh dayn kopf an·shlah·gèn* to bang one's head

Anschluß *an·shloos m* —e connection (*train etc*); **dieser Zug hat Anschluß an den 16.45** *dee·zèr tsook hat an·shloos an dayn 16.45* this train connects with the 16:45

sich anschnallen *zikh an·shna·lèn* vr fasten one's seat belt

Anschrift *an·shrift f* —en address

Anschriftenliste *an·shrif·tèn·lis·tè f* —n mailing list

an|schwellen* *an·shve·lèn* vi swell (up) (*limb etc*)

an|sehen* *an·zay·èn* vt watch (*TV, play*); look at; **kurz an|sehen*** *koorts an·zay·èn* to glance at

an|setzen *an·zet·sèn* vt arrange (*meeting*)

Ansicht *an·zikht f* —en view (*opinion*)

Anspannung *an·shpa·noong f* strain

Anstalten *an·shtal·tèn pl* preparations

anständig *an·shten·dikh* adj respectable; proper; decent

anstatt *an·shtat prep* instead of

ansteckend *an·shte·kènt* adj infectious; contagious

an|stellen *an·shte·lèn* vt turn on (*water*)

Anstoß nehmen* **an** *an·shtōs nay·mèn an* vt object to

an|stoßen* *an·shtō·sèn* vt knock

Anstreicher *an·shtrye·khèr m* — painter (*decorator*)

sich an|strengen *zikh an·shtreng·èn* vr struggle

Antarktis *ant·ark·tis f* Antarctic

Anteil *an·tile m* —e share (*part*)

Antenne *an·te·nè f* —n antenna; aerial

Antibiotikum *an·ti·bee·ō·ti·koom nt* —tika antibiotic

Antihistamin *an·tee·hi·sta·min nt* antihistamine

antik *an·teek* adj period (*furniture*)

Antiquität *an·tee·kvee·tet m* —en antique

Antiquitätenhändler *an·tee·kvee·te·tèn·hend·lèr m* — antique dealer

Antiseptikum *an·ti·zep·ti·koom nt* —tika antiseptic

Antwort *an·vort f* —en answer; reply

antworten *ant·vor·tèn* vi answer; **auf eine Frage antworten** *owf ine·è frah·gè ant·vor·tèn* to reply to a question

Anweisungen *an·vye·zoong·èn pl* instructions

anwesend *an·vay·zènt* adj present

Anzahlung *an·tsah·loong f* —en deposit (*down payment*)

Anzeichen *an·tsye·khèn nt* — indication

Anzeige *an·tsye·gè f* —n advertisement; notice (*poster*); **per Anzeige eine Sekretärin suchen** *per an·tsye·gè ine·è ze·kray·tay·rin zoo·khèn* to advertise for a secretary

an|zeigen *an·tsye·gèn* vt announce

an|ziehen* *an·tsee·èn* vt dress (*child*); **ein Kleid an|ziehen*** *ine klite an·tsee·èn* to put on a dress; **sich an|ziehen*** *zikh an·tsee·èn* to dress oneself

Anzug *an·tsook m* —e suit

an|zünden *an·tsōōn·dèn* vt light (*fire, cigarette*)

Aperitif *a·pe·ri·teef m* —s aperitif

Apfel *ap·fèl m* — apple

Apfelbaum *ap·fèl·bowm m* —e apple tree

Apfelwein *ap·fèl·vine m* —e cider

Apotheke *a·pō·tay·kè f* —n chemist's shop; pharmacy

Apotheker *a·pō·tay·kèr m* — pharmacist; chemist

Apparat *a·pa·raht m* —e appliance

Appetit *a·pay·teet m* appetite

Appetitanreger *a·pay·teet·an·ray·gèr m* — appetizer

Aprikose *a·pri·kō·zè f* —n apricot

April *a·pril m* April

Aquarium *a·kvah·ree·oom nt* —arien aquarium

Äquator *e·kvah·tor m* equator

Araber *ah·ra·bèr m* — Arab

arabisch *a·rah·bish* adj Arabic □ nt Arabisch *a·rah·bish* Arabic

Arbeit *ar·bite f* labor; employment; work; **gute Arbeit** *goo·tè ar·bite* a good piece of work; **unerledigte Ar-**

beit *oon·er·lay·dikh·tè ar·bite* backlog of work

arbeiten *ar·bye·tèn vi* work; **arbeiten gehen*** *ar·bye·tèn gay·èn* to go to work

Arbeiter *ar·bye·tèr m* — laborer; workman; worker

Arbeiter- *ar·bye·tèr pref* working-class

Arbeiterschaft *ar·bye·tèr·shaft f* labor force; work force

Arbeitgeber *ar·bite·gay·bèr m* — employer

Arbeitskräfte *ar·bites·kref·tè pl* manpower

arbeitslos *ar·bites·lōs adj* jobless; unemployed

Arbeitslose(n) *ar·bites·lō·zè(n) pl* the unemployed

Arbeitslosigkeit *ar·bites·lō·zikh·kite f* unemployment

Arbeitsstunden *ar·bites·shtoon·dèn pl* working hours

Arbeitstag *ar·bites·tak m* —e workday

Arbeitszimmer *ar·bites·tsi·mèr nt* — study (*room*)

Architekt *ar·khi·tekt m* —en architect

Architektur *ar·khi·tek·toor f* architecture

Argentinien *ar·gen·tee·nee·èn nt* Argentina

argentinisch *ar·gen·tee·nish adj* Argentine

ärgerlich *er·gèr·likh adj* annoying; **es ist ärgerlich** *es ist er·gèr·likh* it's a nuisance

ärgern *er·gèrn vt* bother; annoy

Ärgernis *er·gèr·nis nt* —se nuisance

Arktis *ark·tis f* Arctic

arm *arm adj* poor

Arm *arm m* —e arm (*of person*)

Armaturenbrett *ar·ma·toor·èn·bret nt* —er dash(board)

Armband *arm·bant nt* —er bracelet

Armbanduhr *arm·bant·oo·èr f* —en watch

Armee *ar·may f* —n army

Ärmel *er·mèl m* — sleeve

Ärmelkanal *er·mèl·ka·nahl m* Channel

arrangieren *a·rang·zhee·rèn vt* arrange (*flowers, furniture*)

Art *art f* —en type; sort; manner (*way, attitude*); kind; **eine Art Bohne** *ine·è art bō·nè* a kind of bean

Arterie *ar·tay·ree·è f* —n artery

Arthritis *ar·tree·tis f* arthritis

artig *ar·tikh adj* good (*well-behaved*)

Artikel *ar·tee·kèl m* — article (*in newspaper*)

Artischocke *ar·ti·sho·kè f* —n globe artichoke

Arznei *arts·nye f* medicine

Arzt *arst m* —e doctor; **der Arzt für Allgemeinmedizin** *arst fōōr al·gè·mine·me·di·tseen* general practitioner, G.P.

Ärztin *erts·tin f* —nen doctor

As *ass nt* —se ace (*cards*)

Asbest *as·best m* asbestos

Asche *a·shè f* —n ash (*cinders*)

Aschenbecher *a·shèn·be·khèr m* — ashtray

Ascheneimer *a·shèn·ime·èr m* — ashcan

asiatisch *a·zee·ah·tish adj* Asian

Asien *ah·zee·èn nt* Asia

Aspirin *as·pi·reen nt* aspirin

Ast *ast m* —e branch

Asthma *ast·ma nt* asthma

Atem *ah·tèm m* breath

Athen *a·tayn nt* Athens

Athlet *at·layt m* —en athlete

Atlantik *at·lan·tik m* Atlantic Ocean

Atlas *at·las m* **Atlanten** atlas

atmen *aht·mèn vi* breathe

Atom- *a·tōm pref* nuclear (*energy, war*)

Aubergine *ō·ber·zhee·nè f* —n eggplant

auch *owkh adv* also; too; as well; **ich auch** *ikh owkh* so do I; **er auch** *er owkh* so is he; **ich war nicht da, und er auch nicht** *ikh var nikht dah oont er owkh nikht* I wasn't there and neither was he

audiovisuell *ow·di·ō·vi·zoo·el adj* audio-visual

Auditorium *ow·di·tō·ree·oom nt* —rien auditorium

auf *owf prep* onto; on; upon; on top of; **auf dem/den Tisch** *owf daym/dayn tish* on the table; **auf deutsch** *owf doytsh* in German; **wie sagt man "dog" auf deutsch** *vee zakt man dog owf doytsh* what's the German for "dog"? □ *adv* **auf owf** on (*water supply*); **er ist noch nicht auf** *er ist nokh nikht owf* he isn't up yet (*out of bed*)

auf|bewahren *owf·bè·vah·rèn vt* keep

aufblasbar *owf·blahs·bar adj* inflatable

auf|blasen* *owf·blah·zèn vt* inflate

auf|bleiben* *owf·blye·bèn vi* stay up (*at night*)

auf|decken *owf·de·kèn vt* uncover

Aufenthalt *owf·ènt·halt m* —e stay (*period*); visit

Aufenthaltsgenehmigung *owf·ènt·halts·gè·nay·mi·goong f* —en residence permit

Auffahrt *owf·fahrt f* —en entrance ramp

auf|fallen* *owf·fa·lèn vi* stand out

Aufführung *owf·fōō·roong f* —en performance

Aufgabe *owf·gah·bè f* —n task; duty (*function*); job

auf|geben* *owf·gay·bèn vi* quit □ *vt* give up (*abandon hope*); **das Rauchen auf|geben** *dass row·khèn owf·gay·bèn* to give up smoking

auf|gehen* *owf·gay·èn vi* rise (*sun*)

aufgeräumt *owf·gè·roymt adj* tidy (*room, papers*)

aufgeregt *owf·gè·raykt adj* excited

auf|halten* *owf·hal·tèn vt* delay; hold up

auf|hängen *owf·heng·èn vt* hang; **ein Plakat auf|hängen** *ine pla·kaht owf·heng·èn* to put up a notice

Aufhängung *owf·heng·oong f* suspension (*on car*)

auf|heben* *owf·hay·bèn vt* pick up (*object*); lift; **etwas bis später auf|heben*** *et·vass biss shpay·tèr owf·hay·bèn* to keep something till later

auf|hören *owf·hur·rèn vi* finish; **auf|hören zu arbeiten** *owf·hur·rèn tsoo ar·bye·tèn* to retire; **auf|hören, etwas zu tun** *owf·hur·rèn et·vass tsoo toon* to stop doing something

auf|kreuzen *owf·kroy·tsèn vi* tack (*sailing*)

Auflage *owf·lah·gè f* —n edition

Auflauf *owf·lowf m* —e soufflé

auf|legen *owf·lay·gèn vi* hang up (*phone*)

auf|leuchten *owf·loykh·tèn vi* flash (*light*)

auf|lösen *owf·lur·zèn vt* dissolve; **sich auf|lösen** *zikh owf·lur·zèn* dissolve

auf|machen *owf·ma·khèn vt* unfasten □ *vi* open (*store, bank*); **sich auf|machen** *zikh owf·ma·khèn* to set off

aufmerksam *owf·merk·zam adj* attentive

auf|nehmen* *owf·nay·mèn vt* tape record; absorb (*fluid*)

auf|passen *owf·pa·sèn vi* pay attention

auf|räumen *owf·roy·mèn vt* put away

aufrecht *owf·rekht adj* upright

aufregend *owf·ray·gènt adj* exciting

Aufregung *owf·ray·goong f —en* excitement

aufrichtig *owf·rikh·tikh adj* sincere

auf|rollen *owf·ro·lèn vt* roll up (*newspaper etc*)

Aufruhr *owf·roor m —e* riot

auf|schließen* *owf·shlee·sèn vt* unlock

Aufschnitt *owf·shnit m* cold meat

auf|schnüren *owf·shnöö·rèn vt* untie (*parcel*)

auf|schrauben *owf·shrow·bèn vt* unscrew

auf|schreiben* *owf·shrye·bèn vt* write down

auf|schürfen *owf·shöör·fèn vt* graze (*skin*)

Aufschwung *owf·shvoong m —e* upturn (*in business*); boom (*economic*)

Aufseher *owf·zay·èr m —* supervisor

Aufseherin *owf·zay·èr·in f —nen* supervisor

auf|setzen *owf·ze·tsèn vt* draw up (*document*)

Aufsichtsrat *owf·zikhts·raht m —e* board (*of directors*)

Aufsichtsratsvorsitzende *owf·zikhts·rahts·fōr·zit·sèn·dè m —n* president (*of company*)

auf|stapeln *owf·shtah·pèln vt* pile up

auf|stehen* *owf·shtay·èn vi* stand up; get up; rise (*person*)

auf|stellen *owf·shte·lèn vt* pitch (*tent*)

Aufstieg *owf·shteek m —e* ascent

auf|tauen *owf·tow·èn vt* defrost (*food*) □ *vt/i* thaw (*frozen food*)

auf|tischen *owf·ti·shèn vt* dish up

auf|wachen *owf·va·khèn vi* wake up

aufwärts *owf·verts adv* upward(s)

auf|wischen *owf·vi·shèn vt* mop

auf|zeichnen *owf·tsyekh·nèn vt* record (*write down*)

auf|ziehen* *owf·tsee·èn vt* rear (*children, cattle*); eine Uhr **auf|ziehen*** *ine·è oor owf·tsee·èn* to wind up a clock

Auge *ow·gè nt —n* eye

Augenblick *ow·gèn·blik m —e* moment; instant; point (*in time*); einen Augenblick! *ine·èn ow·gèn·blik* hold on! (*on phone*); im Augenblick *im ow·gèn·blik* at present

augenblicklich *ow·gèn·blik·likh adv* at the moment

Augenbraue *ow·gèn·brow·è f —n* eyebrow

Augenklappe *ow·gèn·kla·pè f —n* patch (*for eye*)

Augenlid *ow·gèn·leet nt —er* eyelid

Augenwimper *ow·gèn·vim·pèr f —n* eyelash

August *ow·goost m* August

Auktion *owk·tsee·ōn f —en* auction

aus *ows adv* off (*machine, light*); das Licht ist aus *das likht ist ows* the light is out; das Spiel ist aus *dass shpeel ist ows* the match is over □ *prep* aus *ows* from; out of; er lief aus dem Haus *er leef ows daym hows* he ran out of the house; Wasser aus der Leitung *va·sèr ows der lye·toong* water from the faucet; aus Holz *ows holts* made (out) of wood

Ausbackteig *ows·bak·tike m —e* batter (*for frying*)

aus|bilden *ows·bil·dèn vt* train (*apprentice*)

Ausbildung *ows·bil·doong f* training (*for job*)

aus|breiten *ows·brye·tèn vt* spread out **sich aus|dehnen** *zikh ows·day·nèn vr* expand (*material*)

aus|drehen *ows·dray·èn vt* turn off (*light*)

Ausdruck *ows·drook m —e* expression; printout; term (*word*)

aus|drücken *ows·drōō·kèn vt* express

auseinander *ows·ine·an·dèr adv* apart (*separately*)

Auseinandersetzung *ows·ine·an·dèr·zet·soong f —en* argument (*quarrel*)

Ausfall *ows·fal m —e* failure (*mechanical*)

Ausflug *ows·flook m —e* trip (*excursion*); outing; einen Ausflug machen *ine·èn ows·flook ma·khèn* to go on an excursion; einen Ausflug ans Meer machen *ine·èn ows·flook ans mayr ma·khèn* to go on a trip to the beach

Ausfuhr *ows·foor f —en* export

aus|führen *ows·föö·rèn vt* export; jemanden ins Theater aus|führen *yay·man·dèn ins tay·ah·tèr ows·föö·rèn* to take someone out to the theater; einen Befehl aus|führen *ine·èn bè·fayl ows·föö·rèn* to carry out an order

ausführlich *ows·föör·likh adj* in detail; detailed

aus|füllen *ows·föö·lèn vt* fill in/out (*form*); bitte nicht ausfüllen *bi·tè nikht ows·föö·lèn* please leave blank

Ausgabe *ows·gah·bè f —n* issue (*of magazine*)

Ausgaben *ows·gah·bèn pl* expenditure

Ausgang *ows·gang m —e* exit

aus|geben* *ows·gay·bèn vt* spend (*money*); wir haben unser ganzes Geld ausgegeben *veer hah·bèn oon·zèr gan·tsès gelt ows·gè·gay·bèn* all our money's gone; ich gebe Ihnen ein Eis aus *ikh gay·bè ee·nèn ine ise ows* I'll treat you to an ice cream cone

ausgebildet *ows·gè·bil·dèt adj* qualified; skilled (*workers*)

aus|gehen* *ows·gay·èn vi* go out; wir gehen davon aus, daß... *veer gay·èn da·fon ows das* we understand that...

ausgereift *ows·gè·ryeft adj* mature (*wine*)

ausgeschaltet *ows·gè·shal·tèt adj* off (*radio*)

ausgeschieden *ows·gè·shee·dèn adj* out (*team, player*)

ausgezeichnet *ows·gè·tsyekh·nèt adj* excellent

aus|gleichen *ows·glye·khèn vt* balance

aus|graben* *ows·gra·bèn vt* dig up

aus|kommen *ows·ko·mèn vi* get by; mit etwas aus|kommen* *mit et·vass ows·ko·mèn* to make do with something

aus|kugeln *ows·koo·gèln vt* dislocate

Auskunft *ows·koonft f —e* information; information desk

Auskunftsbüro *ows·koonfts·bōō·rō nt —s* information office

aus|laden *ows·lah·dèn vt* unload

Auslage *ows·lah·gè f —n* display

Ausland *ows·lant nt* foreign countries; ins Ausland fahren *ins ows·lant fah·rèn* to go abroad; aus dem Ausland *ows daym ows·lant* overseas (*visitor*)

Ausländer *ows·len·dèr m —* foreigner

Ausländerin *ows·len·dè·rin f —nen* foreigner

ausländisch *ows·len·dish adj* foreign
aus|lassen* *ows·la·sèn vt* leave out
(*omit*); miss out
aus|legen *ows·lay·gèn vt* interpret
aus|lüften *ows·lōōf·tèn vt* air (*clothes*)
aus|machen *ows·ma·khèn vt* put out
(*light*); **die Wärme macht mir nichts
aus** *dee ver·mè makht meer nikhts
ows* I don't mind the heat
Ausnahme *ows·nah·mè f* —n exception
aus|nützen *ows·nŏŏ·tsèn vt* make the
most of
aus|packen *ows·pa·kèn vt* unpack; un-
wrap
aus|pressen *ows·pre·sèn vt* squeeze (*le-
mon*)
Auspuff *ows·poof m* —e exhaust
(*pipe*)
Auspufftopf *ows·poof·topf m* ⁼e muffler (*on car*)
aus|radieren *ows·ra·dee·rèn vt* rub out;
erase
aus|rauben *ows·row·bèn vt* rob (*bank*)
aus|rechnen *ows·rekh·nèn vt* calculate
Ausrede *ows·ray·dè f* —n excuse (*pretext*)
Ausreisegenehmigung *ows·rye·zè·gè·
nay·mi·goong f* —en exit permit
aus|rufen* *ows·roo·fèn vt* exclaim; **aus-
rufen lassen*** *ows·roo·fèn la·sèn* to
page
sich aus|ruhen *zikh ows·roo·èn vr* rest
Ausrüstung *ows·rŏŏs·toong f* equipment
aus|rutschen *ows·root·shèn vi* slip (*trip*)
Aussage *ows·zah·gè f* —n statement
aus|schalten *ows·shal·tèn vt* switch off
aus|scheren *ows·shay·rèn vi* pull out
Ausschlag *ows·shlahk m* ⁼e rash
aus|schließen* *ows·shlee·sèn vt* exclude
ausschließlich *ows·shlees·likh adv* exclusive of
Ausschuß *ows·shoos m* ⁼e committee
Ausschußware *ows·shoos·vah·rè f* —n
reject
aus|schwenken *ows·shveng·kèn vi*
swerve
Aussehen *ows·zay·èn nt* — look (*ap-
pearance*) □ *vi* **aus|sehen*** *ows·zay·èn*
look (*appear*); **aus|sehen* wie** *ows·
zay·èn vee* to look like
Außenbord- *ow·sèn·bort pref* outboard
Außenminister *ow·sèn·mee·nis·tèr m*
— secretary of state
Außenpolitik *ow·sèn·pō·lee·tik f*
foreign policy
Außenseite *ow·sèn·zye·tè f* —n outside
Außenwand *ow·sèn·vant f* ⁼e outside
wall
außer *ow·sèr prep* except (for), ex-
cept(ing); **außer meiner Reichweite**
ow·sèr mine·èr ryekh·vye·tè beyond
my reach; **alle außer ihm** *a·lè ow·sèr
eem* all but him
außerdem *ow·sèr daym adv* besides
(*moreover*)
äußere(r/s) *oy·sè·rè(·rèr/·rès) adj* exterior, external
außergewöhnlich *ow·sèr·gè·wur'n·likh
adj* exceptional; remarkable
außerhalb *ow·sèr·halp prep* out of (*outside*); **außerhalb des Hauses** *ow·sèr·
halp des how·zès* outside the house
äußerlich *oy·sèr·likh adj* exterior
außerordentlich *ow·sèr·or·dènt·likh adj*
extraordinary
äußerst *oy·serst adv* extremely
Aussicht *ows·zikht f* —en prospect;
outlook; view; **er hat gute Aussichten**

zu... *er hat goo·tè ows·zikh·tèn tsoo*
he has a good chance of...
Aussprache *ows·shpra·khè f* pronunciation
aus|sprechen* *ows·shpre·khèn vt* pro-
nounce
Ausstand *ows·shtant m* ⁼e strike
aus|steigen* *ows·shtye·gèn vi* get out;
pull out
aus|stellen *ows·shte·lèn vt* exhibit
Ausstellung *ows·shte·loong f* —en
show; exhibition
Ausstellungsraum *ows·shte·loongs·
rowm m* ⁼e showroom
aus|strecken *ows·shtre·kèn vt* stretch
out
aus|streichen* *ows·shtrye·khèn vt* cross
out
aus|strömen *ows·shtrur'·mèn vi* escape
(*liquid, gas*)
aus|tauschen *ows·tow·shèn vt* exchange
Auster *ows·tèr f* —n oyster
Australien *ows·strah·lee·èn nt* Australia
australisch *ows·strah·lish adj* Australian
Ausverkauf *ows·fer·kowf m* ⁼e sale
(*cheap prices*)
ausverkauft *ows·fer·kowft adj* sold out
Auswahl *ows·vahl f* —en variety;
choice (*range*)
aus|wählen *ows·vay·lèn vt* pick
(*choose*)
Auswanderer *ows·van·dè·rèr m* —
emigrant
aus|wandern *ows·van·dèrn vi* emigrate
Ausweis *ows·vise m* —e identity card;
pass (*permit*)
auswendig *ows·ven·dikh adv* by heart
aus|wringen* *ows·vring·èn vt* wring
(*clothes*)
aus|zahlen *ows·tsah·lèn vt* buy out
(*partner etc*); pay off (*workers*)
aus|ziehen* *ows·tsee·èn vt* take off
(*clothes*); undress; **sich aus|ziehen***
zikh ows·tsee·èn undress
Auszubildende(r) *ows·tsoo·bil·dèn·
dè(r) m/f* —n trainee
Auto *ow·tō nt* —s auto(mobile); car
Autobahn *ow·tō·bahn f* —en freeway;
die gebührenpflichtige Autobahn *gè·
bŏŏ·rèn·pflikh·ti·gè ow·tō·bahn* turnpike
Autobahnausfahrt *ow·tō·bahn·ows·
fahrt f* —en exit ramp
Autofähre *ow·tō·fay·rè f* —n car-ferry
Autofahrer *ow·tō·fah·rèr m* — motorist
Automat *ow·tō·maht m* —en slot
machine
Automatikwagen *ow·tō·mah·tik·vah·
gèn m* — automatic (*car*)
automatisch *ow·tō·mah·tish adj* automatic □ *adv* automatically
Automatisierung *ow·tō·ma·ti·zee·
roong f* automation
Automobilausstellung *ow·tō·mo·beel·
ows·shte·loong f* —en auto show
Autor *ow·tor m* —en author; writer
Autorität *ow·tō·ree·tet f* power (*auth-
ority*)
Autounfall *ow·tō·oon·fal m* ⁼e car acci-
dent
Avocado *a·vō·kah·dō f* —s avocado
Axt *akst f* ⁼e ax

B

Baby *bay·bee nt* —s baby
Babyflasche *bay·bee·fla·shè f* —n
bottle (*baby's*)
Babynahrung *bay·bee·nah·roong f*
baby food

babysitten *bay·bee·si·tèn* vi baby-sit

Babysitter *bay·bee·sit·èr m* — baby-sitter

Babysitterin *bay·bee·si·tè·rin f* **—nen** baby-sitter

Bach *bakh m* **¨e** stream

backen* *ba·kèn* vt bake

Bäcker *be·kèr m* — baker

Bäckerei *be·kè·rye f* **—en** bakery

Backgammon *bak·ga·mon* nt backgammon

Backofen *bak·ō·fèn m* **¨** oven

Backpflaume *bak·pflow·mè f* **—n** prune

Backstein *bak·shtine m* **—e** brick

Bad *baht* nt **¨er** bath

Badeanzug *bah·dè·an·tsook m* **¨e** swimsuit

Badehose *bah·dè·hō·zè f* **—n** swimming trunks

Bademantel *bah·dè·man·tèl m* **¨** robe *(after bath)*

Bademütze *bah·dè·mōōt·sè f* **—n** bathing cap

baden *bah·dèn* vi bathe

Badewanne *bah·dè·va·nè f* **—n** bath *(tub)*

Badezimmer *bah·dè·tsi·mèr* nt — bathroom

Badminton *bet·min·tèn* nt badminton

Bahn *bahn f* **—en** railroad; rink; **per Bahn** *per bahn* by rail

Bahnhof *bahn·hōf m* **¨e** station; depot *(trains)*

Bahnlinie *bahn·lee·nee·è f* **—n** line *(railway)*

Bahnsteig *bahn·shtike m* **—e** platform *(in station)*

Bahnübergang *bahn·ōō·bèr·gang m* **¨e** grade crossing

Bakkarat *ba·ka·rah* nt baccarat

bald *balt* adv soon

Balken *bal·kèn m* — beam *(of wood)*

Balkon *bal·kōn m* **—s** balcony

Ball *bal m* **¨e** ball

Ballett *ba·let* nt **—e** ballet

Ballon *ba·lōn m* **—s** balloon

Ballungsgebiet *ba·loongs·gè·beet* nt **—e** conurbation

Bambus *bam·boos m* bamboo

Banane *ba·nah·nè f* **—n** banana

Band *bant m* **¨e** volume *(book)* □ nt **das Band** *bant* **¨er** ribbon; tape □ f **die Band** *bent* **—s** band *(musical)*

Bande *ban·dè f* **—n** gang

Bandscheibenschaden *bant·shye·bèn·sha·dèn m* **¨** slipped disk

Bank *bank f* **—en** bank *(finance)*; **bei der Bank** *bye der bank* at the bank

Bank *bank f* **¨e** bench *(seat)*

Bankett *bang·ket* nt **—e** banquet

Bankgebühren *bank·gè·bōō·rèn pl* bank charges

Bankier *bang·kyay m* **—s** banker

Bankkonto *bank·kon·tō* nt **—konten** bank account

Banknote *bank·nō·tè f* **—n** banknote

bankrott *bank·rot* adj bankrupt □ m **der Bankrott** *bank·rot* bankruptcy; **Bankrott machen** *bank·rot ma·khèn* to go bankrupt

Banner *ba·nèr* nt — banner

Baptisten- *bap·ti·stèn* pref Baptist

bar *bahr* adj cash; **etwas bar bezahlen** *et·vass bahr bè·tsah·lèn* to pay cash for something

Bar *bar f* **—s** saloon *(bar)*

Bär *ber m* **—en** bear

Barbecue *bar·bi·kyoo* nt **—s** barbecue

Bardame *bahr·dah·mè f* **—n** barmaid

barfuß *bahr·foos* adv barefoot

Bargeld *bar·gelt* nt cash

Barkasse *bar·ka·sè f* **—n** launch

Barmann *bahr·man m* **¨er** barman

Bart *bart m* **¨e** beard

Basar *ba·zahr m* **—e** bazaar

Baseball *bays·bōl* nt baseball

basieren *ba·zee·rèn* vt base

Basis *bah·zis f* **Basen** basis; base

Basketball *bahs·kèt·bal* nt basketball

Batate *ba·tah·tè f* **—n** sweet potato

Batterie *ba·tè·ree f* **—n** battery

bauen *bow·èn* vt construct; build

Bauer *bow·èr m* **—n** farmer

Bauernhof *bow·èrn·hōf m* **¨e** farmyard; farm

Baugutachter *bow·goot·akh·tèr m* — inspector *(of building)*

Baum *bowm m* **¨e** tree

Baumrinde *bowm·rin·dè f* **—n** bark *(of tree)*

Baumstamm *bowm·shtam m* **¨e** log *(of wood)*

Baumwolle *bowm·vo·lè f* cotton *(fabric)*

Baumwollgarn *bowm·vol·garn* nt **—e** cotton *(thread)*

Bausparkasse *bow·shpar·ka·sè f* **—n** savings and loan association

beabsichtigen *bè·ap·zikh·ti·gèn* vi intend; **beabsichtigen, zu tun** *bè·ap·zikh·ti·gèn tsoo toon* to mean to do

beachten *bè·akh·tèn* vt observe; obey

Beamte(r) *bè·am·tè(·tèr) m* **—n** civil servant

beantworten *bè·ant·vor·tèn* vt answer

bearbeiten *bè·ar·bye·tèn* vt process *(application, order)*

beaufsichtigen *bè·owf·zikh·ti·gèn* vt supervise

Becher *bè·khèr m* — carton *(of yogurt etc)*; mug

Becken *bè·kèn* nt — pond *(artificial)*

Bedarfshaltestelle *bè·darfs·hal·tè·shte·lè f* **—n** flag stop

bedauern *bè·dow·èrn* vt regret; be sorry for

bedecken *bè·dè·kèn* vt cover

bedeuten *bè·doy·tèn* vt mean *(signify)*

Bedeutung *bè·doy·toong f* **—en** meaning

bedienen *bè·dee·nèn* vt serve *(customer)*; operate *(machine)*

Bedienung *bè·dee·noong f* **—en** service *(in restaurant)*; service charge

Bedingung *bè·ding·oong f* **—en** condition *(proviso)*; stipulation; **unter der Bedingung, daß...** *oon·tèr der bè·ding·oong dass* on condition that...; **die Bedingungen** *dee bè·ding·oong·èn* terms *(of contract)*

bedingungslos *bè·ding·oongs·lōs* adj unconditional *(offer)*

bedrohen *bè·drō·èn* vt threaten

Bedürfnis *bè·dōōrf·nis* nt **—se** requirement

sich beeilen *zikh bè·ile·èn* vr hurry

beeindrucken *bè·ine·droo·kèn* vt impress *(win approval)*

beeinflussen *bè·ine·floo·sèn* vt influence; affect

beenden *bè·en·dèn* vt end

beerdigen *bè·èr·di·gèn* vt bury *(person)*

Beerdigung *bè·èr·di·goong f* **—en** funeral

Beere *bay·rè f* **—n** berry

Befehl *bè·fayl m* **—e** command; order

befehlen* *bè·fay·lèn* vt order

befestigen *bè·fes·ti·gèn* vt attach; fasten; fix

beflecken *bè·fle·kèn* vt stain

befördern *bè·fur·dèrn vt* promote (*person*); carry (*transport*)
Beförderung *bè·fur·dè·roong f* promotion (*of person*)
begabt *bè·gapt adj* gifted
Begabung *bè·gah·boong f —en* talent; gift (*ability*)
begegnen *bè·gayg·nèn vt* meet
begehen* *bè·gay·èn vt* commit (*crime*)
begeistert *bè·gye·stèrt adj* enthusiastic
Begeisterung *bè·gye·stè·roong f* enthusiasm
beginnen* *bè·gi·nèn vt* start
Begleitbrief *bè·glite·breef m —e* covering letter
begleiten *bè·glye·tèn vt* accompany (*go with*); escort; **jemanden hinaus|begleiten** *yay·man·dèn hi·nows·bè·glye·tèn* to show someone out
Begleiter *bè·glye·tèr m —* escort
begreifen* *bè·grye·fèn vt* understand
begrenzen *bè·gren·tsèn vt* restrict (*speed*)
Begrenzung *bè·gren·tsoong f —en* limit
Begriff *bè·grif m —e* idea; **im Begriff sein*, etwas zu tun** *im bè·grif zine et·vass tsoo toon* to be about to do something
begrüßen *bè·grōō·sèn vt* greet; welcome
Begutachtung *bè·goot·akh·toong f* survey (*of building*)
behalten* *bè·hal·tèn vt* keep (*retain*)
Behälter *bè·hel·tèr m —* container
behandeln *bè·han·dèln vt* handle (*deal with*); treat; **ein Thema behandeln** *ine tay·ma bè·han·dèln* to deal with a subject
Behandlung *bè·hant·loong f —en* treatment
behaupten *bè·howp·tèn vt* maintain; declare (*announce*)
beherrschen *bè·her·shèn vt* control
Beherrschung *bè·her·shoong f* control; **die Beherrschung verlieren*** *dee bè·her·shoong fer·lee·rèn* to lose one's temper
bei *bye prep* near; at, on; during; care of, c/o; **bei mir** *bye meer* at my house
beide *bye·dè adj, pron* both; **alle beide** *a·lè bye·dè* both (of them); **auf beiden Seiten** *owf bye·dèn zye·tèn* on either side
Beifahrersitz *bye·fah·rèr·zits m —e* passenger seat
Beifall *bye·fal m* applause; approval
beige *baysh adj* beige; fawn
Beignet *ben·yay m —s* fritter
Beihilfe *bye·hil·fè f —n* allowance (*state payment*)
Beilage *bye·lah·gè f —n* enclosure; supplement
bei|legen* *bye·lay·gèn vt* enclose; settle (*argument*)
Bein *bine nt —e* leg
beinahe *bye·nah·è adv* almost
Beispiel *bye·shpeel nt —e* example; **zum Beispiel** *tsoom bye·shpeel* for example
beißen* *bye·sèn vt* bite
Beitrag *bye·trahk m —̈e* contribution; subscription (*to club*)
bei|tragen* *bye·trah·gèn vi* contribute
Bekannte(r) *bè·kan·tè(·tèr) m/f —n* acquaintance
bekennen* *bè·ken·èn vt* confess
sich beklagen *zikh bè·klah·gèn vr* complain
bekommen* *bè·ko·mèn vt* get; win; obtain; **Zwiebeln bekommen mir**

nicht *tsvee·bèln bè·ko·mèn meer nikht* onions don't agree with me
beladen *bè·lah·dèn vt* load (*truck, ship*)
belasten *bè·las·tèn vt* burden; **jemandes Konto mit $50 belasten** *yay·man·dès kon·to mit $50 bè·las·tèn* to debit $50 to someone's account
Belastung *bè·las·toong f —en* load; **die Belastungen des modernen Lebens** *dee bè·las·toong·èn des mō·der·nèn lay·bèns* the pressures of modern life; **er war großen Belastungen ausgesetzt** *er vahr grō·sèn bè·las·toong·èn ows·gè·zetst* he was under great pressure
beleben *bè·lay·bèn vt* revive (*person*)
belebt *bè·laypt adj* busy (*place*)
Belegschaft *bè·layk·shaft f* payroll
belegt *bè·laygt adj* occupied
beleidigen *bè·lye·di·gèn vt* offend; insult
Beleidigung *bè·lye·di·goong f —en* insult
Beleuchtung *bè·loykh·toong f* lighting
Belichtungsmesser *bè·likh·toongs·me·sèr m —* light meter
beliebt *bè·leept adj* popular
bellen *bè·lèn vi* bark
Belohnung *bè·lō·noong f —en* reward
bemerken *bè·mer·kèn vt* notice
Bemerkung *bè·mer·koong f —en* comment; remark; **seine Bemerkungen zu dieser Sache** *zine·è bè·mer·koong·èn tsoo dee·zèr za·khè* his reference to this matter
Benehmen *bè·nay·mèn nt* behavior □ **vr sich benehmen*** *zikh bè·nay·mèn* behave
beneiden *bè·nye·dèn vt* envy
Benelux-Staaten *bay·nay·looks·shtah·tèn pl* Benelux
benutzen *bè·noo·tsèn vt* use
Benzin *ben·tseen nt* gas(oline)
Benzinpumpe *ben·tseen·poom·pè f —n* fuel pump
beobachten *bè·ō·bakh·tèn vt* watch
bequem *bè·kvaym adj* comfortable
Bequemlichkeit *bè·kvaym·likh·kite f* comfort (*ease*)
Berater *bè·rah·tèr m —* consultant
berauben *bè·row·bèn vt* rob (*person*)
berechnen *bè·rekh·nèn vt* calculate; charge (*money*)
Bereich *bè·ryekh m —e* area; **im Bereich von** *im bè·ryekh fon* within the scope of
bereit *bè·rite adj* ready; **bereit, etwas zu tun** *bè·rite et·vass tsoo toon* ready to do something; willing to do something
bereit|stellen *bè·rite·shte·lèn vt* put up (*capital*)
Berg *berk m —e* mountain
bergab *berk·ap adv* downhill
Bergarbeiter *berk·ar·bite·èr m* miner
bergauf *berk·owf adv* uphill
Bergsteigen *berk·shtye·gèn nt* mountaineering; **bergsteigen gehen*** *berk·shtye·gèn gay·èn* to go mountaineering
Bergwerk *berk·verk nt —e* mine (*for coal etc*)
Bericht *bè·rikht m —e* report; bulletin
berichten *bè·rikh·tèn vt* report
berichtigen *bè·rikh·ti·gèn vt* correct
Berichtigung *bè·rikh·ti·goong f —en* correction (*alteration*)
Berliner *ber·lee·nèr m —* doughnut
Beruf *bè·roof m —e* profession; occupation (*job*)

beruflich *bė·roof·likh adj* professional

Berufs- *bė·roofs pref* professional (*not amateur*)

beruhigen *bė·roo·i·gėn vt* ease (*pain*); **sich beruhigen** *zikh bė·roo·i·gėn* calm down; settle (*wine*)

Beruhigungsmittel *bė·roo·i·goongs·mi·tėl nt* — sedative; tranquilizer

berühmt *bė·rōōmt adj* famous

berühren *bė·rōō·rėn vt* handle; touch

beschädigen *bė·she·di·gėn vt* damage

beschäftigen *bė·shef·ti·gėn vt* employ (*worker*)

beschäftigt *bė·shef·tikht adj* busy (*person*); **anderweitig beschäftigt** *an·dėr·vye·tikh bė·shef·tikht* otherwise engaged

Beschäftigung *bė·shef·ti·goong f* — employment; occupation

bescheiden *bė·shide·ėn adj* modest

Bescheinigung *bė·shye·ni·goong f* — en certificate

beschleunigen *bė·shloy·ni·gėn vi* accelerate; speed up

beschränken *bė·shreng·kėn vt* restrict

Beschränkung *bė·shreng·koong f* — en restriction

beschreiben* *bė·shrye·bėn vt* describe

Beschreibung *bė·shrye·boong f* — en description

beschützen *bė·shōōt·sėn vt* protect

Beschwerde *bė·shvayr·dė f* — n complaint (*dissatisfaction*)

sich beschweren *zikh bė·shvay·rėn vr* complain

beseitigen *bė·zye·ti·gėn vt* remove (*stain*)

Besen *bay·zėn m* — broom

Besessenheit *bė·ze·sėn·hite f* — en obsession

besetzen *bė·zet·sėn vt* trim (*decorate*)

besetzt *bė·zetst adj* busy (*telephone*)

Besetztzeichen *bė·zetst·tsye·khėn nt* — busy signal

Besetzung *bė·zet·soong f* — en cast (*of play*)

besichtigen *bė·zikh·ti·gėn vt* visit

Besichtigungen *bė·zikh·ti·goong·ėn pl* sightseeing

besiegen *bė·zee·gėn vt* defeat

Besitz *bė·zits m* — e property; estate; ownership

besitzen* *bė·zit·sėn vt* own (*possess*)

Besitzer *bė·zit·sėr m* — owner

besondere(r/s) *bė·zon·dė·rė(·rėr/·rės) adj* particular; special

besonders *bė·zon·dėrs adv* especially; particularly; extra

besorgt *bė·zorkt adj* worried

Besorgung *bė·zor·goong f* — en errand; **eine Besorgung machen** *ine·ė bė·zor·goong ma·khėn* to run an errand

besprechen* *bė·shpre·khėn vt* discuss; **etwas besprechen*** *et·vass bė·shpre·khėn* to talk something over

besprengen *bė·shpreng·ėn vt* sprinkle

bespritzen *bė·shprit·sėn vt* splash

besser *be·sėr adj, adv* better; **er singt besser als Sie** *er zingt be·sėr als zee* he sings better than you; **immer besser** *im·ėr be·sėr* better and better

bessern *be·sėrn vt* improve

Besserung *bė·sė·roong f* — en improvement; **gute Besserung** *goo·tė bė·sė·roong* get well soon

beständig *bė·shten·dikh adj* settled (*weather*)

bestätigen *bė·shtay·ti·gėn vt* confirm (*reservation etc*); witness (*signature*); acknowledge (*letter*)

bestechen* *bė·shte·khėn vt* bribe

Besteck *bė·shtek nt* — e cutlery

bestehen* *bė·shtay·ėn vt* pass (*exam*); **auf etwas bestehen*** *owf et·vass bė·shtay·ėn* to insist on something; **bestehen* aus** *bė·shtay·ėn ows* to consist of

besteigen* *bė·shtye·gėn vt* board (*ship*)

bestellen *bė·shte·lėn vt* reserve (*tickets*); order (*goods, meal*); **neu bestellen** *noy bė·shte·lėn* to reorder

Bestellformular *bė·shtel·for·moo·lahr nt* — e order form

Bestellung *bė·shte·loong f* — en order (*for goods*)

beste(r/s) *bes·tė(·tėr/·tės) adj* best; **das Beste wäre... dass** *bes·tė ve·rė* the best thing would be...; **er ist der Beste** *er ist der bes·tė* he's the best; **er kann es am besten** *er kan ess am bes·tėn* he can do it best

besteuern *bė·shtoy·ėrn vt* tax

Besteuerung *bė·shtoy·ė·roong f* taxation

bestickt *bė·shtikt adj* embroidered

bestimmen *bė·shti·mėn vt* intend

bestimmt *bė·shtimt adj* definite □ *adv* certainly; surely

bestrafen *bė·shtrah·fėn vt* punish

bestreiten* *bė·shtrye·tėn vt* dispute (*fact*)

Besuch *bė·zookh m* — e visit

besuchen *bė·zoo·khėn vt* visit; attend (*meeting etc*)

Besucher *bė·zoo·khėr m* — visitor

Besucherin *bė·zoo·khė·rin f* — nen visitor

Betätigung *bė·tay·ti·goong f* — en activity

betäuben *bė·toy·bėn vt* stun

beten *bay·tėn vi* pray

Beton *bay·tong m* — s concrete □ *pref* **Beton-** *bay·tong* concrete

betonen *bė·tō·nėn vt* emphasize

Betonung *bė·tō·noong f* — en stress; emphasis

Betrag *bė·trahk m* — e amount

betreffen* *bė·tre·fėn vt* concern (*be important to*)

betreffs *bė·trefs prep* concerning

betreten* *bė·tray·tėn vt* enter

Betrieb *bė·treep m* — e business (*firm*); **außer Betrieb** *ow·sėr bė·treep* out of order (*machine*)

Betriebskapital *bė·treeps·ka·pi·tahl nt* working capital

Betriebskosten *bė·treeps·kos·tėn pl* running costs

betrügen* *bė·trōō·gėn vi* cheat

betrunken *bė·troong·kėn adj* drunk

Bett *bet nt* — en bed; **im Bett** *im bet* in bed; **ins Bett gehen*** *ins bet gay·ėn* to go to bed

Bettdecke *bet·de·kė f* — n cover (*blanket*)

betteln *be·tėln vi* beg

Bettlaken *bet·lah·kėn nt* — sheet

Bettler *bet·lėr m* — beggar

Bettlerin *bet·lė·rin f* — nen beggar

Bettzeug *bet·tsoyk nt* bedclothes

beugen *boy·gėn vt* bend (*arm, leg*); **sich beugen** *zikh boy·gėn* bend (*person*)

Beule *boy·lė f* — n lump; bump; dent

beunruhigen *bė·oon·roo·i·gėn vt* disturb

beurteilen *bė·oor·tile·ėn vt* judge

Beutel *boy·tėl m* — bag

Bevölkerung *bė·furl·kė·roong f* population

bevor *bè·fòr conj* before; **bevor ich ins Bett gehe** *bè·fòr ikh ins bet gay·è* before I go to bed

bewachen *bè·va·khèn vt* guard (*prisoner*)

Bewaffnete(r) *bè·vaf·nè·tè(·tèr) m* —n gunman

bewegen *bè·vay·gèn vt* move; **sich bewegen** *zikh bè·vay·gèn* move

Bewegung *bè·vay·goong f* —en movement

bewegungslos *bè·vay·goongs·lòs adj* still (*motionless*)

Beweis *bè·vice m* —e proof

Beweise *bè·vye·zè pl* evidence (*proof*)

beweisen* *bè·vye·zèn vt* prove

sich bewerben *zikh bè·ver·bèn vr* apply; **sich um eine Stelle bewerben*** *zikh oom ine·è shte·lè bè·ver·bèn* to apply for a job

Bewerber *bè·ver·bèr m* — applicant

Bewerberin *bè·ver·bè·rin f* —nen applicant

Bewerbung *bè·ver·boong f* —en application (*for job*)

bewohnen *bè·vò·nèn vt* inhabit

bewundern *bè·voon·dèrn vt* admire

bewußt *bè·voost adj* deliberate

bewußtlos *bè·voost·lòs adj* unconscious

Bewußtsein *bè·voost·zine nt* consciousness; **bei Bewußtsein** *bye bè·voost·zine* conscious

bezahlen *bè·tsah·lèn vt* pay; pay for; settle (*bill*)

bezahlt *bè·tsahlt adj* paid (*vacation*)

Bezahlung *bè·tsah·loong f* —en payment

sich beziehen* auf *zikh bè·tsee·èn owf vr* refer to (*allude to*)

Beziehungen *bè·tsee·oong·èn pl* relations

Bezirk *bè·tsirk m* —e precinct (*administrative area*); district (*administrative*)

mit Bezug auf *mit bè·tsook owf prep* with reference to; **in bezug auf** *in bè·tsook owf* regarding

Bezüge *bè·tsöö·gè pl* earnings

bezweifeln *bè·tsvye·fèln vt* doubt; **das bezweifle ich** *dass bè·tsvye·flè ikh* I doubt it

BH *bay·hah m* —s bra

Bibel *bee·bèl f* Bible

Bibliothek *bib·lee·ò·tayk f* —en library

biegen* *bee·gèn vt* bend

biegsam *beek·zam adj* flexible

Biegung *bee·goong f* —en bend (*in pipe, wire etc*)

Biene *bee·nè f* —n bee

Bier *beer nt* —e beer

bieten* *bee·tèn vt/i* offer; bid (*amount*); **auf etwas bieten*** *owf et·vass bee·tèn* to bid for something

Bietende(r) *bee·tèn·dè(·dèr) m/f* —n bidder

Bikini *bee·kee·nee m* —s bikini

Bilanz *bee·lants f* —en balance sheet

Bilanzbuchhalter *bi·lants·bookh·hal·tèr m* — certified public accountant

Bild *bilt nt* —er picture

Bildkarte *bilt·kar·tè f* —n face card

Bildschirm *bilt·shirm m* —e screen (*TV*)

Bildung *bil·doong f* culture

Billard *bil·yart nt* billiards

billig *bil·likh adj* cheap; inexpensive; **der/die/das billigste** *der/dee/dass bi·likh·stè* the least expensive

billigen *bi·li·gèn vt* approve of

binden* *bin·dèn vt* bind; tie

Bindestrich *bin·dè·shtrikh m* —e hyphen

Biologie *bee·ò·lò·gee f* biology

Birke *bir·kè f* —n birch (*tree*)

Birne *bir·nè f* —n bulb (*light*); pear

bis *biss conj* until; **von Montag bis Freitag** *fon mōn·tahk bis frye·tahk* Monday through Friday; **bis jetzt** *biss yetst* up till now; **bis zu 6** *biss tsoo 6* up to 6; **bis zum Bahnhof** *bis tsoom bahn·hōf* as far as the station

Bischof *bi·shof m* —e bishop

bisher *biss·her adv* till now

Biß *biss m* —e bite (*by animal*)

ein bißchen *ine bis·khèn adj* a little; a bit of; **ein bißchen fahren*** *ine bis·khèn fah·rèn* to go for a drive

Bissen *bi·sèn m* — bite (*of food*)

Bitte *bi·tè f* —n request □ *adv* **bitte** *bi·tè* please; **bitte?** *bi·tè* pardon me?, (I beg your) pardon?

bitten *bi·tèn vi* ask; **um etwas bitten*** *oom et·vas bi·tèn* to ask for something

bitter *bi·tèr adj* bitter; **die bittere Schokolade** *bi·tè·rè shō·kō·lah·dè* plain chocolate

Blähung *blay·oong f* —en wind (*in stomach*)

Blankoscheck *blang·kō·shek m* —s blank check

Blase *blah·zè f* —n bladder; blister (*on skin*); bubble

blasen* *blah·zèn vi* blow

blaß *blass adj* pale

Blatt *blat nt* —er sheet (*of paper*); leaf

blau *blow adj* blue; **das blaue Auge** *blow·è ow·gè* black eye

Blazer *blay·zèr m* — blazer

Blei *blye nt* lead

bleiben* *blye·bèn vi* remain; stay

Bleistift *blye·shtift m* —e pencil

Bleistiftabsätze *blye·shtift·ap·zet·sè pl* stiletto heels

blenden *blen·dèn vt* dazzle

Blick *blik m* —e look; glance

blicken *bli·kèn vi* look

blind *blint adj* blind (*person*)

Blinddarmentzündung *blint·darm·ent·tsöōn·doong f* —en appendicitis

Blindenhund *blin·dèn·hoont m* —e guide dog

Blinker *bling·kèr m* — turn signal (*of car*)

Blitz *blits m* —e lightning

Blitzen *blit·sèn vi* — flash

Blitzlicht *blits·likht m* —er flash (*on camera*)

Blitzlichtwürfel *blits·likht·vōōr·fèl m* — flashcube

Block *blok m* —e block; pad; **3 Blocks weiter** *3 bloks vye·tèr* 3 blocks away (*streets*)

blockieren *blo·kee·rèn vt* block (*road*)

Blockschrift *blok·shrift f* block letters; **in Blockschrift** *in blok·shrift* in capitals

blond *blont adj* blond(e)

bloß *blōs adj* bare

blühen *blōō·èn vi* bloom; **das Geschäft blüht** *dass gè·sheft blōōt* business is booming

Blume *bloo·mè f* —n flower

Blumenbeet *bloo·mèn·bayt nt* —e flowerbed

Blumenhändler *bloo·mèn·hent·lèr m* — florist

Blumenkohl *bloo·mèn·kōl m* —e cauliflower

Bluse *bloo·zè f* —n blouse

Blut *bloot nt* blood

Blutdruck *bloot·drook m* blood pressure

Blüte *blōō·tè f* —n blossom

bluten *bloo·tèn vi* bleed

Blutgruppe *bloot·groo·pè f* —n blood group

Blutvergiftung *bloot·fer·gif·toong f* —en blood poisoning

Bö *bur' f* —en squall

Boden *bō·dèn m* = ground; bottom; land (*soil*); floor

Bogen *bō·gèn m* = arch

Bohnen *bō·nèn pl* beans

Bohnerwachs *bō·nèr·vaks nt* polish (*for floor*)

bohren *bō·rèn vt* drill (*hole*)

Bohrer *bō·rèr m* — drill (*tool*)

böig *bur'·ikh adj* gusty (*wind*)

Boiler *boy·lèr m* — immersion heater

Boje *bō·yè f* —n buoy

Bombe *bom·bè f* —n bomb

Bonbon *bon·bon nt* —s candy

Boot *bōt nt* —e boat

an Bord *an bort adv* on board (*ship, plane*); **an Bord gehen*** *an bort gay·èn* to go aboard; **an Bord des Schiffes** *an bort des shi·fès* aboard the ship

Bordkarte *bort·kar·tè f* —n boarding pass

Bordsteinkante *bort·shtine·kan·tè f* —n curb

borgen *bor·gèn vt* borrow; **etwas von jemandem borgen** *et·vass fon yay·man·dèm bor·gèn* to borrow something from someone

Börse *bur·sè f* —n stock exchange

Börsenmakler *bur·sèn·mah·klèr m* — stockbroker

Börsenmarkt *bur·sèn·markt m* =e stock market

Böschung *bur'·shoong f* —en embankment

böse *bur'·zè adj* wicked; **auf jemanden böse sein*** *owf yay·man·dèn bur'·zè zine* to be angry with someone

botanischer Garten *bō·tah·ni·shèr gar·tèn m* = botanical gardens

Bote *bō·tè m* —n messenger

Botschaft *bōt·shaft f* —en embassy

Botschafter *bōt·shaf·tèr m* — ambassador

Bourbon *bur·bon m* —s bourbon

Boutique *boo·teek f* —n boutique

Bowle *bō·lè f* —n punch (*drink*)

Boxen *bok·sèn nt* boxing

boykottieren *boy·ko·tee·rèn vt* boycott

Brand *brant m* =e blaze; fire; **in Brand stecken** *in brant shte·kèn* to set fire to

Brat- *braht pref* fried; roast

braten* *braht·tèn vt* fry; roast; **das Fleisch brät** *das flyesh brayt* the meat is cooking

Braten *brah·tèn m* — roast meat; joint

Bratensaft *brah·tèn·zaft m* =e gravy

Bratpfanne *braht·pfa·nè f* —n fry(ing) pan; skillet

Bratspieß *braht·shpees m* —e spit (*for roasting*)

Bratwurst *braht·voorst f* =e sausage

Brauch *browkh m* =e custom

brauchen *brow·khèn vt* need; **Sie brauchen nicht (zu) kommen** *zee brow·khèn nikht tsoo ko·mèn* you needn't come

Brauerei *brow·è·rye f* —en brewery

braun *brown adj* brown; **braun werden*** *brown ver·dèn* to tan (*in sun*)

Bräune *broy·nè f* tan (*on skin*)

Brausen *brow·zèn nt* boom (*noise*)

Braut *browt f* =e bride

Bräutigam *broy·ti·gam m* —e bridegroom

Brautkleid *browt·klite nt* —er wedding dress

brechen* *bre·khèn vi* be sick (*vomit*) □ *vt/i* break; **sich den Arm brechen*** *zikh dayn arm bre·khèn* to break one's arm

breit *brite adj* broad; **4 cm. breit** *4 cm. brite* 4 cm. wide

Breite *brite·è f* width

Breitling *brite·ling m* —e whitebait

Bremse *brem·zè f* —n brake

bremsen *brem·zèn vi* brake

Bremsflüssigkeit *bremz·flōō·sikh·kite f* brake fluid

Bremslichter *bremz·likh·tèr pl* stoplights

Bremsschuh *brems·shoo m* —e shoe (*of brake*)

brennen* *bre·nèn vi* burn; **das Haus brennt** *das hows brent* the house is on fire

Brennerei *bre·nè·rye f* —en distillery

Brennspiritus *bren·shpee·ree·toos m* methylated spirits

Brennstoff *bren·shtof m* —e fuel

Brett *bret nt* —er plank; board (*of wood*)

Bridge *bridge nt* bridge (*game*)

Brief *breef m* —e letter (*message*); **der eingeschriebene Brief** *ine·gè·shree·bè·nè breef* registered letter

Briefchen *breef·khèn nt* — sachet

Brieffreund *breef·froynt m* —e pen pal

Brieffreundin *breef·froyn·din f* —nen pen pal

Briefkasten *breef·kas·tèn m* = letter box; mailbox

Briefmarke *breef·mar·kè f* —n stamp (*postage*)

Briefpapier *breef·pa·peer nt* notepaper

Brieftasche *breef·ta·shè f* —n pocketbook; wallet

Briefträger *breef·tray·gèr m* — postman; mailman

Brille *bri·lè f* —n glasses

bringen* *bring·èn vt* bring; **bringen Sie dies zur Post** *bring·èn zee dees tsoor post* take this to the post office; **jemanden zum Bahnhof bringen*** *yay·man·dèn tsoom bahn·hōf bring·èn* to take someone to the station; **to see someone off at the station; jemanden nach Hause bringen*** *yay·man·dèn nakh how·zè bring·èn* to see someone home

Brise *bree·zè f* —n breeze

Brite *bri·tè m* —n Briton; **er ist Brite** *er ist bri·tè* he's British

Britin *bri·tin f* —nen Briton; **sie ist Britin** *zee ist bri·tin* she's British

britisch *bri·tish adj* British

Brokkoli *bro·kō·lee pl* broccoli

Brombeere *brom·bay·rè f* —n blackberry

Bronchitis *bron·khee·tis f* bronchitis

Bronze *brōn·tsè f* bronze

Brosche *bro·shè f* —n brooch

Broschüre *bro·shōō·rè f* —n brochure

Brot *brōt nt* —e bread; loaf

Brötchen *brur't·khèn nt* —roll (*bread*); bun

Bruch *brookh m* =e hernia; fracture (*of arm etc*)

Bruchlandung *brookh·lan·doong f* —en crash-landing

Brücke *brōō·kè f* —n bridge

Bruder *broo·dèr m* = brother

Brühe *brōō·è f* —n stock (*for soup etc*)

brüllen *brōō·lèn vi* roar

Brunnen *broo·nèn m* — well (*for water*); fountain

Brüssel *brŏŏ·sèl nt* Brussels

Brust *broost f -̈e* chest (*of body*); breast

Brustumfang *broost·oom·fang m -̈e* bust measurements

brutto *broo·tō adj* pretax (*profit*); gross (*before deductions*)

Bruttoertragsziffer *broo·tō·er·trahks·tsi·fèr f —n* cash flow

Bruttosozialprodukt *broo·tō·zo·tsee·ahl·prō·dookt nt —e* gross national product, GNP

Bube *boo·bè m —n* jack (*cards*)

Buch *bookh nt -̈er* book

Buche *boo·khè f —n* beech

Buchführung *bookh·fōō·roong f* accountancy

Buchhalter *bookh·hal·tèr m* — accountant

Buchhandlung *bookh·hant·loong f —en* bookstore

Buchprüfer *bookh·prōō·fèr m* — auditor

Büchse *bŏŏk·sè f —n* can (*container*)

Büchsen- *bŏŏk·sèn pref* canned

Büchsenöffner *bŏŏk·sèn·ur'f·nèr m* — can-opener

Buchstabe *bookh·stah·bè m —n* letter (*of alphabet*)

buchstabieren *bookh·shta·bee·rèn vt* spell (*in writing*)

Bucht *bookht f —en* bay (*on coast*)

Buckel *boo·kèl m —s* hump (*on road*)

Budget *bōō·djay nt —s* budget

Bügel *bōō·gèl m —* coathanger

Bügeleisen *bōō·gèl·eye·zèn nt* — iron (*for clothes*)

Bügelfalte *bōō·gèl·fal·tè f —n* crease

bügelfrei *bōō·gèl·frye adj* drip-dry (*shirt etc*)

bügeln *bōō·gèln vt* iron

Bühne *bōō·nè f —n* stage (*in theater*)

Bullauge *bool·ow·gè nt —n* porthole

Bulldozer *bool·dō·zèr m —* bulldozer

Bummelstreik *boo·mèl·shtrike m* slow-down

Bündel *bōōn·dèl nt* — bundle

Bundes- *boon·dès pref* federal

Bundesrepublik *boon·dès·ray·poo·bleek f* West Germany

Bündnis *bōŏnt·nis nt —se* alliance

Bungalow *boong·ga·lo m —s* bungalow

buntes Glasfenster *boon·tès glahs·fen·stèr nt* — stained glass window

Buntstift *boont·shtift m* — crayon

Bürgerkrieg *bōŏr·gèr·kreek m —e* civil war

bürgerlich *bōŏr·gèr·likh adj* middle-class

Bürgermeister *bōŏr·gèr·mye·stèr m* — mayor

Bürgersteig *bōŏr·gèr·shtike m —e* sidewalk

Büro *bōō·rō nt —s* agency; office; bureau

Büroangestellte(r) *bōō·rō·an·gè·shtel·tè(·tèr) m/f —n* office worker; clerk (*in office*)

Bürohochhaus *bōō·rō·hōkh·hows nt -̈er* office-block

Büroklammer *bōō·rō·kla·mèr f —n* paper clip

Bursche *boor·shè m —n* fellow

Bürste *bŏŏr·stè f —n* brush

bürsten *bŏŏr·stèn vt* brush

Bus *boos m —se* bus

Busch *boosh m -̈e* shrub

Busen *boo·zèn m —* bust

Bushaltestelle *boos·hal·tè·shte·lè f —n* bus stop

Büste *bŏŏs·tè f —n* bust (*statue*)

Busverbindung *boos·fer·bin·doong f —en* bus service

Butangas *boo·tahn·gas nt* butane

Butter *boo·tèr f* butter

b.w. *abbrev* P.T.O.

C

Café *ka·fay nt —s* café

Callgirl *kŏl·gurl nt —s* call girl

Camping *kam·ping nt* camping

Campingbett *kam·ping·bet nt —en* camp-bed

Canasta *ka·nas·ta nt* canasta

Cape *kayp nt —s* cape

Cello *tshe·lō nt —s* cello

Cellophan *tse·lo·fahn nt* cellophane

Celsius *tsel·zee·oos adj* Celsius

Cent *tsent m* cent

Chalet *sha·lay nt —s* chalet

Charakter *ka·rak·tèr m —e* character

Charterflug *shar·tèr·flook m -̈e* charter flight

chartern *shar·tèrn vt* charter (*plane, bus*)

Chassis *sha·see nt —* chassis

Chef *shef m —s* head (*chief*); boss

Chemie *khay·mee f* chemistry

chemisch *khay·mish adj* chemical

Chicorée *shi·ko·ray f —s* chicory

Chili *chee·lee m* chili

China *khee·na nt* China

Chinesisch *khee·nay·zish nt* Chinese (*language*) □ *adj* chinesisch *khee·nay·zish* Chinese

Chip *chip m —s* chip (*in gambling*); die Chips *chips* potato chips

Chirurg *khee·roork m —en* surgeon

Chirurgie *khee·roor·gee f* surgery (*operation*)

Choke *chōk m —s* choke (*of car*)

Cholesterin *khŏ·les·tay·reen nt* cholesterol

Chor *kōr m -̈e* choir

Christ *krist m —en* Christian

Chrom *krōm nt* chrome

Chrysantheme *kri·zan·tay·mè f —n* chrysanthemum

Clown *klown m —s* clown

Cocktail *kok·tayl m —s* cocktail

College *ko·lich nt —s* college

Comic-Heft *ko·mik·heft nt —e* comic

Computer *kom·poo·tèr m —* computer

Container *kon·tay·nèr m —* container (*for shipping etc*)

Copyright *ko·pee·rite nt* copyright

Couchtisch *kowch·tish m —e* coffee table

Coupé *koo·pay nt —s* coupé (*car*)

Creme *kraym f —s* cream (*cosmetic*)

cremefarben *kraym·far·bèn adj* cream

Cremespeise *kraym·shpye·zè f —n* mousse

cremig *kray·mikh adj* creamy (*texture*)

Croupier *kroo·pyay m —s* croupier

Crouton *kroo·tong m —s* crouton

Cup *kup m —s* cup (*trophy*)

Curry *ku·ree m —s* curry

Currypulver *ku·ree·pool·vèr nt —* curry powder

D

da *dah adv* there; nicht da *nikht dah* out (*not at home*); ist eine Woche nicht da *er ist ine·è vo·khè nikht dah* he's away for a week; von da an *fon da an* from then on; da kommt sie *dah komt zee* here she comes; **ist er da?** *ist er dah* is he in?; **ist da jemand?** *ist dah yay·mant* is there anyone there? □ *conj da er schlief dah er shleef* as he was asleep (*because*)

Dach *dakh nt* ⁼er roof

Dachboden *dakh·bō·dèn m* — attic

Dachrinne *dakh·ri·nè f* —n gutter (*on building*)

Dachträger *dakh·tray·gèr m* — roof rack

dagegen *da·gay·gèn adv* against it; **haben Sie etwas dagegen, wenn ...?** *hah·bèn zee et·vass da·gay·gèn ven* do you mind if ...?

daher *dah·her conj* and so

damals *dah·mals adv* then

Dame *dah·mè f* —n lady; **meine Dame** *mine·è dah·mè* madam

Damenbinde *dah·mèn·bin·dè f* —n sanitary napkin

Damentoilette *dah·mèn·tō·a·le·tè f* —n powder room

Damespiel *dah·mè·shpeel nt* —e checkers

damit *da·mit conj* so that

Damm *dam m* ⁼e dam

Dampf *dampf m* ⁼e steam

dämpfen *demp·fèn vt* steam (*food*); absorb (*shock*)

Dampfer *damp·fèr m* — steamer (*ship*)

Dampfkochtopf *dampf·kokh·topf m* ⁼e pressure cooker

danach *da·nakh adv* afterward(s)

Däne *day·nè m* —n Dane

Dänemark *day·nè·mark nt* Denmark

Dänin *day·nin f* —nen Dane

dänisch *day·nish adj* Danish □ *nt* Dänisch *day·nish* Danish

dank *dank prep* thanks to □ *m der* Dank *dank* thanks

dankbar *dank·bahr adj* grateful

danke *dang·kè excl* thank you

danken *dang·kèn vi* thank

dann *dan adv* then

Darlehen *dar·lay·èn nt* — loan

Darstellung *dar·shte·loong f* —en version

Dartspiel *dart·shpeel nt* —e game of darts

das *das art the* □ *pron* that; this; whom; **das heißt...** *dass hyest* that is (to say)...

daß *dass conj* that; **ich hoffe, daß...** *ikh ho·fè dass* I hope that...

dasselbe *das·zel·bè adj, pron* (the) same

Datei *da·tye f* —en data file

Daten *dah·tèn pl* data

Datenbank *dah·tèn·bank f* —en data bank, data base

Datenverarbeitung *dah·tèn·fer·ar·bye·toong f* data processing

Dattel *da·tèl f* —n date (*fruit*)

Datum *dah·toom nt* Daten date (*day*); **welches Datum haben wir heute?** *vel·khès dah·toom hah·bèn veer hoy·tè* what's the date today?

Datumsgrenze *dah·tooms·gren·tsè f* date line

dauern *dow·èrn vi* last; **es dauert eine Stunde** *ess dow·èrt ine·è shtoon·dè* it takes an hour

Dauerwelle *dow·èr·ve·lè f* —n perm

Daumen *dow·mèn m* — thumb

DDR *day·day·er f* East Germany

Debatte *de·ba·tè f* —n debate

Debet *de·bèt nt* —s debit

Deck *dek nt* —s deck (*of ship*)

Decke *de·kè f* —n blanket; ceiling

Deckel *de·kèl m* — top; lid

decken *de·kèn vt* cover; **den Tisch decken** *dayn tish de·kèn* to lay the table

Defizit *day·fi·tsit nt* —e deficit; shortfall

Deflation *de·fla·tsee·ōn f* deflation

deformiert *de·for·meert adj* deformed

dehnen *day·nèn vt* stretch; expand; **sich dehnen** *zikh day·nèn* stretch; expand

Deich *dyekh m* —e dike

dein(e) *dine(·è) adj* your (*familiar form*)

deine(r/s) *dine·è(·èr/·ès) pron* yours (*familiar form*)

Delegation *day·lay·ga·tsee·ōn f* —en delegation

delegieren *day·lay·gee·rèn vt* delegate

Demonstration *de·mon·stra·tsee·ōn f* —en demonstration (*political*)

den *dayn pron* whom; for; **der Apfel, den Sie gegessen haben** *der ap·fèl dayn zee gè·ge·sèn hah·bèn* the apple which you ate

denken[*] *deng·kèn vi* think; an etwas denken[*] *an et·vass deng·kèn* to think of something; an jemanden denken[*] *an yay·man·dèn deng·kèn* to think about someone

Denkmal *denk·mahl nt* ⁼er monument

denn *den conj* for; then; than

dennoch *den·nokh conj* nevertheless

deponieren *de·pō·nee·rèn vt* deposit (*money*)

Depot *de·pō nt* —s depot

deprimiert *de·pree·meert adj* depressed (*person*)

der *der art* the; **der vierzehnte Juni** *der fir·zayn·tè yoo·nee* 14th of June; **der Junge da** *der yoong·è dah* that boy □ *pron der der* who

Designer *di·zye·nèr m* — designer

Desinfektionsmittel *des·in·fek·tsee·ōnz·mi·tèl nt* — disinfectant

desinfizieren *des·in·fi·tsee·rèn vt* disinfect

Desodorant *des·ō·do·rant nt* —s deodorant

dessen *de·sèn pron* whose

Dessertlöffel *de·ser·lur'·fèl m* — dessertspoon

Detektiv *day·tek·teef m* —e detective

deutlich *doyt·likh adj* distinct (*clear*)

Deutsch *doytsh nt* German; **auf Deutsch** *owf doytsh* in German

deutsch *doytsh adj* German

Deutsche *doyt·shè m/f* —n German

Deutschland *doytsh·lant nt* Germany; **nach Deutschland** *nakh doytsh·lant* to Germany

Devisen *day·vee·zèn pl* foreign currency

Devisenmarkt *day·vee·zen·markt m* ⁼e foreign exchange market

Dezember *de·tsem·bèr m* December

dezimal *de·tsee·mahl adj* decimal

Dezimalzahl *de·tsee·mahl·tsahl f* —en decimal

Dia *dee·a nt* —s slide (*photo*)

Diabetiker *dee·a·bay·ti·kèr m* — diabetic

Diabetikerin *dee·a·bay·ti·kè·rin f* —nen diabetic

Diagnose *dee·ag·nō·zè f* —n diagnosis

diagonal *dee·a·go·nahl adj* diagonal

Diagramm *dee·a·gram nt* —e diagram

Dialekt *dee·a·lekt m* —e dialect

Diamant *dee·a·mant m* —en diamond

dich *dikh pron* you

dicht *dikht adj* dense (*fog etc*)

Dichtung *dikh·toong f* —en gasket
dick *dik adj* thick; fat (*person*); 3 Meter dick 3 *meh·tèr dik* 3 meters thick
Dickmilch *dick·milkh f* soured milk
die *dee art* the □ *pron* who(m)
Dieb *deep m* —e thief
Diele *dee·lè f* —n hall (*entrance*)
Dienst *deenst m* —e service; im Dienst *im deenst* on duty (*doctor*)
Dienstag *deens·tahk m* Tuesday
Dienstleistungsbranche *deenst·lye·stoongs·bran·shè f* service industry
Dienstmädchen *deenst·mayt·khèn nt* — maid
Dienstzeit *deenst·tsite f* —en office hours
diese(r/s) *dee·zè(·zèr|·zès) adj* this □ *pron* this one; diese *dee·zè* these
Dieselmotor *dee·zèl·mō·tōr m* —en diesel engine
Dieselöl *dee·zèl·url'l nt* diesel fuel
Digital- *di·gi·tahl pref* digital
diktieren *dik·teer·èn vt* dictate (*letter*)
Ding *ding nt* —e thing
Dingi *ding·ee nt* —s dinghy
Diplom *di·plōm nt* —e diploma
Diplomat *di·plo·maht m* —en diplomat
dir *deer pron* (to) you
direkt *dee·rekt adj* direct; direkt nach Venedig fliegen* *dee·rekt nay·dikh flee·gèn* to fly to Venice direct; direkt nach Hause gehen* *dee·rekt nakh how·zè gay·èn* to go straight home
Direktor *dee·rek·tor m* —en director (*of firm*); headmaster; governor (*of institution*); der leitende Direktor *lye·tèn·dè dee·rek·tor* managing director, M.D.
Direktorin *dee·rek·tō·rin f* —nen headmistress
Dirigent *di·ri·gent m* —en conductor (*of orchestra*)
Diskjockey *disk·jo·kay m* —s disc jockey
Disko *di·skō f* —s disco(thèque)
Diskriminierung *dis·kri·mi·nee·roong f* discrimination (*racial etc*)
diskutieren *dis·koo·tee·rèn vt* discuss
disqualifizieren *dis·kva·li·fi·tsee·rèn vt* disqualify
Disziplin *dis·tsi·pleen f* discipline
diversifizieren *dee·ver·see·fi·tsee·rèn vt/i* diversify
Dividende *di·vi·den·dè f* —n dividend
Diwan *dee·van m* —e divan
doch *dokh adv* yes (*in answer to negative question*) □ *conj* all the same
Docht *dokht m* —e wick (*of cigarette lighter*)
Dock *dok nt* —s dock
Doktor *dok·tor m* doctor
Dokument *do·koo·ment nt* document
Dolch *dolkh m* —e dagger
Dollar *do·lar m* —s dollar
dolmetschen *dol·met·shèn vi* interpret
Dolmetscher *dol·met·shèr m* — interpreter
Dolmetscherin *dol·met·shè·rin f* —nen interpreter
Dom *dōm m* —e cathedral
Donner *do·nèr m* thunder
Donnerstag *do·ners·tahk m* Thursday
Doppelbett *do·pèl·bet nt* —er double bed
Doppelschnitte *do·pèl·shni·tè f* —n sandwich
doppelt *do·pèlt adj* double; doppelt soviel kosten *do·pèlt zō·feel ko·stèn* to cost double

Doppelzimmer *do·pèl·tsi·mèr nt* — double room
Dorf *dorf nt* ∸er village
dort *dort adv* there
Dose *dō·zè f* —n box; can; in Dosen *in dō·zèn* canned (*food*)
dösen *dur'·zèn vi* doze
Dosenöffner *dō·zèn·ur'f·nèr m* — can opener
Dosis *dō·sis f* Dosen dosage, dose
Dozent *dō·tsent m* —en professor
Drachen *dra·khèn m* — kite
Draht *draht m* ∸e wire
Drahtseil *draht·zile nt* —e cable (*rope*)
drainieren *dray·nee·rèn vt* drain (*land*)
Drama *drah·ma nt* Dramen drama (*art*)
dramatisch *dra·mah·tish adj* dramatic
drastisch *dra·stish adj* drastic
draußen *drow·sèn adv* outdoors; nach draußen gehen* *nakh drow·sèn gay·èn* to go outside
drehen *dray·èn vt* turn; twist
drei *drye num* three
Dreieck *drye·ek nt* —e triangle
dreißig *drye·sikh num* thirty
dreißigste(r/s) *drye·sikh·stè(·stèr|·stès) adj* thirtieth
dreizehn *drye·tsayn num* thirteen
dreizehnte(r/s) *drye·tsayn·tè(·tèr|·tès) adj* thirteenth
dressieren *dre·see·rèn vt* train (*dog*)
dringend *dring·ènt adj* urgent
drinnen *drin·nèn adv* inside
dritte(r/s) *dri·tè(·tèr|·tès) adj* third
Dritte Welt *dri·tè velt f* Third World
Droge *drō·gè f* —n drug (*narcotic*)
Drogist *dro·gist m* —en druggist
Drohung *drō·oong f* —en threat
drüben *drōō·bèn adv* over there
Druck *drook m* ∸e pressure
drücken *drōō·kèn vt* press; squeeze (*hand*); push (*button*); drücken Sie den Knopf *drōō·kèn zee dayn knopf* press the button
drucken *droo·kèn vt* print (*book, newspaper*)
Drucker *droo·kèr m* — printer
Druckfehler *drook·fay·lèr m* — misprint
Druckknopf *drook·knopf m* ∸e snap fastener
Druckschrift *drook·shrift f* block letters
Drugstore *drug·stōr m* —s drugstore
Drüse *drōō·zè f* —n gland
du *doo pron* you (familiar form)
Dudelsack *doo·dèl·zak m* ∸e (bag-) pipes
Duft *dooft m* ∸e scent (*smell*)
dumm *doom adj* stupid
Dummkopf *doom·kopf m* ∸e idiot
Dumping *dam·ping nt* dumping (*of goods*)
Düne *dōō·nè f* —n dune
dunkel *doong·kèl adj* dark
dünn *dōōn adj* thin; weak (*tea*)
durch *doorkh prep* through □ *adj* done (*meat*)
durch|brennen* *doorkh·bre·nèn vi* blow (*fuse*)
durch|dringen* *doorkh·dring·èn vt* penetrate
Durcheinander *doorkh·ine·an·dèr nt* muddle □ *adj* durcheinander *doorkh·ine·an·dèr* in a muddle
durcheinander|bringen* *doorkh·ine·an·dèr·bring·èn vt* mix up
Durchfall *doorkh·fal m* diarrhea
durch|fallen* *in doorkh·fa·lèn vi* fail (*exam*)

durchgebraten *doorkh·gè·brah·tèn* adj well-done (*steak*)

durchgehender Zug *doorkh·gay·èn·dèr tsook m* -̈e through train

durch|kommen* *doorkh·ko·mèn vi* to get through (*on phone*)

Durchmesser *doorkh·me·sèr m* — diameter

Durchschlag *doorkh·shlahk m* -̈e carbon copy

Durchschnitt *doorkh·shnit m* average

durchschnittlich *doorkh·shnit·likh adj* average

durchsichtig *doorkh·zikh·tikh adj* transparent

durchstechen* *doorkh·shte·khèn vt* pierce

durchsuchen *doorkh·zoo·khèn vt* search

dürfen* *döor·fèn vi* be allowed; **darf ich eintreten?** *darf ikh ine·tray·tèn* may I come in?

Dürre *döo·rè f* -n drought

Durst haben* *doorst hah·bèn vi* to be thirsty

durstig *door·stikh adj* thirsty

Dusche *doo·shè f* -n shower (*bath*)

duschen *doo·shèn vi* to have a shower

Düsenflugzeug *döo·zèn·flook·tsoyk nt* -e jet (*plane*)

düster *döo·stèr adj* drab

duty-free *dyoo·tee free adj* duty-free (*shop*)

Dutzend *doo·tsènt nt* -e dozen; **4 Dutzend Eier** *4 doo·tsènt eye·èr* 4 dozen eggs

dynamisch *döo·nah·mish adj* dynamic (*person*)

Dynamo *döo·na·mō m* -s dynamo

E

Ebbe *e·bè f* -n low tide

eben *ay·bèn adj* level (*surface*); flat; **er ist eben angekommen** *er ist ay·bèn an·gè·ko·mèn* he arrived just now

Ebene *ay·bè·nè f* -n level; plain

Echo *e·kho m* -s echo

echt *ekht adj* real; genuine

Ecke *e·kè f* -n corner (*of streets*)

Eclair *ay·kler nt* -s éclair

edel *ay·dèl adj* vintage (*wine*)

Edelstein *ay·dèl·shtine m* -e jewel; gem

Effekten *e·fek·tèn pl* stocks and bonds

effektiv *e·fek·teef adv* in real terms

EG *ay·gay f* E.E.C.

egal *ay·gahl adv* all the same; **es ist mir egal** *ess ist meer ay·gahl* I don't mind; I don't care; **welcher? - das ist egal** *vel·khèr - dass ist ay·gahl* which one? - either

egoistisch *ay·gō·is·tish adj* selfish

Ehe *ay·è f* -n marriage

ehemalig *ay·è·mah·likh adj* ex-

eher *ay·èr adv* sooner; rather

Ehering *ay·è·ring m* -e wedding ring

ehrgeizig *ayr·gye·tsikh adj* ambitious (*person*)

ehrlich *ayr·likh adj* honest

Ei *eye nt* -er egg; **ein weiches Ei** *ine vye·khès eye* a soft-boiled egg

Eiche *eye·khè f* -n oak

Eichel *eye·khèl f* -n acorn

Eichhörnchen *eyekh·hurn·khèn nt* — squirrel

Eierbecher *eye·èr·be·khèr m* — egg cup

eifersüchtig *ife·èr·zöokh·tikh adj* jealous

eifrig *eye·frikh adj* eager

eigen *ige·èn adj* own

eigenartig *eye·gèn·ar·tikh adj* queer (*strange*)

Eigenschaft *eye·gèn·shaft f* -en quality (*characteristic*)

eigentlich *eye·gènt·likh adv* actually

Eigentum *eye·gèn·toom nt* property

Eigentümer *eye·gèn·töo·mèr m* — owner

Eigentümerin *eye·gèn·töo·mè·rin f* -nen owner

Eil- *ile pref* urgent

Eilbrief *ile·breef m* -e express letter

Eile *ile·è f* haste; rush

eilen *ile·èn vi* rush

eilig *ile·ikh adj* quick; **es eilig haben*** *ess ile·ikh hah·bèn* to be in a hurry

Eimer *ime·èr m* — pail; bucket

einander *ine·an·dèr pron* one another

Einbahnstraße *ine·bahn·shtrah·sè f* -n one-way street

Einband *ine·bant m* -̈e cover (*of book*)

sich ein|bilden *zikh ine·bil·dèn vr* imagine (*wrongly*)

Einbrecher *ine·bre·khèr m* — burglar

ein|bringen* *ine·bring·èn vt* yield (*investment*); bring in (*profit*)

Einbußen *ine·boo·sèn pl* shrinkage

Eindruck *ine·drook m* -̈e impression

eindrucksvoll *ine·drooks·fol adj* impressive

ein(e) *ine(·è) art* a; an

eine(r/s) *ine·è(·èr/·ès) pron* one; **eine(r) von Ihnen** *ine·è(r) fon ee·nèn* either of you

einfach *ine·fakh adj* simple; **die einfache Fahrkarte** *ine·fa·khè fahr·kar·tè* one-way ticket; single ticket

ein|fahren* *ine·fah·rèn vt* to break in (*car*)

Einfahrt *ine·fart f* -en drive (*driveway*)

Einfluß *ine·floos m* -̈e influence

ein|frieren* *ine·free·rèn vt* freeze (*food*)

Einfuhr *ine·foor f* — import

ein|führen *ine·föo·rèn vt* launch (*product*); import

Eingang *ine·gang m* -̈e entrance; entry; gate (*of building*)

Eingangshalle *ine·gangs·ha·lè f* -n lobby (*entrance*)

Eingangsstufe *ine·gangs·shtoo·fè f* -n doorstep

eingebildet *ine·gè·bil·dèt adj* conceited

eingebürgert *ine·gè·böor·gèrt adj* naturalized

eingelegt *ine·gè·laykt adj* in gear

ein(geschaltet) *ine(·gè·shal·tèt) adj* on (*machine*)

einheimisch *ine·hye·mish adj* native

Einheit *ine·hite f* -en unit; **der Preis pro Einheit** *prise prō ine·hite* unit price

einheitlich *ine·hite·likh adj* plain (*not patterned*)

einige(r/s) *ine·i·gè(·gèr/·gès) pron* some; **einige Leute** *ine·i·gè loy·tè* some people; **einige Bücher** *ine·i·gè böo·khèr* a few books; **einige waren…** *ine·i·gè vah·rèn* some (of them) were…; **einige von uns** *ine·i·gè fon oons* several of us

sich einigen auf *zikh ine·i·gèn owf vt* agree on (*price*)

Einkauf *ine·kowf m* -̈e purchase; **die Einkäufe** *ine·koy·fè* shopping

ein|kaufen *ine·kow·fèn vi* shop

ein|kaufen gehen* *ine·kow·fèn gay·èn vi* go shopping

Einkäufer *ine·koy·fĕr m* — buyer (for shop, factory)

Einkäuferin *ine·koy·fĕ·rin f* —nen buyer (for shop, factory)

Einkaufsnetz *ine·kowfs·nets nt* —e string bag

Einkaufstasche *ine·kowfs·ta·shĕ f* —n shopping bag

Einkaufswagen *ine·kowfs·vah·gĕn m* — cart (for purchases)

Einkaufszentrum *ine·kowfs·tsen·troom nt* —zentren shopping center

Einkommen *ine·ko·mĕn nt* — income

ein|laden* *ine·lah·dĕn vt* invite

Einladung *ine·lah·doong f* —en invitation

ein|laufen* *ine·low·fĕn vi* shrink

sich ein|leben *zikh ine·lay·bĕn vr* settle in

einleitend *ine·lye·tĕnt adj* preliminary

Einleitung *ine·lye·toong f* —en introduction (in book)

ein|lösen *ine·lur·zĕn vt* cash (check)

einmal *ine·mahl adv* once; sind Sie schon einmal in London gewesen? *zint zee shōn ine·mahl in lon·don gĕ·vay·zĕn* have you ever been to London?; früher einmal *frōō·ĕr ine·mahl* once (formerly); noch einmal *nokh ine·mahl* once more; auf einmal *owf ine·mahl* all at once

sich ein|mischen *zikh ine·mi·shĕn vr* interfere

einmütig *ine·mōō·tikh adj* unanimous (decision)

Einnahmen *ine·nah·mĕn pl* revenue; receipts (income)

ein|packen *ine·pa·kĕn vt* pack (goods); ein Paket ein|packen *ine pa·kayt ine·pa·kĕn* to wrap up a parcel

ein|planen *ine·plah·nĕn vt* plan (on)

Einrichtungen *ine·rikh·toong·ĕn pl* facilities

eins *ines num* one

einsam *ine·zam adj* lonely (person)

Einsatz *ine·zats m* —e stake (in gambling)

ein|schalten *ine·shal·tĕn vt* switch on (light, TV)

ein|schenken *ine·sheng·kĕn vt* pour (tea, milk)

Einschienenbahn *ine·sheen·ĕn·bahn f* —en monorail

sich ein|schiffen *zikh ine·shi·fĕn vr* embark

ein|schlafen* *ine·shla·fĕn vi* go to sleep

ein|schließen* *ine·shlee·sĕn vt* include

einschließlich *ine·shlees·likh prep* including; vom 6. bis einschließlich 12. *fom 6 bis ine·shlees·likh 12* from 6th to 12th inclusive

Einschränkung *ine·shreng·koong f* —en qualification (restriction)

Einschreiben *ine·shrye·bĕn nt* certified mail

einseitig *ine·zye·tikh adj* unilateral

ein|steigen* *ine·shtye·gĕn vt* board (train, bus)

ein|stellen *ine·shte·lĕn vt* adjust; focus; appoint

Einstellplatz *ine·shtel·plats m* —e car-port

Einstellung *ine·shte·loong f* —en appointment (to job); attitude

Einstellungsgespräch *ine·shte·loongs·gĕ·shprekh nt* —e interview (for job)

Eintopf *ine·topf m* —e stew

einträglich *ine·trayk·likh adj* profitable

ein|treten* *ine·tray·tĕn vi* come in; **ein|treten*** *in ine·tray·tĕn* in enter (room)

Eintrittsgeld *ine·trits·gelt nt* —er entrance fee

Eintrittskarte *ine·trits·kar·tĕ f* —n ticket (for theatre)

Einwand *ine·vant m* —e objection

Einwanderer *ine·van·dĕr·ĕr m* — immigrant

ein|wechseln *ine·vek·sĕln vt* change (money)

ein|weichen *ine·vye·khĕn vt* soak (washing)

ein|wickeln *ine·vi·kĕln vt* wrap

Einwohner *ine·vō·nĕr m* — inhabitant

ein|zahlen *ine·tsah·lĕn vt* bank (money)

Einzelbett *ine·tsĕl·bet nt* —en single bed; zwei Einzelbetten *tsvye ine·tsĕl·be·tĕn* twin beds

Einzelhandel *ine·tsĕl·han·dĕl m* retail

Einzelhandelspreis *ine·tsĕl·han·dĕls·prise m* —e retail price; zum Einzelhandelspreis verkaufen *tsoom ine·tsĕl·han·dĕls·prise fer·kow·fĕn* to sell at retail price

Einzelhändler *ine·tsĕl·hent·lĕr m* — retailer

Einzelhaus *ine·tsĕl·hows nt* —er detached house

Einzelheit *ine·tsĕl·hite f* —en detail

Einzelkind *ine·tsĕl·kint nt* only child

einzeln *ine·tsĕln adj* single (not double); individual □ *adv* individually

Einzelzimmer *ine·tsĕl·tsi·mĕr nt* — single room

einzig *ine·tsikh adj* only

einzigartig *ine·tsikh·ar·tikh adj* unique

Eis *ise nt* ice cream; ice; das Eis am Stiel *ise am shteel* popsicle

Eisbahn *ise·bahn f* —en skating rink

Eisen *eye·zĕn nt* iron (material, golf club)

Eisenbahn *eye·zĕn·bahn f* —en railroad

Eisenwaren *eye·zĕn·vah·rĕn pl* hardware

Eisenwarenhändler *eye·zĕn·vah·rĕn·hent·lĕr m* — ironmonger

Eistüte *ise·tōō·tĕ f* —n cornet (of ice cream)

Eiswürfel *ise·vōōr·fĕl m* — ice cube

eitel *eye·tĕl adj* vain

ekelhaft *ay·kĕl·haft adj* nasty

Ekzem *ek·tsaym nt* —e eczema

Elefant *ay·lay·fant m* —en elephant

elegant *e·lay·gant adj* smart; stylish; elegant

Elektriker *ay·lek·tri·kĕr m* — electrician

elektrisch *ay·lek·trish adj* electric(al)

Elektrizität *ay·lek·tri·tsi·tet f* electricity

Elektronik *ay·lek·trō·nik f* electronics

elektronisch *ay·lek·trō·nish adj* electronic

Elektroschock *e·lek·tro·shok m* —s shock (electric)

Element *e·le·ment nt* —e unit (of machinery, furniture); element

Elend *ay·lĕnt nt* misery

elf *elf num* eleven

Elfenbein *el·fĕn·bine nt* ivory

elfte(r/s) *elf·tĕ(·tĕr/·tĕs) adj* eleventh

Ellbogen *el·bō·gĕn m* — elbow

Eltern *el·tĕrn pl* parents

Email *ay·mye nt* —s enamel

Embargo *em·bar·gō nt* —s embargo

Emission *ay·mi·see·ōn f* issue (of stocks)

emotional *ay·mō·tsee·ō·nahl adj* emotional (person)

Empfang *emp·fang m ⁻e* welcome; reception (*in hotel etc, gathering*)

empfangen* *emp·fang·ën vt* receive (*guest*)

Empfangschef *emp·fangs·shef m —s* receptionist (*in hotel*)

Empfangsdame *emp·fangs·dah·mè f —n* receptionist (*in hotel*)

Empfangsschein *emp·fangs·shine m —e* receipt (*for parcel*)

empfehlen* *emp·fay·lën vt* recommend

empfindlich *emp·fint·likh adj* sensitive

Endbetrag *ent·bè·trahk m ⁻e* amount (*total*)

Ende *en·dè nt* bottom (*of page, list*); end

enden *en·dën vi* end

Endiviensalat *en·dee·vee·ën·za·laht m —e* endive (*curly*)

endlich *ent·likh adv* at last

Endstation *end·shta·tsee·ön f —en* terminal (*buses*)

Endsumme *ent·zoo·mè f —n* sum total

Energie *ay·ner·gee f —n* energy

eng *eng adj* narrow; tight (*clothes*)

Engel *eng·èl m —* angel

England *eng·glant nt* England

Engländer *eng·glen·dèr m —* Englishman

Engländerin *eng·glen·dè·rin f —nen* Englishwoman

Englisch *eng·glish nt* English □ *adj* englisch *eng·glish* English; auf englisch *owf eng·glish* in English

Engpaß *eng·pas m ⁻e* bottleneck

en gros *oñ grō adv* in bulk (*in large quantities*)

Enkel *eng·kèl m —* grandson

Enkelin *eng·kè·lin f —nen* granddaughter

Enkelkind *eng·kèl·kint nt —er* grandchild

enorm *ay·norm adj* enormous

Ensemble *on·som·bèl m —s* ensemble (*clothes*)

Entbindungsheim *ent·bin·doongs·hime nt* maternity hospital

entdecken *ent·de·kën vt* discover

Ente *en·tè f —n* duck

enteisen *ent·eye·zën vt* de-ice

entfalten *ent·fal·tën vt* unfold

entfernen *ent·fer·nën vt* remove

entfernt *ent·fernt adj* distant; 30 Kilometer entfernt *30 ki·lō·may·tèr ent·fernt* 30 kilometers away

Entfernung *ent·fer·noong f —en* distance

Entfernungsmesser *ent·fer·noongs·mesèr m —* range finder (*on camera*)

entführen *ent·foo·rën vt* hijack; kidnap

Entführer *ent·foo·rèr m —* hijacker

enthalten* *ent·hal·tën vt* hold; contain; sich enthalten *zikh ent·hal·tën* abstain (*in voting*)

entkommen* *ent·ko·mën vi* get away; escape (*person*)

entladen* *ent·lah·dën vt* unload (*vehicle*)

entlang *ent·lang prep* along; die Straße entlang *dee shtrah·sè ent·lang* along the street

entlassen* *ent·la·sën vt* dismiss (*from job*)

entmutigt *ent·moo·tikht adj* discouraged

entrahmte Milch *ent·rahm·tè milkh f* skim milk

entschädigen *ent·she·di·gën vt* compensate

sich entscheiden* *zikh ent·shye·dën vr* decide (*between alternatives*)

Entscheidung *ent·shye·doong f —en* decision

sich entschließen* *zikh ent·shlee·sën vr* to make up one's mind

entschlossen *ent·shlo·sën adj* firm (*person*); determined

entschuldigen *ent·shool·di·gën vt* excuse; sich entschuldigen *zikh ent·shool·di·gën* apologize

Entschuldigung *ent·shool·di·goong excl* pardon; excuse me

sich entspannen *zikh ent·shpa·nën vr* relax

entsprechen* *ent·shpre·khën vi* meet (*demand*)

entsprechend *ent·shpre·khènt adj* equivalent to

enttäuscht *ent·toysht adj* disappointed

entweder ... oder ... *ent·vay·dèr ... ō·dèr ... conj* either ... or ...

entwerfen* *ent·ver·fën vt* design

entwickeln *ent·vik·ëln vt* develop (*photo*); sich entwickeln *zikh ent·vik·ëln* develop

Entwicklungsland *ent·vik·loongz·lant nt —er* developing country

Entwurf *ent·voorf m ⁻e* draft (*rough outline*); design (*plan*); einen Entwurf anfertigen von *ine·ën ent·voorf an·fer·ti·gën fon* to plan (*make a design*)

entzückt *ent·tsöökt adj* delighted

Entzündung *ent·tsöön·doong f —en* inflammation

Enzyklopädie *ent·sōō·klō·pe·dee f —n* encyclop(a)edia

Epidemie *ay·pee·day·mee f —n* epidemic

Epilepsie *ay·pee·lep·see f* epilepsy

er *er pron* he; it; er ist es *er ist ess* it's him

erben *er·bën vt* inherit

sich erbrechen* *zikh er·bre·khën vr* vomit

Erbsen *erp·sën pl* peas

Erdbeben *ert·bay·bën nt —* earthquake

Erdbeere *ert·bay·rè f —n* strawberry

Erde *er·dè f* earth; ground (*electrical*); soil

Erdgeschoß *ert·gè·shos nt —e* ground floor; first floor

Erdnuß *ert·noos f ⁻e* groundnut; peanut

Erdöl *ert·url nt —e* oil (*petroleum*)

Erdrutsch *ert·rootsh m —e* landslide

Ereignis *er·ike·nis nt —se* incident (*event*); occasion (*special event*)

erfahren *er·fah·rën adj* experienced

Erfahrung *er·fah·roong f —en* experience (*skill, knowledge*)

erfinden* *er·fin·dën vt* invent

Erfindung *er·fin·doong f —en* invention

Erfolg *er·folk m —e* success; keinen Erfolg haben* *kye·nën er·folk hah·bën* to fail (*person*)

erfolgreich *er·folk·ryekh adj* successful; erfolgreich sein* *er·folk·ryekh zine* to succeed

erforschen *er·for·shën vt* explore

Erfrischungen *er·fri·shoong·ën pl* refreshments

sich ergießen* *zikh er·gee·sën vr* spill

ergreifen* *er·grye·fën vt* grasp (*seize*)

erhalten* *er·hal·tën vt* receive (*letter*)

erhöhen *er·hur·ën vt* increase; raise (*price*)

Erhöhung *er·hur·oong f —en* raise

sich erholen *zikh er·hō·lën vr* get better (*from illness*); recover

erinnern *er·in·èrn* vt remind; **jemanden an etwas erinnern** *yay·man·dèn an et·vass er·in·èrn* to remind someone of something; **sich erinnern an** *zikh er·in·èrn an* to remember

Erinnerung *er·in·è·roong f* —en memory

sich erkälten *zikh er·kel·tèn* vr to catch cold

Erkältung *er·kel·toong f* —en cold (*illness*)

erkennen* *er·ke·nèn* vt recognize

erklären *er·kle·rèn* vt state; explain

Erklärung *er·kle·roong f* —en explanation

sich erkundigen *zikh er·koon·di·gèn* vr ask; **sich nach dem Preis erkundigen** *zikh nakh daym price er·koon·di·gèn* to ask the price

erlauben *er·low·bèn* vt permit (*something*); **jemandem erlauben, etwas zu tun** *yay·man·dèm er·low·bèn et·vass tsoo toon* to permit someone to do something

Erlaubnis *er·lowp·nis f* permission

Erlebnis *er·layp·nis nt* —se experience (*event*)

erledigen *er·lay·di·gèn* vt finish

Erleichterung *er·lyekh·tè·roong f* relief (*from pain, anxiety*)

erleiden* *er·lye·dèn* vt suffer (*pain, grief*)

ermorden *er·mor·dèn* vt murder

ernähren *er·ne·rèn* vt feed

erneuern *er·noy·èrn* vt renew

ernst *ernst adj* serious

Ernte *ern·tè f* —n harvest (*of grain*); crop

ernten *ern·tèn* vt harvest (*grain*)

erotisch *ay·rō·tish adj* erotic

erreichen *er·rye·khèn* vt catch (*train etc*); reach (*with hand, contact*)

Ersatz *er·zats m* substitute; replacement

Ersatzteil *er·zats·tile m* —e spare (*part*)

erscheinen* *er·shine·èn* vi appear

erschießen* *er·shee·sèn* vt shoot (*kill*)

erschöpft *er·shur·pft adj* exhausted

erschrecken *er·shre·kèn* vt frighten; alarm

ersetzen *er·zet·sèn* vt replace (*substitute*); **etwas durch etwas anderes ersetzen** *et·vass doorkh et·vass an·dè·rès er·zet·sèn* to substitute something for something else

erstaunlich *er·shtown·likh adj* astonishing

erste(r/s) *er·stè· (stèr/ stès) adj* first; top (*in rank*); **der erste Stock** *er·stè shtok* second floor; **die Erste Hilfe** *er·stè hil·fè* first aid; **im ersten Gang** *im er·stèn gang* in first (*gear*); **der erste Zug** *der er·stè tsook* the early train

erstechen* *er·shte·khèn* vt stab

Erste-Hilfe-Ausrüstung *er·stè·hil·fè·ows·rōōs·toong f* —en first-aid kit

erstklassig *erst·kla·sikh adj* first-class (*work etc*)

erteilen *er·tile·èn* vt place (*order*)

Ertrag *er·trahk m* —e yield

ertragen* *er·trah·gèn* vt stand; bear (*endure*)

ertrinken* *er·tring·kèn* vi drown

erwachsen *er·vak·sèn adj* grown-up

Erwachsene(r) *er·vak·sè·nè(·nèr) m/f* —n adult

erwähnen *er·vay·nèn* vt mention

Erwähnung *er·vay·noong f* —en reference (*mention*)

erwarten *er·var·tèn* vt expect (*antici-*

pate); **sie erwartet ein Kind** *zee er·var·tet ine kint* she's expecting a baby

erwerben* *er·ver·bèn* vt acquire

erwidern *er·vee·dèrn* vi reply; **er erwiderte, daß... er** *er·vee·dèr·tè dass he answered that...*

erwürgen *er·vōōr·gèn* vt strangle

erzählen *er·tsay·lèn* vt tell (*story*); **jemandem von etwas erzählen** *yay·man·dèm fon et·vass er·tsay·lèn* to tell someone something

Erzeuger *er·tsoy·gèr m* — producer (*agricultural*)

Erzeugnis *er·tsoyk·nis nt* —se produce (*products*)

erziehen* *er·tsee·èn* vt bring up; educate

Erziehung *er·tsee·oong f* education

es *ess pron* it; **ich bin es** *ikh bin ess* it's me; **es regnet** *ess rayg·nèt* it's raining; **es sind 5 Kilometer** *ess zint 5 kee·lō·may·tèr* it's 5 kilometers; **es gibt** *ess gipt* there is/are

Esche *e·shè f* —n ash (*tree*)

Esel *ay·zèl m* — donkey

Esperanto *es·pay·ran·tō nt* Esperanto

Espresso *es·pre·sō m* —s espresso (*coffee*)

Essay *e·say m* —s essay

eßbar *ess·bar adj* edible

essen* *e·sèn* vt eat □ *nt* **das Essen** *e·sèn* food; meal

Essig *e·sikh m* vinegar

Eßlöffel *ess·lur·fèl m* — tablespoon

Eßlokal *es·lo·kahl nt* —e diner

Eßzimmer *ess·tsi·mèr nt* — dining room

Etagenbett *ay·tah·zhèn·bet nt* —en bunk beds

Etappe *ay·tap·è f* —n stage

ethisch *ay·tish adj* ethical

ethnisch *ayt·nish adj* ethnic

Etikett *ay·ti·ket nt* —e ticket; label

Etikette *ay·ti·ke·tè f* etiquette

etikettieren *ay·ti·ke·teer·èn* vt label

etwa *et·va adv* around; about

etwas *et·vass pron* something; **etwas Brot** *et·vass brōt* some bread; **können Sie etwas sehen?** *kur'n·èn zee et·vass zay·èn* can you see anything?; **etwas Größeres** *et·vass grur'·sè·rès* something bigger

euch *oykh pron* you (*plural*)

euer(e) *oy·èr(·è) adj* your (*plural form*)

eure(r/s) *oy·rè(·rèr/·rès) pron* yours (*plural form*)

Europa *oy·rō·pa nt* Europe

europäisch *oy·rō·pay·ish adj* European

Evolution *ay·vō·loo·tsee·ōn f* evolution

Exemplar *ex·em·plahr nt* —e copy (*of book etc*)

Existenz *ek·sis·tents f* existence

existieren *ek·sis·tee·rèn* vi exist

exklusiv *eks·kloo·zeef adj* exclusive (*club, shop*)

Exklusivrechte *eks·kloo·zeef·rekh·tè pl* exclusive rights

exotisch *ek·sō·tish adj* exotic

Expedition *ek·spay·dee·tsee·ōn f* —en expedition

Experiment *ek·spe·ri·ment nt* —e experiment

explodieren *ek·splō·dee·rèn* vi explode

Explosion *eks·plō·zee·ōn f* —en blast; explosion

Exporteur *ek·spor·tur m* —e exporter

per Expreß *per ek·spres adv* express

extravagant *ek·stra·va·gant adj* extravagant

exzentrisch *eks·tsen·trish adj* eccentric

Eyeliner *eye·line·èr m* — eyeliner

F

Fabrik *fa·breek f* —**en** factory
Fach *fakh nt* —**er** subject (*in school*)
Facharzt *fakh·artst m* —**e** consultant (*doctor*)
Fächer *fe·khèr m* — fan (*folding*)
Fachmann *fakh·man m* **Fachleute** expert
Faden *fah·dèn m* — thread
fähig *fay·ikh adj* competent; capable; **zu...fähig** *tsoo...fay·ikh* capable of
Fähigkeit *fay·ikh·kite f* —**en** ability
Fahne *fah·nè f* —**n** flag
Fahrbahn *fahr·bahn f* —**en** roadway
Fähre *fe·rè f* —**n** ferry
fahren* *fah·rèn vt* drive; können Sie Auto fahren? *kur'·nèn zee ow·tō fah·rèn* do you drive?; **jemanden in die Stadt fahren*** *yay·man·dèn in dee shtat fah·rèn* to give someone a ride into town □ *vi* **fahren*** *fah·rèn* go; dieses Auto fährt mit Diesel *dee·zès ow·tō fert mit dee·zèl* this car runs on diesel; die Züge fahren stündlich *dee tsōō·gè fah·rèn shtöönt·likh* the trains run every hour; mit dem Auto in die Stadt fahren* *mit daym ow·tō in dee shtat fah·rèn* to drive to town; wir sind mit dem Zug gefahren *veer zint mit daym tsook gè·fah·rèn* we took the train; das zu schnelle Fahren *tsoo shne·lè fah·rèn* speeding (*in car*)
Fahrer *fah·rèr m* — chauffeur; driver (*of car*)
Fahrerin *fah·rè·rin f* —**nen** driver (*of car*)
Fahrgast *fahr·gast m* —**e** passenger
Fahrkarte *fahr·kar·tè f* —**n** ticket
Fahrkartenschalter *fahr·kar·tèn·shal·tèr m* — ticket office
Fahrplan *fahr·plan m* —**e** timetable (*for trains etc*)
Fahrpreis *fahr·price m* —**e** fare
Fahrprüfung *fahr·prōō·foong f* —**en** driving test
Fahrrad *fahr·raht nt* —**er** bicycle
Fahrschein *fahr·shine m* —**e** ticket
Fahrschüler *fahr·shōō·lèr m* — student driver
Fahrstuhl *fahr·shtool m* —**e** elevator
Fahrt *fahrt f* —**en** journey; drive; ride (*in vehicle*); eine Fahrt mit dem Auto machen *ine·è fahrt mit daym ow·tō ma·khèn* to go for a ride (*by car*)
Fahrzeug *fahr·tsoyk nt* —**e** vehicle
fair *fayr adv* fair
Faktor *fak·tor m* —**en** factor
Faktura *fak·too·ra f* **Fakturen** invoice
Fakultät *fa·kool·tet f* —**en** faculty (*university*)
Fall *fal m* —**e** case (*instance, lawsuit*); fall; auf jeden Fall *owf yay·dèn fal* in any case; für alle Fälle *föör a·lè fe·lè* just in case; im Falle von *im fa·lè fon* in case of; auf alle Fälle *owf a·lè fe·lè* in any case; im schlimmsten Fall *im shlim·stèn fal* in the last resort
Falle *fa·lè f* —**n** trap
fallen* *fa·lèn vi* fall; drop; fallen lassen* *fa·lèn la·sèn* drop (*let fall*)
fällig *fe·likh adj* due (*owing*)
Fallschirm *fal·shirm m* —**e** parachute
falsch *falsh adj* incorrect; false (*name etc*); wrong
Fälschung *fel·shoong f* —**en** forgery
familiär *fa·mee·lee·er adj* familiar (*impertinent*)

Familie *fa·meel·yè f* —**n** family
Fan *fen m* —**s** fan (*supporter*)
fangen* *fang·èn vt* catch (*ball, animal, fish, person*)
Farbe *far·bè f* —**n** color; paint; suit (*cards*)
farbecht *farp·ekht adj* fast (*dye*)
färben *fer·bèn vt* dye
Farbfernsehen *farp·fern·zay·èn nt* — color TV
Farbfilm *farp·film m* —**e** color film
farbig *far·bikh adj* colored (*person*)
Farbstoff *farp·shtof m* —**e** dye
Farce *far·sè f* —**n** farce
Farn *farn m* —**e** fern
Fasan *fa·zahn m* —**e** pheasant
Fasching *fa·shing m* —**e** carnival
Faser *fah·zèr f* —**n** fiber
Faß *fass nt* —**er** barrel (*for beer*)
Faßbier *fass·beer nt* draft beer
fassen *fa·sèn vt* grasp
fast *fast adv* almost; nearly; es hat fast getroffen *ess hat fast gè·tro·fèn* it only just missed
Fastnachtsdienstag *fast·nakhts·deens·tahk m* Shrove Tuesday
faszinierend *fas·tsee·nee·rènt adj* fascinating
faul *fowl adj* rotten (*wood etc*); lazy
faulen *fow·lèn vi* rot
Faust *fowst f* —**e** fist; mit der Faust schlagen* *mit dèr fowst shlah·gèn* to punch
Fausthandschuh *fowst·hant·shoo m* —**e** mitt(en)
Februar *fay·broo·ar m* February
Feder *fay·dèr f* —**n** spring (*coil*); feather
Federbett *fay·dèr·bet nt* —**en** comforter; eiderdown
Fee *fay f* —**n** fairy
Feedback *feed·bak nt* —**s** feedback
fegen *fay·gèn vt* sweep (*floor*)
fehlen *fay·lèn vi* be missing; es fehlen einige Seiten *es fay·lèn ine·i·gè zite·èn* some pages are missing; meine Mutter fehlt mir *mine·è moo·tèr faylt meer* I miss my mother
Fehler *fay·lèr m* — fault (*defect*); mistake; error
fehlerhaft *fay·lèr·haft adj* faulty
Fehlgeburt *fayl·gè·boort f* —**en** miscarriage
Fehlschlag *fayl·shlahk m* —**e** failure
fehl|schlagen* *fayl·shlah·gèn vi* fail (*plan*)
feiern *fye·èrn vi* celebrate
Feiertag *fye·èr·tahk m* —**e** holiday (*day*)
Feige *fye·gè f* —**n** fig
Feigling *fike·ling m* —**e** coward
Feile *file·è f* —**n** file (*tool*)
fein *fine adj* delicate (*dainty*); fine; subtle
Feind *fyent m* —**e** enemy
Feinkostgeschäft *fine·kost·gè·sheft nt* —**e** delicatessen
Feinschmecker *fine·shme·kèr m* — gourmet
Feld *felt nt* —**er** field
Feldbett *felt·bet nt* —**en** cot
Feldstecher *felt·shte·khèr m* — field glasses
Fels *fels m* —**en** rock (*substance*)
Felsblock *fels·blok m* —**e** rock (*boulder*)
Felsen *fel·zèn m* —**e** cliff
feminin *fe·mee·neen adj* feminine
Fenster *fen·stèr nt* — window
Fensterladen *fen·stèr·lah·dèn m* —**e** shutter (*on window*)

Ferien *fay·ree·èn* pl vacation; holiday (*period*)

Feriensaison *fay·ree·èn·zay·zön* f vacation season

Fern- *fern* pref long-distance □ *adj* fern *fern* distant

Fernamt *fern·amt* nt ⁼er exchange (*telephone*)

Ferne *fer·nè* f —n distance

Fernfahrerlokal *fern·fah·rèr·lo·kahl* nt —e truckstop

Ferngespräch *fern·gè·shprekh* nt —e long-distance call

Fernglas *fern·glahs* nt ⁼er binoculars

Fernkurs *fern·koors* m —e correspondence course

Fernmeldewesen *fern·mel·dè·vay·zèn* nt telecommunications

Fernschreiben *fern·shrye·bèn* nt telex

fernschriftlich *fern·shrift·likh* adv by telex; **fernschriftlich mit|teilen** *fern·shrift·likh mit·tile·èn* to telex

Fernsehen *fern·zay·èn* nt television; video; **im Fernsehen senden*** *im fern·zay·èn zen·dèn* to televise; **im Fernsehen** *im fern·zay·èn* on television; on video

Fernseher *fern·zay·èr* m — television (*set*)

Fernsehüberwachungsanlage *fern·zay·öö·bèr·va·khoongs·an·lah·gè* f —n closed circuit television (*for security*)

Fernsprechamt *fern·shprekh·amt* nt ⁼er telephone exchange

Fernsteuerung *fern·shtoy·èr·oong* f —en remote control

Ferse *fer·zè* f —n heel

fertig *fer·tikh* adj ready; finished; **ich bin gleich fertig** *ikh bin glyekh fer·tikh* I shan't be long; **sich fertig machen** *zikh fer·tikh ma·khèn* to get ready; **wenn ich mit meiner Arbeit fertig bin** *ven ikh mit mine·èr ar·bite fer·tikh bin* when I'm through with my work

fest *fest* adj firm (*object, material*); solid (*strong, not liquid*); **fest schlafen*** *fest shlah·fèn* to be fast asleep

Fest *fest* nt —e fête; **das große Fest** *grö·sè fest* gala

Festival *fes·tee·val* nt —s festival

Festland *fest·lant* nt mainland

fest|legen *fest·lay·gèn* vt tie up (*capital*)

fest|machen *fest·ma·khèn* vt fasten

Festmahl *fest·mahl* nt —e feast

fest|setzen *fest·zet·sèn* vt stipulate; fix (*arrange*)

fett *fet* adj greasy (*food*) □ *nt* **das Fett** *fet* fat; grease

fettig *fe·tikh* adj greasy

feucht *foykht* adj damp

Feuer *foy·èr* nt — fire; **haben Sie Feuer?** *hah·bèn zee foy·èr* have you got a light?

Feueralarm *foy·èr·a·larm* m — fire alarm

feuergefährlich *foy·èr·gè·fayr·likh* adj flammable

Feuerlöscher *foy·èr·lur'·shèr* m — fire extinguisher

Feuerrost *foy·èr·rost* m —e grate

Feuerstein *foy·èr·shtine* m —e flint (*in lighter*)

Feuerstelle *foy·èr·shte·lè* f —n hearth

Feuertreppe *foy·èr·tre·pè* f —n fire escape

Feuerwache *foy·èr·va·khè* f —n fire station

Feuerwehr *foy·èr·vayr* f —en fire department

Feuerwehrauto *foy·èr·vayr·ow·tö* nt —s fire engine

Feuerwehrmann *foy·èr·vayr·man* m ⁼er fireman

Feuerwerk *foy·èr·verk* nt fireworks

Feuerzeug *foy·èr·tsoyk* nt —e cigarette lighter

Fiberglas *fee·ber·glahs* nt fiberglass

Fieber *fee·bèr* nt — fever; **Fieber haben*** *fee·bèr hah·bèn* to have a temperature

Figur *fi·goor* f —en figure

Filet *fee·lay* nt —s sirloin; fillet (*of meat, fish*)

Filiale *fee·lee·ah·lè* f —n branch (*of store, bank etc*)

Film *film* m —e film; movie

Filmkamera *film·ka·mè·ra* f —s movie camera

Filter *fil·tèr* m — filter □ *pref* **Filter-** *fil·tèr* filter-tip (*cigarettes*)

Filz *filts* m — felt (*cloth*)

Filzstift *filts·shtift* m —e felt-tip pen

Finale *fee·nah·lè* nt —s finals (*sports*)

Finanz *fee·nants* f finance

Finanzamt *fee·nants·amt* nt ⁼er Internal Revenue

Finanzen *fee·nant·sèn* pl finance

finanziell *fee·nant·see·el* adj financial

finanzieren *fee·nant·see·rèn* vt finance

Finanzjahr *fee·nants·yahr* nt —e fiscal year

Finanzminister *fee·nants·mi·ni·stèr* m — Finance Minister

Finanzministerium *fi·nants·mi·ni·stay·ree·oom* nt Treasury

finden* *fin·dèn* vt find

Finger *fing·èr* m — finger

Fingerknöchel *fing·èr·knur'·khèl* m — knuckle

finnisch *fi·nish* adj Finnish □ *nt* **Finnisch** *fi·nish* Finnish

Finnland *fin·lant* nt Finland

Firma *fir·ma* f **Firmen** firm; company

Fisch *fish* m —e fish

Fischhändler *fish·hent·lèr* m — fishmonger

fit *fit* adj fit (*strong, healthy*)

flach *flakh* adj flat; shallow

Fläche *fle·khè* f —n area (*of surface*)

flämisch *fle·mish* adj Flemish □ *nt* **Flämisch** *fle·mish* Flemish

Flamme *fla·mè* f —n flame

Flasche *fla·shè* f bottle

Flaschenöffner *fla·shèn·ur'·f·nèr* m — bottle opener

flattern *fla·tèrn* vi flap (*sail*)

flau *flow* adj slack (*business*)

Flaum *flowm* m down (*fluff*)

Fleck *flek* m —en patch (*spot*); blot; stain; **der blaue Fleck** *blow·è flek* bruise

Fledermaus *flay·dèr·mows* f ⁼e bat (*animal*)

Fleisch *flyesh* nt meat; flesh

Fleischer *flye·shèr* m — butcher

Fleischerei *flye·shè·rye* f —en butcher's (*shop*)

Fleischwolf *flyesh·volf* m ⁼e mincer

Flicken *fli·kèn* m — patch (*of material*)

Fliege *flee·gè* f —n bow tie; fly

fliegen* *flee·gèn* vi fly □ *nt* **das Fliegen** *flee·gèn* flying

Fliese *flee·zè* f —n tile (*on floor, wall*)

fließen* *flee·sèn* vi flow

fließend *flee·sènt* adv fluently

Flipper *fli·pèr* m pinball

flirten *flir·tèn* vi flirt

Flitterwochen *fli·tèr·vo·khèn* pl honeymoon; **in den Flitterwochen** *in dayn fli·tèr·vo·khèn* on one's honeymoon

Flocke *flo·kè* f —n flake (of snow)

Floh *flō* m ⸚e flea

Flohmarkt *flō·markt* m ⸚e flea market

Flossen *flo·sèn* pl flippers (for swimming)

Flöte *flur'·tè* f —n flute; pipe (musical)

Flotte *flo·tè* f —n fleet

fluchen *floo·khèn* vi swear (curse)

Flug *flook* m ⸚e flight

Flügel *flōo·gèl* m — wing; grand piano

Fluggesellschaft *flook·gè·zel·shaft* f —en airline

Flughafen *flook·hah·fèn* m ⸚ airport

Flugreise *flook·rye·zè* f —n air travel

Flugzeug *flook·tsoyk* nt ⸚e plane; aircraft; **mit dem Flugzeug** *mit daym flook·tsoyk* by plane; by air

Fluor *floo·ōr* nt fluoride.

Flur *floo·èr* m ⸚e hall

Fluß *floos* m ⸚e river

Flußdiagramm *floos·dee·a·gram* nt —e flow chart

flüssig *flōo·sikh* adj liquid

Flüssigkeit *flōo·sikh·kite* f —en liquid

Flußkrebs *floos·krayps* m —e crayfish

flüstern *flōo·stèrn* vi whisper

Flut *floot* f —en flood; **wir hatten eine Flut von Aufträgen** *veer ha·tèn ine·è floot fon owf·tre·gèn* we had a rush of orders; **es ist Flut** *ess ist floot* the tide is in

Flutlicht *floot·likht* nt floodlight

Folge *fol·gè* f —n series; consequence (result)

folgen *fol·gèn* vi follow; **jemandem folgen** *yay·man·dèm fol·gèn* to follow someone

folgend *fol·gènt* adj following

Fönen *fur'·nèn* nt blow-dry

Forelle *fo·re·lè* f —n trout

formell *for·mel* adj formal

Formular *for·moo·lahr* nt —e form (document)

Forschung *for·shoong* f —en research

fort *fort* adv away; gone

fort|bestehen* *fort·bè·shtay·èn* vi survive (custom)

fort|fahren* *fort·fah·rèn* vi depart

Fortschritte *fort·shri·tè* pl progress

Foto *fō·tō* nt —s photo; **ein Foto machen** *ine fō·tō ma·khèn* to take a photo

Fotoapparat *fō·tō·a·pa·raht* m —e camera

Fotograf *fō·tō·grahf* m —en photographer

Fotografie *fō·tō·gra·fee* f —n photography; photograph

fotografieren *fō·tō·gra·fee·rèn* vt photograph

Fotokopie *fō·tō·kō·pee* f —n photocopy

fotokopieren *fō·tō·kō·pee·rèn* vt photocopy

Fracht *frakht* f —en cargo; freight

Frack *frak* m ⸚e tailcoat

Frage *frah·gè* f —n issue (matter); question; **nicht in Frage** *nikht in frah·gè* out of the question; **eine Frage stellen** *ine·è frah·gè shtel·èn* to ask a question

Fragebogen *frah·gè·bō·gèn* m — questionnaire

fragen *frah·gèn* vt/i ask; **jemanden nach der Uhrzeit fragen** *yay·man·dèn nakh der oor·tsite frah·gèn* to ask someone the time; **sich fragen, ob...** *zikh frah·gèn op* to wonder whether...

Fragezeichen *frah·gè·tsye·khèn* nt — question mark

frankieren *frang·kee·rèn* vt stamp (letter)

Frankreich *frank·ryekh* nt France

Fransenkante *fran·zèn·kan·tè* f —n fringe (edging)

Franzose *fran·tsō·zè* m —n Frenchman

Französin *fran·tsur'·zin* f —nen Frenchwoman

französisch *fran·tsur'·zish* adj French □ nt **Französisch** *fran·tsur'·zish* French

Frau *frow* f Mrs, Ms; wife; woman

Fräulein *froy·line* nt Miss

frech *frekh* adj cheeky; insolent

Frechheit *frekh·hite* f —en cheek (impudence)

frei *frye* adj free; clear (not blocked); vacant (seat, toilet); **ein Tag frei** *ine tahk frye* a day off; **im Freien** *im frye·èn* outdoor; open-air

Freibad *frye·bat* nt open-air swimming pool

frei|lassen* *frye·la·sèn* vt release (prisoner)

Freitag *frye·tahk* m Friday

Freizeit *frye·tsite* f spare time; leisure

Freizeitkleidung *frye·tsite·klye·doong* f casual clothes, casual wear

Freizeitschuhe *frye·tsite·shoo·è* pl sneakers

Freizeitzentrum *frye·tsite·tsen·troom* nt —zentren leisure center

fremd *fremt* adj foreign; strange (unknown)

Fremde(r) *frem·dè(·dèr)* m/f —n stranger

Fremdenführer *frem·dèn·fōo·rèr* m — courier

Fremdenverkehrsamt *frem·dèn·fer·kayrs·amt* nt —er tourist office

Fremdenverkehrsgewerbe *frem·dèn·fer·kayrs·gè·ver·bè* nt tourist trade

Fremdsprache *fremt·shprah·khè* f —n foreign language

Freude *froy·dè* f —n joy; **eine kleine Freude** *ine·è kline·è froy·dè* a little treat

sich freuen *zikh froy·èn* vr be glad; **sich freuen auf** *zikh froy·èn owf* to look forward to; **es hat mich gefreut, zu hören...** *ess hat mikh gè·froyt tsoo hur'·rèn* I was glad to hear...

Freund *froynt* m —e friend; boyfriend

Freundin *froyn·din* f —nen friend; girlfriend

freundlich *froynt·likh* adj friendly; kind

Frieden *free·dèn* m peace

Friedhof *freed·hōf* m ⸚e graveyard; cemetery

friedlich *freet·likh* adj peaceful

frieren* *free·rèn* vi freeze

frisch *frish* adj fresh; wet (paint)

Friseur *free·zur* m hairdresser

Friseuse *free·zur'·zè* f hairdresser

Frist *frist* f —en period; deadline

Frisur *free·zoor* f —en hair-style

froh *frō* adj glad

fröhlich *frur'·likh* adj gay (merry)

frontal *fron·tahl* adj head-on

Frosch *frosh* m ⸚e frog

Froschschenkel *frosh·sheng·kèl* pl frogs legs

Frost *frost* m frost

Frostschutzmittel *frost·shoots·mi·tèl* nt — antifreeze

fruchtbar *frookht·bahr adj* fertile (*land*)

Fruchteis *frookht·ice nt* sherbet

Fruchtsaftkonzentrat *frookt·saft·kon·tsen·traht nt —e* concentrate

früh *froo adj* early; **Sie sind früh dran** *zee zint froo dran* you're early; **er ist zu früh gekommen** *er ist tsoo froo ge·ko·men* he came too soon

früher *froo·èr adj* earlier; former; **früher gingen wir** *froo·èr ging·èn veer* we used to go

frühere(r/s) *froo·è·rè(·rèr/·rès) adj* previous

Frühling *froo·ling m* spring (*season*)

Frühstück *froo·shtook nt —e* breakfast; **das kleine Frühstück** *das klye·nè froo·shtook* continental breakfast

Fuchs *fooks m —e* fox

fühlen *foo·lèn vt* feel

führen *foo·rèn vt* lead; run (*a business, country*); stock (*have in shop*); **die Straße führt am Haus vorbei** *dee shtrah·sè foort am hows for·bye* the road runs past the house

Führer *foo·rèr m* leader; guide (*person*)

Führerin *foo·rè·rin f —nen* leader; guide (*person*)

Führerschein *foo·rèr·shine m —e* driver's license

Fuhrpark *foor·park m —s* fleet of vehicles

Führung *foo·roong f —en* guided tour; **in Führung liegen** *in foo·roong lee·gèn* to lead (*in contest*)

füllen *foo·lèn vt* fill up (*cup*); fill

Füller *foo·lèr m —* fountain pen

Füllung *foo·loong f —en* stuffing (*in chicken etc*)

fünf *foonf num* five

fünfte(r/s) *foonf·tè(·tèr/·tès) adj* fifth

fünfzehn *foonf·tsayn num* fifteen

fünfzig *foonf·tsikh num* fifty

Funke *foong·kè m —n* spark

funkeln *foong·kèln vi* sparkle

funktionieren *foonk·tsee·on·eer·èn vi* work (*clock, mechanism*); **gut funktionieren** *goot foonk·tsee·on·eer·èn* to be in working order

für *foor prep* for; **für alle Zeiten** *foor a·lè tsye·tèn* forever; **Benzin für DM50** *ben·tseen foor DM50* DM50 worth of gas

furchtbar *foorkht·bahr adj* terrible

fürchten *foorkh·tèn vt* fear; **sich fürchten vor** *zikh foorkh·tèn for* to be afraid of; to dread

fürchterlich *foorkh·tèr·likh adj* horrible

Furt *foort f —en* ford

Furunkel *foo·roong·kèl m —* boil (*on skin*)

Fusion *foo·zee·ōn f —en* amalgamation; merger

fusionieren *foo·zee·ō·neer·èn vi* merge

Fuß *foos m —e* foot; **zu Fuß gehen** *tsoo foos gay·èn* to walk (*for pleasure, exercise*)

Fußball *foos·bal m* football (*game, ball*); soccer

Fußboden *foos·bō·dèn m —* floor

Fußbremse *foos·brem·zè f —n* footbrake

Fußgänger *foos·geng·èr m —* pedestrian

Fußgängerüberweg *foos·geng·èr·oo·bèr·vayk m —e* pedestrian crossing

Fußgängerzone *foos·geng·èr·tsō·nè f —n* pedestrian precinct

Fußmatte *foos·ma·tè f —n* doormat

Fußpfleger *foos·pflay·gèr m —* podiatrist

Fußpflegerin *foos·pflay·gè·rin f —nen* podiatrist

Fußweg *foos·vayk m —e* footpath

Futter *foo·tèr nt* lining

G

Gabel *gah·bèl f —n* fork

Gabelung *gah·bè·loong f —en* fork (*in road*)

gähnen *gay·nèn vi* yawn

Galerie *ga·le·ree f —n* art gallery (*commercial*); gallery

Galopp *ga·lop m* gallop

galoppieren *ga·lo·pee·rèn vi* gallop

Gang *gang m —e* course (*of meal*); passage; gear (*of car*); **zweiter/dritter Gang** *tsvye·tèr/dri·tèr gang* 2nd/3rd gear; **vierter/erster Gang** *feer·tèr/er·stèr gang* high/low gear

Gangster *gang·stèr m —* gangster

Gans *gans f —e* goose

ganz *gants adj* whole (*complete*); **den ganzen Tag** *dayn gant·sèn tahk* all day; **das ganze Brot** *dass gant·sè brōt* all the bread □ *adv* **ganz** *gants* quite (*absolutely*); **ganz und gar nicht** *gants oont gar nikht* not in the least

ganztägig *gants·te·gikh adj* full-time

gar *gar adj* done (*vegetables*); **nicht gar** *nikht gar* undercooked

Garage *ga·rah·zhè f —n* garage (*for parking*)

Garantie *ga·ran·tee f —n* guarantee; warrant(y)

garantieren *ga·ran·tee·rèn vt* underwrite (*finance*); guarantee

Garderobe *gar·dè·rō·bè f —n* cloakroom; wardrobe

Garn *garn nt —e* thread

Garnele *gar·nay·lè f —n* prawn

gar nicht *gar nikht adv* not at all

Garten *gar·tèn m —* garden

Gartenbohnen *gar·tèn·bō·nèn pl* kidney beans

Gartencenter *gar·tèn·sen·tèr m —* garden center

Gartenkürbis *gar·tèn·koor·bis m —se* marrow (*vegetable*)

Gärtner *gert·nèr m —* gardener

Gas *gahs nt —e* gas

Gashebel *gahs·hay·bèl m —* throttle (*in car*)

Gasherd *gahs·hert m —e* gas stove

Gaspedal *gahs·pay·dahl nt —e* accelerator

Gasse *ga·sè f —n* alley; lane (*in town*)

Gast *gast m —e* guest; **zu Gast haben** *tsoo gast hah·bèn* to entertain (*give hospitality*)

Gastarbeiter *gast·ar·bye·tèr m* foreign worker

Gästehaus *ge·stè·hows m —er* guesthouse

Gästezimmer *ge·stè·tsi·mèr nt —* guest-room

Gastfreundschaft *gast·froynt·shaft f* hospitality

Gastgeber *gast·gay·bèr m —* host

Gastgeberin *gast·gay·bè·rin f —nen* hostess

Gasthaus *gast·hows nt —er* inn

Gaze *gah·zè f —n* gauze

Gebäck *gè·bek nt* pastry (*cake*)

Gebäude *gè·boy·dè nt —* building

geben *gay·bèn vt* give (*give, award*); **jemandem etwas geben** *yay·man·dèm et·vass gay·bèn* to give someone something

Gebet *gè·bayt nt —e* prayer

Gebiet *gè·beet nt* —e region (*administrative*); area

Gebiß *gè·biss nt* —e dentures

Gebläse *gè·blay·zè nt* — defroster

geboren *gè·bō·rèn adj* born; **geboren werden*** *gè·bō·rèn ver·dèn* to be born

Gebot *gè·bōt nt* —e bid

gebraten *gè·brah·tèn adj* fried

gebrauchen *gè·brow·khèn vt* use

Gebrauchsanweisung *gè·browkhs·an·vye·zoong f* —en instructions for use

Gebraucht- *gè·browkht pref* used (*car etc*)

Gebrüll *gè·brōōl nt* roar

Gebühr *gè·bōōr f* —en fee

Gebührenordnung *gè·bōō·rèn·ort·noong f* —en scale of charges

gebührenpflichtige Brücke *gè·bōō·rèn·pflikh·ti·gè brōō·kè f* —n toll bridge

Geburt *gè·boort f* —en birth

Geburtstag *gè·boorts·tahk m* —e birthday

Geburtsurkunde *gè·boorts·oor·koon·dè f* —n birth certificate

Gedächtnis *gè·dekht·nis nt* memory

Gedanke *gè·dang·kè m* —n thought

Gedankenstrich *gè·dank·èn·shtrikh m* —e dash (*in writing*)

Gedeck *gè·dek nt* —e place setting

Gedicht *gè·dikht nt* —e poem

Geduld *gè·doolt f* patience

geduldig *gè·dool·dikh adj* patient

geeignet *gè·ike·nèt adj* suitable

Gefahr *gè·fahr f* —en danger

gefährlich *gè·fer·likh adj* dangerous

gefallen* *gè·fa·lèn vi* please; **er gefällt mir** *gè·fe·lt meer* I like him

Gefallen *gè·fa·lèn m* — favor; **jemandem einen Gefallen tun*** *yay·man·dèm ine·èn gè·fa·lèn toon* to do someone a favor

gefältelt *gè·fel·tèlt adj* pleated

Gefangene(r) *gè·fang·è·nè(·nèr) m/f* —n prisoner

Gefängnis *gè·feng·nis nt* —se prison; **im Gefängnis** *im gè·feng·nis* in prison

Geflügel *gè·flōō·gèl nt* — poultry

Gefrierschutzmittel *gè·freer·shoots·mi·tèl nt* antifreeze

Gefriertruhe *gè·freer·troo·è f* —n freezer

gefroren *gè·frō·rèn adj* frozen (*food*)

Gefühl *gè·fōōl nt* —e feeling

gefühllos *gè·fōōl·lōs adj* numb (*with cold*)

gefüllt *gè·fōōlt adj* stuffed

gegen *gay·gèn prep* versus; against; toward(s)

Gegend *gay·gènt f* —en district (*in country*); region

Gegenreaktion *gay·gèn·ray·ak·tsee·ōn f* backlash

Gegenstand *gay·gèn·shtant m* —e object

Gegenteil *gay·gèn·tile nt* —e opposite; **im Gegenteil** *im gay·gèn·tile* on the contrary

gegenüber *gay·gèn·ōō·bèr prep* opposite; facing; **das Haus gegenüber** *das hows gay·gèn·ōō·bèr* the house opposite; **seine Haltung anderen gegenüber** *zine·è hal·toong an·dè·rèn gay·gèn·ōō·bèr* his attitude towards others

Gegenverkehr *gay·gèn·fer·kayr m* oncoming traffic

gegenwärtig *gay·gèn·ver·tikh adj* present

Gehalt *gè·halt nt* —er pay; salary

Gehässigkeit *gè·he·sikh·kite f* —en spite

geheim *gè·hime adj* secret

Geheimnis *gè·hime·nis nt* —se secret; mystery

Geheimwahl *gè·hime·vahl f* —en ballot

gehen* *gay·èn vi* go; walk; **wie geht es Ihnen?** *vee gayt ess ee·nèn* how are you?; **kaufen gehen*** *kow·fèn gay·èn* to go and buy; **es geht mir besser** *ess gayt meer be·sèr* I feel better; **geht es?** *gayt ess* can you manage?; **will it do?** (*be suitable*); **gehen wir** *gay·èn veer* let's go

Gehirn *gè·hirn nt* —e brain

gehorchen *gè·hor·khèn vi* obey; **jemandem gehorchen** *yay·man·dèm gè·hor·khèn* to obey someone

gehören *gè·hö·rèn vi* belong; **jemandem gehören** *yay·man·dèm gè·hö·rèn* to belong to someone

gehorsam *gè·hor·zahm adj* obedient

Geige *gye·gè f* —n violin

Geisel *gye·zèl f* —n hostage; **jemanden als Geisel nehmen*** *yay·man·dèn als gye·zèl nay·mèn* to take someone hostage

Geist *gyest m* mind; spirit (*soul*)

geizig *gye·tsikh adj* mean (*miserly*)

gekocht *gè·kokht adj* cooked; boiled

gekräuselt *gè·kroy·zèlt adj* gathered

Gelächter *gè·lekh·tèr nt* laughter

gelähmt *gè·laymt adj* paralyzed

Gelände *gè·len·dè nt* grounds (*land*); site (*of building*)

Geländer *gè·len·dèr nt* — handrail (*on stairs*); railings

gelassen *gè·la·sèn adj* calm (*person*)

gelb *gelp adj* yellow

Geld *gelt nt* money

Gelder *gel·dèr pl* funds

Geldgeber *gelt·gay·bèr m* — backer

Geldkassette *gelt·ka·se·tè f* —n strongbox

Geldknappheit *gelt·knap·hite f* —en squeeze (*financial*)

Geldschein *gelt·shine m* —e banknote

Geldstrafe *gelt·shtrah·fè f* —n fine

Gelegenheit *gè·lay·gèn·hite f* —en opportunity; occasion

Gelegenheitskauf *gè·lay·gèn·hites·kowf m* —e bargain (*cheap buy*)

gelegentlich *gè·lay·gènt·likh adv* occasionally

Gelenk *gè·lenk nt* —e joint (*of body*)

gelingen* *gè·ling·èn vi* succeed; **es ist ihm gelungen, es zu tun** *ess ist eem gè·loong·èn ess tsoo toon* he succeeded in doing it

gelten* *gel·tèn vt* be worth; be valid

gemahlen *gè·mah·lèn adj* ground (*coffee*)

Gemälde *gè·mel·dè nt* — painting (*picture*)

Gemäldegalerie *gè·mel·dè·ga·lè·ree f* —n gallery (*art*)

gemein *gè·mine adj* mean (*unkind*)

Gemeinde *gè·mine·dè f* —n community

Gemeinsamer Markt *gè·mine·za·mèr markt m* Common Market

gemischt *gè·misht adj* mixed; assorted

Gemüse *gè·mōō·zè nt* — vegetables

genau *gè·now adj* accurate; precise; exact □ *adv* exactly; **genau hier** *gè·now heer* just here; **genau in der Mitte** *gè·now in der mi·tè* right in the middle

Genauigkeit *gè·now·ikh·kite f* precision

Genehmigung *gè·nay·mi·goong f* —en approval; permit

General *ge·ne·rahl m* —e general (*soldier*)

Generation *ge·ne·ra·tsee·ōn* f —en generation

Generator *ge·ne·rah·tor* m —en generator (*electrical*)

Genesung *gè·nay·zoong* f —en convalescence

Genf *genf* nt Geneva

genießen* *gè·nee·sèn* vt enjoy (*concert, outing*)

Genossenschaft *gè·no·sèn·shaft* f —en co-operative

genug *gè·nook* pron enough

Geographie *gay·o·gra·fee* f geography

Geologie *gay·o·lo·gee* f geology

Geometrie *gay·o·me·tree* f geometry

Gepäck *gè·pek* nt luggage

Gepäckaufbewahrung *gè·pek·owf·bè·vah·roong* f —en baggage checkroom

Gepäckausgabe *gè·pek·ows·gah·bè* f baggage claim

Gepäckkontrolle *gè·pek·kon·tro·lè* f —n baggage check

Gepäcknetz *gè·pek·nets* nt —e luggage rack (*in train*)

Gepäckträger *gè·pek·tray·gèr* m —luggage rack (*on car*); porter (*for luggage*)

Gepäckwagen *gè·pek·vah·gèn* m —baggage car

gepfeffert *gè·pfe·fèrt* adj peppery

gerade *gè·rah·dè* adj straight; eine gerade Zahl *ine·è gè·rah·dè tsahl* an even number; er ist gerade weggegangen *er ist gè·rah·dè vek·gè·gang·èn* he's just left; ich habe es gerade eben geschafft *ikh hah·bè ess gè·rah·dè ay·bèn gè·shaft* I just managed it

geradeaus *gè·rah·dè·ows* adv straight ahead

Geranie *gay·rah·nee·è* f —n geranium

Gerät *gè·ret* nt —e appliance; gadget

aufs Geratewohl *owfs gè·rah·tè·vōl* adv at random

geräuchert *gè·roy·khèrt* adj smoked (*salmon etc*)

Geräusch *gè·roysh* nt —e noise; sound

gerecht *gè·rekht* adj fair (*just*)

Gerechtigkeit *gè·rekh·tikh·kite* f justice

Gericht *gè·rikht* nt —e court (*law*); dish (*food*); vor Gericht stellen *fōr gè·rikht shte·lèn* to try (*in law*)

gering *gè·ring* adj slight (*small*); die geringste Menge *dee gè·ring·stè meng·è* the least amount

geringfügig *gè·ring·fōō·gikh* adj trivial

gern(e) *gern(·è)* adv willingly; etwas gern tun* *et·vass gern toon* to love doing something; ich würde sehr gerne gehen *ikh vōōr·dè zayr ger·nè gay·èn* I'd love to go; ich hätte gern ein Eis *ikh he·tè gern ine ise* I'd like an ice cream; gern haben* *gern hah·bèn* to like; gern geschehen *gern gè·shay·èn* not at all (*don't mention it*)

geröstet *gè·rur·stèt* adj sauté

Geruch *gè·rookh* m —e smell

Gesamtmenge *gè·zamt·meng·è* f —n total

Geschäft *gè·sheft* nt —e shop; deal; business (*dealings, work*); transaction; Geschäfte mit jemandem machen *gè·shef·tè mit yay·man·dèm ma·khèn* to do business with someone; ein Geschäft ab|schließen* *ine gè·sheft ap·shlee·sèn* to make a bargain

geschäftlich *gè·sheft·likh* adv on business

Geschäftsfrau *gè·shefts·frow* f —en businesswoman

Geschäftsführer *gè·shefts·fōō·rèr* m —executive; manager

Geschäftsführerin *gè·shefts·fōō·rè·rin* f —nen manageress

Geschäftsmann *gè·shefts·man* m ⁼er businessman

Geschäftsreise *gè·shefts·rye·zè* f —n business trip

Geschäftsstunden *gè·shefts·shtoon·dèn* pl business hours

geschehen* *gè·shay·èn* vi happen

Geschenk *gè·shenk* nt —e gift

Geschenkgutschein *gè·shenk·goot·shine* m —e gift token

Geschichte *gè·shikh·tè* f —n story; history

Geschick *gè·shik* nt —e skill

geschieden *gè·shee·dèn* adj divorced

Geschirr *gè·shir* nt crockery; harness

Geschirrspülmaschine *gè·shir·shpōōl·ma·shee·nè* f —n dishwasher

Geschirrtuch *gè·shir·tookh* nt ⁼er dishtowel

Geschlecht *gè·shlekht* nt —er gender; sex

Geschlechtsverkehr *gè·shlekhts·fer·kayr* m sexual intercourse

Geschmack *gè·shmak* m ⁼e taste; flavor

geschmacklos *gè·shmak·lōs* adj in poor taste

geschmackvoll *gè·shmak·fol* adj in good taste

geschmort *gè·shmōrt* adj braised

Geschwindigkeit *gè·shvin·dikh·kite* f —en speed

Geschwindigkeitsbegrenzung *gè·shvin·dikh·kites·bè·gren·tsoong* f —en speed limit

Geschwür *gè·shvōōr* nt —e ulcer

Gesellschaft *gè·zel·shaft* f society; wollen Sie uns nicht Gesellschaft leisten? *vol·èn zee oons nikht gè·zel·shaft lye·stèn* do join us

Gesellschaftsraum *gè·zel·shafts·rowm* m ⁼e lounge (*in hotel*)

Gesetz *gè·zets* nt —e law

gesetzlich *gè·zets·likh* adj legal

gesetzwidrig *gè·zets·vee·drikh* adj illegal

Gesicht *gè·zikht* nt —er face

Gesichtscreme *gè·zikhts·kraym* f —s face cream

Gesichtspunkt *gè·zikhts·poonkt* m —e point of view

gespannt *gè·shpant* adj tense

Gespenst *gè·shpenst* nt —er ghost

Gespräch *gè·shprekh* nt —e talk (*conversation*); die Gespräche *gè·shprekh·è* talks (*negotiations*)

Gestalt *gè·shtalt* f —en figure

Geständnis *gè·shtent·nis* nt —se confession

Geste *gè·stè* f —n gesture

gestehen* *gè·shtay·èn* vi confess; etwas gestehen* *et·vass gè·shtay·èn* to confess to something

Gestell *gè·shtel* nt —e frames (*of eyeglasses*); rack (*for wine*)

gestern *ge·stèrn* adv yesterday

gesund *gè·zoont* adj healthy (*person*); Spinat ist gesund *shpi·naht ist gè·zoont* spinach is good for you

Gesundheit *gè·zoont·hite* f health

Gesundheitswesen *gè·zoont·hites·vay·zèn* nt health service

Getränk *gè·trenk* nt —e drink

Getreide *gè·trye·dè* nt grain (*cereal crops*)

Getreideflocken *gè·trye·dè·flo·kèn* pl cereal (*breakfast*)

getrennt *gè·trent adv* separately; under separate cover

Getriebe *gè·tree·bè nt* — gearbox

getrocknet *gè·trok·nèt adj* dried (*fruit, beans*)

Gewächs *gè·veks nt* —e growth

Gewächshaus *gè·veks·hows nt* ⁼er greenhouse

gewähren *gè·vay·rèn vt* grant (*wish*)

Gewalt *gè·valt f* force (*violence*)

Gewalttätigkeit *gè·valt·tay·tikh·kite f* —en violence

Gewehr *gè·vayr nt* —e gun; rifle

Gewerkschaft *gè·verk·shaft f* —en labor union

Gewicht *gè·vikht nt* —e weight

Gewinn *gè·vin m* —e profit; yield (*financial*)

Gewinnbeteiligung *gè·vin·bè·tile·i·goong f* profit-sharing

Gewinnchancen *gè·vin·shan·sèn pl* odds (*in betting*)

gewinnen* *gè·vi·nèn vt* gain (*obtain*) □ *vi* win

Gewinnspanne *gè·vin·shpa·nè f* profit margin

gewiß *gè·viss adj* certain

Gewissen *gè·vis·èn nt* — conscience

Gewitter *gè·vi·tèr nt* — thunderstorm

gewitzt *gè·vitst adj* shrewd

sich gewöhnen an *zikh gè·vur'·nèn an vr* to get used to

Gewohnheit *gè·vōn·hite f* —en habit

gewöhnlich *gè·vur'n·likh adj* usual; ordinary

Gewürz *gè·vōorts nt* —e spice; seasoning

Gewürze *gè·vōor·tsè pl* condiments

Gewürzgurke *gè·vōorts·goor·kè f* —n gherkin

Gewürznelke *gè·vōorts·nel·kè f* —n clove

Gezeiten *gè·tsye·tèn pl* tide

Ghetto *ge·tō nt* —s ghetto

gierig *gee·rikh adj* greedy

gießen* *gee·sèn vt* pour

Gift *gift nt* —e poison

giftig *gif·tikh adj* poisonous

Gin *jin m* gin (*drink*)

Gingan *ging·an m* gingham

Gipfel *gip·fèl m* — peak (*of mountain*)

Gips *gips m* plaster of Paris

Gipsverband *gips·fer·bant m* ⁼e plaster cast (*for limb*)

Girokonto *zhee·rō·kon·tō nt* —ten checking account

Gitarre *gi·ta·rè f* —n guitar

glamourös *gla·moo·rur's adj* glamorous

glänzen *glen·tsèn vi* shine (*metal*)

glänzend *glen·tsent adj* shiny

Glas *glahs nt* ⁼er glass; lens (*of glasses*); jar

Glaswaren *glahs·vah·rèn pl* glass (*glassware*)

glatt *glat adj* smooth

Glaube *glow·bè m* —n faith (*religious*); belief

glauben *glow·bèn vt* believe; **ich glaube schon** *ikh glow·bè shōn* I think so; **glauben an** *glow·bèn an* to believe in; **ich glaube, wir können gehen** *ikh glow·bè veer kur'·nèn gay·èn* we may as well go; **ich glaube daß...** *ikh glow·bè das* I feel that...

gläubig *gloy·bikh adj* religious (*person*)

Gläubiger *gloy·bi·gèr m* — creditor

gleich *glyekh adj* even (*equally matched*); equal; **das gleiche Buch wie** *das glyekh·è bookh vee* the same book as (*similar*); **gleich über**

---

dem Ellenbogen *glyekh ōō·bèr dayn el·èn·bō·gèn* just above the elbow

Gleichgewicht *glyekh·gè·vikht nt* balance; **das Gleichgewicht der Mächte** *glyekh·gè·vikht der mekh·tè* balance of power; **das Gleichgewicht verlieren*** *dass glyekh·gè·vikht fer·lee·rèn* to lose one's balance; **im Gleichgewicht halten** *im glyekh·gè·vikht hal·tèn* to balance

gleichmäßig *glyekh·may·sikh adj* even; steady (*pace*)

gleichwertig *glyekh·ver·tikh adj* equivalent

Gleis *glise nt* —e track (*for trains*)

Gleisanschluß *glyes·an·shloos m* ⁼e junction (*railroad*)

gleiten* *glye·tèn vi* slide; glide

global *glō·bahl adj* global

Globus *glō·boos m* —se globe (*map*)

Glocke *glo·kè f* —n bell

Glück *glōōk nt* happiness; luck; **Glück haben*** *glōōk hah·bèn* to be lucky; **viel Glück!** *feel glōōk* good luck!

glücklich *glōōk·likh adj* happy; fortunate

Glückwünsche *glōōk·vōōn·shè pl* congratulations; **herzliche Glückwünsche!** *herts·li·khè glōōk·vōōn·shè* congratulations!

Glühbirne *glōō·bir·nè f* —n light bulb

glühen *glōō·èn vi* glow

Glyzerin *glōō·tsè·reen nt* glycerin(e)

GmbH *gay·em·bay·hah abbrev* Ltd, Inc

Gold *golt nt* gold

golden *gol·dèn adj* golden; gold

Goldfisch *golt·fish m* —e goldfish

Golf *golf nt* golf

Golfball *golf·bal m* ⁼e golf ball

Golfer *gol·fèr m* — golfer

Golfjunge *golf·yoong·è m* —n caddie

Golfklub *golf·kloop m* —s golf club (*association*)

Golfplatz *golf·plats m* ⁼e golf course

Golfschläger *golf·shlay·gèr m* — golf club

Gosse *go·sè f* —n gutter (*in street*)

Gott *got m* ⁼er god

Gottesdienst *go·tès·deenst m* —e service (*in church*)

Gouverneur *goo·ver·nur m* —e governor (*of colony*)

Grab *grahp m* ⁼er grave

Graben *grah·bèn m* ⁼ ditch □ *vt* graben* *gra·bèn* dig

Grad *grat m* —e degree; **der akademische Grad** *a·ka·day·mish·è grat* degree (*university*)

graduieren *gra·doo·ee·rèn vi* graduate (*from university*)

Gramm *gram nt* — gram

Grammatik *gra·ma·tik f* grammar

Grammatikbuch *gra·ma·tik·bookh nt* ⁼er grammar (*book*)

Granatapfel *gra·naht·ap·fèl m* ⁼ pomegranate

Grand Prix *groñ pree m* — Grand Prix

Graphit *gra·feet m* — lead (*in pencil*)

Gras *grahs nt* ⁼er grass

Gräte *gre·tè f* —n bone (*of fish*)

gratulieren *gra·too·lee·rèn vi* congratulate; **jemandem zu etwas gratulieren** *yay·man·dèm tsoo et·vass gra·too·lee·rèn* to congratulate someone on something

grau *grow adj* gray

grausam *grow·zahm adj* cruel

greifen* *grye·fèn vt* seize; grip; **greifen* zu** *grye·fèn tsoo* to resort to

Grenze *gren·tsè f* —**n** boundary; frontier; border (*of country*)

Griechenland *gree·khèn·lant nt* Greece

griechisch *gree·khish adj* Greek

Griff *grif m* —**e** handle (*of knife*); knob (*on door*)

Grill *gril m* —**s** grill (*gridiron*)

grillen *gri·lèn vt/i* broil

Grillroom *gril·room m* —**s** grillroom

Grillteller *gril·te·lèr m* — mixed grill

Grimasse *gri·ma·sè f* —**n** grimace

Grippe *gri·pè f* flu

grob *gròp adv* roughly □ *adj* coarse (*texture, material*); eine grobe Schätzung *ine·è grò·bè shet·soong* a rough estimate

grollen *gro·lèn vi* rumble □ *nt* das Grollen *gro·lèn* rumble

Gros *gròs nt* — gross

groß *gròs adj* tall; large; great; big; wide (*range*); wie groß sind Sie? *vee gròs zint zee* how tall are you?

großartig *gròs·ahr·tikh adj* magnificent; grand

Großbritannien *gròs·bri·ta·nee·èn nt* Great Britain

Großbuchstabe *gròs·bookh·shtah·bè m* —**n** capital letter

Größe *grur·sè f* —**n** height (*of person*); size

Großeinkauf *gròs·ine·kowf m* —**e** bulk buying

Großhandel *gròs·han·dèl m* wholesale; im Großhandel *im gròs·han·dèl* wholesale (*sell*)

Großhandels- *gròs·han·dèls pref* wholesale (*price*)

Großhändler *gròs·hend·lèr m* — wholesaler

Großmutter *gròs·moo·tèr f* — grandmother

Großraum- *gròs·rowm pref* open-plan

Großstadt *gròs·shtat f* —**e** city

Großvater *gròs·fah·tèr m* — grandfather

groß|ziehen *gròs·tsee·èn vt* raise (*family*)

großzügig *gròs·tsōō·gikh adj* generous

grotesk *grò·tesk adj* grotesque

Grube *groo·bè f* —**n** pit

grün *grōōn adj* green

Grund *groont m* —**e** ground; reason

gründen *grōōn·dèn vt* establish

grundlegend *groont·lay·gènt adj* basic

gründlich *grōōnt·likh adj* thorough (*work*)

Grundschul- *groont·shool pref* primary (*education*)

Grundschule *groont·shoo·lè f* —**n** grade school

Grundschullehrer *groont·shool·lay·rèr m* — teacher (*primary school*)

Grundschullehrerin *groont·shool·lay·rè·rin f* —**nen** teacher (*primary school*)

Grundsteuer *groont·shtoy·èr f* —**n** rates (*local tax*)

Grundstück *groont·shtōōk nt* —**e** land (*property*)

Grundstücksmakler *groont·shtōōks·mah·klèr m* — realtor

grunzen *groon·tsèn vi* grunt

Gruppe *groo·pè f* —**n** group

Gruppenbestellung *groo·pèn·bè·shte·loong f* —**en** block booking

Gruß *groos m* —**e** greeting; mit freundlichen Grüßen *mit froynt·likh·èn grōō·sèn* yours sincerely; viele liebe Grüße von *fee·lè lee·bè grōō·sè fon* love from (*on letter*); mit besten Grüßen *mit bes·tèn grōō·sèn* with best wishes (*on gift*)

grüßen *grōō·sèn vt* greet

Grußkarte *groos·kar·tè f* —**n** greeting card

gucken *koo·kèn vi* look

Gulasch *goo·lash nt* goulash

gültig *gōōl·tikh adj* valid

Gummi *goo·mi m* —**s** rubber (*material*); eraser; elastic

Gummiband *goo·mi·bant nt* —**er** rubber band; elastic band

Gummisauger *goo·mi·zow·gèr m* — nipple (*for bottle*)

Gummistiefel *goo·mi·shtee·fèl m* — wellington boot

gurgeln *goor·gèln vi* gargle

Gurke *goor·kè f* —**n** cucumber

Gürtel- *gōōr·tèl pref* radial ply □ *m* der Gürtel *gōōr·tèl* belt (*for waist*)

Gürtelrose *gōōr·tèl·rò·zè f* shingles (*illness*)

Gußeisen *goos·eye·zèn nt* cast iron

gut *goot adv* well; all right (*yes*) □ *adj* good; gut im Golf sein* *goot im golf zine* to be good at golf; guten Morgen/guten Tag! *goo·tèn mor·gèn/goo·tèn tahk* good morning/good afternoon!; guten Abend/gute Nacht! *goo·tèn ah·bènt/goo·tè nakht* good evening/good night!; alles Gute *a·lès goo·tè* with best wishes (*on letter*); sehr gut! *zayr goot* (that's) fine!

gutaussehend *goot·ows·zay·ènt adj* handsome (*person*)

Güter *gōō·tèr pl* goods

Güterzug *gōō·tèr·tsook m* —**e** freight train

Gutschein *goot·shine m* —**e** voucher; coupon

gut|schreiben *goot·shrye·bèn vt* credit

gut|tun *goot·toon vi* do good; das wird Ihnen guttun *dass virt ee·nèn goot·toon* it'll do you good

Gymnastik *gōōm·na·stik f* gymnastics

H

H *hah nt* B flat (*music*)

Den Haag *dayn hahk m* Hague (the)

Haar *hahr nt* —**e** hair (*single strand*)

Haarbürste *hahr·bōōr·stè f* —**n** hairbrush

Haare *hah·rè pl* hair; sich die Haare schneiden lassen* *zikh dee hah·rè shnye·dèn la·sèn* to have a haircut

Haarklemme *hahr·kle·mè f* —**n** bobby pin; hairpin

Haarnadelkurve *hahr·nah·dèl·koor·vè f* —**n** hairpin curve

Haarschnellkur *hahr·shnel·koor f* —**s** conditioner (*for hair*)

Haarspray *hahr·shpray nt* —**s** hair spray

Haartrockner *hahr·trok·nèr m* — hairdrier

haben* *hah·bèn vt* have; ich hätte gern ein… *ikh he·tè gern ine* I should like a…

hacken *ha·kèn vt* mince

Hackfleisch *hak·flyesh nt* ground beef

Hafen *hah·fèn m* — harbor; port (*for ships*)

Hafenmeister *hah·fèn·mye·stèr m* — harbor master

Hafer *hah·fèr m* — oats

Haferbrei *hah·fèr·brye m* porridge

Haftpflichtversicherung *haft·pflikht·fer·zi·kher·oong f* —**en** third party insurance

Hagel *hah·gèl m* hail

es hagelt *ess hah·gèlt vi* it's hailing

Hahn *hahn m* ⁼e tap (*for water*); faucet; cock(erel)

Hai *hye m* —e shark

Haken *hah·kèn m* — hook; tick (*mark*); peg (*for coat*); Haken und Öse *hah·kèn oont ur'·zè* hook and eye

halb *halp adj* half; ein halbes Dutzend *ine hal·bès doot·sènt* a half dozen; dreieinhalb Kilometer *drye·ine·halp kee·lō·may·tèr* three and a half kilometers; auf halbem Weg *owf hal·bèm vayk* halfway; eine halbe Stunde *ine·è hal·bè shtoon·dè* half an hour; halb offen *halp o·fèn* half open; der halbe Fahrpreis *der hal·bè fahr·price* half-fare; zum halben Preis *tsoom hal·bèn price* half-price

halbdunkel *halp·doong·kèl adj* dim (*room*)

Halbfinale *halp·fee·nah·lè nt* semifinal

halbieren *hal·bee·rèn vt* halve (*divide in two*)

Halbtags- *halp·tahks pref* part-time

Halbzeit *halp·tsite f* —en half-time

Hälfte *helf·tè f* —n half; auf die Hälfte reduzieren *owf dee helf·tè ray·doot·see·rèn* to halve (*to reduce by half*)

Hallenbad *ha·lèn·bat nt* ⁼er indoor pool

hallo *ha·lō excl* hello

Hals *hals m* ⁼e neck; throat

Halsband *hals·bant nt* ⁼er collar (*for dog*)

Halskette *hals·ke·tè f* —n necklace

Halsschmerzen *hals·shmer·tsèn pl* sore throat

haltbar *halt·bar adj* durable (*fabric, article*)

halten* *hal·tèn vt* hold; keep; Halten verboten *hal·tèn fer·bō·tèn* no stopping (*road sign*); ich halte nichts von der Idee *ikh hal·tè nikhts fon der ee·day* I'm not in favor of that idea; etwas sauber halten* *et·vass zow·bèr hal·tèn* to keep something tidy; Milch hält sich nicht gut *milkh helt zikh nikht goot* milk doesn't keep very well

Haltestelle *hal·tè·shte·lè f* —n bus stop

Hamburger *ham·boor·gèr m* — hamburger

Hammelfleisch *ha·mèl·flyesh nt* mutton

Hammer *ha·mèr m* ⁼ hammer

Hämorrhoiden *he·mo·rō·ee·dèn pl* hemorrhoids

Hand *hant f* ⁼e hand; jemandem die Hand geben; *yay·man·dèm dee hant gay·bèn* to shake hands with someone; von Hand *fon hant* by hand

Handbremse *hant·brem·zè f* —n handbrake

Handbuch *hant·bookh nt* ⁼er handbook

Handcreme *hant·kraym f* —s hand cream

Handel *han·dèl m* — trade; commerce

handeln *han·dèln vi* act; trade; als X handeln *als X han·dèln* to act as X; mit etwas handeln *mit et·vass han·dèln* to deal in something; es handelt sich um *ess han·dèlt zikh oom* it's a question of

Handeln *han·dèln nt* — action (*movement*)

Handels- *han·dèls pref* commercial

Handelsbank *han·dèls·bank f* —en commercial bank

Handelsbilanz *han·dèls·bee·lants f* —en balance of trade

Handelsgesellschaft *han·dèls·gè·zel·shaft f* —en corporation (*firm*)

Handelskammer *han·dèls·ka·mèr f* Chamber of Commerce

Handelsname *han·dèls·nah·mè m* —n trade name

Handfläche *hant·fle·khè f* —n palm (*of hand*)

handgearbeitet *hant·gè·ar·bye·tèt adj* handmade

Handgelenk *hant·gè·lenk nt* —e wrist

Handgepäck *hant·gè·pek nt* hand-luggage

Handikap *han·di·kap nt* —s handicap (*golf*)

Händler *hent·lèr m* — trader; dealer

Handlung *hant·loong f* —en plot (*in play*)

Handschellen *hant·she·lèn pl* handcuffs

Handschrift *hant·shrift f* —en writing

Handschuh *hant·shoo m* —e glove

Handschuhfach *hant·shoo·fakh nt* ⁼er glove compartment

Handtasche *hant·ta·shè f* —n purse

Handtuch *hant·tookh nt* ⁼er towel

Handwerk *hant·verk nt* —e craft

Handwerker *hant·ver·kèr m* — craftsman

Hang *hang m* ⁼e slope; hill

Hängematte *heng·è·ma·tè f* —n hammock

hängen *heng·en vt* hang □ *vi* hängen* *heng·èn* hang

Hardware *hard·wayr f* hardware (*computing*)

Harfe *har·fè f* —n harp

harmlos *harm·lōs adj* harmless

hart *hart adj* hard; rough (*not gentle*)

hartgekocht *hart·gè·kokht adj* hard-boiled

Hase *hah·zè m* —n hare

Haß *hass m* hatred

hassen *ha·sèn vt* hate

häßlich *hes·likh adj* ugly (*object, person*)

Haufen *how·fèn m* — heap

häufig *hoy·fikh adj* frequent; common

Haupt- *howpt pref* major; main

Hauptbuch *howpt·bookh nt* ⁼er ledger

Hauptgericht *howpt·gè·rikht nt* —e entrée

hauptsächlich *howpt·sekh·likh adv* mainly

Hauptschlüssel *howpt·shlōō·sèl m* — master key

Hauptstadt *howpt·shtat f* ⁼e capital (*city*)

Hauptstraße *howpt·shtrah·sè f* —n main street

Hauptverkehrszeit *howpt·fer·kayrs·tsite f* peak hours

Haus *hows nt* ⁼er house; home; auf Kosten des Hauses *owf kos·tèn des how·zès* on the house; zu Hause *tsoo how·zè* at home; nach Hause gehen* *nakh how·zè gay·èn* to go home; im Haus *im hows* indoors (*be*); ins Haus *ins hows* indoors (*go*)

Hausarbeit *hows·ar·bite f* housework

Häuschen *hoys·khèn nt* — cottage

Hausdiener *hows·dee·nèr m* — valet (*in hotel*)

Hausfrau *hows·frow f* —en housewife

Haushalt *hows·halt m* —e household

Haushälterin *hows·hel·tè·rin f* —nen housekeeper

Hausmeister *hows·mye·stèr m* — caretaker

Hausschuh *hows·shoo m* —e slipper
Haustier *hows·teer nt* —e pet
Haut *howt f* ⁼e hide (*leather*); skin
Hautausschlag *howt·ows·shlak m* ⁼e rash
Hebamme *hay·ba·mè f* —n midwife
Hebel *hay·bèl m* — lever
heben* *hay·bèn vt* raise
Hecke *he·kè f* —n hedge
Hecktür *hek·tŏŏr f* —en tailgate (*of car*)
Hecktürmodell *hek·tŏŏr·mo·del nt* — hatchback (*car*)
Hefe *hay·fè f* yeast
Heft *heft nt* —e exercise book
Heftklammer *heft·kla·mèr f* —n staple
Heftmaschine *heft·ma·shee·nè f* —n stapler
Heftpflaster *heft·pfla·stèr nt* — band-aid
heikel *hye·kèl adj* delicate (*situation*)
heilen *hye·lèn vt* cure □ *vi* heal (*wound*)
heilig *hye·likh adj* holy
Heiligabend *hye·likh·ah·bènt m* Christmas Eve
Heilige *hye·li·gè m/f* —n saint
Heilmittel *hile·mi·tèl nt* — remedy
Heim *hime nt* —e home (*institution*); hostel
Heimatadresse *hye·mat·a·dre·sè f* —n home address
Heimweh *hime·vay nt* homesickness; **Heimweh haben*** *hime·vay hah·bèn* to be homesick
Heimwerken *hime·ver·kèn nt* do-it-yourself
heiraten *hye·rah·tèn vt* marry; **sie haben gestern geheiratet** *zee hah·bèn ge·stern gè·hye·rah·tèt* they were married yesterday
heiß *hise adj* hot
heißen* *hye·sèn vi* to be called; **wie heißen Sie?** *vee hye·sèn zee* what is your name?; **ich heiße Paul** *ikh hye·sè Paul* my name is Paul
heiß|laufen* *hise·low·fèn vi* overheat (*engine*)
Heißwassergerät *hise·va·sèr·gè·ret nt* —e water heater
Heizdecke *hites·de·kè f* —n electric blanket
Heizgerät *hites·gè·ret nt* —e heater
Heizkörper *hites·kur·pèr m* — radiator
Heizöl *hites·url nt* —e oil (*for heating*)
Heizplatte *hites·pla·tè f* —n hotplate
Heizung *hye·tsoong f* heating
helfen* *hel·fèn vi* help; **können Sie mir helfen?** *kur'·nèn zee meer hel·fèn* can you help me?
hell *hel adj* light (*pale*); bright
hellbraun *hel·brown adj* tan
Helm *helm m* —e helmet
Hemd *hemt nt* —en shirt
Henkel *heng·kèl m* — handle (*of cup*)
Henne *he·nè f* —n hen
herab *her·ap adv* down(wards)
herab|setzen *her·ap·ze·tsèn vt* reduce (*price*)
herauf *her·owf adv* up(wards)
heraus *her·ows adv* out
heraus|bekommen *her·ows·bè·ko·mèn vt* get out; **sein Geld wieder heraus|bekommen*** *zine gelt vee·dèr her·rows·bè·ko·mèn* to break even
heraus|bringen* *her·ows·bring·èn vt* release (*book, film*)
heraus|finden* *her·ows·fin·dèn vt* find out
heraus|geben* *her·ows·gay·bèn vt* give

back; **er hat mir zuwenig herausgegeben** *er hat meer tsoo·vay·nikh her·ows·gè·gay·bèn* he gave me short change
heraus|gehen* *her·ows·gay·èn vi* go out; come out (*stain*)
heraus|kommen* *her·ows·ko·mèn vi* come out (*person, sun*)
heraus|ziehen* *her·ows·tsee·èn vt* pull out
Herbst *herpst m* fall (*season*)
Herde *her·dè f* —n flock
herein *her·ine adv* in
Hering *hay·ring m* —e herring; peg
Hermelin *her·mè·leen m* ermine (*fur*)
Herr *her m* —en gentleman; master; Mr; **mein Herr** *mine her* sir
Herrenartikel *he·rèn·ar·tee·kèl pl* haberdashery
Herrenbekleidung *her·rèn·bè·klye·doong f* menswear
herrlich *her·likh adj* marvellous
Herrscher *her·shèr m* — ruler (*leader*)
her|stellen *her·shte·lèn vt* manufacture; produce; **serienweise her|stellen** *zay·ree·èn·vye·zè her·shte·lèn* to mass-produce
Hersteller *her·shte·lèr m* — producer; manufacturer
Herstellung *her·shte·loong f* manufacturing
herüber *her·ŏŏ·bèr adv* over
herum *her·oom adv* (a)round; **hier herum** *her·oom* about here
herum|gehen* *her·oom·gay·èn vi* go round; **um ein Feld herum|gehen*** *oom ine felt her·oom·gay·èn* to go round a field
herunter *her·oon·tèr adv* down(wards)
herunter|kommen* *her·oon·tèr·ko·mèn vi* to come down; **er kam die Straße herunter** *er kahm dee strah·sè her·oon·tèr* he came down the street
Herz *herts nt* heart; hearts (*cards*)
Herzanfall *herts·an·fal m* ⁼e heart attack
Herzmuschel *herts·moo·shèl f* —n cockle
Herzog *her·tsŏk m* ⁼e duke
Heu *hoy nt* hay
Heulen *hoy·lèn nt* roar (*of engine*) □ *vi* heulen *hoy·lèn* roar
Heuschnupfen *hoy·shnoop·fèn m* hay fever
heute *hoy·tè adv* today; **heute abend** *hoy·tè ah·bènt* tonight
heutzutage *hoyt·tsoo·tah·gè adv* nowadays
hier *heer adv* here
hierher *heer·hayr adv* this way; **hierher bitte** *heer·hayr bi·tè* this way please; **kommen Sie hierher** *ko·mèn zee heer·hayr* come over here
hiesig *hee·zikh adj* local
Hi-Fi *hye·fye nt* — hi-fi
Hilfe *hil·fè f* help; **Hilfe!** *hil·fè* help!
Himbeere *him·bay·rè f* —n raspberry
Himmel *hi·mèl m* — sky
hin *hin adv* there
hinab *hin·ap adv* down
hinauf *hin·owf adv* up
hinauf|gehen* *hin·owf·gay·èn vi* go up; **einen Berg hinauf|gehen*** *ine·èn berk hin·owf·gay·èn* to go up a hill
hinaus *hin·ows adv* out
hinaus|gehen* *hin·ows·foo·rèn vi* lead out; **diese Tür führt in den Garten hinaus** *dee·zè tŏŏr fŏŏrt in dayn gar·tèn hin·ows* this door leads into the garden

hinaus|gehen* *hin·ows·gay·èn* vi go out

Hindernis *hin·dèr·nis* nt **-se** obstacle

hinein *hin·ine* adv in

hinein|gehen* *hin·ine·gay·èn* vi go in

hinein|stecken *hin·ine·shte·kèn* vt put in; plug in

hin|fallen* *hin·fa·lèn* vi fall over; fall down

hin|gehen* *hin·gay·èn* vi go (there); **er ist hingegangen** *er ist hin·gè·gang·èn* he went there

hinken *hing·kèn* vi limp

hin|legen *hin·lay·gèn* vt lay down; **sich hin|legen** *zikh hin·lay·gèn* to lie down

hin|richten *hin·rikh·tèn* vt execute (kill)

hin|sehen* *hin·zay·èn* vi look; **auf etwas hin|sehen*** *owf et·vass hin·zay·èn* to look towards something

hinten *hin·tèn* adv behind; **nach hinten** *nakh hin·tèn* back (backwards)

Hinter- *hin·tèr* pref rear (wheel) □ prep behind; **hinter der Mauer** *hin·tèr der mow·èr* behind the wall

hintere(r/s) *hin·tè·rè(·rèr/·rès)* adj rear; back; **das hintere Ende** *hin·tè·rè en·dè* back (of hall, room)

Hintergrund *hin·tèr·groont* m **-e** background

hinter|lassen* *hin·tèr·la·sèn* vt leave; **eine Nachricht hinter|lassen*** *ine·è nakh·rikht hin·tèr·la·sèn* to leave a message

Hinterteil *hin·tèr·tile* nt **-e** bottom (of person)

hinüber *hin·ōō·bèr* adv across; over

hinunter *hin·oon·tèr* adv down

hinunter|gehen* *hin·oon·tèr·gay·èn* vi go down; **er ging die Straße hinunter** *er ging dee strah·sè hin·oon·tèr* he went down the street

hinzu|fügen *hin·tsoo·fōō·gèn* vt add (comment)

Hirn *hirn* nt brains (as food)

Hitze *hit·sè* f heat

Hobby *ho·bee* nt **-s** hobby

Hobel *ho·bèl* m — plane (tool)

Hoch- *hōkh* pref overhead (railway) □ adj hoch *hōkh* high; **6 Meter hoch** *6 may·tèr hōkh* 6 meters high

hochachtungsvoll *hōkh·akh·toongs·fol* adv yours faithfully

hochentwickelt *hōkh·ent·vi·kèlt* adj sophisticated (machine)

Hochhaus *hōkh·hows* nt **-er** apartment house

Hochsaison *hōkh·ze·zong* f **-s** high season

Höchst- *hur·kst* pref maximum

höchstens *hur·kh·stèns* adv at the most

Hochstuhl *hōkh·shtool* m **-e** highchair

Hochwasser *hōkh·va·sèr* nt — high tide

hoch|werfen* *hōkh·ver·fèn* vt throw up; **eine Münze hoch|werfen*** *ine·è mōōn·tsè hōkh·ver·fèn* to toss a coin

hochwertig *hōkh·ver·tikh* adj high-class

Hochzeit *hōkh·tsite* f **-en** wedding

Hochzeitsgeschenk *hōkh·tsites·gè·shenk* nt **-e** wedding gift

Hocker *ho·kèr* m — stool

Hockey *ho·kee* nt hockey

Hof *hōf* m **-e** yard (of building); courtyard

hoffen *ho·fèn* vi hope

hoffentlich *ho·fènt·likh* adv I hope so; **hoffentlich nicht** *ho·fènt·likh nikht* I hope not

Hoffnung *hof·noong* f **-en** hope

höflich *hur'f·likh* adj polite

Höhe *hur'·è* f **-n** altitude; height (of object)

Höhensonne *hur'·en·zo·nè* f **-n** sunlamp

höher *hur'·èr* adj higher; **höher stellen** *hur'·èr shte·lèn* to turn up (heat, volume)

hohe(r/s) *hō·è(·èr/·ès)* adj high; **der hohe Berg** *der hō·è berk* the high mountain; **mit hohen Absätzen** *mit hō·èn tip'zet·sèn* high-heeled

hohl *hōl* adj hollow

Höhle *hur'·lè* f **-n** cave

holen *hō·lèn* vt get; fetch; **sich holen** *zikh hō·lèn* get (catch: illness)

Holland *ho·lant* nt Holland

Holländisch *ho·len·dish* nt Dutch □ adj holländisch *ho·len·dish* Dutch

Holz *holts* nt **-er** wood (material)

hölzern *hur'l·tsèrn* adj wooden

Holzhammer *holts·ha·mèr* m **-** mallet

homogenisiert *hō·mō·gay·nee·zeert* adj homogenized

Honig *hō·nikh* m **-e** honey

Honorar *hō·nō·rahr* nt **-e** fee

hören *hur'·rèn* vt/i hear; **ich höre Sie nicht** *ikh hur'·rè zee nikht* I can't hear (you)

Hörer *hur·èr* m — receiver (phone)

Hörgerät *hur·gè·ret* nt — hearing aid

Horizont *hō·ree·tsont* m — horizon

horizontal *hō·ree·tson·tahl* adj horizontal

Horn *horn* nt **-er** horn (of animal)

Hörnchen *hurn·khèn* nt — croissant

Horrorfilm *ho·ror·film* m **-e** horror movie

Hose *hō·zè* f **-n** pants

Hosenanzug *hō·zèn·an·tsook* m **-e** pant(s) suit; trouser-suit

Hosenträger *hō·zèn·tray·gèr* pl suspenders

Hot Dog *hot dok* m **-s** hot dog

Hotel *hō·tel* nt **-s** hotel

Hoteljunge *hō·tel·yoong·è* m **-n** bellboy

hübsch *hōōpsh* adj pretty (woman, child)

Hubschrauber *hoop·shrow·bèr* m — helicopter

Hüfte *hōōf·tè* f **-n** hip

Hüfthalter *hōōft·hal·tèr* m — girdle (corset)

Hügel *hōō·gèl* m — hill

hügelig *hōō·gè·likh* adj hilly

Huhn *hoon* nt **-er** chicken

Hühnerauge *hōō·nèr·ow·gè* nt **-n** corn (on foot)

Hühnerbein *hōō·nèr·bine* nt **-e** chicken leg

Hummer *hoo·mèr* m — lobster

Humor *hoo·mōr* m humor; **der Sinn für Humor** *zin fōōr hoo·mōr* sense of humor

Hund *hoont* m **-e** dog

hundert *hoon·dèrt* num hundred; **hundertfünfundachtzig** *hoon·dèrt·fōōnf·oont·akh·tsikh* a hundred (and) eighty-five; **einhundert Leute** *ine·hoon·dèrt loy·tè* a hundred people; **Hunderte von Büchern** *hoon·dèr·tè fon bōō·khèrn* hundreds of books

hundertste(r/s) *hoon·dèrt·stè (·stèr/·stès)* adj hundredth

Hunger *hoong·èr* m hunger; **Hunger haben*** *hoong·èr hah·bèn* to be hungry

hungrig *hoong·grikh* adj hungry

Hupe *hoo·pè* f **-n** horn (of car)

hupen *hoo·pèn* vi to sound one's horn

hüpfen *hōōp·fèn vi* hop

Husten *hoo·stèn m* cough □ *vi* husten *hoo·stèn* cough

Hustenpastillen *hoo·stèn·pa·stil·èn pl* cough drops

Hustensaft *hoo·stèn·zaft m* ⁻e cough medicine

Hut *hoot m* ⁻e hat

Hutständer *hoot·shten·dèr m* — hat stand

Hütte *hōō·tè f* —n hut

Hüttenkäse *hōō·tèn·kay·zè m* — cottage cheese

hygienisch *hōō·gee·ay·nish adj* hygienic

Hymne *hōōm·nè f* —n hymn

Hypothek *hōō·po·tayk f* —en mortgage

hypothekarisch belasten *hōō·po·tay·kah·rish be·las·tèn vt* mortgage

hysterisch *hōō·stay·rish adj* hysterical

I

ich *ikh pron* I; **ich bin es** *ikh bin ess* it's me

ideal *i·day·ahl adj* ideal

Idee *i·day f* —n idea

identifizieren *i·den·ti·fi·tsee·rèn vt* identify

identisch *i·den·tish adj* identical

Idiotenhügel *i·dee·ō·tèn·hōō·gèl m* — beginners' slope

ihm *eem pron* (to) him; (to) it; **geben Sie es ihm** *gay·bèn zee ess eem* give it to him

ihn *een pron* him; it

ihnen *ee·nèn pron* (to) them; **zeigen Sie ihnen die Bücher** *tsye·gèn zee ee·nèn dee bōō·khèr* show them the books; **er sprach mit ihnen** *er shprakh mit ee·nèn* he spoke to them

Ihnen *ee·nèn pron* (to) you (*polite form*)

ihr *eer pron* to her; to it; you (*plural form*); **geben Sie es ihr** *gay·bèn zee ess eer* give it to her

ihr(e) *eer(·è) adj* her; its; their; **Ihr(e)** *eer(·è)* your (*polite form*)

ihr(r/s) *eer·è·(rèr/·ès) pron* hers; its; theirs; **Ihre(r/s)** *eer·è·(·èr/·ès)* yours (*polite form*)

Illustration *i·loo·stra·tsee·ōn f* —en illustration

Imbiß *im·biss m* —e snack

Imbißstube *im·biss·shtoo·bè f* —n snack bar

immer *i·mèr adv* always

Immobilien *i·mō·bee·lee·èn pl* real estate

Immobilienmakler *i·mō·bee·lee·èn·mahk·lèr m* — realtor

Impfung *imp·foong f* —en inoculation

Importeur *im·por·tur m* —e importer

in *in prep* in; into; **er wird in 2 Tagen zurück sein** *er virt in 2 tah·gèn tsoo·rōōk zine* he'll be back in 2 days; **in der Stadt** *in der shtat* in town; **in Frankreich** *in frank·ryekh* in/to France; **in der Schweiz** *in der shvites* in Switzerland; **in der Schachtel** *in der shakh·tèl* inside the box; **in dem Zug** *in daym tsook* on the train; **im Mai** *im mye* in May; **in der Schule** *in der shoo·lè* at school; **in London an·halten** *in lon·don an·hal·tèn* to stop in London; **im Fernsehen** *im fern·zay·èn* on television; **in die Schweiz** *in dee shvites* to Switzerland; **in die Schule/Stadt** *in dee shoo·lè/shtat* to school/town

inbegriffen *in·bè·gri·fèn adj* included

indes(sen) *in·des(·èn) adv* meanwhile

Index *in·deks m* —e index

Indianer *in·dee·ah·nèr m* — Indian (*American*)

Indien *in·dee·èn nt* India

indirekt *in·dee·rekt adj* indirect (*route*)

indisch *in·dish adj* Indian

indossieren *in·do·see·rèn vt* endorse (*document*)

Industrie *in·doos·tree f* —n industry □ *pref* Industrie- *in·doos·tree* industrial

Industriegelände *in·doos·tree·ge·len·dè nt* — industrial area

Infektion *in·fek·tsee·ōn f* —en infection

Inflation *in·fla·tsee·ōn f* —en inflation (*economic*)

Inflationsrate *in·fla·see·ōnz·rah·tè f* rate of inflation; **der Inflationsrate angeglichen** *der in·fla·tsee·ōns·rah·tè an·ge·gli·khèn* indexed (*interest rates etc*)

Ingenieur *in·zhay·nyur m* —e engineer

Ingwer *ing·vèr m* ginger

Inhalt *in·halt m* —e contents

Inhaltsverzeichnis *in·halts·fer·tsyekh·nis m* —se contents (*list in book*)

Initialen *i·ni·tsee·ah·lèn pl* initials

inklusive *in·kloo·zee·vè adj* inclusive (*costs*)

inkompetent *in·kom·pay·tent adj* inefficient

Innen- *in·èn pref* interior

Innenwand *in·èn·vant f* ⁻e inside wall

Innere *in·è·rè nt* inside □ *adj* innere(r/s) *in·è·rè·(·èr/·ès)* internal

innerhalb *in·èr·halp prep* within; **er hat es innerhalb von 2 Tagen gemacht** *er hat ess in·èr·halp fon 2 tah·gèn gè·makht* he did it in 2 days

inoffiziell *in·o·fi·tsee·el adj* unofficial

Input *in·poot m* input (*computing*)

Insekt *in·zekt nt* —en insect

Insektenbekämpfungsmittel *in·zek·tèn·bè·kemp·foongs·mi·tèl nt* — insect repellent

Insel *in·zèl f* —n island

insgesamt *ins·gè·zamt adv* altogether

Inspektion *in·shpek·tsee·ōn f* —en inspection; service (*for car*)

Institut *in·sti·toot nt* —e institute

Instrument *in·stroo·ment nt* —e instrument (*musical*)

Insulin *in·zoo·leen nt* insulin

Inszenierung *in·tsay·nee·roong f* —en production (*of play*)

intelligent *in·te·li·gent adj* intelligent; bright (*clever*)

Intelligenz *in·te·li·gents f* intelligence

interessant *in·tè·re·sant adj* interesting

Interesse *in·tè·re·sè nt* —n interest

interessieren *in·tè·re·see·rèn vt* interest; **sich interessieren für** *zikh in·tè·re·see·rèn fōōr* to be interested in

interessiert *in·tè·re·seert adj* interested

international *in·ter·na·tsee·ō·nahl adj* international

Inventar *in·ven·tahr nt* —e inventory

investieren *in·ve·stee·rèn vt* invest

Investition *in·ve·sti·tsee·ōn f* —en investment

inzwischen *in·tsvi·shèn adv* meanwhile

Irak *i·rahk m* Iraq

Iran *i·rahn m* Iran

irgend *ir·gènt adv* at all; **irgend etwas** *ir·gènt et·vass* anything at all; **irgend jemand** *ir·gènt yay·mant* anybody at all; **kann irgend jemand von euch singen?** *kan ir·gènt yay·mant fon*

oykh zing·èn can any of you sing?;
können Sie irgend jemanden sehen?
kur'n·èn zee ir·gènt yay·man·dèn zay·
èn can you see anybody?
irgendein(e) *ir·gènt·ine(·è)* pron some;
any; **geben Sie mir irgendein Buch**
gay·bèn zee meer ir·gènt·ine bookh
give me any book
irgendwo *ir·gènt·vō adv* somewhere;
someplace
irisch *ee·rish adj* Irish
Irland *eer·lant nt* Ireland
Island *ees·lant nt* Iceland
Israel *is·ra·el nt* Israel
Italien *i·tahl·yèn nt* Italy
italienisch *i·tal·yay·nish adj* Italian □
Italienisch *i·tal·yay·nish* Italian

J

ja *ya adv* yes
Jacht *yakht f* —en yacht
Jacke *ya·kè f* —n jacket; jerkin
jagen *yah·gèn vt* hunt; chase
jäh *yay adj* steep (*slope*)
Jahr *yahr nt* —e year
Jahrestag *yah·rès·tahk m* —e anniver-
sary; **der hundertste Jahrestag** *hoon·*
dèrt·stè yah·rès·tahk centenary
Jahreszeit *yah·rès·tsite f* —en season
Jahrgang *yahr·gang m* —e vintage
Jahrhundert *yahr·hoon·dèrt nt* —e
century
jährlich *yayr·likh adj* annual; yearly
Jahrmarkt *yahr·markt m* —e funfair
Jahrzehnt *yahr·tsaynt nt* —e decade
Jakobsmuschel *yah·kops·moo·shèl f*
—n scallop
Jalousie *zha·loo·zee f* —n blind (*at*
window)
Januar *yan·oo·ar m* January
Japan *ya·pahn nt* Japan
Japanisch *ya·pah·nish nt* Japanese
□ *adj* japanisch *ya·pah·nish* Japanese
Jazz *jaz m* jazz
Jeans *jeenz pl* jeans
Jeansstoff *jeens·shtof m* denim
jede(r/s) *yay·dè(·dèr/·dès) adj* each;
every
jedenfalls *yay·dèn·fals adv* anyway
(*nonetheless*)
jedoch *yay·dokh conj* however; **er ist**
jedoch glücklich *er ist yay·dokh*
glöök·likh he's happy, though
Jeep *jeep m* —s jeep
jemals *yay·mals adv* ever
jemand *yay·mant pron* somebody,
someone
jene(r/s) *yay·nè(·nèr/·nès) pron, adj*
that (one) (*remote*)
jenseits *yayn·zites prep* beyond; **jenseits**
der Mauer *yayn·zites der mow·èr*
beyond the wall
Jersey *jer·zee m* jersey (*fabric*)
jetzig *yet·sikh adj* present
jetzt *yetst adv* now
Jod *yōt nt* iodine
Joga *yō·ga m* yoga
Joggen *jo·gèn m* jogging
Joghurt *yog·oort m* yogurt
Johannisbeere *yō·ha·nis·bay·rè f* —n
currant; **die rote Johannisbeere** *rō·tè*
yō·ha·nis·bay·rè red currant; **die**
schwarze Johannisbeere *shvart·sè yō·*
ha·nis·bay·rè black currant
Joker *jō·kèr m* —s joker (*cards*)
Journalist *joor·na·list m* —en journalist
Jubiläum *yoo·bi·lay·oom nt* Jubiläen
jubilee
jucken *yoo·kèn vi* itch

Juckreiz *yook·rites m* —e itch
Jude *yoo·dè m* —n Jew
jüdisch *yōō·dish adj* Jewish
Judo *yoo·dō·nt* judo
Jugend *yoo·gènt f* youth (*period*)
Jugendherberge *yoo·gènt·her·ber·gè f*
—n youth hostel
Jugendklub *yoo·gènt·kloop m* —s
youth club
Jugendliche(r) *yoo·gènt·li·khè(r) m/f*
teenager
Jugoslawien *yoo·go·sla·vee·èn nt* Yu-
goslavia
jugoslawisch *yoo·go·sla·vish adj* Yu-
goslav(ian)
Juli *yoo·lee m* July
Jumbo *jum·bō m* —s jumbo jet
jung *yoong adj* young
Junge *yoong·è m* —n boy
Junggeselle *yoong·gè·ze·lè m* —n
bachelor
Juni *yoo·nee m* June
Juwelier *yoo·vè·leer m* —e jeweler

K

Kabarett *ka·ba·ret nt* —s cabaret
Kabel *kah·bèl nt* — cable; lead (*elec-
trical*)
Kabeljau *kah·bèl·yow m* —s cod
Kabriolett *ka·bree·ō·let nt* —s convert-
ible (*car*)
Käfer *kay·fèr m* — beetle
Kaffee *ka·fay m* coffee
Kaffeekanne *ka·fay·ka·nè f* —n cof-
feepot
Kaffeemaschine *ka·fay·ma·shee·nè f*
—n percolator
Kaffeepause *ka·fay·pow·zè f* —n cof-
fee break
Kaffeetasse *ka·fay·ta·sè f* —n coffee
cup
Käfig *kay·fikh m* —e cage
kahl *kahl adj* bald
Kai *kye m* —s wharf; quayside
Kaiser *kye·zèr m* — emperor
Kajüte *ka·yōō·tè f* —n cabin (*in ship*)
Kakao *ka·kow m* —s cocoa
Kaktus *kak·toos m* —se cactus
Kalb *kalp nt* —er calf
Kalbfleisch *kalp·flyesh nt* veal
Kaldaunen *kal·dow·nèn pl* tripe
Kalender *ka·len·dèr m* — calendar
Kalorie *ka·lō·ree f* —n calorie
kalt *kalt adj* cold; **mir ist kalt** *meer ist*
kalt I'm cold
Kalzium *kal·tsee·oom nt* calcium
Kamel *ka·mayl nt* —e camel
Kamera *ka·mè·ra f* —s camera (*TV*)
Kamin *ka·meen m* —e fireplace
Kaminsims *ka·meen·zims m* —e
mantelpiece
Kamm *kam m* —e comb; ridge
kämmen *kè·mèn vt* comb
Kampagne *kam·pa·nyè f* —n campaign
Kampf *kampf m* —e battle; struggle;
fight
kämpfen *kemp·fèn vi* fight; struggle
Kampfrichter *kampf·rikh·tèr m* — ref-
eree
Kanada *ka·na·da nt* Canada
kanadisch *ka·nah·dish adj* Canadian
Kanal *ka·nahl m* —e canal
Kandidat *kan·dee·daht m* —en candi-
date (*for election*)
Kandidatin *kan·dee·dah·tin f* —nen
candidate (*for election*)
kandiert *kan·deert adj* glacé
Kaninchen *ka·neen·khèn nt* — rabbit
Kanone *ka·nō·nè f* —n cannon
Kantine *kan·tee·nè f* —n canteen

Kanu *kah·noo nt* —s canoe; **Kanu fahren** *kah·noo fah·rèn* to go canoeing

Kanzler *kants·lèr m* — chancellor (*in Germany, Austria*)

Kapelle *ka·pe·lè f* —n chapel

Kapital *ka·pi·tahl nt* —ien capital (*finance*)

Kapitalanleger *ka·pee·tahl·an·lay·gèr m* — investor

Kapitaleinkommen *ka·pi·tahl·ine·ko·mèn nt* — unearned income

Kapitalismus *ka·pi·ta·lis·moos m* capitalism

Kapitalist *ka·pi·ta·list m* —en capitalist

Kapitän *ka·pi·tayn m* —e captain

Kapitel *ka·pi·tèl nt* — chapter

Kappe *ka·pè f* —n cap (*hat*)

Kapsel *kap·sèl f* —n capsule (*of medicine*)

Kapuze *ka·poot·sè f* —n hood

Karaffe *ka·ra·fè f* —n decanter; carafe

Karamelbonbon *ka·ra·mel·bon·bon nt* —s toffee

Karamelle *ka·ra·me·lè f* —n caramel

Karat *ka·raht nt* — carat

Karate *ka·rah·tè nt* karate

Karfreitag *kahr·frye·tahk m* Good Friday

Karibische Meer *ka·ree·bi·shè mayr nt* Caribbean (Sea)

kariert *ka·reert adj* check(er)ed (*patterned*)

Karneval *kar·ne·val m* —s carnival

Karo *ka·rō nt* diamonds (*cards*)

Karren *ka·rèn m* — wagon

Karriere *ka·ree·ay·rè f* —n career

Karte *kar·tè f* —n card; ticket (*for train, plane, boat*); chart (*map*)

Kartei *kar·tye f* —en card index

Kartell *kar·tel nt* —e cartel

Kartengeber *kar·tèn·gay·bèr m* — dealer (*cards*)

Kartenspiel *kar·tèn·shpeel nt* —e card game

Kartoffel *kar·to·fèl f* —n potato

Kartoffelbrei *kar·to·fèl·brye m* mashed potatoes

Karton *kar·tōng m* —s box (*cardboard*)

Karussell *ka·roo·sel nt* —s merry-go-round

Kaschmir *kash·meer m* cashmere

Käse *kay·zè m* — cheese

Käsekuchen *kay·zè·koo·khèn m* — cheesecake

Kaserne *ka·zer·nè f* —n barracks

Kasino *ka·zee·no nt* —s casino

Kasse *ka·sè f* —n cashdesk; checkout (*in store*); box office; till (*cash register*)

Kasserolle *ka·sè·ro·lè f* —n casserole (*food*)

Kassette *ka·se·tè f* —n cassette; cartridge (*of tape, for camera*)

Kassettenrecorder *ka·se·tèn·ray·kor·dèr m* — cassette-recorder

Kassierer *ka·see·rèr m* — teller; cashier

Kassiererin *ka·see·rè·rin f* —nen teller; cashier

Kastanie *kas·tah·nee·è f* —n chestnut

kastanienbraun *kas·tahn·yèn·brown adj* maroon

Katalog *ka·ta·lōk m* —e catalog

Katastrophe *ka·ta·strō·fè f* —n disaster

Kater *kah·tèr m* hangover

katholisch *ka·tō·lish adj* catholic

Katze *kat·sè f* —n cat

kauen *kow·èn vt* chew

kaufen *kow·fèn vt* buy

Käufer *koy·fèr m* — buyer (*customer*)

Käuferin *koy·fè·rin f* —nen buyer (*customer*)

Kaufhaus *kowf·hows nt* ⁼er department store

Kaufmann *kowf·man m* ⁼er merchant; grocer

Kaugummi *kow·goo·mi nt* —s chewing gum

kaum *kowm adv* scarcely

Kaution *kow·tsee·ōn f* —en deposit (*for key etc*); bail (*for prisoner*); **gegen Kaution** *gay·gèn kow·tsee·ōn* on bail

Kaviar *kah·vi·ar m* caviar(e)

Kebab *kay·bap m* —s kebab

Kehlkopfentzündung *kayl·kopf·ent·tsöōn·doong f* —en laryngitis

Kehrschaufel *kayr·show·fèl f* —n dustpan

Keilriemen *kile·ree·mèn m* — fanbelt

Keim *kime m* —e germ

kein(e) *kine(·è) adj* no, not a(n); **wir haben kein Brot** *veer hah·bèn kine·brōt* we haven't any bread

keine(r/s) *kine·è(·èr/·ès) pron* nobody; neither; none; **wir haben keinen/keine/keines** *veer hah·bèn kine·èn/kine·è/kine·ès* we haven't any

keineswegs *kine·ès·vayks adv* not at all

Keks *kayks m* —e biscuit (*sweet*)

Keller *ke·lèr m* — cellar

Kellner *kel·nèr m* — waiter; steward (*at club*)

Kellnerin *kel·nè·rin f* —nen waitress

Kenia *ken·ya m* Kenya

kennen* *ken·èn vt* know (*person*)

kennen|lernen *ken·èn·ler·nèn vt* meet (*make acquaintance of*)

Kenner *ken·èr m* — connoisseur

Kenntnis *kent·niss f* —se knowledge

Keramik *kay·rah·mik f* pottery

Kerosin *ke·rō·zeen nt* kerosene

Kerze *kert·sè f* —n candle

Kessel *ke·sèl m* — kettle

Ketchup *ke·chap nt* ketchup

Kette *ke·tè f* —n chain; range (*of mountains*)

Kettenladen *ke·tèn·lah·dèn m* ⁼ chain store

keuchen *koy·khèn vi* pant

Keuchhusten *koykh·hoo·stèn m* whooping cough

Keule *koy·lè f* —n drumstick (*of chicken*)

kicken *ki·kèn vt* kick (*ball*)

Kiefer *kee·fèr f* pine (*tree*)

Kiefer(knochen) *kee·fèr(·knokh·èn) m* — jaw

Kiefernholz *kee·fèrn·holts nt* pine

Kies *kees m* gravel

Kiesel *kee·zèl m* — pebble

Kilo *kee·lō nt* —s kilo; **$3 das Kilo** *$3 dass kee·lō* $3 per kilo

Kilogramm *kee·lō·gram nt* — kilogram

Kilometer *kee·lō·may·tèr m* — kilometer; **Kilometer pro Stunde** *kee·lō·may·tèr prō shtoon·dè* ≈ miles per hour, m.p.h.

Kilometerzähler *kee·lō·may·tèr·tsay·lèr m* ≈ odometer

Kilowatt *kee·lō·vat nt* — kilowatt

Kilt *kilt m* —s kilt

Kind *kint nt* —er child

Kinderarzt *kin·dèr·artst m* ⁼e pediatrician

Kinderärztin *kin·dèr·èrts·tin f* —nen pediatrician

Kinderbett *kin·dèr·bet nt* —en crib (*baby's*)

Kinderkrippe *kin·dèr·kri·pè f* —n day nursery

Kinderwagen *kin·dèr·vah·gèn m —* pram; baby buggy, baby carriage

Kinderzimmer *kin·dèr·tsi·mèr nt —* nursery

Kinn *kin nt* —**e** chin

Kino *kee·nō nt* —**s** cinema

Kiosk *kee·osk m* —**e** stand (*for newspapers*)

kippen *ki·pèn vt* tip (*tilt*)

Kirche *kir·khè f* —**n** church

Kirchenschiff *kirkh·èn·shif nt* —**e** nave

Kirchhof *kirkh·hōf m* —**e** churchyard

Kirsch *kirsh m* kirsch

Kirschbaum *kirsh·bowm m* —**e** cherry (*tree*)

Kirsche *kir·shè f* —**n** cherry

Kissen *ki·sèn nt* —cushion

Kiste *kis·tè f* —**n** crate; case (*of wine*)

Kittel *ki·tèl m* —smock

Kittelschürze *ki·tèl·shŏŏr·tsè f* —**n** overall

kitzeln *kit·tsèln vt* tickle

Klage *klah·gè f* —**n** complaint

Klammer *kla·mèr f* —**n** bracket (*in writing*)

Klappe *kla·pè f* —**n** flap

Klappstuhl *klap·shtool m* —**e** folding chair

Klapptisch *klap·tish m* —**e** folding table

Klaps *klaps m* —**e** smack; **einen Klaps geben*** *ine·èn klaps gay·bèn* to smack

klar *klahr adj* clear; plain; definite (*distinct*)

Klasse *kla·sè f* —**n** class; grade; **erster Klasse fahren*** *er·stèr kla·sè fah·rèn* to travel first class; **zweite Klasse** *tsvye·tè kla·sè* second-class; **ein Fahrschein zweiter Klasse** *ine fahr·shine tsvye·tèr kla·sè* a second-class ticket

klassisch *kla·sish adj* classical (*music, art*)

Klatsch *klatsh m* gossip (*chatter*)

klatschen *klat·shèn vi* clap

Klausel *klow·zèl f* —**n** clause (*in contract*)

Klavier *kla·veer nt* —**e** piano

kleben *klay·bèn vt* glue; stick

klebrig *klay·brikh adj* sticky

Klebstoff *klayp·shtof m* glue

Klebstreifen *klayp·shtrye·fèn m* adhesive tape

Kleid *klite nt* —**er** dress

sich kleiden *zikh klye·dèn vr* dress (*oneself*)

Kleider *klye·dèr pl* clothes

Kleiderbügel *klye·dèr·bŏŏ·gèl m* —coat hanger

Kleiderschrank *klye·dèr·shrank m* —**e** wardrobe (*furniture*)

Kleidung *klye·doong f* outfit (*clothes*)

Kleidungsstück *klye·doongs·shtŏŏk nt* —**e** garment

klein *kline adj* short (*person*); little; small

Kleinbus *kline·boos m* —**se** minibus

Kleingeld *kline·gelt nt* change (*money*)

klein|schneiden* *kline·shnye·dèn vt* chop (*food*)

Kleister *klye·stèr m* paste (*glue*)

Klempner *klemp·nèr m* —plumber

klettern auf *kle·tèrn owf vt* climb (*tree, wall*); **über etwas klettern** *ŏŏ·bèr et·vass kle·tèrn* to climb over something

Klima *klee·ma nt* —**s** climate

Klimaanlage *klee·ma·an·lah·gè f* —**n** air-conditioning

klimatisiert *klee·ma·ti·zeert adj* air-conditioned

Klinge *kling·è f* —**n** blade (*of knife*)

Klingel *kling·èl f* —**n** bell (*electric*)

klingeln *kling·èln vi* ring

Klinik *klee·nik f* —**en** clinic; **die psychiatrische Klinik** *psŏŏ·khee·ah·tri·shè klee·nik* mental hospital

Klinke *kling·kè f* —**n** handle (*of door*)

klopfen *klop·fèn vi* knock (*engine*); **klopfen an** *klop·fèn an* tap; **an die Tür klopfen** *an dee tŏŏr klop·fèn* to knock (at) the door

Kloß *klōs m* —**e** dumpling

Kloster *klōs·tèr nt* — monastery; convent

Klub *kloop m* —**s** club (*society*)

klug *klook adj* clever (*person*)

Klumpen *kloom·pèn m* —lump (*in sauce*)

Knacks *knaks m* —**e** crack (*noise*)

Knall *knal m* —**e** bang (*of gun etc*)

knallen *kna·lèn vi* bang (*gun etc*); **gegen etwas knallen** *gay·gèn et·vass kna·lèn* to crash into something

Knallfrosch *knal·frosh m* —**e** cracker (*paper toy*)

knapp *knap adj* tight (*schedule*)

Knäuel *knoy·èl m* —ball (*of string, wool*)

kneifen* *knye·fèn vt* pinch

Kneipe *knye·pè f* —**n** pub

Knie *knee nt* —knee; **auf jemandes Knien sitzen*** *owf yay·man·dès knee·èn zit·sèn* to sit on someone's knee; **auf Knien liegen*** *owf knee·èn lee·gèn* to kneel

Knoblauch *knōp·lowkh m* garlic

Knoblauchwurst *knōp·lowkh·voorst f* —**e** garlic sausage

Knoblauchzehe *knōp·lowkh·tsay·è f* —**n** clove of garlic

Knöchel *knur·khèl m* —ankle

Knochen *kno·khèn m* —bone

Knopf *knopf m* —**e** button; knob (*on radio etc*)

Knospe *knos·pè f* —**n** bud

Knoten *knō·tèn m* —knot; **einen Knoten machen** *ine·èn knō·tèn makh·èn* to tie a knot □ *vt* **knoten** *knō·tèn* knot

knurren *knoo·rèn vi* growl

knusprig *knoos·prikh adj* crisp

Koch *kokh m* —**e** chef; cook

kochen *ko·khèn vi* boil □ *vt* cook

Kochherd *kokh·hert m* —**e** stove; cooker

Köchin *kur·khin f* —**nen** cook

Kochtopf *kokh·topf m* —**e** saucepan

Kodein *ko·day·een nt* codeine

Köder *kur·dèr m* —bait (*in fishing*)

koffeinfrei *ko·fe·een·frye adj* decaffeinated

Koffer *ko·fèr m* —suitcase

Kofferkuli *ko·fèr·koo·lee m* —**s** luggage cart

Kofferraum *ko·fèr·rowm m* —**e** trunk (*in car*)

Kognak *kon·yak m* —**s** cognac; brandy

Kohl *kōl m* —**e** cabbage

Kohle *kō·lè f* coal

Kohlenstoff *kō·lèn·shtof m* carbon

Kohlepapier *kō·lè·pa·peer nt* carbon paper

Kohlrabi *kōl·rah·bee m* —**s** kohlrabi

Kohlrübe *kōl·rŏŏ·bè f* —**n** swede

Koje *kō·yè f* —**n** berth (*in ship*); bunk

Kokosnuß *kō·kos·noos f* —**e** coconut

Kolben *kol·bèn m* —piston

Kolik *ko·leek f* —**en** colic

Kollege *ko·lay·gè m* —**n** colleague

Kollegin *ko·lay·gin f* —**nen** colleague

Kölnischwasser *kur·l·nish·va·sèr nt* cologne

Kombiwagen *kom·bee·vah·gèn m* — station wagon

Komiker *kō·mi·kèr m* — comedian

komisch *kō·mish adj* funny (*amusing*)

Komma *ko·ma nt* —s comma; decimal point; 3 Komma 4 *3 ko·ma 4* 3 point 4

kommen* *ko·mèn vi* come (*arrive*); wieder zu sich kommen* *vee·dèr tsoo zikh ko·mèn* to revive; to come around (*recover*); wie kommen wir dorthin? *vee ko·mèn veer dort·hin* how do we get there?; kommen Sie noch zu uns mit *ko·mèn zee nokh tsoo oons mit* come back to our place; auf eine Straße kommen* *owf ine·è shtrah·sè ko·mèn* to get onto a road

kommerzialisiert *ko·mer·tsee·a·lee·zeert adj* commercialized (*resort*)

auf Kommission *owf ko·mi·see·ōn adv* on sale or return

Kommunist *ko·moo·nist m* —en Communist

Kommunistin *ko·moo·nis·tin f* —nen Communist

kommunistisch *ko·moo·nis·tish adj* Communist

Komödie *ko·mur'·dee·è f* —n comedy

Kompaß *kom·pas m* —e compass

Kompliment *kom·plee·ment nt* —e compliment

kompliziert *kom·plee·tseert adj* complex; elaborate; complicated

Komponist *kom·pō·nist m* —en composer

Kondensmilch *kon·dens·milkh f* condensed milk; evaporated milk

Konditor *kon·dee·tor m* —en confectioner

Kondom *kon·dōm nt* —e prophylactic (*contraceptive*)

Konfektions- *kon·fek·tsee·ōns pref* ready-made (*clothes*); ready-to-wear

Konferenz *kon·fè·rents f* —en conference (*meeting*)

König *kur'·nikh m* —e king

Königin *kur'·ni·gin f* —nen queen

königlich *kur'·nik·likh adj* royal

Konkurrent *kon·koo·rent m* —en competitor

Konkurrenzfirma *kon·koo·rents·fir·ma f* —firmen rival firm

können* *kur'·nèn vi* be able; ich kann *ikh kan* I can; Sie können *zee kur'·nèn* you can; etwas tun können* *et·vass toon kur'n·èn* to be able to do something; etwas nicht tun können* *et·vass nikht toon kur'·nèn* to be unable to do something; es könnte regnen *es kur'n·tè rayg·nèn* it might rain; wir könnten es tun *veer kur'n·tèn ess toon* we could do it; könnte ich... haben *kur'n·tè ich... hah·bèn* could I have... □ *vt* können* *kur'·nèn* know (*language*)

konservativ *kon·zer·va·teef adj* conservative

Konservatorium *kon·zer·va·tō·ree·oom nt* —torien academy of music

Konservierungsmittel *kon·zer·vee·roongs·mi·tèl nt* — preservative

Konsul *kon·sool m* —e consul

Konsulat *kon·soo·laht nt* —e consulate

Konsumgüter *kon·zoom·gōō·tèr pl* consumer goods

Kontaktlinsen *kon·takt·lin·zèn pl* contact lenses

Kontinent *kon·tee·nènt m* —e continent

kontinental *kon·tee·nen·tahl adj* continental

Kontinentaleuropa *kon·tee·nen·tahl·oy·rō·pah nt* the Continent

Kontingent *kon·ting·gent nt* —e quota (*of goods*)

Konto *kon·tō nt* Konten account; ein Konto bei Smiths haben* *ine kon·tō bye Smiths hah·bèn* to bank with Smiths

Kontoüberziehung *kon·tō·ōō·bèr·tsee·oong f* —en overdraft

Kontrollabschnitt *kon·trol·ap·shnit m* —e counterfoil

Kontrolleur *kon·tro·lur m* —e inspector (*of tickets*)

kontrollieren *kon·tro·lee·rèn vt* check (*passport, ticket*); inspect (*ticket*)

Kontrollturm *kon·trol·toorm m* —e control tower

Konzert *kon·tsert nt* —e concert

Konzessionär *kon·tse·see·ō·nayr m* —e concessionaire

Kopenhagen *kō·pèn·hah·gèn nt* Copenhagen

Köper *kur'·pèr m* twill

Kopf *kopf m* —e head

Kopfhaut *kopf·howt f* scalp

Kopfhörer *kopf·hur'·rèr pl* headphones

Kopfkissen *kopf·ki·sèn nt* — pillow

Kopfkissenbezug *kopf·ki·sèn·bè·tsook m* —e pillowcase, pillowslip

Kopfsalat *kopf·za·laht m* — lettuce

Kopfschmerzen *kopf·shmer·tsèn pl* headache; Kopfschmerzen haben* *kopf·shmer·tsèn hah·bèn* to have a headache

Kopfsprung *kopf·shproong m* —e dive

Kopfstütze *kopf·shtöōt·sè f* —n headrest

Kopie *ko·pee f* —n copy (*imitation*)

kopieren *ko·pee·rèn vt* copy

Koralle *ko·ra·lè f* —n coral

Korb *korp m* —e hamper; basket

Korbgeflecht *korp·gè·flekht nt* —e wicker

Kordsamt *kort·zamt m* cord (*fabric*); corduroy

Korinthe *kō·rin·tè f* —n currant

Kork *kork m* —e cork

Korken *kor·kèn m* — cork (*of bottle*)

Korkenzieher *kor·kèn·tsee·èr m* — corkscrew

Körper *kur·pèr m* — body

körperbehindert *kur·pèr·bè·hin·dèrt adj* disabled

körperlich *kur·pèr·likh adj* physical

Körperschaftsteuer *kur·pèr·shafts·shtoy·èr f* —n corporation tax

korrekt *ko·rekt adj* correct (*proper*)

Korrespondenz *ko·res·pon·dents f* —en correspondence (*mail*)

korrupt *ko·roopt adj* corrupt

Korruption *ko·roop·tsee·ōn f* corruption

Korsett *kor·zet nt* —s corset

koscher *kō·shèr adj* kosher

Kosmetika *kos·may·ti·ka pl* cosmetics

kosmetische Chirurgie *kos·may·ti·shè khi·roor·gee f* cosmetic surgery

Kosten *kos·tèn pl* costs (*of production etc*); expense □ *vt* kosten *kos·tèn* cost; wieviel kostet das? *vee·feel kos·tèt dass* how much is it?

kostenlos *kos·tèn·lōs adj* free (*costing nothing*)

Kostenvoranschlag *kos·tèn·fōr·an·shlahk m* —e estimate

köstlich *kur'st·likh adj* delicious

Kostüm *kos·tōōm nt* —e fancy dress; costume (*theatrical*); suit (*women's*)

Kotelett *kot·let* nt —s cutlet

Kotflügel *kōt·flōō·gèl* m — fender (on car); mudguard

Krabbe *kra·bè* f —n shrimp

Krach *krakh* m —e crash (noise); row

Kräcker *kre·kèr* m — biscuit (savory); cracker (crisp wafer)

Kraft *kraft* f strength

Kraftbrühe *kraft·brōō·è* f —n consommé

Kraftfahrzeugbrief *kraft·fahr·tsoyk·breef* m —e logbook (of car)

Kraftfahrzeugkennzeichen *kraft·fahr·tsoyk·ken·tsye·khen* nt — license number (on car)

kräftig *kref·tikh* adj strong (person); powerful

Kragen *krah·gèn* m — collar

Kragenknopf *krah·gèn·knopf* m —e stud (for collar)

Krampf *krampf* m —e cramp

Kran *krahn* m —e crane (machine)

krank *krank* adj ill; sick

Krankenhaus *krang·kèn·hows* nt —er hospital

Krankenkasse *krang·kèn·ka·sè* f —n medical insurance

Krankenschwester *krang·kèn·shve·stèr* f —n nurse

Krankenwagen *krang·kèn·vah·gèn* m — ambulance

Kranke(r) *krang·kè(·kèr)* m/f —n invalid

Krankheit *krank·hite* f —en disease; sickness; illness

kratzen *kra·tsèn* vt scratch

Kraulen *krow·lèn* nt crawl (swimming)

Kräuter *kroy·tèr* pl herbs

Krautsalat *krowt·za·lat* m —e coleslaw

Krawatte *kra·va·tè* f —n (neck)tie

Krebs *krayps* m —e crab; cancer

Kredit *kray·deet* m —e credit; auf Kredit *owf kray·deet* on credit; jemandem Kredit geben* *yay·man·dèm kray·deet gay·bèn* to give somebody credit

Kreditbeschränkung *kray·deet·bè·shreng·koong* f —en credit squeeze

Kreditkarte *kray·deet·kar·tè* f —n credit card

Kreide *krye·dè* f chalk

Kreis *krise* m —e circle; round

Kreisverkehr *krise·fer·kayr* m traffic circle

Krepp *krep* m seersucker

Kresse *kre·sè* f watercress; cress

Kreuz *kroyts* m —e cross; clubs (in cards)

Kreuzfahrt *kroyts·fahrt* f —en cruise; eine Kreuzfahrt machen *ine·è kroyts·fahrt ma·khèn* to go on a cruise

Kreuzung *kroy·tsoong* f —en junction (in road); interchange; crossroads

kriechen* *kree·khèn* vi crawl

Krieg *kreek* m —e war

kriminell *kree·mi·nel* adj criminal

Krise *kree·zè* f —n crisis

Kristall *kri·stal* nt crystal (glass)

Kritik *kri·teek* f —en review (of book etc)

kritisieren *kri·ti·zee·rèn* vt criticize

Krocket *kro·ket* nt croquet

Krokette *kro·ke·tè* f —n croquette

Krokodil *krō·kō·deel* nt —e crocodile

Krokus *krō·koos* m —se crocus

Krone *krō·nè* f —n crown

Krönung *krur·noong* f —en coronation

Krug *krook* m —e jug; pitcher

Krümel *krōō·mèl* m — crumb

krumm *kroom* adj crooked

Krüppel *krōō·pèl* m — cripple

Kruste *kroo·stè* f —n crust

Küche *kōō·khè* f —n kitchen; cooking; cuisine

Kuchen *kōō·khèn* m — flan; cake

Kugel *koo·gèl* f —n bullet

Kugelschreiber *koo·gèl·shrye·bèr* m — pen

Kuh *koo* f —e cow

kühl *kōōl* adj cool

kühlen *kōō·lèn* vt chill (wine, food)

Kühler *kōō·lèr* m — radiator (of car)

Kühlschrank *kōōl·shrank* m —e refrigerator; icebox

Kühlung *kōō·loong* f cooling system

kühn *kōōn* adj ambitious (plan)

kultivieren *kool·tee·vee·rèn* vt cultivate (land)

kultiviert *kool·ti·veert* adj sophisticated (person)

Kulturbeutel *kool·toor·boy·tèl* m — washbag

sich kümmern um *zikh kōō·mèrn oom* vr to look after; sich um etwas kümmern *zikh oom et·vass kōō·mèrn* to see to something

Kunde *koon·dè* m —n customer; client

Kundgebung *koont·gay·boong* f —en rally (political)

kündigen *kōōn·di·gèn* vi resign

Kündigung *kōōn·di·goong* f —en resignation

Kundin *koon·din* f —nen customer; client

Kunst- *koonst* pref synthetic □ f die Kunst *koonst* art

Kunstgalerie *koonst·ga·lè·ree* f —n art gallery

Künstler *kōōnst·lèr* m — artist

Künstlerin *kōōnst·lè·rin* f —nen artist

künstlich *kōōnst·likh* adj artificial; man-made

Kunststück *koonst·shtōōk* nt —e trick (clever act)

Kunstwerk *koonst·verk* nt —e work of art

Kupfer *koop·fèr* nt copper (metal)

Kupplung *koo·ploong* f —en clutch (of car)

Kurbel *koor·bèl* f —n handle (for winding)

Kürbis *kōōr·bis* m —se squash (gourd); pumpkin

Kurort *koor·ort* m —e spa

Kursus *koor·zoos* m **Kurse** course (lessons)

Kurve *koor·vè* f —n curve; corner (bend in road); turn; eine Kurve nehmen* *ine·è koor·vè nay·mèn* to corner; eine Kurve machen *ine·è koor·vè ma·khèn* to bend (road)

kurz *koorts* adj short; brief

Kurze(r) *koort·sèr* m —n short drink

in Kürze *in kōōr·tsè* adv shortly (soon)

kurzfristig *koorts·fris·tikh* adj short term

kürzlich *kōōrts·likh* adv recently

Kurzschrift *koorts·shrift* f shorthand

kurzsichtig *koorts·zikh·tikh* adj nearsighted

Kurzwaren *koorts·vah·rèn* pl notions

Kurzwelle *koorts·ve·lè* f —n short wave

Kusine *koo·zee·nè* f —n cousin

Kuß *koos* m —e kiss

küssen *kōō·sèn* vt kiss; sich küssen *zikh kōō·sèn* to kiss (each other)

Küste *kōō·stè* f —n coast; seaside

Küstenbadestadt *kōō·stèn·bah·dè·shtat* f —e seaside resort küstennah *kōō·stèn·nah adj* offshore (*island*)

Küstenwache *kōō·stèn·va·khê f —n* coastguard

L

Labor *la·bōr nt —s* laboratory

Lächeln *lekh·èln nt* smile □ *vi* lächeln *lekh·èln* smile

Lachen *la·khèn nt* laugh □ *vi* lachen *la·khèn* laugh

lächerlich *le·khèr·likh adj* ridiculous

Lachs *laks m —e* salmon

Lack *lak m —e* varnish

Lackleder *lak·lay·dèr nt* patent leather

laden* *lah·dèn vt* load (*gun, camera*)

Laden *lah·dèn m* shop, store

Ladendiebstahl *lah·dèn·deep·shtahl m —e* shoplifting

Ladenkette *lah·dèn·ke·tè f —n* chain (*of shops*); multiple store

Ladentisch *lah·dèn·tish m —e* counter (*in shop*)

Lage *lah·gè f —n* position (*circumstance*); situation (*place*)

Lager *lah·gèr nt —* camp; store (*warehouse*) □ *pl* die Lager *lah·gèr* bearings (*in car*)

Lagerhaus *lah·gèr·hows nt —²er* warehouse

lagern *lah·gèrn vt* lay down (*wine*); store

Lagerraum *lah·gèr·rowm m —²e* store room

Lakritze *la·krits·è f* licorice

Lamm *lam nt —²er* lamb

Lammkeule *lam·koy·lè f —n* leg of lamb

Lampe *lam·pè f —n* lamp

Lampenschirm *lam·pèn·shirm m —e* lampshade

Land *lant nt —²er* country; land; auf dem Land *owf daym lant* in the country; an Land *an lant* ashore

Landebahn *lan·dè·bahn f —en* landing strip

landen *lan·dèn vi* land (*plane*)

Landkarte *lant·kar·tè f —n* map (*of country*)

ländlich *lent·likh adj* rural

Landschaft *lant·shaft f —en* countryside

Landsmann *lants·man m* Landsleute fellow countryman

Landstraße *lant·shtrah·sè f —n* highway

Landstreicher *lant·strye·khèr m —* tramp

Landung *lan·doong f —en* landing (*of plane*)

Landungsbrücke *lan·doongs·brōō·kè f —n* gangway (*bridge*)

Landvermesser *lant·fer·me·sèr m —* surveyor (*of land*)

Landwirtschaft *lant·virt·shaft f* agriculture

landwirtschaftlich *lant·virt·shaft·likh adj* agricultural

lang *lang adj* long; eine Stunde lang laufen* *ine·è shtoon·dè lang low·fèn* to walk for an hour; 6 Meter/Monate lang *6 may·tèr/mō·na·tè lang* 6 meters/months long

lange *lang·è adv* a long time; wie lange dauert das Programm? *vee lang·è dow·èrt dass prō·gram* how long is the program?

Länge *leng·è f —n* length

langfristig *lang·fri·stikh adj* long-term

länglich *leng·likh adj* oblong

langsam *lang·zam adj* slow; langsamer fahren* *lang·zam·èr fah·rèn* to slow down

sich langweilen *zikh lang·vye·lèn vr* be bored; ich langweile mich *ikh lang·vye·lè mikh* I'm bored

langweilig *lang·vye·likh adj* boring

Langwelle *lang·ve·lè f —n* long wave

Lanolin *la·nō·leen nt* lanolin

Lappen *la·pèn m —* rag; cloth (*cleaning*)

Lärm *lerm m —e* noise (*loud*)

lassen* *la·sèn vt* let (*allow*); lassen Sie mich nur machen *la·sèn zee mikh noor ma·khèn* leave it to me; lassen Sie Ihren Mantel hier *la·sèn zee eer·èn man·tèl heer* leave your coat here; etwas machen lassen* *et·vass ma·khèn la·sèn* to have something done; jemanden etwas tun lassen* *yay·man·dèn et·vass toon la·sèn* to let someone do something

Last *last f —en* load

lästig *le·stikh adj* annoying; er ist lästig *er ist le·stikh* he's a nuisance

Lastwagen *last·vah·gèn m —* truck (*vehicle*)

Latein *la·tine nt* Latin

Lateinamerika *la·tine·a·may·ri·ka nt* Latin America

Laterne *la·ter·nè f —n* streetlight

Laternenpfahl *la·ter·nèn·pfahl m —²e* lamppost

Latzhosen *lats·hō·zèn pl* dungarees

laufen* *low·fèn vi* run; wann läuft der Film? *van loyft der film* when is the movie on?

Laufgitter *lowf·gi·tèr nt —* playpen

Laufmasche *lowf·ma·shè f —n* run (*in stocking*)

Laune *low·nè f —n* mood; guter Laune *goo·tèr low·nè* in a good mood; schlechter Laune *shlekh·tèr low·nè* in a bad temper

laut *lowt adj* noisy; loud □ *adv* loudly; aloud (*read*)

läuten *loy·tèn vt* ring (*doorbell*)

lauter *low·tèr adv* nothing but

Lautsprecher *lowt·shpre·khèr m —* (loud)speaker

Lautstärke *lowt·shter·kè f* volume (*sound*)

Lawine *la·vee·nè f —n* avalanche

Leben *lay·bèn nt —* life □ *vi* leben *lay·bèn* live

lebend *lay·bènt adj* live (*alive*)

lebendig *lay·ben·dikh adj* alive

Lebenshaltungskosten *lay·bèns·hal·toongs·kos·tèn pl* cost of living

Lebensmittel *lay·bèns·mi·tèl pl* groceries

Lebensmittelgeschäft *lay·bèns·mi·tèl·ge·sheft nt —e* grocery shop

Lebensmittelvergiftung *lay·bèns·mi·tèl·fer·gif·toong f —en* food poisoning

Lebensstandard *lay·bèns·shtan·dart m* standard of living

Lebensversicherung *lay·bèns·fer·zikh·è·roong f —en* life insurance

Leber *lay·bèr f —n* liver

Leberwurst *lay·bèr·voorst f* liver sausage

lebhaft *layp·haft adj* lively

Leck *lek nt —e* leak (*water*)

lecken *le·kèn vi* leak □ *vt* lick

Leder *lay·dèr nt —* leather

ledig *lay·dikh adj* single (*not married*)

leer *layr adj* empty; flat (*battery*); blank

leeren *lay·rèn vt* empty

Leerlauf *layr·lowf* m neutral (*gear*)

Leerung *lay·roong* f —en collection (*of mail*)

legal *lay·gahl* adj legal

legen *lay·gèn* vt lay; **sich die Haare legen lassen** *zikh dee hah·rè lay·gèn la·sèn* to have one's hair set

Lehm *laym* m clay

lehnen *lay·nèn* vt/i lean; **sich gegen etwas lehnen** *zikh gay·gèn et·vass lay·nèn* to lean against something

Lehnstuhl *layn·shtool* m easy-chair

Lehrbuch *layr·bookh* nt =er textbook

Lehrer *lay·rèr* m — teacher; instructor

Lehrerin *lay·rè·rin* f —nen teacher; instructress

Lehrling *layr·ling* m —e apprentice

Lehrplan *layr·plan* m =e syllabus

Leibwächter *lipe·vekh·tèr* m — bodyguard (*person*)

Leiche *lye·khè* f —n body (*corpse*)

leicht *lyekht* adv easily □ adj light (*not heavy*); easy

Leichtindustrie *lyekht·in·doo·stree* f light industry

Leid *lite* nt grief; **es tut mir leid** *ess toot meer lite* (I'm) sorry

leiden *lye·dèn* vi suffer

Leidenschaft *lye·dèn·shaft* f —en passion

leider *lye·dèr* adv unfortunately; **leider nicht** *lye·dèr nikht* I'm afraid not

leihen *lye·èn* vt rent (*car*); lend; loan

Leihgebühr *lye·gè·bühr* f —en rental

Leine *lye·nè* f —n leash

Leinen *lye·nèn* nt linen (*cloth*)

Leinwand *line·vant* f =e screen (*movie*)

leise *lye·zè* adv quietly (*speak*) □ adj soft (*not loud*); faint (*sound etc*); **leiser stellen** *lye·zèr shte·lèn* to turn down (*volume*)

leisten *lye·stèn* vt achieve; **das kann ich mir nicht leisten** *dass kan ikh meer nikht lye·stèn* I can't afford it

Leistung *lye·stoong* f power (*of machine*); performance

leiten *lye·tèn* vt manage (*business*)

Leiter *lye·tèr* f —n ladder

Leitung *lye·toong* f —en management (*of business*)

Leitungswasser *lye·toongs·va·sèr* nt tap-water

lenken *leng·kèn* vt steer (*car*)

Lenkrad *lenk·raht* nt =er steering-wheel

Lenksäule *lenk·zoy·lè* f —n steering column

Lenkstange *lenk·shtang·è* f —n handlebar(s)

Lenkung *leng·koong* f —en steering (*in car*)

lernen *ler·nèn* vt learn

Lese *lay·zè* f —n harvest (*of grapes*)

Lesen *lay·zèn* nt reading □ vt **lesen** *lay·zèn* harvest (*grapes*) □ vt/i **lesen** *lay·zèn* read

letzte(r/s) *let·stè(·stèr/·stès)* adj last; final; **letzte Nacht/Woche** *let·stè nakht/vo·khè* last night/week; **in letzter Zeit** *in let·stèr tsite* lately

leuchten *loykh·tèn* vi blaze (*lights*)

Leuchtturm *loykht·toorm* m =e lighthouse

leugnen *loyg·nèn* vt deny

Leute *loy·tè* pl people

Licht *likht* nt —er light; **die Lichter an|machen** *dee likh·tèr an·ma·khèn* to switch on the lights (*car*)

Lichtmaschine *likht·ma·shee·nè* f —n alternator (*in car*)

Lidschatten *leet·sha·tèn* m — eyeshadow

lieb *leep* adj sweet (*kind*); dear

Liebe *lee·bè* f love

lieben *lee·bèn* vt love

lieber *lee·bèr* adv rather; **ich würde lieber ins Kino gehen** *ikh vöör·dè lee·bèr ins kee·no gay·èn* I'd rather go to the movies

Lieblings- *leep·lings* pref favorite

Lied *leet* nt —er song

liefern *lee·fèrn* vt deliver (*goods*); supply

Lieferung *lee·fè·roong* f —en delivery (*of goods*)

Lieferwagen *lee·fèr·vah·gèn* m — van

liegen *lee·gèn* vi lie

Liegestuhl *lee·gè·shtool* m =e deck-chair

Liegewagenplatz *lee·gè·vah·gèn·plats* m =e couchette

Lift *lift* m —s elevator

Likör *lee·kur* m —e liqueur

Lilie *lee·lee·è* f —n lily

Limonade *lee·mô·nah·dè* f lemonade

Limone *li·mô·nè* f —n lime (*fruit*)

Limonensaft *li·mô·nèn·zaft* m lime juice

Limousine *li·moo·zee·nè* f —n limousine; sedan (*car*)

Lineal *li·nay·ahl* nt —e ruler (*for measuring*)

Linie *lee·nee·è* f —n line; **die punktierte Linie** *poonk·teer·tè lee·nee·è* dotted line

Linienflug *lee·nee·èn·flook* m =e scheduled flight

linke(r/s) *ling·kè(r/s)* adj left(-hand)

links *links* adv (to the) left; on the left; **links ab|biegen** *links ap·bee·gèn* to turn left

linkshändig *links·hen·dikh* adj left-handed

Linkssteuerung *links·shtoy·èr·oong* f left-hand drive

Linoleum *li·nô·le·oom* nt linoleum

Linse *lin·zè* f —n lens (*of camera*)

Linsen *lin·zèn* pl lentils

Lippe *li·pè* f —n lip

Lippenstift *li·pèn·shtift* m —e lipstick

Liquidation *li·kvi·da·tsee·ôn* f liquidation; **in Liquidation gehen** *in li·kvi·da·tsee·ôn gay·èn* to go into liquidation

Liste *li·stè* f —n list

Listenpreis *li·stèn·prise* m —e list price

Liter *lee·tèr* nt — liter

Literatur *li·tè·ra·toor* f —en literature

LKW *el·kah·vay* m —s truck

LKW-Fahrer *el·kah·vay·fah·rèr* m — trucker

Loch *lokh* nt =er hole

lochen *lo·khèn* vt punch (*ticket etc*)

Locke *lo·kè* f —n curl

Lockenwickel *lo·kèn·vi·kèl* m — curler (*for hair*)

locker *lo·kèr* adj slack; loose

lockig *lo·kikh* adj curly

Löffel *lur·fèl* m — spoon

Löffelvoll *lur·fèl·fol* m — spoonful

Lohn *lôn* m =e wage, wages

Lohnempfänger *lôn·emp·feng·èr* m — wage earner

lohnend *lô·nènt* adj worthwhile (*activity*)

Lohnsteuer *lôn·stoy·èr* f income tax

Lohnstopp *lôn·shtop* m —s wage freeze

Lokal *lo·kahl* nt —e bar (*drinking establishment*)

Lokomotive *lō·kō·mō·tee·vè* f —n engine (*of train*)

los *lōs adj* loose; **was ist los?** *vass ist lōs* what's wrong?

Los *lōs nt* —e lot (*at auction*)

los|binden* *lōs·bin·dèn vt* untie (*animal*)

löschen *lur'·shèn vt* extinguish

lösen *lur'·zèn vt* solve (*problem*)

Lösung *lur'·zoong f* —en solution

Lotion *lō·tsee·ōn f* —en lotion

Lotterie *lo·tè·ree f* —n lottery

Löwe *lur'·vè m* —n lion

LP *el·pay f* —s LP

Lücke *lŏŏ·kè f* —n gap; space

Luft *looft f* ⸚e air

luftdicht *looft·dikht adj* airtight

lüften *lŏŏf·tèn vt* air (*room*)

Luftfahrt *looft·fahrt f* aviation

Luftfilter *looft·fil·tèr m* — air filter

Luftfracht *looft·frakht f* air freight

Luftkissenfahrzeug *looft·ki·sèn·fahr·tsoyk nt* —e hovercraft

Luftmatratze *looft·ma·trat·sè f* —n air bed; air-mattress

Luftpost *looft·post f* air mail; **per Luftpost** *per looft·post* by air mail

Luftpostbrief *looft·post·breef m* —e air letter

Luftwaffe *looft·va·fè f* —n air force

Lüge *lŏŏ·gè f* —n lie (*untruth*)

lügen *lŏŏ·gèn vi* lie (*tell a lie*)

Lunge *loong·è f* —n lung

Lungenentzündung *loong·èn·ent·tsŏŏn·doong f* pneumonia

Lust *loost f* pleasure; **ich habe Lust auf ein Bier** *ikh hah·bè loost owf ine beer* I feel like a beer

lustig *loos·tikh adj* merry; **sich über jemanden lustig machen** *zikh ŏŏ·bèr yay·man·dèn loos·tikh ma·khèn* to laugh at somebody

Lutscher *loot·shèr m* — lollipop

luxuriös *look·soo·ree·ur's adj* luxurious

Luxus *lŏŏk·soos m* luxury **— pref** Luxus- *look·soos* luxury (*car, hotel*); de luxe

Lyrik *lŏŏ·rik f* poetry

M

Machbarkeit *makh·bahr·kite f* feasibility

Machbarkeitsstudie *makh·bahr·kites·shtoo·dee·è f* —n feasibility study

machen *ma·khèn vt* make; do; get (*prepare: food*); **das macht nichts** *dass makht nikhts* it doesn't matter; **macht nichts** *makht nikhts* never mind; **eine Prüfung machen** *ine·è prŏŏ·foong ma·khèn* to take an exam; **die Betten machen** *dee be·tèn ma·khèn* to make the beds; **jemanden traurig machen** *yay·man·dèn trow·rikh ma·khèn* to make someone sad

Macht *makht f* ⸚e power

mächtig *mekh·tikh adj* powerful (*person*)

Mädchen *mayt·khèn nt* — girl

Mädchenname *mayt·khèn·nah·mè m* —n maiden name

Madeira *ma·day·ra m* Madeira (*wine*)

Madrid *ma·drit nt* Madrid

Magen *mah·gèn m* ⸚ stomach

Magenbeschwerden *mah·gèn·bè·shver·dèn pl* stomach trouble

Magenschmerzen *mah·gèn·shmert·sèn pl* stomach ache; **ich habe Magenschmerzen** *ikh hah·bè mah·gèn·shmert·sèn* I have (a) stomach ache

Magenverstimmung *mah·gèn·fer·shti·moong f* —en indigestion

mager *mah·gèr adj* lean (*meat*)

Magie *ma·gee f* magic

magisch *mah·gish adj* magic

Magnat *mag·naht m* —en tycoon

Magnet *mag·nayt m* —e magnet

Magnetband *mag·nayt·bant nt* ⸚er magnetic tape

Mahagoni *ma·ha·gō·nee nt* mahogany

mähen *may·èn vt* mow

mahlen* *mah·lèn vt* grind

Mahlzeit *mahl·tsite f* —en meal

Mähmaschine *may·ma·shee·nè f* —n mower

Mai *mye m* May

Mais *mise m* sweet corn; corn (*cereal crop*)

Maiskolben *mise·kol·bèn pl* corn-on-the-cob

Maismehl *mise·mayl nt* —e cornstarch

Majoran *mah·yo·rahn m* marjoram

Makadam *ma·ka·dam m* tarmac

Makkaroni *ma·ka·rō·nee pl* macaroni

Makler *mahk·lèr m* — broker

Makrele *ma·kray·lè f* —n mackerel

Mal *mal nt* —e time; **das erste Mal** *dass er·stè mahl* the first time

malen *mah·lèn vt* paint

Maler *mah·lèr m* — painter

malerisch *mah·lèr·ish adj* quaint

Malta *mal·ta nt* Malta

Malz *malts nt* malt

man *man pron* one; **man sollte... man zol·tè** one should...; **man sagt, daß... man zahkt dass** they say that... (*people in general*)

Management *ma·nage·ment nt* management

manche(r/s) *man·khè(·khèr/khès) pron* a good many

manchmal *mankh·mal adv* sometimes

Mandarine *man·da·ree·nè f* —n tangerine

Mandel *man·dèl f* —n almond

Mandelentzündung *man·dèl·ent·tsŏŏn·doong f* —en tonsillitis

Mangel *mang·èl m* ⸚ shortage

Manieren *ma·neer·èn pl* manners

Maniküre *ma·nee·kŏŏ·rè f* —n manicure

Mann *man m* ⸚er man; husband

Mannequin *ma·nè·kan nt* —e model (*mannequin*)

männlich *men·likh adj* masculine; male

Mannschaft *man·shaft f* —en team; crew (*of ship, plane*)

Manschette *man·she·tè f* —n cuff (*of shirt*)

Manschettenknopf *man·she·tèn·knopf m* ⸚e cuff link

Mantel *man·tèl m* ⸚ (over)coat

manuell *man·oo·el adj* manual

Märchen *mer·khèn nt* — fairy tale

Margarine *mar·ga·ree·nè f* margarine

Marine *ma·ree·nè f* navy

marineblau *ma·ree·nè·blow adj* navy blue

Mark *mark f* — mark (*currency*)

Marke *mar·kè f* —n brand (*of product*); make; counter (*gambling*); token (*for machine*)

Markenname *mar·kèn·nah·mè m* —n brand name

Marketing *mar·kè·ting nt* marketing; **der Leiter des Marketing** *der lye·tèr dess mar·kè·ting* marketing manager

markieren *mar·kee·rèn vt* mark

Markt *markt m* ⸚e market; **der Markt für X ist gut** *der markt fŏŏr X ist goot* there is a good market for X

Marktforschung *markt·for·shoong f* market research

Marktplatz *markt·plats m ∹e* marketplace

Markttag *markt·tahk m ∹e* market-day

Marktwert *markt·vert m* market value

Marmelade *mar·mè·lah·dè f —n* jam; preserve(s)

Marmor *mar·mor m* marble (*material*)

marokkanisch *ma·ro·kah·nish adj* Moroccan

Marokko *ma·ro·kō nt* Morocco

Marsch *marsh m ∹e* march

marschieren *mar·shee·rèn vi* march

Martini *mar·tee·nee m —s* martini (*Brit*)

Martini-Cocktail *mar·tee·nee kok·tayl m —s* martini (*US*)

März *merts m* March

Marzipan *mar·tsee·pahn nt* marzipan

Marzipanmasse *mar·tsi·pahn·ma·sè f* almond paste

Maschine *ma·shee·nè f —n* machine

maschinegeschrieben *ma·shee·nè·gè·shree·bèn adj* typewritten

Maschinerie *ma·shee·nè·ree f* machinery

Masern *mah·zèrn pl* measles

Maserung *mah·zè·roong f* grain (*in wood*)

Maske *mas·kè f —n* mask

maskieren *mas·kee·rèn vt* mask

Maß *mahs nt —e* measure

Massage *ma·sah·zhè f* massage

Maßband *mahs·bant nt ∹er* tape measure

Maße *mah·sè pl* measurements

Massenproduktion *ma·sèn·prō·dook·tsee·ōn f* mass production

Masseur *ma·sur m* masseur

Masseuse *ma·sur'·zè f —n* masseuse

maßgeschneidert *mahs·gè·shnye·dèrt adj* custom-made; made-to-measure

massieren *ma·see·rèn vt* massage

massiv *ma·seef adj* solid (*not hollow*); in massivem Gold *in ma·see·vèm golt* in solid gold

Maßstab *mahs·shtahp m ∹e* scale (*of map*)

Mastbaum *mast·bowm m ∹e* mast (*ship's*)

Material *ma·tay·ree·ahl nt —ien* material

Mathematik *ma·tay·mah·teek f* mathematics

Matratze *ma·trats·è f —n* mattress

Matrose *ma·trō·zè m —n* sailor

Matte *ma·tè f —n* mat

Mauer *mow·èr f —n* wall (*outside*)

Maul *mowl nt ∹er* mouth (*of animal*)

Maus *mows f ∹e* mouse

mauve *mōv adj* mauve

maximieren *mak·see·mee·rèn vt* maximize

Maximum *mak·see·moom nt* **Maxima** maximum

Mayonnaise *ma·yo·nay·zè f* mayonnaise

Mechaniker *me·khah·ni·kèr m —* mechanic

Medien *may·dee·èn pl* media

Medikament *me·di·ka·ment nt —e* drug; medicine (*pills etc*)

medizinisch *may·di·tseen·ish adj* medical

Meer *mayr nt —e* sea

Meeresfrüchte *may·rès·frōōkh·tè pl* seafood

Meeresspiegel *may·rès·shpee·gèl m* sea level

Mehl *mayl nt* flour

mehr *mayr adj* more; wir haben keine Milch mehr *veer hah·bèn kine·è milkh mayr* we've run out of milk; mehr Käse/Leute *mayr kay·zè/loy·tè* more cheese/people; mehr oder weniger *mayr ō·dèr vay·ni·gèr* more or less; kein Benzin mehr haben* *kine ben·tseen mayr hah·bèn* to be out of gasoline

mehrere *mayr·rè·rè adj* several

Mehrheit *mayr·hite f —en* majority; mit einer Mehrheit von 5 Stimmen gewählt *mit ine·èr mayr·hite fon 5 shti·mèn gè·vaylt* elected by a majority of 5

mehrsprachig *mayr·shprah·khik adj* multilingual

mehrstöckig *mayr·shtur'·kikh adj* multilevel

Mehrwertsteuer *mayr·vert·shtoy·èr f —n* value-added tax

Meile *mile·è f —n* mile

Meilenzahl *mile·èn·tsahl f* mileage

mein(e) *mine(·è) adj* my; mein Vater *mine fah·tèr* my father; meine Mutter *mine·è moo·tèr* my mother; meine Brüder/Schwestern *mine·è brōō·dèr/shve·stèrn* my brothers/sisters

meine(r/s) *mine·è(r/·ès) pron* mine

meinetwegen *mine·èt·vay·gèn adv* for my sake

Meinung *mye·noong f —en* opinion; meiner Meinung nach *mine·èr mye·noong nakh* in my opinion; seine Meinung ändern *zine·è mine·oong en·dèrn* to change one's mind

meiste(r/s) *mye·stè'(·stèr/·stès) pron* most; die meisten Leute *dee mye·stèn loy·tè* most people; die meisten Wagen *dee mye·stèn vah·gèn* the most cars; er hat das meiste *er hat das mye·stè* he has the most

Meister *mye·stèr m —* champion

Meisterstück *mye·stèr·shtōōk nt —e* masterpiece

Melasse *ma·la·sè f* molasses

melden *mel·dèn vt* report (*tell about*); sich bei der Abfertigung melden *zikh bye der ap·fer·ti·goong mel·dèn* to check in (*at airport*)

Melodie *may·lo·dee f —n* tune

Melone *may·lō·nè f —n* melon; derby

Menge *meng·è f —n* quantity; crowd; eine große Menge X *ine·è grō·sè meng·è X* a large amount of X

Mensch *mensh m —en* man (*human race*); person

menschlich *mensh·likh adj* human

Menthol- *men·tōl pref* mentholated

Meringe *me·ring·è f —n* meringue

merkwürdig *merk·vōōr·dikh adj* curious (*strange*)

Messe *me·sè f —n* fair (*commercial*); mass (*church*)

messen* *me·sèn vt/i* measure

Messer *me·sèr nt —* knife

Meßgerät *mess·gè·ret nt —e* gauge (*device*)

Messing *me·sing nt* brass

Metall *may·tal nt —e* metal

Meter *may·tèr m —* meter (*measure*)

Methode *may·tō·dè f —n* method

Methodist *may·tō·dist m —en* Methodist

metrisch *may·trish adj* metric

Metzger *mets·gèr m —* butcher

mexikanisch *mek·si·kah·nish adj* Mexican

Mexiko *mek·si·kō nt* Mexico

mich *mikh pron* me; ich wusch mich *ikh voosh mikh* I washed myself

Miesmuschel *mees·moo·shèl f —n* mussel

Miete *mee·tè f —n* lease; rent

mieten *mee·tèn vt* hire; rent (*house etc*)

Mieter *mee·tèr m —* tenant

Mieterin *mee·tè·rin f —nen* tenant

Mietwagen *meet·vah·gèn m —* rental car

Migräne *mi·gray·nè f —n* migraine

Mikrochip *mee·krö·chip nt —s* microchip

Mikrocomputer *mee·krö·kom·pyoo·tèr m —* microcomputer

Mikrofiche *mee·krö·feesh nt —s* microfiche

Mikrofilm *mee·krö·film m —e* microfilm

Mikrophon *mee·krö·fön m —e* microphone

Mikroprozessor *mee·krö·pro·tses·or m —en* microprocessor

Mikrowellenofen *mee·krö·vel·èn·ö·fèn m —* microwave oven

Milch *milkh f* milk

Milchgeschäft *milkh·gè·sheft nt —e* dairy store

Milchkaffee *milkh·ka·fay m* coffee with milk

Milchmann *milkh·man m ⁼er* milkman

Milchmixgetränk *milkh·miks·gè·trenk nt —e* milkshake

Milchpulver *milkh·pool·vèr nt* dried milk

mild *milt adj* mild

Militärakademie *mi·li·ter·a·ka·day·mee f —n* military academy

militärisch *mi·li·tay·rish adj* military

Milliarde *mi·lee·ar·dè f —n* billion

Milligramm *mi·li·gram nt —* milligram

Milliliter *mi·li·lee·tèr nt —* milliliter

Millimeter *mi·li·may·tèr m —* millimeter

Million *mi·lee·ôn f —en* million

Millionär *mi·lee·ö·nayr m —e* millionaire

millionstel *mi·lee·ön·stèl adj* millionth

Minderheit *min·dèr·hite f —en* minority

minderjährig *min·dèr·yay·rikh adj* under age

minderwertig *min·dèr·ver·tikh adj* inferior; substandard

Mindest- *min·dèst pref* minimum

Mindestpreis *min·dèst·prise m —e* upset price

Mineralwasser *mi·nay·rahl·va·sèr nt* mineral water

Minestrone *mi·nes·trö·ne f* minestrone (soup)

Minicomputer *mi·ni·kom·pyoo·tèr m —* minicomputer

Minimum *mi·ni·moom nt* **Minima** minimum

Minirock *mi·ni·rok m ⁼e* miniskirt

Minister *mi·nis·tèr m —* minister (in government)

Ministerium *min·is·tay·ree·oom nt —rien* ministry (government)

minus *mee·noos prep* minus; **bei 2 Grad minus** *bye 2 grat mee·noos* at minus 2 degrees

Minute *mi·noo·tè f —n* minute

Minze *min·tsè f* mint (*herb*)

mir *meer pron* (to) me; **geben Sie es mir** *gay·bèn zee es meer* give it to me

Mischung *mi·shoong f —en* mixture

mißbilligen *mis·bi·li·gèn vt* disapprove of

mit *mit prep* with

mit|bringen* *mit·bring·èn vt* bring (*person*)

Miteigentum *mit·ige·èn·toom nt* joint ownership

mitfühlend *mit·füö·lènt adj* sympathetic

Mitgefühl *mit·gè·füöl nt* sympathy

Mitglied *mit·gleet nt —er* member; **Mitglied werden* von** *mit·gleet ver·dèn fon* to join (*club*)

Mitleid *mit·lite nt* pity

zum Mitnehmen *tsoom mit·nay·mèn adv* carryout (*food*)

mit|nehmen* *mit·nay·mèn vt* give a ride to

Mittag *mi·tahk m* midday

Mittagessen *mi·tak·e·sèn nt —* lunch

mittags *mi·tahks adv* at midday

Mittagsstunde *mi·taks·shtoon·dè f —n* lunch hour

Mitte *mi·tè f —n* middle; **genau in der Mitte** *gè·now in der mi·tè* right in the middle

Mittel *mi·tèl nt —* means; **das empfängnisverhütende Mittel** *emp·feng·nis·fer·hüö·tèn·dè mi·tèl* contraceptive; **ein Mittel gegen** *ine mi·tèl gay·gèn* a remedy for □ *pl* **die Mittel** *mi·tèl* resources

mittelmäßig *mi·tèl·may·sikh adj* poor (*mediocre*)

Mittelmeer *mi·tèl·mayr nt* the Mediterranean (Sea) □ *pref* **Mittelmeer-** *mi·tèl·mayr* Mediterranean

mittels *mi·tèls prep* by means of

Mittelstreifen *mi·tèl·shtrye·fèn m —* median strip

Mittelwelle *mi·tèl·ve·lè f* medium wave

mitten *mi·tèn adv* in the middle; **mitten in der Nacht** *mi·tèn in der nakht* in the middle of the night

Mitternacht *mi·tèr·nakht f* midnight; **um Mitternacht** *oom mi·tèr·nakht* at midnight

mittlere(r/s) *mit·lè·rè(·rèr/·rès) adj* medium; **in den mittleren Jahren** *in dayn mit·lè·rèn yah·rèn* middle-aged

Mittwoch *mit·vokh m* Wednesday

Mixer *mik·sèr m —* mixer

Möbel *mur'·bèl pl* furniture

Möbelstück *mur'·bèl·shtöök nt —e* piece of furniture

Möbelwagen *mur'·bèl·vah·gèn m —* moving van

möblieren *mur'·blee·rèn vt* furnish (*room etc*)

Mode *mö·dè f —n* fashion

Modell *mo·del nt —e* model

modern *mo·dern adj* modern

modernisieren *mo·dern·ee·zee·rèn vt* modernize

Modeschmuck *mö·dè·shmook m* costume jewelry

Modeschöpfer *mö·dè·shur'p·fèr m —* designer (*of clothes*)

Modeschöpferin *mö·dè·shur'p·fè·rin f —nen* designer (*of clothes*)

modisch *mö·dish adj* fashionable

mögen* *mur'·gèn vt* like; **ich möchte zu einem Arzt** *ikh mur'kh·tè tsoo ine·èm artst* I want to see a doctor; **möchten Sie eine Tasse Kaffee?** *mur'kh·tèn zee ine·è ta·sè ka·fay* would you like a cup of coffee?; **ich möchte gehen** *ikh mur'kh·tè gay·èn* I'd like to go

möglich *mur'g·likh adj* possible; **alles Mögliche tun*** *a·lès mur'g·li·khè toon* to do all one possibly can

Möglichkeit *mur'g·likh·kite f —en* possibility

Mohair *mö·hayr m* mohair

mohammedanisch *mo·ham·e·dah·nish adj* Muslim

Möhre *mur'·rè f* —**n** carrot

Mole *mô·lè f* —**n** jetty

Molekül *mo·lay·kool nt* —**e** molecule

Moment *mo·ment m* —**e** moment

Monaco *mô·na·kô nt* Monaco

Monat *mô·nat m* —**e** month

monatlich *mô·nat·likh adj* monthly

Monatszeitschrift *mô·nats·tsite·shrift f* —**en** monthly

Mönch *mur'nkh m* —**e** monk

Mond *mônt m* —**e** moon

monetär *mo·nay·tayr adj* monetary

Monitor *mo·ni·tor m* —**en** monitor (*TV*)

Mono- *mô·nô pref* mono; **in Mono** *in mô·nô* in mono

Monopol *mo·no·pôl nt* —**e** monopoly

Montag *môn·tahk m* Monday

Montageband *mon·tah·zhè·bant nt* —**er** assembly line

montieren *mon·tee·rèn vt* assemble (*parts of machine*)

Moped *mô·pet m* —**s** moped

Mord *mort m* —**e** murder

Mörder *mur·dèr m* —**-** killer

Mörderin *mur·dè·rin f* —**nen** killer

morgen *mor·gèn adv* tomorrow □ *m* **der Morgen** *mor·gèn* morning

Morgendämmerung *mor·gèn·de·mè·roong f* dawn

Morgenrock *mor·gèn·rok m* —**-e** dressing gown

Moschee *mo·shay f* —**n** mosque

Moselwein *mo·zèl·vine m* —**e** moselle (*wine*)

Moskau *mos·kow nt* Moscow

Moskitonetz *mos·kee·tô·nets nt* —**e** mosquito net

Moslem *mos·lem m* —**s** Muslim

Motel *mô·tel nt* —**s** motel

Motor *mô·tor m* —**en** motor; engine

Motorboot *mô·tôr·bôt nt* —**e** motorboat

Motorhaube *mô·tôr·how·bè f* —**n** hood (*of car*)

Motorjacht *mô·tôr·yakht f* —**en** cabin cruiser

Motorrad *mô·tôr·rat nt* —**-er** motorbike

Motorradfahrer *mô·tôr·rat·fah·rèr m* —**-** motorcyclist

Motorroller *mô·tôr·ro·lèr m* —**-** scooter

Motorschaden *mô·tor·shah·dèn m* —**-** engine trouble

müde *mōō·dè adj* tired

muffig *moo·fikh adj* stale (*smell, taste*)

Mühe *mōō·è f* bother (*effort*); **machen Sie sich bitte keine Mühe** *ma·khèn zee zikh bi·tè kine·è mōō·è* please don't bother; **sich mit etwas viel Mühe geben*** *zikh mit et·vass feel mōō·è gay·bèn* to take trouble over something

Mühle *mōō·lè f* —**n** mill

Mull *mool m* lint

Mülleimer *mōōl·ime·èr m* —**-** bin (*for refuse*)

Müllplatz *mōōl·plats m* —**-e** dump (*for rubbish*)

multinational *mool·ti·na·tsee·o·nahl adj* multinational

Multiplikation *mool·ti·pli·ka·tsee·ôn f* —**en** multiplication

multiplizieren *mool·ti·pli·tseer·èn vt* multiply; **9 mit 4 multiplizieren** *9 mit 4 mool·ti·pli·tseer·èn* to multiply 9 by 4

Mumps *moomps m* mumps

München *mün·khèn nt* Munich

Mund *moont m* —**-er** mouth

mündlich *mōōnt·likh adj* verbal (*agreement*)

munter *moon·tèr adj* lively

Münze *mōōn·tsè f* —**n** coin

Murmel *moor·mèl f* —**n** marble (*ball*)

Museum *moo·zay·oom nt* **Museen** museum

Musik *moo·zeek f* music

Musikbox *moo·zeek·box f* —**en** jukebox

Musiker *moo·zi·kèr m* —**-** musician

Muskel *moos·kèl m* —**n** muscle

müssen *mōō·sèn vi* to have to; **ich muß gehen** *ikh moos gay·èn* I need to go; I must go; **sie muß es tun** *zee moos ess toon* she has to do it; **er müßte gewinnen** *er mōōs·tè gè·vi·nèn* he ought to win

Muster *moo·stèr nt* —**-** sample (*of goods*); design (*pattern*)

Mut *moot m* nerve; courage

mutig *moo·tikh adj* brave

Mutter *moo·tèr f* —**-** mother

Mutterleib *moo·tèr·lipe m* womb

Mutti *moo·tee f* —**s** mom(my)

MwSt *may·vert·shtoy·èr f* value-added tax

N

nach *nakh prep* after; according to; **nach London gehen*** *nakh lon·don gay·èn* to go to London; **nach Frankreich** *nakh frank·ryekh* to France; **mit etwas nach jemandem werfen*** *mit et·vass nakh yay·man·dèm ver·fèn* to throw something at someone; **wie kommt man nach London?** *vee komt man nakh lon·don* which is the way to London?; **nach London abreisen** *nakh lon·don ap·rye·zèn* to leave for London

nach|ahmen *nakh·ah·mèn vt* copy; imitate

Nachbar *nakh·bar m* —**n** neighbor

Nachbarin *nakh·ba·rin f* —**nen** neighbor

Nachbestellung *nakh·bè·shte·loong f* —**en** repeat order

nachdem *nakh·daym conj* after; **nachdem wir weggegangen waren** *nakh·daym veer vek·gè·gang·èn vah·rèn* after we had left

nach|denken* *nakh·deng·kèn vi* think

nacheinander *nakh·ine·an·dèr adv* one after the other

Nachfrage *nakh·frah·gè f* demand (*for goods*)

nach|geben* *nakh·gay·bèn vt* give in (*yield*)

nach|gehen* *nakh·gay·èn vi* lose (*clock, watch*); **meine Uhr geht nach** *mine·è oor gayt nakh* my watch is slow

nachher *nakh·her adv* afterwards

Nachlaß *nakh·las m* —**-e** reduction (*in price*); **3% Nachlaß** *3% nakh·las* 3% off

nach|laufen* *nakh·low·fèn vi* run after

Nachmittag *nakh·mi·tahk m* —**e** afternoon

nachmittags *nakh·mi·tahks adv* p.m.; in the afternoon

per Nachnahme *per nakh·nah·mè adv* cash on delivery

Nachname *nakh·nah·mè m* —**n** surname

nach|prüfen *nakh·prōō·fèn vt* check

Nachricht *nakh·rikht f* —**en** note (*letter*); message

Nachrichten *nakh·rikh·tèn pl* news

nach|schlagen* *nakh·shlah·gĕn vt* look up (*word*); nach|schlagen* in *nakh·shlah·gĕn in* refer to (*consult*)

nach|schneiden* *nakh·shnye·dĕn vt* trim (*hair*)

nach|sehen* *nakh·zay·ĕn vt* check (*train time etc*)

nach|senden* *nakh·zen·dĕn vt* redirect; forward (*letter*)

nächste(r/s) *nekh·stĕ(·stĕr/·stĕs) adj* next (*stop, station, week*); der nächste Verwandte *nekh·stĕ fer·van·tĕ* next of kin

Nacht *nakht f* ̈e night; von einer Nacht *fon ine·ĕr nakht* overnight (*a stay*); über Nacht *ōō·bĕr nakht* overnight

Nachteil *nakh·tile m* —e disadvantage; handicap; im Nachteil *im nakh·tile* at a disadvantage

Nachtfalter *nakht·fal·tĕr m* — moth

Nachthemd *nakht·hemt nt* —en nightgown

Nachtisch *kline* m dessert

Nachtlokal *nakht·lō·kahl nt* —e night club

Nachtportier *nakht·por·tyay m* —s night porter

Nackenrolle *na·kĕn·ro·lĕ f* —n bolster

nackt *nakt adj* nude; naked; bare (*person, head*)

Nadel *nah·dĕl f* —n needle

Nagel *nah·gĕl m* ̈ nail; stud; der kleine Nagel *kline·ĕ nah·gĕl* tack

Nagelbürste *nah·gĕl·bōōr·stĕ f* —n nailbrush

Nagelfeile *nah·gĕl·fye·lĕ f* —n nailfile; emery board

Nagellack *nah·gĕl·lack m* —e nail polish

nageln *nah·gĕln vt* nail

Nagelnecessaire *nah·gĕl·nay·se·sayr nt* —s manicure set

nah *nah adv* near

nahe *nah·ĕ adj* close (*near*)

Nähe *nay·ĕ f* proximity; in der Nähe des Hauses *in der nay·ĕ des how·zĕs* near (to) the house; mit Läden in günstiger Nähe *mit lay·dĕn in gōōn·sti·gĕr nay·ĕ* convenient to stores; in der Nähe von *in der nay·ĕ fon* close to; in unmittelbarer Nähe des Meeres *in oon·mi·tĕl·bah·rĕr nay·ĕ dess me·rĕs* within easy reach of the sea; in der Nähe *in der nay·ĕ* nearby

nahen *nah·ĕn vi* approach (*season*)

nähen *nay·ĕn vt* sew

Nahe Osten *nah·ĕ os·tĕn m* Middle East

sich nähern *zikh nay·ĕrn vr* approach (*person*); sich einem Ort nähern *zikh ine·ĕm ort nay·ĕrn* to approach a place

Nähmaschine *nay·ma·shee·nĕ f* —n sewing machine

Name *nah·mĕ m* —n name; im Namen von *im nah·mĕn fon* on behalf of

Narbe *nar·bĕ f* —n scar

Narkose *nar·kō·zĕ f* —n anesthetic

Nase *nah·zĕ f* —n nose

Nasenbluten *nah·zĕn·bloo·tĕn nt* nosebleed

naß *nass adj* wet (*clothes*)

Naßmop *nas·mop m* —s mop

Nation *na·tsee·ōn f* —en nation

national *na·tsee·o·nahl adj* national

Nationalhymne *na·tsee·o·nahl·hōōm·nĕ f* —n national anthem

Nationaltracht *na·tsee·o·nahl·trakht f* —en national dress

Natur *na·toor f* nature □ *pref* Natur-

na·toor natural (*connected with nature*)

Naturjoghurt *na·toor·yō·goort nt* plain yogurt

natürlich *na·tōōr·likh adj* natural □ *adv* naturally; of course

Nebel *nay·bĕl m* — mist; fog

Nebellampe *nay·bĕl·lam·pĕ f* —n fog light

neben *nay·bĕn prep* by (*next to*); beside □ *pref* Neben- *nay·bĕn* minor (*road*)

Nebenanschluß *nay·bĕn·an·shloos m* ̈e extension (*phone*)

neblig *nay·blikh adj* foggy

Neffe *ne·fĕ m* —n nephew

Negativ *ne·ga·teef nt* —e negative (*of photo*)

nehmen* *nay·mĕn vt* take (*remove, acquire*); nehmen Sie sich *nay·mĕn zee zikh* help yourself; nehmen Sie Zucker? *nay·mĕn zee tsoo·kĕr* do you take sugar?

Neid *nite m* envy

neidisch *nye·dish adj* envious

sich neigen *zikh nye·gĕn vr* lean

Neigung *nye·goong f* —en slope (*angle*)

nein *nine adv* no (*as answer*)

Nelke *nel·kĕ f* —n carnation

nennen* *nen·ĕn vt* quote (*price*)

Nennwert *nen·vert m* par (*business*); über dem Nennwert *ōō·bĕr daym nen·vert* above par

Neonbeleuchtung *nay·on·bĕ·loykh·toong f* strip-lighting

Neonröhre *nay·on·rur·rĕ f* —n fluorescent light

Nerv *nerf m* —en nerve

Nervenzusammenbruch *ner·fĕn·tsoo·za·mĕn·brookh m* ̈e nervous breakdown

Nerz *nerts m* mink (*fur*)

Nerzmantel *nerts·man·tĕl m* ̈ mink coat

Nest *nest nt* —er nest

nett *net adj* nice

Netto- *ne·tō pref* net (*income, price*)

Nettogewicht *ne·tō·gĕ·vikht nt* —e net weight

Nettolohn *ne·tō·lōn m* take-home pay

Netz *nets nt* —e net

neu *noy adj* new

Neue(r) *noy·ĕ(·ĕr) m/f* —n recruit

neuer *noy·ĕr adj* later (*version*)

Neu(e)ste(s) *noy·(ĕ·)stĕ(s) nt* — the latest news □ *adj* neueste(r/s) *noy·ĕ·stĕ(·stĕr/·stĕs*) recent

neugierig *noy·gee·rikh adj* curious (*inquisitive*)

Neujahrstag *noy·yahrs·tahk m* —e New Year's Day

neulich *noy·likh adv* the other day

neun *noyn num* nine

neunte(r/s) *noyn·tĕ(·tĕr/·tĕs) adj* ninth

neunzehn *noyn·tsayn num* nineteen

neunzig *noyn·tsikh num* ninety

neutral *noy·trahl adj* neutral

nicht- *nikht pref* non- □ *adv* nicht *nikht* not; er hat es nicht getan *er hat es nikht gĕ·tahn* he did not do it; Sie kennen ihn, nicht wahr? *zee ke·nĕn een nikht vahr* you know him, don't you?

Nichte *nikh·tĕ f* —n niece

Nichterscheinen *nikht·er·shye·nĕn nt* absenteeism

Nichtraucher *nikht·row·khĕr m* — nonsmoker (*person*)

Nichtraucherabteil *nikht·row·khĕr·ap·tile nt* —e nonsmoker (*compartment*)

nichts *nikhts pron* nothing; ich kann nichts sehen *ikh kan nikhts zay·èn* I can't see anything; ich kann nichts dafür *ikh kan nikhts da·fōōr* I can't help it

nicken *ni·kèn vi* nod

Nickerchen *ni·kèr·khèn nt* — nap (*sleep*)

nie *nee adv* never

nieder|knien *nee·dèr·knee·èn vi* to kneel down

Niederlande *nee·dèr·lan·dè pl* Low Countries

nieder|setzen *nee·dèr·zet·sèn vt* put down

niedlich *neet·lich adj* sweet (*cute, pretty*)

niedrig *need·rikh adj* low

niedriger *nee·dri·gèr adj* lower

Niedrigwasser *nee·drikh·va·ser nt* low tide

niemand *nee·mant pron* no one; nobody; ich sehe niemanden *ikh zay·è nee·man·dèn* I can't see anybody

Niere *nee·rè f —n* kidney

Nierenfett *nee·rèn·fet nt* suet

Nieselregen *nee·zèl·ray·gèn m* drizzle

Niesen *nee·zèn nt* sneeze □ *vi* niesen *nee·zèn* sneeze

nirgends *nir·gènts adv* nowhere; ich kann es nirgends sehen *ikh kan ess nir·gènts zay·èn* I can't see it anywhere

Niveau *nee·vō nt —s* grade

noch *nokh adv* still (*up to this time*); yet; sogar noch schneller *zō·gar nokh shne·lèr* even faster; ist noch Suppe da? *ist nokh zoo·pè dah* is there any more soup?; noch nicht *nokh nikht* not yet; ich möchte noch etwas *ikh mur'kh·tè nokh et·vass* I'd like (some) more; noch einmal *nokh ine·mahl* again; noch ein Bier, bitte *ine beer bi·tè* another beer please!

Nockenwelle *no·kèn·ve·lè f —n* camshaft

nominell *no·mi·nel adj* nominal (*fee*)

Nonne *no·nè f —n* nun

Nordamerika *nort·a·may·ri·ka nt* North America

Norden *nor·dèn m* north

nördlich *nurt·likh adv* north □ *adj* northern

Nordosten *nort·o·stèn m* northeast

Nordpol *nort·pōl m* North Pole

Nordsee *nort·zay f* North Sea

Nordwesten *nort·ve·stèn m* northwest

Norm *norm f —en* standard

normal *nor·mahl adj* normal; regular (*usual, size*) □ *pref* Normal- *nor·mahl* standard (*size*)

normalerweise *nor·mah·lèr·vye·zè adv* normally (*usually*)

Not *nōt f —e* need

Notausgang *nōt·ows·gang m —e* emergency exit

Notbremse *nōt·brem·zè f —n* emergency brake

Note *nō·tè f —n* note (*music*); mark (*in school*)

Notfall *nōt·fal m —e* emergency

notieren *nō·tee·rèn vt* list

nötig *nur'·tikh adj* necessary

Notiz *nō·teetz f —en* memo(randum)

Notlandung *nōt·lan·doong f —en* emergency landing

notwendig *nōt·ven·dikh adj* essential (*necessary*)

Nougat *noo·gat m* nougat

November *nō·vem·bèr m* November

nüchtern *nōōkh·tèrn adj* sober

Nudelholz *noo·dèl·holts nt —er* rolling pin

Nudeln *noo·dèln pl* pasta; noodles

Null *nool f* nil; zero; nought □ *adj* null und nichtig *nool oont nikh·tikh* null and void

Nummer *noo·mèr f —n* act (*at circus etc*)

Nummernschild *noo·mèrn·shilt nt —er* license plate

nur *noor adv* only; nicht nur *nikht noor* not only; es war nur ein Fehler *ess vahr noor ine fay·lèr* it was just a mistake; es sind nur 4 da *ess zint noor 4 dah* there are only 4; nur zu! *noor tsoo* go ahead!

Nuß *noos f —e* nut

Nutzen *noot·sèn m —* use; wir ziehen keinen Nutzen daraus *veer tsee·èn kine·èn noot·sèn dah·rows* it's of no benefit (to us)

nützlich *nōōts·likh adj* useful

nutzlos *noots·lōs adj* useless

Nylon *nye·lon nt* nylon

O

ob *op conj* whether; so tun*, als ob *zō toon als op* to pretend

oben *ō·bèn adv* upstairs; overhead; this side up; oben sehen Sie... *ō·bèn zay·èn zee* above, you can see...; dort oben *dort ō·bèn* up there

Ober *ō·bèr m —* waiter

obere(r/s) *ō·bè·rè(·èr/·ès) adj* upper; top; das obere Teil *ō·bè·rè tile* top (*of ladder*)

Oberfläche *ō·bèr·fle·khè f —n* top (*of table*); surface

Oberschule *ō·bèr·shoo·lè f —n* high school

obskur *op·skoor adj* obscure

Obst *ōpst nt* fruit

Obstgarten *ōpst·gar·tèn m —* orchard

Obstsalat *ōpst·za·laht m —e* fruit salad

obwohl *op·vōl conj* although; obwohl Sie denken könnten... *op·vōl zee deng·kèn kur'n·tèn* though you may think...

oder *ō·dèr conj* or; er ist nicht gekommen, oder? *er ist nikht gè·ko·mèn ō·dèr* he didn't come, did he?

Ofen *ō·fèn m —* oven

offen *o·fèn adj* open

offensichtlich *o·fèn·zikht·likh adj* obvious □ *adv* obviously; apparently

öffentlich *ur'f·ènt·likh adj* public; die öffentliche Hand *ur'f·ènt·li·khè hant* public sector; der öffentliche Sector *ur'·fènt·li·khè zek·tōr* public sector

Öffentlichkeit *ur'·fènt·likh·kite f* public; in der Öffentlichkeit *in der ur'·fènt·likh·kite* in public

offiziell *o·fee·tsee·el adj* official

Offizier *o·fee·tseer m —e* officer (*in army etc*)

öffnen *ur'f·nèn vt* open (*window etc*); undo

oft *oft adv* often; wie oft? *vee oft* how many times?

ohne *ō·nè prep* without

Ohnmacht *ōn·makht f* faint; in Ohnmacht fallen* *in ōn·makht fa·lèn* to faint

Ohr *ōr nt —en* ear

Ohrenschmalz *ō·rèn·shmalts nt* wax (*in ear*)

Ohrenschmerzen *ō·rèn·shmer·tsèn pl* earache

Ohrring *ōr·ring m —e* earring

Ohrwatten *ōr·va·tèn pl* earplugs

okay ō·kay *adv* O.K., okay (*agreement*)

Oktober ok·tō·bèr *m* October

Öl url'l *nt* —e oil

Ölbohrinsel url'l·bōr·in·zèl *f* —n oil-rig

Ölfilter url'l·fil·tèr *nt* — oil filter

Olive o·lee·vè *f* —n olive

Olivenöl o·lee·vèn·url'l *nt* —e olive oil

Ölmeßstab url'l·mess·shtahp *m* —e dip-stick

Öltanker url'l·tang·kèr *m* — oil tanker

Ölwanne url'l·va·nè *f* —n oil pan (*in car*)

Omelett o·mè·let *nt* —s omelet

Onkel ong·kèl *m* — uncle

OPEC-Staaten ō·pek·shtah·tèn *pl* OPEC

Oper ō·pèr *f* —n opera

Operation o·pay·ra·tsee·ōn *f* —en operation

Opfer op·fèr *nt* — victim (*of accident etc*)

Optiker op·ti·kèr *m* — optician

optimistisch op·tee·mis·tish *adj* optimistic

Orange ō·ran·zhè *f* —n orange □ *adj* orange ō·ran·zhè orange

Orangeade ō·ran·zhah·dè *f* orangeade

Orangenmarmelade ō·ran·zhèn·mar·me·la·dè *f* marmalade

Orangensaft ō·ran·zhèn·zaft *m* orange juice

Orchester or·kes·tèr *m* — orchestra

Orchestersitze or·kes·tèr·zit·sè *pl* orchestra (*in theater*)

ordentlich or·dènt·likh *adj* tidy (*person*); neat; er machte es ganz ordentlich *er makh·tè ess gants or·dènt·likh* he did it all right (*satisfactorily*)

ordnen ort·nèn *vt* put in order

Ordnung ort·noong *f* order; nicht in Ordnung *nikht in ort·noong* to go wrong (*machine*); er ist in Ordnung *er ist in ort·noong* he's all right (*safe, fit*); das ist in Ordnung *dass ist in ort·noong* it's OK

Organisation or·ga·nee·za·tsee·ōn *f* —en organization

organisieren or·ga·nee·zee·rèn *vt* organize

Orgel or·gèl *f* —n organ (*instrument*)

orientalisch o·ree·en·tah·lish *adj* oriental

sich orientieren zikh ō·ree·en·tee·rèn *vr* to take one's bearings

Original- o·ree·gee·nahl *pref* original (*earliest*) □ *nt* das Original o·ree·gee·nahl original

originell o·ree·gee·nel *adj* original (*creative*)

Orkan or·kahn *m* —e hurricane

Ort ort *m* —e place; an Ort und Stelle *an ort oont shte·lè* on the spot

örtlich urt·likh *adj* local

Ortsgespräch orts·gè·shprekh *nt* —e local call (*on phone*)

Osten os·tèn *m* east; der Ferne Osten *fer·nè os·tèn* the Far East; nach Osten *nakh os·tèn* east

Osterei ōs·tèr·eye *nt* —er Easter egg

Osterglocke ō·stèr·glo·kè *f* —n daffodil

Ostern ōs·tèrn *nt* Easter; zu Ostern *tsoo ōs·tèrn* at Easter

Österreich ur'·stè·ryekh *nt* Austria

österreichisch ur'·stè·rye·khish *adj* Austrian

östlich ur'st·likh *adj* eastern

oval o·val *adj* oval

Overall ō·ver·ol *m* —s overalls

Ouvertüre ō·ver·tōō·rè *f* —n overture

Ozean ō·tsay·ahn *m* —e ocean

P

Paar pahr *nt* —e pair; couple (*persons*); ein Paar Schuhe *ine pahr shoo·è* a pair of shoes; ein paar *ine pahr* a couple of (*a few*); ein paar Äpfel *ine pahr ep·fèl* some apples

Päckchen pek·khèn *nt* — packet

packen pa·kèn *vt* grab; seinen Koffer packen *zine·èn ko·fèr pa·kèn* to pack one's suitcase

Packpapier pak·pa·peer *nt* wrapping paper

Paddel pa·dèl *nt* — paddle (*oar*)

Page pah·zhè *m* —n pageboy

Paket pa·kayt *nt* —e parcel; packet

Palast pa·last *m* —e palace

Palästina pa·les·tee·na *nt* Palestine

palästinensisch pa·les·ti·nen·zish *adj* Palestinian

Palme pal·mè *f* —n palm-tree

Pampelmuse pam·pèl·moo·zè *f* —n grapefruit

Pampelmusensaft pam·pèl·moo·zèn·zaft *m* grapefruit juice

Panik pah·nik *f* panic; in Panik geraten[*] *in pah·nik gè·rah·tèn* to panic

Panne pa·nè *f* —n breakdown (*of car*); eine Panne haben[*] *ine·è pa·nè hah·bèn* to break down (*car*)

Panzer pan·tsèr *m* — tank (*military*)

Papa pa·pa *m* —s dad(dy)

Papier pa·peer *nt* —e paper; die Papiere *pa·pee·rè* papers (*passport etc*)

Papierkorb pa·peer·korp *m* —e waste paper basket

Papierkrieg pa·peer·kreek *m* red tape

Papiertaschentuch pa·peer·ta·shèn·tookh *nt* —er kleenex; tissue (*handkerchief*)

Pappe pa·pè *f* —n cardboard

Pappel pa·pèl *f* —n poplar

Pappkarton pap·kar·ton *m* —s carton (*box*)

Paprika pa·pree·ka *m* paprika

Paprikaschote pa·pree·ka·shō·tè *f* —n pepper (*capsicum*); die grüne/rote Paprikaschote *grōō·nè/rō·tè pa·pree·ka·shō·tè* green/red pepper

Papst pahpst *m* —e pope

Par par *m* par (*golf*)

Paraffin pa·ra·feen *nt* kerosene

parallel pa·ra·lel *adj* parallel

Parfüm par·fōōm *nt* perfume

Park park *m* —s park

Parka par·ka *m* —s parka

parken par·kèn *vt/i* park; kann man hier parken? *kan man heer par·kèn* can I park here?

Parkett par·ket *nt* stalls (*in theatre*)

Parkhaus park·hows *nt* —er multilevel parking lot

Parklichter park·likht·èr *pl* sidelights (*on car*)

Parkplatz park·plats *m* —e parking lot

Parkscheibe park·shye·bè *f* —n parking disk

Parkuhr park·oo·èr *f* —en parking meter

Parlament par·la·ment *nt* —e parliament

Parlamentswahlen par·la·ments·wah·lèn *pl* general election

Partei par·tye *f* —en party (*political*)

Partie par·tee *f* —n part; eine Partie Tennis *ine·è par·tee te·nis* a game of tennis

Partner part·nèr *m* — associate; partner

Partnerin *part·nèr·in f* —**nen** partner

Party *pahr·tee f* —**s** party (*celebration*)

Paß *pas m* ̈-**e** passport; pass (*in mountains*)

Passage *pa·sah·zhè f* —**n** arcade

Passagier *pa·sa·zheer m* —**e** passenger

Passagierschiff *pa·sa·zheer·shif nt* —**e** liner (*ship*)

passen *pa·sèn vi* fit; suit; **passen zu** (*pa·sèn tsoo*) match; **es paßt (mir) gut** *ess past (meer) goot* it fits (me); **dies paßt gut zu Ihrem Kleid** *dees past goot tsoo ee·rèm klite* this goes with your dress; **paßt Ihnen Donnerstag?** *past ee·nèn do·nèrs·tahk* does Thursday suit you?

passend *pa·sènt adj* proper (*appropriate*)

passieren *pa·see·rèn vi* happen; **was ist ihm passiert?** *vass ist eem pa·seert* what happened to him?

Passiva *pa·see·vah pl* liabilities (*on balance sheet*)

Paßkontrolle *pas·kon·tro·lè f* —**n** passport control

Pastete *pas·tay·tè f* pâté; pie (*meat*)

pasteurisiert *pas·tur·ee·zeert adj* pasteurized

Pastille *pa·sti·lè f* —**n** pastille

Pastinak *pas·tee·nak m* —**e** parsnip

Pate *pah·tè m* —**n** godfather

Patent *pa·tent nt* —**e** patent

Patient *pa·tsee·ent m* —**en** patient

Patientin *pa·tsee·en·tin f* —**nen** patient

Patin *pah·tin f* —**nen** godmother

Patrone *pa·trö·nè f* —**n** cartridge (*for gun*)

Pauschalangebot *pow·shahl·an·gè·böt nt* —**e** package deal

Pauschale *pow·shah·lè f* —**n** flat rate

Pauschalreise *pow·shahl·rye·zè f* —**n** package holiday

Pause *pow·zè f* —**n** pause; break; intermission (*in performance*)

Pazifik *pa·tsee·fik m* Pacific Ocean

Pech *pekh nt* bad luck

Pedal *pay·dahl nt* —**e** pedal

peinlich *pine·likh adj* embarrassing

Peitsche *pye·tshè f* —**n** whip

pellen *pe·lèn vt* peel; **sich pellen** *zikh pe·lèn* peel (*person*)

Pelz *pelts m* fur

Pendelverkehr *pen·dèl·fer·kayr m* shuttle (service) (*airline*)

Pendler *pend·lèr m* —commuter

Penis *pay·nis m* —**se** penis

Penizillin *pe·nee·tsi·leen nt* penicillin

Pension *pen·zee·ön f* —**en** pension (*from company*); boarding house

Penthouse *pent·hows nt* penthouse

Periode *pay·ree·ö·dè f* period (*menstruation*)

Perle *per·lè f* —**n** bead; pearl

persisch *per·zish adj* Persian

Person *per·zön f* —**en** person

Personal *per·zö·nahl nt* staff

Personalabteilung *per·zö·nahl·ap·tile·oong f* —**en** personnel department

Personalchef *per·zö·nahl·shef m* —**s** personnel manager

Personenzug *per·zö·nèn·tsook m* ̈-**e** stopping train

persönlich *per·zur'n·likh adj* personal □ *adv* personally; in person

Perücke *pay·rőő·kè f* —**n** wig

pessimistisch *pe·see·mis·tish adj* pessimistic

Petersilie *pay·tèr·zeel·yè f* parsley

Pfad *pfaht m* —**e** path

Pfannkuchen *pfan·koo·khèn m* — pancake

Pfarrer *pfa·rèr m* — vicar; minister (*of religion*)

Pfeffer *pfe·fèr m* pepper

Pfefferkuchen *pfe·fèr·koo·khèn m* — gingerbread

Pfefferminz *pfe·fèr·mints nt* —**e** (pepper)mint (*confectionery*)

Pfefferminzlikör *pfe·fèr·mints·lee·kur m* —**e** crème de menthe

Pfefferminztee *pfe·fèr·mints·tay m* mint tea

Pfefferstreuer *pfe·fèr·shtroy·èr m* — pepper pot

Pfeife *pfye·fè f* —**n** pipe (*for smoking*); whistle (*object*)

pfeifen* *pfye·fèn vi* whistle

Pfeil *pfile m* —**e** arrow; dart

Pfennig *pfe·nikh nt* —**e** pfennig

Pferd *pfert nt* —**e** horse

Pferderennen *pfer·dè·re·nèn nt* — the races; horse-racing

Pfiff *pfif m* whistle (*sound*)

Pfingsten *pfing·stèn* Whitsun

Pfingstsonntag *pfingst·zon·tahk m* Whitsunday

Pfirsich *pfir·zikh m* —**e** peach

Pflanze *pflant·sè f* —**n** plant

pflanzen *pflant·sèn vt* plant

Pflaster *pflas·tèr m* — bandaid

Pflaume *pflow·mè f* —**n** plum

pflegen *pflay·gèn vt* look after; nurse (*patient*)

Pflicht *pflikht f* —**en** duty (*obligation*)

pflücken *pflőő·kèn vt* pick (*flower*)

Pflug *pflook m* ̈-**e** plow

Pforte *pfor·tè f* —**n** gate (*of garden*)

Pförtner *pfurt·nèr m* — porter (*doorkeeper*)

Pfosten *pfos·tèn m* — post (*pole*)

Pfote *pfo·tè f* —**n** paw

Pfund *pfoont nt* — pound; **das Pfund Sterling** *pfoont ster·ling* sterling

Pfütze *pfőőt·sè f* —**n** puddle

Phantasie *fan·ta·zee f* imagination

Phrase *frah·zè f* —**n** phrase

Physik *főő·zik f* physics

Picke *pi·kè f* —**n** pickaxe

Pickel *pi·kèl m* — pimple

picken *pi·kèn vt* peck

Picknick *pik·nik nt* —**s** picnic; **ein Picknick machen** *ine pik·nik ma·khèn* to go on a picnic

Pier *peer m* —**s** pier

Pik *peek nt* spades (*cards*)

pikant *pi·kant adj* savory (*not sweet*)

Pille *pi·lè f* pill; **die Pille nehmen*** *dee pi·lè nay·mèn* to be on the pill

Pilot *pee·löt m* —**en** pilot

Pils *pils nt* lager

Pilz *pilts m* —**e** mushroom

Pingpong *ping·pong nt* ping-pong

Pinsel *pin·zèl m* — brush (*for painting*)

Pinzette *pin·tse·tè f* —**n** tweezers

Piste *pis·tè f* — runway

Pizza *pit·sa f* **Pizzen** pizza

Plage *plah·gè f* —**n** bother (*nuisance*)

Plakat *pla·kaht nt* —**e** poster

Plakette *pla·ke·tè f* —**n** badge (*of metal*)

Plan *plahn m* ̈-**e** plan; scheme

planen *plah·nèn vt* plan

Planet *pla·nayt m* —**en** planet

Planetarium *pla·nay·tah·ree·oom nt* **Planetarien** planetarium

Planschbecken *plansh·be·kèn nt* — wading pool

Planung *plah·noong f* planning (*economic*)

Plastik *pla·stik nt* plastic □ *pref* Plastik- *pla·stik* plastic

Plastiktüte *pla·stik·tōō·tè f* —n plastic bag; polyethylene bag

plastisch *pla·stish adj* plastic; **die plastische Chirurgie** *pla·sti·shè khee·roor·gee* plastic surgery

Platane *pla·tah·nè f* —n plane (*tree*)

Platin *plah·teen nt* platinum

platt *plat adj* flat

Plattenspieler *pla·tèn·shpee·lèr m* —record-player

Plattform *plat·form f* —en platform

Platz *plats m* —̈e place (*seat*); room (*space*); square (*in town*); court (*tennis etc*); course (*for golf*); field (*for football etc*)

Plätzchen *plets·khèn* — cookie

platzen *plat·sèn vi* bounce (*check*); burst

pleite *plye·tè adj* broke (*penniless*)

Plombe *plom·bè f* —n filling (*in tooth*)

plötzlich *plur·ts·likh adj* sudden

plus *ploos prep* plus

pochiert *po·sheert adj* poached

Pocken *po·kèn pl* smallpox

Podium *pō·dee·oom nt* **Podien** platform (*in hall*)

Poker *pō·kèr nt* poker (*card game*)

Pol *pōl m* —e terminal (*electricity*)

Polaroid- *pō·la·rō·eet pref* Polaroid

Pole *pō·lè m* —n Pole

Polen *pō·lèn nt* Poland

Police *po·lee·sè f* —n policy (*insurance*)

polieren *po·lee·rèn vt* polish

Polin *pō·lin f* —nen Pole

Polio *pō·lee·ō f* polio

Politik *po·li·teek f* policy; politics

Politiker *po·li·ti·kèr m* — politician

politisch *po·li·tish adj* political

Polizei *po·li·tsye f* police

Polizeiauto *po·li·tsye·ow·tō nt* —s police car

Polizeibeamte(r) *po·li·tsye·bè·am·tè(r) m* —n officer (*police*)

Polizeiinspektor *po·li·tsye·in·shpek·tor m* —en inspector (*police*)

Polizeiwache *po·li·tsye·va·khè f* —n police station

Polizist *po·li·tsist m* —en policeman

Polizistin *po·li·tsis·tin f* —nen policewoman

Polnisch *pol·nish nt* Polish □ *adj* polnisch *pol·nish* Polish

Polo *pō·lō nt* polo

Polyäthylen *pō·lōō·e·tōō·layn nt* polyethylene

Polyester *pō·lōō·es·tèr m* polyester

Pommes Frites *pom fret pl* french fried potatoes, french fries

Pony *po·nee nt* —s pony

Ponyfransen *po·nee·fran·zèn pl* fringe (*hair*); bangs

Poolbillard *pool·bil·yart nt* pool (*game*)

Pop *pop adj* pop (*music, art*)

Popcorn *pop·korn nt* popcorn

Popelin *po·pè·leen m* poplin

Popgruppe *pop·groo·pè f* —n pop group

Popkonzert *pop·kon·tsert nt* —e pop concert

Porree *po·ray m* —s leek

Portemonnaie *port·mo·nay nt* —s purse (*for money*)

Portier *por·tee·ay m* —s doorman (*in hotel*)

Portion *por·tsee·ōn f* —en helping

Porto *por·tō nt* postage

Portugal *por·too·gal nt* Portugal

portugiesisch *por·too·gee·zish adj* Portuguese □ *nt* **Portugiesisch** *por·too·gee·zish* Portuguese

Portwein *port·vine m* port (*wine*)

Porzellan *por·tse·lahn nt* —e china; porcelain

positiv *pō·zi·teef adj* positive

Post *post f* mail; post; Post Office; **mit der Post schicken** *mit der post shi·kèn* to mail

Post- *post pref* postal

Postamt *post·amt nt* —̈er post office

Postanweisung *post·an·vye·zoong f* —en money order; postal order

Postbezirk *post·bè·tsirk m* —e zone (*postal*)

Posten *pos·tèn m* — item

Postfach *post·fakh nt* —̈er box number; post-office box

Postkarte *post·kar·tè f* —n postcard

postlagernd *post·lah·gèrnt adv* general delivery

Postleitzahl *post·lite·tsahl f* —en zip code; post-code

Postort *post·ort m* —e postal district

Prag *prahk nt* Prague

prächtig *prekh·tikh adj* splendid

prahlen *prah·lèn vi* boast

praktisch *prak·tish adj* handy (*convenient*); practical

Prämie *pray·mee·è f* —n premium; bonus (*on salary*)

Präsident *pre·zi·dent m* —en president (*of country*)

Praxis *prak·sis f* **Praxen** doctor's office

Preis *price m* —e prize; price

Preisangebot *price·an·gè·bōt f* —n quotation (*price*)

Preiselbeere *price·èl·bay·rè f* —n cranberry

Preisklasse *price·kla·sè f* —n price range

Preisliste *price·lis·tè f* —n price list

Premiere *prè·mee·ay·rè f* —n première

Premierminister *prè·mee·ay·mee·nis·tèr m* — prime minister, P.M.

presbyterianisch *pres·bōō·tay·ree·ah·nish adj* Presbyterian

Presse *pre·sè f* press

Pressekampagne *pre·sè·kam·pan·yè f* —n press-campaign

Pressesprecher *pre·sè·shpre·khèr m* — public relations officer

Prestige *pres·tee·zhè nt* prestige

Priester *prees·tèr m* — priest

prima *pree·ma adj* great (*excellent*)

Prinz *prints m* —en prince

Prinzessin *print·ses·in f* —nen princess

Prise *pree·zè f* —n pinch (*of salt etc*)

privat *pree·vaht adj* personal; private □ *adv* in private

Privatbereich *pree·vaht·bè·ryekh m* private sector

Privatklinik *pree·vaht·klee·nik f* —en nursing home

Privatlehrer *pri·vaht·lay·rèr m* — tutor

Privatlehrerin *pri·vaht·lay·rè·rin f* —nen tutor

Privatsekretär *pree·vaht·zay·kray·ter m* —e personal assistant, P.A.

Privatsektor *pree·vaht·zek·tōr m* private sector

Privatunternehmen *pree·vaht·oon·tèr·nay·mèn nt* private enterprise

Privatunternehmertum *pree·vaht·oon·tèr·nay·mèr·toom nt* private enterprise

Privatunterricht *pree·vaht·oon·tèr·rikht m* private lesson

pro *prō prep* per; **pro Stunde** *prō shtoon·dè* per hour; **zweimal pro Tag** *tsvye·mal prō tahk* twice a day; **pro**

Kopf *prŏ kopf* per person; pro Jahr *prŏ yahr* per annum

Probe *prŏ·bĕ f* —n test (*trial, check*); specimen; rehearsal; **auf die Probe stellen** *owf dee prŏ·bĕ shte·lĕn* to test (*ability*); **auf Probe** *owf prŏ·bĕ* on approval

Probeabzug *prŏ·bĕ·ap·tsook m ⁼e* proof (*of photo*)

Probefahrt *prŏ·bĕ·fahrt f* —en test-drive

probieren *prŏ·bee·rĕn vt* taste (*try*); sample (*wine*)

Problem *prŏ·blaym nt* —e problem

Produkt *pro·dookt nt* —e product

Produktion *pro·dook·tsee·ŏn f* —en production; output

Produktionsmittel *pro·dook·tsee·ŏns·mi·tĕl pl* capital goods

Produktivität *pro·dook·tee·vee·tet f* productivity

Produzent *prŏ·doot·sent m* —en producer (*of movie*)

produzieren *prŏ·doot·see·rĕn vt* produce (*movie*)

Professor *prŏ·fe·sor m* —en professor (*in Britain*)

Profiterole *pro·fee·tĕ·rŏl f* —s profiterole

Programm *prŏ·gram nt* —e schedule; program (*brochure, computer*)

programmieren *prŏ·gra·mee·rĕn vt* program □ *nt* **das Programmieren** *prŏ·gra·mee·rĕn* computer programming

Programmierer *prŏ·gra·mee·rĕr m* — programmer (*person*)

Programmiererin *prŏ·gra·mee·rĕr·in f* —nen programmer (*person*)

Projekt *prŏ·yekt nt* —e project (*plan*)

Projektor *prŏ·yek·tor m* —en projector

Promenade *pro·mè·nah·dĕ f* —n promenade (*by sea*)

propagieren *prŏ·pa·gee·rĕn vt* push (*product*)

Propfen *prop·fĕn m* — stopper

Prospekt *prŏ·spekt m* —e prospectus

Prost! *prŏst excl* cheers!

Protein *prŏ·tay·een nt* protein

Protest *prŏ·test m* —e protest

protestantisch *prŏ·tes·tan·tish adj* Protestant

protestieren *prŏ·tes·tee·rĕn vi* protest

Prototyp *prŏ·tŏ·tŏŏp m* —en prototype

Provinz *prŏ·vints f* province (*region*)

Provision *prŏ·vee·zee·ŏn f* —en commission (*sum received*)

provisorisch *pro·vi·zŏ·rish adj* temporary

Prozent *prŏ·tsent nt* per cent; **20 Prozent** *20 prŏ·tsent* 20 per cent

Prozentsatz *prŏ·tsent·zats m ⁼e* percentage

Prozeß *prŏ·tses m* —e process (*method*); trial (*in law*)

prüfen *prü·fĕn vt* inspect; audit; check (*oil, water etc*)

Prüfung *prŏŏ·foong f* —en examination

Psychiater *psŏŏ·khee·ah·tĕr m* — psychiatrist

Psychiaterin *psŏŏ·khee·ah·tè·rin f* —nen psychiatrist

psychiatrisch *psŏŏ·khee·ah·trish adj* psychiatric

Psychologe *psŏŏ·khŏ·lŏ·gĕ m* —n psychologist

Psychologie *psŏŏ·khŏ·lŏ·gee f* psychology

Psychologin *psŏŏ·khŏ·lŏ·gin f* —nen psychologist

psychologisch *psŏŏ·khŏ·lŏ·gish adj* psychological

Publikum *poob·li·koom nt* public

Puder *poo·dèr m* powder (*cosmetic*)

Pullover *poo·lŏ·vèr m* — jersey (*sweater*); pullover

Pulver *pool·vèr nt* powder

Pulverkaffee *pool·vèr·ka·fay m* instant coffee

Pumpe *poom·pè f* —n pump

pumpen *poom·pèn vt* pump

Punkt *poonkt m* —e period (*punctuation*); point (*dot, sport: in score, subject*); full stop; **er antwortete ihm Punkt für Punkt** *er ant·vor·tè·tè eem poonkt fŏŏr poonkt* he answered him point by point

pünktlich *pŏŏnkt·likh adj* on schedule (*train*); punctual

Puppe *poo·pè f* —n doll

pur *poor adj* straight (*drink*)

Püree *pŏŏ·ray nt* purée

Putz *poots m* plaster (*for wall*)

putzen *poot·sèn vt* clean; polish; **sich die Nase putzen** *zikh dee nah·zè poot·sèn* to blow one's nose

Putzfrau *poots·frow f* —en cleaning lady

Puzzle *poo·zèl nt* —s puzzle (*jigsaw*)

Pyjama *pŏŏ·zhah·ma m* —s pajamas

Pyramide *pŏŏ·ra·mee·dè f* —n pyramid

Q

Quadrat *kva·draht nt* —e square; **3 Meter im Quadrat** *3 may·tèr im kva·draht* 3 meters square

quadratisch *kva·drah·tish adj* square

Quadratmeter *kva·draht·may·tèr m* square meter

Qual *kvahl f* —en distress; agony

Qualifikation *kva·li·fi·ka·tsee·ŏn f* —en qualification (*diploma etc*)

sich qualifizieren für *zikh kva·li·fi·tsee·rèn fŏŏr vr* qualify for (*in sports*)

Qualität *kva·li·tayt f* —en quality

Qualitätswaren *kva·li·tayts·vah·rèn pl* quality goods

Qualle *kva·lè f* —n jellyfish

Quarantäne *kva·ran·tay·nè f* —n quarantine; **einen Hund unter Quarantäne stellen** *ine·èn hoont oon·tèr kva·ran·tay·nè shtel·èn* to put a dog in quarantine

Quarz *kvarts m* quartz

Quatsch *kvatch m* rubbish (*nonsense*)

Quelle *kve·lè f* —n spring (*of water*); source

quer *kver adv* diagonally; **wir fuhren quer durch Frankreich** *vayr foo·rèn kvayr doorkh frank·ryekh* we drove across France

Quiche *keesh f* —s quiche

Quittung *kvi·toong f* —en receipt

Quiz *kvis nt* — quiz

R

Rabatt *ra·bat m* —e discount; **auf Rabatt** *owf ra·bat* at a discount

Rabattmarke *ra·bat·mar·kè f* —n trading stamp

Rabbiner *rah·bee·nèr m* — rabbi

Rad *raht nt ⁼er* wheel; bicycle

Radar *ra·dahr nt* radar

Radarfalle *ra·dahr·fa·lè f* —n radar trap

rad|fahren* *raht·fah·rèn vi* cycle □ *nt*
das Radfahren *raht·fah·rèn* cycling
Radfahrer *raht·fah·rèr m* — cyclist
Radfahrerin *raht·fah·rè·rin f* —**nen**
cyclist
Radiergummi *ra·deer·goo·mi m* —**s**
eraser
Radieschen *ra·dees·khèn nt* — radish
Radio *rah·dee·ō nt* —**s** radio (*radio
set*); im Radio *im rah·dee·ō* on the
radio
Raffinerie *ra·fee·ne·ree f* —**n** refinery
raffinieren *ra·fi·nee·rèn vt* refine
Rahmen *rah·mèn m* — frame (*of pic-
ture*)
Rakete *ra·kay·tè f* —**n** rocket
Rallye *ra·lee f* —**s** rally (*sporting*)
Rampe *ram·pè f* —**n** ramp
Rand *rant m* —**er** verge; border; edge
Rang *rang m* —**e** circle (*in theater*);
rank (*status*); der erste Rang *er·stè
rang* dress circle
rar *rahr adj* scarce
rasch *rash adj* quick
Rasen *rah·zèn m* — lawn (*grass*)
Rasenmäher *rah·zèn·may·èr m* — lawn
mower
Rasentennis *rah·zèn·te·nis nt* lawn ten-
nis
Rasierapparat *ra·zeer·a·pa·raht m* —**e**
shaver; razor
Rasiercreme *ra·zeer·kraym f* —**s** shav-
ing cream
sich rasieren *zikh ra·zee·rèn vr* shave
Rasierklinge *ra·zeer·kling·è f* razor
blade
Rasierpinsel *ra·zeer·pin·zèl m* — shaving brush
Rasierseife *ra·zeer·zye·fè f* —**n** shaving
soap
Rasierwasser *ra·zeer·va·sèr nt* — aftershave (lotion)
Rasse *ra·sè f* —**n** race
Rassen- *ra·sèn pref* racial
Rast *rast f* —**en** rest
Rat *raht m* advice
Rate *rah·tè f* —**n** installment
raten* *rah·tèn vi* guess; advise; jemandem raten*, etwas zu tun *yay·man·
dèm rah·tèn et·vass tsoo toon* to ad-
vise someone to do something
Rathaus *raht·hows nt* —**er** town hall;
city hall
rationalisieren *ra·tsee·ō·na·lee·zee·rèn
vt* rationalize
Rationalisierung *ra·tsee·ō·na·lee·zee·
roong f* —**en** rationalization
Rätsel *ret·sèl nt* — puzzle
Ratte *ra·tè f* —**n** rat
Raub *rowp m* robbery
rauben *row·bèn vt* rob
Rauch *rowkh m* smoke
rauchen *row·khèn vt/i* smoke; rauchen
Sie? *row·khèn zee* do you smoke?
Raucher *row·khèr m* — smoker (*per-
son*)
Raucherabteil *row·khèr·ap·tile nt* —**e**
smoker (*compartment*)
Rauh *row nt* —**s** rough (*golf*) □ *adj*
rauh *row* rough
Raum *rowm m* space (*room*)
räumen *roy·mèn vt* clear (*road*)
Räumlichkeiten *roym·likh·kite·èn pl*
premises
Raumschiff *rowm·shif nt* —**e** space-
craft
Ravioli *ra·vee·ō·lee pl* ravioli
Razzia *ra·tsee·a f* **Razzien** raid (*by
police*)
Reaktion *ray·ak·tsee·ōn f* —**en** reac-
tion

Reaktor *ray·ak·tor m* —**en** reactor
realisieren *ray·a·lee·zee·rèn vt* realize
(*assets*)
Rebe *ray·bè f* —**n** vine
Rebhuhn *rep·hoon nt* —**er** partridge
Rechen *re·khèn m* — rake
Rechenaufgabe *re·khèn·owf·gah·bè f*
—**n** sum (*problem*)
Rechenschieber *rekh·èn·shee·bèr m* —
slide rule
Rechnen *rekh·nèn nt* arithmetic □ *vt/i*
rechnen *rekh·nèn* calculate; rechnen
Sie mit 10 Minuten, um dort hinzukommen *rekh·nèn zee mit 10 mee·
noo·tèn oom dort hin·tsoo·ko·mèn*
allow 10 minutes to get there
Rechner *rekh·nèr m* — calculator
Rechnung *rekh·noong f* —**en** check;
bill (*account*); etwas in Rechnung
stellen *et·vass in rekh·noong shte·lèn*
to make a charge for something
recht *rekht adj* right (*morally good*)
□ *nt* das Recht *rekht* right (*entitle-
ment*); Recht und Ordnung *rekht
oont ort·noong* law and order
Rechte *rekh·tè f* right (*right-hand side*)
□ *adj* rechte(r/s) *rekh·tè(·tèr/·tès*)
right (*not left*)
rechts *rekhts adv* on the right; rechts
ab|biegen* *rekhts ap·bee·gèn* to turn
right; nach rechts *nakh rekhts* to the
right
Rechtsanwalt *rekhts·an·valt m* —**e** lawyer; counselor; attorney
rechtshändig *rekhts·hen·dikh adj* right-
handed
rechtzeitig *rekht·tsye·tikh adv* on time;
gerade noch rechtzeitig *gè·rah·dè
nokh rekht·tsye·tikh* just in time
Rede *ray·dè f* —**n** speech (*oration*);
das ist doch nicht der Rede wert *dass
ist dokh nikht der ray·dè vert* don't
mention it
reden *ray·dèn vi* speak; Unsinn reden
oon·zin ray·dèn to talk nonsense
Reduktion *ray·dook·tsee·ōn f* —**en** reduction
reduzieren *ray·doo·tsee·rèn vt* reduce
reduziert *ray·doo·tseert adj* cut-rate
Reedereivertreter *ray·dè·rye·fer·tray·
tèr m* — shipping agent
Referenz *ray·fay·rents f* —**en** reference (*testimonial*)
reflektieren *ray·flek·tee·rèn vt* reflect
Reformkost *ray·form·kost f* health
foods
Regal *ray·gahl nt* —**e** shelf
Regatta *ray·ga·ta f* **Regatten** regatta
Regel *ray·gèl f* —**n** rule (*regulation*)
regelmäßig *ray·gèl·may·sikh adj* regular
regeln *ray·gèln vt* direct (*traffic*)
Regen *ray·gèn m* rain
Regenbogen *ray·gèn·bō·gèn m* —**¨** rainbow
Regenmantel *ray·gèn·man·tèl m* —**¨** raincoat
Regie *ray·zhee f* —**n** production (*of
play*); die Regie führen bei *dee ray·
zhee föö·rèn bye* to produce (*play*)
regieren *ray·gee·rèn vt* govern (*country*); rule
Regierung *ray·gee·roong f* —**en** government
Regisseur *ray·zhee·sur m* —**e** director
(*of film*); producer (*of play*)
Register *ray·gi·ster nt* — register
regnen *rayg·nèn vi* rain; es regnet *ess
rayg·nèt* it's raining
regnerisch *rayg·nè·risch adj* wet
(*weather, day*); rainy

Reh *ray nt* —e deer
Rehfleisch *ray·flyesh nt* venison
Reibe *rye·bě f* —n grater
reiben* *rye·běn vt* rub; grate (*food*)
reich *ryekh adj* rich; wealthy; **sie sind reicher als wir** *zee zint rye·kher als veer* they are better off than us
Reich *ryekh nt* —e empire
reichen *rye·khěn vt* pass (*hand on: object*); **reicht es?** *ryekht ess* will it do? (*be enough*); **jemandem etwas reichen** *yay·man·děm et·vass rye·khěn* to hand someone something; **reichen Sie mir bitte den Zucker** *rye·khěn zee meer bi·tě dayn tsoo·kěr* please pass the sugar
reichlich *ryekh·likh adj* ample; **danke, das ist reichlich** *dang·kě dass ist ryekh·likh* thank you, that's plenty
Reichtum *ryekh·toom m* wealth
Reichweite *ryekh·vye·tě f* —n range (*of missile*); **außer Reichweite** *ow·sěr ryekh·vye·tě* out of reach
reif *rife adj* ripe; mature (*cheese*)
Reifen *rye·fěn m* — hoop; tire; **der laufflächenerneuerte Reifen** *lowf·fle·khěn·er·noy·ěr·tě rye·fěn* retread
Reifenpanne *rye·fěn·pa·ně f* —n blowout; puncture
Reihe *rye·ě f* —n row; **Sie sind an der Reihe** *zee zint an der rye·ě* it's your turn
Reihenfolge *rye·ěn·fol·gě f* —n order (*in series*)
rein *rine adj* pure
Reinemachefrau *rine·ě·ma·khě·frow f* —en cleaner (*of house etc*)
reinigen *rye·ni·gěn vt* clean; chemisch reinigen *khay·mish rye·ni·gěn* to dry-clean; **einen Anzug reinigen lassen*** *ine·ěn an·tsook rye·ni·gěn la·sěn* to have a suit cleaned
Reinigung *rye·ni·goong f* —en cleaner's; **die chemische Reinigung** *khay·mi·shě rye·ni·goong* dry-cleaner's
Reis *rice m* rice
Reise *rye·zě f* —n trip (*journey*)
Reisebüro *rye·zě·bōō·rō nt* —s travel agency
Reiseführer *rye·zě·fōō·rěr m* — guidebook
Reisen *rye·zěn nt* — travel □ *vi* **reisen** *rye·zěn* travel
Reisende(r) *rye·zěn·dě(·děr) m/f* —n traveler
Reisepaß *rye·zě·pas m* ⁝e passport
Reisescheck *rye·zě·shek m* —s traveler's check
Reisetasche *rye·zě·ta·shě f* —n grip (*case*); carryall
Reiseveranstalter *rye·zě·fer·an·shtal·těr m* — travel agent
Reiseziel *rye·zě·tseel nt* —e destination
reißen* *rye·sěn vi* rip
Reißer *rye·sěr m* — thriller
Reißnagel *rice·nah·gěl m* ⁝ thumbtack
Reißverschluß *rice·fer·shloos m* ⁝e zipper
Reißzwecke *rice·tsve·kě f* —n thumbtack
Reiten *rye·těn nt* riding □ *vt* **reiten*** *rye·těn* to ride; **reiten gehen*** *rye·těn gay·ěn* to go (horseback) riding
Reitpeitsche *rite·pye·tshě f* —n crop (*whip*)
Reiz *ryets m* —e charm
reizend *rye·tsěnt adj* charming
Rekord *ray·kort m* —e record (*in sports*) □ *pref* **Rekord-** *ray·kort* record (*production, crop etc*)

Rektor *rek·tor m* —en principal (*of school etc*)
Rektorin *rek·tō·rin f* —nen principal (*of school etc*)
relativ *ray·la·teef adj* relative
relevant *ray·lay·vant adj* relevant; **relevant für** *ray·lay·vant fōōr* relevant to
Religion *ray·lee·gee·ōn f* —en religion
Remouladensoße *ray·moo·lah·děn·zō·sě f* —n tartar sauce
Rennbahn *ren·bahn f* —en racecourse; track (*sports*)
Rennen *re·něn nt* — race (*sport*)
Rennpferd *ren·pfert nt* —e racehorse
Rennreiter *ren·rye·těr m* — jockey
Rennstrecke *ren·shtre·kě f* —n race track
rentabel *ren·tah·běl adj* profitable; profit-making
Rentabilität *ren·ta·bi·lee·tet f* profitability
Rente *ren·tě f* —n annuity; pension (*from State*); superannuation
Rentenfonds *ren·těn·fong m* — pension fund
Rentner *rent·něr m* — pensioner; retiree
Rentnerin *rent·něr·in f* —nen pensioner; retiree
in Reparatur *in ray·pa·ra·toor adv* under repair
Reparaturwerkstatt *ray·pa·ra·toor·verk·shtat f* ⁝en garage (*service station*)
reparieren *ray·pa·ree·rěn vt* repair
Reportage *ray·por·tah·zhě f* —n report (*in press*)
Reporter *ray·por·těr m* — reporter (*press*)
Republik *ray·poo·bleek f* —en republic
republikanisch *ray·poo·bli·kah·nish adj* republican
Reserven *ray·zer·věn pl* reserves
Reserverad *ray·zer·vě·raht nt* ⁝er spare wheel
reservieren lassen* *ray·zer·vee·rěn la·sěn vt* book (*seat*)
Reservierung *ray·zer·vee·roong f* —en reservation
Rest *rest m* —e remainder; **der ganze Rest** *der gan·tsě rest ist* the rest; **der Rest ist für Sie!** *der rest ist fōōr zee* keep the change!
Restaurant *res·tō·rant nt* —s restaurant
Resultat *ray·zool·taht nt* —e result
retten *re·těn vt* save (*person*); rescue
Rettung *re·toong f* —en rescue
Rettungsboot *re·toongs·bōt nt* —e lifeboat
Rettungsgürtel *re·toongs·gōōr·těl m* — lifebelt
Rettungsschwimmer *re·toongs·shvi·měr m* — lifeguard
revidieren *ray·vi·dee·rěn vt* revise (*estimate etc*)
Revolution *ray·vo·loo·tsee·ōn f* —en revolution (*political*)
Revue *rě·vōō f* —n revue
Rezept *ray·tsept nt* —e prescription; recipe
Rezeption *re·tsep·tsee·ōn f* —en reception desk
Rezession *ray·tse·see·ōn f* —en recession
R-Gespräch *er·gě·shprekh nt* —e collect call
Rhabarber *ra·bar·běr m* rhubarb
Rhein *rine m* Rhine
Rheinwein *rine·vine m* —e Rhine wine

Rheumatismus *roy·ma·tis·moos m* rheumatism

Rhone *rō·nè f* Rhone

Rhythmus *rōōt·moos m* **Rhythmen** rhythm

richten *rikh·tèn vt* point (*gun*); ein Gewehr auf jemanden richten *ine gè·vayr owf yay·man·dèn rikh·tèn* to aim a gun at someone

Richter *rikh·tèr m* — judge

richtig *rikh·tikh adj* correct (*accurate*); right; proper; es ist die richtige Zeit für Erdbeeren *ess ist dee rikh·ti·gè tsite fōōr ert·bay·rèn* strawberries are in season; ja, das ist richtig *ya dass ist rikh·tikh* yes, that's right □ *adv* richtig *rikh·tikh* properly

Richtung *rikh·toong f* —en direction; in Richtung X *in rikh·toong X* in the direction of X

riechen* *ree·khèn vt/i* smell; nach Knoblauch riechen* *nakh knop·lowkh ree·khèn* to smell of garlic

Riegel *ree·gèl m* — bolt; latch

Riemen *ree·mèn m* — strap

Riese *ree·zè m* —n giant

riesig *ree·zikh adj* massive

Rindfleisch *rint·flyesh nt* beef

Rindvieh *rint·fee nt* cattle

Ring *ring m* —e ring

Ringen *ring·èn nt* wrestling

Ringrichter *ring·rikh·tèr m* — referee (*boxing*)

Ringstraße *ring·shtrah·sè f* —n beltway

Rippchen *rip·khèn nt* — spare rib

Rippe *ri·pè f* —n rib

Risiko *ree·zi·kō nt* **Risiken** risk

riskieren *ris·kee·rèn vt* risk

Risotto *ri·zo·tō m* —s risotto

Riß *ris m* —e tear; split

Ritt *rit m* —e ride (*on horse*)

Rivale *ri·vah·lè m* —n rival

Rivalin *ri·vah·lin f* —nen rival

Rizinusöl *ree·tsee·noos·ur'l nt* castor oil

Robe *rō·bè f* —n gown

Roboter *ro·bo·tèr m* — robot

Rochen *ro·khèn m* — skate (*fish*)

Rock *rok m* —e skirt

Rock 'n' Roll *rok èn rōl m* rock ('n' roll)

Roggen *ro·gèn m* rye

Roggenbrot *ro·gèn·brōt m* rye bread

Roggenwhiskey *ro·gèn·vis·kee m* rye (whiskey)

roh *rō adj* raw □ *pref* Roh- *rō* crude (*oil etc*)

Rohr *rōr m* —e pipe (*tube*)

Rohstoffe *rō·shto·fè pl* raw material

Rollbrett *rol·bret m* —er skateboard

Rolle *ro·lè f* —n roll; part (*in play*)

rollen *ro·lèn vt* roll

Rollkragen *rol·krah·gèn m* — polo neck

Rollschuhe *rol·shoo·è pl* roller skates

Rollsteg *rol·shtayk m* —e moving walkway

Rollstuhl *rol·shtool m* —e wheelchair

Rolltreppe *rol·tre·pè f* —n escalator

Rom *rōm nt* Rome

Roman *rō·mahn m* —e novel (*book*)

Romane *rō·mah·nè pl* fiction

romantisch *ro·man·tish adj* romantic

römisch *rur'·mish adj* Roman

römisch-katholisch *rur'·mish·ka·tō·lish adj* Roman Catholic

röntgen *rur'nt·gèn vt* X-ray

Röntgenaufnahme *rur'nt·gèn·owf·nah·mè f* —n X-ray (*photo*)

rosa *rō·za adj* pink

Rose *rō·zè f* —n rose

Rosé *ro·zay m* —s rosé

Rosenkohl *rō·zèn·kōl m* Brussels sprouts

Rosine *ro·zee·nè f* —n raisin

Rost *rost m* rust

rosten *ros·tèn vi* rust; nicht rostend *nikht ros·tènt* rustproof

rostfrei *rost·frye adj* stainless (*steel*)

rostig *ros·tikh adj* rusty

rot *rōt adj* red; rot werden* *rōt ver·dèn* to blush

rothaarig *rōt·hah·rikh adj* red-haired

Rotlicht *rōt·likht nt* —er red light (*traffic light*)

Roulett *roo·let nt* roulette

Routine *roo·tee·nè f* —n routine

routinemäßig *roo·tee·nè·may·sikh adj* routine

Rowdy *row·dee m* **Rowdies** vandal

Rübe *rōō·bè f* —n rutabaga; die rote Rübe *rō·tè rōō·bè* beet

Rubin *roo·been m* —e ruby

im Rückblick *im rōōk·blik adv* in retrospect

Rücken *rōō·kèn m* — back

Rückenlehne *rōō·kèn·lay·nè f* —n back (*of chair*)

Rückenschmerzen *rōō·kèn·shmer·tsèn pl* backache

Rückfahrkarte *rōōk·fahr·kar·tè f* —n round trip (ticket)

Rückgang *rōōk·gang m* —e slump

Rückgrat *rōōk·graht nt* —e spine (*backbone*)

Rückkehr *rōōk·kayr f* return (*going/coming back*)

Rucksack *rook·zak m* —e rucksack; back pack

Rückseite *rōōk·zye·tè f* —n back (*reverse side*)

Rücksicht *rōōk·zikht f* consideration; ohne Rücksicht auf *ō·nè rōōk·zikht owf* regardless of

Rückspiegel *rōōk·shpee·gèl m* — rear view mirror

Rückstand *rōōk·shtant m* —e arrears

Rückstau *rōōk·shtow m* —s traffic jam

Rückstrahler *rōōk·shtrah·lèr m* — reflector (*on cycle, car*)

rück|vergüten *rōōk·fer·gōō·tèn vt* refund

rückwärts *rōōk·verts adv* backwards

Rückwärtsgang *rōōk·verts·gang m* reverse (*gear*)

Ruder *roo·dèr nt* — oar; rudder

Rudern *roo·dèrn nt* rowing (*sport*) □ *vi* rudern *roo·dèrn* row

Ruf *roof m* —e shout; reputation

rufen* *roo·fèn vi* shout

Rugby *rug·bee nt* rugby

Ruhe *roo·è f* rest (*repose*); peace (*calm*); Ruhe! *roo·è* be quiet!

Ruhestand *roo·è·shtant m* retirement; im Ruhestand *im roo·è·shtant* retired

ruhig *roo·ikh adj* calm (*sea, day*); quiet (*place*); peaceful □ *adv* quietly (*walk, work*)

rühren *rōō·rèn vt* stir

Rührkuchen *rōōr·koo·khèn m* — sponge (*cake*)

Ruine *roo·ee·nè f* —n ruin

Rum *room m* rum

Rumänien *roo·may·nee·èn nt* Romania

rumänisch *roo·may·nish adj* Romanian □ *nt* Rumänisch *roo·may·nish* Romanian (*language*)

Rummelplatz *roo·mèl·plats m* —e fairground

Rumpsteak *roomp·stayk nt* —s rump steak

rund *roont adj* round; **die runde Zahl** *roon·dè tsahl* round figure/number

Runde *roon·dè f* —**n** lap (*of track*); round (*in sport, of talks*)

Rundfahrt *roont·fahrt f* —**en** tour; **eine Rundfahrt machen durch** *ine·è roont·fahrt ma·khèn doorkh* to tour (*town*)

Rundfunk *roont·foonk m* radio

rundlich *roont·likh adj* plump

Rundreise *roont·rye·zè f* —**n** round trip

Runzel *roon·tsèl f* —**n** wrinkle

Russisch *roo·sish nt* Russian (*language*) □ *adj* **russisch** *roo·sish* Russian

Rußland *roos·lant nt* Russia

Rutschbahn *rootsh·bahn f* —**en** slide (*chute*)

rutschen *root·shèn vi* slide

rutschig *root·shikh adj* slippery

S

Saal *zahl m* **Säle** hall (*room*)

Saccharin *zakh·a·reen nt* saccharin

Sache *za·khè f* —**n** thing

Sachen *za·khèn pl* stuff (*things*); belongings

Sack *zak m* —**e** sack

Sackgasse *zak·ga·sè f* —**n** dead end; cul-de-sac; blind alley

Saft *zaft m* —**e** juice

sagen *zah·gèn vt* say; tell (*fact, news*); **jemandem sagen, er solle etwas tun** *yay·man·dèm zah·gèn er zol·lè et·vass toon* to tell someone to do something

Sahne *zah·nè f* cream

Sahnequark *zah·nè·kvark m* —**s** cream cheese

Saite *zye·tè f* —**n** string (*of instrument*)

Salat *za·laht m* —**e** salad; **der grüne Salat** *grōō·nè za·laht* green salad

Salatsoße *za·laht·zō·sè f* —**n** vinaigrette (*sauce*); salad dressing

Salbe *zal·bè f* —**n** ointment

Salbei *zal·bye m* sage (*herb*)

saldieren *zal·dee·rèn vt* balance (*accounts*)

Saldo *zal·dō m* **Salden** balance (*remainder owed*); bank balance

Salz *zalts nt* —**e** salt

salzig *zal·tsikh adj* salty

Salzstreuer *zalts·shtroy·èr m* — salt cellar

Samen *zah·mèn m* — seed

sammeln *za·mèln vt* gather (*assemble*); collect

Sammlung *zam·loong f* —**en** collection

Samstag *zams·tahk m* Saturday

Samt *zamt m* velvet

Sanatorium *za·na·tō·ree·oom nt* —**rien** sanitarium

Sand *zant m* sand

Sandale *zan·dah·lè f* —**n** sandal

Sandbank *zant·bank f* —**e** sandbank

sanft *zanft adj* gentle

Sänger *zeng·èr m* — singer

Sängerin *zeng·è·rin f* —**nen** singer

Sanktionen *zank·tsee·ō·nèn pl* sanctions

Sardelle *zar·de·lè f* —**n** anchovy

Sardine *zar·dee·nè f* —**n** sardine

Sardinien *zar·dee·nee·èn nt* Sardinia

Sarg *zark m* —**e** coffin

sarkastisch *zar·ka·stish adj* sarcastic

Satellit *za·tè·leet m* —**en** satellite

Satin *za·tañ m* satin

Satire *za·tee·rè f* —**n** satire (*play*)

satt *zat adj* full; **ich habe es satt** *ikh*

hah·bè es zat I'm tired of it; I'm fed up

Sattel *za·tèl m* — saddle

sättigen *ze·ti·gèn vt* saturate (*market*)

sättigend *ze·ti·gènt adj* filling (*food*)

Satz *zats m* —**e** set (*collection*); grounds (*of coffee*); sentence

sauber *zow·bèr adj* clean

sauber|machen *zow·bèr·ma·khèn vt* clean

sauer *zow·èr adj* sour; spoiled (*milk*)

Sauerstoff *zow·èr·shtof m* oxygen

saugen *zow·gèn vt* suck

Sauger *zow·gèr m* — nipple (*on bottle*)

saugfähig *zowk·fay·ikh adj* absorbent

Säuglingstrage *zoyg·lings·trah·gè f* —**n** portable crib

Säule *zoy·lè f* —**n** pillar

Saum *zowm m* —**e** seam; hem

Sauna *zow·na f* —**s** sauna

Säure *zoy·rè f* —**n** acid

Scampi *skam·pi pl* scampi

schäbig *she·bikh adj* shabby

Schach *shakh nt* chess

Schachtel *shakh·tèl f* —**n** box; pack

schade *shah·dè adj* a pity; **wie schade!** *vee shah·dè* what a shame!

Schädel *shay·dèl m* — skull

Schaden *shah·dèn m* —**e** damage

Schadensersatz *shah·dèns·er·zats m* damages; compensation

schädlich *shet·likh adj* harmful

Schaf *shahf nt* —**e** sheep

Schaffell *shahf·fel nt* —**e** sheepskin

schaffen* *sha·fèn vt* create; **es schaffen, etwas zu tun** *es sha·fèn et·vass tsoo toon* to manage to do something

Schaffner *shaf·nèr m* — conductor (*on bus*)

schal *shahl adj* flat (*beer*)

Schal *shahl m* — scarf

Schale *shah·lè f* —**n** shell; peel

schälen *shay·lèn vt* peel

Schalldämpfer *shal·demp·fèr m* — muffler (*on car*)

Schallplatte *shal·pla·tè f* —**n** disk; record

Schalotte *sha·lo·tè f* —**n** scallion

schalten *shal·tèn vi* to shift gear

Schalter *shal·tèr m* — switch

Schaltiere *shahl·tee·rè pl* shellfish (*on menu*)

Schaltknüppel *shalt·knōō·pèl m* — gearshift

sich schämen *zikh she·mèn vr* to be ashamed

Schande *shan·dè f* —**n** shame

scharf *sharf adj* hot (*spicy*); sharp

schärfen *sher·fèn vt* sharpen

scharlachrot *shar·lakh·rōt adj* scarlet

Schatten *sha·tèn m* — shadow; shade

schattig *sha·tikh adj* shady

Schatz *shats m* —**e** treasure; darling

schätzen *shet·sèn vt* value; estimate; **zu schätzen wissen*** *tsoo shet·sèn vi·sèn* to appreciate

Schätzung *shet·soong f* —**en** estimate

Schaubild *show·bilt nt* —**er** graph

schauen *show·èn vi* look

Schauer *show·èr m* — shower (*rain*)

Schaufel *show·fèl f* —**n** shovel

Schaufenster *show·fen·stèr nt* — shop window

Schaufensterbummel *show·fen·stèr·boo·mèl m* — window shopping

Schaukel *show·kèl f* —**n** swing

schaukeln *show·kèln vt* swing

Schaum *showm m* —**e** foam □ *pref* **Schaum-** *showm* sparkling (*wine*)

Schauspiel *show·shpeel nt* —**e** play

Schauspieler *show·shpee·lèr m* — actor

Schauspielerin *show·shpee·lè·rin f* —**nen** actress

Scheck *shek m* —s check (*banking*)

Scheckbuch *shek·bookh nt* ⁼**er** checkbook

Scheibe *shye·bè f* —**n** plate (*of glass, metal*); slice; disk; in Scheiben schneiden* *in shye·bèn shnye·dèn* to slice

Scheibenbremsen *shye·bèn·brem·zèn pl* disc brakes

Scheibenwaschanlage *shye·bèn·vash·an·lah·gè f* —**n** windshield washer

Scheibenwischer *shye·bèn·vi·shèr m* — windshield wiper

Scheidung *shye·doong f* —**en** divorce

Schein *shine m* —**e** note; bill (*bank note*)

scheinen* *shye·nèn vi* shine (*sun etc*); seem; die Sonne scheint *dee zo·nè shyent* the sun is out; er scheint krank zu sein *er shyent krank tsoo zine* he appears to be ill

Scheinwerfer *shine·ver·fèr m* — headlight; floodlight; spotlight

Scheitel *shye·tèl m* — part (*in hair*)

Schellfisch *shel·fish m* —**e** haddock

schenken *sheng·kèn vt* give

Schere *shay·rè f* —**n** (pair of) scissors

Scheune *shoy·nè f* —**n** barn

Schicht *shikht f* —**en** shift (*of workmen*); layer

schick *shik adj* fancy

schicken *shi·kèn vt* send

Schiebedach *shee·bè·dakh nt* ⁼**er** sunroof

schieben* *shee·bèn vt* push

Schiedsrichter *sheets·rikh·tèr m* — referee (*football*); umpire

Schieferplatte *shee·fèr·pla·tè f* —**n** slate

Schienbein *sheen·bine nt* —**e** shin

Schiene *shee·nè f* —**n** splint

Schienen *shee·nèn pl* rails (*for train*)

schießen* *shee·sèn vt/i* score (*goal*); shoot

Schiff *shif nt* —**e** ship; mit dem Schiff fahren* *mit dem shif fah·rèn* to go by sea

Schiffahrtsgesellschaft *shif·fahrts·gè·zel·shaft f* —**en** shipping company

Schiffbau *shif·bow m* shipbuilding

Schild *shilt nt* —**er** sign (*notice*)

Schildkrötensuppe *shilt·krur·tèn·zoo·pè f* turtle soup

schimpfen *shimp·fèn vt/i* grumble; scold

Schinken *shing·kèn m* — ham

Schinkenbrot *shing·kèn·bröt nt* —**e** ham sandwich

Schirm *shirm m* —**e** peak (*of cap*); umbrella; screen (*partition*)

Schirmständer *shirm·shten·dèr m* — umbrella stand

Schlacht *shlakht f* —**en** battle

Schlaf *shlahf m* sleep

schlafen* *shlah·fèn vi* sleep; in der Wohnung können 3 Personen schlafen *in der vö·noong kur·nèn 3 per·zö·nèn shlah·fèn* the apartment sleeps three

schlafend *shlah·fènt adj* asleep

Schlafsaal *shlahf·zahl m* —**säle** dormitory (*room*)

Schlafsack *shlahf·zak m* ⁼**e** sleeping bag

Schlaftablette *shlahf·ta·ble·tè f* —**n** sleeping pill

Schlafwagen *shlahf·vah·gèn m* — sleeping car

Schlafwagenplatz *shlahf·vah·gèn·plats m* ⁼**e** berth (*in train*)

Schlafzimmer *shlahf·tsi·mèr nt* — bedroom

Schlag *shlahk m* ⁼**e** stroke (*golf*); blow (*knock*)

Schlaganfall *shlahk·an·fal m* ⁼**e** stroke (*illness*)

schlagen* *shlah·gèn vt* hit; whip (*cream, eggs*); beat; K.o. schlagen* *kah·ö shlah·gèn* to knock out; die Uhr schlug drei *dee oo·èr shlook drye* the clock struck three

Schläger *shlay·gèr m* — paddle (*table tennis etc*); racket (*tennis*)

Schlagsahne *shlahk·zah·nè f* whipped cream

Schlagzeile *shlahk·tsile·è f* —**n** headline

Schlamm *shlam m* mud

schlammig *shla·mikh adj* muddy (*water*)

Schlange *shlang·è f* —**n** line (*people waiting*); snake; Schlange stehen* *shlang·è shtay·èn* to stand in line

sich schlängeln *zikh shleng·èln vr* twist (*road*)

schlank *shlank adj* slim

Schlankheitskur *shlank·hites·koor f* —**en** diet (*slimming*); eine Schlankheitskur machen *ine·è shlank·hites·koor ma·khèn* to be on a diet

schlau *shlow adj* clever (*plan*); smart

Schlauch *shlowkh m* ⁼**e** hose (*pipe*)

Schlauchboot *shlowkh·böt nt* —**e** dinghy (*inflatable*)

schlecht *shlekht adj* bad (*not good*); das schlechteste Buch *dass shlekh·tès·tè bookh* the worst book; mir ist schlecht *meer ist shlekht* I feel sick □ *adv* schlecht *shlekht* badly (*not well*); er machte es am schlechtesten *er makh·tè ess am shlekh·tès·tèn* he did it worst

Schleier *shlye·èr m* — veil

Schleife *shlye·fè f* —**n** bow (*ribbon*)

schlendern *shlen·dèrn vi* wander

Schleppe *shle·pè f* —**n** train (*on dress*)

schleppen *shle·pèn vt* drag

Schleppkahn *shlep·kahn m* ⁼**e** barge

Schleppstange *shlep·shtang·è f* —**n** tow-bar (*on car*)

Schleudern *shloy·dèrn nt* skid □ *vi* schleudern *shloy·dèrn* skid

Schleuse *shloy·zè f* —**n** lock (*in canal*)

schließen* *shlee·sèn vt/i* shut; die Tür schloß sich *dee töör shlos zikh* the door closed; um wieviel Uhr schließen die Läden? *oom vee·feel oor shlee·sèn dee lay·dèn* when do the shops close?

Schließfach *shlees·fakh nt* ⁼**er** locker

schließlich *shlees·likh adv* finally; eventually

schlimm *shlim adj* bad

Schlinge *shling·è f* —**n** sling (*for arm*); loop

Schlitten *shli·tèn m* — sleigh; sled(ge)

Schlittschuh *shlit·shoo m* —**e** skate (*for ice*); Schlittschuh laufen* *shlit·shoo low·fèn* to skate

Schlitz *shlits m* —**e** slot

Schloß *shloss nt* ⁼**er** castle; lock (*on door*)

Schluckauf *shlook·owf m* hiccup

schlucken *shloo·kèn vt/i* swallow

Schlüpfer *shlöop·fèr m* — panties

Schlüssel *shlöö·sèl m* — key

Schlüsselloch *shlöö·sèl·lokh nt* ⁼**er** keyhole

Schlüsselring *schlōō·sèl·ring m* —e key ring

Schlußverkauf *shloos·fer·kowf m* ꞋꞋe clearance sale

schmecken *shme·kèn vt/i* taste

Schmeißfliege *shmice·flee·gè f* —n bluebottle

schmelzen* *shmel·tsèn vi* melt

Schmerz *shmerts m* —en pain; ache

schmerzend *shmer·tsènt adj* sore *(painful)*

schmerzhaft *shmerts·haft adj* painful

schmerzstillendes Mittel *shmerts·shtil·èn·dès mi·tèl nt* painkiller

Schmetterling *shme·tèr·ling m* —e butterfly

schmieren *shmee·rèn vt* lubricate

Schmierfett *shmeer·fet nt* — grease *(lubricant)*

sich schminken *zikh shming·kèn vr* to make (oneself) up

Schmortopf *shmor·topf m* ꞋꞋe casserole *(dish)*

Schmuck *shmook m* jewelry; ornament; decorations

schmücken *shmōō·kèn vt* decorate *(adorn)*

schmuggeln *shmoo·gèln vt* smuggle

Schmuggelware *shmoo·gèl·vah·rè f* contraband

Schmutz *shmoots m* dirt

Schmutzfänger *shmoots·feng·èr m* — mud-flap

schmutzig *shmoot·tsikh adj* muddy *(clothes)*; dirty

Schnalle *shna·lè f* —n buckle

schnappen *shna·pèn vt* snatch

Schnappverschluß *shnap·fer·shloos m* ꞋꞋe clasp

schnarchen *shnar·khèn vi* snore

Schnecke *shne·kè f* —n snail

Schnee *shnay f* snow

Schneeball *shnay·bal m* ꞋꞋe snowball

Schneebesen *shnay·bay·zèn m* — whisk

Schneemann *shnay·man m* ꞋꞋer snowman

Schneepflug *shnay·pflook m* ꞋꞋe snowplow

Schneeregen *shnay·ray·gèn m* sleet

Schneesturm *shnay·shtoorm m* ꞋꞋe blizzard

Schneewehe *shnay·vay·è f* —n snowdrift

Schneide *shnye·dè f* —n edge *(of blade)*

schneiden* *shnye·dèn vt* cut; sich schneiden* *zikh shnye·dèn* to cut oneself; sich die Haare schneiden lassen* *zikh dee hah·rè shnye·dèn la·sèn* to get one's hair cut

Schneider *shnye·dèr m* — tailor

schneien *shnye·èn vi* snow; es schneit *ess shnite* it's snowing

schnell *shnel adj, adv* fast; mach schnell! *makh shnel* be quick!

Schnell- *shnel- pref* high-speed

Schnellboot *shnel·bōt nt* —e speedboat

Schnellgang *shnel·gang m* ꞋꞋe overdrive

Schnellstraße *shnel·shtrah·sè f* —n divided highway; expressway

Schnellzug *shnel·tsook m* ꞋꞋe express train

Schnittlauch *shnit·lowkh m* chives

Schnittmuster *shnit·moos·tèr nt* — pattern *(dressmaking)*

Schnittwunde *shnit·voon·dè f* —n cut *(wound)*

Schnitzel *shnit·sèl nt* — escalope

Schnorchel *shnor·khèl m* — snorkel

Schnuller *shnoo·lèr m* — pacifier

Schnupftabak *shnoopf·ta·bak m* snuff

Schnur *shnoor f* ꞋꞋe string; cord *(twine)*; wire *(electrical)*

Schnürsenkel *shnōōr·seng·kèl m* — shoelace

Schock *shok m* —s shock

Schokolade *sho·ko·lah·dè f* chocolate

Scholle *sho·lè f* —n plaice

schon *shōn adv* already; wir kennen uns schon *veer ke·nèn oons shōn* we've met before

schön *shur'n adj* lovely; fine *(weather)*; beautiful; es war sehr schön *ess vahr zayr shur'n* we had a good time

Schönheit *shur'n·hite f* beauty

Schöpflöffel *shur'pf·lur'·fèl m* — ladle

Schorf *shorf m* —e scab

Schornstein *shorn·shtine m* —e chimney

Schoß *shōss m* ꞋꞋe lap *(of person)*

Schotte *sho·tè m* —n Scot

Schottenstoff *sho·tèn·shtof m* tartan

Schottin *sho·tin f* —nen Scot

schottisch *sho·tish adj* Scottish

Schottland *shot·lant nt* Scotland

schräg *shrayk adj* sloping; slanting

schrammen *shra·mèn vt* scrape

Schrank *shrank m* ꞋꞋe cupboard; closet

Schranke *shrang·kè f* —n barrier

Schraube *shrow·bè f* —n screw

Schraubenschlüssel *shrow·bèn·shlōō·sèl m* — wrench

Schraubenzieher *shrow·bèn·tsee·èr m* — screwdriver

schrecklich *shrek·likh adj* awful; terrible

Schrei *shrye m* —e cry

Schreibblock *shripe·blok m* ꞋꞋe pad *(notepaper)*

schreiben* *shrye·bèn vi* write

Schreibmaschine *shripe·ma·shee·nè f* —n typewriter

Schreibpapier *shripe·pa·peer nt* writing paper

Schreibtisch *shripe·tish m* —e desk *(in office)*

Schreibwaren *shripe·vah·rèn pl* stationery

Schreibwarengeschäft *shripe·vah·rèn·gè·sheft nt* — stationer's *(shop)*

schreien* *shrye·èn vi* scream; call *(shout)*

Schrift *shrift f* print

schriftlich *shrift·likh adv* in writing

Schritt *shrit m* —e pace; step; Schritt halten* mit *shrit hal·tèn mit* to keep pace with; Schritte unternehmen*, etwas zu tun *shri·tè oon·tèr·nay·mèn et·vass tsoo toon* to take steps to do something

Schubkarre *shoop·ka·rè f* —n wheelbarrow

Schublade *shoop·lah·dè f* —n drawer

schüchtern *shōōkh·tèrn adj* shy

Schuh *shoo m* —e shoe

Schuhcreme *shoo·kraym f* polish *(for shoes)*

Schuhgeschäft *shoo·gè·sheft nt* —e shoeshop

Schulaufgaben *shool·owf·gah·bèn pl* homework

Schuld *shoolt f* —en debt; guilt; fault *(blame)*; die Schuld geben* *dee shoolt gay·bèn* to blame *(reproach)*

schulden *shool·dèn vt* owe *(money)*; er schuldet mir $5 *er shool·dèt meer $5* he owes me $5

schuldig *shool·dikh adj* guilty

schuld sein* *shoolt zine vi* to be to

blame; **wer ist schuld daran?** *ver ist shoolt da·ran* whose fault is it?
Schule *shōo·lè f* —**n** school; **die höhere Schule** *hur'·è·rè shoo·lè* secondary school
Schüler *shōo·lèr m* — pupil
Schülerin *shōo·lèr·in f* —**nen** pupil
Schulter *shool·tèr f* —**n** shoulder
Schuppe *shoo·pè f* —**n** scale *(of fish)*
□ *pl* **Schuppen** *shoo·pèn* dandruff
Schuppen *shoo·pèn m* — shed
Schürze *shōōr·tsè f* —**n** apron
Schuß *shoos m* —**e** shot *(from gun)*
Schüssel *shōo·sèl f* —**n** basin; bowl *(for food)*
Schußwaffe *shoos·va·fè f* —**n** firearm
schütteln *shōo·tèln vt* shake
Schutz *shoots m* safeguard
Schutzbrille *shoots·bri·lè f* —**n** goggles
schützen *shōo·tsèn vt* guard *(protect)*
Schutzimpfung *shoots·imp·foong f* —**en** vaccination
schwach *shvakh adj* weak *(person)*; dim *(light)*; **schwächer werden*** *shve·khèr ver·dèn* to fade; **mir ist schwach** *meer ist shvakh* I feel faint
Schwager *shvah·gèr m* —**˙** brother-in-law
Schwägerin *shvay·gè·rin f* —**nen** sister-in-law
Schwamm *shvam m* —**e** sponge
Schwan *shvahn m* —**e** swan
schwanger *shvang·èr adj* pregnant
schwanken *shvang·kèn vi* sway
Schwanz *shvants m* —**e** tail
schwarz *shvarts adj* black; **ein schwarzer Kaffee** *ine shvart·sèr ka·fay* a black coffee
Schwarzmarkt *shvarts·markt m* —**e** black market
schwatzen *shva·tsèn vi* gossip
Schwede *shvay·dè m* —**n** Swede
Schweden *shvay·dèn nt* Sweden
Schwedin *shvay·din f* —**nen** Swede
schwedisch *shvay·dish adj* Swedish
□ *nt* **Schwedisch** *shvay·dish* Swedish
schweigen* *shvye·gèn vi* be silent
Schwein *shvine m* —**e** pig
Schweinefleisch *shvine·è·flyesh nt* pork
Schweinekotelett *shvine·è·kot·let nt* —**s** pork chop
Schweineschmalz *shvine·è·shmalts nt* lard
Schweinsleder *shvines·lay·dèr nt* pigskin
Schweiß *shvice m* sweat
schweißen *shvye·sèn vt* weld
Schweiz *shvites f* Switzerland; **in die Schweiz** *in dee shvites* to Switzerland; **in der Schweiz** *in der shvites* in Switzerland
schweizerisch *shvye·tsè·rish adj* Swiss
Schwellung *shve·loong f* —**en** swelling *(lump)*
schwer *shvayr adj* rich *(food)*; heavy; difficult
Schwert *shvert nt* —**er** sword
Schwester *shve·stèr f* —**n** sister
Schwestergesellschaft *shves·tèr·gè·zel·shaft f* —**en** affiliated company
Schwiegermutter *shvee·gèr·moo·tèr f* —**˙** mother-in-law
Schwiegersohn *shvee·gèr·zōn m* —**e** son-in-law
Schwiegertochter *shvee·gèr·tokh·tèr f* —**˙** daughter-in-law
Schwiegervater *shvee·gèr·fah·tèr m* —**˙** father-in-law
schwierig *shvee·rikh adj* hard; difficult
Schwierigkeit *shvee·rikh·kite f* —**en** difficulty □ *pl* **Schwierigkeiten** *shvee·rikh·kite·èn* trouble *(problems)*; in

Schwierigkeiten sein* *in shvee·rikh·kite·èn zine* to be in trouble
Schwimmbad *shvim·baht nt* —**er** swimming pool
Schwimmbecken *shvim·be·kèn nt* — pool *(swimming)*
schwimmen* *shvi·mèn vi* swim; **schwimmen gehen*** *shvi·mèn gay·èn* to go swimming □ *nt* **Schwimmen** *shvi·mèn* swimming
Schwimmer *shvi·mèr m* — float *(fishing)*
Schwimmkork *shvim·kork m* —**e** float *(for swimming)*
Schwimmweste *shvim·ve·stè f* —**n** life preserver; life jacket
schwind(e)lig *shvind·likh adj* dizzy *(person)*
schwingen* *shving·èn vi* swing
schwitzen *shvit·sèn vi* sweat; perspire
schwören *shvur'·rèn vt/i* swear; **er schwört, daß...** *er shvurt dass* he swears that...
schwül *shvōōl adj* close *(stuffy)*
Science-Fiction *f* science fiction
Scotch *skotsh m* Scotch *(liquor)*
sechs *zeks num* six
sechste(r/s) *zeks·tè(·tèr/·tès) adj* sixth
sechzehn *zekh·tsayn num* sixteen
sechzehnte(r/s) *zekh·tsayn·tè(·tèr/·tès) adj* sixteenth
sechzig *zekh·tsikh num* sixty
See *zay f* —**n** sea
See *zay m* —**n** lake
seekrank *zay·krank adj* seasick
Seele *zay·lè f* —**n** soul
Seenot *zay·nōt f* distress; **ein Schiff in Seenot** *ine shif in zay·nōt* a ship in distress
Seezunge *zay·tsoong·è f* —**n** sole *(fish)*
Segel *zay·gèl nt* — sail
Segelboot *zay·gèl·bōt nt* —**e** sailboat
Segelfliegen *zay·gèl·flee·gèn nt* gliding *(sport)*
Segelflugzeug *zay·gèl·flook·tsoyk nt* —**e** glider
Segeln *zay·gèln nt* yachting □ *vi* **segeln** *zay·gèln* sail; **segeln gehen*** *zay·gèln gay·èn* to go yachting
Segeltuch *zay·gèl·tookh nt* canvas
segnen *zayk·nèn vt* bless
sehen* *zay·èn vt/i* see; **ich kann keinen Unterschied zwischen ihnen** *ikh zay·è kye·nèn oon·tèr·sheed tsvi·shèn ee·nèn* I can't tell the difference between them; **zu sehen sein*** *tsoo zay·èn zine* to show *(be visible)*; **schlecht sehen*** *shlekht zay·èn* to have poor sight
Sehenswürdigkeiten *zay·èns·vōōr·dikh·kite·èn pl* sights *(of town)*
Sehkraft *zay·kraft f* eyesight
sehr *zehr adv* very; **ich habe es sehr gerne** *ikh hah·bè ess zehr ger·nè* I like it very much
Seide *zye·dè f* —**n** silk
Seidenkleid *zye·dèn·klite nt* —**er** silk dress
Seidenpapier *zye·dèn·pa·peer nt* —**e** tissue paper
Seife *zye·fè f* —**n** soap
Seifenflocken *zye·fèn·flo·kèn pl* soap-flakes
Seifenpulver *zye·fèn·pool·vèr nt* — soap powder
Seil *zile nt* —**e** rope
sein* *zine vi* be; **ich bin** *ikh bin* I am; **Sie sind** *zee zint* you are; **er ist** *er ist* he is; **wir sind** *veer zint* we are; **sie sind** *zee zint* they are; **ich/er war** *ikh/er vahr* I/he was; **wir sind in Paris ge-**

wesen *veer zint in pa·rees gè·vay·zèn* we have been to Paris; **er ist Arzt** *er ist artst* he is a doctor

sein(e) *zine(·è) adj* his; its

seine(r/s) *zine·è(·èr/·ès) pron* his; its

seit *zite prep* since; **seit er...** *zite er* ever since he...; **ich bin schon seit 4 Uhr hier** *ikh bin shôn zite 4 oor heer* I've been here since 4 o'clock; **seit wir ankamen** *zite veer an·kah·mèn* since we arrived

seitdem *zite·daym adv, conj* since; **seitdem ist er da** *zite·daym ist er da* he's been there ever since

Seite *zye·tè f —n* page; side; **die rechte Seite** *dee rekh·tè zye·tè* the right side (*of cloth etc*)

Seitenstraße *zye·tèn·shtrah·sè f —n* side-street

Seitenstreifen *zye·tèn·shtrye·fèn m —* berm

seither *zite·her adv, conj* since

Sekretär *zay·kray·tayr m —e* secretary

Sekretärin *zay·kray·tay·rin f —nen* secretary

Sekt *zekt m —e* champagne

Sektor *zek·tôr m* sector (*economy*)

sekundär *zay·koon·dayr adj* secondary (*importance*)

Sekunde *ze·koon·dè f —n* second (*time*)

selbe(r/s) *zel·bè(·bèr/·bès) adj* same

selbst *zelpst pron* myself; yourself; yourselves; himself; herself; ourselves; itself; themselves; **ich machte es selbst** *ikh makh·tè ès zelpst* I did it myself; **sie taten es selbst** *zee tah·tèn ès zelpst* they did it themselves; **er hat es selbst getan** *er hat ess zelpst gè·tahn* he did it himself

selbständig *zelp·shten·dikh adj* self-employed

mit Selbstbedienung *mit zelpst·bè·dee·noong adj* self-service

Selbstbedienungsrestaurant *zelpst·bè·dee·noongs·re·stô·rant nt —s* cafeteria

Selbstkostenpreis *zelpst·kos·tèn·prise m —e □ etwas zum Selbstkostenpreis kaufen* *et·vass tsoom zelpst·kos·tèn·prise kow·fèn* to buy something at cost

Selbstmord *zelpst·mort m —e* suicide

selbstsicher *zelpst·zi·khèr adj* confident

selbstverständlich *zelpst·fer·stent·likh adv* of course

Selbstwählfernverkehr *zelpst·vayl·fern·fer·kayr m* automatic long-distance dialing

Sellerie *ze·lè·ree f* celeriac

selten *zel·tèn adj* rare □ *adv* seldom

seltsam *zelt·zam adj* strange (*unusual*); peculiar

Senat *zay·naht m* senate (*political*)

Senator *zay·nah·tor m —en* senator

senden *zen·dèn vt* broadcast

senden* *zen·dèn vt* send

Sender *zen·dèr m —* station (*radio*); transmitter

Sendeturm *zen·dè·toorm m ᵘe* mast (*radio*)

Sendung *zen·doong f —en* program (*radio, TV*); broadcast; shipment

Senf *zenf m* mustard

senkrecht *zenk·rekht adj* vertical

separat *zay·pa·raht adj* self-contained (*apartment*); separate

September *zep·tem·bèr m* September

servieren *zer·vee·rèn vt* serve (*food*)

Serviette *zer·vee·è·tè f —n* serviette

Sessel *ze·sèl m —* armchair

Sessellift *ze·sèl·lift m —s* chair-lift

Set *set nt —s* place mat

setzen *zet·sèn vt* place; put; **setzen Sie es auf meine Rechnung** *zet·sèn zee ess owf mine·è rekh·noong* charge it to my account; **setzen auf** *zet·sèn owf* to back (*bet on*); **sich setzen** *zikh zet·sèn* to sit down; **setzen Sie sich bitte** *zet·sèn zee zikh bi·tè* please take a seat

seufzen *zoyf·tsèn vi* sigh

sexy *sek·see adj* sexy

Shampoo *sham·poo nt —s* shampoo

Shorts *shorts pl* shorts

Show *shô f —s* show (*in theater*)

Showgeschäft *shô·gè·sheft nt* show business

sich *zikh pron* oneself; **sie waschen sich** *zee va·shèn zikh* they wash themselves

sicher *zi·khèr adj* sure; safe (*out of danger*); definite; **das geht sicher** *das gayt zi·khèr* it's sure to work; **er wird sicher kommen** *er virt zi·khèr ko·mèn* I expect he'll come

Sicherheit *zi·khèr·hite f —en* security (*for loan*); safety

Sicherheitsdienst *zi·khèr·hites·deenst m —e* security

Sicherheitsgurt *zi·khèr·hites·goort m —e* seat belt; safety belt

Sicherheitsnadel *zi·khèr·hites·nah·dèl f —n* safety pin

Sicherung *zikh·è·roong f —en* fuse

sichtbar *zikht·bar adj* visible

sie *zee pron* she; her; they; them; **sie sind es** *zee zint ess* it's them!; **kaufen Sie sie** *kow·fèn zee zee* buy them

Sie *zee pron* you (*polite form*)

Sieb *zeep nt —e* sieve; colander

sieben *zee·bèn vt* strain (*tea etc*); sieve □ *num* seven

siebte(r/s) *zeep·tè(·tèr/·tès) adj* seventh

siebzehn *zeep·tsayn num* seventeen

siebzehnte(r/s) *zeep·tsayn·tè(·tèr/·tès) adj* seventeenth

siebzig *zeep·tsikh num* seventy

sieden* *zee·dèn vi* simmer

Siedlung *zeet·loong f —en* development (*housing*)

Sieg *zeek m —e* victory

Sieger *zee·gèr m —* winner

Siegerin *zee·gè·rin f —nen* winner

Signal *zig·nahl nt —e* signal

Silbe *zil·bè f —n* syllable

Silber *zil·bèr nt* silver

Silbergeld *zil·bèr·gelt nt* silver (*money*)

silbern *zil·bèrn adj* silver

Silvester *zil·ve·stèr nt* New Year's Eve

singen* *zing·èn vt/i* sing

sinken* *zing·kèn vi* sink □ *nt* **das Sinken** *zing·kèn* fall (*decrease*)

Sinn *zin m —e* sense; mind; feeling; point; **Sinn ergeben*** *zin er·gay·bèn* to make sense (*expression*)

Sirene *zee·ray·nè f —n* siren

Sirup *see·roop m* treacle; syrup; **gelbe Sirup** *gel·bè see·roop* (golden) syrup

Situation *zi·too·a·tsee·ôn f —en* situation (*circumstances*)

sitzen* *zi·tsèn vi* sit

Sitzplatz *zits·plats m ᵘe* seat

Sizilien *zee·tsee·lee·èn nt* Sicily

Skala *skah·la f* **Skalen** scale (*on thermometer*)

Skandinavien *skan·dee·nah·vee·èn nt* Scandinavia

skandinavisch *skan·dee·nah·vish adj* Scandinavian

Ski *shee m* — ski; **Ski fahren*** *shee fah·rèn* to ski

Skifahren *shee·fah·rèn nt* skiing; **Skifahren gehen*** *shee·fah·rèn gay·èn* to go skiing

Skihose *shee·hō·zè f* —n ski pants

Skiläufer *shee·loy·fèr m* — skier

Skiläuferin *shee·loy·fè·rin f* —nen skier

Skilift *shee·lift m* —s ski lift

Skipiste *shee·pis·tè f* —n ski run

Skistiefel *shee·shtee·fèl m* —s ski boot

Skizze *ski·tsè f* —n sketch (*drawing*)

skizzieren *ski·tsee·rèn vt* sketch

Sklave *sklah·vè m* —n slave

Sklavin *sklah·vin f* —nen slave

Skulptur *skoolp·toor f* —en sculpture

Slang *sleng m* slang

Slip *slip m* —s briefs; panties

Smaragd *sma·rakt m* —e emerald

Smoking *smō·king m* —s tuxedo

Smokingjacke *smō·king·ya·kè f* —n dinner jacket

Snob *snop m* —s snob

so *zō adv* thus (*in this way*); **so groß wie** *zō grōs vee* as big as; **nicht so schnell** *nikht zō shnel* less quickly; **so froh, daß...** *zō frō dass* so pleased that...; **so viel** *zō feel* so much; **so viele** *zō fee·lè* such a lot of; **so many** *zō fee·lè* such a lot of; **so viele** *zō fee·lè* such a lot of; **so bald** *zō·balt* conj as soon as; **sobald es hell war** *zō·balt ess hel vahr* as soon as it was light

Socke *zo·kè f* —n sock

Soda *zō·da nt* soda (*chemical*)

Sodawasser *zō·da·va·sèr nt* soda water

Sodbrennen *zōt·bre·nèn nt* — heartburn

Sofa *zō·fa nt* —s sofa; couch

sofort *zō·fort adv* at once; immediately

sofortig *zō·for·tikh adj* instant

sogar *zō·gar adv* even; **sogar ein Kind könnte das** *zō·gar ine kint kur'n·tè dass* even a child could do it

Sohle *zō·lè f* —n sole

Sohn *zōn m* —e son

Sojabohnen *zō·ya·bō·nèn pl* soy beans

Sojasoße *zō·ya·zō·sè f* —n soy sauce

solang(e) *wie* *zō·lang·è vee* conj as long as (*provided that*)

solche(r/s) *zolkh·è(·èr/·ès) adj* such; **ein solches Buch** *ine zol·khès bookh* such a book; **solche Bücher** *zol·khè bōō·khèr* such books

Soldat *zol·daht m* —en soldier

sollen *zo·lèn vi* to be (supposed to); **soll ich es tun?** *zol ikh ess toon* shall I do it?; **sollen wir morgen kommen?** *zo·lèn veer mor·gèn ko·mèn* shall we come tomorrow?; **Sie sollen es heute machen** *zee zo·lèn ess hoy·tè ma·khèn* you're supposed to do it today; **wann soll der Zug ankommen?** *van zol der tsook an·ko·mèn* when is the train due?; **ich sollte es tun** *ikh zol·tè es toon* I ought to do it; **was soll's?** *vass zols* what's the point?; **wir sollten es kaufen** *veer zol·tèn ess kow·fèn* we should buy it

Sommer *zo·mèr m* — summer

sonderbar *zon·dèr·bahr adj* odd (*strange*)

sondern *zon·dèrn conj* but; **nicht dies, sondern das** *nikht dees zon·dèrn dass* not this, but that

Sonnabend *zon·ah·bènt m* —e Saturday

Sonne *zo·nè f* —n sun; **in der Sonne liegen*** *in der zo·nè lee·gèn* to sunbathe

Sonnen- *zo·nèn pref* solar

Sonnenaufgang *zo·nèn·owf·gang m* —e sunrise

Sonnenblende *zo·nèn·blen·dè f* —n sun visor (*in car*)

Sonnenbrand *zo·nèn·brant m* sunburn (*painful*)

Sonnenbräune *zo·nèn·broy·nè f* suntan

Sonnenbrille *zo·nèn·bri·lè f* —n sunglasses

sonnengebräunt *zo·nèn·gè·broynt adj* sun-tanned; sunburned

Sonnenhut *zo·nèn·hoot m* —e sun-hat

Sonnenkleid *zo·nèn·klite nt* —er sun dress

Sonnenöl *zo·nèn·ur'l nt* suntan oil

Sonnenschein *zo·nèn·shine m* sunshine

Sonnenschirm *zo·nèn·shirm m* —e parasol; umbrella (*on table*)

Sonnenstich *zo·nèn·shtikh m* —e sunstroke

Sonnenuntergang *zo·nèn·oon·tèr·gang m* —e sunset

sonnenverbrannt *zo·nèn·fer·brant adj* sunburned (*painfully*)

sonnig *zo·nikh adj* sunny

Sonntag *zon·tahk m* —e Sunday

sonst *zonst adv* otherwise; else; **sonst nichts** *zonst nikhts* nothing else

Sorge *zor·gè f* —n concern (*anxiety*); worry; care (*carefulness*)

sorgen für *zor·gèn fōōr vt* look after; provide for; take care of (*children etc*)

sorgfältig *zork·fel·tikh adj* careful (*cautious*)

Sortiment *zor·tee·ment f* —e range (*variety*)

SOS *ess·ō·ess nt* SOS

Soße *zō·sè f* —n dressing (*salad*); sauce

Sos-signal *ess·ō·ess·zig·nahl nt* —e Mayday

soviel *zō·feel adv* so much; **soviel wie** *zō·feel vee* as much as

soweit *zō·vite conj* as far as; **soweit ich weiß** *zo·vite ikh vice* as far as I know

sowjetisch *sov·ye·tish adj* Soviet

Sowjetunion *sov·yet·oo·nyōn f* Soviet Union

sozial *zo·tsee·al adj* social

Sozialarbeiter *zō·tsee·al·ar·bye·tèr m* — social worker

Sozialarbeiterin *zō·tsee·al·ar·bye·tè·rin f* —nen social worker

Sozialismus *zō·tsee·a·lis·moos m* socialism

Sozialist *zō·tsee·a·list m* —en socialist

sozialistisch *zō·tsee·a·li·stish adj* socialist

Sozialversicherung *zō·tsee·al·fer·zi·khè·roong f* social security

Sozialversorgung *zo·tsee·al·fer·zor·goong f* social services

Spaghetti *shpa·ge·tee pl* spaghetti

spalten *shpal·tèn vt* split (*tear*)

Spanien *shpah·nee·èn nt* Spain

Spanisch *shpah·nish nt* Spanish □ *adj* spanisch *shpah·nish* Spanish

Spannung *shpa·noong f* —en voltage

Sparbuch *shpar·bookh nt* —er bankbook

sparen *shpah·rèn vt* save (*money*)

Spargel *shpar·gèl m* asparagus

Sparkasse *shpar·ka·sè f* —n savings bank

Sparkonto *shpar·kon·tō nt* —konten savings account

sparsam *shpar·zam adj* economical

Spaß *shpahs m* —e fun; joke; **es machte viel Spaß** *es makh·tè feel shpahs* it was great fun

spät *shpayt adj* late; **wie spät ist es?** *vee shpayt ist ess* what's the time?

Spatel *shpah·tél m* — spatula

Spaten *shpah·tèn m* — spade

später *shpay·tèr adj, adv* later; **4 Jahre später** *4 yah·rè shpay·tèr* 4 years after

Spatz *shpats m* —**en** sparrow

spazieren gehen* *shpa·tsee·rèn·gay·èn vi* to go for a walk □ *nt* **das Spazierengehen** *shpa·tsee·rèn·gay·èn* walking

Spaziergang *shpa·tseer·gang m* ¨e stroll; walk; **einen Spaziergang machen** *ine·èn shpa·tseer·gang ma·khèn* to go for a stroll

Spazierstock *shpa·tseer·shtok m* ¨e walking stick

Speck *shpek m* bacon

Speichel *shpye·khèl m* saliva

Speicher *shpye·khèr m* —s loft

Speisekammer *shpye·zè·kam·èr f* —n larder

Speisekarte *shpye·zè·kar·tè f* —n menu; **nach der Speisekarte** *nakh der shpye·zè·kar·tè* à la carte

Speisewagen *shpye·zè·vah·gèn m* — dining car; club car

Spende *shpen·dè f* —**en** donation (*money*)

spenden *shpen·dèn vt* donate (*funds*)

Sperre *shpe·rè f* —**n** barrier (*fence*)

sperren *shpe·rèn vt* stop (*check*)

Sperrholz *shper·holts nt* plywood

Spesen *shpay·zèn pl* (business) expenses

Spesenkonto *shpay·zèn·kon·tō nt* —**konten** expense account

sich spezialisieren auf *zikh shpe·tsee·a·lee·zee·rènowf vr* to specialize in

spezifisch *shpe·tsee·fish adj* specific

spezifiziert *shpe·tsi·fi·tseert adj* itemized (*bill etc*)

Spiegel *shpee·gèl m* — mirror

Spiegelei *shpee·gèl·eye nt* —**er** fried egg

spiegeln *shpee·gèln vt* reflect (*in mirror*)

Spiel *shpeel nt* —**e** pack (*of cards*); game; **auf dem Spiel stehen*** *owf daym shpeel shtay·èn* to be at stake

spielen *shpee·lèn vi* gamble □ *vt/i* play; **den Hamlet spielen** *dayn ham·let shpee·lèn* to act Hamlet; **Fußball spielen** *foos·bal shpee·lèn* to play football; **Geige spielen** *gye·gè shpee·lèn* to play the violin; **spielen mit** *shpee·lèn mit* to play with

Spielen *shpee·lèn nt* gambling

Spieler *shpee·lèr m* — gambler; player (*in sport*)

Spielerin *shpee·lè·rin f* —**nen** player (*in sport*)

Spielfilm *shpeel·film m* —**e** feature film

Spielgruppe *shpeel·groo·pè f* —**n** playgroup

Spielkarte *shpeel·kar·tè f* —**n** playing card

Spielplatz *shpeel·plats m* ¨e playground

Spielstand *shpeel·shtant m* score

Spielwarenladen *shpeel·vah·rèn·lah·dèn m* ¨ toyshop

Spielzeug *shpeel·tsoyk nt* —**e** toy

Spieß *shpees m* —**e** skewer

Spinat *shpi·naht m* spinach

Spinne *shpi·nè f* —**n** spider

spinnen* *shpi·nèn vt* spin (*wool*)

Spion *shpee·ōn m* —**e** spy

Spionin *shpee·ō·nin f* —**nen** spy

Spirituosen *shpi·ri·too·ō·zèn pl* spirits (*alcohol*)

Spitze *shpit·sè f* —**n** lace; point (*tip*)

Split *shplit m* grit

Splitter *shpli·tèr m* — flake; splinter

Sport *shport m* **Sportarten** sport(s)

Sportjackett *shport·ya·ket nt* —**s** sport coat, sport jacket

Sportkleidung *shport·klye·doong f* sportswear

Sportplatz *shport·plats m* ¨e playing field

Sportwagen *shport·vah·gèn m* — stroller; sport(s) car

Sprache *shprah·khè f* —**n** speech; language

Sprachführer *shprakh·füö·rèr m* — phrase book

Sprachlabor *shprakh·la·bōr nt* —**s** language laboratory

Spray *shpray m* —**s** spray (*of liquid*)

Spraydose *shpray·dō·zè f* —**n** aerosol

Sprechanlage *shprekh·an·lah·gè f* —**n** intercom

sprechen* *shpre·khèn vt/i* speak; **sprechen Sie Englisch?** *shpre·khèn zee eng·lish* do you speak English?; **mit jemandem über etwas sprechen*** *mit yay·man·dèm üö·bèr et·vass shpre·khèn* to speak/talk to someone about something

Sprecher *shpre·khèr m* — spokesman

Sprechzimmer *shprekh·tsi·mèr nt* — consulting room; doctor's office

springen* *shpring·èn vi* jump; bounce (*ball*); **das Glas ist gesprungen** *das glahs ist gè·shproong·èn* the glass cracked

Springrollo *shpring·ro·lō nt* —**s** window shade

Spritze *shprit·sè f* —**n** injection

spritzen *shprit·sèn vi* splash □ *vt* spray (*liquid*)

Spritzer *shprit·sèr m* — splash

sprudelnd *shproo·dèlnt adj* fizzy

Sprühdose *shprüö·dō·zè f* —**n** spray (*container*)

Sprung *shproong m* ¨e jump; crack; **einen Sprung in ein Glas machen** *ine·èn shproong in ine glahs ma·khèn* to crack a glass

Sprungbrett *shproong·bret nt* —**er** divingboard

spucken *shpoo·kèn vi* spit

spülen *shpüö·lèn vi* flush the toilet □ *vt* rinse

Spüllappen *shpüöl·la·pèn m* — dishcloth

Spülschüssel *shpüöl·shüö·sèl f* —**n** bowl (*for washing*)

Spülstein *shpüöl·shtine m* —**e** sink (*basin*)

Spülung *shpüö·loong f* —**en** rinse (*hair conditioner*)

Spur *shpoor f* —**en** trace (*mark*); track (*of animal*); lane (*of road*)

Squash *skvosh nt* squash (*sport*)

Staat *shtaht m* —**en** state

staatliche Schule *shtaht·li·khè shoo·lè f* public school

Staatsangehörigkeit *shtahts·an·gè·hur·rikh·kite f* —**en** nationality

Staatsbürger *shtahts·büör·gèr m* — subject (*person*)

Staatsbürgerin *shtahts·büör·gè·rin f* —**nen** subject (*person*)

Staatsdienst *shtahts·deenst m* civil service

Staatsstreich *shtahts·shtryekh m* —**e** coup d'état

Stäbchen *shtep·khèn pl* chopsticks

stabil *shta·beel* adj stable

Stachelbeere *shta·khèl·bay·rè* f —n gooseberry

Stacheldraht *shta·khèl·draht* m ˸e barbed wire

Stadion *shtah·dee·on* nt Stadien stadium

Stadium *shtah·dee·oom* nt Stadien stage (*period*)

Stadt *shtat* f ˸e town

Stadtgemeinde *shtat·gè·mine·dè* f —n borough

städtisch *shte·tish* adj urban; municipal

Stadtplan *shtat·plahn* m ˸e map (*of town*)

Stadtrand *shtat·rant* m suburbs; outskirts

Stadtrat *shtat·raht* m ˸e council (*of town*)

Stadtteil *shtat·tile* m —e district (*of town*)

Stadtzentrum *shtat·tsen·troom* nt —zentren town center

Stahl *shtahl* m steel

Stahlkammer *shtahl·ka·mèr* f —n strongroom

Stall *shtal* m ˸e stable

Stamm *shtam* m ˸e trunk (*of tree*); tribe

Stand *shtant* m ˸e stall; stand (*for taxis*); auf den neuesten Stand bringen* *owf dayn noy·èst·èn shtant bring·èn* to update

Standard- *shtan·dart* pref standard (*model*)

Ständer *shten·dèr* m — rack (*for dishes*)

ständig *shten·dikh* adj permanent □ adv permanently; continuously

Standuhr *shtant·oo·èr* f —en grandfather clock

Stange *shtang·è* f —n pole (*wooden*); bar (*rod*)

Stangenbohnen *shtang·èn·bō·nèn* pl pole beans

Stangensellerie *shtang·èn·ze·lè·ree* m —s celery

Stapel *shtah·pèl* m — pile; vom Stapel lassen* *fom shtah·pèl la·sèn* to launch (*ship*)

Star *star* m —s star (*celebrity*)

stark *shtark* adj strong (*structure, material*); es riecht stark *ess reekht shtark* it has a strong smell

Stärke *shter·kè* f strength (*of girder, rope etc*); starch

starren *shtar·rèn* vi stare; auf jemanden starren *owf yay·man·dèn shtar·rèn* to stare at somebody

Starthilfekabel *shtart·hilf·è·kah·bèl* pl jumper cables

Station *shta·tsee·ōn* f —en ward (*in hospital*)

Statistik *shta·ti·stik* f —en statistic; statistics

statistisch *shta·ti·stish* adj statistical

Stativ *shta·teef* nt —e tripod

statt *shtat* prep instead of

statt|finden* *shtat·fin·dèn* vi take place

Statue *stah·too·è* f —n statue

Staub *shtowp* m dust

staubig *shtow·bikh* adj dusty

Staubsauger *shtowp·zow·gèr* m — vacuum cleaner

Steak *stayk* nt —s steak

stechen* *shte·khèn* vt sting; prick

Stechmücke *shtekh·mōō·kè* f —n mosquito; gnat

Steckdose *shtek·dō·zè* f —n socket (*electrical*)

Stecker *shte·kèr* m — plug (*electric*)

Stecknadel *shtek·nah·dèl* f —n pin

stehen* *shtay·èn* vi stand; dieser Hut steht Ihnen gut *dee·zèr hoot shtayt ee·nèn goot* that hat suits you

stehen|bleiben* *shtay·èn·blye·bèn* vi stop (*person*)

Stehlampe *shtay·lam·pè* f —n floor lamp

stehlen* *shtay·lèn* vt steal; jemandem etwas stehlen* *yay·man·dèm et·vass shtay·lèn* to steal something from someone

steif *shtife* adj stiff

steigen* *shtye·gèn* vi rise (*prices*); increase; go uphill; steigen* auf *shtye·gèn owf* to mount

Steigerung *shtye·gè·roong* f —en rise (*in prices, wages*)

steil *shtile* adj steep

Steilkurs *shtile·koors* m —e crash course

Stein *shtine* m —e stone

Steinbruch *shtine·brookh* m ˸e quarry

Steinbutt *shtine·boot* m —e turbot

steinig *shtye·nikh* adj stony

Stelle *shte·lè* f —n job (*employment*); place; spot (*locality*); point (*in space*); die freie Stelle *frye·è shte·lè* vacancy (*job*); an der richtigen Stelle *an der rikh·ti·gèn shte·lè* in place; nicht an der richtigen Stelle *nikht an der rikh·ti·gèn shte·lè* out of place (*object*); die undichte Stelle *oon·dikh·tè shte·lè* leak (*gas etc*)

stellen* *shte·lèn* vt set (*alarm*); put; eine Frage stellen *ine·è frah·gè shte·lèn* to ask a question

stellvertretend *shtel·fer·tray·tènt* adj acting

Stellvertreter *shtel·fer·tray·tèr* m — deputy (*second-in-command*)

Stempel *shtem·pèl* m — hallmark; stamp (*rubber*)

stempeln *shtem·pèln* vt stamp (*visa*)

Stengel *shteng·èl* m — stem

Stenotypistin *shtay·nō·tōō·pist·in* f —nen shorthand typist; stenographer

Steppdecke *shtep·dek·è* f —n quilt

sterben* *shter·bèn* vi die

Stereo *ste·ray·ō* nt stereo; in Stereo *in ste·ray·ō* in stereo

stereo(phonisch) *ste·ray·ō(·fō·nish)* adj stereo(phonic)

steril *shte·reel* adj sterile

sterilisieren *shte·ri·li·zee·rèn* vt sterilize (*disinfect*)

Stern *shtern* m —e star

Steuer *shtoy·èr* f —n tax

steuerfrei *shtoy·èr·frye* adj tax-free

steuern *shtoy·èrn* vt steer (*boat*)

steuerpflichtig *shtoy·èr·pflikh·tikh* adj taxable

Steuerung *shtoy·èr·oong* f —en controls

Steward *styoo·art* m —s steward

Stewardeß *styoo·ar·dess* f —en flight attendant; stewardess

Stich *shtikh* m —e bite (*by insect*); stitch (*sewing*); sting; trick (*in cards*); jemanden im Stich lassen* *yay·man·dèn im shtikh la·sèn* to let someone down

Stiche *shti·khè* pl stitch (*pain*)

Stichprobe *shtikh·prō·bè* f —n spot check

Stickerei *shti·kè·rye* f —en embroidery

stickig *shti·kikh* adj stuffy

Stiefbruder *shteef·broo·dèr* m ˸ stepbrother

Stiefel *shtee·fèl* m — boot

Stiefmutter *shteef·moo·tèr f =* stepmother

Stiefschwester *shteef·shve·stèr f —n* stepsister

Stiefsohn *shteef·zōn m =e* stepson

Stieftochter *shteef·tokh·tèr f =* stepdaughter

Stiefvater *shteef·fah·tèr m =* stepfather

Stier *shteer m —e* bull

Stierkampf *shteer·kampf m =e* bullfight

Stil *shteel m —e* style

still *shtil adj* silent; quiet (*person*)

Stille *shti·lè f* silence

Stimme *shti·mè f —n* voice; vote

stimmen *shti·mèn vt* tune (*instrument*); **stimmen für** *shti·mèn fōōr* to vote for

Stimmung *shti·moong f —en* mood; atmosphere

Stipendium *shti·pen·dee·oom nt —dien* grant (*to student*)

Stirn *shtirn f —en* forehead

Stock *shtok m =e* cane (*walking stick*); stick; floor; **der erste Stock** *er·stè shtok* second floor

Stockung *shto·koong f —en* tie-up (*traffic*)

Stockwerk *shtok·verk nt —e* story (*in building*)

Stoff *shtof m —e* fabric; material

stöhnen *shtur'·nèn vi* groan; moan □ *nt* **das Stöhnen** *shtur'·nèn* groan; moan

Stola *shtō·la f Stolen* stole (*wrap*)

stolpern *shtol·pèrn vi* trip (*stumble*)

stolz *shtolts adj* proud; **stolz auf** *shtolts owf* proud of

Stolz *shtolts m* pride

stopfen *shtop·fèn vt* darn

stoppen *shto·pèn vt* stop (*car etc*)

Stoppuhr *shtop·oo·èr f —en* stop watch

Stöpsel *shtur'p·sèl m —* plug (*for basin etc*)

stören *shtur'·rèn vt* disturb (*interrupt*); **bitte nicht stören** *bi·tè nikht shtur'·rèn* do not disturb

Störungssucher *shtur'·roongs·zoo·khèr m —* trouble-shooter (*technical*)

Stoß *shtōs m =e* gust; bump (*knock*)

Stoßdämpfer *shtōs·demp·fèr m —* shock absorber

stoßen* *shtō·sèn vt* bump

Stoßstange *shtōs·shtang·è f —n* bumper (*on car*)

Stoßzeit *shtōs·tsite f —en* rush hour

Strafe *shtrah·fè f —n* punishment

strafen *shtrah·fèn vt* punish

straff *shtraf adj* tight (*rope*)

Strafzettel *shtrahf·tse·tèl m —* parking-ticket

Strahl *shtrahl m —en* ray; beam (*of light*)

Strand *shtrant m =e* shore (*of sea*); beach

Strandpromenade *shtrant·pro·mè·nah·dè f —n* front (*seaside*)

strapazierfähig *shtra·pa·tseer·fay·ikh adj* tough (*material*)

Straße *shtrah·sè f —n* road; street

Straßenbahn *shtrah·sèn·bahn f —en* tram(car); streetcar

Straßenbauarbeiten *shtrah·sèn·bow·ar·bye·tèn pl* road works

Straßenkarte *shtrah·sèn·kar·tè f —n* road map

Straßenlaterne *shtrah·sèn·la·ter·nè f —n* streetlamp

Straßensperre *shtrah·sèn·shpe·rè f —n* road block

Straßentest *shtrah·sèn·test m —s* road test

Straßenverkehrsordnung *shtrah·sèn·fer·kayrs·ort·noong f —en* Highway Code

Strauch *shtrowkh m =er* bush

Strauß *shtrows m =e* bunch (*of flowers*)

Strecke *shtre·kè f —n* route

streicheln *shtrye·khèln vt* stroke

streichen* *shtrye·khèn vt* paint

Streichholz *shtryekh·holts nt =er* match

Streichholzschachtel *shtryekh·holts·shakh·tèl f —n* matchbox

Streifen *shtrye·fèn m —* strip (*length*); stripe; streak

Streik *shtrike m —s* strike (*industrial*); walkout; **der wilde Streik** *vil·dè shtrike* unofficial strike; **vom Streik betroffen** *fom shtrike bè·tro·fèn* strikebound

Streikbrecher *shtrike·bre·khèr m —* strike-breaker

streiken *shtrye·kèn vi* strike (*workers*)

Streikende(r) *shtrye·kèn·dè(·dèr) m/f —n* striker

Streikposten *shtrike·pos·tèn m —* picket

Streit *shtrite m —e* dispute; quarrel; disagreement

sich streiten* *zikh shtrye·tèn vr* quarrel; argue; **sich mit jemandem streiten*** *zikh mit yay·man·dèm shtrye·tèn* to quarrel with somebody

streng *shtreng adj* positive (*definite*); strict; harsh (*severe*)

Streß *shtres m* stress (*tension*)

Strichgegend *shtrikh·gay·gènt f —en* red light district

Strickanleitung *shtrik·an·lye·toong f —en* pattern (*knitting*)

stricken *shtri·kèn vt/i* knit

Strickjacke *shtrik·ya·kè f —n* cardigan

Stricknadel *shtrik·nah·dèl f —n* knitting needle

Strickwaren *shtrik·vah·rèn pl* knitwear

Stripperin *shtri·pè·rin f —nen* stripper

Striptease *shtrip·teez nt* striptease

Stroh *shtrō nt* straw

Strom *shtrōm m* power (*electricity*)

Stromausfall *shtrōm·ows·fal m =e* power failure

strömen *shtrur'·mèn vi* pour

Stromkreis *shtrōm·krise m —e* circuit (*electric*)

stromlinienförmig *shtrōm·leen·yèn·fur·mikh adj* streamlined (*car*)

Strömung *shtrur'·moong f —en* current (*of water, air*)

Strudel *shtroo·dèl m —* whirlpool

Struktur *shtrook·toor f —en* structure

Strumpf *shtroompf m =e* stocking

Strumpfhose *shtroompf·hō·zè f —n* panty hose; tights

Stück *shtōōk nt —e* piece; cut (*of meat*); track (*on record*); plot (*of land*); **das Stück Zucker** *shtōōk tsoo·kèr* lump of sugar; **das Stück Seife** *shtōōk zye·fè* bar of soap

Stückchen *shtōōk·khèn nt —* scrap (*bit*)

Student *shtoo·dent m —en* student

Studentin *shtoo·den·tin f —nen* student

studieren *shtoo·dee·rèn vt/i* study

Studio *shtoo·dee·ō nt —s* studio

Studium *shtoo·dee·oom nt Studien* study; **sein Studium genießen*** *zine shtoo·dee·oom gè·nee·sèn* to enjoy one's studies

Stufe *shtoo·fè f —n* step (*stair*)

Stuhl *shtool m -̈e* chair
stumm *shtoom adj* dumb
stumpf *shtoompf adj* blunt (*knife*)
Stunde *shtoon·dě f -n* hour; lesson
stündlich *shtöont·likh adv* hourly
stur *shtoor adj* stubborn
Sturm *shtoorm m -̈e* storm; gale
stürmisch *shtöör·mish adj* stormy; rough (*sea*)
stürzen *shtöör·tsen vi.*slump
Sturzhelm *shtoorts·helm m -e* crash helmet
stutzen *shtoot·sĕn vt* trim (*hedge*)
Stützpunkt *shtöots·poonkt m -e* base (*military*)
Substanz *zoop·stants f -en* substance
Subvention *soop·ven·tsee·ôn f -en* grant (*to institution*); subsidy
subventionieren *zoop·ven·tsee·ô·nee·rĕn vt* subsidize
suchen *zoo·khĕn vt* look for; search for
Süchtige(r) *zöökh·ti·gĕ(·gĕr) m/f -n* addict
Südafrika *zööt·a·fri·ka nt* South Africa
südafrikanisch *zööt·a·fri·kah·nish adj* South African
Südamerika *zööt·a·may·ri·ka nt* South America
südamerikanisch *zööt·a·may·ri·kah·nish adj* South American
Süden *zöö·dĕn m* south; nach Süden *nakh zöö·dĕn* south
südlich *zööt·likh adj* southern
Südosten *zööt·o·stĕn m* southeast
Südpol *zööt·pôl m* South Pole
Südwesten *zööt·ve·stĕn m* southwest
Sultanine *zool·ta·nee·nĕ f -n* sultana
Summe *zoo·mĕ f -n* sum (*total amount*)
Sumpf *zoompf m -̈e* swamp; bog
Supermarkt *zoo·pĕr·markt m -̈e* supermarket; der große Supermarkt *grö·sĕ zoo·pĕr·markt* superstore
Supertanker *zoo·pĕr·tang·kĕr m —* supertanker
Suppe *zoo·pĕ f -n* soup
Surfboard *zurf·bort nt —s* surf board
Surfen *zur·fĕn nt* surfing □ *vi surfen gehen* zur·fĕn gay·ĕn* to go surfing
suspendieren *zoos·pen·dee·rĕn vt* suspend (*worker*)
süß *zöös adj* sweet
Süßwaren *söös·vah·rĕn pl* confectionery
Sweatshirt *swet·shurt nt —s* sweatshirt
Symbol *zöm·bôl nt —e* symbol
symbolisieren *zöm·bô·li·zee·rĕn vt* represent (*symbolize*)
symmetrisch *zöö·may·trish adj* symmetrical
Symphonie *zöm·fô·nee f -n* symphony
Symposium *zöm·pô·zee·oom nt* **Symposien** symposium
Symptom *zöömp·tôm nt —e* symptom
Synagoge *zöö·na·gô·gĕ f -n* synagogue
Synchrongetriebe *zöön·krôn·gĕ·tree·bĕ nt —* synchromesh
Syrien *zöö·ree·ĕn nt* Syria
syrisch *zöö·rish adj* Syrian
System *zöos·taym nt —e* system
Systemanalytiker *zöos·taym·a·na·löö·ti·kĕr m —* systems analyst
systematisch *zöos·tay·mah·tish adj* systematic
Szene *stsay·nĕ f -n* scene

T

Tabak *ta·bak m —e* tobacco

Tabakhändler *ta·bak·hent·lĕr m —* tobacconist
Tabakladen *ta·bak·lah·dĕn m -̈* tobacconist's (shop)
Tabelle *ta·be·lĕ f -n* chart (*diagram, table*)
Tablett *ta·blet nt —s* tray
Tablette *ta·ble·tĕ f -n* tablet (*medicine*); pill
Tachometer *takh·o·may·tĕr m —* speedometer
Tafel *tah·fĕl f -n* table; board; die Tafel Schokolade *tah·fĕl shô·kô·lah·dĕ* bar of chocolate
Tag *tahk m —e* day; jeden Tag *yay·dĕn tahk* every day, day by day; am Tag zuvor *am tahk tsoo·fôr* the day before; am Tag danach *am tahk da·nakh* the next day; eines Tages *ine·ĕs tah·gĕs* one day
Tagebuch *tah·gĕ·bookh nt -̈er* diary
Tagesordnung *tah·gĕs·ort·noong f —en* agenda
Tagesrückfahrkarte *tah·gĕs·röök·fahr·kar·tĕ f -n* one-day excursion
Tageszeitung *tah·gĕs·tsye·toong f —en* daily (*newspaper*)
täglich *teg·likh adj* daily
Taille *tal·yĕ f -n* waist
Taktik *tak·tik f -en* tactics
taktvoll *takt·fol adj* discreet
Tal *tahl nt -̈er* valley
Talkumpuder *talk·oom·poo·dĕr m* talc(um powder)
Tampon *tam·pon m —s* tampon
Tango *tan·gô m —s* tango
Tank *tank m —s* tank (*of car*)
Tankschiff *tank·shif nt —e* tanker (*ship*)
Tankstelle *tank·shte·lĕ f -n* filling station; gas station; die Großtankstelle *grôs·tank·shte·lĕ* service station; die Tankstelle und Raststätte *tank·shte·lĕ oont rast·shte·tĕ* service area
Tankwagen *tank·vah·gĕn m —* tanker (*truck*)
Tanne *ta·nĕ f -n* fir (*tree*)
Tante *tan·tĕ f -n* aunt(ie)
Tanz *tants m -̈e* dance
Tanzabend *tants·ah·bĕnt m —e* dance (*ball*)
tanzen *tan·tsĕn vi* dance
Tapete *ta·pay·tĕ f -n* wallpaper
tapezieren *ta·pay·tsee·rĕn vt* paper (*wall*)
tapfer *tap·fĕr adj* brave
Tarif *ta·reef m —e* rate (*price*); tariff (*list of charges*)
Tasche *ta·shĕ f -n* bag; pocket
Taschenbuch *ta·shĕn·bookh nt -̈er* paperback
Taschengeld *ta·shĕn·gelt nt* pocket money
Taschenlampe *ta·shĕn·lam·pĕ f -n* flashlight
Taschenmesser *ta·shĕn·me·sĕr m —* penknife; pocketknife
Taschentuch *ta·shĕn·tookh nt -̈er* handkerchief
Tasse *ta·sĕ f -n* cup
Taste *ta·stĕ f -n* key (*of piano, typewriter*)
Tat *taht f —en* action (*act*)
tätig *tay·tikh adj* active
Tätigkeit *tay·tikh·kite f —en* activity; occupation
Tatsache *taht·za·khĕ f -n* fact
tatsächlich *taht·zekh·likh adv* in fact
tätscheln *tet·shĕln vt* pat
taub *towb adj* deaf
Taube *tow·bĕ f -n* pigeon; dove

tauchen *tow·khèn vi* dive □ *vt* dip *(into liquid)*

tauen *tow·èn vi* thaw *(ice)*

Taufe *tow·fè f* —**n** baptism

täuschen *toy·shèn vt* deceive

tauschen *tow·shèn vt* exchange

tausend *tow·zènt num* thousand

tausendste(r/s) *tow·zènt·stè (·stèr/·stès) adj* thousandth

Taxi *tak·see nt* —**s** taxi; **mit dem Taxi fahren*** *mit daym tak·see fah·rèn* to go by taxi

Taxistand *tak·see·shtant m* ¨**e** taxi stand

Team *teem nt* —**s** team

Technik *tekh·nik f* technology; technique

Techniker *tekh·ni·kèr m* — technician

Technikerin *tekh·ni·kè·rin f* —**nen** technician

technisch *tekh·nish adj* technical

technologisch *tekh·no·lō·gish adj* technological

Tee *tay m* tea □ *nt das Tee tee* —**s** tee *(in golf)*

Teebeutel *tay·boy·tèl m* — tea bag

Teekanne *tay·ka·nè f* —**n** teapot

Teelöffel *tay·lur'·fèl m* — teaspoon

Teer *tayr m* tar

Teesieb *tay·zeep nt* —**e** tea strainer

Teestube *tay·shtoo·bè f* —**n** tearoom

Teetasse *tay·ta·sè f* —**n** teacup

Teich *tyekh m* —**e** pond *(natural)*

Teig *tike m* dough; pastry

Teil *tile m* —**e** part

teilen *tye·lèn vt* divide *(apportion)*; share *(money, room)*; **8 durch 4 teilen** *8 doorkh 4 tye·lèn* to divide 8 by 4

Teilnahme *tile·nah·mè f* participation

teil|nehmen* *tile·nay·mèn vi* participate

teilweise *tile·vye·zè adv* partly

Teilzahlungskauf *tile·tsah·loongs·kowf m* installment plan

Teint *tang m* —**s** complexion

Telefon *tay·lay·fōn nt* —**e** telephone; **er ist am Telefon** *er ist am tay·lay·fōn* he's on the phone

Telefonanruf *tay·lay·fōn·an·roof m* —**e** telephone call

Telefonbuch *tay·lay·fōn·bookh nt* ¨**er** telephone directory

Telefongespräch *tay·lay·fōn·gè·shprekh nt* —**e** phone-call

telefonieren *tay·lay·fō·nee·rèn vi* telephone

telefonisch *tay·lay·fō·nish adv* by telephone

Telefonist *tay·lay·fō·nist m* —**en** telephone operator

Telefonistin *tay·lay·fō·nis·tin f* —**nen** telephone operator

Telefonnummer *tay·lay·fōn·noo·mèr f* —**n** telephone number

Telefonzelle *tay·lay·fōn·tse·lè f* —**n** telephone booth

Telegramm *tay·lay·gram nt* —**e** telegram

telegraphieren *tay·lay·gra·fee·rèn vt* telegraph

Teleobjektiv *tay·lay·op·yek·teef nt* —**e** telephoto lens

Telephonist *tay·lay·fō·nist m* —**en** switchboard operator

Telephonistin *tay·lay·fō·nis·tin f* —**nen** switchboard operator

Teleskop *tay·lay·skōp nt* —**e** telescope

Teller *te·lèr m* — plate

Tempel *tem·pèl m* — temple *(building)*

Temperatur *tem·pay·ra·toor f* —**en** temperature; **jemandes Temperatur messen*** *yay·man·dès tem·pay·ra·toor me·sèn* to take someone's temperature

Tempo *tem·pō nt* pace *(speed)*; **in einem Tempo von** *in ine'·em tem·pō fon* at the rate of

Tendenz *ten·dents f* —**en** trend *(tendency)*; **die Tendenz haben***, **etwas zu tun** *dee ten·dents hah·bèn et·vass tsoo toon* to tend to do something

Tennis *te·niss nt* tennis

Tennisplatz *te·niss·plats m* ¨**e** tennis court

Tennisschläger *te·niss·shlay·gèr m* — tennis racket

Teppich *te·pikh m* —**e** carpet

Teppichboden *te·pikh·bō·dèn m* ¨ wall-to-wall carpet(ing)

Termin *ter·meen m* —**e** date; deadline; appointment *(rendezvous)*

Terminal *ter·mee·nal nt* —**s** terminal

Terminkalender *ter·meen·ka·len·dèr m* — diary

Terrasse *te·ra·sè f* —**n** patio; terrace *(of café)*

Terrorismus *te·ro·ris·moos m* terrorism

Terrorist *te·ro·rist m* —**en** terrorist

Terroristin *te·ro·ris·tin f* —**nen** terrorist

Terylene *te·rōō·layn nt* terylene; dacron

Tesafilm *tay·za·film m* Scotch tape

Test *test m* —**s** test *(in school etc)*

Testament *tes·ta·ment nt* —**e** will *(testament)*

testen *tes·tèn vt* test

teuer *toy·èr adj* expensive

Text *tekst m* —**e** text

Textilien *teks·tee·lee·èn pl* textiles

Textur *teks·toor f* texture

Theater *tay·ah·tèr nt* — theater; fuss; **ins Theater gehen*** *ins tay·ah·tèr gay·èn* to go to the theater; **Theater machen** *tay·ah·tèr ma·khèn* to make a fuss

Theaterstück *tay·ah·tèr·shtōōk nt* —**e** play *(theatrical)*

Theke *tay·kè f* —**n** bar *(counter)*

Thema *tay·ma nt* **Themen** topic; subject

Theorie *tay·ō·ree f* —**n** theory

Thermometer *ter·mō·may·tèr nt* — thermometer

Thermosflasche *ter·mos·fla·shè f* —**n** Thermos

Thunfisch *toon·fish m* tuna fish

Thymian *tōō·mi·ahn m* thyme

ticken *ti·kèn vi* tick *(clock)*

tief *teef adj* deep; low *(in pitch)*

Tiefe *tee·fè f* depth

Tiefkühltruhe *teef·kōōl·troo·è f* —**n** deepfreeze

Tier *teer nt* —**e** animal

Tierarzt *teer·artst m* ¨**e** vet(erinary surgeon)

Tierwelt *teer·velt f* wildlife

Tiger *tee·gèr m* — tiger

Tinte *tin·tè f* —**n** ink

tippen *ti·pèn vt* type *(letter)*

Tisch *tish m* —**e** table; **den Tisch decken** *dayn tish de·kèn* to set the table

Tischdecke *tish·de·kè f* —**n** tablecloth

Tischtennis *tish·te·nis nt* table tennis

Tischwäsche *tish·ve·shè f* linen *(for table)*

Titel *tee·tèl m* — title

T-Kreuzung *tay·kroy·tsoong f* —**en** T-junction *(on road)*

Toast *tōst* m toast; einen Toast auf je-manden aus|bringen* *ine·èn tōst owf yay·man·dèn ows·bring·èn* to pro-pose a toast to someone
Toaster *tōs·tèr* m — toaster
Tochter *tokh·tèr* f ˝ daughter □ *pref* **Tochter-** *tokh·tèr* subsidiary
Tochtergesellschaft *tokh·tèr·gè·zel·shaft* f —en subsidiary (*company*)
Tod *tōt* m —e death
tödlich *tur't·likh* adj fatal
Toilette *tō·a·le·tè* f —n toilet; rest-room
Toiletten *tō·a·le·tèn* pl public conveni-ences
Toilettenartikel *tō·a·le·tèn·ar·tee·kèl* pl toiletries
Toilettenpapier *tō·a·le·tèn·pa·peer* nt toilet paper
Toilettentisch *tō·a·le·tèn·tish* m —e dressing table
Toilettenwasser *tō·a·le·tèn·va·sèr* nt toilet water
Tollwut *tol·voot* f rabies
Tomate *tō·mah·tè* f —n tomato
Ton *tōn* m tone; clay
Tonband *tōn·bant* nt ˝er tape (*mag-netic*)
Tonbandbegleiter *tōn·bant·bè·glye·tèr* m — audio-guide
Tonbandgerät *tōn·bant·gè·ret* nt —e tape recorder
Tonic *to·nik* nt tonic water
Tonikum *tō·ni·koom* nt **Tonika** tonic (*medicine*)
Tonleiter *tōn·lye·tèr* f —n scale (*mu-sic*)
Tonne *to·nè* f —n ton
Tonspur *tōn·shpoor* f —en sound track
Topf *topf* m ˝e pot; pan (*saucepan*)
Töpfchen *tur'pf·khèn* nt — pot(ty)
Töpferei *tur'p·fè·rye* f —en pottery (*workshop*)
Topfkratzer *topf·kra·tsèr* m — scourer
Topinambur *tō·pi·nam·boor* m —s Jerusalem artichoke
Tor *tōr* nt —e gate; goal (*sport*)
Torte *tor·tè* f —n gateau; tart
Tortelett *tor·tè·let* nt —s pie
tot *tōt* adj dead (*person*)
töten *tur'·tèn* vt kill
Totenschein *tō·tèn·shine* m —e death certificate
Tour *toor* f —en tour; auf Touren brin-gen* *owf too·rèn bring·èn* to rev
Tourismus *too·ris·moos* m tourism
Tourist *too·rist* m —en tourist
Touristenklasse *too·ris·tèn·kla·sè* f tourist class
Touristin *too·ris·tin* f —nen tourist
traben *trah·bèn* vi trot (*horse*)
Tracht *trakht* f —en costume
Tradition *tra·di·tsee·ōn* f —en tradition
Tragbahre *trahk·bah·rè* f —n stretcher
tragbar *trahk·bahr* adj portable
tragen* *trah·gèn* vt wear (*clothes*); bear (*weight*); carry (*in hands, arms*)
Trägerkleid *tre·gèr·klite* nt —er jump-er (*dress*)
trägerlos *tre·gèr·lōs* adj strapless
Tragtasche *trahk·ta·shè* f —n bag (*paper carrier*)
Trainer *tray·nèr* m — coach (*instruc-tor*)
Trainerin *tray·nèr·in* f —nen coach (*instructress*)
trainieren *tray·nee·rèn* vi train (*athlete*)
Training *tray·ning* nt training (*for sports*)
Trainingsanzug *tray·nings·an·tsook* m ˝e track suit

Traktor *trak·tor* m —en tractor
trampen *tram·pèn* vi hitchhike
tranchieren *tron·shee·rèn* vt carve (*meat*)
Träne *tray·nè* f —n tear; in Tränen aufgelöst *in tray·nèn owf·gè·lur'st* in tears
transatlantisch *tranz·at·lan·tish* adj transatlantic
Transistor *tran·zis·tor* m —en transis-tor
im Transit *im tran·zit* adv in transit
Transithalle *tran·zit·ha·lè* f —n transit lounge
Transitvisum *tran·zit·vee·zoom* nt —visa transit visa
Transport *trans·port* m transport
transportieren *trans·por·tee·rèn* vt transport
Traube *trow·bè* f —n grape
Traum *trowm* m ˝e dream
träumen *troy·mèn* vi dream; träumen von *troy·mèn fon* to dream of
traurig *trow·rikh* adj sorry; sad
Trauung *trow·oong* f —en wedding ceremony
Trauzeuge *trow·tsoy·gè* m —n best man
treffen* *tre·fèn* vt meet; eine Entschei-dung treffen* *ine·è ent·shye·doong tre·fèn* to take a decision
treiben* *trye·bèn* vi drift (*boat*); float □ vt drive; go in for
trennen *tre·nèn* vt divide (*separate*)
Trennwand *tren·vant* f ˝e partition (*wall*)
Treppe *tre·pè* f —n flight of steps; stairs
Treppenabsatz *tre·pèn·ap·zats* m ˝e landing (*on stairs*)
Treppenhaus *tre·pèn·hows* nt ˝er stair-case
Tresor *tray·zor* m —e safe
Tretboot *trayt·bōt* nt —e pedalo
treten* *tray·tèn* vi step □ vt kick
Trick *trik* m —s trick (*malicious*); mit einem Trick betrügen* *mit ine·èm trik bè·trōō·gèn* to trick
Trifle *trye·fèl* m —s trifle (*dessert*)
Trimester *tri·mes·tèr* m — term (*of school etc*)
trinken* *tring·kèn* vt drink; etwas trin-ken* *et·vass tring·kèn* to have a drink
Trinkgeld *trink·gelt* nt —er tip (*money given*)
Trinkwasser *trink·vass·èr* nt drinking water
Tritt *trit* m —e step; kick
Trittleiter *trit·lye·tèr* f —n stepladder
trocken *tro·kèn* adj dry
trocken|schleudern *tro·kèn·shloy·dèrn* vt spin-dry
trocknen *trok·nèn* vt dry
Trommel *tro·mèl* f —n drum
Trompete *trom·pay·tè* f —n trumpet
Tropen *trō·pèn* pl tropics
tropfen *trop·fèn* vi drip □ m der Trop-fen *trop·fèn* drip; drop (*of liquid*)
tropfnaß auf|hängen *tropf·nass owf·heng·èn* vt drip-dry
tropisch *trō·pish* adj tropical
trotz *trots* prep in spite of
trotzdem *trots·daym* adv even so; all the same
trüb *trōōp* adj dull (*day, weather*)
Trüffel *trōō·fèl* f —n truffle (*fungus*)
Trumpf *troompf* m —e trump (*cards*)
Trupp *troop* m —s troop
Trust *trust* m —s trust (*company*)
Truthahn *troot·hahn* m ˝e turkey

tschechisch *che·khish* adj Czech(oslo-vakian)

Tschechoslowakei *che·kho·slo·va·kye f* Czechoslovakia

T-Shirt *tee·shirt nt* —s T-shirt

Tube *too·bè f* —n tube

Tuch *tookh nt* ̈er cloth; scarf; towel; shawl

tüchtig *tōōkh·tikh* adj efficient

Tulpe *tool·pè f* —n tulip

tun* *toon vt* do; put; **das tut nichts dass toon nikhts** that doesn't matter

Tunesien *too·nay·zyen nt* Tunisia

tunesisch *too·nay·zish* adj Tunisian

Tunnel *too·nèl m* —s tunnel

Tür *tōōr f* —en door

Türkei *tōōr·kye f* Turkey

türkis *tōōr·kees* adj turquoise

türkisch *tōōr·kish* adj Turkish

Türklingel *tōōr·kling·èl f* —n doorbell

Türklinke *tōōr·kling·kè f* —n door handle, doorknob

Turm *toorm m* ̈e tower

Turnen *toor·nèn nt* gymnastics

Turnhalle *toorn·ha·lè f* —n gym(nasium)

Turnschuhe *toorn·shoo·è pl* plimsolls

Tüte *tōō·tè f* —n bag (*paper*)

typisch *typ·pish* adj typical

U

u.A.w.g. *abbrev* R.S.V.P.

U-Bahn *oo·bahn f* —en subway (*railway*); underground (*railway*)

übel *ōō·bèl* adj bad; **mir ist übel meer ist ōō·bèl** I feel sick

Übelkeit *ōō·bèl·kite f* —en sickness (*nausea*)

üben *ōō·bèn vt/i* practice

über *ōō·bèr prep* over; above; **über London fahren* ōō·bèr lon·don fah·rèn** to go to London (*via*); **über etwas sprechen* ōō·bèr et·vass shpre·khèn** to talk about something; **über die Straße gehen* ōō·bèr dee shtrah·sè gay·èn** to walk across the road

überall *ōō·bèr·al* adv everywhere

überbacken *ōō·bèr·ba·kèn* adj au gratin

überbelichtet *ōō·bèr·bè·likh·tèt* adj overexposed (*photo*)

Überblick *ōō·bèr·blik m* —e review

Überdosis *ōō·bèr·dō·zis f* —dosen overdose

übereinander *ōō·bèr·ine·an·dèr* adv one upon the other

überein|stimmen *ōō·bèr·ine·shti·mèn vi* agree; **mit jemandem nicht überein|stimmen mit yay·man·dèm nikht ōō·bèr·ine·shti·mèn** to disagree with somebody

überfahren* *ōō·bèr·fah·rèn vt* to run down (*car etc*)

Überfahrt *ōō·bèr·fahrt f* —en crossing (*voyage*)

Überfall *ōō·bèr·fal m* ̈e raid (*by criminals*)

überfallen* *ōō·bèr·fa·lèn vt* attack

überfällig *ōō·bèr·fe·likh* adj overdue

Überfluß *ōō·bèr·flooss m* ̈e excess

überflüssig *ōō·bèr·flōō·sikh* adj superfluous

Überführung *ōō·bèr·fōō·roong f* —en overpass

überfüllt *ōō·bèr·fōōlt* adj crowded

übergeben* *ōō·bèr·gay·bèn vt* present (*give*)

Übergewicht *ōō·bèr·gè·vikht nt* excess baggage

überhaupt *ōō·bèr·howpt* adv at all

überholen *ōō·bèr·hō·lèn vt* pass (*car*)

Überholspur *ōō·bèr·hōl·shpoor f* —en outside lane (*in road*)

überleben *ōō·bèr·lay·bèn vi* survive

überlegen *ōō·bèr·lay·gèn vt* consider

übermorgen *ōō·bèr·mor·gèn* adv the day after tomorrow

übernachten *ōō·bèr·nakh·tèn vi* to stay the night

Übernahme *ōō·bèr·nah·mè f* —n take-over

Übernahmeangebot *ōō·bèr·nah·mè·an·ge·bōt nt* —e take-over bid

übernehmen* *ōō·bèr·nay·mèn vt* adopt (*proposal*); accept (*responsibility*); **eine Firma übernehmen* ine·è fir·ma ōō·bèr·nay·mèn** to take over a firm

überprüfen *ōō·bèr·prōō·fèn vt* check (*examine*)

überqueren *ōō·bèr·kvay·rèn vt* cross (*road, sea*)

überraschen *ōō·bèr·ra·shèn vt* surprise

überrascht *ōō·bèr·rasht* adj surprised

Überraschung *ōō·bèr·ra·shoong f* —en surprise

überreden *ōō·bèr·ray·dèn vt* persuade

überschreiten* *ōō·bèr·shrye·tèn vt* exceed

Überschuß *ōō·bèr·shoos m* ̈e surplus

in Übersee *in ōō·bèr·zay* adv overseas

Überseekoffer *ōō·bèr·zay·ko·fèr m* — trunk (*for clothes etc*)

übersehen* *ōō·bèr·zay·èn vt* ignore (*person*)

übersenden* *ōō·bèr·zen·dèn vt* send

übersetzen *ōō·bèr·zet·sèn vt* translate

Übersetzung *ōō·bèr·zet·soong f* —en translation

Überstunden *ōō·bèr·shtoon·dèn pl* overtime

übertreiben* *ōō·bèr·trye·bèn vt* exaggerate

Übertreibung *ōō·bèr·trye·boong f* —en exaggeration

übertrieben *ōō·bèr·tree·bèn* adj unreasonable (*demand, price*)

übertrumpfen *ōō·bèr·troomp·fèn vt* trump

überwachen *ōō·bèr·wa·khèn vt* supervise

überweisen* *ōō·bèr·vye·zèn vt* transfer (*money*)

Überweisung *ōō·bèr·vye·zoong f* —en remittance

überzeugen *ōōoo·bèr·tsoy·gèn vt* convince

üblich *ōō·blikh* adj usual

übrig *ōō·brikh* adj left over; **es war etwas übrig ess vahr et·vass ōō·brikh** some (of it) was left

übrig|bleiben* *ōō·brikh·blye·bèn vi* remain (*be left over*)

übrigens *ōō·bri·gèns* adv by the way

Übung *ōō·boong f* —en exercise; practice

UdSSR *oo·day·ess·ess·ehr f* U.S.S.R.

Ufer *oo·fèr nt* — bank (*of river*); shore (*of lake*)

Uhr *oor f* —en clock; **um 3 Uhr oom 3 oor** at 3 o'clock; **es ist 4 Uhr es ist 4 oor** it's 4 o'clock

UKW *oo·ka·vay abbrev* V.H.F.

Ulme *ool·mè f* —n elm

Ultimatum *ool·ti·mah·toom nt* Ultimaten ultimatum

um *oom prep* around; **um Weihnachten herum oom vye·nakh·tèn he·room** near (to) Christmas; **um 4 Uhr oom 4 oor** at 4 o'clock; **um etwas zu tun oom et·vass tsoo toon** in order to do something

um|adressieren *oom·a·dre·see·rèn vt* readdress

umarmen *oom·ar·mèn vt* embrace

um|drehen *oom·dray·èn vt* turn around; **er drehte sich um** *er dray·tè zikh oom* he turned (around); **etwas um|drehen** *et·vass oom·dray·èn* to turn something inside out; to turn something over; to turn something upside down

Umdrehung *oom·dray·oong f* **—en** rev (*in engine*)

um|fallen* *oom·fa·lèn vi* fall down

umgeben* *oom·gay·bèn vt* surround

Umgebung *oom·gay·boong f* surroundings; neighborhood

Umgehungsstraße *oom·gay·oongs·shtrah·sè f* **—n** bypass; beltway

umgekehrt *oom·gè·kayrt adv* vice versa

Umhang *oom·hang m* **⁼e** cloak

Umhangtuch *oom·hang·tookh nt* **⁼er** wrap (*shawl*)

um|kehren *oom·kay·rèn vi* turn back

Umkleidekabine *oom·klye·dè·ka·bee·nè f* **—n** cubicle

um|leiten *oom·lye·tèn vt* divert; reroute

um|lernen *oom·ler·nèn vi* retrain

Umorganisation *oom·or·ga·ni·za·tsee·ōn f* **—en** reorganization

um|organisieren *oom·or·ga·ni·zee·rèn vt* reorganize

Umrechnungskurs *oom·rekh·noongs·koors m* rate of exchange

Umriß *oom·riss m* **—e** outline (*summary*)

Umsatz *oom·zats m* **⁼e** volume of sales; turnover (*money*)

Umschlag *oom·shlahk m* **⁼e** envelope

um|schulen *oom·shoo·lèn vt* retrain

Umschulung *oom·shoo·loong f* **—en** retraining

sich um|sehen* *zikh oom·zay·èn vr* to look about/around

Umstände *oom·shten·dè pl* circumstances

Umstandskleid *oom·shtants·klite nt* **—er** maternity dress

um|steigen* *oom·shtye·gèn vi* change (*trains etc*); **in Marseille um|steigen** *in mar·say oom·shtye·gèn* to change trains at Marseilles

um|stellen *oom·shte·lèn vt* adapt; **auf Computer um|stellen** *owf kom·poo·tèr oom·shtel·èn* to computerize (*system*)

um|tauschen *oom·tow·shèn vt* change (*exchange*)

um|verteilen *oom·fer·tye·lèn vt* redistribute

Umverteilung *oom·fer·tye·loong f* **—en** redistribution

Umweg *oom·vayk m* **—e** detour

Umwelt *oom·velt f* **—en** environment

Umweltverschmutzung *oom·velt·fer·shmoot·soong f* pollution

um|werfen* *oom·ver·fèn vt* knock over/down

um|ziehen* *oom·tsee·èn vi* move (*change residence*); **sich um|ziehen** *zikh oom·tsee·èn* to change one's clothes

Umzug *oom·tsook m* **⁼e** parade

unabhängig *oon·ap·heng·ikh adj* independent

Unabhängigkeit *oon·ap·heng·ikh·kite f* independence

unangenehm *oon·an·gè·naym adj* unpleasant

unanständig *oon·an·shten·dikh adj* indecent

unartig *oon·ar·tikh adj* bad (*naughty*)

unbedingt *oon·bè·dingt adv* absolutely; **etwas unbedingt wollen** *et·vass oon·bè·dingt vo·lèn* to want something badly

unbegrenzt *oon·bè·grentst adj* unlimited

unbekannt *oon·bè·kant adj* unknown

unbequem *oon·bè·kvaym adj* uncomfortable

unbewaffnet *oon·bè·vaf·nèt adj* unarmed (*person*)

unbezahlt *oon·bè·tsahlt adj* unpaid (*debt*)

und *oont conj* and

unecht *oon·ekht adj* fake

unehelich *oon·ay·è·likh adj* illegitimate

unehrlich *oon·ayr·likh adj* dishonest

unerläßlich *oon·èr·les·likh adj* vital (*essential*)

unerträglich *oon·er·trayk·likh adj* unbearable (*pain*)

Unfall *oon·fal m* **⁼e** accident

unfreundlich *oon·froynt·likh adj* unfriendly; unkind

Ungar *oon·gar m* Hungarian

ungarisch *oon·ga·rish adj* Hungarian

Ungarn *oon·garn nt* Hungary

ungeduldig *oon·gè·dool·dikh adj* impatient

ungefähr *oon·gè·fayr adj* approximate; **ungefähr $10** *oon·gè·fayr $10* about $10

ungefüttert *oon·gè·fōō·tert adj* unlined (*clothes*)

Ungeheuer *oon·gè·hoy·èr nt* **—** monster

ungehorsam *oon·gè·hor·zam adj* disobedient

ungelernte Arbeiter *oon·gè·lern·tè ar·bye·tèr pl* unskilled labor

ungerade *oon·gè·rah·dè adj* odd (*number*)

ungeschickt *oon·gè·shikt adj* clumsy (*person*)

ungewöhnlich *oon·gè·vur'n·likh adj* unusual

ungezogen *oon·gè·tsō·gèn adj* naughty

unglaublich *oon·glowp·likh adj* incredible

unglücklich *oon·glōōk·likh adj* unhappy; unfortunate (*event*)

unglückselig *oon·glōōk·zay·likh adj* unlucky

ungültig *oon·gōōl·tikh adj* void (*contract*)

ungünstig *oon·gōōn·stikh adj* inconvenient (*time, place*)

unhöflich *oon·hur'f·likh adj* rude

Uniform *oo·ni·form f* **—en** uniform

Uniformrock *oo·ni·form·rok m* **⁼e** tunic (*of uniform*)

Universität *oo·ni·ver·si·tayt f* **—en** university

Unkosten *oon·kos·tèn pl* costs; **allgemeine Unkosten** *al·gè·mye·nè oon·kos·tèn* overhead

Unkraut *oon·krowt nt* **⁼er** weed

unlauter *oon·low·tèr adj* unfair (*competition*)

unmittelbar *oon·mi·tèl·bar adj* immediate

unmöglich *oon·mur'·glikh adj* impossible

unnatürlich *oon·na·tōōr·likh adj* unnatural

unnötig *oon·nur'·tikh adj* unnecessary

unökonomisch *oon·ur'·ko·nō·mish adj* uneconomical

unordentlich *oon·or·dènt·likh adj* untidy

Unordnung *oon·ort·noong f* mess; **etwas in Unordnung bringen*** *et·vass in oon·ort·noong bring·èn* to make a mess of something

unparteiisch *oon·par·tye·ish adj* unbiased

unpassend *oon·pa·sènt adj* unsuitable

unpersönlich *oon·per·zur'n·likh adj* impersonal

unpraktisch *oon·prak·tish adj* inconvenient

unrecht haben* *oon·rekht hah·bèn vi* be wrong

unreif *oon·rife adj* unripe

Unruhe *oon·roo·è f* unrest

uns *oons pron* us

unschlagbar *oon·shlak·bar adj* unbeatable (*offer*)

unschuldig *oon·shool·dikh adj* innocent

unser(e) *oon·zèr(·è) adj* our

unsere(r/s) *oon·zè·rè(·rèr/·rès) pron* ours

unsicher *oon·sikh·èr adj* uncertain (*fact*)

unsichtbar *oon·zikht·bahr adj* invisible

Unsinn *oon·zin m* nonsense

unten *oon·tèn adv* downstairs; below; **nach unten** *nakh oon·tèn* downward(s); downstairs

unter *oon·tèr prep* under(neath); among; **unter dem/den Tisch** *oon·tèr daym/dayn tish* under the table; **unter einem Kilometer** *oon·tèr ine·èm ki·lô·may·tèr* under a kilometer; **mein Zimmer liegt unter seinem** *mine tsi·mèr leekt oon·tèr zine·èm* my room is below his

Unterausschuß *oon·tèr·ows·shoos m -e* subcommittee

unterbelichtet *oon·tèr·bè·likh·tèt adj* underexposed

unterbewerten *oon·tèr·bè·ver·tèn vt* undervalue

unterbezahlt *oon·tèr·bè·tsahlt adj* underpaid

unterbrechen* *oon·tèr·bre·khèn vt* interrupt

unterbringen* *oon·tèr·bring·èn vt* accommodate

unterentwickelt *oon·tèr·ent·vi·kèlt adj* underdeveloped (*country*)

Unterführung *oon·tèr·foo·roong f -en* subway (*underground passage*); underpass (*for pedestrians*)

Untergebene(r) *oon·tèr·gay·bè·nè(r) m/f -n* subordinate

untergeordnet *oon·tèr·gè·ort·nèt adj* subordinate

Untergeschoß *oon·tèr·gè·shos nt -e* basement

Unterhalt *oon·tèr·halt m* keep; upkeep; **seinen Unterhalt verdienen** *zine·èn oon·tèr·halt fer·dee·nèn* to earn one's keep

unterhalten* *oon·tèr·hal·tèn vt* entertain (*amuse*)

Unterhaltung *oon·tèr·hal·toong f* entertainment; maintenance (*of building*); conversation

Unterhaltungsmusik *oon·tèr·hal·toongs·moo·zeek f* light music

Unterhemd *oon·tèr·hemt nt -en* undershirt

Unterhose *oon·tèr·hô·zè f -n* shorts (*underwear*); underpants

unterirdisch *oon·tèr·ir·dish adj* underground (*pipe etc*)

Unterkontrahent *oon·tèr·kon·tra·hent m -en* subcontractor

Unterkunft *oon·tèr·koonft f* accommodations

Unterlagen *oon·tèr·lah·gèn pl* record (*register*)

Unterleib *oon·tèr·lipe m -er* abdomen

Untermieter *oon·tèr·mee·tèr m -* lodger

unternehmen* *oon·tèr·nay·mèn vt* undertake □ *nt das Unternehmen* *oon·tèr·nay·mèn* project (*venture*); operation (*enterprise*)

Unternehmensleitung *oon·tèr·nay·mèns·lye·toong f -en* management (*managers*)

Unternehmer *oon·tèr·nay·mèr m -* contractor

Unternehmung *oon·tèr·nay·moong f -en* undertaking (*enterprise*)

unterrichten *oon·tèr·rikh·tèn vt* teach; inform

Unterrock *oon·tèr·rok m -e* slip (*underskirt*); petticoat

unterscheiden* *oon·tèr·shye·dèn vt* distinguish

Unterschied *oon·tèr·sheet m -e* difference

unterschiedlich *oon·tèr·sheet·likh adj* varying

unterschreiben* *oon·tèr·shrye·bèn vt* sign

Unterschrift *oon·tèr·shrift f -en* signature

Unterseeboot *oon·tèr·zay·bôt nt -e* submarine

Untersetzer *oon·tèr·zet·sèr m -* tablemat

Unterstand *oon·tèr·shtant m -e* shelter (*for waiting under*)

unterste(r/s) *oon·tèr·stè(·stèr/·stès) adj* bottom

sich unter\|stellen *zikh oon·tèr·shte·lèn vr* shelter (*from rain etc*)

unterstreichen* *oon·tèr·shtrye·khèn vt* underline

unterstützen* *oon·tèr·shtôôt·sèn vt* back; support

Unterstützung *oon·tèr·shtôôt·soong f -en* backing; support (*moral, financial*)

untersuchen *oon·tèr·zoo·khèn vt* examine (*inspect*)

Untersuchung *oon·tèr·zoo·khoong f -en* test (*medical*); examination (*inspection, also medical*)

Untertasse *oon·tèr·ta·sè m -n* saucer

Untertitel *oon·tèr·tee·tèl m -* subtitle (*of movie*)

Untervertrag *oon·tèr·fer·trahk m -e* subcontract

Unterwäsche *oon·tèr·ve·shè f* underwear

unterwegs *oon·tèr·vayks adv* on the way

unterzeichnen *oon·tèr·tsyekh·nèn vt* sign (*document*)

ununterbrochen *oon·oon·tèr·bro·khèn adj* continuous

unverändert *oon·fer·en·dèrt adj* unchanged

unvermeidlich *oon·fer·mite·likh adj* unavoidable; inevitable

unverpackt *oon·fer·pakt adj* in bulk (*unpackaged*)

unvollständig *oon·fol·shten·dikh adj* incomplete

unwahrscheinlich *oon·vahr·shine·likh adj* unlikely

unwirtschaftlich *oon·virt·shaft·likh adj* uneconomic

unwissend *oon·vi·sènt adj* ignorant

unzerbrechlich *oon·tser·brekh·likh adj* unbreakable

unzivilisiert *oon·tsi·vi·li·zeert adj* uncivilized (*tribe*)

Urlaub *oor·lowp m* leave (*holiday*); **auf Urlaub** *owf oor·lowp* on holiday; on leave

Urlauber *oor·low·bèr m* vacationer

Urlaubsort *oor·lowps·ort m* — resort

Ursache *oor·za·khè f* —n cause

Ursprung *oor·shproong m* —e origin

ursprünglich *oor·shprööng·likh adv* originally (*at first*)

Urteil *oor·tile nt* —e judgement; verdict

V

vage *vah·gè adj* vague

Vanille *va·nil·lè f* vanilla

Vanilleeis *va·nil·lè·ise nt* vanilla ice cream

variabel *va·ree·ah·bèl adj* variable

Variable *va·ree·ah·blè f* —n variable

Varietévorführung *va·ree·ay·tay·for·föö·roong f* —en variety show

Vase *va·zè f* —n vase

Vaseline *va·zay·lee·nè f* petroleum jelly; vaseline

Vater *fah·tèr m* ﹦ father

Vatikan *va·ti·kahn m* Vatican

V-Ausschnitt *fow·ows·shnit m* —e V-neck

vegetarisch *ve·gay·tah·rish adj* vegetarian

Vene *vay·nè f* —n vein

Venedig *ve·nay·dikh nt* Venice

Ventil *ven·teel nt* —e valve

Ventilator *ven·ti·la·tor m* —en ventilator; fan (*electric, in car*)

Venusmuschel *vay·noos·moo·shèl f* —n clam

verabreden *fer·ap·ray·dèn vt* agree; **sich verabreden** *zikh fer·ap·ray·dèn* arrange to meet

Verabredung *fer·ap·ray·doong f* —en date (*appointment*)

Veranda *ve·ran·da f* —s veranda

verändern *fer·en·dèrn vt* change

Veränderung *fer·en·dè·roong f* —en change

veranlassen* *fer·an·la·sèn vt* cause

veranstalten *fer·an·shtal·tèn vt* organize

verantwortlich *fer·ant·vort·likh adj* responsible; **verantwortlich sein* für** *fer·ant·vort·likh zine föör* to be in charge of; **dafür sind Sie verantwortlich** *da·föör zint zee fer·ant·vort·likh* this is your responsibility

Verantwortung *fer·ant·vor·toong f* responsibility

verantwortungsbewußt *fer·ant·vor·toongs·bè·voost adj* responsible

verarbeiten *fer·ar·bye·tèn vt* process

Verband *fer·bant m* ﹦e association; syndicate; bandage

verbessern *fer·be·sèrn vt* improve

Verbesserung *fer·be·sè·roong f* —en improvement

sich verbeugen *zikh fer·boy·gèn vr* bow

Verbeugung *fer·boy·goong f* —en bow

verbieten* *fer·bee·tèn vt* ban; forbid; prohibit; **jemandem verbieten*, etwas zu tun** *yay·man·dèm fer·bee·tèn et·vass tsoo toon* to forbid someone to do something; **es ist verboten** *ess ist fer·bô·tèn* it is forbidden

verbinden* *fer·bin·dèn vt* connect (*join*); **jemanden verbinden*** *yay·man·dèn fer·bin·dèn* to put someone

through (*on phone*); **verbinden Sie mich bitte mit Herrn X** *fer·bin·dèn zee mikh bi·tè mit hern X* put me through to Mr X

Verbindung *fer·bin·doong f* —en service (*bus etc*); line (*telephone*); **mit jemandem in Verbindung stehen*** *mit yay·man·dèm in fer·bin·doong shtay·èn* to communicate with someone; **in Verbindung mit** *in fer·bin·doong mit* in touch with; **sich in Verbindung setzen mit** *zikh in fer·bin·doong zet·sèn mit* to contact

verblassen *fer·bla·sèn vi* fade

Verbot *fer·bôt nt* —e ban

verboten *fer·bô·tèn adj* forbidden; out of bounds

Verbraucher *fer·brow·khèr m* — consumer

Verbrauchssteuern *fer·browkhs·shtoy·èrn pl* excise duties

Verbrechen *fer·bre·khèn nt* — crime

verbreiten *fer·brye·tèn vt* spread (*news*)

verbrennen* *fer·bre·nèn vt* burn; **ich habe mir den Arm verbrannt** *ikh hah·bè meer dayn arm fer·brant* I've burned my arm

Verbrennungsofen *fer·bre·noongs·ô·fèn m* ﹦ incinerator

verbringen* *fer·bring·èn vt* spend (*time*)

verbrühen *fer·bröö·èn vt* scald

verdammen *fer·dam·èn vt* condemn

verdampfen *fer·dampf·èn vi* evaporate

verdaulich *fer·dow·likh adj* digestible

verderben* *fer·der·bèn vi* go bad (*food*) □ *vt* spoil (*damage*)

verdienen *fer·dee·nèn vt* deserve; earn; **Geld verdienen** *gelt fer·dee·nèn* to make money

Verdienst *fer·deenst m* —e earnings

verdoppeln *fer·do·pèln vt* double

verdorben *fer·dor·bèn adj* spoiled

verdünnen *fer·döön·èn vt* dilute

Verein *fer·ine m* —e society

vereinigen *fer·ine·i·gèn vt* unite

Vereinigtes Königreich *fer·ine·ikh·tès kur·nikh·ryekh nt* United Kingdom

Vereinigte Nationen *fer·ine·ikh·tè na·tsee·ô·nèn pl* United Nations Organization

Vereinigte Staaten (von Amerika) *fer·ine·ikh·tè shtah·tèn (fon a·me·ri·ka) pl* United States (of America)

Vereinigung *fer·ine·i·goong f* —en union

Verfahren *fer·fah·rèn nt* — procedure; process

verfehlen *fer·fay·lèn vt* miss (*target*)

verfügbar *fer·fôôk·bar adj* available

Verfügung *fer·föö·goong f* disposal; **zur Verfügung** *tsoor fer·föö·goong* at one's disposal

vergangene(r/s) *fer·gang·è·nè(·nèr/·nès) adj* past

Vergangenheit *fer·gang·èn·hite f* past

Vergaser *fer·gah·zèr m* — carburetor

vergeben* *fer·gay·bèn vt* allocate (*duties*); forgive

vergebens *fer·gay·bèns adv* in vain

vergelten* *fer·gel·tèn vt* repay (*person*)

vergessen* *fer·ge·sèn vt* forget; **ich habe meinen Schirm vergessen** *ikh hah·bè mine·èn shirm fer·ge·sèn* I've left my umbrella

vergleichen* *fer·glye·khèn vt* compare; **sich vergleichen** *zikh fer·glye·khèn* to settle out of court

Vergnügen *fer·gnöö·gèn nt* enjoyment; pleasure

Vergnügungsdampfer *fer·gnōō·goongs·damp·fèr m* — pleasure boat

Vergnügungspark *fer·gnōō·goongs·park m* —**s** amusement park

vergoldet *fer·gol·dèt adj* gold-plated

vergriffen *fer·gri·fèn adj* out of print/stock

vergrößern *fer·grur'·sèrn vt* expand (*business*); enlarge

Vergrößerung *fer·grur'·sè·roong f* —**en** increase (*in size*)

Vergütung *fer·gōō·toong f* —**en** refund

verhaften *fer·haf·tèn vt* arrest

sich verhalten* *zikh fer·hal·tèn vr* act (*behave*)

Verhältnis *fer·helt·nis nt* —**se** relationship; ratio; **über seine Verhältnisse** *ōō·bèr zine·è fer·helt·ni·sè* beyond his means

verhandeln *fer·han·dèln vi* negotiate; **mit einer Firma verhandeln** *mit ine·èr feer·ma fer·han·dèln* to deal with a firm

Verhandlungen *fer·hant·loong·èn pl* negotiations

verheiratet *fer·hye·rah·tèt adj* married

verhungern *fer·hoong·èrn vi* starve

Verhütungsmittel *ver·hōō·toongs·mi·tèl nt* contraceptive

Verkauf *fer·kowf m* —**e** sale

verkaufen *fer·kow·fèn vt* sell

Verkäufer *fer·koy·fèr m* — sales assistant; vendor

Verkäuferin *fer·koy·fè·rin f* —**nen** sales assistant

verkäuflich *fer·koyf·likh adj* negotiable

Verkaufsautomat *fer·kowfs·ow·tō·maht m* —**en** vending machine

Verkaufsleiter *fer·kowfs·lye·tèr m* — sales manager

Verkehr *fer·kayr m* traffic (*cars*)

Verkehrsampel *fer·kayrs·am·pèl f* —**n** traffic lights

Verkehrsinsel *fer·kayrs·in·zèl f* —**n** island (*traffic*)

Verkehrspolizist *fer·kayrs·po·li·tsist m* —**en** traffic policeman

Verkehrsstau *fer·kayrs·shtow f* —**s** traffic jam

Verkehrszeichen *fer·kayrs·tsye·khèn nt* — road sign

verkehrt *fer·kayrt adj* wrong; **verkehrt herum** *fer·kayrt he·room* upside down

verklagen *fer·klah·gèn vt* sue

verkleidet *fer·klye·dèt adj* in disguise

Verkleidung *fer·klye·doong f* —**en** disguise

sich verklemmen *zikh fer·kle·mèn vr* jam (*machine*)

verkürzen *fer·kōōr·tsèn vt* shorten

verlangen *fer·lang·èn vt* demand

verlängern *fer·leng·èrn vt* renew (*subscription, passport*)

verlassen* *fer·la·sèn vt* leave (*room, club, school*); **sich verlassen* auf** *zikh fer·la·sèn owf* rely on (*person*)

sich verlaufen* *zikh fer·low·fèn vr* lose one's way

verlegen *fer·lay·gèn adj* embarrassed

Verleger *fer·lay·gèr m* — publisher

Verlegerin *fer·lay·gè·rin f* —**nen** publisher

verletzen *fer·let·sèn vt* injure

Verletzung *fer·let·soong f* —**en** injury

sich verlieben *zikh fer·lee·bèn vr* fall in love

verliebt *fer·leept adj* in love

verlieren* *fer·lee·rèn vt* lose

Verlies *fer·lees nt* —**e** dungeon

verlobt *fer·lōpt adj* engaged (*betrothed*)

Verlobte(r) *fer·lōp·tè(·tèr) m/f* —**n** fiancé(e)

Verlobung *fer·lō·boong f* —**en** engagement (*betrothal*)

Verlobungsring *fer·lō·boongs·ring m* —**e** engagement ring

Verlust *fer·loost m* —**e** loss

vermeiden* *fer·mye·dèn vt* avoid

Vermessung *fer·me·soong f* —**en** survey (*of land*)

vermieten *fer·mee·tèn vt* rent; **zu vermieten** *tsoo fer·mee·tèn* to let (*on sign*)

vermindern *fer·min·dèrn vt* decrease

vermischen *fer·mi·shèn vt* blend; mix; **sich vermischen** *zikh fer·mi·shèn* mix

vermissen *fer·mi·sèn vt* miss

vermißt *fer·mist adj* missing (*person*)

Vermittler *fer·mit·lèr m* — mediator; trouble-shooter (*political*)

Vermittlung *fer·mit·loong f* —**en** telephone exchange; operator

Vermögen *fer·mur'·gèn nt* fortune (*wealth*)

vermuten *fer·moo·tèn vt* guess

vermutlich *fer·moot·likh adv* presumably

vernünftig *fer·nōōnf·tikh adj* reasonable; sensible; wise (*decision*)

veröffentlichen *fer·ur'f·ènt·li·khèn vt* publish

verpacken *fer·pa·kèn vt* pack

Verpackung *fer·pa·koong f* —**en** wrapper (*paper*); packing (*material*)

sich verpflichten *zikh fer·pflikh·tèn vr* undertake

Verpflichtung *fer·pflikh·toong f* —**en** obligation

Verrenkung *fer·reng·koong f* —**en** sprain

verrückt *fer·rōōkt adj* crazy

versagen *fer·zah·gèn vi* fail (*brakes*); ◻ *nt* **das Versagen** *fer·zah·gèn* failure (*of brakes*)

Versager *fer·zah·gèr m* — failure (*person*)

sich versammeln *zikh fer·za·mèln vr* gather (*crowd*)

Versammlung *fer·zam·loong f* —**en** meeting

Versandhaus *fer·zant·hows nt* —**¨er** mail order firm; **etwas bei einem Versandhaus kaufen** *et·vass bye ine·èm fer·zant·hows kow·fèn* to buy something by mail order

versäumen *fer·zoy·mèn vt* miss (*train*)

verschieben* *fer·shee·bèn vt* postpone

verschieden *fer·shee·dèn adj* various; different

verschiffen *fer·shi·fèn vt* ship (*goods*)

verschließen* *fer·shlee·sèn vt* lock

Verschluß *fer·shloos m* —**¨e** lock; shutter (*in camera*); top (*of bottle*)

verschnüren *fer·shnōō·rèn vt* tie up

verschuldet *fer·shool·dèt adj* in debt

verschütten *fer·shōō·tèn vt* spill

verschwenden *fer·shven·dèn vt* waste

Verschwendung *fer·shven·doong f* waste

verschwinden* *fer·shvin·dèn vi* disappear

verschwunden *fer·shvoon·dèn adj* missing (*object*)

Versehen *fer·zay·èn nt* — oversight; **aus Versehen** *ows fer·zay·èn* by mistake; in error

Versicherer *fer·zi·khè·rèr m* — underwriter

versichern *fer·zi·khèrn vt* insure

versichert *fer·zi·khèrt adj* insured

Versicherung *fer·zi·khè·roong f* **—en** insurance

Versicherungsgesellschaft *fer·zi·khè·roongs·gè·zel·shaft f* **—en** insurance company

Versicherungspolice *fer·zi·khè·roongs·po·lee·sè f* **—n** insurance policy

versnobt *fer·snopt adj* snobbish

versorgen *fer·zor·gèn* v keep (*feed and clothe*); jemanden mit etwas versorgen *yay·man·dèn mit et·vass fer·zor·gèn* to provide someone with something; to supply someone with something

Verspätung *fer·shpay·toong f* **—en** delay (*to train, plane*); der Zug hat Verspätung *der tsook hat fer·shpay·toong* the train has been delayed

Versprechen *fer·shpre·khèn nt* **—** promise □ *vt* **versprechen*** *fer·shpre·khèn* promise

verstaatlichen *fer·shtaht·li·khèn vt* nationalize

Verstand *fer·shtant m* intelligence

Verständnis *fer·shtent·nis nt* understanding

verstärken *fer·shter·kèn vt* strengthen

Verstärker *fer·shter·kèr m* **—** amplifier

verstauchen *fer·shtow·khèn vt* sprain

verstecken *fer·shte·kèn vt* hide; sich verstecken *zikh fer·shte·kèn* hide

verstehen* *fer·shtay·èn vt* understand

verstopfen *fer·shtop·fèn vt* plug; block (*pipe*)

Verstopfung *fer·shtop·foong f* **—en** blockage; Verstopfung haben* *fer·shtop·foong hah·bèn* to be constipated

verstreichen* *fer·shtrye·khèn vt* spread (*butter*)

Versuch *fer·zookh m* **—e** attempt

versuchen *fer·zoo·khèn vt* try; tempt; versuchen, etwas zu tun *fer·zoo·khèn et·vass tsoo toon* to try to do something

Versuchung *fer·zoo·khoong f* **—en** temptation

sich vertagen *zikh fer·tah·gèn vr* adjourn

Vertagung *fer·tah·goong f* **—en** adjournment

verteidigen *fer·tye·di·gèn vt* defend

Verteidiger *fer·tye·di·gèr m* **—** back (*in sports*)

Verteidigung *fer·tye·di·goong f* defense

verteilen *fer·tile·èn vt* allocate (*funds*); spread (*payments*)

Verteiler *fer·tye·lèr m* **—** distributor (*in car*)

Vertrag *fer·trak m* **—e** contract

vertrauen *fer·trow·èn vt* trust; jemandem vertrauen *yay·man·dèm fer·trow·èn* to trust someone

Vertrauen *fer·trow·èn nt* confidence (*trust*); Vertrauen zu *fer·trow·èn tsoo* confidence in; im Vertrauen *im fer·trow·èn* in confidence

vertraulich *fer·trow·likh adj* confidential

vertraut *fer·trowt adj* familiar

vertreiben* *fer·trye·bèn vt* market (*product*)

vertreten* *fer·tray·tèn vt* represent (*act as deputy for*)

Vertreter *fer·tray·tèr m* **—** representative

verursachen *fer·oor·za·khèn vt* cause

vervollständigen *fer·fol·shten·di·gèn vt* complete

verwalten *fer·val·tèn vt* manage

Verwaltung *fer·val·toong f* **—en** administration

Verwandte(r) *fer·van·tè(·tèr) m/f* **—n** relation; relative

verwechseln *fer·vek·sèln vt* confuse; eine Sache mit einer anderen verwechseln *ine·è za·khè mit ine·èr an·dè·rèn fer·vek·sèln* to confuse one thing with another

verweigern *fer·vye·gèrn vt* refuse

Verwendung *fer·ven·doong f* **—en** use

verwirren *fer·vi·rèn vt* tangle

verwirrt *fer·virt adj* confused (*muddled*)

verwöhnen *fer·vur·nèn vt* spoil

verzeihen* *fer·tsye·èn vt* forgive

Verzeihung! *fer·tsye·oong excl* sorry; excuse me

verzollen *fer·tsol·èn vt* declare (*customs*); nichts zu verzollen *nikhts tsoo fer·tsol·èn* nothing to declare

verzweifelt *fer·tsvye·fèlt adj* desperate

Veto *vay·tō nt* **—s** veto; sein Veto einlegen gegen *zine vay·tō ine·lay·gèn gay·gèn* to veto

Vetter *fet·èr m* cousin

via *vee·a prep* via

Viadukt *fer·van·a·dookt m* **—e** viaduct

Videoband *vi·day·ō·bant nt* **—er** videotape

Videokassette *vee·day·ō·ka·set·tè f* **—n** videocassette

Videorekorder *vee·day·ō·re·kor·dèr m* **—** videocassette recorder

Vieh *feeh nt* cattle

viel *feel adj* much; haben Sie viel? *hah·bèn zee feel* have you got much?; nicht viel *nikht feel* not much; viel besser *feel be·sèr* a lot better

viele *fee·lè pron* many; zu viele Bücher *tsoo fee·lè bōō·khèr* too many books; es gibt ziemlich viele *ess gipt tseem·likh fee·lè* there are quite a few

vielleicht *fee·lyekht adv* perhaps; possibly; er wird vielleicht kommen *er virt fee·lyekht ko·mèn* perhaps he'll come

vier *feer num* four

vierte(r/s) *feer·tè(·tèr/·tès) adj* fourth

Viertel *fir·tèl nt* **—** quarter; (ein) Viertel vor 4 *(ine) fir·tèl fōr 4* (a) quarter to 4; (ein) Viertel nach 4 *(ine) fir·tèl nakh 4* (a) quarter past 4

Viertelstunde *fir·tèl·shtoon·dè f* **—n** quarter of an hour

vierzehn *feer·tsayn num* fourteen

vierzig *feer·tsikh num* forty

Villa *vi·la f* Villen villa; mansion

Vinyl *vee·nōōl nt* vinyl

violett *vee·ō·let adj* purple

Viper *vee·pèr f* **—n** adder (*snake*)

Visum *vee·zoom nt* Visa visa, visé

Vitamin *vi·ta·meen nt* **—e** vitamin

Vizepräsident *vee·tsè·pray·zee·dent m* **—en** vice president

Vogel *fō·gèl m* **—** bird

Volk *folk nt* **—er** people; nation

Volkslied *folks·leet nt* **—er** folk song

Volkstanz *folks·tants m* **—e** folk dance

Volkswirtschaft *folks·virt·shaft f* economics

Volkswirtschaftler *folks·virt·shaft·lèr m* **—** economist

voll *fol adj* full; voll von *fol fon* full of

völlig *fur·likh adv* wholly

Vollkaskoversicherung *fol·kas·ko·fer·zi·khè·roong f* **—en** comprehensive insurance

vollkommen *fol·ko·mèn adj* perfect

Vollkornbrot *fol·korn·bröt nt* whole-wheat bread
Vollmilchschokolade *fol·milkh·sho·ko·lah·dé f* milk chocolate
vollständig *fol·shten·dikh adj* complete
volltanken *fol·tang·kén vt/i* fill up (*car*)
Volumen *vo·loo·mèn nt —mina* volume (*capacity*); **Whisky mit 70 Volumenprozent Alkohol** *vis·kee mit 70 vo·loo·mèn·prō·tsent al·kō·hōl* a 70° proof whiskey
von *fon prep* from; of; **von einer Wand fallen*** *fon ine·èr vant fal·èn* to fall off a wall; **ein Freund von mir** *ine froynt fon meer* a friend of mine; **3 von ihnen** *3 fon ee·nèn* 3 of them
vor *för prep* before; **vor Mittag** *för mi·tahk* before noon; **vor dem König** *för daym kur·nikh* before the king (*position*); **etwas vor sich sehen*** *et·vass för zikh zay·èn* to see something ahead; **rot vor Wut** *röt för voot* red with anger; **vor 4 Jahren** *för 4 yah·rèn* 4 years ago
voran|kommen* *för·an·ko·mèn vi* move (*traffic*)
Vorarbeiter *för·ar·bye·tèr m —* foreman
voraus *för·ows adv* ahead; **im voraus** *im för·ows* in advance; **den anderen voraus** *dayn an·dè·rèn för·ows* ahead of the others
vorausbezahlt *för·ows·bè·tsahlt adj* prepaid
voraus|denken* *för·ows·deng·kén vt* think ahead
vorausgesetzt *för·ows·gè·zetst conj* provided; providing; **vorausgesetzt, daß er kommt** *för·ows·gè·zetst dass er komt* provided (that) he comes
voraus|planen *för·ows·plah·nèn vi* plan ahead
Voraussage *för·ows·zah·gè f —n* prediction
voraus|sagen *för·ows·zah·gèn vt* predict
Vorbau *för·bow m —ten* porch
Vorbehalt *för·bè·halt m —e* reservation (*doubt*); proviso
vorbei *för·bye adv* past
vorbei|gehen* *för·bye·gay·èn vi* pass by; **vorbei|gehen an** *för·bye·gay·èn an* pass (*place*)
vor|bereiten *för·bè·rye·tèn vt* prepare
Vorbereitung *för·bè·rye·toong f —en* preparation
vor|bestellen *för·bè·shte·lèn vt* reserve (*seat, room*)
Vorbestellung *för·bè·shte·loong f —en* reservation (*of seats, rooms etc*)
vor|datieren *för·da·tee·rèn vt* postdate
Vorder- *för·dèr pref* front
Vorderradantrieb *för·dèr·raht·an·treep m* front-wheel drive
Vorderseite *för·dèr·zye·tè f —n* front (*foremost part*)
Vorfahr *för·fahr m —en* ancestor
Vorfahrt *för·fahrt f* right of way (*on road*); **die Vorfahrt beachten** *dee för·fahrt bè·akh·tèn* to yield (*when driving*)
vor|führen *för·föö·rèn vt* demonstrate (*appliance etc*)
Vorführung *för·föö·roong f —en* demonstration
vor|geben* *för·gay·bèn vt* pretend
vor|gehen* *för·gay·èn vi* go on ahead; gain (*clock*); **meine Uhr geht vor** *mine·è oor gayt för* my watch is fast
vorgekocht *för·gè·kokht adj* ready-cooked

vorgesetzt *för·gè·zetst adj* senior (*in rank*)
Vorgesetzte(r) *för·gè·zet·stè(·stèr) m/f* —n superior
vorgestern *för·ge·stèrn adv* the day before yesterday
vor|haben* *för·hah·bèn vt* intend
vorhanden *för·han·dèn adj* available
Vorhang *för·hang m —e* curtain; drape
Vorhängeschloß *för·heng·è·shlos nt —e* padlock
vorher *för·her adv* before; **am Tag vorher** *am tahk för·her* on the previous day
Vorhersage *för·her·zah·gè f —n* forecast
Vorladung *för·lah·doong f —en* summons
Vorlage *för·lah·gè f —n* presentation
Vorlauf *för·lowf m —e* heat (*sports*)
vor|legen *för·lay·gèn vt* submit (*proposal*)
Vorleger *för·lay·gèr m —* rug
Vorlesung *för·lay·zoong f —en* lecture
vormittags *för·mi·tahks adv* a.m.
Vormund *för·moont m —er* guardian
vorn *förn adv* at the front; **der Sitz ist zu weit vorn** *der zits ist tsoo vite förn* the seat is too far forward
Vorname *för·nah·mè m —n* first name
vorne *för·nè adv* in front
Vorort *för·ort m —e* suburb
Vorrat *för·raht m —e* stock (*supply*)
vorrätig *för·ray·tikh adj* in stock
vorsätzlich *för·zets·likh adv* deliberately
Vorschau *för·show f —en* preview
Vorschlag *för·shlahk m —e* proposal; suggestion
vor|schlagen* *för·shlah·gèn vt* propose; suggest
Vorschrift *för·shrift f —en* regulation (*rule*)
Vorschuß *för·shoos m —e* advance (*loan*); **als Vorschuß geben*** *als för·shoos gay·bèn* to advance (*money*)
Vorsicht *för·zikht f* care; **Vorsicht!** *för·zikht* look out!; be careful!; **Vorsicht! Stufe!** *för·zikht shtoo·fè* mind the step
Vorsitzende(r) *för·zit·sèn·dè(·dèr) m* —n chairman; **der stellvertretende Vorsitzende** *shtel·fer·tray·tèn·dè för·zit·sèn·dè* vice chairman
Vorspeise *för·shpye·zè f —n* hors d'œuvre
vorstädtisch *för·shte·tish adj* suburban
vor|stellen *för·shte·lèn vt* introduce (*person*); **sich vor|stellen** *zikh för·shte·lèn* imagine
Vorstellung *för·shte·loong f —en* introduction (*social*); performance (*of play*)
Vorteil *för·tile m —e* advantage; benefit
Vortrag *för·trahk m —e* talk (*lecture*)
vorüber *för·öö·bèr adv* past; over
vorübergehend *för·öö·bèr·gay·ènt adv* for the time being
Vorurteil *för·oor·tile nt —e* prejudice
Vorverkaufskasse *för·fer·kowfs·ka·sè f —n* ticket office
vorwärts *för·verts adv* forward(s)
vor|ziehen* *för·tsee·èn vt* prefer
Vorzug *för·tsook m —e* preference
Vorzugsaktien *för·tsooks·ak·tsee·èn pl* preferred stock
Vulkan *vool·kahn m —e* volcano

W

Waage *vah·gè* f —n scales (*for weighing*)

waagerecht *vah·gè·rekht* adj level (*horizontal*)

Wache *va·khè* f —n guard

Wachs *vaks* nt —e wax

wachsen* *vak·sèn* vi expand (*business*); grow

Wachstum *vaks·toom* nt growth

Wachtel *vakh·tèl* f —n quail

wackeln *va·kèln* vi wobble (*chair etc*)

Wackelpeter *va·kèl·pay·tèr* m — jello

Waffe *va·fè* f —n weapon

Waffel *va·fèl* f —n wafer; waffle

Wagen *vah·gèn* m — car

wagen *vah·gèn* vt dare; es wagen, etwas zu tun *ess vah·gèn et·vass tsoo toon* to dare to do something

Wagenheber *vah·gèn·hay·bèr* m — jack (*for car*)

Waggon *va·gon* m —s freight car; coach (*of train*)

Wahl *vahl* f —en choice; election; die engere Wahl *eng·è·rè vahl* short list

wählen *vay·lèn* vt dial (*number*); choose; elect □ vi vote

wahr *vahr* adj true

während *ve·rènt* prep during □ conj while

Wahrheit *vahr·hite* f —en truth

wahrscheinlich *vahr·shine·likh* adj likely; probable; es ist wahrscheinlich, daß er kommt *ess ist vahr·shine·likh dass er komt* he's likely to come □ adv wahrscheinlich *vahr·shine·likh* probably

Währung *vay·roong* f —en currency

Wahrzeichen *vahr·tsye·khèn* nt — landmark

Waise *vye·zè* f —n orphan

Wal *vahl* m —e whale

Wald *valt* m —er wood; forest

Waldhuhn *valt·hoon* nt —er grouse (*bird*)

Wales *waylz* nt Wales

walisisch *va·lee·zish* adj Welsh □ nt Walisisch *va·lee·zish* Welsh

Walnuß *val·noos* f —e walnut

Walzer *val·tsèr* m — waltz

Wand *vant* f —e wall (*inside*)

Wandern *van·dèrn* nt hiking

wandern gehen* *van·dèrn gay·èn* vi go hiking

Wanderung *van·dè·roong* f —en hike

Wange *vang·è* f —n cheek

wann *van* conj when (*in questions*)

Ware *vah·rè* f —n commodity

Warenlager *vah·rèn·lah·gèr* nt — stock (*in shop*)

Warenumschlag *vah·rèn·oom·shlahk* m — turnover (*in goods*)

Warenzeichen *vah·rèn·tsye·khèn* nt — trade mark; das eingetragene Warenzeichen *ine·gè·trah·gè·nè vah·rèn·tsye·khèn* registered trademark

warm *varm* adj warm; mir ist warm *meer ist varm* I'm warm

wärmen *ver·mèn* vt warm

Wärmflasche *verm·fla·shè* f —n hot-water bottle

warnen *var·nèn* vt warn; jemanden vor etwas warnen *yay·man·dèn fōr et·vass var·nèn* to warn someone of something

Warschau *var·show* nt Warsaw

Wartehalle *var·tè·ha·lè* f —n lounge (*at airport*)

Warteliste *var·tè·lis·tè* f —n waiting list

warten *var·tèn* vi wait; auf jemanden warten *owf yay·man·dèn var·tèn* to wait for someone; jemanden warten lassen* *yay·man·dèn var·tèn la·sèn* to keep someone waiting

Wartesaal *var·tè·zahl* m —säle waiting room (*at station*)

Wartung *var·toong* f maintenance

warum *va·room* adv why

Warze *var·tsè* f —n wart

was *vass* pron what; machen Sie, was ich Ihnen sage *ma·khèn zee vass ikh ee·nèn zah·gè* do as I say; was für eine Unordnung! *vass fōōr ine·è oon·ord·noong* what a mess! (*in room*); was wollen Sie? *vass vo·lèn zee* what do you want?; ich sah, was passiert ist *ikh zah vass pa·seert ist* I saw what happened

waschbar *vash·bar* adj washable

Waschbecken *vash·be·kèn* nt — washbasin, washbowl

Wäsche *ve·shè* f linen (*for beds*); washing (*clothes*); die schmutzige Wäsche *shmoo·tsi·gè ve·shè* laundry; die Wäsche waschen* *dee ve·shè va·shèn* to do the washing

Wäscheklammer *ve·shè·kla·mèr* f —n clothespin

Wäscheleine *ve·shè·line·è* f —n clothesline

waschen* *va·shèn* vt wash; sich waschen* *zikh va·shèn* to wash (oneself), to wash up

Wäscherei *ve·shè·rye* f —en laundry (*place*)

Wäscheständer *ve·shè·shten·dèr* m — clotheshorse

Waschlappen *vash·la·pèn* m — washcloth; facecloth

Waschmaschine *vash·ma·shee·nè* f —n washing machine

Waschmittel *vash·mi·tèl* nt — detergent

Waschpulver *vash·pool·vèr* nt detergent

Waschraum *vash·rowm* m —e washroom

Waschsalon *vash·za·long* m —s laundromat

Wasser *va·sèr* nt water; das destillierte Wasser *de·sti·leer·tè va·sèr* distilled water

Wasserfall *va·sèr·fal* m —e waterfall

Wassermelone *va·sèr·may·lō·nè* f —n watermelon

Wasserski laufen* *va·sèr·shee low·fèn* vi to go water-skiing

Wasserskilaufen *va·sèr·shee·low·fèn* nt water-skiing

wasserundurchlässig *va·sèr·oon·doorkh·le·sikh* adj waterproof

waten *vah·tèn* vi paddle

Watt *vat* nt — watt

Watte *va·tè* f cotton batting; absorbent cotton

weben *vay·bèn* vt weave

Wechsel *wek·sèl* m — draft (*financial*); exchange (*between currencies*)

Wechselkurs *vek·sèl·koors* m —e exchange rate

wechseln *vek·sèln* vt change

wecken *ve·kèn* vt wake; wecken Sie mich bitte um 7 Uhr *ve·kèn zee mikh bi·tè oom 7 oor* call me at 7 a.m. (*in hotel etc*)

Wecker *ve·kèr* m — alarm (clock)

wedeln mit *vay·dèln mit* vi wag (*tail*)

weder ... noch *vay·dèr ... nokh* conj neither ... nor

Weg *vayk* m —e path; lane (*in coun-*

try); **auf dem Weg nach** *owf daym vayk nakh* bound for (*ship*); **im Weg stehen*** *im vayk shtay·èn* to be in the way; **nach dem Weg nach Paris fragen** *nakh daym vayk nakh pa·rees frah·gèn* to ask the way to Paris

weg *vek adv* away; **von zu Hause weg** *fon tsoo how·zè vek* away from home

wegen *vay·gèn prep* because of

weg|geben* *vek·gay·bèn vt* give away

weg|gehen* *vek·gay·èn vi* go (away)

weg|laufen* *vek·low·fèn vi* run away

weg|nehmen* *vek·nay·mèn vt* take away; **er hat es mir weggenommen** *er hat ess meer vek·ge·no·mèn* he took it from me

Wegweiser *vayk·vye·zèr m —* signpost

Wegwerf- *vek·verf pref* disposable

weg|werfen* *vek·ver·fèn vt* to throw away

weh tun* *vay toon vi* ache; hurt; **sich weh tun*** *zikh vay toon* to hurt oneself; **Sie haben sich weh getan** *zee hah·bèn zikh vay ge·tahn* you've hurt yourself/yourselves

weiblich *vipe·likh adj* female

weich *vyekh adj* soft (*not hard*)

sich weigern *zikh vye·gèrn vr* refuse

Weihnachten *vye·nakh·tèn nt* Christmas

Weihnachtsbaum *vye·nakhts·bowm m ̈-e* Christmas tree

Weihnachtskarte *vye·nakhts·kar·tè f —n* Christmas card

Weihnachtslied *vye·nakhts·leet nt —er* carol

Weihnachtsmärchen *vye·nakhts·mer·khèn nt* pantomime

Weihnachtstag *vye·nakhts·tahk m —e* Christmas Day

weil *vile conj* because

Weile *vye·lè f —n* while; spell (*period*)

Wein *vine m —e* wine

Weinberg *vine·berk m —e* vineyard

weinen *vye·nèn vi* cry

Weinglas *vine·glas nt ̈-er* wineglass

Weinkarte *vine·kar·tè f —n* wine list

Weinkeller *vine·ke·lèr m —* wine cellar

Weinkellner *vine·kel·nèr m —* wine waiter

weise *vye·zè adj* wise (*person*) □ *f* **die Weise** *vye·zè adj* way (*manner*); **auf eine andere Weise** *owf ine·è an·dè·rè vye·zè* (in) a different way

weiß *vice adj* white

Weißes Haus *vye·sès hows nt* White House

Weißling *vice·ling m —e* whiting

weit *vite adj* far; loose (*clothing*) □ *adv* far; **am weitesten** *am vye·tè·stèn* farthest; furthest; **bei weitem** *bye vye·tèm* far (*much*); **wie weit ist es nach...?** *vee vite ist ess nakh* how far is it to...?; **das ist weit** *dass ist vite* it's a long way

weiter *vye·tèr adv* farther; further; **und so weiter, usw** *oont zō vye·tèr etc*; **weiter tun*** *vye·tèr toon* to continue to do

weiter|gehen* *vye·tèr·gay·èn vi* continue (*road etc*)

weiter|machen *vye·tèr·ma·khèn vt/i* continue

Weiterverkauf *vye·tèr·fer·kowf m* resale; **nicht zum Weiterverkauf bestimmt** *nikht tsoom vye·tèr·fer·kowf bè·shtimt* not for resale

weiter|verkaufen *vye·tèr·fer·kow·fèn vt* resell

weitsichtig *vite·zikh·tikh adj* farsighted

Weitwinkelobjectiv *vite·ving·kèl·op·yek·teef nt —e* wide-angle lens

Weizen *vye·tsèn m* wheat

welche(r/s *vel·khè(·khèr/·khès) adj* which; what; **welches Buch?** *vel·khès bookh* which book?; what book?; **welche Sprachen?** *vel·khè shprah·khèn* which languages?; what languages?* □ *pron* **welche(r/s)** *vel·khè (·khèr/·khès)* which one; **ich weiß nicht, welches ich nehmen soll** *ikh vice nikht vel·khès ikh nay·mèn zol* I don't know which to take

Wellblech *vel·blekh nt* corrugated iron

Welle *ve·lè f —n* wave

wellig *ve·likh adj* wavy (*hair*)

Wellpappe *vel·pa·pè f* corrugated paper

Welt *velt f —en* world

Weltall *velt·al nt* universe

Weltkrieg *velt·kreek m —e* world war

Weltmacht *velt·makht f ̈-e* world power

Weltraum *velt·rowm m* space (*universe*)

wem *vaym pron* to whom; **ich weiß, wem das gehört** *ikh vice vaym dass gè·hurt* I know whose it is; **wem gehört dieses Buch?** *vaym gè·hurt dee·zès bookh* whose book is this?

Wende *ven·dè f* —n U-turn (*in car*)

wenig *vay·nikh adj* little; **ein wenig** *ine vay·nikh* a little; **etwas zu wenig haben*** *et·vass tsoo vay·nikh hah·bèn* to be short of something; **er hat weniger** *er hat vay·ni·gèr* he has less; **weniger als** *vay·ni·gèr als* less than; **weniger Fleisch** *vay·ni·gèr flyesh* less meat; **das wenigste Geld** *dass vay·nikh·stè gelt* the least money; **er hat am wenigsten** *er hat am vay·nikh·stèn* he has the least

wenige *vay·ni·gè adj* few; **es gibt nur wenige** *ess gipt noor vay·ni·gè* there are very few

wenigstens *vay·nikh·stèns adv* at least

wenn *ven conj* if; when (*with present tense*); **wenn wir nicht kommen** *ven veer nikht ko·mèn* unless we come

wer *ver pron* who; **wer von Ihnen?** *ver fon ee·nèn* which one of you?

Werbeagentur *ver·bè·a·gen·toor f —en* advertising agency

Werbekampagne *ver·bè·kam·pan·yè f —n* publicity campaign

werben* für *ver·bèn fōor vt* promote (*product*)

Werbespot *ver·bè·shpot m —s* commercial (*ad*)

Werbespruch *ver·bè·shprookh m ̈-e* jingle (*advertising*); slogan

Werbung *ver·boong f* promotion (*of product*); advertising; publicity; **Werbung machen für** *ver·boong ma·khèn fōor* to advertise (*product*)

werden* *ver·dèn vi* become; **schlecht werden*** *shlekht ver·dèn* to go bad; **Profi werden*** *prō·fi ver·dèn* to turn professional; **sie würde kommen, wenn...** *zee vōōr·dè ko·mèn ven* she would come if...; **ich werde es tun** *ikh ver·dè ess toon* I'm going to do it; **er wird es tun** *er virt ess toon* he will do it; **müde werden*** *mōō·dè ver·dèn* to get tired; **erwachsen werden*** *er·vak·sèn ver·dèn* to grow up

werfen* *ver·fèn vt* throw

Werft *verft f —en* shipyard

Werk *verk nt —e* plant (*factory*); work (*art, literature*)

Werkbank *verk·bank f* ⁼e bench (*work table*)

Werkstatt *verk·shtat f* ⁼en workshop

Werktag *verk·tak m* —e workday

Werkzeug *verk·tsoyk nt* —e tool

Wermut *ver·moot m* —s vermouth

Wert *vert m* —e value; im Wert steigen* *im vert shtye·gèn* to appreciate (*in value*) □ *adj* wert *vert* worth; DM5 wert sein* *DM5 vert zine* to be worth DM5; es ist der Mühe wert *ess ist der müö·è vert* it's worth it

Wertgegenstände *vert·gay·gèn·shten·dè pl* valuables

wertlos *vert·lōs adj* worthless

wertvoll *vert·fol adj* valuable; precious (*jewel etc*)

im wesentlichen *im vay·zènt·li·khèn adv* basically

wessen *ve·sèn pron* whose

Weste *ve·stè f* —n vest

Westen *ve·stèn m* west; nach Westen *nakh ve·stèn* west

Western *ves·tèrn m* — western (*movie*)

westlich *vest·likh adj* western

Wettbewerb *vet·bè·verp m* —e competition

Wette *ve·tè f* —n bet

wetten *ve·tèn vi* bet

Wetter *ve·tèr nt* weather

Wetterbericht *ve·tèr·bè·rikht m* —e forecast (*weather*)

Wetterveränderung *ve·tèr·fer·en·dè·roong f* —en change in the weather

Wettervorhersage *ve·tèr·fōr·her·zah·gè f* —n weather forecast

Wettkampf *vet·kampf m* ⁼e match (*sport*)

Whisky *vi·skee m* —s whiskey; ein Whisky Soda *ine vi·skee zō·da* a whiskey and soda

wichtig *vikh·tikh adj* important

Wichtigkeit *vikh·tikh·kite f* importance

wickeln *vi·kèln vt* wind

widerlich *vee·dèr·likh adj* disgusting

widersprechen* *vee·dèr·shpre·khèn vi* contradict

widerstandsfähig *vee·dèr·shtants·fay·ikh adj* hard-wearing

Widerstandsfähigkeit *vee·dèr·shtants·fay·ikh·kite f* resistance (*to illness*)

widerstehen* *vee·dèr·shtay·èn vi* resist

wie *vee conj* like □ *adv* how; wie war es? *vee var es* how was it?; wie lange? *vee lang·è* how long?; wie lange sind Sie schon hier? *vee lang·è zint zee shōn heer* how long have you been here?; wie viele? *vee fee·lè* how many?; wie geht's? *vee gayts* how are you getting on?; wie ist es? *vee ist ess* what's it like?; wie heißt es? *vee hyest ess* what's it called?

wieder *vee·dèr adv* again

wiederholen *vee·dèr·hō·lèn vt* revise (*school work*); repeat; könnten Sie das wiederholen? *kur'n·tèn zee dass vee·dèr·hō·lèn* could you say that again?

Wiederholung *vee·dèr·hō·loong f* —en repetition

auf Wiedersehen *owf vee·dèr·zay·èn excl* goodbye

Wiege *vee·gè f* —n cradle

wiegen* *vee·gèn vt* weigh

wiegen *vee·gèn vt* rock

Wien *veen nt* Vienna

wieviel *vee·feel adv* how much

Wild *vilt nt* game (*hunting*) □ *adj* wild *vilt* fierce; wild (*animal*)

Wildleder *vilt·lay·dèr nt* suede

wildwachsend *vilt·vak·sènt adj* wild (*flower*)

willkommen *vil·ko·mèn adj* welcome

willkürlich *vil·kōōr·likh adj* random

Wimperntusche *vim·pern·too·shè f* mascara

Wind *vint m* —e wind (*breeze*)

Windel *vin·dèl f* — diaper

windig *vin·dikh adj* windy (*place*)

Windmühle *vint·mōō·lè f* —n windmill

Windpocken *vint·po·kèn pl* chicken pox

Windschutzscheibe *vint·shoots·shye·bè f* —n windshield

windsurfen *vint·sur·fèn vi* to go windsurfing

Windsurfing *vint·sur·fing nt* windsurfing

winken *ving·kèn vi* wave

Winter *vin·tèr m* — winter

Wintergarten *vin·tèr·gar·tèn m* ⁼ conservatory (*greenhouse*)

Wintersport *vin·tèr·shport m* winter sports

Wippe *vi·pè f* —n seesaw

wir *veer pron* we; wir sind's *veer zints* it's us

Wirbelwind *vir·bèl·vint m* —e whirlwind

wirken *vir·kèn vi* work (*medicine*)

wirklich *virk·likh adj* real □ *adv* really; das ist wirklich ein Problem *dass ist virk·likh ine pro·blaym* it's a real problem

wirksam *virk·zahm adj* effective (*remedy etc*); wirksam werden* *virk·zahm ver·dèn* to take effect

Wirkung *vir·koong f* —en effect

Wirt *virt m* —e landlord

Wirtin *vir·tin f* —nen landlady

Wirtschaft *virt·shaft f* economy (*of country*)

wirtschaftlich *virt·shaft·likh adj* economic; economical (*use, method*)

Wirtshaus *virts·hows nt* ⁼er inn

wischen *vish·èn vt* wipe

wissen* *vi·sèn vt* know (*fact*); wissen*, wie man etwas macht *vi·sèn, vee man et·vass makht* to know how to do something

Wissenschaft *vi·sèn·shaft f* —en science

Wissenschaftler *vi·sèn·shaft·lèr m* — scientist

Wissenschaftlerin *vi·sèn·shaft·lè·rin f* —nen scientist

wissenschaftlich *vi·sèn·shaft·likh adj* scientific

Witwe *vit·vè f* —n widow

Witwer *vit·vèr m* — widower

Witz *vits m* —e joke

wo *vō conj* where

Woche *vo·khè f* —n week

Wochenende *vo·khèn·en·dè nt* —n weekend

Wochentag *vo·khèn·tahk m* —e weekday

wöchentlich *vur'·khènt·likh adv* weekly

Wochenzeitschrift *vo·khèn·tsite·shrift f* —en weekly (*periodical*)

Wodka *vod·ka m* —s vodka

woher *vō·her adv* where... from; woher kommen Sie? *vō·her ko·mèn zee* where are you from?

wohin *vō·hin adv* where; ich bringe Sie, wohin Sie wollen *ikh bring·è zee vō·hin zee vo·lèn* I'll take you anywhere you like; wohin gehen Sie? *vō·hin gay·èn zee* where are you going?

wohl *vōl adv* well; wohl sein* *vōl zine* to be well

wohlhabend *vōl·hah·bènt adj* prosperous

wohlklingend *vōl·kling·ènt adj* sweet (*music*)

Wohn- *vōn pref* residential (*area*)

Wohnblock *vōn·blok m* —s apartment block

wohnen *vō·nèn vi* stay; live

Wohnheim *vōn·hime nt* —e dormitory (*of college*)

Wohnsiedlung *vōn·zeet·loong f* —en development (*housing*)

Wohnung *vō·noong f* —en apartment; residence; **Wohnungen** *vō·noong·èn* housing

Wohnwagen *vōn·vah·gèn m* — trailer (*home on wheels*)

Wohnzimmer *vōn·tsi·mèr nt* — sitting room; living room

Wolf *volf m* —e wolf

Wolke *vol·kè f* —n cloud

Wolkenkratzer *vol·kèn·krat·sèr m* — skyscraper

wolkig *vol·kikh adj* cloudy

Woll- *vol pref* woolen

Wolle *vo·lè f* wool

wollen* *vo·lèn vt* want (*wish for*); **etwas tun wollen*** *et·vass toon vo·lèn* to want to do something; **was wollen Sie?** *vass vo·lèn zee* what would you like?; **er will weggehen** *er vil vek·gay·èn* he wants to leave

worauf *vō·rowf adv* on which; whereupon; **der Stuhl, worauf** *der shtool vō·rowf* the chair on which

Wort *vort nt* —er word; **Wort für Wort** *vort fōōr vort* word for word

Wörterbuch *vur·tèr·bookh nt* —er dictionary

Wörterverzeichnis *vur·tèr·fer·tsyekh·nis nt* —se vocabulary (*list of words*)

Wortschatz *vort·shats m* vocabulary

Wrack *vrak m* —s wreck (*ship*); **zum Wrack machen** *tsoom vrak ma·khèn* to wreck (*ship*)

Wunde *voon·dè f* —n wound (*injury*)

wunderbar *voon·dèr·bahr adj* marvelous; wonderful

Wunsch *voonsh m* —e wish; desire

wünschen *vōōn·shèn vt* want; **ich wünschte, ich könnte...** *ikh vōōnsh·tè ikh kur'n·tè* I wish I could...; **sich etwas wünschen** *zikh et·vass vōōn·shèn* to wish for something

Würfel *vōōr·fèl m* — dice; cube

würfeln *vōōr·fèln vt/i* throw; **eine Sechs würfeln** *ine·è zeks vōōr·fèln* to throw a 6 (*dice*)

Wurm *voorm m* —er worm

Wurst *voorst f* —e sausage

Wurzel *voor·tsèl f* —n root

würzig *vōōrt·sikh adj* spicy

Wüste *vōō·stè f* —n desert

Wut *voot f* anger

wütend *vōō·tènt adj* angry (*person*)

X

Xerokopie *kse·ro·ko·pee f* —n Xerox

xerokopieren *kse·ro·ko·pee·rèn vt* Xerox

Y

Yachthafen *yakht·hah·fèn m* — marina

Z

zäh *tsay adj* tough (*meat etc*)

Zahl *tsahl f* —en number (*figure*)

zahlbar *tsahl·bahr adj* payable

zahlen *tsah·lèn vt* pay; **zahlen bitte** *tsah·lèn bi·tè* can I have the check please?

zählen *tsay·lèn vt* count (*objects, people*); **bis 10 zählen** *bis 10 tsay·lèn* to count up to 10

zahlender Gast *tsah·lèn·dèr gast m* —e paying guest

Zähler *tsay·lèr m* — meter

Zahlung *tsah·loong f* —en payment; **in Zahlung** *in tsah·loong* as a trade-in

Zahlungsbilanz *tsah·loongs·bee·lants f* —en balance of payments

Zahlungsempfänger *tsah·loongs·emp·feng·èr m* — payee

zahm *tsahm adj* tame (*animal*)

Zahn *tsahn m* —e tooth

Zahnarzt *tsahn·artst m* —e dentist

Zahnärztin *tsahn·erts·tin f* —nen dentist

Zahnbürste *tsahn·bōōr·stè f* —n toothbrush

Zahnfleisch *tsahn·flyesh nt* gum (*of teeth*)

Zahnpasta *tsahn·pa·sta f* toothpaste

Zahnschmerzen *tsahn·shmer·tsèn pl* toothache; **Zahnschmerzen haben*** *tsahn·shmer·tsèn hah·bèn* to have a toothache

Zange *tsang·è f* —n pliers

Zäpfchen *tsepf·khèn nt* — suppository

Zapfsäule *tsapf·zoy·lè f* —n gas pump

zart *tsart adj* tender (*meat, vegetables*); delicate

zärtlich *tsert·likh adj* affectionate

Zauberer *tsow·bè·rèr m* — conjuror

Zaum *tsowm m* —e bridle

Zaun *tsown m* —e fence

z.B. *tsoom bye·shpeel abbrev* e.g.

Zebra *tsay·bra nt* —s zebra

Zebrastreifen *tsay·bra·shtrye·fèn m* — crosswalk

Zeder *tsay·dèr f* —n cedar

Zehe *tsay·è f* —n toe

zehn *tsayn num* ten

zehnte(r/s) *tsayn·tè(·tèr/·tès) adj* tenth

Zeichen *tsye·khèn nt* — sign; mark

Zeichengeschichte *tsye·khèn·gè·shikh·tè f* —n cartoon

Zeichentrickfilm *tsye·khèn·trik·film m* —e cartoon (*animated*)

zeichnen *tsyekh·nèn vt* draw (*picture*)

Zeichner *tsyekh·nèr m* — draftsman

Zeichnung *tsyekh·noong f* —en picture; drawing

zeigen *tsye·gèn vt* show; **auf etwas zeigen** *owf et·vass tsye·gèn* to point at something; to point something out

Zeiger *tsye·gèr m* — hand (*of clock*)

Zeit *tsite f* time; **von Zeit zu Zeit** *fon tsite tsoo tsite* from time to time

Zeitalter *tsite·al·tèr nt* — age (*era*)

zeitgenössisch *tsite·gè·nur·sish adj* contemporary (*modern*)

Zeitkarte *tsite·kar·tè f* —n season ticket; commutation ticket

Zeitraum *tsite·rowm m* period (*of time*)

Zeitschrift *tsite·shrift f* —en magazine (*journal*)

Zeitung *tsye·toong f* —en (news)paper

Zeitungshändler *tsye·toongs·hent·lèr m* — newsdealer

Zeitungsstand *tsye·toongs·shtant m* —e newsstand

Zeitzone *tsite·tsō·nè f* —n time zone

Zelle *tse·lè f* —n cell

Zelt *tselt nt* —e tent

Zeltboden *tselt·bō·dèn m* —: groundcloth

zelten *tsel·tèn vi* camp; **zelten gehen*** *tsel·tèn gay·èn* to go camping

Zeltpflock *tselt·pflok m ˦e* tent stake

Zeltplatz *tselt·plats m ˦e* campsite

Zeltstange *tselt·shtang·è f* **–n** tent pole

Zement *tse·ment m* **—** cement

Zentiliter *tsen·tee·lee·tèr nt* **—** centiliter

Zentimeter *tsen·tee·may·tèr m* **—** centimeter

zentral *tsen·trahl adj* central

Zentrale *tsen·trah·lè f* **–n** head office; switchboard

Zentralheizung *tsen·trahl·hye·tsoong f* **–en** central heating

Zentrum *tsen·troom nt* **Zentren** center; **ins Zentrum** *ins tsen·troom* downtown; **das Zentrum von Chicago** *dass tsen·troom fon shi·kah·gō* downtown Chicago

zerbrechen* *tser·bre·khèn vt/i* break

zerbrechlich *tser·brekh·likh adj* fragile

zerdrücken *tser·dröö·kèn vt* crush

Zeremonie *tsay·ray·mo·nee f* **–n** ceremony

zerfressen* *tser·fre·sèn vt* corrode

zerknittert *tser·kni·tèrt adj* creased

zerlumpt *tser·loompt adj* ragged (*clothes*)

Zero *zay·rō f* **—** zero (*in roulette*)

zerquetschen *tser·kvet·shèn vt* squash (*crush*)

zerreißen* *tser·rye·sèn vt* tear; rip □ *vi* tear

zerren *tse·rèn vt* strain (*muscle*)

zerschmettern *tser·shme·tèrn vt* smash

zerstampfen *tser·shtam·pfèn vt* mash

zerstören *tser·stur·èn vt* destroy

Zettel *tse·tèl m* **—** slip (*of paper*)

Zeug *tsoyk nt* stuff (*substance*)

Zeuge *tsoy·gè m* **–n** witness

Zeugenaussage *tsoy·gèn·ows·zah·gè f* **–n** evidence (*of witness*)

Zeugin *tsoy·gin f* **–nen** witness

Zeugnis *tsoyg·niss nt* **–se** certificate; reference

Zichorie *tsi·khō·ree·è f* **–n** chicory (*for coffee*)

Ziege *tsee·gè f* **–n** goat

Ziegel *tsee·gèl m* **—** brick; tile (*on roof*)

Ziegenleder *tsee·gèn·lay·dèr nt* kid (*leather*)

ziehen* *tsee·èn vt* grow (*plants*); tow (*trailer*) □ *vt/i* pull; **sich einen Zahn ziehen lassen*** *zikh ine·èn tsahn tsee·èn la·sèn* to have a tooth taken out

Ziel *tseel nt* **–e** goal; target

zielen *tsee·lèn vi* aim (*gun etc*)

Zielscheibe *tseel·shye·bè f* **–n** target

ziemlich *tseem·likh adv* quite; fairly (*rather*); **ziemlich gut** *tseem·likh goot* fair (*average*); **ziemlich viele** *tseem·likh fee·lè* quite a few

zierlich *tseer·likh adj* dainty

Ziffer *tsi·fèr f* **–n** figure (*number*)

Zigarette *tsi·ga·re·tè f* **–n** cigarette

Zigarettenetui *tsi·ga·re·tèn·et·vee nt* **–s** cigarette case

Zigarre *tsi·ga·rè f* **–n** cigar

Zigeuner *tsi·goy·nèr m* **—** gypsy

Zigeunerin *tsi·goy·nè·rin f* **–nen** gypsy

Zimmer *tsi·mèr nt* **—** room; **das freie Zimmer** *frye·è tsi·mèr* vacancy (*in hotel etc*)

Zimmer- *tsi·mèr pref* indoor (*games*)

Zimmermann *tsi·mèr·man m* **–er** carpenter

Zimmerservice *tsi·mèr·sur·vees m* room service

Zimt *tsimt nt* cinnamon

Zink *tsink nt* zinc

Zinn *tsin nt* tin (*substance*)

Zinsen *tsin·zèn pl* interest (*on investment*)

Zinseszins *tsin·zès·tsins m* compound interest

Zinssatz *tsins·zats m ˦e* interest rate

Zirkus *tsir·kooss m* **–se** circus

Zitat *tsi·taht nt* **–e** quotation (*passage*)

zitieren *tsi·teer·èn vt* quote (*passage*)

Zitrone *tsi·trō·nè f* **–n** lemon

Zitronenpresse *tsi·trō·nèn·pre·sè f* **–n** lemon-squeezer

Zitronensaft *tsi·trō·nèn·zaft m* lemon juice

zittern *tsi·tèrn vi* shiver; shake

Zivilisation *tsee·vee·lee·zat·see·ōn f* **–en** civilization

zögern *zur·gèrn vi* hesitate

Zoll *tsol m* customs; customs duty; toll (*on road etc*)

Zollbeamte(r) *tsol·bè·am·tè(r) m* **–n** customs officer

zollfrei *tsol·frye adj* duty-free (*goods*)

Zone *tsō·nè f* **–n** zone

Zoo *tsō m* **–s** zoo

Zoom *zoom nt* **–s** zoom lens

Zopf *tsopf m ˦e* plait (*of hair etc*)

zu *tsoo prep* to; **ich habe vergessen, ... zu tun** *ikh hah·bè fer·ge·sèn ... tsoo toon* I forgot to do ... □ *adj zu tsoo* off (*water supply*); **zu sein*** *tsoo zine* to be shut (*door*) □ *adv zu tsoo* too; **er ist zu groß** *er ist tsoo grōs* he's too big

Zubehör *tsoo·bè·hur nt* accessories

zu|bereiten *tsoo·bè·rye·tèn vt* prepare (*meal*)

Zucchini *tsoo·kee·nee pl* zucchini

Zucker *tsoo·kèr m* **—** sugar

Zuckerdose *tsoo·kèr·dō·zè f* **–n** sugar bowl

Zuckerguß *tsoo·kèr·goos m* icing (*on cake*)

Zuckerkrankheit *tsoo·kèr·krank·hite f* diabetes

zuerst *tsoo·erst adv* at first; first

Zufall *tsoo·fal m ˦e* chance; coincidence

zufällig *tsoo·fe·likh adv* by chance □ *adj* accidental

zufrieden *tsoo·free·dèn adj* pleased; content(ed)

zufrieden|stellen *tsoo·free·dèn·shte·lèn vt* satisfy

zufriedenstellend *tsoo·free·dèn·shte·lènt adj* satisfactory

Zug *tsook m ˦e* train; draft (*wind*); stroke (*swimming*)

Zugabe *tsoo·gah·bè f* **–n** encore; **Zugabe!** *tsoo·gah·bè* encore!

Zugang *tsoo·gang m* **–e** access

zugänglich *tsoo·geng·likh adj* accessible

Züge *tsöō·gè pl* features

zu|gehen* *tsoo·gay·èn vi* shut (*door, window*)

Zügel *tsöō·gèl m* **—** rein

Zugführer *tsook·föö·rèr m* **—** conductor (*on train*)

Zuhause *tsoo·how·zè nt* home

zu|hören *tsoo·hur·èn vt/i* listen (to)

zu|jubeln *tsoo·yoo·bèln vt* cheer

zu|kommen* *tsoo·ko·mèn vi* come up; **auf jemanden zu|kommen*** *owf yay·man·dèn tsoo·ko·mèn* to come towards someone

Zukunft *tsoo·koonft f* future

zu|machen *tsoo·ma·khèn vt* shut; fasten

Zunahme *tsoo·nah·mè f* **—n** increase (*in number*); growth (*in amount etc*)

Zündflamme *tsoONt·fla·mè f* **—n** pilot light (*gas*)

Zündkerze *tsoONt·kert·sè f* **—n** spark plug

Zündschlüssel *tsoONt·shlOO·sèl m* **—** ignition key

Zündung *tsoON·doong f* ignition (*car*)

Zuneigung *tsoo·nye·goong f* **—en** affection

Zunge *tsoong·è f* **—n** tongue

zunichte machen *tsoo·nikh·tè ma·khèn vt* wreck (*plans*)

zu|riegeln *tsoo·ree·gèln vt* bolt (*door, gate*)

zurück *tsoo·rOOk adv* backward (*glance*)

zurück|bleiben* *tsoo·rOOk·blye·bèn vi* stay behind

zurück|blicken *tsoo·rOOk·bli·kèn vi* look behind

zurück|bringen* *tsoo·rOOk·bring·èn vt* bring/take back

zurück|datieren *tsoo·rOOk·da·tee·rèn vt* backdate (*letter*)

zurück|geben* *tsoo·rOOk·gay·bèn vt* give back

zurückgeblieben *tsoo·rOOk·gè·blee·bèn adj* backward (*child*)

zurück|gehen* *tsoo·rOOk·gay·èn vi* go back

zurück|kehren *tsoo·rOOk·kay·rèn vi* return (*come back*)

zurück|kommen* *tsoo·rOOk·ko·mèn vi* come back

zurück|legen *tsoo·rOOk·lay·gèn vt* travel (*a distance*); replace (*put back*)

zurück|rufen* *tsoo·rOOk·roo·fèn vt* call back

zurück|senden* *tsoo·rOOk·zen·dèn vt* return (*send back*)

zurück|setzen *tsoo·rOOk·zet·sèn vt* put back; den Wagen zurück|setzen *den vah·gèn tsoo·rOOk·zet·sèn* to back the car

zurück|stellen *tsoo·rOOk·shte·lèn vt* put back (*replace*)

zurück|zahlen *tsoo·rOOk·tsah·lèn vt* pay back (*money*)

zusammen *tsoo·za·mèn adv* together

zusammen|arbeiten *tsoo·za·mèn·ar·bye·tèn vi* co-operate; collaborate

zusammen|brechen* *tsoo·za·mèn·bre·khèn vi* collapse (*person*)

zusammen|fallen* *tsoo·za·mèn·fa·lèn vi* coincide

zusammen|falten *tsoo·za·mèn·fal·tèn vt* fold

Zusammenfassung *tsoo·za·mèn·fa·soong f* **—en** summary

Zusammenstoß *tsoo·za·mèn·shtOs m* **—e** collision

zusammen|stoßen* *tsoo·za·mèn·shtO·sèn vi* collide

zusammen|zählen *tsoo·za·mèn·tsay·lèn vt* add (up) (*numbers*)

zusätzlich *tsoo·zets·likh adj* extra

Zuschauer *tsoo·show·èr pl* audience (*in theater*)

Zuschlag *tsoo·shlahk m* **—e** surcharge

zu|schlagen* *tsoo·shlah·gèn vt* bang (*door*)

zu|sehen* *tsoo·say·èn vi* watch; bei einem Wettkampf zu|sehen *bye ine·èm vet·kampf tsoo·zay·èn* to watch a match

Zustand *tsoo·shtant m* **—e** state (*condition*)

zuständig *tsoo·shten·dikh adj* responsible

zu|stellen *tsoo·shte·lèn vt* deliver (*mail*)

Zustellung *tsoo·shte·loong f* **—en** delivery (*of mail*)

zu|stimmen *tsoo·shti·mèn vi* agree; jemandem zu|stimmen *yay·man·dèm tsoo·shti·mèn* to agree with somebody

Zutaten *tsoo·tah·tèn pl* ingredients

Zutritt *tsoo·trit m* admission

zuverlässig *tsoo·fer·le·sikh adj* reliable (*person*)

Zuverlässigkeit *tsoo·fer·le·sikh·kite f* reliability (*of person*)

zuviel *tsoo·feel adv* too much

zuwenig *tsoo·vay·nikh adv* too little

sich zu|ziehen* *zikh tsoo·tsee·èn vr* catch (*illness*)

zuzüglich *tsoo·tsOOk·likh prep* extra

zwanglos *tsvang·lOs adj* informal (*party*); zwanglose Kleidung *tsvang·lO·zè klye·doong* dress: informal

zwanzig *tsvan·tsikh num* twenty

Zweck *tsvek m* **—e** purpose; es hat keinen Zweck *ess hat kine·èn tsvek* it's no use

zwei *tsvye num* two

zweieinhalb *tsvye·ine·halp num* two and a half

Zweifel *tsvye·fèl m* **—** doubt; ohne Zweifel *O·nè tsvye·fèl* without (a) doubt

zweifelhaft *tsvye·fèl·haft adj* doubtful

zweifellos *tsvye·fèl·lOs adj* no doubt

Zweig *tsvike m* **—e** twig; branch (*of tree*)

zweimal *tsvye·mahl adv* twice

zweisprachig *tsvye·shprah·khikh adj* bilingual

Zweiteiler *tsvye·tile·èr m* **—** two-piece

zweite(r/s) *tsvye·tè(·tèr/tès) adj* second; der zweite Stock *tsvye·tè shtok* third floor

Zwetschge *tsvetsh·gè f* **—n** plum

Zwiebel *tsvee·bèl f* **—n** bulb; onion

Zwillinge *tsvi·ling·è pl* twins

zwingen* *tsving·èn vt* force (*compel*)

zwinkern *tsving·kèrn vi* blink; wink

zwischen *tsvi·shèn prep* between

Zwischenlandung *tsvi·shèn·lan·doong f* **—en** stopover (*air travel*)

Zwischensumme *tsvi·shèn·zoo·mè f* **—n** subtotal

zwölf *tsvur·lf num* twelve

zwölfte(r/s) *tsvur·lf·tè(·tèr/·tès) adj* twelfth

Zylinder *tsOO·lin·dèr m* **—** top hat; cylinder

ENGLISH–GERMAN DICTIONARY

a *art* ein(e) *ine(·è)*; twice a day zwei-mal pro Tag *tsvye·mal prō tahk*; $40 a week $40 pro Woche *$40 prō vo·khè*

abbey *n* die Abtei *ap·tye*

abbreviation *n* die Abkürzung *ap·kōōr·tsoong*

abdomen *n* der Unterleib *oon·tèr·lipe*

ability *n* die Fähigkeit *fay·ikh·kite*

able *adj* □ to be able to do something etwas tun können* *et·vass toon kur'n·èn*

aboard *adv* □ to go aboard an Bord gehen* *an bort gay·èn* □ *prep* aboard the ship an Bord des Schiffes *an bort des shi·fès*

abolish *vt* ab|schaffen *ap·sha·fèn*

about *prep* □ about $10 ungefähr $10 *oon·gè·fayr $10*; about here hier herum *heer hè·room*; to talk about something über etwas sprechen* *ōō·bèr et·vass shpre·khèn* □ *adv* things lying about Sachen die überall her-umliegen *za·khèn dee ōō·bèr·al he·room·lee·gèn*; to look about sich um|-sehen* *zikh oom·zay·èn*; to be about to do something im Begriff sein*, et-was zu tun *im bè·grif zine et·vass tsoo toon*

above *prep* □ the house is above the valley das Haus liegt über dem Tal *dass hows leekt ōō·bèr daym tahl* □ *adv* above, you can see... oben se-hen Sie... *ō·bèn zay·èn zee*

abroad *adv* im Ausland *im ows·lant*; to go abroad ins Ausland fahren* *ins ows·lant fah·rèn*

abrupt *adj* (*person*) abrupt *a·broopt*; (*slope*) jäh *yay*

abscess *n* der Abszeß *aps·tses*

absent *adj* abwesend *ap·vay·zènt*

absenteeism *n* das Nichterscheinen *nikht·èr·shye·nèn*

absolute *adj* absolut *ap·zō·loot*

absorb *vt* (*fluid*) auf|nehmen* *owf·nay·mèn*; (*shock*) dämpfen *demp·fèn*

absorbent *adj* saugfähig *zowk·fay·ikh*

absorbent cotton *n* die Watte *va·tè*

abstain *vi* (*in voting*) sich enthalten* *zikh ent·hal·tèn*

abstract *adj* abstrakt *ap·strakt*

absurd *adj* absurd *ap·zoort*

academy *n* □ academy of music das Konservatorium *kon·zer·va·tō·ree·oom*; military academy die Militär-akademie *mi·li·ter·a·ka·day·mee*

accelerate *vi* beschleunigen *bè·shloy·ni·gèn*

accelerator *n* das Gaspedal *gahs·pay·dahl*

accent *n* der Akzent *ak·tsent*

accept *vt* an|nehmen* *an·nay·mèn*; (*responsibility*) über|nehmen* *ōō·bèr·nay·mèn*

acceptance *n* die Annahme *an·nah·mè*

access *n* der Zugang *tsoo·gang*

accessible *adj* zugänglich *tsoo·geng·likh*

accessories *pl* das Zubehör *tsoo·bè·hur*

accident *n* der Unfall *oon·fal*; by accident zufällig *tsoo·fe·likh* I13, Ea4

accidental *adj* zufällig *tsoo·fe·likh*

accommodations *n* die Unterkunft *oon·tèr·koonft* A4

accompany *vt* (*go with*) begleiten *bè·glye·tèn*

according to *prep* nach *nakh*

account *n* das Konto *kon·tō*

accountancy *n* die Buchführung *bookh·fōō·roong*

accountant *n* der Buchhalter *bookh·hal·tèr*

accrue *vi* sich an|sammeln *zikh an·za·mèln*

accumulate *vi* sich an|häufen *zikh an·hoy·fèn*

accurate *adj* genau *gè·now*

accuse *vt* an|klagen *an·klah·gèn*

ace *n* (*cards*) das As *ass*

ache *n* der Schmerz *shmerts* □ *vi* weh tun* *vay toon*

acid *n* die Säure *zoy·rè*

acknowledge *vt* (*letter*) bestätigen *bè·shtay·ti·gèn*

acne *n* die Akne *ak·nè*

acorn *n* die Eichel *eye·khèl*

acquaintance *n* der/die Bekannte *bè·kan·tè*

acquire *vt* erwerben* *er·ver·bèn*

acquisition *n* die Anschaffung *an·sha·foong*

acre *n* der Morgen *mor·gèn*

across *prep* □ to walk across the road über die Straße gehen* *ōō·bèr dee shtrah·sè gay·èn*; I saw him from across the road ich sah ihn auf der anderen Straßenseite *ikh zah een owf der an·dè·rèn shtrah·sèn·zye·tè*; we drove across France wir fuhren quer durch Frankreich *veer foo·rèn kvayr doorkh frank·ryekh*

acrylic *adj* Acryl–*a·krōōl*

act *n* (*of play*) der Akt *akt*; (*at circus etc*) die Nummer *noo·mèr* □ *vi* (*behave*) sich verhalten* *zikh fer·hal·tèn* □ *vt* to act Hamlet den Hamlet spie-len *dayn ham·let shpee·lèn*; to act as X als X handeln *als X han·dèln*

acting *adj* stellvertretend *shtel·fer·tray·tènt*

action *n* (*movement*) das Handeln *han·dèln*; (*act*) die Tat *taht*

active *adj* (*energetic*) aktiv *ak·teef*; (*volcano*) tätig *tay·tikh*

activity *n* die Betätigung *bè·tay·ti·goong*

actor *n* der Schauspieler *show·shpee·lèr*

actress *n* die Schauspielerin *show·shpee·lè·rin*

actually *adv* eigentlich *eye·gènt·likh*

adapt *vt* um|stellen *oom·shte·lèn*

adapter, adaptor *n* (*electrical*) der Adapter *a·dap·tèr*

add *vt* (*comment*) hinzu|fügen *hin·tsoo·fōō·gèn*; add (up) (*numbers*) zu-sammen|zählen *tsoo·za·mèn·tsay·lèn*

adder *n* (*snake*) die Viper *vee·pèr*

addict *n* der/die Süchtige *zōōkh·ti·gè*

addition *n* die Addition *a·di·tsee·ōn*

address *n* die Anschrift *an·shrift* □ *vt* (*letter*) adressieren *a·dre·see·rèn* T207, F2, S30, Ea12

adhesive tape *n* (*for wound*) das Heftpflaster *heft·pfla·stèr*

adjourn *vi* sich vertagen *zikh fer·tah·gèn*

adjournment *n* die Vertagung *fer·tah·goong*

adjust vt ein|stellen *ine·shte·lèn*
administration n die Verwaltung *fer· val·toong*
admire vt bewundern *bè·voon·dèrn*
admission n der Zutritt *tsoo·trit*
admission fee n das Eintrittsgeld *ine· trits·gelt* L14
adopt vt (child) adoptieren *a·dop·tee· rèn*; (proposal) übernehmen* *öö· bèr·nay·mèn*
Adriatic (Sea) n Adria (f) *a·dree·a*
adult n der/die Erwachsene *er·vak·sè· nè* □ adj für Erwachsene *föör er·vak· sè·nè*
advance vt (money) als Vorschuß geben* *als för·shoos gay·bèn* □ vi Fortschritte machen *fort·shri·tè ma· khèn* □ n (loan) der Vorschuß *för· shoos*; in advance im voraus *im för· ows* M10
advantage n der Vorteil *för·tile*
adventure n das Abenteuer *ah·bèn· toy·èr*
advertise vt (product) Werbung machen für *ver·boong ma·khèn föör* □ vi to advertise for a secretary per Anzeige eine Sekretärin suchen *per an·tsye·gè ine·è ze·kray·tay·rin zoo· khèn* Bm19
advertisement n die Anzeige *an·tsye· gè*
advertising n die Werbung *ver·boong*
advertising agency n die Werbeagentur *ver·bè·a·gen·toor*
advice n der Rat *raht*
advise vt raten* *rah·tèn*; to advise someone to do something jemandem raten*, etwas zu tun *yay·man·dèm rah·tèn et·vass tsoo toon*
aerial n die Antenne *an·te·nè*
aerosol n die Spraydose *shpray·dö·zè*
affair n (matter) die Angelegenheit *an· gè·lay·gèn·hite*; affairs die Angelegenheiten (pl) *an·gè·lay·gèn·hite·èn*
affect vt beeinflussen *bè·ine·floo·sèn*
affection n die Zuneigung *tsoo·nye· goong*
affectionate adj zärtlich *tsert·likh*
affiliated company n die Schwestergesellschaft *shves·tèr·gè·zel·shaft*
afford vt □ I can't afford it das kann ich mir nicht leisten *dass kan ikh meer nikht lye·stèn*; to be able to afford a new car sich ein neues Auto leisten können* *zikh ine noy·ès ow·tö lye·stèn kur'·nèn*
afraid adj □ to be afraid of something vor etwas Angst haben* *för et·vass angst hah·bèn*; I'm afraid not leider nicht *lye·dèr nikht*; I'm afraid I can't do it ich kann es leider nicht machen *ikh kan ess lye·dèr nikht ma·khèn*
Africa n Afrika (nt) *a·fri·ka*
African adj afrikanisch *a·fri·kah·nish*
after prep, adv nach *nakh*; to come after someone/something etwas/jemandem folgen *et·vass/yay·man·dèm fol·gèn*; 4 years after 4 Jahre später *4 yah·rè shpay·tèr* □ conj after nachdem *nakh·daym*; after we had left nachdem wir weggegangen waren *nakh·daym veer vek·gè·gang·èn vah· rèn*
afternoon n der Nachmittag *nakh·mi· tahk*
aftershave (lotion) n das Rasierwasser *ra·zeer·va·sèr*
afterward(s) adv danach *da·nakh*
again adv noch einmal *nokh ine·mahl*; wieder *vee·dèr*
against prep gegen *gay·gèn*

age n (of person) das Alter *al·tèr*; (era) das Zeitalter *tsite·al·tèr*; under age minderjährig *min·dèr·yay·rikh*
agency n (office) das Büro *bōō·rö*
agenda n die Tagesordnung *tah·gès· ort·noong*
agent n der Agent *a·gent*; the Renault agent der Renault-Konzessionär *re· nō·kon·tse·see·ö·nayr*
aggressive adj aggressiv *a·gre·seef*
agile adj agil *a·geel*
ago adv □ 4 years ago vor 4 Jahren *för 4 yah·rèn*
agony n die Qual *kvahl*
agree vt/i □ to agree with somebody jemandem zu|stimmen *yay·man·dèm tsoo·shti·mèn*; to agree on (price) sich einigen auf *zikh ine·i·gèn owf*; onions don't agree with me Zwiebeln bekommen mir nicht *tsvee·bèln bè· ko·mèn meer nikht*
agreement n die Abmachung *ap·ma· khoong*
agricultural adj landwirtschaftlich *lant· virt·shaft·likh*
agriculture n die Landwirtschaft *lant· virt·shaft*
ahead adv □ to see something ahead etwas vor sich sehen* *et·vass för zikh zay·èn*; to plan ahead voraus|planen *för·ows·plah·nèn*; to think ahead voraus|denken* *för·ows·deng·kèn* □ prep ahead of the others den anderen voraus *dayn an·dè·rèn för·ows*
aim vt/i (gun etc) zielen *tsee·lèn*; to aim a gun at someone ein Gewehr auf jemanden richten *ine gè·vayr owf yay· man·dèn rikh·tèn* □ n aim (intention) die Absicht *ap·zikht*
air n die Luft *looft*; by air mit dem Flugzeug *mit daym flook·tsoyk* □ vt air (room) lüften *lööf·tèn*; (clothes) aus|lüften *ows·lööf·tèn*
air bed n die Luftmatratze *looft·ma· trat·sè*
air bus n der Airbus *er·boos*
air-conditioned adj klimatisiert *klee· ma·ti·zeert*
air-conditioning n die Klimaanlage *klee·ma·an·lah·gè* A47
aircraft n das Flugzeug *flook·tsoyk*
air filter n der Luftfilter *looft·fil·tèr*
air force n die Luftwaffe *looft·va·fè*
air freight n die Luftfracht *looft·frakht*
air letter n der Luftpostbrief *looft· post·breef*
airline n die Fluggesellschaft *flook·gè· zel·shaft*
air mail n □ by air mail per Luftpost *per looft·post*
air-mattress n die Luftmatratze *looft· ma·trat·sè*
airplane n das Flugzeug *flook·tsoyk*
airport n der Flughafen *flook·hah·fèn* T37, 95
airtight adj luftdicht *looft·dikht*
air travel n die Flugreise *flook·rye·zè*
à la carte adv nach der Speisekarte *nakh der shpye·zè·kar·tè*
alarm n (signal, apparatus) die Alarmanlage *a·larm·an·lah·gè* □ vt erschrecken *er·shre·kèn*
alarm (clock) n der Wecker *ve·kèr*
album n das Album *al·boom*
alcohol n der Alkohol *al·kö·hōl*
alcoholic adj (drink) alkoholisch *al·kö· hö·lish* □ n der Alkoholiker *al·kö· hö·li·kèr*
alcove n der Alkoven *al·kö·vèn*
Algeria n Algerien (nt) *al·gay·ree·èn*
Algerian adj algerisch *al·gay·rish*

Algiers n Algier (nt) al·zheer
alike adj ähnlich lay·ben·dikh
alive adj lebendig lay·ben·dikh
all adj (with singular noun) alle(r/s)
a·le(·ler/·les); (with plural noun) alle
a·le; all day den ganzen Tag dayn
gant·sèn tahk; all the tables alle Tische a·le ti·she; all the bread das
ganze Brot das gant·se bröt; all
passengers alle Passagiere a·le pa·sa·
zhee·re □ pron all (singular) alles a·
les; (plural) alle a·le; all you need alles, was Sie brauchen a·les vass zee
brow·khen; all of them know that...
alle wissen, daß... a·le vi·sèn dass
Allah n Allah (m) ah·la
allergic to adj allergisch gegen a·ler·
gish gay·gèn I43
allergy n die Allergie a·ler·gee
alley n die Gasse ga·sè
alliance n das Bündnis böont·nis
allocate vt (funds) verteilen fer·tile·èn;
(duties) vergeben* fer·gay·bèn
allow vt □ to allow someone to go jemandem erlauben, zu gehen yay·
man·dèm er·low·bèn tsoo gay·èn; we
will allow $10 wir planen $10 ein
veer plah·nèn $10 ine; allow 10 min-
utes to get there rechnen Sie mit 10
Minuten, um dort hinzukommen
rekh·nèn zee mit 10 mee·noo·tèn oom
dort hin·tsoo·ko·mèn
allowance n (state payment) die Beihilfe bye·hil·fè
alloy n die Legierung lay·gee·roong
all right adv (yes) gut goot; he's all
right (safe, fit) er ist in Ordnung er
ist in ort·noong; he did it all right
(satisfactorily) er machte es ganz ordentlich er makh·tè ess gants or·dènt·
likh
almond n die Mandel man·dèl
almond paste n die Marzipanmasse
mar·tsi·pahn·ma·sè
almost adv fast fast
alone adj allein a·line
along prep □ along the street die
Straße entlang dee shtrah·sè ent·lang
aloud adv (read) laut lowt
alphabet n das Alphabet al·fa·bayt
alpine adj alpin al·peen
Alps pl die Alpen (pl) al·pèn
already adv schon shön
also adv auch owkh
altar n der Altar al·tahr
alter vt ändern en·dèrn
alternator n (in car) die Lichtmaschine
likht·ma·shee·nè
although conj obwohl op·völ
altitude n die Höhe hur·è
aluminum n das Aluminium a·loo·
mee·nee·oom
always adv immer i·mèr
a.m. adv vormittags för·mi·tahks
am vi □ I am ich bin ikh bin
amalgamation n die Fusion foo·zee·ön
amateur n der Amateur a·ma·tur
ambassador n der Botschafter böt·
shaf·tèr
amber n (traffic light) das Gelb gelp
ambition n (aim) die Ambition am·bi·
tsee·ön
ambitious adj (person) ehrgeizig ayr·
gye·tsikh; (plan) kühn köön
ambulance n der Krankenwagen
krang·kèn·vah·gèn I14, Ea8
amenities pl (of a building) die Annehmlichkeiten
(pl) an·naym·likh·kye·tèn
America n Amerika (nt) a·may·ri·ka
American adj amerikanisch a·may·ri·
kah·nish; he's American er ist Ame-

rikaner er ist a·may·ri·kah·nèr; she's
American sie ist Amerikanerin zee ist
a·may·ri·kah·nè·rin
amethyst n der Amethyst a·may·töost
among prep unter oon·tèr
amount n (total) der Endbetrag ent·bè·
trahk; a large amount of X eine
große Menge X ine·è grö·sè meng·è
X □ vi it amounts to DM4 das be-
läuft sich auf DM4 dass bè·loyft zikh
owf DM4
amp n das Ampere am·payr
amplifier n der Verstärker fer·shter·
kèr
amuse vt amüsieren a·mōō·zee·rèn
amusement park n der Vergnügungspark fer·gnōō·goongs·park C9
an art ein(e) ine(·è)
analysis n die Analyse a·na·lōō·zè
analyze vt analysieren a·na·lōō·zee·rèn
ancestor n der Vorfahr för·fahr
anchor n der Anker ang·kèr
anchovy n die Sardelle zar·de·lè
and conj und oont; better and better
immer besser im·èr be·sèr; to go and
buy kaufen gehen* kow·fèn gay·èn
anemic adj anämisch a·ne·mish
anesthetic n die Narkose nar·kō·zè
angel n der Engel eng·èl
anger n die Wut voot
angler n der Angler ang·lèr
angling n das Angeln ang·èln
angora n (fabric) das Angora ang·gö·
ra
angry adj (person) wütend vōō·tènt; to
be angry with someone auf jemanden
böse sein* owf yay·man·dèn bur'·zè
zine
animal n das Tier teer
ankle n der Knöchel knur'·khèl
anniversary n der Jahrestag yah·rès·
tahk
announce vt an|zeigen an·tsye·gèn
annoy vt ärgern er·gèrn
annual adj jährlich yayr·likh
annuity n die Rente ren·tè
anorak n der Anorak a·no·rak
another adj □ another beer please!
noch ein Bier, bitte nokh ine beer bi·
tè; I want to see another shirt ich
möchte ein anderes Hemd sehen ikh
mur'kh·tè ine an·dè·rès hemt zay·èn
answer n die Antwort ant·vort □ vi
antworten ant·vor·tèn □ vt to answer
a question eine Frage beantworten
ine·è frah·gè bè·ant·vor·tèn; to an-
swer the phone das Telefon ab|neh-
men* dass tay·lay·fön ap·nay·mèn;
he answered that... er erwiderte,
daß... er er·vee·dèr·tè dass
ant n die Ameise ah·mye·zè
Antarctic n die Antarktis ant·ark·tis
antenna n die Antenne an·te·nè
antibiotic n das Antibiotikum an·ti·
bee·ö·ti·koom
antifreeze n das Frostschutzmittel
frost·shoots·mi·tèl
antihistamine n das Antihistamin an·
tee·hi·sta·min
antique n die Antiquität an·tee·kvee·
tet
antique dealer n der Antiquitätenhändler an·tee·kvee·te·tèn·hend·lèr
antiseptic n das Antiseptikum an·ti·
zep·ti·koom
any adj □ give me any book geben Sie
mir irgendein Buch gay·bèn zee meer
ir·gènt·ine bookh; we haven't any
bread wir haben kein Brot veer hah·
bèn kine bröt; have you any bread?
haben Sie Brot? hah·bèn zee bröt; is

there any more soup? ist noch Suppe da? *ist nokh zoo·pĕ dah* □ *pron* we haven't any wir haben keinen/keine/keines *veer hah·bĕn kine·ĕn/kine·ĕ/kine·ĕs*; can any of you sing? kann irgend jemand von euch singen? *kan ir·gĕnt yay·mant fon oykh zing·ĕn*

anybody, anyone *pron* □ can you see anybody? können Sie jemanden sehen? *kur'n·ĕn zee ir·gĕnt yay·man·dĕn zay·ĕn*; I can't see anybody ich kann niemand sehen *ikh kan nee·mant zay·ĕn*; anybody at all irgend jemand *ir·gĕnt yay·mant*

anything *pron* □ can you see anything? können Sie etwas sehen? *kur'n·ĕn zee et·vass zay·ĕn*; I can't see anything ich kann nichts sehen *ikh kan nikhts zay·ĕn*; anything at all irgend etwas *ir·gĕnt et·vass*

anyway *adv* (*nonetheless*) jedenfalls *yay·dĕn·fals*

anywhere *adv* □ I'll take you anywhere you like ich bringe Sie, wohin Sie wollen *ikh bring·ĕ zee vō·hin zee vo·lĕn*; I can't see it anywhere ich kann es nirgends sehen *ikh kan es nir·gĕnts zay·ĕn*

apart *adv* (*separately*) auseinander *ows·ine·an·dĕr*

apartment *n* die Wohnung *vō·noong*

ape *n* der Affe *a·fĕ*

aperitif *n* der Aperitif *a·pe·ri·teef*

apologize *vi* sich entschuldigen *zikh ent·shool·di·gĕn*

apparently *adv* offensichtlich *o·fĕn·zikht·likh*

appear *vi* erscheinen* *er·shine·ĕn*; he appears to be ill er scheint krank zu sein *er shyent krank tsoo zine*; it appears that... es hat den Anschein, daß... *ess hat dayn an·shine dass*

appendicitis *n* die Blinddarmentzündung *blint·darm·ent·tsōōn·doong*

appetite *n* der Appetit *a·pay·teet*

appetizer *n* der Appetitanreger *a·pay·teet·an·ray·gĕr*

applause *n* der Beifall *bye·fal*

apple *n* der Apfel *ap·fĕl* S34

apple tree *n* der Apfelbaum *ap·fĕl·bowm*

appliance *n* das Gerät *gĕ·ret*

application *n* (*for job*) die Bewerbung *bĕ·ver·boong*

apply *vi* □ to apply for a job sich um eine Stelle bewerben* *zikh oom ine·ĕ shte·lĕ bĕ·ver·bĕn*

appoint *vt* ein|stellen *ine·shte·lĕn*

appointment *n* (*rendezvous*) der Termin *ter·meen*; (*to job*) die Einstellung *ine·shte·loong* Sn32, Bm9, I10

appreciate *vt* zu schätzen wissen* *tsoo shet·sĕn vi·sĕn* □ *vi* (*in value*) im Wert steigen* *im vert shtye·gĕn*

apprentice *n* der Lehrling *layr·ling*

approach *vi* (*person*) sich nähern *zikh nay·ĕrn*; (*season*) nahen *nah·ĕn* □ *vt* to approach a place sich einem Ort nähern *zikh ine·ĕm ort nay·ĕrn*

approval *n* der Beifall *bye·fal*; on approval auf Probe *owf prō·bĕ*

approve of *vt* billigen *bi·li·gĕn*

approximate *adj* ungefähr *oon·gĕ·fer*

apricot *n* die Aprikose *a·pri·kō·zĕ*

April *n* April (*m*) *a·pril*

apron *n* die Schürze *shōōr·tsĕ*

aquarium *n* das Aquarium *a·kvah·ree·oom*

Arab *n* der Araber *ah·ra·bĕr*

Arabic *adj* arabisch *a·rah·bish* □ *n* Arabisch (*nt*) *a·rah·bish*

arcade *n* die Passage *pa·sah·zhĕ*

arch *n* der Bogen *bō·gĕn*

architect *n* der Architekt *ar·khi·tekt*

architecture *n* die Architektur *ar·khi·tek·toor*

Arctic *n* die Arktis *ark·tis*

are *vi* □ we are wir sind *veer zint*; you are Sie sind *zee zint*; they are sie sind *zee zint*

area *n* (*of surface*) die Fläche *fle·khĕ*; (*region*) das Gebiet *gĕ·beet*

Argentina *n* Argentinien (*nt*) *ar·gen·tee·nee·ĕn*

Argentine *adj* argentinisch *ar·gen·tee·nish*

argue *vi* (*quarrel*) sich streiten* *zikh shtrye·tĕn*

argument *n* (*quarrel*) die Auseinandersetzung *ows·ine·an·dĕr·zet·soong*

arithmetic *n* das Rechnen *rekh·nĕn*

arm *n* (*of person*) der Arm *arm* I24, 25

armchair *n* der Sessel *ze·sĕl*

arms *pl* die Waffen (*pl*) *va·fĕn*

army *n* die Armee *ar·may*

around *adv* □ to look around sich nach allen Seiten um|sehen* *zikh nakh a·lĕn zye·tĕn oom·zay·ĕn*; things lying around herumliegende Sachen *he·room·lee·gĕn·dĕ za·khĕn* □ *prep* to go around the world um die Welt reisen *oom dee velt rye·zĕn*; the scarf around her neck der Schal um ihren Hals *der shahl oom ee·rĕn hals*; around $10 etwa $10 *et·va $10*

arrange *vt* (*flowers, furniture*) arrangieren *a·rang·zhee·rĕn*; (*meeting*) an|setzen *an·zet·sĕn*

arrears *pl* die Rückstände (*pl*) *rōōk·shten·dĕ*; to be in arrears with a payment mit einer Zahlung im Rückstand sein* *mit ine·ĕr tsah·loong im rōōk·shtant zine*

arrest *vt* verhaften *fer·haf·tĕn*

arrival *n* die Ankunft *an·koonft*

arrive *vi* an|kommen* *an·ko·mĕn*

arrow *n* der Pfeil *pfile*

art *n* die Kunst *koonst*

artery *n* die Arterie *ar·tay·ree·ĕ*

art gallery *n* die Kunstgalerie *koonst·ga·lĕ·ree*; (*commercial*) die Galerie *ga·le·ree*

arthritis *n* die Arthritis *ar·tree·tis*

artichoke *n* die Artischocke *ar·ti·sho·kĕ*; Jerusalem artichoke der Topinambur *to·pi·nam·boor*

article *n* (*in newspaper*) der Artikel *ar·tee·kĕl*; (*thing*) der Gegenstand *gay·gĕn·shtant*

artificial *adj* künstlich *kōōnst·likh*

artist *n* der Künstler *kōōnst·lĕr*, die Künstlerin *kōōnst·lĕ·rin*

as *conj* □ as he was asleep (*because*) da er schlief *dah er shleef*; (*while*) während er schlief *vay·rĕnt er shleef*; he arrived as we left er ist angekommen, als wir weggingen *er ist an·gĕ·ko·mĕn als veer vek·ging·ĕn*; do as I say machen Sie, was ich Ihnen sage *ma·khĕn zee vass ikh ee·nĕn zah·gĕ*; as big as so groß wie *zō grōs vee*; as for this was dies angeht *vass dees an·gayt*; as if, as though als ob *als op*; as well (*too*) auch *owkh*; as much/many as soviel wie *zō feel vee*

asbestos *n* der Asbest *as·best*

ash *n* (*tree*) die Esche *e·shĕ*; (*cinders*) die Asche *a·shĕ*

ashamed *adj* □ to be ashamed sich schämen *zikh she·mĕn*

ashcan *n* der Ascheneimer *a·shĕn·ime·ĕr*

ashore *adv* an Land *an lant*

ashtray *n* der Aschenbecher *a·shĕn·be·khĕr* A43

Asia *n* Asien (*nt*) *ah·zee·ĕn*

Asian *adj* asiatisch *a·zee·ah·tish*

ask *vt/i* fragen *frah·gĕn*; **to ask a question** eine Frage stellen *ine·ĕ frah·gĕ shte·lĕn*; **to ask someone the time** jemanden nach der Uhrzeit fragen *yay·man·dĕn nakh der oor·tsite frah·gĕn*; **to ask for something** um etwas bitten* *oom et·vass bi·tĕn*; **to ask the price** sich nach dem Preis erkundigen *zikh nakh daym price er·koon·di·gĕn*

asleep *adj* schlafend *shlah·fĕnt*

asparagus *n* der Spargel *shpar·gĕl*

aspirin *n* das Aspirin *as·pi·reen*

assemble *vt* (*parts of machine*) montieren *mon·tee·rĕn*

assembly line *n* das Montageband *mon·tah·zhĕ·bant*

asset *n* (*financial*) der Aktivposten *ak·teef·pos·tĕn*

assistant *n* (*in shop*) der Verkäufer *fer·koy·fĕr*, die Verkäuferin *fer·koy·fĕ·rin*

associate *n* der Partner *part·nĕr*

association *n* der Verband *fer·bant*

assorted *adj* gemischt *gĕ·misht*

assume *vt* (*suppose*) an|nehmen* *an·nay·mĕn*

asthma *n* das Asthma *ast·ma* I1

at *prep* □ **at 4 o'clock** um 4 Uhr *oom 4 oor*; **at my house** bei mir *bye meer*; **at school** in der Schule *in der shoo·lĕ*; **to throw something at someone** mit etwas nach jemandem werfen* *mit et·vass nakh yay·man·dĕm ver·fĕn*; **not at all** gar nicht *gar nikht*; **at once** sofort *zō·fort*

Athens *n* Athen (*nt*) *a·tayn*

athlete *n* der Athlet *at·layt*

Atlantic Ocean *n* der Atlantik *at·lan·tik*

atlas *n* der Atlas *at·las*

attach *vt* befestigen *bĕ·fes·ti·gĕn*

attack *vt* überfallen* *ōō·bĕr·fa·lĕn* □ *n* der Angriff *an·grif*

attempt *vt* versuchen *fer·zoo·khĕn* □ *n* der Versuch *fer·zookh*

attend *vt* (*meeting etc*) besuchen *bĕ·zoo·khĕn*

attic *n* der Dachboden *dakh·bō·dĕn*

attitude *n* die Einstellung *ine·shte·loong*

attorney *n* der Rechtsanwalt *rekhts·an·valt*

aubergine *n* die Aubergine *ō·ber·zhee·nĕ*

auction *n* die Auktion *owk·tsee·ōn*

audience *n* (*in theatre*) die Zuschauer (*pl*) *tsoo·show·ĕr*

audio-guide *n* der Tonbandbegleiter *tōn·bant·bĕ·glye·tĕr* L4

audio-visual *adj* audiovisuell *ow·di·ō·vi·zoo·el*

audit *vt* prüfen *prōō·fĕn*

auditor *n* der Buchprüfer *bookh·prōō·fĕr*

auditorium *n* das Auditorium *ow·di·tō·ree·oom*

au gratin *adj* überbacken *ōō·bĕr·ba·kĕn*

August *n* August (*m*) *ow·goost*

aunt(ie) *n* die Tante *tan·tĕ*

Australia *n* Australien (*nt*) *ow·strah·lee·ĕn*

Australian *adj* australisch *ow·strah·lish*; **he's Australian** er ist Australier *er ist ow·strah·lee·ĕr*; **she's Aus-**

tralian sie ist Australierin *zee ist ow·strah·lee·rin*

Austria *n* Österreich (*nt*) *ur·stĕ·ryekh*

Austrian *adj* österreichisch *ur·stĕ·rye·khish*; **he's Austrian** er ist Österreicher *er ist ur·stĕ·rye·khĕr*; **she's Austrian** sie ist Österreicherin *zee ist ur·stĕ·rye·khĕ·rin*

author *n* der Autor *ow·tor*

automatic *adj* automatisch *ow·tō·mah·tish* □ *n* (*car*) der Automatikwagen *ow·tō·mah·tik·vah·gĕn*

automatically *adv* automatisch *ow·tō·mah·tish*

automation *n* die Automatisierung *ow·tō·ma·ti·zee·roong*

auto(mobile) *n* das Auto *ow·tō*

auto show *n* die Automobilausstellung *ow·tō·mo·beel·ows·shte·loong*

autumn *n* der Herbst *herpst*

available *adj* verfügbar *fer·fōōk·bar*

avalanche *n* die Lawine *la·vee·nĕ*

avenue *n* die Allee *a·lay*

average *adj* durchschnittlich *doorkh·shnit·likh* □ *n* der Durchschnitt *doorkh·shnit* Bm27

aviation *n* die Luftfahrt *looft·fahrt*

avocado *n* die Avocado *a·vō·kah·dō*

avoid *vt* vermeiden* *fer·mye·dĕn*

away *adv* □ **away from home** von zu Hause weg *fon tsoo how·zĕ vek*; **he's away for a week** er ist eine Woche nicht da *er ist ine·ĕ vo·khĕ nikht da*; **30 kilometers away** 30 Kilometer entfernt *30 ki·lō·may·tĕr ent·fernt*

awful *adj* schrecklich *shrek·likh*

ax *n* die Axt *akst*

axle *n* die Achse *ak·sĕ*

B

baby *n* das Baby *bay·bee* C12, 18

baby buggy, baby carriage *n* der Kinderwagen *kin·dĕr·vah·gĕn*

baby food *n* die Babynahrung *bay·bee·nah·roong*

baby-sit *vi* babysitten *bay·bee·si·tĕn* C5

baby-sitter *n* der Babysitter *bay·bee·si·tĕr*, die Babysitterin *bay·bee·si·tĕ·rin* C4

baccarat *n* das Bakkarat *ba·ka·rah*

bachelor *n* der Junggeselle *yoong·gĕ·ze·lĕ*

back *n* der Rücken *rōō·kĕn*; (*of chair*) die Rückenlehne *rōō·kĕn·lay·nĕ*; (*reverse side*) die Rückseite *rōōk·zye·tĕ*; (*of hall, room*) das hintere Ende *hin·tĕ·rĕ en·dĕ*; (*in sports*) der Verteidiger *fer·tye·di·gĕr* □ *adv* (*backwards*) nach hinten *nakh hin·tĕn*; **to come back** zurück|kommen* *tsoo·rōōk·ko·mĕn*; **to go back** zurück|gehen* *tsoo·rōōk·gay·ĕn* □ *vt* back (*support*) unterstützen *oon·tĕr·shtōōt·sĕn*; (*bet on*) setzen auf *zet·sĕn owf*; **to back the car** den Wagen zurück|setzen *den vah·gĕn tsoo·rōōk·zet·sĕn*

backache *n* die Rückenschmerzen (*pl*) *rōō·kĕn·shmer·tsĕn*

backdate *vt* (*letter*) zurück|datieren *tsoo·rōōk·da·tee·rĕn*

backer *n* der Geldgeber *gelt·gay·bĕr*

backgammon *n* das Backgammon *bak·ga·mon*

background *n* der Hintergrund *hin·tĕr·groont*

backing *n* die Unterstützung *oon·tĕr·shtōōt·soong*

backlash *n* die Gegenreaktion *gay·gĕn·ray·ak·tsee·ōn*

backlog n □ backlog of work unerledigte Arbeit (f) *oon·er·lay·dikh·tè ar·bite*

back pack n der Rucksack *rook·zak*

backward adj (glance) zurück *tsoo·rŏŏk*; (child) zurückgeblieben *tsoo·rŏŏk·gè·blee·bèn*

backwards adv rückwärts *rŏŏk·verts*

bacon n der Speck *shpek*

bad adj (not good) schlecht *shlekht*; (naughty) unartig *oon·ar·tikh*; to go bad (food) verderben* *fer·der·bèn*; a bad debt uneinbringliche Schulden (pl) *oon·ine·bring·li·khèn shool·dèn*

badge n (of metal) die Plakette *pla·ke·tè*; (of cloth) das Abzeichen *ap·tsye·khèn*

badly adv (not well) schlecht *shlekht*; to want something badly etwas unbedingt wollen* *et·vass oon·bè·dingt vo·lèn*

badminton n das Badminton *bet·min·tèn*

bag n (of paper) die Tüte *tōō·tè*; (paper carrier) die Tragtasche *trahk·ta·shè*; (handbag) die Tasche *ta·shè*; bags (luggage) das Gepäck *gè·pek* B78, T22f

baggage n das Gepäck *gè·pek*

baggage car n der Gepäckwagen *gè·pek·vah·gèn*

baggage check n die Gepäckkontrolle *gè·pek·kon·tro·lè*

baggage checkroom n die Gepäckaufbewahrung *gè·pek·owf·bè·vah·roong* T25, 33

baggage claim n die Gepäckausgabe *gè·pek·ows·gah·bè*

baggage room n die Gepäckaufbewahrung *gè·pek·owf·bè·vah·roong*

bail n (for prisoner) die Kaution *kow·tsee·ōn*; on bail gegen Kaution *gay·gèn kow·tsee·ōn*

bait n (in fishing) der Köder *kur'·dèr*

bake vt backen* *ba·kèn*

baker n der Bäcker *be·kèr* S32

bakery n die Bäckerei *be·kè·rye*

balance n das Gleichgewicht *glyekh·gè·vikht*; (remainder owed) der Saldo *zal·dō*; balance of power das Gleichgewicht der Mächte *glyekh·gè·vikht der mekh·tè*; balance of payments die Zahlungsbilanz *tsah·loongz·bee·lants*; balance of trade die Handelsbilanz *han·dèls·bee·lants*; to lose one's balance das Gleichgewicht verlieren* *dass glyekh·gè·vikht fer·lee·rèn* □ vt balance in Gleichgewicht halten* *im glyekh·gè·vikht hal·tèn*; (accounts) saldieren *zal·dee·rèn* □ vi ausgeglichen sein* *ows·gè·gli·khèn zine*

balance sheet n die Bilanz *bee·lants*

balcony n der Balkon *bal·kōn*

bald adj kahl *kahl*

ball n der Ball *bal*; (of string, wool) der Knäuel *knoy·èl*

ballet n das Ballett *ba·let*

balloon n der Ballon *ba·lōn*

ballot n die Geheimwahl *gè·hime·vahl*

bamboo n der Bambus *bam·boos*

ban vt verbieten* *fer·bee·tèn* □ n das Verbot *fer·bōt*

banana n die Banane *ba·nah·nè*

band n (musical) die Band *bent*

bandage n der Verband *fer·bant*

bandaid n das Heftpflaster *heft·pfla·stèr*

bang n (of gun etc) der Knall *knal*; (of door) das Zuschlagen *tsoo·shlah·gèn*; (blow) der Schlag *shlahk* □ vt (door) zu|schlagen* *tsoo·shlah·gèn*;

to bang one's head sich den Kopf an|schlagen* *zikh dayn kopf an·shlah·gèn* □ vi bang (gun etc) knallen *kna·lèn*

bangs pl die Ponyfransen (pl) *po·nee·fran·zèn*

bank n (of river, lake) das Ufer *oo·fèr*; (finance) die Bank *bank* □ vt (money) ein|zahlen *ine·tsah·lèn* □ vi to bank with Smiths ein Konto bei Smiths haben* *ine kon·tō bye Smiths hah·bèn* M30f

bank account n das Bankkonto *bank·kon·tō*

bank balance n der Saldo *zal·dō*

bank bill n der Wechsel *vek·sèl*

bankbook n das Sparbuch *shpahr·bookh*

bank charges pl die Bankgebühren (pl) *bank·gè·bŏŏ·rèn*

banker n der Bankier *bang·kyay*

bank loan n das Darlehen *dar·lay·èn*

bank manager n der Filialleiter der Bank *fee·lyahl·lye·tèr der bank*

bank note n der Geldschein *gelt·shine*

bankrupt adj bankrott *bank·rot*; to go bankrupt Bankrott machen *bank·rot ma·khèn*

bankruptcy n der Bankrott *bank·rot*

banner n das Banner *ba·nèr*

banquet n das Bankett *bang·ket*

baptism n die Taufe *tow·fè*

Baptist adj Baptisten- *bap·ti·stèn*

bar n (metal) die Stange *shtang·è*; (counter) die Theke *tay·kè*; (drinking establishment) das Lokal *lo·kahl*; bar of soap das Stück Seife *shtŏŏk zye·fè*; bar of chocolate die Tafel Schokolade *tah·fèl shō·kô·lah·dè*

barbecue n das Barbecue *bar·bi·kyoo*

barbed wire n der Stacheldraht *shta·khèl·draht*

barber n der Friseur *free·zur*

bare adj (person, head) nackt *nakt*; to go barefoot barfuß gehen* *bahr·foos gay·èn*

bargain n (cheap buy) der Gelegenheitskauf *gè·lay·gèn·hites·kowf*; to make a bargain ein Geschäft ab|schließen* *ine gè·sheft ap·shlee·sèn*

bargaining n (negotiation) das Verhandeln *fer·han·dèln*

barge n der Schleppkahn *shlep·kahn*

bark n (of tree) die Baumrinde *bowm·rin·dè*; (of dog) das Bellen *be·lèn* □ vi bellen *be·lèn*

barmaid n die Bardame *bahr·dah·mè*

barman n der Barmann *bahr·man*

barn n die Scheune *shoy·nè*

barracks pl die Kaserne *ka·zer·nè*

barrel n (for beer) das Faß *fass* E59

barrier n (fence) die Sperre *shpe·rè*

bartender n der Barmann *bahr·man*

base n die Basis *bah·zis*; (military) der Stützpunkt *shtŏŏts·poonkt* □ vt basieren *ba·zee·rèn*

baseball n Baseball (nt) *bays·bōl*

basement n das Untergeschoß *oon·tèr·gè·shos*

basic adj grundlegend *groont·lay·gènt*

basically adv im wesentlichen *im vay·zènt·li·khèn*

basin n (dish) die Schüssel *shŏŏ·sèl*; (for washing) das Waschbecken *vash·be·kèn*

basis n die Basis *bah·zis*

basket n der Korb *korp*

basketball n Basketball (nt) *bahs·kèt·bal*

bat n (table tennis etc) der Schläger

shlay·gèr; (animal) die Fledermaus flay·dèr·mows

bath n das Bad baht; (tub) die Badewanne bah·dè·va·nè A4

bathe vt/i baden bah·dèn

bathing cap n die Bademütze bah·dè·mōōt·sè

bathing suit n der Badeanzug bah·dè·an·tsook

bathroom n das Badezimmer bah·dè·tsi·mèr; (lavatory) die Toilette tō·a·le·tè A17

batter n (for frying) der Ausbackteig ows·bak·tike

battery n die Batterie ba·tè·ree T169

battle n der Kampf kampf

bay n (on coast) die Bucht bookht

bazaar n der Basar ba·zahr

be vi sein* zine; I am ich bin ikh bin; you are Sie sind zee zint; he is er ist er ist; we are wir sind veer zint; they are sie sind zee zint; how are you? wie geht es Ihnen? vee gayt ess ee·nèn; I am hungry ich habe Hunger ikh hah·bè hoong·èr; how much is it? wieviel kostet das? vee·feel kos·tèt dass; we are going to the beach wir gehen zum Strand veer gay·èn tsoom shtrant; we have been to Paris wir sind in Paris gewesen veer zint in pa·rees gè·vay·zèn; he is a doctor er ist Arzt er ist artst

beach n der Strand shtrant L21

bead n die Perle per·lè

beam n (of wood) der Balken bal·kèn; (of light) der Strahl shtrahl

beans npl die Bohnen (pl) bō·nèn

bear n der Bär ber □ vt (weight) tragen* trah·gèn; (endure) ertragen* er·trah·gèn

beard n der Bart bart

bearings npl (in car) die Lager (pl) lah·gèr; to take one's bearings sich orientieren zikh ō·ree·en·tee·rèn

beat vt/i schlagen* shlah·gèn

beautiful adj schön shur'n

beauty n die Schönheit shur'n·hite

because conj weil vile; because of wegen vay·gèn

become vi werden* ver·dèn

bed n das Bett bet; in bed im Bett im bet; to go to bed ins Bett gehen* ins bet gay·èn A4, C7, I52

bedclothes npl das Bettzeug bet·tsoyk

bedding n das Bettzeug bet·tsoyk

bedroom n das Schlafzimmer shlahf·tsi·mèr A4

bee n die Biene bee·nè

beech n die Buche boo·khè

beef n das Rindfleisch rint·flyesh E29

beer n das Bier beer E59

beet n die rote Rübe rō·tè rōō·bè

beetle n der Käfer kay·fèr

before prep (in time) vor fōr; before noon vor Mittag fōr mi·tahk; before the king (position) vor dem König fōr daym kur'·nikh □ adv before vorher fōr·her; we've met before wir kennen uns schon vom kne·nèn oons shōn □ conj before bevor bè·fōr; before I go to bed bevor ich ins Bett gehe bè·fōr ikh ins bet gay·è

beg vi betteln bet·lèn

beggar n der Bettler bet·lèr, die Bettlerin bet·lè·rin

begin vt/i anfangen* an·fang·èn

beginner n der Anfänger an·feng·èr, die Anfängerin an·feng·è·rin

behalf n □ on behalf of im Namen von im nah·mèn fon

behave vi sich benehmen* zikh bè·nay·mèn

behavior n das Benehmen bè·nay·mèn

behind adv hinten hin·tèn; to look behind zurück|blicken tsoo·rōōk·bli·kèn; to stand behind dahinter stehen* dah·hin·tèr shtay·èn □ prep behind the wall hinter der Mauer hin·tèr der mow·èr; to be behind schedule im Verzug sein* im fer·tsook zine

beige adj beige baysh

belief n der Glaube glow·bè

believe vt/i glauben glow·bèn; to believe in glauben an glow·bèn an

bell n die Glocke glo·kè; (electric) die Klingel kling·èl

bellboy n der Hoteljunge hō·tel·yoong·è

belong vi □ to belong to someone jemandem gehören yay·man·dèm gè·hur'·rèn; to belong to a club einem Klub an|gehören ine·èm kloop an·gè·hur'·rèn

belongings npl die Sachen (pl) za·khèn

below adv unten oon·tèn; to look below nach unten sehen* nahkh oon·tèn zay·èn □ prep my room is below his mein Zimmer liegt unter seinem mine tsi·mèr leekt oon·tèr zine·èm

belt n (for waist) der Gürtel gōōr·tèl S85

beltway n die Umgehungsstraße oom·gay·oongs·shtrah·sè

bench n (seat) die Bank bank; (work table) die Werkbank verk·bank

bend n (in pipe, wire etc) die Biegung bee·goong; (in road) die Kurve koor·vè □ vt biegen* bee·gèn; (arm, leg) beugen boy·gèn □ vi (person) sich beugen zikh boy·gèn; (road) eine Kurve machen ine·è koor·vè ma·khèn T199

beneath = **below**

benefit n der Vorteil fōr·tile; it's of no benefit (to us) wir ziehen keinen Nutzen daraus veer tsee·èn kine·èn noot·sèn dah·rows

Benelux n die Benelux-Staaten (pl) bay·nay·looks·shtah·tèn

berm n der Seitenstreifen zye·tèn·shtrye·fèn

berry n die Beere bay·rè

berth n (in ship) die Koje kō·yè; (in train) der Schlafwagenplatz shlahf·vah·gèn·plats

beside prep neben nay·bèn

besides adv (moreover) außerdem ow·sèr·daym □ prep besides him außer ihm ow·sèr eem

best adj beste(r/s) bes·tè(·tèr/·tès) □ n he's the best er ist der Beste er ist der bes·tè □ adv he can do it best er kann es am besten er kann es am bes·tèn

best man n der Trauzeuge trow·tsoy·gè

bet vt/i wetten ve·tèn □ n die Wette ve·tè

better adj besser be·sèr □ adv he sings better than you er singt besser als Sie er zingt be·sèr als zee; to get better (from illness) sich erholen zikh er·hō·lèn; they are better off than us (richer) sie sind reicher als wir zee zint rye·khèr als veer

between prep zwischen tsvi·shèn

beyond prep jenseits yayn·zites; beyond the wall jenseits der Mauer yayn·zites der mow·èr; beyond my reach außer meiner Reichweite ow·sèr mine·èr ryekh·vye·tè; beyond his means über seine Verhältnisse ōō·bèr zine·è fer·helt·ni·sè

Bible *n* die Bibel *bee·bèl*

bicycle *n* das Fahrrad *fahr·raht*

bid *vt* (*amount*) bieten* *bee·tèn* □ *vi* to bid for something auf etwas bieten* *owf et·vass bee·tèn* □ *n* bid das Gebot *gè·bôt*

bidder *n* der/die Bietende *bee·tèn·dè*

big *adj* groß *grôs*

bikini *n* der Bikini *bee·kee·nee*

bilingual *adj* zweisprachig *tsvye·shprah·khikh*

bill *n* (*account*) die Rechnung *rekh·noong*; (*bank note*) der Schein *shine* M14, A21, E44

billiards *n* Billard *bil·yart*

billion *n* die Milliarde *mi·lee·ar·dè*

bin *n* (*for refuse*) der Mülleimer *mööl·ime·èr*

bind *vt* (*tie*) binden* *bin·dèn*

binoculars *pl* das Fernglas *fern·glass*

biology *n* die Biologie *bee·ô·lô·gee*

birch *n* (*tree*) die Birke *bir·kè*

bird *n* der Vogel *fô·gèl* L40

birth *n* die Geburt *gè·boort*

birth certificate *n* die Geburtsurkunde *gè·boorts·oor·koon·dè*

birthday *n* der Geburtstag *gè·boorts·tahk*

biscuit *n* (*sweet*) der Keks *kayks*; (*savory*) der Kräcker *kre·kèr*

bishop *n* der Bischof *bi·shof*

bit *n* (*piece*) das Stück *shtöök*; a bit of ein bißchen *ine bis·khèn*

bite *vt* beißen* *bye·sèn* □ *n* (*by animal*) der Biß *bis*; (*by insect*) der Stich *shtikh*; (*of food*) der Bissen *bi·sèn* S43

bitter *adj* bitter *bi·tèr*

black *adj* schwarz *shvarts*; a black coffee ein schwarzer Kaffee *ine shvart·sèr ka·fay*

blackberry *n* die Brombeere *brom·bay·rè*

blackbird *n* die Amsel *am·zèl*

black currant *n* die schwarze Johannisbeere *shvart·sè yô·ha·nis·bay·rè*

black eye *n* das blaue Auge *blow·è ow·gè*

blackjack *n* Siebzehn und Vier (*nt*) *zeep·tsayn oont feer*

black market *n* der Schwarzmarkt *shvarts·markt*

bladder *n* die Blase *blah·zè*

blade *n* (*of knife*) die Klinge *kling·è*

blame *vt* (*reproach*) die Schuld geben* *dee shoolt gay·bèn*; to be to blame schuld sein* *shoolt zine*

blank *adj* leer *layr*; blank check der Blankoscheck *blang·kô·shek*; please leave blank bitte nicht ausfüllen *bi·tè nikht ows·föö·lèn*

blanket *n* die Decke *de·kè* A44

blast *n* (*explosion*) die Explosion *eks·plô·zee·ôn*

blaze *n* (*fire*) der Brand *brant* □ *vi* brennen* *bre·nèn*; (*lights*) leuchten *loykh·tèn*

blazer *n* der Blazer *blay·zèr*

bleed *vi* bluten *bloo·tèn*

blend *vt* vermischen *fer·mi·shèn* □ *n* die Mischung *mi·shoong*

bless *vt* segnen *zayk·nèn*

blind *adj* (*person*) blind *blint* □ *n* (*at window*) die Jalousie *zha·loo·zee*

blind alley *n* die Sackgasse *zak·ga·sè*

blind corner *n* die unübersichtliche Kurve *oon·öö·bèr·zikht·li·khè koor·vè*

blink *vi* zwinkern *tsving·kèrn*

blister *n* (*on skin*) die Blase *blah·zè*

blizzard *n* der Schneesturm *shnay·shtoorm*

block *n* (*of stone*) der Block *blok*; 3 blocks away (*streets*) 3 Blocks weiter *3 bloks vye·tèr*; apartment block der Wohnblock *vôn·blok* □ *vt* block (*road*) verstopfen *fer·shtop·fèn*; block letters die Blockschrift *blok·shrift*; block booking die Gruppenbestellung *groo·pèn·bè·shte·loong*

blockage *n* die Verstopfung *fer·shtop·foong*

blond(e) *adj* blond *blont*

blood *n* das Blut *bloot*

blood group *n* die Blutgruppe *bloot·groo·pè* I50, 51

blood poisoning *n* die Blutvergiftung *bloot·fer·gif·toong*

blood pressure *n* der Blutdruck *bloot·drook* I44

bloom *n* (*flower*) die Blume *bloo·mè* □ *vi* blühen *blöö·èn*

blossom *n* die Blüte *blöö·tè*

blot *n* der Fleck *flek* □ *vt* (*ink*) ablöschen *ap·lur·shèn*

blouse *n* die Bluse *bloo·zè* S21

blow *n* (*knock*) der Schlag *shlahk* □ *vi* (*wind*) blasen* *blah·zèn*; (*fuse*) durchbrennen* *doorkh·bre·nèn* □ *vt* to blow one's nose sich die Nase putzen *zikh dee nah·zè poot·sèn*

blow-dry *n* Fönen (*nt*) *fur·nèn*

blow-out *n* die Reifenpanne *rye·fèn·pa·nè*

blue *adj* blau *blow*

bluebottle *n* die Schmeißfliege *shmice·flee·gè*

blue chips *pl* die erstklassige Effekten (*pl*) *erst·kla·si·gè e·fek·tèn*

blueprint *n* der Plan *plahn*

blunt *adj* (*knife*) stumpf *shtoompf*

blush *vi* rot werden* *rôt ver·dèn*

board *n* (*of wood*) das Brett *bret*; (*for notices*) das Anschlagbrett *an·shlahk·bret*; (*of directors*) der Aufsichtsrat *owf·zikhts·raht*; on board (*ship, plane*) an Bord *an bort* □ *vt* board (*train, bus*) einsteigen* in *ine·shtye·gèn in*; (*ship*) besteigen* *bè·shtye·gèn*

boarding house *n* die Pension *pen·see·ôn*

boarding pass *n* die Bordkarte *bort·kar·tè*

boast *vi* prahlen *prah·lèn*

boat *n* das Boot *bôt*

bobby pin *n* die Haarklemme *hahr·kle·mè*

body *n* der Körper *kur·pèr*; (*corpse*) die Leiche *lye·khè*

bodyguard *n* (*person*) der Leibwächter *lipe·vekh·tèr*

bog *n* der Sumpf *zoompf*

boil *vt*/*i* kochen *ko·khèn* □ *n* (*on skin*) der Furunkel *foo·roon·kèl*

bold *adj* mutig *moo·tikh*

bolster *n* die Nackenrolle *na·kèn·ro·lè*

bolt *n* der Riegel *ree·gèl* □ *vt* (*door, gate*) zuriegeln *tsoo·ree·gèln*

bomb *n* die Bombe *bom·bè*

bone *n* der Knochen *kno·khèn*; (*of fish*) die Gräte *gre·tè*

bonfire *n* das Freudenfeuer *froy·dèn·foy·èr*

bonus *n* (*on salary*) die Prämie *pre·mee·è*

book *n* das Buch *bookh* □ *vt* (*seat*) reservieren lassen* *ray·zer·vee·rèn la·sèn*

boom *n* (*noise*) das Brausen *brow·zèn*;

(*economic*) der Aufschwung *owf·shvoong* □ *vi* business is booming das Geschäft blüht *dass ge·sheft bloot*

boost *vt* (*sales*) an|kurbeln *an·koor·beln*

boot *n* der Stiefel *shtee·fèl*

booth *n* (*telephone*) die Telefonzelle *tay·lay·fōn·tse·lè*

border *n* (*edge*) der Rand *rant*; (*of country*) die Grenze *gren·tsè*

bored *adj* □ I'm bored ich langweile mich *ikh lang·vile·è mikh*

boring *adj* langweilig *lang·vile·ikh*

born *adj* geboren *gè·bō·rèn*; to be born geboren werden* *gè·bō·rèn ver·dèn*

borough *n* die Stadtgemeinde *shtat·gè·mine·dè*

borrow *vt* borgen *bor·gèn*; to borrow something from someone etwas von jemandem borgen *et·vass fon yay·man·dèm bor·gèn*

boss *n* der Chef *shef*

botanical gardens *pl* der botanische Garten *bō·tah·ni·shè gar·tèn*

both *adj* beide *bye·dè* □ *pron* both (of them) alle beide *a·lè bye·dè*

bother *vt* (*annoy*) ärgern *er·gèrn* □ *vi* please don't bother machen Sie sich bitte keine Mühe *ma·khèn zee zikh bi·tè kine·è mōō·è* □ *n* bother (*nuisance*) die Plage *plah·gè*; (*effort*) die Mühe *mōō·è*

bottle *n* die Flasche *fla·shè*; (*baby's*) die Babyflasche *bay·bee·fla·shè* E13, C2

bottleneck *n* der Engpaß *eng·pas*

bottle opener *n* der Flaschenöffner *fla·shèn·ur'f·nèr*

bottom *n* der Boden *bō·dèn*; (*of page, list*) das Ende *en·dè*; (*of person*) das Hinterteil *hin·tèr·tile* □ *adj* unterste(r/s) *oon·tèr·stè(·stèr/·stès)*

bounce *vi* (*ball*) springen* *shpring·èn*; (*check*) platzen *plat·sèn*

bound *adj* □ bound for (*ship*) auf dem Weg nach *owf daym vayk nakh* □ *n* out of bounds verboten *fer·bō·tèn*

boundary *n* die Grenze *gren·tsè*

bourbon *n* der Bourbon *bur·bon*

boutique *n* die Boutique *boo·teek*

bow¹ *vi* sich verbeugen *zikh fer·boy·gèn* □ *n* die Verbeugung *fer·boy·goong*

bow² *n* (*ribbon*) die Schleife *shlye·fè*

bowl *n* (*for food*) die Schüssel *shōō·sèl*; (*for washing*) die Spülschüssel *shpōōl·shōō·sèl*

bow tie *n* die Fliege *flee·gè*

box *n* die Schachtel *shakh·tèl*; (*cardboard*) der Karton *kar·tōng*

boxing *n* Boxen (*nt*) *bok·sèn*

box number *n* das Postfach *post·fakh*

box office *n* die Kasse *ka·sè*

boy *n* der Junge *yoong·è* S114

boycott *vt* boykottieren *boy·ko·tee·rèn*

boyfriend *n* der Freund *froynt*

bra *n* der BH *bay·hah*

bracelet *n* das Armband *arm·bant*

bracken *n* der Adlerfarn *ahd·lèr·farn*

bracket *n* (*in writing*) die Klammer *kla·mèr*

brain *n* das Gehirn *gè·hirn*; **brains** (*as food*) das Hirn *hirn*

braised *adj* geschmort *gè·shmort*

brake *n* die Bremse *brem·zè* □ *vi* bremsen *brem·zèn* T165

brake fluid *n* die Bremsflüssigkeit *bremz·flōō·sikh·kite*

branch *n* (*of tree*) der Zweig *tsvyek*; (*of store, bank etc*) die Filiale *fee·lee·ah·lè*

brand *n* (*of product*) die Marke *mar·kè*

brand name *n* der Markenname *mar·kèn·nah·mè*

brandy *n* der Kognak *kon·yak*

brass *n* das Messing *me·sing*

brave *adj* mutig *moo·tikh*

bread *n* das Brot *brōt* E31

break *n* (*pause*) die Pause *pow·zè* □ *vt* brechen* *bre·khèn*; (*object*) zerbrechen* *tser·bre·khèn*; to break in (*car*) ein|fahren* *ine·fah·rèn*; to break one's arm sich den Arm brechen* *zikh dayn arm bre·khèn* □ *vi* break zerbrechen* *tser·bre·khèn*; to break down (*car*) eine Panne haben* *ine·è pa·nè hah·bèn* T157

breakdown *n* (*of car*) die Panne *pa·nè*

break even *vi* sein Geld wieder heraus|bekommen* *zine gelt vee·dèr hè·rows·bè·ko·mèn*

breakfast *n* das Frühstück *frōō·shtōōk* A9

breast *n* die Brust *broost*

breath *n* der Atem *ah·tèm*

breathe *vi* atmen *aht·mèn*

breeze *n* die Brise *bree·zè*

brewery *n* die Brauerei *brow·èr·eye*

bribe *vt* bestechen* *bè·shte·khèn*

brick *n* der Backstein *bak·shtine*

bride *n* die Braut *browt*

bridegroom *n* der Bräutigam *broy·ti·gam*

bridge *n* die Brücke *brōō·kè*; (*game*) das Bridge *bridge*

bridle *n* der Zaum *tsowm*

brief *adj* kurz *koorts*

briefcase *n* der Aktenkoffer *ak·tèn·ko·fèr*

briefs *pl* der Slip *slip*

bright *adj* hell *hel*; (*clever*) intelligent *in·te·lee·gent*

bring *vt* (*thing*) bringen* *bring·èn*; (*person*) mit|bringen* *mit·bring·èn*; to bring in (*profit*) ein|bringen* *ine·bring·èn*

Britain *n* Großbritannien (*nt*) *grōs·bri·tan·yèn*

British *adj* britisch *bri·tish*; he's British er ist Brite *er ist bri·tè*; she's British sie ist Britin *zee ist bri·tin*

broad *adj* breit *brite*

broadcast *vt* senden *zen·dèn* □ *n* die Sendung *zen·doong*

broccoli *n* der Brokkoli (*pl*) *bro·kō·lee*

brochure *n* die Broschüre *bro·shōō·rè* Bm24

broil *vt* grillen *gri·lèn*

broke *adj* (*penniless*) pleite *plye·tè*

broker *n* der Makler *mahk·lèr*

bronchitis *n* die Bronchitis *bron·khee·tis*

bronze *n* die Bronze *brōn·tsè*

brooch *n* die Brosche *bro·shè* S92

broom *n* der Besen *bay·zèn*

brother *n* der Bruder *broo·dèr*

brother-in-law *n* der Schwager *shvah·gèr*

brown *adj* braun *brown*

bruise *n* der blaue Fleck *blow·è flek*

brush *n* (*for cleaning*) die Bürste *bōōr·stè*; (*for painting*) der Pinsel *pin·zèl* □ *vt* bürsten *bōōr·stèn*

Brussels *n* Brüssel (*nt*) *brōō·sèl*

Brussels sprouts *pl* der Rosenkohl *rō·zèn·kōl*

bubble *n* die Blase *blah·zè*

bucket *n* der Eimer *ime·èr*

buckle *n* die Schnalle *shna·lè*

bud *n* die Knospe *knos·pè*

budget *n* das Budget *bōō·djay*

bug *n* (*insect*) der Käfer *kay·fèr*

build vt (*house*) bauen *bow·èn*
building n das Gebäude *gè·boy·dè* L11
bulb n die Zwiebel *tsvee·bèl*; (*light*) die Birne *bir·nè*
bulk n □ in bulk (*in large quantities*) en gros *oñ grō*; (*unpackaged*) unverpackt *oon·fer·pakt*; bulk buying der Großeinkauf *grōs·ine·kowf*
bull n der Stier *shteer*
bulldozer n der Bulldozer *bool·dō·zèr*
bullet n die Kugel *koo·gèl*
bulletin n der Bericht *bè·rikht*
bulletin board n das Anschlagbrett *an·shlahk·bret*
bullfight n der Stierkampf *shteer·kampf*
bump n (*knock*) der Stoß *shtōs*; (*lump*) die Beule *boy·lè* □ vt stoßen* *shtō·sèn*
bumper n (*on car*) die Stoßstange *shtōs·shtang·è*
bun n das Brötchen *brur't·khèn*
bunch n (*of flowers*) der Strauß *shtrows*
bundle n das Bündel *bōōn·dèl*
bungalow n der Bungalow *boon·ga·lō*
bunk n die Koje *kō·yè*; bunk beds das Etagenbett *ay·tah·zhèn·bet*
buoy n die Boje *bō·yè*
buoyant adj (*market*) fest *fest*
bureau n (*office*) das Büro *bōō·rō*
burglar n der Einbrecher *ine·bre·khèr*
burn n vt verbrennen* *fer·bre·nèn*; I've burned my arm ich habe mir den Arm verbrannt *ikh hah·bè meer dayn arm fer·brant*
burst vi platzen *plat·sèn* □ vt platzen lassen* *plat·sèn la·sèn*
bury vt (*person*) beerdigen *bè·ayr·di·gèn*
bus n der Bus *boos* T82f, F16
bush n der Strauch *shtrowkh*
business n (*dealings, work*) das Geschäft *gè·sheft*; (*firm*) der Betrieb *bè·treep*; on business geschäftlich *gè·sheft·likh*; to do business with someone Geschäfte mit jemandem machen *gè·shef·tè mit yay·man·dèm ma·khèn*
business expenses pl die Spesen (*pl*) *shpay·zèn*
business hours pl die Geschäftsstunden (*pl*) *gè·shefts·shtoon·dèn*
businessman n der Geschäftsmann *gè·shefts·man* Mc48
business trip n die Geschäftsreise *gè·shefts·rye·zè* Bm12
businesswoman n die Geschäftsfrau *gè·shefts·frow*
bus service n die Busverbindung *boos·fer·bin·doong*
bus stop n die Bushaltestelle *boos·hal·tè·shte·lè*
bust n der Busen *boo·zèn*; (*statue*) die Büste *bōōs·tè*
busy adj (*person*) beschäftigt *bè·shef·tikht*; (*place*) belebt *bè·laypt*; (*telephone*) besetzt *bè·zetst*
busy signal n das Besetztzeichen *bè·zetst·tsye·khèn*
but conj aber *ah·bèr*; not this, but that nicht dies, sondern das *nikht dees zon·dèrn dass* □ prep all but him alle außer ihm *a·le ow·sèr eem*
butane n das Butangas *boo·tahn·gas*
butcher n der Fleischer *flye·shèr*; butcher's (*shop*) die Fleischerei *flye·shè·rye* S32
butter n die Butter *boo·tèr* E32, S33
butterfly n der Schmetterling *shme·tèr·ling*

button n der Knopf *knopf* Sn74
buy vt kaufen *kow·fèn*; to buy out (*partner etc*) aus|zahlen *ows·tsah·lèn* S7
buyer n (*customer*) der Käufer *koy·fèr*, die Käuferin *koy·fè·rin*; (*for shop, factory*) der Einkäufer *ine·koy·fèr*, die Einkäuferin *ine·koy·fè·rin* Bm3
by prep (*next to*) neben *nay·bèn*; to go by London (*via*) über London fahren* *ōō·bèr lon·don fah·rèn*; by air/train/car mit dem Flugzeug/Zug/Auto *mit daym flook·tsoyk/tsook/ow·tō*; we'll be there by 4 o'clock wir werden bis 4 Uhr da sein *veer ver·dèn biss 4 oor dah zine* □ adv a plane flew by ein Flugzeug ist vorbeigeflogen *ine flook·tsoyk ist fōr·bye·gè·flō·gèn*
bypass n die Umgehungsstraße *oom·gay·oongs·shtrah·sè*

C

cab n (*taxi*) das Taxi *tak·si*
cabaret n das Kabarett *ka·ba·ret*
cabbage n der Kohl *kōl*
cabin n (*in ship*) die Kajüte *ka·yōō·tè*
cabin cruiser n der Motorjacht *mō·tōr·yakht*
cable n (*rope*) das Drahtseil *draht·zile*; (*electric*) das Kabel *kah·bèl*
cactus n der Kaktus *kak·toos*
caddie n der Golfjunge *golf·yoong·è*
café n das Café *ka·fay*
cafeteria n das Selbstbedienungsrestaurant *zelpst·bè·dee·noongs·re·stō·rant*
cage n der Käfig *kay·fikh*
cake n der Kuchen *koo·khèn*
calcium n das Kalzium *kal·tsee·oom*
calculate vt aus|rechnen *ows·rekh·nèn*
calculator n der Rechner *rekh·nèr*
calendar n der Kalender *ka·len·dèr*
calf n das Kalb *kalp*
call n (*shout*) der Ruf *roof*; (*on phone*) der Anruf *an·roof* □ vi (*shout*) schreien* *shrye·èn* □ vt rufen* *roo·fèn*; (*summon*) herbei|rufen* *her·bye·roo·fèn*; call me at 7 a.m. (*in hotel etc*) wecken Sie mich bitte um 7 Uhr *ve·kèn zee mikh bi·tè oom 7 oor*; to be called heißen* *hye·sèn*
call girl n das Callgirl *kōl·gurl*
calm adj (*sea, day*) ruhig *roo·ikh*; (*person*) gelassen *gè·la·sèn*
calorie n die Kalorie *ka·lō·ree*
camel n das Kamel *ka·mel*
camera n der Fotoapparat *fō·tō·a·pa·raht*; (*TV*) die Kamera *ka·mè·ra* S50f
camp vi zelten *tsel·tèn* A84f
campaign n die Kampagne *kam·pa·nyè*
camp-bed n das Campingbett *kam·ping·bet*
camping n das Camping *kam·ping*; to go camping zelten gehen* *tsel·tèn gay·èn*
camp(ing) site n der Zeltplatz *tselt·plats*
camshaft n die Nockenwelle *no·kèn·ve·lè*
can[1] n (*container*) die Büchse *bōōk·sè* T|60, S36
can[2] vi können* *kur·nèn*; I can ich kann *ikh kan*; you can Sie können *zee kur'nèn*; he/she can er/sie kann *er/zee kan*; we can wir können *veer kur'nèn*
Canada n Kanada (*nt*) *ka·na·da*

Canadian *adj* kanadisch *ka·nah·dish*; he's Canadian er ist Kanadier *er ist ka·nah·dee·èr*; she's Canadian sie ist Kanadierin *zee ist ka·nah·dee·rin*

canal *n* der Kanal *ka·nahl*

canasta *n* das Canasta *ka·nas·ta*

cancel *vt* ab|sagen *ap·zah·gèn*

cancer *n* der Krebs *krayps*

candidate *n* (*for election*) der Kandidat *kan·dee·daht*, die Kandidatin *kan·dee·dah·tin*

candle *n* die Kerze *ker·tsè*

candy *n* die Bonbons (*pl*) *boñ·boñs*

cane *n* (*walking stick*) der Stock *shtok*

canned *adj* Büchsen- *böök·sèn*

cannon *n* die Kanone *ka·nō·nè*

canoe *n* das Kanu *kah·noo*

canoeing *n* □ to go canoeing Kanu fahren* *kah·noo fah·rèn*

can-opener *n* der Büchsenöffner *böök·sèn·ur'f·nèr*

canteen *n* die Kantine *kan·tee·nè*

canvas *n* das Segeltuch *zay·gèl·tookh*

cap *n* (*hat*) die Kappe *ka·pè*

capable *adj* fähig *fay·ikh*; capable of zu…fähig *tsoo…fay·ikh*

cape *n* das Cape *kayp*

capital *n* (*city*) die Hauptstadt *howpt·shtat*; (*finance*) das Kapital *ka·pi·tahl*; in capitals in Blockschrift *in blok·shrift*; capital A Groß-A *grōs·ah*

capital goods *pl* die Produktionsmittel (*pl*) *pro·dook·tsee·ōns·mi·tèl*

capitalism *n* der Kapitalismus *ka·pi·ta·lis·moos*

capitalist *n* der Kapitalist *ka·pi·ta·list*

capital letter *n* der Großbuchstabe *grōs·bookh·shtah·bè*

capsule *n* (*of medicine*) die Kapsel *kap·sèl*

captain *n* der Kapitän *ka·pi·tayn*; (*of plane*) der Pilot *pee·lōt*

capture *vt* fassen *fa·sèn*

car *n* das Auto *ow·tō*; (*of train*) der Wagen *vah·gèn* T104f, 157, A28

carafe *n* die Karaffe *ka·ra·fè* E13

caramel *n* die Karamelle *ka·ra·me·lè*

carat *n* das Karat *ka·raht*

carbon *n* der Kohlenstoff *kō·lèn·shtof*

carbon copy *n* der Durchschlag *doorkh·shlahk*

carbon paper *n* das Kohlepapier *kōl·è·pa·peer*

carburetor *n* der Vergaser *fer·gah·zèr*

card *n* (*post*) die Karte *kar·tè* Bm2

cardboard *n* die Pappe *pa·pè*

card game *n* das Kartenspiel *kar·tèn·shpeel*

cardigan *n* die Strickjacke *shtrik·ya·kè*

card index *n* die Kartei *kar·tye*

care *n* (*carefulness*) die Sorge *zor·gè* □ *vi* I don't care es ist mir egal *ess ist meer a·gal*; to take care of (*children etc*) sorgen für *zor·gèn föör*

career *n* die Karriere *ka·ree·ay·rè*

careful *adj* (*cautious*) sorgfältig *zork·fel·tikh*; be careful! Vorsicht! *för·zikht*

care of, c/o *prep* bei *bye*

caretaker *n* der Hausmeister *hows·mye·stèr*

car-ferry *n* die Autofähre *ow·tō·fay·rè*

cargo *n* die Fracht *frakht*

Caribbean (Sea) *n* das Karibische Meer *ka·ree·bi·shè mayr*

carnation *n* die Nelke *nel·kè*

carnival *n* der Karneval *kar·ne·val*

carol *n* das Weihnachtslied *vye·nakhts·leet*

carpenter *n* der Zimmermann *tsi·mèr·man*

carpet *n* der Teppich *te·pikh*

carport *n* der Einstellplatz *ine·shtel·plats*

carrot *n* die Möhre *mur'·rè*

carry *vt* (*in hands, arms*) tragen* *trah·gèn*; (*transport*) befördern *bè·fur·dèrn*; to carry out an order einen Befehl aus|führen *ine·èn bè·fayl ows·föö·rèn*

carryall *n* die Reisetasche *rye·zè·ta·shè*

carryout *adj* (*food*) zum Mitnehmen *tsoom mit·nay·mèn*

cart *n* der Einkaufswagen *ine·kowfs·vah·gèn*

carton *n* (*box*) der Pappkarton *pap·kar·ton*; (*of yogurt etc*) der Becher *be·khèr*

cartoon *n* die Zeichengeschichte *tsye·khèn·gè·shikh·tè*; (*animated*) der Zeichentrickfilm *tsye·khèn·trik·film*

cartridge *n* (*for gun*) die Patrone *pa·trō·nè*; (*of tape, for camera*) die Kassette *ka·se·tè*

carve *vt* (*meat*) tranchieren *tron·shee·rèn*

case *n* der Koffer *ko·fèr*; (*of wine*) die Kiste *kis·tè*; (*instance, knowledge*) der Fall *fal*; just in case für alle Fälle *föör a·lè fe·lè*; in case of im Falle von *im fal·è fon*; in any case auf alle Fälle *owf a·lè fe·lè*

cash *vt* (*check*) ein|lösen *ine·lur'·zèn* □ *n* das Bargeld *bar·gelt*; to pay cash for something etwas bar bezahlen *et·vass bahr bè·tsah·lèn*; cash on delivery per Nachnahme *per nahkh·nah·mè* M27, L57

cashdesk *n* die Kasse *ka·sè*

cash flow *n* die Bruttoertragsziffer *broo·to·er·trahks·tsi·fèr*

cashier *n* der Kassierer *ka·see·rèr*, die Kassiererin *ka·see·rè·rin*

cashmere *n* der Kaschmir *kash·meer*

casino *n* das Kasino *ka·zee·no*

casserole *n* (*food*) die Kasserolle *ka·sè·ro·lè*; (*dish*) der Schmortopf *shmor·topf*

cassette *n* die Kassette *ka·se·tè*

cassette-recorder *n* der Kassettenrecorder *ka·se·tèn·ray·kor·dèr*

cast *n* (*of play*) die Besetzung *bè·ze·tsoong*

cast iron *n* das Gußeisen *goos·eye·zèn*

castle *n* das Schloß *shloss* T86

castor oil *n* das Rizinusöl *ree·tsee·noos·ur'l*

casual clothes, casual wear *n* die Freizeitkleidung *frye·tsite·klye·doong*

cat *n* die Katze *kat·sè*

catalog *n* der Katalog *ka·ta·lōk* Bm20

catch *vt* (*ball, animal, fish, person*) fangen* *fang·èn*; (*train etc*) erreichen *er·rye·khèn*; (*illness*) sich zu|ziehen* *zikh tsoo·tsee·èn*; to catch cold sich erkälten *zikh er·kel·tèn*

cathedral *n* der Dom *dōm* F12

catholic *adj* katholisch *ka·tō·lish*

cattle *pl* das Rindvieh *rint·fee*

cauliflower *n* der Blumenkohl *bloo·mèn·kōl*

cause *n* die Ursache *oor·za·khè* □ *vt* verursachen *fer·oor·za·khèn*

cave *n* die Höhle *hur'·lè*

caviar(e) *n* der Kaviar *kah·vi·ar*

cedar *n* die Zeder *tsay·dèr*

ceiling *n* die Decke *de·kè*

celebrate *vt/i* feiern *fye·èrn*

celeriac *n* die Sellerie *ze·le·ree*

celery *n* die Stangensellerie *shtang·èn·ze·le·ree*

cell n (in prison) die Zelle tse·lè

cellar n der Keller ke·lèr

cello n das Cello tshe·lō

cellophane n das Cellophan tse·lo·fahn

Celsius adj Celsius tsel·zee·oos

cement n der Zement tse·ment

cemetery n der Friedhof freed·hóf

cent n der Cent tsent

centenary n der hundertste Jahrestag hoon·dèrt·stè yah·rès·tahk

center n das Zentrum tsen·troom

centigrade adj Celsius tsel·zee·oos

centiliter n das Zentiliter tsen·tee·lee·tèr

centimeter n der Zentimeter tsen·tee·may·tèr

central adj zentral tsen·trahl

central heating n die Zentralheizung tsen·trahl·hye·tsoong

century n das Jahrhundert yahr·hoon·dèrt

cereal n (breakfast) die Getreideflocken (pl) gè·trye·dè·flo·kèn

ceremony n die Zeremonie tsay·ray·mo·nee

certain adj (person) sicher zi·khèr; (fact) gewiß gè·viss

certainly adv bestimmt bè·shtimt

certificate n die Bescheinigung bè·shye·ni·goong

certified mail n das Einschreiben ine·shrye·bèn

certified public accountant n der Bilanzbuchhalter bi·lants·bookh·hal·tèr

chain n die Kette ke·tè; (of shops) die Ladenkette lah·dèn·ke·tè

chain store n der Kettenladen ke·tèn·lah·dèn

chair n der Stuhl shtool; (armchair) der Sessel ze·sèl

chair-lift n der Sessellift ze·sèl·lift

chairman n der Vorsitzende fōr·zit·sèn·dè

chalet n das Chalet sha·lay

chalk n die Kreide krye·dè

Chamber of Commerce n die Handelskammer han·dèls·ka·mèr

champagne n der Sekt zekt

champion n der Meister mye·stèr

chance n □ by chance zufällig tsoo·fe·likh; he has a good chance of... er hat gute Aussichten zu... er hat goo·tè ows·zikh·tèn tsoo

chancellor n (in Germany, Austria) der Kanzler kants·lèr

change vi sich ändern zikh en·dèrn □ vt wechseln vek·sèln; (money) ein|wechseln ine·vek·sèln; (alter) ändern en·dèrn; (exchange) um|tauschen oom·tow·shèn; to change one's clothes sich um|ziehen zikh oom·tsee·èn; to change trains at Marseilles in Marseille um|steigen* in mar·say oom·shtye·gèn □ n change (transformation) die Veränderung fer·en·dè·roong; (money) das Kleingeld kline·gelt; a change in the weather eine Wetterveränderung ve·tèr·fer·en·dè·roong M21f

Channel n der Ärmelkanal er·mèl·ka·nahl

chapel n die Kapelle ka·pe·lè

chapter n das Kapitel ka·pi·tèl

character n (nature) der Charakter ka·rak·tèr

charge n (accusation) die Anklage an·klah·gè; to make a charge for something etwas in Rechnung stellen et·vass in rekh·noong shte·lèn; free of charge kostenlos kos·tèn·lōs; to be in charge of verantwortlich sein* für

fer·ant·vort·likh zine fōōr □ vt charge (money) berechnen bè·rekh·nèn; charge it to my account setzen Sie es auf meine Rechnung zet·sèn zee ess owf mine·è rekh·noong

charm n der Reiz ryets

charming adj reizend rye·tsènt

chart n (map) die Karte kar·tè; (diagram, table) die Tabelle ta·be·lè

charter vt (plane, bus) chartern shar·tèrn

charter flight n der Charterflug shar·tèr·flook

chase vt jagen yah·gèn

chassis n das Chassis sha·see

chauffeur n der Fahrer fah·rèr

cheap adj billig bi·likh S16, Sn18

cheat vt betrügen* bè·trōō·gèn

check n (banking) der Scheck shek; (bill) die Rechnung rekh·noong; can I have the check please? zahlen bitte tsah·lèn bi·tè □ vt check (examine) überprüfen ōō·bèr·prōō·fèn; (oil, water etc) prüfen prōō·fèn; (passport, ticket) kontrollieren kon·tro·lee·rèn; (train time etc) nach|sehen* nakh·zay·èn; to check in (at hotel) sich an|melden zikh an·mel·dèn; (at airport) sich bei der Abfertigung melden zikh bye der ap·fer·ti·goong mel·dèn; to check out sich ab|melden zikh ap·mel·dèn M24, 27

checkbook n das Scheckbuch shek·bookh

check(er)ed adj (patterned) kariert ka·reert

checkers pl das Damespiel dah·mè·shpeel

checking account n das Girokonto zhee·rō·kon·tō

checkout n (in store) die Kasse ka·sè

checkroom n die Gepäckaufbewahrung gè·pek·owf·bè·vah·roong

cheek n die Wange vang·è; (impudence) die Frechheit frekh·hite

cheeky adj frech frekh

cheer vt zu|jubeln tsoo·yoo·bèln; cheers! Prost! prōst

cheese n der Käse kay·zè E27, 35, 41, S33

cheesecake n der Käsekuchen kay·zè·koo·khèn

chef n der Koch kokh

chemical adj chemisch khay·mish

chemist n (pharmacist) der Apotheker a·po·tay·kèr; chemist's shop der Apotheke a·po·tay·kè

chemistry n die Chemie khay·mee

cherry n die Kirsche kir·shè; (tree) der Kirschbaum kirsh·bowm

chess n das Schach shakh

chest n (of body) die Brust broost

chestnut n die Kastanie kas·tah·nee·è

chew vt kauen kow·èn

chewing gum n das Kaugummi kow·goo·mi

chicken n das Huhn hoon

chicken pox n die Windpocken (pl) vint·po·kèn

chicory n (for coffee) die Zichorie tsi·khō·ree·è; (vegetable) die Chicorée shi·ko·ray

chief n (boss) der Chef shef

child n das Kind kint T13, S46, C1f, 14

chili n der Chili chee·lee

chill vt (wine, food) kühlen kōō·lèn

chimney n der Schornstein shorn·shtine

chin n das Kinn kin

china n das Porzellan por·tse·lahn

China n China (nt) khee·na

Chinese adj chinesisch *khee·nay·zish*; he's Chinese er ist Chinese *er ist khee·nay·zè*; she's Chinese sie ist Chinesin *zee ist khee·nay·zin* □ n Chinese (*language*) Chinesisch (*nt*) *khee·nay·zish*

chip n (*electronics*) das Chip *chip*; (*in gambling*) der Chip *chip*

chips pl die Chips (*pl*) *chips*

chives pl der Schnittlauch *shnit·lowkh*

chocolate n die Schokolade *sho·ko·lah·dè*

choice n die Wahl *vahl*; (*range*) die Auswahl *ows·vahl*

choir n der Chor *kór*

choke n (*of car*) der Choke *chók*

cholesterol n das Cholesterin *khö·les·tay·reen*

choose vt wählen *ve·lèn*

chop vt (*food*) klein|schneiden* *kline·shnye·dèn* □ n **pork chop** das Schweinekotelett *shvine·è·kot·let* S39

chopsticks pl die Stäbchen (*pl*) *shtep·khèn*

Christian n der Christ *krist*

Christian name n der Vorname *för·nah·mè*

Christmas n Weihnachten (*nt*) *vye·nakh·tèn*

Christmas card n die Weihnachtskarte *vye·nakhts·kar·tè*

Christmas Day n der Weihnachtstag *vye·nakhts·tahk*

Christmas Eve n der Heiligabend *hye·likh·ah·bènt*

Christmas tree n der Weihnachtsbaum *vye·nakhts·bowm*

chrome n das Chrom *króm*

chrysanthemum n die Chrysantheme *kri·zan·tay·mè*

church n die Kirche *kir·khè* L4, Sn86

churchyard n der Kirchhof *kirkh·höf*

cider n der Apfelwein *ap·fèl·vine*

cigar n die Zigarre *tsi·ga·rè*

cigarette n die Zigarette *tsi·ga·re·tè*

cigarette case n das Zigarettenetui *tsi·ga·re·tèn·et·vee*

cigarette lighter n das Feuerzeug *foy·èr·tsoyk*

cinema n das Kino *kee·nö*

cinnamon n der Zimt *tsimt*

circle n der Kreis *krise*; (*in theater*) der Rang *rang*

circuit n (*electric*) der Stromkreis *shtröm·krise*

circumstances pl die Umstände (*pl*) *oom·shten·dè*

circus n der Zirkus *tsir·kooss*

city n die Großstadt *grös·shtat*; **city center** das Stadtzentrum *shtat·tsen·troom*

city hall n das Rathaus *raht·hows*

civilization n die Zivilisation *tsee·vee·lee·zat·see·ön*

civil servant n der Beamte *bè·am·tè*

civil service n der Staatsdienst *shtahts·deenst*

civil war n der Bürgerkrieg *bôör·gèr·kreek*

claim vt (*lost property, baggage*) ab|holen *ap·hö·lèn*

clam n die Venusmuschel *vay·noos·moo·shèl*

clap vi klatschen *klat·shèn*

claret n roter Bordeauxwein (*m*) *rö·tèr bor·dö·vine*

clasp n der Schnappverschluß *shnap·fer·shlooss*

class n die Klasse *kla·sè*; **to travel first class** erster Klasse fahren* *er·stèr kla·sè fah·rèn*; **a second class ticket**

ein Fahrschein zweiter Klasse *ine fahr·shine tsvye·tèr kla·sè*

classical adj (*music, art*) klassisch *kla·sish*

clause n (*in contract*) die Klausel *klow·zèl*

clay n der Lehm *laym*

clean adj sauber *zow·bèr* □ vt sauber|machen *zow·bèr·ma·khèn*; **to have a suit cleaned** einen Anzug reinigen lassen* *ine·èn an·tsook rye·ni·gèn la·sèn*

cleaner n (*of house etc*) die Reinemachefrau *rine·è·ma·khè·frow*

cleaner's n die Reinigung *rye·ni·goong*

clear adj klar *klahr*; (*not blocked*) frei *frye* □ vt (*road*) räumen *roy·mèn*; (*pipe*) reinigen *rye·ni·gèn*

clerk n (*in office*) der Büroangestellte *böö·rö·an·gè·shtel·tè*; (*in store*) der Verkäufer *fer·koy·fèr*, die Verkäuferin *fer·koy·fè·rin*

clever adj (*person*) klug *klook*; (*plan*) schlau *shlow*

client n der Kunde *koon·dè*, die Kundin *koon·din*

cliff n der Felsen *fel·zèn*

climate n das Klima *klee·ma*

climb vt (*tree, wall*) klettern auf *kle·tèrn owf*; **to climb over something** über etwas klettern *öö·bèr et·vass kle·tèrn*

clinic n die Klinik *klee·nik*

cloak n der Umhang *oom·hang*

cloakroom n die Garderobe *gar·dè·rö·bè*

clock n die Uhr *oor*

close[1] adj (*near*) nahe *nah·è*; (*stuffy*) schwül *shvööl*; **close to** in der Nähe von *in der nay·è fon*; **close by** in der Nähe *in der nay·è*

close[2] vt schließen* *shlee·sèn* □ vi the door closed die Tür schloß sich *dee töör shlos zikh*; **when do the shops close?** um wieviel Uhr schließen die Läden? *oom vee·feel oor shlee·sèn dee lay·dèn* T36

closed circuit television n die Fernsehüberwachungsanlage *fern·zay·öö·bèr·va·khoongs·an·lah·gè*

closet n der Schrank *shrank*

cloth n (*cleaning*) der Lappen *la·pèn*

clothes pl die Kleider (*pl*) *klye·dèr* Sn72

clotheshorse n der Wäscheständer *ve·shè·shten·dèr*

clothesline n die Wäscheleine *ve·shè·line·è*

clothespin n die Wäscheklammer *ve·shè·kla·mèr*

cloud n die Wolke *vol·kè*

cloudy adj wolkig *vol·kikh*

clove n die Gewürznelke *gè·vöörts·nel·kè*; **clove of garlic** die Knoblauchzehe *knöp·lowkh·tsay·è*

clown n der Clown *klown*

club n (*society*) der Klub *kloop*; **clubs** (*in cards*) Kreuz (*nt*) *kroyts*

club car n der Speisewagen *shpye·zè·vah·gèn*

clumsy adj (*person*) ungeschickt *oon·gè·shikt*

clutch n (*of car*) die Kupplung *koo·ploong*

coach n (*of train*) der Waggon *va·gon*; (*bus*) der Bus *boos*; (*instructor*) der Trainer *tray·nèr*, die Trainerin *tray·nèr·in* B78

coal n die Kohle *kö·lè*

coarse adj (*texture, material*) grob *gröp*

coast n die Küste *köö·stè*

coastguard *n* die Küstenwache *kōō·stèn·va·khè*

coat *n* der Mantel *man·tèl*

coat hanger *n* der Kleiderbügel *klye·dèr·bōō·gèl*

cock(erel) *n* der Hahn *hahn*

cockle *n* die Herzmuschel *herts·moo·shèl*

cocktail *n* der Cocktail *kok·tayl*

cocoa *n* der Kakao *ka·kow*

coconut *n* die Kokosnuß *kō·kos·noos*

cod *n* der Kabeljau *kah·bèl·yow*

codeine *n* das Kodein *ko·day·een*

coffee *n* der Kaffee *ka·fay*; **coffee with milk** der Milchkaffee *milkh·ka·fay* B62, E43, 62

coffee break *n* die Kaffeepause *ka·fay·pow·zè*

coffee cup *n* die Kaffeetasse *ka·fay·ta·sè*

coffeepot *n* die Kaffeekanne *ka·fay·ka·nè*

coffee table *n* der Couchtisch *kowch·tish*

coffin *n* der Sarg *zark*

cognac *n* der Kognak *kon·yak*

coin *n* die Münze *mōōn·tsè*

coincide *vi* zusammen|fallen* *tsoo·za·mèn·fa·lèn*

coincidence *n* der Zufall *tsoo·fal*

colander *n* das Sieb *zeep*

cold *adj* kalt *kalt*; **cold meat** der Aufschnitt *owf·shnit*; **I'm cold** mir ist kalt *meer ist kalt* □ **cold** *(illness)* die Erkältung *er·kel·toong* S43

coleslaw *n* der Krautsalat *krowt·za·lat*

colic *n* die Kolik *ko·leek*

collaborate *vi* zusammen|arbeiten *tsoo·za·mèn·ar·bye·tèn*

collapse *vi (person)* zusammen|brechen* *tsoo·za·mèn·bre·khèn*

collar *n* der Kragen *krah·gèn*; *(for dog)* das Halsband *hals·bant*

colleague *n* der Kollege *ko·lay·gè*, die Kollegin *ko·lay·gin*

collect *vt* sammeln *za·mèln* S92

collect call *n* das R-Gespräch *er·ge·shprekh*

collection *n (of mail)* die Leerung *lay·roong*

college *n* das College *ko·lich*

collide *vi* zusammen|stoßen* *tsoo·za·mèn·shtō·sèn*

collision *n* der Zusammenstoß *tsoo·za·mèn·shtōs*

cologne *n* das Kölnischwasser *kurl·nish·va·sèr*

color *n* die Farbe *far·bè*; **color TV** das Farbfernsehen *farp·fern·zay·èn*

colored *adj (person)* farbig *far·bikh*

comb *n* der Kamm *kam* □ *vt* kämmen *ke·mèn*

come *vi (arrive)* kommen* *ko·mèn*; **to come in** ein|treten* *ine·tray·tèn*; **to come off** ab|gehen* *ap·gay·èn*; **to come out** *(person, sun)* heraus|kommen* *he·rows·ko·mèn*; *(stain)* heraus|gehen* *he·rows·gay·èn*; **to come around** *(recover)* wieder zu sich kommen* *vee·dèr tsoo zikh ko·mèn*

comedian *n* der Komiker *kō·mi·kèr*

comedy *n* die Komödie *ko·mur·dee·è*

comfort *n (ease)* die Bequemlichkeit *bè·kvaym·likh·kite*

comfortable *adj* bequem *bè·kvaym*

comforter *n* das Federbett *fay·dèr·bet*

comfort station *n* die öffentliche Toilette *ur·fènt·li·khè twa·le·tè*

comic *n* das Comic-Heft *ko·mik·heft*

comma *n* das Komma *ko·ma*

command *n* der Befehl *bè·fayl*

comment *n* die Bemerkung *bè·mer·koong*

commerce *n* der Handel *han·dèl*

commercial *adj* Handels- *han·dèls* □ *n (ad)* der Werbespot *ver·bè·shpot*

commercialized *adj (resort)* kommerzialisiert *ko·mer·tsee·a·lee·zeert*

commission *n (sum received)* die Provision *prō·vee·zee·ōn*

commit *vt (crime)* begehen* *bè·gay·èn*

committee *n* der Ausschuß *ows·shoos*

commodity *n* die Ware *vah·rè*

common *adj (ordinary, frequent)* häufig *hoy·fikh*

Common Market *n* der Gemeinsame Markt *gè·mine·za·mè markt*

communicate *vi* □ **to communicate with someone** mit jemandem in Verbindung stehen* *mit yay·man·dèm in fer·bin·doong shtay·èn*

Communist *n* der Kommunist *ko·moo·nist*, die Kommunistin *ko·moo·nis·tin* □ *adj* kommunistisch *ko·moo·nis·tish*

commutation ticket *n* die Zeitkarte *tsite·kar·tè*

commuter *n* der Pendler *pend·lèr*

company *n (firm)* die Firma *fir·ma*

compare *vt* vergleichen* *fer·glye·khèn*

compartment *n (on train)* das Abteil *ap·tile*

compass *n* der Kompaß *kom·pas*

compensation *n* der Schadenersatz *shah·dèn·er·zats*

competent *adj* fähig *fay·ikh*

competition *n* der Wettbewerb *vet·be·verp*

competitor *n* der Konkurrent *kon·koo·rent*

complain *vi* sich beklagen *zikh bè·klah·gèn*; **to complain about** sich beschweren über *zikh bè·shvay·rèn ōō·ber*

complaint *n (dissatisfaction)* die Beschwerde *bè·shvayr·dè*

complete *adj* vollständig *fol·shten·dikh* □ *vt* vervollständigen *fer·fol·shten·di·gèn*

completely *adv* völlig *fur·likh*

complex *adj* kompliziert *kom·plee·tseert*

complexion *n* der Teint *tang*

complicated *adj* kompliziert *kom·plee·tseert*

compliment *n* das Kompliment *kom·plee·ment*

component *n (for car etc)* das Teil *tile*

composer *n* der Komponist *kom·pō·nist*

compound interest *n* der Zinsezins *tsin·zè·tsins*

comprehensive insurance *n* die Vollkaskoversicherung *fol·kas·ko·fer·zi·khè·roong* T112

computer *n* der Computer *kom·poo·tèr*

computerize *vt (system)* auf Computer um|stellen *owf kom·poo·tèr oom·shtel·èn*

computer programming *n* das Programmieren *pro·gra·mee·rèn*

conceited *adj* eingebildet *ine·gè·bil·dèt*

concern *n (anxiety)* die Sorge *zor·gè* □ *vt (be important to)* betreffen* *bè·tre·fèn*; **that doesn't concern you** das geht Sie nichts an *das gayt zee nikhts an*

concert *n* das Konzert *kon·tsert* L43

concrete *n* der Beton *bay·tong* □ *adj* Beton- *bay·tong*

condemn *vt* verdammen *fer·dam·èn*

condensed milk *n* die Kondensmilch *kon·dens·milkh*

condiments *pl* die Gewürze (*pl*) *gè·vöör·tsè*

condition *n* (*state*) der Zustand *tsoo·shtant*; (*proviso*) die Bedingung *bè·ding·oong*; on condition that… unter der Bedingung, daß… *oon·tèr der bè·ding·oong dass* L37

conditioner *n* (*for hair*) die Haarschnellkur *hahr·shnel·koor*

conductor *n* (*on bus*) der Schaffner *shaf·nèr*; (*of orchestra*) der Dirigent *di·ri·gent*; (*on train*) der Zugführer *tsook·föö·rèr*

cone *n* (*for ice cream*) die Eistüte *ise·töö·tè*

confectioner *n* der Konditor *kon·dee·tor*

confectionery *n* die Süßwaren (*pl*) *süss·vah·rèn*

conference *n* (*meeting*) die Konferenz *kon·fè·rents* Bm14

confess *vt* bekennen* *be·ken·èn* □ *vi* gestehen* *ge·shtay·èn*; to confess to something etwas gestehen* *et·vass ge·shtay·èn*

confession *n* das Geständnis *ge·shtent·nis*

confidence *n* (*trust*) das Vertrauen *fer·trow·èn*; confidence in Vertrauen zu *fer·trow·èn tsoo*; in confidence im Vertrauen *im fer·trow·èn*

confident *adj* selbstsicher *zelpst·zi·khèr*

confidential *adj* vertraulich *fer·trow·likh*

confirm *vt* (*reservation etc*) bestätigen *be·shtay·ti·gèn*

confuse *vt* verwechseln *fer·vek·sèln*; to confuse one thing with another eine Sache mit einer anderen verwechseln *ine·è za·khè mit ine·èr an·dè·rèn fer·vek·sèln*

confused *adj* (*muddled*) verwirrt *fer·virt*

congratulate *vt* □ to congratulate someone on something jemandem zu etwas gratulieren *yay·man·dèm tsoo et·vass gra·too·lee·rèn*

congratulations *pl* die Glückwünsche (*pl*) *glöök·vöön·shè*; congratulations! herzliche Glückwünsche! *herts·li·khè glöök·vöön·shè*

conjuror *n* der Zauberer *tsow·bè·rèr*

connect *vt* (*join*) verbinden* *fer·bin·dèn*; this train connects with the 16:45 dieser Zug hat Anschluß an den 16.45 *dee·zèr tsook hat an·shloos an dayn 16.45*

connection *n* (*train etc*) der Anschluß *an·shloos*

connoisseur *n* der Kenner *ken·èr*

conscience *n* das Gewissen *gè·vis·èn*

conscious *adj* bei Bewußtsein *bye bè·voost·zine*

consequence *n* (*result*) die Folge *fol·gè*

conservative *adj* konservativ *kon·ser·va·teef*

conservatory *n* (*greenhouse*) der Wintergarten *vin·tèr·gar·tèn*

consider *vt* überlegen *öö·bèr·lay·gèn*

consist of *vt* bestehen* aus *bè·shtay·èn ows*

consommé *n* die Kraftbrühe *kraft·bröö·è*

constipated *adj* □ to be constipated Verstopfung haben* *fer·shtop·foong hah·bèn*

construct *vt* bauen *bow·èn*

consul *n* der Konsul *kon·sool*

consulate *n* das Konsulat *kon·soo·laht* Sn85

consult *vt* um Rat fragen *oom raht frah·gèn*

consultant *n* (*doctor*) der Facharzt *fakh·artst*; (*other specialist*) der Berater *bè·rah·tèr*

consulting room *n* das Sprechzimmer *shprekh·tsi·mèr*

consumer *n* der Verbraucher *fer·brow·khèr*

consumer goods *pl* die Konsumgüter (*pl*) *kon·zoom·göö·tèr*

contact *vt* sich in Verbindung setzen mit *zikh in fer·bin·doong zet·sèn mit*

contact lenses *pl* die Kontaktlinsen (*pl*) *kon·takt·lin·zèn*

contagious *adj* ansteckend *an·shte·kent*

contain *vt* enthalten* *ent·hal·tèn*

container *n* der Behälter *be·hel·tèr*; (*for shipping etc*) der Container *kon·tay·nèr*

contemporary *adj* (*modern*) zeitgenössisch *tsite·gè·nur·sish*

content(ed) *adj* zufrieden *tsoo·free·dèn*

contents *pl* der Inhalt *in·halt*; (*table in book*) das Inhaltsverzeichnis *in·halts·fer·tsyekh·nis*

contest *n* (*competition*) der Wettbewerb *vet·bè·verp*

contestant *n* der Bewerber *bè·ver·bèr*, die Bewerberin *bè·ver·bè·rin*

continent *n* der Kontinent *kon·tee·nènt*; the Continent Kontinentaleuropa (*nt*) *kon·tee·nen·tahl·oy·rö·pah*

continental *adj* kontinental *kon·tee·nen·tahl*

continental breakfast *n* das kleine Frühstück *das klye·nè fröö·shtöök*

continual *adj* andauernd *an·dow·èrnt*

continue *vt* fort|fahren* mit *fort·fah·rèn mit* □ *vi* (*road etc*) weiter|gehen* *vye·tèr·gay·èn*; to continue to do weiter tun* *vye·tèr toon*

continuous *adj* ununterbrochen *oon·oon·tèr·bro·khèn*

continuously *adv* ständig *shten·dikh*

contraband *n* die Schmuggelware *shmoo·gèl·vah·rè*

contraceptive *n* das empfängnisverhütende Mittel *emp·feng·nis·fer·höö·tèn·dè mi·tèl*

contract *n* der Vertrag *fer·trak*

contractor *n* der Unternehmer *oon·tèr·nay·mèr*

contrary *n* □ on the contrary im Gegenteil *im gay·gèn·tile*

contribute *vi* bei|tragen* *bye·trah·gèn*

control *vt* beherrschen *bè·her·shèn* □ *n* circumstances beyond our control nicht in unserer Hand liegende Umstände *nikht in oon·zè·rèr hant lee·gèn·dè oom·shten·dè*

control tower *n* der Kontrollturm *kon·trol·toorm*

controls *pl* die Steuerung *shtoy·èr·oong*

conurbation *n* das Ballungsgebiet *ba·loongs·gè·beet*

convalescence *n* die Genesung *gè·nay·zoong*

convenient *adj* praktisch *prak·tish*; convenient to stores mit Läden in günstiger Nähe *mit lay·dèn in göon·sti·gèr nay·è*

convent *n* das Kloster *klö·stèr*

conversation *n* die Unterhaltung *oon·tèr·hal·toong*

convertible *n* (*car*) das Kabriolett *kah·bree·ö·lay*

convince vt überzeugen *ōō·bèr·tsoy· gèn*

cook vt kochen *ko·khèn* □ vi the meat is cooking das Fleisch brät *das flyesh brayt* □ n cook der Koch *kokh*, die Köchin *kur'·khin*

cooker n der Kochherd *kokh·hert*

cookie n das Plätzchen *plets·khèn*

cooking n die Küche *kōō·khè*

cool adj kühl *kōōl*

cooling system n die Kühlung *kōō· loong*

co-operate vi zusammen|arbeiten *tsoo· za·mèn·ar·bye·tèn*

co-operative n die Genossenschaft *gè· no·sèn·shaft*

Copenhagen n Kopenhagen (nt) *kō· pèn·hah·gèn*

copper n (metal) das Kupfer *koop·fèr*

copy n (of book etc) das Exemplar *ex· em·plahr*; (imitation) die Kopie *ko· pee* □ vt kopieren *ko·pee·rèn*; (imitate) nach|ahmen *nakh·ah·mèn* Bm24

copyright n das Copyright *ko·pee·rite*

coral n die Koralle *ko·ra·lè*

cord n (twine) die Schnur *shnoor*; (fabric) der Kordsamt *kort·zamt*

cordial n das Fruchtsaftkonzentrat *frookt·saft·kon·tsèn·traht*

corduroy n der Kordsamt *kort·zamt*

cork n der Kork *kork*; (of bottle) der Korken *kor·kèn*

corkscrew n der Korkenzieher *kor· kèn·tsee·èr*

corn n (cereal crop) der Mais *mise*; (on foot) das Hühnerauge *hü·nèr·ow·gè*

corned beef n das Corned Beef *kor· nèt·beef*

corner n (of streets) die Ecke *e·kè*; (bend in road) die Kurve *koor·vè* □ vi eine Kurve nehmen* *ine·è koor· vè nay·mèn*

cornet n (of ice cream) die Eistüte *ise· tōō·tè*

cornflakes pl die Cornflakes (pl) *corn· flakes*

corn-on-the-cob n die Maiskolben (pl) *mise·kol·bèn*

cornstarch n das Maismehl *mise·mayl*

coronation n die Krönung *krur'·noong*

corporation n (firm) die Handelsgesellschaft *han·dèls·gè·zel·shaft*; (of town) die Gemeinde *gè·mine·dè*

corporation tax n die Körperschaftssteuer *kur·pèr·shafts·shtoy·èr*

correct adj (accurate) richtig *rikh·tikh*; (proper) korrekt *ko·rekt* □ vt berichtigen *bè·rikh·ti·gèn*

correction n (alteration) die Berichtigung *bè·rikh·ti·goong*

correspondence n (mail) die Korrespondenz *ko·res·pon·dents*

correspondence course n der Fernkurs *fern·koors*

corridor n der Gang *gang*

corrode vt zerfressen* *tser·fre·sèn*

corrugated iron n das Wellblech *vel· blekh*

corrugated paper n die Wellpappe *vel· pa·pè*

corrupt adj korrupt *ko·roopt*

corruption n die Korruption *ko·roop· tsee·ōn*

corset n das Korsett *kor·zet*

cosmetics pl die Kosmetika (pl) *kos· may·ti·ka*

cosmetic surgery n die kosmetische Chirurgie *kos·may·ti·shè khi·roor·gee*

cosmopolitan adj international *in·ter· na·tsee·ō·nahl*

cost n der Preis *prise*; to buy something at cost etwas zum Selbstkostenpreis kaufen *et·vass tsoom selpst·kos·tèn· prise kow·fèn* □ vt cost kosten *kos· tèn* S5

cost of living n die Lebenshaltungskosten (pl) *lay·bèns·hal·toongs·kos·tèn*

costs pl (of production etc) die Kosten (pl) *ko·stèn* Bm25f

costume n (theatrical) das Kostüm *kos· tōōm*

costume jewelry n der Modeschmuck *mō·dè·shmook*

cot n das Feldbett *felt·bet*

cottage n das Häuschen *hoys·khèn*

cottage cheese n der Hüttenkäse *hōō· tèn·kay·zè*

cotton n (fabric) die Baumwolle *bowm·vo·lè*; (thread) das Baumwollgarn *bowm·vol·garn*

cotton batting n die Watte *va·tè*

couch n das Sofa *zō·fa*

couchette n der Liegewagenplatz *lee· gè·vah·gèn·plats*

cough n der Husten *hoo·stèn* □ vi husten *hoo·stèn* S43

cough drops pl die Hustenpastillen (pl) *hoo·stèn·pa·stil·èn*

cough medicine n der Hustensaft *hoo· stèn·zaft*

could vi □ we could do it wir könnten es tun *veer kur'n·tèn ess toon*; could I have... könnte ich...haben *kur'n·tè ikh...hah·bèn*

council n (of town) der Stadtrat *shtat· raht*

counselor n der Rechtsanwalt *rekhts· an·valt*

count vt (objects, people) zählen *tsay· lèn* □ vi to count up to 10 bis 10 zählen *bis 10 tsay·lèn*

counter n (in shop) der Ladentisch *lah·dèn·tish*; (gambling) die Marke *mar·kè*

counterfoil n der Kontrollabschnitt *kon·trol·ap·shnit*

country n (nation) das Land *lant*; in the country auf dem Land *owf daym lant* Mc13, 14, 50

countryside n die Landschaft *lant·shaft*

coup d'état n der Staatsstreich *shtahts· shtryekh*

coupé n (car) das Coupé *koo·pay*

couple n (persons) das Paar *pahr*; a couple of (a few) ein paar *ine pahr*

coupon n der Gutschein *goot·shine*

courage n der Mut *moot*

courgettes pl die Zucchini (pl) *tsoo· kee·nee*

courier n der Fremdenführer *frem· dèn·fōō·rèr*

course n (lessons) der Kursus *koor· zoos*; (of meal) der Gang *gang*; (for golf) der Platz *plats*; course of treatment die Behandlung *bè·hant·loong*

court n (law) das Gericht *gè·rikht*; (tennis etc) der Platz *plats*

courtyard n der Hof *hóf*

cousin n der Vetter *fet·èr*, die Kusine *koo·zee·nè*

cover n (of book) der Einband *ine· bant*; (blanket) der Bettdecke *bet·dè· kè*; (insurance) die Versicherung *fer· zi·khèr·oong*; under separate cover getrennt *gè·trent* □ vt cover bedecken *bè·de·kèn*; (distance) zurück|legen *tsoo·rōōk·lay·gèn*

cover charge n die Kosten für ein Gedeck *ko·sten fōōr ine gè·dek*

covering letter n der Begleitbrief *bè· glite·breef*

cow *n* die Kuh *koo*
coward *n* der Feigling *fíke·ling*
cowboy *n* der Cowboy *kow·boy*
crab *n* die Krabbe *kra·bè*
crack *n* (split) der Riß *ris*; (noise) der Knacks *knaks* □ *vt* to crack a glass einen Sprung in ein Glas machen *ine·èn shproong in ine glahs ma·khèn* □ *vi* the glass cracked das Glas ist gesprungen *das glahs ist gè·shproong·èn*
cracker *n* (crisp wafer) der Kräcker *kre·kèr*; (paper toy) der Knallfrosch *knal·frosh*
cradle *n* die Wiege *vee·gè*
craft *n* das Handwerk *hant·verk*
craftsman *n* der Handwerker *hant·ver·kèr*
cramp *n* der Krampf *krampf*
cranberry *n* die Preiselbeere *prise·èl·bay·rè*
crane *n* (machine) der Kran *krahn*
crash *n* (noise) der Krach *krakh*; (collision) der Zusammenstoß *tsoo·za·mèn·shtôs* □ *vt* to crash one's car einen Autounfall haben* *ine·èn ow·tô·oon·fal hah·bèn* □ *vi* to crash into something gegen etwas knallen *gay·gèn et·vass kna·lèn*
crash course *n* der Steilkurs *shtíle·koors*
crash helmet *n* der Sturzhelm *shtoorts·helm*
crash-landing *n* die Bruchlandung *brookh·lan·doong*
crate *n* die Kiste *kis·tè*
crawfish, crayfish *n* (freshwater) der Flußkrebs *floos·krayps*; (saltwater) die Languste *lang·goo·stè*
crawl *vi* kriechen* *kree·khèn* □ *n* (swimming) das Kraulen *krow·lèn*
crayon *n* der Buntstift *boont·shtift*
crazy *adj* verrückt *fer·rôokt*
cream *n* die Sahne *zah·nè*; (cosmetic) die Creme *kraym* □ *adj* cremefarben *kraym·far·bèn*
cream cheese *n* der Sahnequark *zah·nè·kvark*
creamy *adj* (texture) cremig *kray·mikh*
crease *n* die Bügelfalte *bōō·gèl·fal·tè*
creased *adj* zerknittert *tser·kni·tèrt*
create *vt* schaffen* *sha·fèn*
crèche *n* die Kinderkrippe *kin·dèr·kri·pè*
credit *n* der Kredit *kray·deet*; on credit auf Kredit *owf kray·deet*; to give somebody credit jemandem Kredit geben* *yay·man·dèm kray·deet gay·bèn* □ *vt* to credit DM50 to someone's account DM50 auf jemandes Konto gut|schreiben* *DM50 owf yay·man·dès kon·tô goot·shrye·bèn*
credit card *n* die Kreditkarte *kray·deet·kar·tè* T155, M13
creditor *n* der Gläubiger *gloy·bi·gèr*
credit squeeze *n* die Kreditbeschränkung *kray·deet·bè·shreng·koong*
crème de menthe *n* der Pfefferminzlikör *pfe·fer·mints·lee·kur*
cress *n* die Kresse *kre·sè*
crew *n* (of ship, plane) die Mannschaft *man·shaft*
crib *n* (baby's) das Kinderbett *kin·dèr·bet* C12
cricket *n* (sport) das Cricket *kri·kèt*
crime *n* das Verbrechen *fer·bre·khèn*
criminal *adj* kriminell *kree·mi·nel*
cripple *n* der Krüppel *krōō·pèl*
crisis *n* die Krise *kree·zè*
crisp *adj* knusprig *knoos·prikh*
criticize *vt* kritisieren *kri·ti·zee·rèn*

crockery *n* das Geschirr *gè·shir*
crocodile *n* das Krokodil *krō·kô·deel*
crocus *n* der Krokus *krō·koos*
croissant *n* das Hörnchen *hur'n·khèn*
crooked *adj* krumm *kroom*
crop *n* (harvest) die Ernte *ern·tè*; (whip) die Reitpeitsche *ríte·pye·tshè*
croquet *n* das Krocket *kro·ket*
croquette *n* die Krokette *kro·ke·tè*
cross *n* das Kreuz *kroyts* □ *vt* (road, sea) überqueren *ōō·bèr·kvay·rèn*; to cross out aus|streichen* *ows·shtrye·khèn*
crossing *n* (voyage) die Überfahrt *ōō·bèr·fahrt*
crossroads *n* die Kreuzung *kroy·tsoong*
crosswalk *n* der Zebrastreifen *tsay·bra·shtrye·fèn*
croupier *n* der Croupier *kroo·pyay*
crouton *n* der Crouton *kroo·tong*
crowd *n* die Menge *meng·è*
crowded *adj* überfüllt *ōō·bèr·fōolt*
crown *n* die Krone *krō·nè*
crude *adj* (oil etc) Roh- *rō*
cruel *adj* grausam *grow·zahm*
cruise *n* die Kreuzfahrt *kroyts·fahrt*; to go on a cruise eine Kreuzfahrt machen *ine·è kroyts·fahrt ma·khèn*
crumb *n* der Krümel *krōō·mèl*
crush *vt* zerdrücken *tser·drōō·kèn*
crust *n* die Kruste *kroo·stè*
crutch *n* der Unterleib *oon·tèr·lipe*
cry *vi* weinen *vye·nèn* □ *n* der Schrei *shrye*
crystal *n* (glass) das Kristall *kri·stal*
cube *n* der Würfel *vōōr·fèl*
cubicle *n* die Umkleidekabine *oom·klye·dè·ka·bee·nè*
cucumber *n* die Gurke *goor·kè*
cuddle *vt* herzen *hayr·tsèn*
cuff *n* (of shirt) die Manschette *man·she·tè*
cuff link *n* der Manschettenknopf *man·she·tèn·knopf*
cuisine *n* die Küche *kōō·khè*
cul-de-sac *n* die Sackgasse *zak·ga·sè*
cultivate *vt* (land) kultivieren *kool·tee·vee·rèn*; (crop) an|bauen *an·bow·èn*
culture *n* die Bildung *bil·doong*
cup *n* die Tasse *ta·sè*; (trophy) der Cup *kup*
cupboard *n* der Schrank *shrank*
curb *n* die Bordsteinkante *bort·shtine·kan·tè*
cure *vt* heilen *hye·lèn*
curious *adj* (inquisitive) neugierig *noy·gee·rikh*; (strange) merkwürdig *merk·vōōr·dikh*
curl *n* die Locke *lo·kè*
curler *n* (for hair) der Lockenwickel *lo·kèn·vi·kèl*
curly *adj* lockig *lo·kikh*
currant *n* die Korinthe *kô·rin·tè*
currency *n* die Währung *vay·roong*; foreign currency die Devisen (pl) *day·vee·zèn*
current *n* (of water, air) die Strömung *shtrur·moong*
curry *n* das Curry *ku·ree*
curry powder *n* das Currypulver *ku·ree·pool·vèr*
curtain *n* der Vorhang *fōr·hang*
curve *n* die Kurve *koor·vè*
cushion *n* das Kissen *ki·sèn*
custard *n* der Vanillepudding *va·ni·lè·poo·ding*
custom *n* der Brauch *browkh*
customer *n* der Kunde *koon·dè*, die Kundin *koon·din*
custom-made *adj* maßgeschneidert *mahss·gè·shnye·dèrt*

customs n der Zoll *tsol*

customs duty n der Zoll *tsol*

customs officer n der Zollbeamte *tsol·bè·am·tè*

cut vt schneiden* *shnye·dèn*; (reduce) herunter|setzen *her·oon·tèr·zet·sèn*; (dilute) verdünnen *fer·dōōn·èn*; to cut oneself sich schneiden* *zikh shnye·dèn* □ n cut (wound) die Schnittwunde *shnit·voon·dè*; (of meat) das Stück *shtōōk*

cute adj (pretty) niedlich *need·likh*

cutlery n das Besteck *bè·shtek*

cutlet n das Kotelett *kot·let*

cut-rate adj reduziert *ray·doo·tseert*

cycle vi rad|fahren* *raht·fah·rèn*

cycling n das Radfahren *raht·fah·rèn*; to go cycling rad|fahren* *raht·fah·rèn*

cyclist n der Radfahrer *raht·fah·rèr*, die Radfahrerin *raht·fah·rè·rin*

cylinder n der Zylinder *tsoo·lin·dèr*

Czechoslovakia n die Tschechoslowakei *che·kho·slo·va·kye*

Czech(oslovakian) adj tschechisch *che·khish*

D

dacron n das Terylene *te·rōō·layn*

dad(dy) n der Papa *pa·pa*

daffodil n die Osterglocke *ō·stèr·glo·kè*

dagger n der Dolch *dolkh*

daily adj täglich *teg·likh* □ n (newspaper) die Tageszeitung *tah·gès·tsye·toong*

dainty adj zierlich *tseer·likh*

dairy store n das Milchgeschäft *milkh·gè·sheft*

dam n der Damm *dam*

damage n der Schaden *shah·dèn*; damages der Schadensersatz *shah·dèns·er·zats* □ vt damage beschädigen *bè·she·di·gèn* Sn48

damp adj feucht *foykht*

dance vi tanzen *tan·tsèn* □ n der Tanz *tants*; (ball) der Tanzabend *tants·ah·bènt* L42

dandruff n die Schuppen (pl) *shoo·pèn*

danger n die Gefahr *gè·fahr*

dangerous adj gefährlich *gè·fer·likh*

Danish adj dänisch *day·nish*; he's Danish er ist Däne *er ist day·nè*; she's Danish sie ist Dänin *zee ist day·nin* □ n Danish (nt) *day·nish*

dare vi □ to dare to do something es wagen, etwas zu tun *ess vah·gèn et·vass tsoo toon*

dark adj dunkel *doong·kèl*

darling n der Schatz *shats*

darn vt stopfen *shtop·fèn*

dart n (to throw) der Pfeil *pfile*; (on clothes) der Abnäher *ap·nay·èr*; game of darts das Dartspiel *dart·shpeel*

dash n (in writing) der Gedankenstrich *gè·dank·èn·shtrikh*

dash(board) n das Armaturenbrett *ar·ma·toor·èn·bret*

data pl die Daten (pl) *dah·tèn*

data bank, data base n die Datenbank *dah·tèn·bank*

data file n die Datei *da·tye*

data processing n die Datenverarbeitung *dah·tèn·fer·ar·bye·toong*

date n (day) das Datum *dah·toom*; (appointment) die Verabredung *fer·ap·ray·doong*; (fruit) die Dattel *da·tèl*; what's the date today? welches Datum haben wir heute? *vel·khès dah·toom hah·bèn veer hoy·tè*; out of date altmodisch *alt·mō·dish*

date line n die Datumsgrenze *dah·tooms·gren·tsè*

daughter n die Tochter *tokh·tèr* C11, 17

daughter-in-law n die Schwiegertochter *shvee·gèr·tokh·tèr*

dawn n die Morgendämmerung *mor·gèn·de·mè·roong*

day n der Tag *tahk*; every day, day by day jeden Tag *yay·dèn tahk*; the day before am Tag zuvor *am tahk tsoo·fōr*; the next or following day am Tag danach *am tahk da·nakh* T108, Mc42

day nursery n die Kinderkrippe *kin·dèr·kri·pè* C4

dazzle vt blenden *blen·dèn*

dead adj (person) tot *tōt*; (battery) leer *layr*

dead end n die Sackgasse *zak·ga·sè*

deaf adj taub *towb*

deal n das Geschäft *gè·sheft* □ vi to deal with a firm mit einer Firma verhandeln *mit ine·èr feer·ma bè·han·dèln*; to deal with a subject ein Thema behandeln *ine tay·ma bè·han·dèln*; to deal in something mit etwas handeln *mit et·vass han·dèln*

dealer n der Händler *hent·lèr*; (cards) der Kartengeber *kar·tèn·gay·bèr*

dear adj lieb *leep*; (expensive) teuer *toy·èr*; Dear Sir sehr geehrte Herren! *zehr gè·er·tè her·rèn*; Dear Madam sehr geehrte Damen! *zehr gè·er·tè dah·mèn*; Dear Mr. Smith sehr geehrter Herr Smith! *zehr gè·er·tèr her Smith*

death n der Tod *tōt*

death certificate n der Totenschein *tō·tèn·shine*

debate n die Debatte *de·ba·tè*

debit n das Debet *de·bèt* □ vt to debit $50 to someone's account jemandes Konto mit $50 belasten *yay·man·dès kon·tō mit $50 bè·las·tèn*

debt n die Schuld *shoolt*; to be in debt verschuldet sein* *fer·shool·dèt zine*

decade n das Jahrzehnt *yahr·tsaynt*

decaffeinated adj koffeinfrei *ko·fe·een·frye*

decanter n die Karaffe *ka·ra·fè*

deceive vt täuschen *toy·shèn*

December n Dezember (m) *de·tsem·bèr*

decent adj anständig *an·shten·dikh*

decide vi (between alternatives) sich entscheiden* *zikh ent·shye·dèn*

decimal adj dezimal *de·tsee·mahl* □ n die Dezimalzahl *de·tsee·mahl·tsahl*

decimal point n das Komma *ko·ma*

decision n die Entscheidung *ent·shye·doong*

deck n (of ship) das Deck *dek*; (of cards) der Pack *pak*

deckchair n der Liegestuhl *lee·gè·shtool* L23

declare vt (announce) behaupten *bè·howp·tèn*; (customs) verzollen *fer·tsol·èn*; nothing to declare nichts zu verzollen *nikhts tsoo fer·tsol·èn*

decorate vt (adorn) schmücken *shmōō·kèn*; (paint) streichen* *shtrye·khèn*

decorations pl der Schmuck *shmook*

decrease vt vermindern *fer·min·dèrn*

deduct vt ab|ziehen* *ap·tsee·èn*

deep adj tief *teef*

deepfreeze n die Tiefkühltruhe *teef·kōōl·troo·è*

deer n das Reh *ray*

defeat vt besiegen *bè·zee·gèn* □ n der Sieg *zeek*

defect n der Fehler *fay·lèr*

defective adj fehlerhaft *fay·lèr·haft*

defend vt verteidigen *fer·tye·di·gèn*

defense n die Verteidigung *fer·tye·di·goong*

deficit n das Deficit *day·fi·tsit*

definite adj (distinct) klar *klahr*; (certain) sicher *zi·khèr*

definitely adv bestimmt *bè·shtimt*

deflation n die Deflation *de·fla·tsee·ön*

deformed adj deformiert *de·for·meert*

defrost vt (food) auf|tauen *owf·tow·èn*; (refrigerator) ab|tauen *ap·tow·èn*

defroster n das Gebläse *gè·blay·zè*

degree n der Grad *grat*; (university) der akademische Grad *a·ka·day·mish·è grat*

de-ice vt enteisen *ent·eye·zèn*

delay vt (hold up) auf|halten* *owf·hal·tèn*; (postpone) verschieben* *fer·shee·bèn*; the train has been delayed der Zug hat Verspätung *der tsook hat fer·shpay·toong* □ n delay (to train, plane) die Verspätung *fer·shpay·toong*

delegate vt delegieren *day·lay·gee·rèn*

delegation n die Delegation *day·lay·ga·tsee·ön*

deliberate adj bewußt *bè·voost*

deliberately adv vorsätzlich *för·zets·likh*

delicate adj (not robust) zart *tsart*; (dainty) fein *fine*; (situation) heikel *hye·kèl*

delicatessen n das Feinkostgeschäft *fine·kost·gè·sheft*

delicious adj köstlich *kur'st·likh*

delighted adj entzückt *ent·tsöökt*

deliver vt (mail) zu|stellen *tsoo·shte·lèn*; (goods) liefern *lee·fèrn*

delivery n (of mail) die Zustellung *tsoo·shte·loong*; (of goods) die Lieferung *lee·fè·roong*

de luxe adj Luxus- *look·zoos*

demand vt verlangen *fer·lang·èn* □ n (for goods) die Nachfrage *nakh·frah·gè*

demonstrate vt (appliance etc) vor|führen *for·föö·rèn*

demonstration n die Vorführung *for·föö·roong*; (political) die Demonstration *de·mon·stra·tsee·ön*

denim n der Jeansstoff *jeens·shtof*

Denmark n Dänemark (nt) *de·nè·mark*

dense adj (fog etc) dicht *dikht*

dent n die Beule *boy·lè*

dentist n der Zahnarzt *tsahn·artst*, die Zahnärztin *tsahn·erts·tin*

dentures pl das Gebiß *gè·biss* I67

deny vt leugnen *loyg·nèn*

deodorant n das Desodorant *des·ō·do·rant*

department n (in store) die Abteilung *ap·tye·loong*

department store n das Kaufhaus *kowf·hows*

departure board n der Abflugtafel *ap·flook·tah·fèl*

departure lounge n die Abflughalle *ap·flook·hal·lè*

depend vi □ it depends es kommt darauf an *es komt da·rowf an*; to depend on ab|hängen* von *ap·heng·èn fon*

deposit n (down payment) die Anzahlung *an·tsah·loong*; (for key etc) die Kaution *kow·tsee·ön* □ vt (money) deponieren *de·pō·nee·rèn* M9

depot n das Depot *de·pō*; (trains) der Bahnhof *bahn·hôf*

depressed adj (person) deprimiert *de·pree·meert*

depth n die Tiefe *tee·fè*

deputy n (second-in-command) der Stellvertreter *shtel·fer·tray·tèr*

derby n die Melone *may·lō·nè*

describe vt beschreiben* *bè·shrye·bèn*

description n die Beschreibung *bè·shrye·boong*

desert n die Wüste *vöö·stè*

deserve vt verdienen *fer·dee·nèn*

design n (plan) der Entwurf *ent·voorf*; (pattern) das Muster *moo·stèr* □ vt entwerfen* *ent·ver·fèn*

designer n der Designer *di·zye·nèr*; (of clothes) der Modeschöpfer *mō·dè·shur'p·fèr*, die Modeschöpferin *mō·dè·shur'p·fè·rin*

desire n der Wunsch *voonsh*

desk n (in office) der Schreibtisch *shripe·tish*; (reception) die Rezeption *ray·tsep·tsee·ön*

desperate adj verzweifelt *fer·tsvye·fèlt*

despite prep trotz *trots*

dessert n der Nachtisch *nakh·tish* E40

dessertspoon n der Dessertlöffel *de·ser·lur'·fèl*

destination n das Reiseziel *rize·è·tseel*

destroy vt zerstören *tser·stur'èn*

detached house n das Einzelhaus *ine·tsèl·hows*

detail n die Einzelheit *ine·tsèl·hite*; in detail ausführlich *ows·föör·likh*

detailed adj ausführlich *ows·föör·likh*

detective n der Detektiv *day·tek·teef*

detergent n das Waschmittel *vash·mi·tèl*

determined adj entschlossen *ent·shlo·sèn*

detour n der Umweg *oom·vayk*; to make a detour einen Umweg machen *ine·èn oom·vayk ma·khèn*

devaluation n die Abwertung *ap·ver·toong*

devalue vt (currency) ab|werten *ap·ver·tèn*

develop vi sich entwickeln *zikh ent·vik·èln* □ vt (photo) entwickeln *ent·vik·èln*

developing country n das Entwicklungsland *ent·vik·loongz·lant*

development n (housing) die Wohnsiedlung *vōn·zeet·loong*

diabetes n die Zuckerkrankheit *tsoo·kèr·krank·hite*

diabetic n der Diabetiker *dee·a·bay·ti·kèr*, die Diabetikerin *dee·a·bay·ti·kè·rin*

diagnosis n die Diagnose *dee·ag·nō·zè*

diagonal adj diagonal *dee·a·go·nahl*

diagram n das Diagramm *dee·a·gram*

dial vt (number) wählen *vay·lèn* Sn13

dialect n der Dialekt *dee·a·lekt*

dial tone n das Amtszeichen *amts·tsye·khèn*

diameter n der Durchmesser *doorkh·me·sèr*

diamond n der Diamant *dee·a·mant*; diamonds (cards) das Karo *ka·rō*

diaper n die Windel *vin·dèl* C19

diarrhea n der Durchfall *doorkh·fal*

diary n der Terminkalender *ter·meen·ka·len·dèr*

dice n der Würfel *vöör·fèl*

dictate vt (letter) diktieren *dik·teer·èn*

dictionary n das Wörterbuch *vur·tèr·bookh*

die vi sterben* *shter·bèn*

diesel n das Dieselöl *dee·zèl·ur'l*

diesel engine n der Dieselmotor *dee·zèl·mō·tôr*

diesel fuel n das Dieselöl *dee·zĕl·ur'l*
diet n (*slimming*) die Schlankheitskur
  shlank·hites·koor; **to be on a diet**
  eine Schlankheitskur machen *ine·ĕ
  shlank·hites·koor ma·khĕn*
difference n der Unterschied *oon·tĕr·
  sheet*
different adj verschieden *fer·shee·dĕn*;
  different from anders als *ahn·dĕrs als*
difficult adj schwierig *shvee·rikh*
difficulty n die Schwierigkeit *shvee·
  rikh·kite*; **with difficulty** nur schwer
  noor shvayr
dig vt graben* *gra·bĕn*; **to dig up** aus|
  graben* *ows·gra·bĕn*
digital adj Digital- *di·gi·tahl*
dike n der Deich *dyekh*
dilute vt verdünnen *fer·dōōn·ĕn*
dim adj (*light*) schwach *shvakh*;
  (*room*) halbdunkel *halp·doong·kĕl*
  □ vt (*headlights*) ab|blenden
dimensions pl die Maße (pl) *mah·sĕ*
dimmer n der Abblendschalter *ap·
  blent·shal·tĕr*
diner n das Eßlokal *es·lo·kahl*
dinghy n das Dingi *ding·ee*; (*inflatable*)
  das Schlauchboot *shlowkh·bōt*
dining car n der Speisewagen *shpye·zĕ·
  vah·gĕn*
dining room n das Eßzimmer *ess·tsi·
  mĕr*
dinner n das Abendessen *ah·bĕnt·e·sĕn*
dinner jacket n die Smokingjacke *smō·
  king·ya·kĕ*
dinner party n die Abendgesellschaft
  ah·bĕnt·gĕ·zel·shaft
dip vt (*into liquid*) tauchen *tow·khĕn*
diploma n das Diplom *di·plōm*
diplomat n der Diplomat *di·plo·maht*
dipstick n der Ölmeßstab *url'l·mess·
  shtahp*
direct adj direkt *dee·rekt* □ adv **to fly
  to Venice direct** direkt nach Venedig
  fliegen* *dee·rekt nakh vĕ·nay·dikh
  flee·gĕn* □ vt **direct** (*traffic*) regeln
  ray·gĕln
direction n die Richtung *rikh·toong*; **in
  the direction of X** in Richtung X *in
  rikh·toong X*; **directions** (*to a place*)
  die Angaben (pl) *an·gah·bĕn*; **directions for use** die Gebrauchsanweisung *gĕ·browkhs·an·vye·zoong*
director n (*of firm*) der Direktor *dee·
  rek·tor*; (*of film*) der Regisseur *ray·
  zhee·sur* Bm3
directory n das Adreßbuch *a·dress·
  bookh*; (*telephone*) das Telefonbuch
  tay·lay·fōn·bookh Sn22
dirt n der Schmutz *shmoots*
dirty adj schmutzig *shmoo·tsikh*
disabled adj körperbehindert *kur·pĕr·
  bĕ·hin·dĕrt* I2f
disadvantage n der Nachteil *nakh·tile*;
  at a disadvantage im Nachteil *im
  nakh·tile*
disagree vi □ **to disagree with some-
  body** mit jemandem nicht überein|
  stimmen *mit yay·man·dĕm nikht ōō·
  bĕr·ine·shti·mĕn*; **eggs disagree with
  me** Eier bekommen mir nicht *eye·ĕr
  bĕ·ko·mĕn meer nikht*
disagreement n der Streit *shtrite*
disappear vi verschwinden* *fer·shvin·
  dĕn*
disappointed adj enttäuscht *ent·toysht*
disapprove vi □ **to disapprove of something** etwas mißbilligen *et·vass mis·
  bi·li·gĕn*
disaster n die Katastrophe *ka·ta·strō·fĕ*
disc brakes pl die Scheibenbremsen
  (pl) *shye·bĕn·brem·zĕn*

discipline n die Disziplin *dis·tsi·pleen*
disc jockey n der Diskjockey *disk·jo·
  kay*
disco(thèque) n die Disko *di·skō*
discount n der Rabatt *ra·bat*; **at a discount** auf Rabatt *owf ra·bat* M5f
discouraged adj entmutigt *ent·moo·
  tikht*
discover vt entdecken *ent·de·kĕn*
discreet adj taktvoll *takt·fol*
discrimination n (*racial etc*) die Diskriminierung *dis·kri·mi·nee·roong*
discuss vt besprechen* *bĕ·shpre·khĕn*
disease n die Krankheit *krank·hite*
disguise n die Verkleidung *fer·klye·
  doong*; **in disguise** verkleidet *fer·
  klye·dĕt*
disgust n die Abscheu *ap·shoy*
disgusted adj angeekelt *an·gĕ·ay·kĕlt*
dish n die Schüssel *shōō·sĕl*; (*food*) das
  Gericht *gĕ·rikht* E20
dishcloth n der Spüllappen *shpōōl·la·
  pĕn*
dishonest adj unehrlich *oon·ayr·likh*
dishtowel n das Geschirrtuch *gĕ·shir·
  tookh*
dish up vt auf|tischen *owf·ti·shĕn*
dishwasher n die Geschirrspülmaschine *gĕ·shir·shpōōl·ma·shee·nĕ*
disinfect vt desinfizieren *des·in·fi·tsee·
  rĕn*
disinfectant n das Desinfektionsmittel
  des·in·fek·tsee·ōnz·mi·tĕl
disk n die Scheibe *shye·bĕ*; (*record*)
  die Schallplatte *shal·pla·tĕ*; **slipped
  disk** der Bandscheibenschaden *bant·
  shye·bĕn·sha·dĕn*
dislocate vt aus|kugeln *ows·koo·gĕln*
dismiss vt (*from job*) entlassen* *ent·la·
  sĕn*
disobedient adj ungehorsam *oon·gĕ·
  hor·zam*
dispatch vt ab|schicken *ap·shi·kĕn*
disposable adj Wegwerf- *vek·verf*
dispute vt (*fact*) bestreiten* *bĕ·shtrye·
  tĕn* □ n der Streit *shtrite*
disqualify vt disqualifizieren *dis·kva·li·
  fi·tsee·rĕn*
dissolve vt auf|lösen *owf·lur'·zĕn* □ vi
  sich auf|lösen *zikh owf·lur'·zĕn*
distance n die Entfernung *ent·fer·
  noong*; **in the distance** in der Ferne
  in der fer·nĕ
distant adj fern *fern*
distilled water n das destillierte Wasser *de·sti·leer·tĕ va·sĕr*
distillery n die Brennerei *bre·nĕ·rye*
distinct adj (*clear*) deutlich *doyt·likh*
distinguish vt unterscheiden* *oon·tĕr·
  shye·dĕn*
distract vt ab|lenken *ap·lenk·ĕn*
distress n die Qual *kvahl*; **a ship in distress** ein Schiff in Seenot *ine shif in
  zay·nōt*
distributor n (*in car*) der Verteiler *fer·
  tye·lĕr*; (*commercial*) der Großhändler *grōs·hent·lĕr*
district n (*of town*) der Stadtteil *shtat·
  tile*; (*in country*) die Gegend *gay·
  gĕnt*; (*administrative*) der Bezirk *bĕ·
  tsirk*
disturb vt (*interrupt*) stören *shtur'·rĕn*;
  do not disturb bitte nicht stören *bi·tĕ
  nikht shtur'·rĕn*
ditch n der Graben *grah·bĕn*
divan n der Diwan *dee·van*
dive vi tauchen *tow·khĕn* □ n der
  Kopfsprung *kopf·shproong*
diversify vt/i diversifizieren *dee·ver·
  see·fi·tsee·rĕn*
divert vt um|leiten *oom·lye·tĕn*

divide vt (separate) trennen tre·nèn;
(apportion) teilen tye·lèn; **to divide 8
by 4** 8 durch 4 teilen 8 doorkh 4 tye·
lèn

divided highway n die Schnellstraße
shnel·shtrah·sè

dividend n die Dividende di·vi·den·dè

divingboard n das Sprungbrett
shproong·bret

divorce n die Scheidung shye·doong

divorced adj geschieden ge·shee·dèn

dizzy adj (person) schwind(e)lig
shvind·likh

do vt/i tun* toon; **will it do?** (be
enough) reicht es? ryekht ess; (be
suitable) geht es? gayt ess; **you know
him, don't you?** Sie kennen ihn,
nicht wahr? zee ke·nèn een nikht
vahr; **he didn't come, did he?** er ist
nicht gekommen, oder? er ist nikht
gè·ko·mèn ō·dèr

dock n das Dock dok

doctor n der Arzt ahrtst, die Ärztin
erts·tin; **it's Doctor Smith** es ist der
Doktor Smith ess ist der dok·tor
Smith I8f

doctor's office n das Sprechzimmer
shprekh·tsi·mèr

document n das Dokument do·koo·
ment Bm24

dog n der Hund hoont

do-it-yourself n das Heimwerken
hime·ver·kèn

doll n die Puppe poo·pè

dollar n der Dollar do·lar

dollar bill n der Dollarschein do·lar·
shine

donate vt (funds) spenden shpen·dèn

donation n (money) die Spende shpen·
dè

done adj (meat) durch doorkh; (vegetables) gar gar

donkey n der Esel ay·zèl

door n die Tür töör Sn60

doorbell n die Türklingel töör·kling·èl

door handle, doorknob n die Türklinke töör·kling·kè

doorman n (in hotel) der Portier por·
tee·ay

doormat n die Fußmatte fōōs·ma·tè

doorstep n die Eingangsstufe ine·
gangs·shtoo·fè

door-to-door salesman n der Vertreter
fer·tray·tèr

dormitory n (room) der Schlafsaal
shlahf·zahl; (of college) das Wohnheim vōn·hime

dosage, dose n die Dosis dō·sis

dot n der Punkt poonkt

dotted line n die punktierte Linie
poonk·teer·tè lee·nee·è

double vt verdoppeln fer·do·pèln □ adv
to cost double doppelt soviel kosten
do·pèlt zō·feel ko·stèn □ adj double
doppelt do·pèlt

double bed n das Doppelbett do·pèl·
bet

double-parking n das Parken in der
zweiten Reihe par·kèn in der tsvye·
tèn rye·è

double room n das Doppelzimmer do·
pèl·tsi·mèr

doubt n der Zweifel tsvye·fèl; **no doubt**
zweifellos tsvye·fèl·lōs; **without (a)
doubt** ohne Zweifel ō·nè tsvye·fèl
□ vt **doubt** bezweifeln bè·tsvye·fèln; **I
doubt it** das bezweifle ich dass bè·
tsvye·flè ikh

doubtful adj zweifelhaft tsvye·fèl·haft

dough n der Teig tike

doughnut n der Berliner ber·lee·nèr

dove n die Taube tow·bè

down n (fluff) der Flaum flowm □ adv
to come down herunter|kommen*
her·oon·tèr·ko·mèn; **to go down** hin-
unter|gehen* hin·oon·tèr·gay·èn
□ prep **he came down the street** er
kam die Straße herunter er kahm dee
strah·sè her·oon·tèr; **he went down
the street** er ging die Straße hinunter
er ging dee strah·sè hin·oon·tèr

downhill adv bergab berk·ap

down payment n die Anzahlung an·
tsah·loong

downstairs adv (go) nach unten nakh
oon·tèn; (be) unten oon·tèn

downstream adv flußabwärts floos·ap·
verts

downtown adv ins Zentrum ins tsen·
troom □ adj **downtown Chicago** das
Zentrum von Chicago dass tsen·
troom fon shi·kah·gō

downward(s) adv nach unten nakh
oon·tèn

doze vi dösen dur'·zèn

dozen n das Dutzend doo·tsènd; **4
dozen eggs** 4 Dutzend Eier 4 doo·
tsènt eye·èr

drab adj düster dōō·stèr

draft n (wind) der Zug tsook; (financial) der Wechsel vek·sèl; (rough
outline) der Entwurf ent·voorf

draft beer n das Faßbier fahs·beer

draftsman n der Zeichner tsyekh·nèr

drag vt schleppen shle·pèn

drain n der Abfluß ap·floos □ vt (land)
drainieren dray·nee·rèn; (vegetables)
ab|gießen* ap·gee·sèn; (sump, pool)
ab|lassen* ap·la·sèn

drainboard n der Ablauf ap·lowf

drainpipe n das Abflußrohr ap·flooss·
rōr

drama n (art) das Drama drah·ma

dramatic adj dramatisch dra·mah·tish

drape n der Vorhang for·hang

drastic adj drastisch dra·stish

draw vt (picture) zeichnen tsyekh·nèn;
to draw out (money) ab|heben* ap·
hay·bèn; **to draw up** (document)
auf|setzen owf·ze·tsen

drawer n die Schublade shoop·lah·dè

drawing n die Zeichnung tsyekh·noong

drawing pin n die Reißzwecke rice·
tsve·kè

dread vt sich fürchten vor zikh föörkh·
tèn for

dream n der Traum trowm □ vi träumen troy·mèn; **to dream of** or **about**
träumen von troy·mèn fon

dress n das Kleid klite □ vt (child) an|-
ziehen* an·tsee·èn □ vi (oneself) sich
kleiden zikh klye·dèn; **to dress for
dinner** sich zum Essen um|ziehen*
zikh tsoom e·sèn oom·tsee·èn S62

dress circle n der erste Rang er·stè
rang

dressing n (salad) die Soße zō·sè; (stuffing) die Füllung fōō·loong

dressing gown n der Morgenrock mor·
gèn·rok

dressing table n der Toilettentisch twa·
le·tèn·tish

dried adj (fruit, beans) getrocknet gè·
trok·nèt; **dried milk** das Milchpulver
milkh·pool·vèr

drift vi (boat) treiben* trye·bèn

drill n (tool) der Bohrer bō·rèr □ vt
(hole) bohren bō·rèn

drink vt trinken* tring·kèn □ n das Getränk gè·trenk; **have a drink!** trinken
Sie doch etwas! tring·kèn zee dokh
et·vass L53

drinking water n das Trinkwasser *trink·vass·èr* A92

drip n der Tropfen *trop·fèn* □ vi tropfen *trop·fèn*

drip-dry vt tropfnaß auf|hängen *tropfnass·owf·heng·èn* □ adj (shirt etc) bügelfrei *bōō·gèl·frye*

drive vt/i fahren* *fah·rèn*; do you drive? können Sie Auto fahren? *kur'n·èn zee ow·tō fah·rèn*; to drive to town mit dem Auto in die Stadt fahren* *mit daym ow·tō in dee shtat fah·rèn* □ n drive (journey) die Fahrt *fart*; (driveway) die Einfahrt *ine·fart*; to go for a drive ein bißchen fahren* *ine bis·khèn fah·rèn*; left-hand drive die Linkssteuerung *links·shtoy·èr·oong*; front-wheel drive der Vorderradantrieb *for·dèr·rat·an·treep*

driver n (of car) der Fahrer *fah·rèr*, die Fahrerin *fah·rè·rin*

driver's license n der Führerschein *fōō·rèr·shine* T11

drizzle n der Nieselregen *nee·zèl·ray·gèn*

drop n (of liquid) der Tropfen *trop·fèn* □ vt (let fall) fallen lassen* *fa·lèn la·sèn* □ vi (fall) fallen* *fa·lèn*

drought n die Dürre *dōō·rè*

drown vi ertrinken* *er·tring·kèn*

drug n (medicine) das Medikament *me·di·ka·ment*; (narcotic) die Droge *drō·gè* I46

druggist n der Drogist *dro·gist*

drugstore n der Drugstore *drug·store*

drum n die Trommel *tro·mèl*

drumstick n (of chicken) die Keule *koy·lè*

drunk adj betrunken *bè·troong·kèn*

dry adj trocken *tro·kèn* □ vt trocknen *trok·nèn*

dry-clean vt chemisch reinigen *khay·mish rye·ni·gèn* S90

dry-cleaner's n die chemische Reinigung *khay·mi·shè rye·ni·goong*

duck n die Ente *en·tè*

due adj (owing) fällig *fe·likh*; when is the train due? wann soll der Zug ankommen? *van zol der tsook an·ko·mèn*

duke n der Herzog *her·tsōk*

dull adj (day, weather) trüb *trōōp*; (boring) langweilig *lang·vye·likh*

dumb adj stumm *shtoom*; (stupid) dumm *doom*

dump n (for rubbish) der Müllplatz *mōōl·plats*

dumping n (of goods) das Dumping *dam·ping*

dumpling n der Kloß *klōs*

dune n die Düne *dōō·nè*

dungarees pl die Latzhosen (pl) *lats·hō·zèn*

dungeon n das Verlies *fer·lees*

durable adj (fabric, article) haltbar *halt·bar*

during prep während *ve·rènt*

dusk n die Abenddämmerung *ah·bènt·de·mè·roong*

dust n der Staub *shtowp* □ vt (furniture) ab|stauben *ap·shtow·bèn*

dustpan n die Kehrschaufel *kayr·show·fèl*

dusty adj staubig *shtow·bikh*

Dutch adj holländisch *ho·len·dish*; he's Dutch er ist Holländer *er ist ho·len·dèr*; she's Dutch sie ist Holländerin *zee ist ho·len·dè·rin* □ n Dutch Holländisch (nt) *ho·len·dish*

duty n (obligation) die Pflicht *pflikht*; (function) die Aufgabe *owf·gah·bè*;

(tax) der Zoll *tsol*; on duty (doctor) im Dienst *im deenst*; off duty nicht im Dienst *nikht im deenst*

duty-free adj (goods) zollfrei *tsol·frye*; (shop) duty-free *dyoo·tee free* T42, S8

dye n der Farbstoff *farp·shtof* □ vt färben *fer·bèn*

dynamic adj (person) dynamisch *dōō·nah·mish*

dynamo n der Dynamo *dōō·na·mō*

E

each adj, pron jede(r/s) *yay·dè(·dèr/·dès)*

eager adj eifrig *eye·frikh*; to be eager to do something darauf erpicht sein*, etwas zu tun *da·rowf er·pikht zine et·vass tsoo toon*

eagle n der Adler *aht·lèr*

ear n das Ohr *ōr*

earache n die Ohrenschmerzen (pl) *ō·rèn·shmer·tsèn*; to have an earache Ohrenschmerzen haben* *ō·rèn·shmer·tsèn hah·bèn*

earlier adj, adv früher *frōō·èr*

early adj, adv früh *frōō*; you're early Sie sind früh dran *zee zint frōō dran*; the early train der erste Zug *der er·stè tsook*

earn vt verdienen *fer·dee·nèn*

earnings pl die Bezüge (pl) *bè·tsōō·gè*

earplugs pl die Ohrwatten (pl) *ōr·va·tèn*

earring n der Ohrring *ōr·ring*

earth n die Erde *er·dè*

earthquake n das Erdbeben *ert·bay·bèn*

ease vt (pain) beruhigen *bè·roo·i·gèn*

easily adv leicht *lyekht*

east n der Osten *os·tèn* □ adv nach Osten *nakh os·tèn*

Easter n Ostern (nt) *ōs·tèrn*; at Easter zu Ostern *tsoo ōs·tèrn*

Easter egg n das Osterei *ōs·tèr·eye*

eastern adj östlich *ur'st·likh*

East Germany n die DDR *day·day·er*

easy adj leicht *lyekht*

eat vt essen* *e·sèn*

eau-de-Cologne n das Kölnisch Wasser *kur'l·nish va·sèr*

eccentric adj exzentrisch *eks·tsen·trish*

echo n das Echo *e·khō*

éclair n das Eclair *ay·kler*

economic adj wirtschaftlich *virt·shaft·likh*

economical adj (use, method) wirtschaftlich *virt·shaft·likh*

economics n die Volkswirtschaft *folks·virt·shaft*

economist n der Volkswirtschaftler *folks·virt·shaft·lèr*

economy n (of country) die Wirtschaft *virt·shaft*

eczema n das Ekzem *ek·tsaym*

edge n der Rand *rant*; (of blade) die Schneide *shnye·dè*

edition n die Auflage *owf·lah·gè*

educate vt erziehen* *er·tsee·èn*

education n die Erziehung *er·tsee·oong*

E.E.C. n die EG *ay·gay*

eels pl die Aale (pl) *ah·lè*

effect n die Wirkung *vir·koong*; to take effect wirksam werden* *virk·zahm ver·dèn*

effective adj (remedy etc) wirksam *virk·zahm*

efficient adj tüchtig *tōōkh·tikh*

effort n die Mühe *mōō·è*

e.g.

e.g. *abbrev* z.B. *tsoom bye·shpeel*
egg *n* das Ei *eye* S34
egg cup *n* der Eierbecher *eye·èr·be·khèr*
eggplant *n* die Aubergine *ō·ber·zhee·ne*
Egypt *n* Ägypten (*nt*) *e·gōōp·tèn*
Egyptian *adj* ägyptisch *e·gōōp·tish*
eiderdown *n* das Federbett *fay·der·bet*
eight *num* acht *akht*
eighteen *num* achtzehn *akh·tsayn*
eighth *adj* achte(r/s) *akh·tè(·tèr/·tès)*
eighties *pl* (*decade*) die achtziger Jahre *dee akh·tsi·gèr yah·rè*
eighty *num* achtzig *akh·tsikh*
either *pron* □ either of you eine(r) von Ihnen *ine·è(r) fon ee·nèn*; which one? - either welcher? - das ist egal *vel·khèr - dass is ay·gahl* □ *adj* on either side auf beiden Seiten *owf bye·dèn zye·tèn* □ *conj* either ... or ... entweder ... oder ... *ent·vay·dèr ... ō·dèr ...*
elaborate *adj* kompliziert *kom·pli·tseert*
elastic *n* der Gummi *goo·mi*
elastic band *n* das Gummiband *goo·mi·bant*
elbow *n* der Ellbogen *el·bō·gèn*
elder *adj* ältere(r/s) *el·tè·rè(·rèr/·rès)*
eldest *adj* älteste(r/s) *el·tè·stè(·stèr/·stès)*
elect *vt* wählen *vay·lèn*
election *n* die Wahl *vahl*
electric(al) *adj* elektrisch *ay·lek·trish*
electric blanket *n* die Heizdecke *hites·de·kè*
electrician *n* der Elektriker *ay·lek·tri·kèr*
electricity *n* die Elektrizität *ay·lek·tri·tsi·tet*
electronic *adj* elektronisch *ay·lek·trō·nish*
electronics *n* die Elektronik *ay·lek·trō·nik*
elegant *adj* elegant *ay·lay·gant*
element *n* das Element *ay·lay·ment*
elephant *n* der Elefant *ay·lay·fant*
elevator *n* der Lift *lift* A30
eleven *num* elf *elf*
eleventh *adj* elfte(r/s) *elf·tè(·tèr/·tès)*
elm *n* die Ulme *ool·mè*
else *adj* □ somewhere else anderswo *an·dèrs·vō*; someone else jemand anders *yay·mant an·dèrs*
embankment *n* die Böschung *bur·shoong*
embargo *n* das Embargo *em·bar·gō*
embark *vi* sich ein|schiffen *zikh ine·shi·fèn*
embarrassed *adj* verlegen *fer·lay·gèn*
embassy *n* die Botschaft *bōt·shaft*
embrace *vt* umarmen *oom·ar·mèn*
embroidered *adj* bestickt *bè·shtikt*
embroidery *n* die Stickerei *shti·kè·rye*
emerald *n* der Smaragd *sma·rakt*
emergency *n* der Notfall *nōt·fal* Ea9
emergency exit *n* der Notausgang *nōt·ows·gang*
emergency landing *n* die Notlandung *nōt·lan·doong*
emery board *n* die Nagelfeile *nah·gèl·file·è*
emigrate *vi* aus|wandern *ows·van·dèrn*
emotion *n* das Gefühl *gè·fōōl*
emotional *adj* (*person*) emotional *ay·mō·tsee·ō·nahl*
emperor *n* der Kaiser *kye·zèr*
emphasis *n* die Betonung *bè·tō·noong*
emphasize *vt* betonen *bè·tō·nèn*
empire *n* das Reich *ryekh*

employ *vt* (*worker*) beschäftigen *bè·shef·ti·gèn*
employee *n* der/die Angestellte *an·gè·shtel·tè*
employer *n* der Arbeitgeber *ar·bite·gay·bèr*
employment *n* die Arbeit *ar·bite*
empty *adj* leer *layr* □ *vt* leeren *lay·rèn*
enamel *n* die Email *ay·mye*
enclosure *n* (*in letter*) die Anlage *an·lah·gè*
encore *n* die Zugabe *tsoo·gah·bè*; en-core! Zugabe! *tsoo·gah·bè*
encyclop(a)edia *n* die Enzyklopädie *ent·sōō·klō·pe·dee*
end *n* das Ende *en·dè* □ *vt* beenden *bè·en·dèn* □ *vi* enden *en·dèn*
endive *n* (*smooth*) das Chicorée *shi·ko·ray*; (*curly*) der Endiviensalat *en·dee·vee·èn·za·laht*
endorse *vt* (*document*) indossieren *in·do·see·rèn*
enemy *n* der Feind *fyent*
energetic *adj* aktiv *ak·teef*
energy *n* die Energie *ay·ner·gee*
engaged *adj* (*betrothed*) verlobt *fer·lōpt*; (*busy*) beschäftigt *bè·shef·tikht*
engagement *n* (*betrothal*) die Verlobung *fer·lō·boong*
engagement ring *n* der Verlobungsring *fer·lō·boonks·ring*
engine *n* (*motor*) der Motor *mō·tōr*; (*of train*) die Lokomotive *lō·kō·mō·tee·vè* T170
engineer *n* der Ingenieur *in·zhay·nyur*
England *n* England (*nt*) *eng·glant*
English *adj* englisch *eng·glish*; he's English er ist Engländer *er ist eng·glen·dèr*; she's English sie ist Engländerin *zee ist eng·glen·dè·rin* □ *n* English Englisch (*nt*) *eng·glish*; in English auf englisch *owf eng·glish*
enjoy *vt* (*concert, outing*) genießen* *gè·nee·sèn*; to enjoy oneself sich amüsieren *zikh a·mōō·zee·rèn*
enjoyment *n* das Vergnügen *fer·gnōō·gèn*
enlarge *vt* vergrössern *fer·grur·sèrn*
enormous *adj* enorm *ay·norm*
enough *pron, adj* genug *gè·nook* S41
ensemble *n* (*clothes*) das Ensemble *on·som·bèl*
enter *n* (*room*) ein|treten* in *ine·tray·tèn in* □ *vi* ein|treten* *ine·tray·tèn*
enterprise *n* das Unternehmen *oon·tèr·nay·mèn*; private enterprise das Privatunternehmertum *pree·vaht·oon·tèr·nay·mèr·toom*
entertain *vt* (*amuse*) unterhalten* *oon·tèr·hal·tèn*; (*give hospitality*) zu Gast haben* *tsoo gast hah·bèn*
entertainment *n* (*show*) die Unterhaltung *oon·tèr·hal·toong*
enthusiasm *n* die Begeisterung *bè·gye·stè·roong*
enthusiastic *adj* begeistert *bè·gye·stèrt*
entrance *n* (*way in*) der Eingang *ine·gang*
entrance fee *n* das Eintrittsgeld *ine·trits·gelt*
entrée *n* das Hauptgericht *howpt·gè·rikht*
entry *n* (*way in*) der Eingang *ine·gang*
envelope *n* der Umschlag *oom·shlahk* S99
envious *adj* neidisch *nye·dish*
environment *n* die Umwelt *oom·velt*
envy *vt* beneiden *bè·nye·dèn* □ *n* der Neid *nite*
epidemic *n* die Epidemie *ay·pee·day·mee*

epilepsy n die Epilepsie *ay·pee·lep·see*
equal adj gleich *glyekh*
equator n der Äquator *e·kvah·tor*
equipment n die Ausrüstung *ows·rōōs·toong* L34
equivalent adj gleichwertig *glyekh·ver·tikh*; **equivalent to** entsprechend *ent·shpre·khènt*
erase vt aus|radieren *ows·ra·dee·rèn*
eraser n der Radiergummi *ra·deer·goo·mi*
ermine n (fur) der Hermelin *her·mè·leen*
erotic adj erotisch *ay·rō·tish*
errand n die Besorgung *bè·zor·goong*; **to do** or **run an errand** eine Besorgung machen *ine·è bè·zor·goong ma·khèn*
error n der Fehler *fay·lèr*; **in error** aus Versehen *ows fer·zay·èn*
escalator n die Rolltreppe *rol·tre·pè*
escalope n das Schnitzel *shnit·sèl*
escape vi (person) entkommen* *ent·ko·mèn*; (liquid, gas) aus|strömen *ows·shtrur'·mèn*
escort vt begleiten *bè·glye·tèn* □ n der Begleiter *bè·glye·tèr*
especially adv besonders *bè·zon·dèrs*
Esperanto n Esperanto (nt) *es·pay·ran·tō*
espresso (coffee) n der Espresso *es·pre·sō*
essay n der Essay *e·say*
essential adj (necessary) notwendig *nōt·ven·dikh*
establish vt gründen *grōōn·dèn*
estate n (property) der Besitz *bè·zits*
estimate vt schätzen *shet·sèn* □ n der Kostenvoranschlag *kos·tèn·fōr·an·shlahk* M8, Bm25
etc abbrev usw *oont zō vye·tèr*
ethical adj ethisch *ay·tish*
ethnic adj ethnisch *ayt·nish*
etiquette n die Etikette *ay·ti·ke·tè*
Europe n Europa (nt) *oy·rō·pa*
European adj europäisch *oy·rō·pay·ish*
evaporate vi verdampfen *fer·damp·fèn*
evaporated milk n die Kondensmilch *kon·dens·milkh*
even adj (level) eben *ay·bèn*; (equally matched) gleich *glyekh*; **an even number** eine gerade Zahl *ine·è gè·rah·dè tsahl* □ adv **even faster** sogar noch schneller *zō·gar nokh shne·lèr*; **even a child** could so ist sogar ein Kind könnte das *zō·gar ine kint kur'n·tè dass*; **even so** trotzdem *trots·daym*
evening n der Abend *ah·bènt*; **in the evening** am Abend *am ah·bènt* F23
evening dress n (woman's) das Abendkleid *ah·bènt·klite*; (man's) der Abendanzug *ah·bènt·an·tsook* S63
evening paper n die Abendzeitung *ah·bènt·tsye·toong*
event n das Ereignis *er·ige·nis*
eventually adv schließlich *shlees·likh*
ever adv jemals *yay·mals*; **have you ever been to London?** sind Sie schon einmal in London gewesen? *zint zee shōn ine·mahl in lon·don gè·vay·zèn*; **ever since he...** seit er... *zite er*; **he's been there ever since** seitdem ist er da *zite·daym ist er da*
every adj jede(r/s) *yay·dè(·dèr/·dès)*; **every other day** alle zwei Tage *a·lè tsvye tah·gè*; **every 6th day** alle sechs Tage *a·lè zeks tah·gè*
everybody, everyone pron alle *a·lè*
everything pron alles *a·lès*
everywhere adv überall *ōō·bèr·al*

evidence n (proof) die Beweise (pl) *bè·vye·zè*; (of witness) die Zeugenaussage *tsoy·gèn·ows·zah·gè*
evil adj böse *bur'·zè*
evolution n die Evolution *ay·vō·loo·tsee·ōn*
ex- pref ehemalig *ay·è·mah·likh*
exact adj genau *gè·now*
exactly adv genau *gè·now*
exaggerate vt/i übertreiben* *ōō·bèr·trye·bèn*
exaggeration n die Übertreibung *ōō·bèr·trye·boong*
examination n (exam) die Prüfung *prōō·foong*; (inspection, also medical) die Untersuchung *oon·tèr·zoo·khoong*
examine vt (inspect) untersuchen *oon·tèr·zoo·khèn*
example n das Beispiel *bye·shpeel*; **for example** zum Beispiel *tsoom bye·shpeel*
exceed vt überschreiten* *ōō·bèr·shrye·tèn*
excellent adj ausgezeichnet *ows·gè·tsyekh·nèt*
except (for), except(ing) prep außer *ow·sèr*
exception n die Ausnahme *ows·nah·mè*
exceptional adj außergewöhnlich *ow·sèr·gè·wur'n·likh*
excess n der Überschuß *ōō·bèr·shoos*
excess baggage n das Übergewicht *ōō·bèr·gè·vikht*
exchange vt tauschen *tow·shèn*; **to exchange something for something** etwas gegen etwas aus|tauschen *et·vass gay·gèn et·vass ows·tow·shèn* □ n exchange (between currencies) der Wechsel *vek·sèl*; (telephone) das Fernamt *fern·amt*
exchange rate n der Wechselkurs *vek·sèl·koors* M25
excise duties pl die Verbrauchssteuern (pl) *fer·browkhs·shtoy·èrn*
excited adj aufgeregt *owf·gè·raykt*
excitement n die Aufregung *owf·ray·goong*
exciting adj aufregend *owf·ray·gènt*
exclaim vi aus|rufen* *ows·roo·fèn*
exclude vt aus|schließen* *ows·shlee·sèn*
exclusive adj (club, shop) exklusiv *eks·kloo·zeef*; **exclusive rights** die Alleinrechte (pl) *eks·klōō·zeef·rekh·tè*; **exclusive of...** ausschließlich... *ows·shlees·likh*
excursion n der Ausflug *ows·flook*; **to go on an excursion** einen Ausflug machen *ine·èn ows·flook ma·khèn* L6
excuse vt entschuldigen *ent·shool·di·gèn*; **excuse me** Entschuldigung *ent·shool·di·goong* □ n **excuse** (pretext) die Ausrede *ows·ray·dè* L1
execute vt (kill) hin|richten *hin·rikh·tèn*
executive n der Geschäftsführer *gè·shefts·fōō·rèr*
exercise n (movement) Bewegung (f) *bè·vay·goong*; (written) die Übung *ōō·boong*
exercise book n das Heft *heft*
exhaust n (fumes) die Abgase (pl) *ap·gah·zè*; (pipe) der Auspuff *ows·poof*
exhausted adj erschöpft *er·shur'pft*
exhibition n die Ausstellung *ows·shte·loong*
exist vi existieren *ek·sis·tee·rèn*
existence n die Existenz *ek·sis·tents*
exit n der Ausgang *ows·gang*

exit permit n die Ausreisegenehmigung *ows·rye·zè·gè·nay·mi·goong*

exotic adj exotisch *ek·sô·tish*

expand vt (material) dehnen *day·nèn*; (business) vergrößern *fer·grur'·sèrn* □ vi (material) sich aus|dehnen *zikh ows·day·nèn*; (business) wachsen* *vak·sèn*

expect vt (anticipate) erwarten *er·var·tèn*; I expect he'll come er wird sicher kommen *er virt zi·khèr ko·mèn*; I expect so ich glaube schon *ikh glow·bè shôn*; she's expecting a baby sie erwartet ein Kind *zee er·var·tet in kint*

expedition n die Expedition *ek·spay·dee·tsee·ôn*

expenditure n die Ausgaben (pl) *ows·gah·bèn*

expense n (cost) die Kosten (pl) *kos·tèn*; expenses die Spesen (pl) *shpay·zèn*

expense account n das Spesenkonto *shpay·zèn·kon·tô*

expensive adj teuer *toy·èr*

experience n (event) das Erlebnis *er·layp·nis*; (skill, knowledge) die Erfahrung *er·fah·roong*

experienced adj erfahren *er·fah·rèn*

experiment n das Experiment *ek·spe·ri·ment*

expert n der Fachmann *fakh·man*

expire vi ab|laufen* *ap·low·fèn*

explain vt erklären *er·kle·rèn*

explanation n die Erklärung *er·kle·roong*

explode vi explodieren *ek·splô·dee·rèn*

explore vt erforschen *er·for·shèn*

explosion n die Explosion *ek·splô·zee·ôn*

export n die Ausfuhr *ows·foor* □ vt aus|führen *ows·füü·rèn*

exporter n der Exporteur *ek·spor·tur*

express vt aus|drücken *ows·drük·èn* □ adv to send something express etwas per Expreß schicken *et·vass per ek·spres shi·kèn*

expression n der Ausdruck *ows·drook*

express letter n der Eilbrief *ile·breef*

express train n der Schnellzug *shnel·tsook*

expressway n die Schnellstraße *shnel·shtrah·sè*

extension n (building) der Anbau *an·bow*; (phone) der Nebenanschluß *nay·bèn·an·shloos*

exterior, external adj äußere(r/s) *oy·sè·rè(·rèr/·rès)*

extra adj zusätzlich *tsoo·zets·likh*; postage zuzüglich Porto *tsoo·tsöök·likh por·tô* □ adv extra besonders *bè·zon·dèrs*

extraordinary adj außerordentlich *ow·sèr·or·dènt·likh*

extravagant adj extravagant *ek·stra·va·gant*

extremely adv äußerst *oy·serst*

eye n das Auge *ow·gè*

eyebrow n die Augenbraue *ow·gèn·brow·è*

eyeglasses pl die Brille *bri·lè*

eyelash n die Augenwimper *ow·gèn·vim·pèr*

eyelid n das Augenlid *ow·gèn·leet*

eyeliner n der Eyeliner *eye·line·èr*

eyeshadow n der Lidschatten *leet·sha·tèn*

eyesight n die Sehkraft *zay·kraft*

F

fabric n der Stoff *shtof* Sn67

face n das Gesicht *gè·zikht*

face card n die Bildkarte *bilt·kar·tè*

facecloth n der Waschlappen *vash·la·pèn*

face cream n die Gesichtscreme *gè·zikhts·kraym*

facilities pl die Einrichtungen (pl) *ine·rikh·toong·èn*

facing prep gegenüber *gay·gèn·öö·bèr*

fact n die Tatsache *taht·za·khè*; in fact tatsächlich *taht·zekh·likh*

factor n der Faktor *fak·tor*

factory n die Fabrik *fa·breek*

faculty n (university) die Fakultät *fa·kool·tet*

fade vi schwächer werden* *shve·khèr ver·dèn*; (color) verblassen *fer·bla·sèn*

Fahrenheit adj Fahrenheit *fah·rèn·hite*

fail vi (person) keinen Erfolg haben* *kye·nèn er·folk hah·bèn*; (plan) fehl|schlagen* *fayl·shlah·gèn*; (brakes) versagen *fer·zah·gèn* □ vt (exam) durch|fallen* in *doorkh·fa·lèn in* □ n without fail auf jeden Fall *owf yay·dèn fal*

failure n der Fehlschlag *fayl·shlahk*; (person) der Versager *fer·zah·gèr*; (mechanical) der Ausfall *ows·fal*; (of brakes) das Versagen *fer·zah·gèn*

faint vi in Ohnmacht fallen* *in ôn·makht fa·lèn* □ adj (sound etc) leise *lye·zè*; I feel faint mir ist schwach *meer ist shvakh*

fair adj (just) gerecht *gè·rekht*; (hair) blond *blont*; (average) ziemlich gut *tseem·likh goot* □ adv to play fair fair spielen *fayr shpee·lèn* □ n fair (commercial) die Messe *me·sè*

fairground n der Rummelplatz *roo·mèl·plats*

fairly adv (rather) ziemlich *tseem·likh*

fairy n die Fee *fay*

faith n (in person) das Vertrauen *fer·trow·èn*; (religious) der Glaube *glow·bè*

faithfully adv □ yours faithfully hochachtungsvoll *hôkh·akh·toongs·fol*

fake adj unecht *oon·ekht*

fall vi (person) fallen* *fa·lèn*; (prices etc) sinken* *zing·kèn*; to fall down hin|fallen* *hin·fa·lèn*; to fall in love sich verlieben *zikh fer·lee·bèn* □ n fall der Fall *fal*; (decrease) das Sinken *zing·kèn*; (season) der Herbst *herpst*

false adj (name etc) falsch *falsh*; false teeth das Gebiß *gè·bis*

familiar adj (impertinent) familiär *fa·mee·lee·er*; to be familiar with something mit etwas vertraut sein* *mit et·vass fer·trowt zine*

family n die Familie *fa·meel·yè*

famous adj berühmt *bè·röömt*

fan n (folding) der Fächer *fè·khèr*; (electric, in car) der Ventilator *ven·tee·lah·tor*; (supporter) der Fan *fen*

fanbelt n der Keilriemen *kile·ree·mèn*

fancy adj schick *shik*

fancy dress n das Kostüm *kos·tööm*

far adj weit *vite*; (much) bei weitem *bye vye·tèm*; how far is it to...? wie weit ist es nach...? *vee vite ist ess nakh*; as far as the station bis zum Bahnhof *bis tsoom bahn·hôf*; as far as I know soweit ich weiß *zo·vite ikh vice*; the Far East der Ferne Osten *fer·nè os·tèn*

farce n die Farce *far·sè*

fare n der Fahrpreis *fahr·price*

farm n der Bauernhof *bow·èrn·hôf*

farmer *n* der Bauer *bow·èr*

farmyard *n* der Bauernhof *bow·èrn·hôf*

farsighted *adj* weitsichtig *vīte·zikh·tikh*

farther *adv* weiter *vye·tèr*

farthest *adv* am weitesten *am vye·tè·stèn*

fascinating *adj* faszinierend *fas·tsee·nee·rènt*

fashion *n* die Mode *mō·dè*

fashionable *adj* modisch *mō·dish*

fast *adj, adv* schnell *shnel*; *(dye)* farbecht *farp·ekht*; my watch is fast meine Uhr geht vor *mine·è oor gayt fōr*; to be fast asleep fest schlafen* *fest shla·fèn*

fasten *vt* befestigen *bè·fes·ti·gèn*; fasten seat belts bitte anschnallen *bi·tè an·shna·lèn*

fat *adj (person)* dick *dik* □ *n* das Fett *fet*

fatal *adj* tödlich *tur't·likh*

father *n* der Vater *fah·tèr*; yes, Father *(priest)* ja, Herr Pfarrer *yah her pfa·rèr*

father-in-law *n* der Schwiegervater *shvee·gèr·fah·tèr*

faucet *n* der Hahn *hahn*

fault *n (defect)* der Fehler *fay·lèr*; *(blame)* die Schuld *shoolt*; whose fault is it? wer ist schuld daran? *ver ist shoolt da·ran*

faulty *adj* fehlerhaft *fay·lèr·haft*

favor *n* der Gefallen *gè·fa·lèn*; to do someone a favor jemandem einen Gefallen tun* *yay·man·dèm ine·èn gè·fa·lèn toon*; I'm not in favor of that idea ich halte nichts von der Idee *ikh hal·tè nikhts fon dèr ee·day*

favorite *adj* Lieblings- *leep·lings*

fawn *adj* beige *baysh*

fear *f* die Angst *angst*

feasibility *n* die Machbarkeit *makh·bahr·kīte*

feasibility study *n* die Machbarkeitsstudie *makh·bahr·kītes·shtoo·dee·è*

feast *n* das Festmahl *fest·mahl*

feather *n* die Feder *fay·dèr*

feature film *n* der Spielfilm *shpeel·film*

features *pl* die Züge *(pl)* *tsöö·gè*

February *n* Februar *(m)* *fay·broo·ar*

federal *adj* Bundes- *boon·dès*

fed up *adj* □ I'm fed up ich habe es satt *ikh hah·bè es zat*

fee *n* das Honorar *hô·nô·rahr*

feed *vt* ernähren *er·ne·rèn* □ *vi* essen* *e·sèn*

feedback *n* das Feedback *feed·bak*

feel *vt (touch)* fühlen *fōō·lèn*; I feel that... ich glaube daß... *ikh glow·bè dass* □ *vi* it feels soft es fühlt sich weich an *ess fōōlt zikh vyekh an*; I feel hungry ich habe Hunger *ikh hah·bè hoong·èr*; I feel better es geht mir besser *ess gayt meer be·sèr*; I feel like a beer ich habe Lust auf ein Bier *ikh hah·bè loost owf īne beer*

feeling *n* das Gefühl *gè·fōōl*

fellow *n* der Bursche *boor·shè*; fellow countryman der Landsmann *lants·man*

felt *n (cloth)* der Filz *filts*

felt-tip pen *n* der Filzstift *filts·shtift*

female *adj* weiblich *vipe·likh*

feminine *adj* feminin *fe·mee·neen*

fence *n* der Zaun *tsown*

fender *n (on car)* der Kotflügel *kōt·flōō·gèl*

fern *n* der Farn *farn*

ferry *n* die Fähre *fe·rè*

fertile *adj (land)* fruchtbar *frookht·bahr*

festival *n* das Festival *fes·tee·val*

fetch *vt* holen *hô·lèn*

fête *n* das Fest *fest*

fever *n* das Fieber *fee·bèr*

few *adj* wenige *vay·ni·gè*; a few books einige Bücher *ine·i·gè bōō·khèr* □ pron there are very few es gibt nur wenige *ess gipt noor vay·ni·gè*; there are quite a few es gibt ziemlich viele *ess gipt tseem·likh fee·lè*

fiancé(e) *n* der/die Verlobte *fer·lōp·tè*

fiber *n* die Faser *fah·zèr* S67

fiberglass *n* das Fiberglas *fee·bèr·glahs*

fiction *n* Romane *(pl)* rô·mah·nè

field *n* das Feld *felt*; *(for football etc)* der Platz *plats*

field glasses *pl* der Feldstecher *felt·shte·khèr*

fierce *adj* wild *vilt*

fifteen *num* fünfzehn *fōōnf·tsayn*

fifth *adj* fünfte *(r/s)* *fōōnf·tè(·tèr/·tès)*

fifty *num* fünfzig *fōōnf·tsikh*

fig *n* die Feige *fye·gè*

fight *vi* kämpfen *kemp·fèn* □ *n* der Kampf *kampf*

figure *n (of human)* die Gestalt *gè·shtalt*; *(number)* die Ziffer *tsi·fèr*; to have a nice figure eine gute Figur haben* *ine·è goo·tè fi·goor hah·bèn* □ *vt* **figure** *(suppose)* schätzen *shet·sèn*

file *n (tool)* die Feile *file·è*; *(dossier)* die Akte *ak·tè*

filing cabinet *n* der Aktenschrank *ak·tèn·shrank*

fill *vt* füllen *fōō·lèn*; to fill in/out *(form)* aus|füllen *ows·fōō·lèn*; to fill up *(cup)* füllen *fōō·lèn*; fill it up! *(car)* volltanken bitte! *fol·tang·kèn bi·tè*

fillet *n (of meat, fish)* das Filet *fee·lay*

filling *n (of food)* sättigend *ze·ti·gènt* □ *n (in tooth)* die Plombe *plom·bè* I61

filling station *n* die Tankstelle *tank·shte·lè*

film *n* der Film *film* L43, S50f

filter *n* der Filter *fil·tèr* S103

filter-tip *adj (cigarettes)* Filter- *fil·tèr*

final *adj* letzte *(r/s)* *let·stè(·stèr/·stès)*

finally *adv* schließlich *shlees·likh*

finals *pl (sports)* das Finale *fee·nah·lè*

finance *n* die Finanzen *(pl)* *fee·nant·sèn* □ *vt* finanzieren *fee·nant·see·rèn*

Finance Minister *n* der Finanzminister *fee·nants·mi·ni·stèr*

financial *adj* finanziell *fee·nant·see·el*

find *vt* finden* *fin·dèn*; to find out heraus|finden* *he·rows·fin·dèn*

fine *adj (delicate)* fein *fine*; *(weather)* schön *shur'n*; (that's) fine! sehr gut! *zayr goot* □ *n* die Geldstrafe *gelt·shtrah·fè*

finger *n* der Finger *fing·èr*

finish *vt* erledigen *er·lay·di·gèn* □ *vi* auf|hören *owf·hur'·rèn*

Finland *n* Finnland *(nt)* *fin·lant*

Finnish *adj* finnisch *fi·nish* □ *n* Finnisch *(nt)* *fi·nish*

fire *n* das Feuer *foy·èr*; *(accident)* der Brand *brant*; the house is on fire das Haus brennt *dass hows brent*; to set fire to in Brand stecken *in brant shte·kèn* □ *vt* to fire a gun ein Gewehr ab|schießen* *īne gè·vayr ap·shee·sèn*; to fire someone *(dismiss)* jemanden entlassen* *yay·man·dèn ent·la·sèn* Ea5

fire alarm *n* der Feueralarm *foy·èr·a·larm*

firearm *n* die Schußwaffe *shoos·va·fè*

fire department n die Feuerwehr *foy·ėr·vayr* Ea8

fire engine n das Feuerwehrauto *foy·ėr·vayr·ow·tŏ*

fire escape n die Feuertreppe *foy·ėr·tre·pė*

fire extinguisher n der Feuerlöscher *foy·ėr·lur'·shėr*

fireman n der Feuerwehrmann *foy·ėr·vayr·man*

fireplace n der Kamin *ka·meen*

fire station n die Feuerwache *foy·ėr·va·khė*

fireworks pl das Feuerwerk *foy·ėr·verk*

firm n die Firma *fïr·ma* □ adj (object, material) fest *fest*; (person) entschlossen *ent·shlo·sėn* Bm17, 19

first adj erste(r/s) *er·stė(·stėr/·stės)* □ adv zuerst *tsoo·erst*; in first (gear) im ersten Gang *im er·stėn gang*; at first zuerst *tsoo·erst*

first aid n die Erste Hilfe *er·stė hil·fė*

first-aid kit n die Erste-Hilfe-Ausrüstung *er·stė·hil·fė·ows·rōōs·toong*

first-class adj (work etc) erstklassig *erst·kla·sikh*; to travel first class erster Klasse fahren* *er·stėr kla·sė fah·rėn*

first floor n das Erdgeschoß *erd·gė·shos* A5

first name n der Vorname *fŏr·nah·mė*

fir (tree) n die Tanne *ta·nė*

fiscal adj Finanz- *fee·nants*

fiscal year n das Finanzjahr *fee·nants·yahr*

fish n der Fisch *fish*; (as food) Fisch (m) *fish* E29

fishing n das Angeln *ang·ėln*; to go fishing angeln gehen* *ang·ėln gay·ėn* L33

fishing rod n die Angelrute *ang·ėl·roo·tė*

fishmonger n der Fischhändler *fish·hent·lėr*

fist n die Faust *fowst*

fit adj (strong, healthy) fit *fit*; (suitable) geeignet *gė·ike·nėt* □ vt/i it fits (me) es paßt (mir) gut *ess past (meer) goot* □ n fit (seizure) der Anfall *an·fal*

five num fünf *fōōnf*

fix vt (fasten) befestigen *bė·fes·ti·gėn*; (arrange) fest|setzen *fest·zet·sėn*; (mend) reparieren *ray·pa·ree·rėn*; (prepare) vor|bereiten *fŏr·bė·rye·tėn*

fizzy adj sprudelnd *shproo·dėlnt*

flag n die Fahne *fah·nė*

flag stop n die Bedarfshaltestelle *bė·darfs·hal·tė·shte·lė*

flake n der Splitter *shpli·tėr*; (of snow) die Flocke *flo·kė*

flame n die Flamme *fla·mė*

flammable adj feuergefährlich *foy·ėr·gė·fayr·likh*

flan n der Kuchen *koo·khėn*

flannel n (facecloth) der Waschlappen *vash·la·pėn*

flap n die Klappe *kla·pė* □ vi (sail) flattern *fla·tėrn*

flash n das Blitzen *blit·sėn*; (on camera) das Blitzlicht *blits·likht* □ vi (light) auf|leuchten *owf·loykh·tėn* S51

flashbulb n die Blitzbirne *blits·bir·nė*

flashcube n der Blitzlichtwürfel *blits·likht·vōōr·fėl*

flashlight n die Taschenlampe *ta·shėn·lam·pė*

flask n die Thermosflasche *ter·mos·fla·shė*

flat adj eben *ay·bėn*; (deflated) platt *plat*; (battery) leer *layr*; (beer) schal

shahl; B flat (music) das H *hah*; flat rate die Pauschale *pow·shah·lė* T168

flavor n der Geschmack *gė·shmak*

flea n der Floh *flŏ*

flea market n der Flohmarkt *flŏ·markt*

fleet n die Flotte *flo·tė*; fleet of vehicles der Fuhrpark *foor·park*

Flemish adj flämisch *fle·mish* □ n Flämisch (nt) der *fle·mish*

flesh n das Fleisch *flyesh*

flexible adj biegsam *beek·zam*

flight n der Flug *flook*; flight of steps die Treppe *tre·pė* T2f, 38f

flight attendant n der Steward *styoo·art*, die Stewardeß *styoo·ar·dess*

flint n (in lighter) der Feuerstein *foy·ėr·shtine*

flippers pl (for swimming) die Flossen (pl) *flo·sėn*

flirt vi flirten *flir·tėn*

float vi treiben* *trye·bėn* □ n (for swimming) der Schwimmkork *shvim·kork*; (for fishing) der Schwimmer *shvi·mėr*

flock n die Herde *her·dė*

flood n die Flut *floot*

floodlight n der Scheinwerfer *shine·ver·fėr*

floodlit adj mit Flutlicht beleuchtet *mit floot·likht bė·loykh·tėt*

floor n der Boden *bŏ·dėn*; 1st floor (Brit), 2nd floor (US) der erste Stock *er·stė shtok* A5

floor lamp n die Stehlampe *shtay·lam·pė*

florist n der Blumenhändler *bloo·mėn·hent·lėr*

flour n das Mehl *mayl*

flow vi fließen* *flee·sėn*

flow chart n das Flußdiagramm *floos·dee·a·gram*

flower n die Blume *bloo·mė*

flowerbed n das Blumenbeet *bloo·mėn·bayt*

flu n die Grippe *gri·pė*

fluent adj he speaks fluent German er spricht fließend deutsch *er shprikht flee·sėnt doytsh*

fluorescent light n die Neonröhre *nay·on·rur·rė*

fluoride n das Fluor *floo·ŏr*

flush vt to flush the toilet spülen *shpōō·lėn*

flute n die Flöte *flur'·tė*

fly n die Fliege *flee·gė* □ vi fliegen* *flee·gėn*

fly in vt das Fliegen *flee·gėn*

flyover n (road) die Überführung *ōō·bėr·fōō·roong*

foam n der Schaum *showm*

focus vt ein|stellen *ine·shte·lėn*

fog n der Nebel *nay·bėl*

foggy adj neblig *nay·blikh*

fog light n die Nebellampe *nay·bėl·lam·pė*

foil n (for food) die Alufolie *ah·loo·fŏ·lee·ė*

fold vt zusammen|falten *tsoo·za·mėn·fal·tėn*

folding chair n der Klappstuhl *klap·shtool*

folding table n der Klapptisch *klap·tish*

folk dance n der Volkstanz *folks·tants*

folk song n das Volkslied *folks·leet*

follow vt/i folgen *fol·gėn*

following adj folgend *fol·gėnt*

food n das Essen *e·sėn* Mc50

food poisoning n die Lebensmittelvergiftung *lay·bėns·mi·tėl·fer·gif·toong* I38

foot n der Fuß *foos*; (*of animal*) die Pfote *pfŏ·tè*

football n (soccer) Fußball (m) *foos·bal*; (ball) der Fußball *foos·bal*

footbrake n die Fußbremse *foos·brem·zè*

footpath n der Fußweg *foos·vayk*

for prep für *fŏŏr*; to leave for London nach London ab|reisen *nahkh lon·don ap·rye·zèn*; to walk for an hour eine Stunde lang laufen* *ine·è shtoon·dè lang low·fèn*; what's the German for "dog"? wie sagt man "dog" auf deutsch? *vee zakt man dog owf doytsh*

forbid vt verbieten* *fer·bee·tèn*; to forbid someone to do something jemandem verbieten*, etwas zu tun *yay·man·dèm fer·bee·tèn et·vass tsoo toon*; it is forbidden es ist verboten *ess ist fer·bŏ·tèn*

force n (violence) die Gewalt *gè·valt* □ vt (compel) zwingen* *tsving·èn*

ford n die Furt *foort*

forecast n die Vorhersage *fŏr·her·zah·gè*; (weather) der Wetterbericht *ve·tèr·bè·rikht*

forehead n die Stirn *shtirn*

foreign adj ausländisch *ows·len·dish*

foreigner n der Ausländer *ows·len·dèr*, die Ausländerin *ows·len·dè·rin* T183

foreign exchange market n der Devisenmarkt *day·vee·zen·markt*

foreign policy n die Außenpolitik *ow·sèn·pŏ·lee·tik*

foreman n der Vorarbeiter *fŏr·ar·bye·tèr*

forename n der Vorname *fŏr·nah·mè*

forest n der Wald *valt*

forever adv für alle Zeiten *fŏŏr·a·lè tsye·tèn*

forgery n die Fälschung *fel·shoong*

forget vt vergessen* *fer·ge·sèn*

forgive vt vergeben* *fer·gay·bèn*

fork n die Gabel *gah·bèl*; (in road) die Gabelung *gah·bè·loong*

form n die Form *form*; (document) das Formular *for·moo·lahr*

formal adj formell *for·mel*

fortnight n zwei Wochen *tsvye vo·khèn*

fortune n (wealth) das Vermögen *fer·mur·gèn*

forty num vierzig *feer·tsikh*

forward vt (letter) nach|senden* *nakh·zen·dèn*

forward(s) adv vorwärts *fŏr·verts*; the seat is too far forward der Sitz ist zu weit vorn *der zits ist tsoo vite fŏrn*

fountain n der Brunnen *broo·nèn*

fountain pen n der Füller *fŏŏ·lèr*

four num vier *feer*

fourteen num vierzehn *feer·tsayn*

fourth adj vierte(r/s) *feer·tè(·tèr/·tès)*

fox n der Fuchs *fooks*

fracture n (of arm etc) der Bruch *brookh*

fragile adj zerbrechlich *tser·brekh·likh*

frame n (of picture) der Rahmen *rah·mèn*; frames (of eyeglasses) das Gestell *gè·shtel*

France n Frankreich (nt) *frank·ryekh*

free adj frei *frye*; (costing nothing) kostenlos *kos·tèn·lŏs* Bm10

freeway n die Autobahn *ow·tŏ·bahn*

freeze vi frieren* *free·rèn* □ vt (food) ein|frieren* *ine·free·rèn*

freezer n die Gefriertruhe *gè·freer·troo·è*

freight n (goods) die Fracht *frakht* Bm26

freight train n der Güterzug *gŏŏ·tèr·tsook*

French adj französisch *fran·tsur·zish*; he's French er ist Franzose *er ist fran·tsŏ·zè*; she's French sie ist Französin *zee ist fran·tsur·zin* □ n French Französisch (nt) *fran·tsur·zish*

french fried potatoes, french fries pl die Pommes Frites (pl) *pom freet*

frequent adj häufig *hoy·fikh*

fresh adj frisch *frish*; (impudent) frech *frekh*

Friday n Freitag (m) *frye·tahk*

fridge n der Kühlschrank *kŏŏl·shrank*

fried adj Brat- *braht*; a fried egg ein Spiegelei (nt) *shpee·gèl·eye*

friend n der Freund *froynt*, die Freundin *froyn·din*

friendly adj freundlich *froynt·likh*

frighten vt erschrecken *er·shre·kèn*

fringe n (hair) die Ponyfransen (pl) *pŏ·nee·fran·zèn*; (edging) die Fransenkante *fran·zèn·kan·tè*

fritter n der Beignet *ben·yay*

frog n der Frosch *frosh*

frogs legs pl die Froschschenkel (pl) *frosh·sheng·kèl*

from prep von *fon*; from 8 o'clock ab 8 Uhr *ap 8 oor*; water from the faucet Wasser aus der Leitung *va·sèr ows der lye·toong*

front adj Vorder- *fŏr·dèr* □ n (foremost part) die Vorderseite *fŏr·dèr·zye·tè*; (seaside) die Strandpromenade *shtrant·pro·mè·nah·dè*; at the front vorn *fŏrn*; to sit in front vorne sitzen* *fŏr·nè zit·sèn*

frontier n die Grenze *gren·tsè*

front-wheel drive n der Vorderradantrieb *fŏr·dèr·raht·an·treep*

frost n der Frost *frost*

frozen adj (food) gefroren *gè·frŏ·rèn*

fruit n das Obst *ŏpst*

fruit salad n der Obstsalat *ŏpst·za·laht*

fry vt braten* *brah·tèn*

fry(ing) pan n die Bratpfanne *braht·pfa·nè*

fuel n der Brennstoff *bren·shtof*

fuel pump n die Benzinpumpe *ben·tseen·poom·pè*

full adj voll *fol*; full of voll von *fol fon*; full of work voll von Arbeit

full stop n der Punkt *poonkt*

full-time adj, adv ganztägig *gants·te·gikh*

fun n □ it was great fun es machte viel Spaß *es makh·tè feel shpahs*

funds pl die Gelder (pl) *gel·dèr*

funeral n die Beerdigung *bè·er·di·goong*

funny adj (amusing) komisch *kŏ·mish*

fur n Pelz (m) *pelts*

furnish vt (room etc) möblieren *mur·blee·rèn*

furniture n die Möbel (pl) *mur·bèl*

further adv weiter *vye·tèr*

furthest adv am weitesten *am vye·tè·stèn*

fuse n die Sicherung *zikh·è·roong* A81

fuss n das Theater *tay·ah·tèr*; to make a fuss Theater machen *tay·ah·tèr ma·khèn*

future n die Zukunft *tsoo·koonft*

G

gadget n das Gerät *gè·rayt*

gain vt (obtain) gewinnen* *gè·vi·nèn* □ vi (clock) vor|gehen* *fŏr·gay·èn*

gala n das große Fest *grŏ·sè fest*

gale n der Sturm *shtoorm*

gallery *n* die Galerie *ga·lě·ree*; (*art*) die Gemäldegalerie *gě·mel·dě·ga·lě·ree*

gallon *n* die Gallone *ga·lō·ně*

gallop *vi* galoppieren *ga·lo·pee·rěn* □ *n* der Galopp *ga·lop*

gamble *vi* spielen *shpee·lěn*

gambler *n* der Spieler *shpee·lěr*

gambling *n* das Spielen *shpee·lěn*

game *n* das Spiel *shpeel*; (*hunting*) das Wild *vilt*; **a game of tennis** eine Partie Tennis *ine·ě par·tee te·nis*

gang *n* die Bande *ban·dě*

gangster *n* der Gangster *gang·stěr*

gangway *n* (*passage*) der Gang *gang*; (*bridge*) die Landungsbrücke *lan·doongs·brŏŏ·kě*

gap *n* die Lücke *lŏŏ·kě*

garage *n* (*for parking*) die Garage *ga·rah·zhě*; (*service station*) die Reparaturwerkstatt *re·pa·ra·toor·verk·shtat*

garbage *n* der Abfall *ap·fal*

garbage can *n* der Abfalleimer *ap·fal·ime·ěr*

garden *n* der Garten *gar·těn*

garden center *n* das Gartencenter *gar·těn·sen·těr*

gardener *n* der Gärtner *gert·něr*

gargle *vi* gurgeln *goor·gěln*

garlic *n* der Knoblauch *knōp·lowkh*

garlic sausage *n* die Knoblauchwurst *knōp·lowkh·voorst*

garment *n* das Kleidungsstück *klye·doongs·shtŏŏk*

gas *n* das Gas *gas*; **gas stove** der Gasherd *gas·hert*

gasket *n* die Dichtung *dikh·toong*

gas(oline) *n* das Benzin *ben·tseen* T147, 162

gas station *n* die Tankstelle *tank·shte·lě*

gate *n* (*of garden*) die Pforte *pfor·tě*; (*of building*) der Eingang *ine·gang*

gateau *n* die Torte *tor·tě*

gather *vt* (*assemble*) sammeln *za·měln* □ *vi* (*crowd*) sich versammeln *zikh fer·za·měln*

gathered *adj* gekräuselt *gě·kroy·zělt*

gauge *n* (*device*) das Meßgerät *mess·gě·ret*

gauze *n* die Gaze *gah·zě*

gay *adj* (*merry*) fröhlich *frur·likh*

gear *n* (*equipment*) die Ausrüstung *ows·rŏŏ·stoong*; (*of car*) der Gang *gang*; **in gear** eingelegt *ine·gě·laykt*; **2nd/3rd gear** zweiter/dritter Gang *tsvye·těr/dri·těr gang*; **high/low gear** vierter/erster Gang *feer·těr/er·stěr gang*

gearbox *n* das Getriebe *gě·tree·bě*

gearshift *n* der Schaltknüppel *shalt·knŏŏ·pěl*

gem *n* der Edelstein *ay·děl·shtine*

gender *n* das Geschlecht *gě·shlekht*

general *adj* allgemein *al·gě·mine* □ *n* (*soldier*) der General *ge·ne·rahl*; **in general** im allgemeinen *im al·gě·mine·ěn*

general delivery *adv* postlagernd *post·lah·gěrnt* Sn8

general election *n* die Parlamentswahlen (*pl*) *par·la·ments·wah·lěn*

general knowledge *n* das Allgemeinwissen *al·gě·mine·vi·sěn*

generally *adv* im allgemeinen *im al·gě·mine·ěn*

general practitioner, G.P. *n* der Arzt für Allgemeinmedizin *artst fŏŏr al·gě·mine·me·di·tseen*

generation *n* die Generation *ge·ne·ra·tsee·ōn*

generator *n* (*electrical*) der Generator *ge·ne·rah·tor*

generous *adj* großzügig *grōs·tsŏŏ·gikh*

Geneva *n* Genf (*nt*) *genf*

gentle *adj* sanft *zanft*

gentleman *n* der Herr *her*

genuine *adj* echt *ekht*

geography *n* die Geographie *gay·o·gra·fee*

geology *n* die Geologie *gay·o·lo·gee*

geometry *n* die Geometrie *gay·o·me·tree*

geranium *n* die Geranie *gay·rah·nee·ě*

germ *n* der Keim *kime*

German *adj* deutsch *doytsh*; **he's German** er ist Deutsche *er ist doyt·shě*; **she's German** sie ist Deutsche *zee ist doyt·shě* □ *n* German Deutsch (*nt*) *doytsh*; **in German** auf Deutsch *owf doytsh*

Germany *n* Deutschland (*nt*) *doytsh·lant*; **to Germany** nach Deutschland *nakh doytsh·lant*

gesture *n* die Geste *ge·stě*

get *vt* (*obtain, receive*) bekommen* *bě·ko·měn*; (*fetch*) holen *hō·lěn*; (*prepare: food*) machen *ma·khěn*; (*catch: illness*) sich holen *zikh hō·lěn*; **to have got(ten)** (*possess*) haben* *hah·běn*; **to get tired** müde werden* *mŏŏ·dě ver·děn*; **to get ready** sich fertig machen *zikh fer·tikh ma·khěn*; **how do we get there?** wie kommen wir dorthin? *vee ko·měn veer dort·hin*; **to get home** nach Hause kommen* *nakh how·zě ko·měn*; **to get one's hair cut** sich die Haare schneiden lassen* *zikh dee hah·rě shnye·děn la·sěn*; **to get away** (*escape*) entkommen* *ent·ko·měn*; **how are you getting on?** wie geht's? *vee gayts*; **to get onto a road** auf eine Straße kommen* *owf ine·ě shtrah·sě ko·měn*; **to get through** (*on phone*) durch|kommen* *doorkh·ko·měn*; **to get up** auf|stehen* *owf·shtay·ěn*

gherkin *n* die Gewürzgurke *gě·vŏŏrts·goor·kě*

ghetto *n* das Ghetto *ge·tō*

ghost *n* das Gespenst *gě·shpenst*

giant *n* der Riese *ree·zě*

gift *n* das Geschenk *gě·shenk*; (*ability*) die Begabung *bě·gah·boong*

gifted *adj* begabt *bě·gapt*

gift token *n* der Geschenkgutschein *gě·shenk·goot·shine*

gift-wrap *vt* als Geschenk verpacken *als gě·shenk fer·pa·kěn*

gin *n* (*drink*) der Gin *jin*

ginger *n* der Ingwer *ing·věr*

ginger ale *n* das Ginger Ale

gingerbread *n* der Pfefferkuchen *pfe·fěr·koo·khěn*

gingham *n* der Gingan *ging·an*

gipsy *n* der Zigeuner *tsi·goy·něr*, die Zigeunerin *tsi·goy·ně·rin*

girdle *n* (*corset*) der Hüfthalter *hŏŏft·hal·těr*

girl *n* das Mädchen *mayt·khěn* S114

girlfriend *n* die Freundin *froyn·din*

give *vt* geben* *gay·běn*; **to give someone something** jemandem etwas geben* *yay·man·děm et·vass gay·běn*; **to give away** weg|geben* *vek·gay·běn*; **to give back** zurück|geben* *tsoo·rŏŏk·gay·běn*; **to give in** (*yield*) nach|geben* *nakh·gay·běn*; **to give up** (*abandon hope*) auf|geben* *owf·gay·běn*; **to give up smoking** das Rauchen auf|geben* *dass row·khěn owf·gay·běn*; **to give way** (*traffic*) dem Gegenverkehr Vorfahrt lassen* *daym gay·gèn·fer·kayr för·fahrt la·sèn*

glacé *adj* kandiert *kan·deert*

glad *adj* froh *frō*; **I was glad to hear…** es hat mich gefreut, zu hören… *ess hat mikh gè·froyt tsoo hur·rèn*

glamorous *adj* glamurös *gla·moo·rur's*

glance *n* der Blick *blik* □ *vi* **to glance at** kurz an|sehen* *koorts an·zay·èn*

gland *n* die Drüse *drōō·zè*

glare *n* (*of light*) das grelle Licht *gre·lè likht*

glass *n* das Glas *glahs*; (*glassware*) die Glaswaren (*pl*) *glahs·vah·rèn* B64, E15

glasses *pl* die Brille *bri·lè* B77

glide *vi* gleiten* *glye·tèn*

glider *n* das Segelflugzeug *zay·gèl·flook·tsoyk*

gliding *n* (*sport*) das Segelfliegen *zay·gèl·flee·gèn*

global *adj* global *glō·bahl*

globe *n* (*map*) der Globus *glō·boos*

globe artichoke *n* die Artischocke *ar·ti·sho·kè*

glove *n* der Handschuh *hant·shoo*

glove compartment *n* das Handschuhfach *hant·shoo·fakh*

glow *vi* glühen *glōō·èn*

glue *n* der Klebstoff *klayp·shtof* □ *vt* kleben *klay·bèn*

glycerin(e) *n* das Glyzerin *glōō·tsè·reen*

gnat *n* die Stechmücke *shtekh·mōō·kè*

go *vi* gehen* *gay·èn*; (*leave*) weg|gehen* *vek·gay·èn*; (*clock, machine*) gehen* *gay·èn*; **to go shopping** ein|kaufen gehen* *ine·kow·fèn gay·èn*; **to go bad** schlecht werden* *shlekht ver·dèn*; **how did it go?** wie war es? *vee vahr ess*; **the books go here** die Bücher gehören hierhin *dee bōō·khèr gè·hur·èn heer·hin*; **it won't go in** es paßt nicht hinein *ess past nikht hin·ine*; **all our money's gone** wir haben unser ganzes Geld ausgegeben *veer hah·bèn oon·zèr gan·tsès gelt ows·gè·gay·bèn*; **I'm going to do it** ich werde es tun *ikh ver·dè ess toon*; **go ahead!** nur zu! *noor tsoo*; **to go away** weg|gehen* *vek·gay·èn*; **to go back** zurück|gehen* *tsoo·rōōk·gay·èn*; **to go down** hinunter|gehen* *hin·oon·tèr·gay·èn*; **to go in** hinein|gehen* *hin·ine·gay·èn*; **to go out** hinaus|gehen* *hin·ows·gay·èn*; **to go out with somebody** mit jemandem aus|gehen* *mit yay·man·dèm ows·gay·èn*; **this goes with your dress** dies paßt gut zu Ihrem Kleid *dees past goot tsoo ee·rèm klite*; **we will have to go without milk** wir müssen ohne Milch aus|kommen *veer mōō·sèn ō·nè milkh ows·ko·mèn*

goal *n* (*sport*) das Tor *tōr*; (*aim*) das Ziel *tseel*

goat *n* die Ziege *tsee·gè*

god *n* der Gott *got*

godfather *n* der Pate *pah·tin*

godmother *n* die Patin *pah·tin*

goggles *pl* die Schutzbrille *shoots·bri·lè*

gold *n* das Gold *golt* □ *adj* golden *gol·dèn*; **gold-plated** vergoldet *fer·gol·dèt* S95, 96

golden *adj* golden *gol·dèn*

goldfish *n* der Goldfisch *golt·fish*

golf *n* Golf (*nt*) *golf* L30

golf ball *n* der Golfball *golf·bal*

golf club *n* der Golfschläger *golf·shlay·*

gèr; (*association*) der Golfklub *golf·kloop*

golf course *n* der Golfplatz *golf·plats*

golfer *n* der Golfer *gol·fèr*

good *adj* gut *goot*; (*well-behaved*) artig *ar·tikh*; **to be good at golf** gut im Golf sein* *goot im golf zine*; **spinach is good for you** Spinat ist gesund *shpi·naht ist gè·zoont*; **it'll do you good** das wird Ihnen guttun *dass virt ee·nèn goot·toon*; **good morning/good afternoon!** guten Morgen/guten Tag! *goo·tèn mor·gèn/goo·tèn tahk*; **good evening/good night!** guten Abend/gute Nacht! *goo·tèn a·bènt/goo·tè nakht*

goodbye *excl* auf Wiedersehen *owf vee·dèr·zay·èn*

Good Friday *n* der Karfreitag *kahr·frye·tahk*

goods *pl* die Güter (*pl*) *gōō·tèr*

goose *n* die Gans *gans*

gooseberry *n* die Stachelbeere *shta·khèl·bay·rè*

gossip *vi* schwatzen *shva·tsèn* □ *n* (*chatter*) der Klatsch *klatsh*

goulash *n* das Gulasch *goo·lash*

gourmet *n* der Feinschmecker *fine·shme·kèr*

govern *vt* (*country*) regieren *ray·gee·rèn*

government *n* die Regierung *ray·gee·roong*

governor *n* (*of colony*) der Gouverneur *goo·ver·nur*; (*of institution*) der Direktor *dee·rek·tor*

gown *n* die Robe *rō·bè*

grab *vt* packen *pa·kèn*

graceful *adj* anmutig *an·moo·tikh*

grade *n* das Niveau *nee·vō*; (*class*) die Klasse *kla·sè*

grade crossing *n* der Bahnübergang *bahn·ōō·bèr·gang*

grade school *n* die Grundschule *groont·shoo·lè*

gradual *adj* allmählich *al·may·likh*

gradually *adv* allmählich *al·may·likh*

graduate *n* (*from university*) der Akademiker *a·ka·day·mi·kèr*, die Akademikerin *a·ka·day·mi·kè·rin* □ *vi* graduieren *gra·doo·ee·rèn*

grain *n* (*cereal crops*) das Getreide *gè·trye·dè*; (*wood*) die Maserung *mah·zè·roong*

gram *n* das Gramm *gram*

grammar *n* die Grammatik *gra·ma·tik*; **grammar (book)** das Grammatikbuch *gra·ma·tik·bookh*

grand *adj* großartig *grōs·ar·tikh*

grandchild *n* das Enkelkind *eng·kèl·kint*

granddaughter *n* die Enkelin *eng·kè·lin*

grandfather *n* der Großvater *grōs·fah·tèr*

grandfather clock *n* die Standuhr *shtant·oo·èr*

grandmother *n* die Großmutter *grōs·moo·tèr*

grand piano *n* der Flügel *flōō·gèl*

Grand Prix *n* der Grand Prix *groñ pree*

grandson *n* der Enkel *eng·kèl*

grant *n* (*to student*) das Stipendium *shti·pen·dee·oom*; (*to institution*) die Subvention *soop·ven·tsee·ōn* □ *vt* (*wish*) gewähren *gè·vay·rèn*

grape *n* die Traube *trow·bè*

grapefruit *n* die Pampelmuse *pam·pèl·moo·zè*

grapefruit juice *n* der Pampelmusensaft *pam·pèl·moo·zèn·zaft*

graph 186

graph n das Schaubild *show·bilt*
grasp vt (seize) ergreifen* *er·grye·fên*
grass n das Gras *grahs*
grate n der Feuerrost *foy·êr·rost* □ vt (food) reiben* *rye·bên*
grateful adj dankbar *dank·bahr*
grater n die Reibe *rye·bê*
grave n das Grab *grahp*
gravel n der Kies *kees*
graveyard n der Friedhof *freed·hôf*
gravy n der Bratensaft *brah·tên·zaft*
gray adj grau *grow*
graze n die Abschürfung *ap·shoor·foong* □ vt (skin) auf|schürfen *owf·shôôr·fên*
grease n das Fett *fet*; (lubricant) das Schmierfett *shmeer·fet*
greasy adj (surface) fettig *fe·tikh*; (food) fett *fet*
great adj groß *grōs*; (excellent) prima *pree·ma*
Great Britain n Großbritannien (nt) *grōs·bri·ta·nee·ên*
Greece n Griechenland (nt) *gree·khên·lant*
greedy adj gierig *gee·rikh*
Greek adj griechisch *gree·khish*
green adj grün *grōōn*
green card n die grüne Versicherungskarte *grōō·nê fer·zi·khê·roongs·kar·tê*
greenhouse n das Gewächshaus *gê·veks·hows*
green salad n der grüne Salat *grōō·nê za·laht*
greet vt grüßen *grōō·sên*
greeting n der Gruß *groos*
greeting card n die Grußkarte *groos·kar·tê*
grey adj grau *grow*
grief n das Leid *lite*
grill n (gridiron) der Grill *gril* □ vt grillen *gri·lên*
grillroom n der Grillroom *gril·room*
grimace n die Grimasse *gri·ma·sê*
grind vt mahlen* *mah·lên*
grip vt packen *pa·kên* □ n (case) die Reisetasche *rye·zê·ta·shê*
grit n der Splitt *shplit*
groan vi stöhnen *shtur·nên* □ n das Stöhnen *shtur·nên*
grocer n der Kaufmann *kowf·man*
groceries pl die Lebensmittel (pl) *lay·bêns·mi·têl*
grocery shop n das Lebensmittelgeschäft *lay·bêns·mi·têl·gê·sheft*
gross adj das Gros *grōs* □ adj (before deductions) brutto *broo·tō*
gross national product, GNP n das Bruttosozialprodukt *broo·tō·zo·tsee·ahl·prō·dookt*
grotesque adj grotesk *grō·tesk*
ground n der Boden *bō·dên*; (electrical) die Erde *er·dê* □ adj (coffee) gemahlen *gê·mah·lên*; ground beef das Hackfleisch *hak·flyesh* S34
groundcloth n der Zeltboden *tselt·bō·dên*
ground floor n das Erdgeschoß *ert·gê·shos*
groundnut n die Erdnuß *ert·noos*
grounds pl (land) das Gelände *gê·len·dê*; (of coffee) der Satz *zats*
group n die Gruppe *groo·pê* M5
grouse n (bird) das Waldhuhn *walt·hoon*
grow vi wachsen* *vak·sên* □ vt (plants) ziehen* *tsee·ên*; to grow up erwachsen werden* *er·vak·sên ver·dên*
growl vi knurren *knoo·rên*
grown-up adj erwachsen *er·vak·sên*

growth n das Wachstum *vaks·toom*; (in amount etc) die Zunahme *tsoo·nah·mê*; (anatomical) das Gewächs *gê·veks*
grumble vi schimpfen *shimp·fên*
grunt vi grunzen *groon·tsên*
guarantee n die Garantie *ga·ran·tee* □ vt garantieren *ga·ran·tee·rên*
guard vt (prisoner) bewachen *bê·va·khên*; (protect) schützen *shōō·tsên* □ n die Wache *va·khê*
guardian n der Vormund *fōr·moont*
guess vt vermuten *fer·moo·tên* □ vi raten* *rah·tên*
guest n der Gast *gast*
guest-house n das Gästehaus *ge·stê·hows*
guest-room n das Gästezimmer *ge·stê·tsi·mêr*
guide n (person) der Führer *fōō·rêr*, die Führerin *fōō·rê·rin* L10
guidebook n der Reiseführer *rye·zê·fōō·rêr* L4
guide dog n der Blindenhund *blin·dên·hoont*
guided tour n die Führung *fōō·roong* L6
guilt n die Schuld *shoolt*
guilty adj schuldig *shool·dikh*
guinea fowl n das Perlhuhn *perl·hoon*
guitar n die Gitarre *gi·ta·rê*
gum n (of teeth) das Zahnfleisch *tsahn·flyesh*; (chewing gum) der Kaugummi *kow·goo·mee* I66
gun n das Gewehr *gê·vayr*
gunman n der Bewaffnete *bê·vaf·nê·tê*
gust n der Stoß *shtōs*
gusty adj (wind) böig *bur·ikh*
gutter n (in street) die Gosse *go·sê*; (on building) die Dachrinne *dakh·ri·nê*
gym(nasium) n die Turnhalle *toorn·ha·lê*
gymnastics n die Gymnastik *gōōm·na·stik*
gypsy n der Zigeuner *tsi·goy·nêr*, die Zigeunerin *tsi·goy·nê·rin*

H

haberdashery n die Herrenartikel (pl) *he·rên·ar·tee·kêl*
habit n die Gewohnheit *gê·vôn·hite*
haddock n der Schellfisch *shel·fish*
Hague (the) n Den Haag (m) *dayn hahk*
hail n der Hagel *hah·gêl* □ vi it's hailing es hagelt *ess hah·gêlt*
hair n die Haare (pl) *hah·rê*; (single strand) das Haar *hahr* Sn34f
hairbrush n die Haarbürste *hahr·bōōr·stê*
haircut n (style) die Frisur *free·zoor*; to have a haircut sich die Haare schneiden lassen* *zikh dee hah·rê shnye·dên la·sên*
hairdresser n der Friseur *free·zur*, die Friseuse *free·zur·zê*
hair-drier n der Haartrockner *hahr·trok·nêr*
hairpin n die Haarklemme *hahr·kle·mê*
hairpin curve n die Haarnadelkurve *hahr·nah·dêl·koor·vê*
hair spray n das Haarspray *hahr·shpray*
hair-style n die Frisur *free·zoor*
half n die Hälfte *helf·tê*; half an hour eine halbe Stunde *ine·ê hal·bê shtoon·dê*; two and a half zweieinhalb *tsvye·ine·halp*; to cut something in half etwas halbieren *et·vass hal·*

bee·rèn □ *adj* a half dozen ein halbes Dutzend *ine hal·bès doot·sènt*; **three and a half kilometers** dreieinhalb Kilometer *drye·ine·halp kee·lô·may·tèr* □ *adv* half halb *halp*; **half open** halb offen *halp o·fèn*

half-fare *n* der halbe Fahrpreis *der hal·bè fahr·price*

half-hour *n* die halbe Stunde *hal·bè shtoon·dè*

half-price *adj* zum halben Preis *tsoom hal·bèn price*

half-time *n* die Halbzeit *halp·tsite*

halfway *adv* auf halbem Weg *owf hal·bèm vayk*

hall *n* (entrance) die Diele *dee·lè*; (room) der Saal *zahl*

hallmark *n* der Stempel *shtem·pèl*

halve *vt* (divide in two) halbieren *hal·bee·rèn*; (reduce by half) auf die Hälfte reduzieren *owf dee helf·tè ray·doot·see·rèn*

ham *n* der Schinken *shing·kèn* S34

hamburger *n* der Hamburger *ham·boor·gèr*

hammer *n* der Hammer *ha·mèr*

hammock *n* die Hängematte *heng·è·ma·tè*

hamper *n* der Korb *korp*

hand *n* die Hand *hant*; (of clock) der Zeiger *tsye·gèr*; **by hand** von Hand *fon hant* □ *vt* to hand someone something jemandem etwas reichen *yay·man·dèm et·vass rye·khèn*

handbag *n* die Handtasche *hant·ta·shè*

handbook *n* das Handbuch *hant·bookh*

hand-brake *n* die Handbremse *hant·brem·zè*

hand cream *n* die Handcreme *hant·kraym*

handcuffs *pl* die Handschellen (pl) *hant·she·lèn*

handicap *n* der Nachteil *nakh·tile*; (golf) das Handikap *han·di·kap*

handkerchief *n* das Taschentuch *ta·shèn·tookh*

handle *n* (of door) die Klinke *kling·kè*; (of cup) der Henkel *heng·kèl*; (of knife) der Griff *grif*; (for winding) die Kurbel *koor·bèl* □ *vt* (touch) berühren *bè·rōō·rèn*; (deal with) behandeln *bè·han·dèln*; **handle with care** Vorsicht - zerbrechlich *fōr·zikht tser·brekh·likh*

handlebar(s) *n* die Lenkstange *lenk·shtang·è*

hand-luggage *n* das Handgepäck *hant·gè·pek*

handmade *adj* handgearbeitet *hant·gè·ar·bye·tèt* S116

handrail *n* (on stairs) das Geländer *gè·len·dèr*

handsome *adj* (person) gutaussehend *goot·ows·zay·ent*

handy *adj* (convenient) praktisch *prak·tish*

hang *vt* auf|hängen *owf·heng·èn*; (criminal) hängen *heng·en* □ *vi* hängen* *heng·èn*; **hang on!** (on phone) einen Augenblick! *ine·èn ow·gèn·blik*; **to hang up** (phone) auf|legen *owf·lay·gèn*

hangover *n* der Kater *kah·tèr*

happen *vi* geschehen* *gè·shay·èn*; **what happened to him?** was ist ihm passiert? *vass ist eem pa·seert*

happiness *n* das Glück *glook*

happy *adj* glücklich *glook·likh*

harbor *n* der Hafen *hah·fèn*

harbor master *n* der Hafenmeister *hah·fèn·mye·stèr*

hard *adj* hart *hart*; (difficult) schwierig *shvee·rikh*

hard-boiled *adj* hartgekocht *hart·gè·kokht*

hardware *n* die Eisenwaren (pl) *eye·zèn·vah·rèn*; (computing) die Hardware *hard·wayr*

hard-wearing *adj* widerstandsfähig *vee·dèr·shtants·fay·ikh*

hare *n* der Hase *hah·zè*

harmful *adj* schädlich *shet·likh*

harmless *adj* harmlos *harm·lōs*

harness *n* das Geschirr *gè·shir*

harp *n* die Harfe *har·fè*

harsh *adj* (severe) streng *shtreng*

harvest *n* (of grain) die Ernte *ern·tè*; (of grapes) die Lese *lay·zè* □ *vt* (grain) ernten *ern·tèn*; (grapes) lesen* *lay·zèn*

haste *n* die Eile *ile·è*

hat *n* der Hut *hoot* S13

hatchback *n* (car) das Hecktürmodell *hek·tōōr·mo·del*

hate *vt* hassen *ha·sèn*

hatred *n* der Haß *hass*

hat stand *n* der Hutständer *hoot·shten·dèr*

have *vt* haben* *hah·bèn*; (meal) essen* *e·sèn*; **to have a shower** duschen *doo·shèn*; **to have a drink** etwas trinken* *et·vass tring·kèn*; **she has to do it** sie muß es tun *zee mooss ess toon*; **to have something done** etwas machen lassen* *et·vass ma·khèn la·sèn*

hay *n* das Heu *hoy*

hay fever *n* der Heuschnupfen *hoy·shnoop·fèn* S43

he *pron* er *er*

head *n* der Kopf *kopf*; (chief) der Chef *shef*

headache *n* die Kopfschmerzen (pl) *kopf·shmer·tsèn*; **to have a headache** Kopfschmerzen haben* *kopf·shmer·tsèn hah·bèn* S43, I33

headlight *n* der Scheinwerfer *shine·ver·fèr*

headline *n* die Schlagzeile *shlahk·tsile·è*

headmaster *n* der Direktor *dee·rek·tor*

headmistress *n* die Direktorin *dee·rek·tō·rin*

head office *n* die Zentrale *tsen·trah·lè*

head-on *adj* frontal *fron·tahl*

headphones *pl* die Kopfhörer (pl) *kopf·hur·rèr*

headrest *n* die Kopfstütze *kopf·shtōōt·sè*

heal *vi* (wound) heilen *hile·èn*

health *n* die Gesundheit *gè·zoont·hite*

health foods *pl* die Reformkost *ray·form·kost*

health service *n* das Gesundheitswesen *gè·zoont·hites·vay·zèn*

healthy *adj* (person) gesund *gè·zoont*

heap *n* der Haufen *how·fèn*

hear *vt/i* hören *hur·rèn*; **I can't hear (you)** ich höre Sie nicht *ikh hur·rè zee nikht*

hearing aid *n* das Hörgerät *hur·gè·ret*

heart *n* das Herz *herts*; **by heart** auswendig *ows·ven·dikh*; **hearts** (cards) Herz (nt) *herts* I1

heart attack *n* der Herzanfall *herts·an·fal*

heartburn *n* das Sodbrennen *zōt·bre·nèn*

hearth *n* die Feuerstelle *foy·èr·shte·lè*

heat *n* die Hitze *hit·sè*; (sports) der Vorlauf *fōr·lowf*

heater n das Heizgerät *hites·gė·ret*

heating n die Heizung *hye·tsoong* A47f

heavy adj schwer *shvayr*

hedge n die Hecke *he·kė*

heel n die Ferse *fer·zė*; (of shoe) der Absatz *ap·zats*

height n (of object) die Höhe *hur'·ė*; (of person) die Größe *grur'·sė*

helicopter n der Hubschrauber *hoop·shrow·bėr*

hello excl hallo *ha·lō*

helmet n der Helm *helm*

help n die Hilfe *hil·fė*; help! Hilfe! *hil·fė* □ vt help helfen* *hel·fėn*; can you help me? können Sie mir helfen? *kur'·nėn zee meer hel·fėn*; I can't help it ich kann nichts dafür *ikh kan nikhts da·főőr*

helping n die Portion *por·tsee·ōn*

hem n der Saum *zowm*

hemorrhoids pl die Hämorrhoiden (pl) *he·mo·rō·ee·dėn*

hen n die Henne *he·nė*

her pron sie *zee*; it's her sie ist es *zee ist ess*; give it to her geben Sie es ihr *gay·bėn zee ess eer* □ adj ihr(e) *eer·(ė)*

herbs pl die Kräuter (pl) *kroy·tėr*

here adv here *heer*; here she comes da kommt sie *dah komt zee*

hernia n der Bruch *brookh*

herring n der Hering *hay·ring*

hers pron ihre(r/s) *ee·rė·(rėr/rės)*

herself pron selbst *zelpst*; she did it herself sie hat es selbst getan *zee hat ess zelpst gė·tahn*; she dressed herself sie zog sich an *zee tsōk zikh an*

hesitate vi zögern *zur'·gėrn*; to hesitate to do something zögern, etwas zu tun *zur'·gėrn et·vass tsoo toon*

hiccup n der Schluckauf *shlook·owf*

hide n (leather) die Haut *howt* □ vt verstecken *fer·shte·kėn* □ vi sich verstecken *zikh fer·shte·kėn*

hi-fi adj Hi-Fi- *hye·fye* □ n das Hi-Fi *hye·fye*

high adj, adv hoch *hōkh*; the mountain is high der Berg ist hoch *der berk ist hōkh*; the high mountain der hohe Berg *der hō·ė berk*; 6 meters high 6 Meter hoch *6 may·tėr hōkh*

highchair n der Hochstuhl *hōkh·shtool* C3

high-class adj hochwertig *hōkh·ver·tikh*

higher adj höher *hur'·ėr*

high-heeled adj mit hohen Absätzen *mit hō·ėn ap·zet·sėn*

high school n die Oberschule *ō·bėr·shoo·lė*

high-speed adj Schnell- *shnel·*

high tide n das Hochwasser *hōkh·va·sėr*

highway n die Landstraße *lant·shtrah·sė*

Highway Code n die Straßenverkehrsordnung *shtrah·sėn·fer·kayrs·ort·noong*

hijack vt entführen *ent·főő·rėn*

hijacker n der Entführer *ent·főő·rėr*

hike n die Wanderung *van·dė·roong*

hiking n das Wandern *van·dėrn*; to go hiking wandern gehen* *van·dėrn gay·ėn*

hill n der Hügel *hőő·gėl*; (slope) der Hang *hang*

hilly adj hügelig *hőő·gė·likh*

him pron ihn *een*; it's him er ist es *er ist ess*; give it to him geben Sie es ihm *gay·bėn zee ess eem*

himself pron selbst *zelpst*; he did it

himself er hat es selbst getan *er hat ess zelpst gė·tahn*; he dresses himself er zieht sich an *er tseet zikh an*

hip n die Hüfte *hőőf·tė*

hire vt mieten *mee·tėn*; to hire something out etwas vermieten *et·vass fer·mee·tėn*

his adj sein(e) *zine·(ė)* □ pron seine(r/s) *zine·ė·(ėr/·ės)*

history n die Geschichte *gė·shikh·tė*

hit vt schlagen* *shlah·gėn*; (with car) an|fahren* *an·fah·rėn* □ n (blow) der Schlag *shlahk*

hitchhike vi per Anhalter fahren* *per an·hal·tėr fah·rėn*

hitchhiker n der Anhalter *an·hal·tėr*, die Anhalterin *an·hal·tė·rin*

hobby n das Hobby *ho·bee*

hockey n Hockey (nt) *ho·kee*

hold vt halten* *hal·tėn*; (contain) enthalten* *ent·hal·tėn*; hold on! (on phone) einen Augenblick! *ine·ėn ow·gėn·blik*; to hold up (delay) auf|halten* *owf·hal·tėn*

hole n das Loch *lokh*

holiday n (day) der Feiertag *fye·ėr·tahk*; (period) die Ferien (pl) *fay·ree·ėn*; on holiday auf Urlaub *owf oor·lowp*

Holland n Holland (nt) *ho·lant*

hollow adj hohl *hōl*

holy adj heilig *hile·ikh*

home n das Haus *hows*; (institution) das Heim *hime*; at home zu Hause *tsoo how·zė*; to go home nach Hause gehen* *nakh how·zė gay·ėn*

home address n die Heimatadresse *hye·mat·a·dre·sė*

homesick adj □ to be homesick Heimweh haben* *hime·vay hah·bėn*

homework n die Schulaufgaben (pl) *shool·owf·gah·bėn*

homogenized adj homogenisiert *hō·mō·gay·nee·zeert*

honest adj ehrlich *ayr·likh*

honey n der Honig *hō·nikh*

honeymoon n die Flitterwochen (pl) *fli·tėr·vo·khėn*; on one's honeymoon in den Flitterwochen *in dayn fli·tėr·vo·khėn*

hood n die Kapuze *ka·poot·sė*; (of car) die Motorhaube *mō·tōr·how·bė*

hook n der Haken *hah·kėn*; hook and eye Haken und Öse *hah·kėn oont ur'·zė*

hoop n der Reifen *rye·fėn*

hoot vi (horn) hupen *hoo·pėn*

hop vi hüpfen *hőőp·fėn*

hope n die Hoffnung *hof·noong* □ vi hoffen *ho·fėn*; I hope so/not hoffentlich (nicht) *ho·fėnt·likh (nikht)*

horizon n der Horizont *ho·ree·tsont*

horizontal adj horizontal *hō·ree·tson·tahl*

horn n (of animal) das Horn *horn*; (of car) die Hupe *hoo·pė*

horrible adj fürchterlich *főőrkh·tėr·likh*

horror movie n der Horrorfilm *ho·ror·film*

hors d'œuvre n die Vorspeise *főr·shpye·zė*

horse n das Pferd *pfert*

horseback riding n Reiten (nt) *rye·tėn*; to go horseback riding reiten gehen* *rye·tėn gay·ėn*

horse-racing n die Pferderennen (pl) *pfer·dė·re·nėn*

hose n (pipe) der Schlauch *shlowkh*

hospital n das Krankenhaus *krang·kėn·hows* I54, Ea7

hospitality *n* die Gastfreundschaft *gast·froynt·shaft*

host *n* der Gastgeber *gast·gay·bèr*

hostage *n* die Geisel *gye·zèl*; **to take someone hostage** jemanden als Geisel nehmen* *yay·man·dèn als gye·zèl nay·mèn*

hostel *n* das Heim *hime*

hostess *n* die Gastgeberin *gast·gay·bè·rin*

hot *adj* heiß *hise*; (spicy) scharf *sharf*

hot dog *n* der Hot Dog *hot dok*

hotel *n* das Hotel *hō·tel* T115, A29

hotplate *n* die Heizplatte *hites·pla·tè*

hot-water bottle *n* die Wärmflasche *verm·fla·shè*

hour *n* die Stunde *shtoon·dè*

hourly *adv* stündlich *shtōōnt·likh*

house *n* das Haus *hows*; **on the house** auf Kosten des Hauses *owf kos·tèn des how·zès* A59f

housecoat *n* der Morgenrock *mor·gèn·rok*

household *n* der Haushalt *hows·halt*

housekeeper *n* die Haushälterin *hows·hel·tè·rin*

housewife *n* die Hausfrau *hows·frow*

housework *n* die Hausarbeit *hows·ar·bite*

housing *n* Wohnungen (pl) *vō·noong·èn*

hovercraft *n* das Luftkissenfahrzeug *looft·ki·sèn·fahr·tsoyk*

how *adv* wie *vee*; **how long?** wie lange? *vee lang·è*; **how long have you been here?** wie lange sind Sie schon hier? *vee lang·è zint zee shōn heer*; **how many?** wie viele? *vee fee·lè*; **how much?** wieviel? *vee·feel*

however *conj* jedoch *yay·dokh*

hug *vt* umarmen *oom·ar·mèn*

hullo *excl* hallo *ha·lō*

human *adj* menschlich *mensh·likh*

hump *n* (on road) der Buckel *boo·kèl*

hundred *num* hundert *hoon·dèrt*; **a hundred (and) eighty five** hundertfünfundachtzig *hoon·dèrt·fōōnf·oont·akh·tsikh*; **a hundred people** einhundert Leute *ine·hoon·dèrt loy·tè*; **hundreds of books** Hunderte von Büchern *hoon·dèr·tè fon bōō·khèrn*

hundredth *adj* hunderste(r/s) *hoon·dèr·stè(·stèr/·stès)*

Hungarian *adj* ungarisch *oon·ga·rish* □ *n* der Ungar *oon·gar*

Hungary *n* Ungarn (nt) *oon·garn*

hunger *n* der Hunger *hoong·èr*

hungry *adj* hungrig *hoong·grikh*; **to be hungry** Hunger haben* *hoong·èr hah·bèn*

hunt *vt* jagen *yah·gèn*

hurricane *n* der Orkan *or·kahn*

hurry *vi* sich beeilen *zikh bè·ile·èn* □ *n* **to be in a hurry** es eilig haben* *ess ile·ikh hah·bèn* B70, Sn69

hurt *vi* weh tun* *vay toon*; **to hurt oneself** sich weh tun* *zikh vay toon*

husband *n* der Mann *man* T111, S111

hut *n* die Hütte *hōō·tè*

hygienic *adj* hygienisch *hōō·gee·ay·nish*

hymn *n* die Hymne *hōōm·nè*

hyphen *n* der Bindestrich *bin·dè·shtrikh*

hysterical *adj* hysterisch *hōō·stay·rish*

I

I *pron* ich *ikh*

ice *n* das Eis *ise* A94

icebox *n* der Kühlschrank *kōōl·shrank*

ice cream *n* das Eis *ise*

ice cube *n* der Eiswürfel *ise·vōōr·fèl*

Iceland *n* Island (nt) *ees·lant*

icing *n* (on cake) der Zuckerguß *tsoo·kèr·goos*

idea *n* die Idee *i·day*

ideal *adj* ideal *i·day·ahl*

identical *adj* identisch *i·den·tish*

identify *vt* identifizieren *i·den·ti·fi·tsee·rèn*

identity card *n* der Ausweis *ows·vise*

idiot *n* der Dummkopf *doom·kopf*

if *conj* wenn *ven*

ignition *n* (car) die Zündung *tsōōn·doong*

ignition key *n* der Zündschlüssel *tsōōnt·shlōō·sèl*

ignorant *adj* unwissend *oon·vi·sènt*

ignore *vt* (person) übersehen* *ōō·bèr·zay·èn*

ill *adj* krank *krank*

illegal *adj* gesetzwidrig *gè·zets·vee·drikh*

illegitimate *adj* unehelich *oon·ay·è·likh*

illness *n* die Krankheit *krank·hite*

illustration *n* die Illustration *i·loo·stra·tsee·ōn*

imagination *n* die Phantasie *fan·ta·zee*

imagine *vt* sich vor|stellen *zikh for·shte·lèn*; (wrongly) sich ein|bilden *zikh ine·bil·dèn*

imitate *vt* nach|ahmen *nakh·ah·mèn*

immediate *adj* unmittelbar *oon·mi·tèl·bar*

immediately *adv* sofort *zō·fort*

immersion heater *n* der Boiler *boy·lèr*

immigrant *n* der Einwanderer *ine·van·dèr·èr*

impatient *adj* ungeduldig *oon·gè·dool·dikh*

imperfect *adj* fehlerhaft *fay·lèr·haft*

impersonal *adj* unpersönlich *oon·per·zur'n·likh*

import *n* die Einfuhr *ine·foor* □ *vt* ein|führen *ine·fōō·rèn*

importance *n* die Wichtigkeit *vikh·tikh·kite*

important *adj* wichtig *vikh·tikh* L2

importer *n* der Importeur *im·por·tur*

impossible *adj* unmöglich *oon·mur'·glikh*

impress *vt* (win approval) beeindrucken *bè·ine·droo·kèn*

impression *n* der Eindruck *ine·drook*

impressive *adj* eindrucksvoll *ine·drooks·fol*

improve *vt* verbessern *fer·be·sèrn* □ *vi* sich bessern *zikh be·sèrn*

improvement *n* die Verbesserung *fer·be·sèr·oong*

in *prep* in *in*; **in May** im Mai *im mye*; **he did it in 2 days** er hat es innerhalb von 2 Tagen gemacht *er hat es in·èr·halp fon 2 tah·gèn gè·makht*; **he'll be back in 2 days** er wird in 2 Tagen zurück sein *er virt in 2 tah·gèn tsoo·rōōk zine*; **in town** in der Stadt *in der shtat*; **in France** in Frankreich *in frank·ryekh*; **in Switzerland** in der Schweiz *in der shvites*; **in German** auf deutsch *owf doytsh* □ *adv* **is he in?** ist er da? *ist er dah*

incentive *n* der Anreiz *an·rites*

inch *n* der Zoll *tsol*

incident *n* (event) das Ereignis *er·ike·nis*

incinerator *n* der Verbrennungsofen *fer·bre·noongs·ō·fèn*

include *vt* ein|schließen* *ine·shlee·sèn*

including *prep* einschließlich *ine·shlees·likh*

inclusive adj (costs) inklusive in·kloo·zee·ve; **from 6th to 12th inclusive** vom 6. bis einschließlich 12. fom 6 bis ine·shlees·likh 12 □ adv **inclusive of tip** Bedienung inbegriffen bė·dee·noong in·bė·gri·fėn

income n das Einkommen ine·ko·mėn

income tax n die Lohnsteuer lōn·stoy·ėr

incomplete adj unvollständig oon·fol·shten·dikh

inconvenient adj unpraktisch oon·prak·tish; (time, place) ungünstig oon·göön·stikh

incorrect adj falsch falsh

increase n er·hur'·ėn □ vi steigen* shtye·gėn □ n (in size) die Vergrößerung fer·grur'·sė·roong; (in number) die Zunahme tsoo·nah·mė

incredible adj unglaublich oon·glowp·likh

indecent adj unanständig oon·an·shten·dikh

independence n die Unabhängigkeit oon·ap·heng·ikh·kite

independent adj unabhängig oon·ap·heng·ikh

index n der Index in·deks

indexed adj (interest rates etc) der Inflationsrate angeglichen in·fla·tsee·ōns·rah·tė an·gė·gli·khėn

India n Indien (nt) in·dee·ėn

Indian adj indisch in·dish □ n (American) der Indianer in·de·ah·nėr

indicator n (of car) der Blinker bling·kėr

indigestible adj schwer verdaulich shvayr fer·dow·likh

indigestion n die Magenverstimmung mah·gėn·fer·shti·moong

indirect adj (route) indirekt in·dee·rekt

individual adj einzeln ine·tsėln

individually adv einzeln ine·tsėln

indoor adj (games) Zimmer- tsi·mėr

indoors adv (be) im Haus im hows; (go) ins Haus ins hows

industrial adj Industrie- in·doos·tree

industry n die Industrie in·doos·tree

inefficient adj inkompetent in·kom·pay·tent

inevitable adj unvermeidlich oon·fer·mite·likh

inexpensive adj billig bi·likh

infection n die Infektion in·fek·tsee·ōn

infectious adj ansteckend an·shte·kėnt

inferior adj minderwertig min·dėr·ver·tikh

inflammation n die Entzündung en·tsōōn·doong

inflatable adj aufblasbar owf·blahs·bar

inflate vt auf|blasen* owf·blah·zėn

inflation n (economic) die Inflation in·fla·tsee·ōn

influence n der Einfluß ine·floos

inform vt unterrichten oon·tėr·rikh·tėn

informal adj (party) zwanglos tsvang·lōs; dress: **informal** zwanglose Kleidung tsvang·lō·zė klye·doong

information n die Auskunft ows·koonft

information desk n die Auskunft ows·koonft

information office n das Auskunftsbüro ows·koonfts·bōō·rō T51

ingredients pl die Zutaten (pl) tsoo·tah·tėn

inhabit vt bewohnen bė·vō·nėn

inhabitant n der Einwohner ine·vō·nėr

inherit vt erben er·bėn

initials pl die Initialen (pl) i·ni·tsee·ah·lėn

injection n die Spritze shpri·tsė

injure vt verletzen fer·let·sėn

injury n die Verletzung fer·le·tsoong

ink n die Tinte tin·tė

inn n das Gasthaus gast·hows

innocent adj unschuldig oon·shool·dikh

inoculation n die Impfung imp·foong

input n (computing) der Input in·poot

insect n das Insekt in·zekt S43

insect repellent n das Insektenbekämpfungsmittel in·zek·tėn·bė·kemp·foongs·mi·tėl

inside n das Innere in·e·rė □ adj **the inside wall** die Innenwand i·nėn·vant □ prep **inside the box** in der Schachtel in der shakh·tėl □ adv **to be inside** drinnen sein* dri·nėn zine; **to go inside** hinein|gehen* hin·ine·gay·ėn; **to turn something inside out** etwas um-|drehen et·vass oom·dray·ėn

insist vi □ **to insist on something** auf etwas bestehen* owf et·vass bė·shtay·ėn

insolent adj frech frekh

inspect vt prüfen prōō·fėn

inspector n (police) der Polizeiinspektor po·lee·tsye·in·shpek·tor; (of building) der Baugutachter bow·goot·akh·tėr

instalment n die Rate rah·tė M11

instalment plan n der Teilzahlungskauf tile·tsah·loongs·kowf

instant adj sofortig zō·for·tikh; **instant coffee** der Pulverkaffee pool·vėr·ka·fay □ n **instant** der Augenblick ow·gėn·blik

instead of prep statt shtat

institute n das Institut in·sti·toot

instructions pl die Anweisungen (pl) an·vye·zoong·ėn; **instructions for use** die Gebrauchsanweisung gė·browkhs·an·vye·zoong

instructor n der Lehrer lay·rėr

instructress n die Lehrerin lay·rė·rin

instrument n (tool) das Gerät gė·ret; (musical) das Instrument in·stroo·ment

insulin n das Insulin in·zoo·leen

insult n die Beleidigung bė·lye·di·goong □ vt beleidigen bė·lye·di·gėn

insurance n die Versicherung fer·zi·khė·roong

insurance company n die Versicherungsgesellschaft fer·zi·khė·roongs·gė·zel·shaft T181, 208

insurance policy n die Versicherungspolice fer·zi·khė·roongs·po·lee·sė

insure vt/i versichern fer·zi·khėrn

insured adj versichert fer·zi·khėrt

intelligence n die Intelligenz in·te·lee·gents

intelligent adj intelligent in·te·lee·gent

intend vt bestimmen bė·shti·mėn; **to intend to do something** beabsichtigen, etwas zu tun bė·ap·zikh·ti·gėn et·vass tsoo toon

intention n die Absicht ap·zikht

interchange n (on roads) die Kreuzung kroy·tsoong

intercom n die Sprechanlage shprekh·an·lah·gė

interest n das Interesse in·tė·re·sė; (hobby) das Hobby ho·bi; (on investment) die Zinsen (pl) tsin·zėn □ vt interessieren in·tė·re·see·rėn Bm30

interested adj interessiert in·tė·re·seert; **to be interested in** sich interessieren für zikh in·tė·re·see·rėn fōōr

interesting adj interessant in·tė·re·sant

interest rate n der Zinssatz tsins·zats

J

interfere *vi* sich ein|mischen *zikh ine·mi·shèn*

interior *adj* Innen- *in·èn*

intermission *n* (*in performance*) die Pause *pow·zè*

internal *adj* innere(r/s) *in·èr·è(·èr/·ès)*

Internal Revenue *n* das Finanzamt *fee·nants·amt*

international *adj* international *in·ter·na·tsee·ô·nahl*

interpret *vt* aus|legen *ows·lay·gèn* □ *vi* dolmetschen *dol·met·shèn*

interpreter *n* der Dolmetscher *dol·met·shèr*, die Dolmetscherin *dol·met·shè·rin*

interrupt *vt/i* unterbrechen* *oon·tèr·bre·khèn*

intersection *n* (*of roads*) die Kreuzung *kroy·tsoong*

interview *n* (*for job*) das Einstellungsgespräch *ine·shte·loongs·gè·shprekh*

into *prep* in *in*

introduce *vt* (*person*) vor|stellen *fôr·shte·lèn* Mc35

introduction *n* (*in book*) die Einleitung *ine·lye·toong*; (*social*) die Vorstellung *fôr·shte·loong*

invalid *n* der/die Kranke *krang·kè*

invent *vt* erfinden* *er·fin·dèn*

invention *n* die Erfindung *er·fin·doong*

inventory *n* das Inventar *in·ven·tahr*

invest *vt* investieren *in·ve·stee·rèn* □ *vi* to invest in Geld an|legen *gelt an·lay·gèn*

investment *n* die Investition *in·ve·sti·tsee·ôn*

investor *n* der Kapitalanleger *ka·pee·tahl·an·lay·gèr*

invisible *adj* unsichtbar *oon·zikht·bahr*

invitation *n* die Einladung *ine·lah·doong*

invite *vt* ein|laden* *ine·lah·dèn*

invoice *n* die Faktura *fak·too·ra*

iodine *n* das Jod *yôt*

Iran *n* der Iran *i·rahn*

Iraq *n* der Irak *i·rahk*

Ireland *n* Irland (*nt*) *eer·lant*

Irish *adj* irisch *ee·rish*

iron *n* (*material, golf club*) das Eisen *eye·zèn*; (*for clothes*) das Bügeleisen *bōō·gel·eye·zèn* □ *vt* bügeln *bōō·gèln*

ironmonger *n* der Eisenwarenhändler *eye·zèn·vah·rèn·hent·lèr*

is *vi* □ **she/he** is sie/er ist *zee·er ist*

island *n* die Insel *in·zèl*; (*traffic*) die Verkehrsinsel *fer·kayrs·in·zèl*

Israel *n* Israel (*nt*) *is·ra·el*

issue *n* (*matter*) die Frage *frah·gè*; (*of magazine*) die Ausgabe *ows·gah·bè*; (*of stocks*) die Emission *ay·mi·see·ôn*

it *pron* □ **it's blue** er/sie/es ist blau *er/zee/ess ist blow*; **take it** nehmen Sie ihn/sie/es *nay·mèn zee een/zee/ess*; **it's me** ich bin es *ikh bin ess*; **it's raining** es regnet *ess rayg·nèt*; **it's 5 kilometers** es sind 5 kilometer *ess zint 5 kee·lô·may·tèr*

Italian *adj* italienisch *i·tal·yay·nish* □ *n* Italienisch (*nt*) *i·tal·yay·nish*

Italy *n* Italien (*nt*) *i·tahl·yèn*

itch *n* der Juckreiz *yook·rites* □ *vi* jucken *yoo·kèn*

item *n* der Posten *pos·tèn*

itemized *adj* (*bill etc*) spezifiziert *shpe·tsi·fi·tseert*

its *adj* sein(e) *zine(·è)*, ihr(e) *eer(·è)*

ivory *n* das Elfenbein *el·fèn·bine*

jack *n* (*for car*) der Wagenheber *vah·gèn·hay·bèr*; (*cards*) der Bube *boo·bè*

jacket *n* die Jacke *ya·kè*

jail *n* das Gefängnis *gè·feng·nis*; **in jail** im Gefängnis *im gè·feng·nis*

jam *vi* (*machine*) sich verklemmen *zikh fer·kle·mèn* □ *n* die Marmelade *mar·mè·lah·dè*; (*in traffic*) der Verkehrsstau *fer·kers·shtow*

janitor *n* der Hausmeister *hows·mye·stèr*

January *n* Januar (*m*) *yan·oo·ar*

Japan *n* Japan (*nt*) *ya·pahn*

Japanese *adj* japanisch *ya·pah·nish*; **he's Japanese** er ist Japaner *er ist ya·pah·nèr*; **she's Japanese** sie ist Japanerin *zee ist ya·pah·nè·rin* □ *n* Japanese Japanisch (*nt*) *ya·pah·nish*

jar *n* das Glas *glahs*

jaw *n* der Kiefer(knochen) *kee·fèr(·knokh·èn)*

jazz *n* der Jazz *jaz* L42

jealous *adj* eifersüchtig *ife·èr·zōōkh·tikh*

jeans *pl* die Jeans (*pl*) *jeenz*

jeep *n* der Jeep *jeep*

jellyfish *n* die Qualle *kva·lè*

jerkin *n* die Jacke *ya·kè*

jersey *n* (*fabric*) der Jersey *jer·zee*; (*sweater*) der Pullover *poo·lô·vèr*

jet *n* (*plane*) das Düsenflugzeug *dōō·zèn·flook·tsoyg*

jetty *n* die Mole *mô·lè*

Jew *n* der Jude *yoo·dè*

jewel *n* der Edelstein *ay·dèl·shtine*

jeweler *n* der Juwelier *yoo·vè·leer*

jewelry *n* der Schmuck *shmook* S91

Jewish *adj* jüdisch *yōō·dish*

jigsaw (puzzle) *n* das Puzzelspiel *pooz·èl·shpeel*

jingle *n* (*advertising*) der Werbespruch *ver·bè·shprookh*

job *n* (*employment*) die Stelle *shte·lè*; (*task*) die Aufgabe *owf·gah·bè*

jockey *n* der Rennreiter *ren·rye·tèr*

jogging *n* das Joggen *jo·gèn*; **to go jogging** Dauerlauf machen *dow·èr·lowf makh·èn*

join *vt* verbinden* *fer·bin·dèn*; (*club*) Mitglied werden* von *mit·gleet ver·dèn fon*; **do join us** wollen Sie uns nicht Gesellschaft leisten? *vol·èn zee oons nikht gè·zel·shaft lye·stèn*

joint *n* (*of body*) das Gelenk *gè·lenk*; (*of meat*) der Braten *brah·tèn*

joint ownership *n* das Miteigentum *mit·ige·èn·toom*

joint-stock company *n* die Aktiengesellschaft *ak·tsee·èn·gè·zel·shaft*

joke *n* der Witz *vits*

joker *n* (*cards*) der Joker *jô·kèr*

journalist *n* der Journalist *joor·na·list*

journey *n* die Fahrt *fahrt*

joy *n* die Freude *froy·dè*

jubilee *n* das Jubiläum *yoo·bi·lay·oom*

judge *n* der Richter *rikh·tèr* □ *vt* beurteilen *bè·oor·tile·èn*

judo *n* das Judo *yoo·dô*

jug *n* der Krug *krook*

juice *n* der Saft *zaft* E65f

jukebox *n* die Musikbox *moo·zeek·box*

July *n* Juli (*m*) *yoo·lee*

jumbo jet *n* der Jumbo *jum·bô*

jump *vt/i* springen* *shpring·èn*; **to jump (over) a wall** über eine Mauer hinüber|springen* *ōō·bèr ine·è mow·èr hin·ōō·bèr·shpring·èn*

jumper *n* (*dress*) das Trägerkleid *tre·gèr·klite*

jumper cables pl die Starthilfekabel (pl) shtart·hilf·e·kah·bèl

junction n (in road) die Kreuzung kroy·tsoong; (railway) der Gleisanschluß glyes·an·shloos

June n Juni (m) yoo·nee

junior adj (class, pupil) Grund- groont

junket n die Dickmilch dick·milkh

just adv □ just here genau hier gè·now heer; he's just left er ist gerade weggegangen er ist gè·rah·dè vek·gè·gang·èn; it was just a mistake es war nur ein Fehler ess vahr noor ine fay·lèr; I just managed it ich habe es gerade eben geschafft ikh hah·bè ess gè·rah·dè ay·bèn gè·shaft; just above the elbow gleich über dem Ellenbogen glyekh ōō·bèr dayn el·èn·bō·gèn; it only just missed es hat fast getroffen ess hat fast gè·trof·fèn; he arrived just now er ist eben angekommen er ist ay·bèn an·gè·ko·mèn

justice n die Gerechtigkeit gè·rekh·tikh·kite

K

karate n das Karate ka·rah·tè

kebab n der Kebab kay·bap

keep n der Unterhalt oon·tèr·halt; to earn one's keep seinen Unterhalt verdienen zy·nèn oon·tèr·halt fer·dee·nèn □ vt keep (retain) behalten* bè·hal·tèn; (feed and clothe) versorgen fer·zor·gèn; to keep something till later etwas bis später auf|heben* et·vass biss shpay·tèr owf·hay·bèn; to keep something in the refrigerator etwas im Kühlschrank auf|bewahren et·vass im kōōl·shrank owf·bè·vah·rèn; keep the change! der Rest ist für Sie! der rest ist fōōr zee; to keep something tidy etwas sauber halten* et·vass zow·bèr hal·tèn □ vi milk doesn't keep very well Milch hält sich nicht gut milkh helt zikh nikht goot

Kenya n Kenia (nt) ken·ya

kerosene n das Kerosin ke·rō·zeen

ketchup n das Ketchup ke·chap

kettle n der Kessel ke·sèl

key n der Schlüssel shlōō·sèl; (of piano, typewriter) die Taste ta·stè B77, T174, A41, Sn59

keyhole n das Schlüsselloch shlōō·sèl·lokh

key ring n der Schlüsselring shlōō·sèl·ring

kick n der Tritt trit □ vt (person) treten* tray·tèn; (ball) kicken ki·kèn

kid n (leather) das Ziegenleder tsee·gèn·lay·dèr

kidnap vt entführen ent·fōō·rèn

kidney n die Niere nee·rè

kidney beans pl die Gartenbohnen (pl) gar·tèn·bō·nèn

kill vt töten tur·tèn

killer n der Mörder mur·dèr, die Mörderin mur·dè·rin

kilo n das Kilo kee·lō

kilogram n das Kilogramm kee·lō·gram

kilometer n der Kilometer kee·lō·may·tèr

kilowatt n das Kilowatt kee·lō·vat

kilt n der Kilt kilt

kind n (type) die Art art; a kind of bean eine Art Bohne ine·è art bō·nè □ adj kind freundlich froynt·likh

king n der König kur·nikh

kirsch n der Kirsch kirsh

kiss vt küssen kōō·sèn; to kiss (each

other) sich küssen zikh kōō·sèn □ n kiss der Kuß kooss

kitchen n die Küche kōō·khè

kite n der Drachen dra·khèn

kleenex n das Papiertaschentuch pa·peer·ta·shèn·tookh

knee n das Knie knee; to sit on someone's knee auf jemandes Knien sitzen* owf yay·man·dès knee·èn zit·sèn

kneel vi auf Knien liegen* owf knee·èn lee·gèn; to kneel down nieder|knien nee·dèr·knee·èn

knife n das Messer me·sèr

knit vt/i stricken shtri·kèn

knitting needle n die Stricknadel shtrik·nah·dèl

knitwear n die Strickwaren (pl) shtrik·vah·rèn

knob n (on door) der Griff grif; (on radio etc) der Knopf knopf

knock vt an|stoßen* an·shtō·sèn; to knock (at) the door an die Tür klopfen an dee tōōr klop·fèn; to knock down um|werfen* oom·ver·fèn; to knock out K.o. schlagen* kah·ō shlah·gèn □ vi knock (engine) klopfen klop·fèn

knot vt knoten knō·tèn □ n der Knoten knō·tèn; to tie a knot einen Knoten machen ine·èn knō·tèn makh·èn

know vt (person) kennen* ke·nèn; (fact) wissen* vi·sèn; (language) können* kur·nèn; to know how to do something wissen*, wie man etwas macht vi·sèn, vee man èt·vass makht

knowledge n die Kenntnis kent·niss

knuckle n der Fingerknöchel fing·èr·knur·khèl

kohlrabi n der Kohlrabi kōl·rah·bee

kosher adj koscher kō·shèr

L

label n das Etikett ay·ti·ket □ vt etikettieren ay·ti·ke·teer·èn

labor n die Arbeit ar·bite

laboratory n das Labor la·bōr

laborer n der Arbeiter ar·bye·tèr

labor force n die Arbeiterschaft ar·bye·tèr·shaft

labor union n die Gewerkschaft gè·verk·shaft

lace n die Spitze shpit·sè; (of shoe) der Schnürsenkel shnōōr·zeng·kèl

ladder n die Leiter lye·tèr

ladle n der Schöpflöffel shur·pf·lur·fèl

lady n die Dame dah·mè

lager n das Pils pils

lake n der See zay

lamb n das Lamm lam S40

lambswool n die Lambswool lams·wool

lamp n die Lampe lam·pè

lamppost n der Laternenpfahl la·ter·nèn·pfahl

lampshade n der Lampenschirm lam·pèn·shirm

land n das Land lant; (soil) der Boden bō·dèn; (property) das Grundstück groont·shtōōk □ vi (from ship) an Land gehen* an lant gay·èn; (plane) landen lan·dèn

landing n (of plane) die Landung lan·doong; (on stairs) der Treppenabsatz tre·pèn·ap·zats

landing strip n die Landebahn lan·dè·bahn

landlady n die Wirtin vir·tin

landlord n der Wirt virt

landmark n das Wahrzeichen *vahr·tsye·khèn*

landslide n der Erdrutsch *ert·rootsh*

lane n (*in country*) der Weg *vayk*; (*in town*) die Gasse *ga·sè*; (*of road*) die Spur *shpoor*

language n die Sprache *shprah·khè*

language laboratory n das Sprachlabor *shprahkh·la·bōr*

lanolin n das Lanolin *la·nō·leen*

lap n (*of track*) die Runde *roon·dè*; (*of person*) der Schoß *shōss*

lard n das Schweineschmalz *shvine·è·shmalts*

larder n die Speisekammer *shpye·zè·kam·èr*

large adj groß *grōss*

laryngitis n die Kehlkopfentzündung *kayl·kopf·ent·tsöōn·doong*

last adj letzt *letst*; **last night/week** letzte Nacht/Woche *let·stè nakht/vo·khè* □ adv last als letzter *als let·stèr*; at last endlich *ent·likh* □ vi last dauern *dow·èrn*

latch n der Riegel *ree·gèl*

late adj, adv spät *shpayt*; **the latest news** die Neu(e)ste *noy·(è·)stè*; **the late king** der verstorbene König *der fer·shtor·bè·nè kur'·nikh*

lately adv in letzter Zeit *in let·stèr tsite*

later adj (*date etc*) später *shpay·tèr*; (*version*) neuer *noy·èr* □ adv (*to come etc*) später *shpay·tèr*

Latin[1] n Latein (nt) *la·tine* □ adj lateinisch *la·tine·ish*

Latin America n Lateinamerika (nt) *la·tine·a·may·ri·ka*

Latin American adj lateinamerikanisch *la·tine·a·may·ri·kah·nish*

laugh vi lachen *la·khèn*; **to laugh at somebody** sich über jemanden lustig machen *zikh ōō·bèr yay·man·dèn loos·tikh ma·khèn* □ n laugh das Lachen *la·khèn*

laughter n das Gelächter *gè·lekh·tèr*

launch n die Barkasse *bar·ka·sè* □ vt (*ship*) vom Stapel lassen* *fom shtah·pèl la·sèn*; (*product*) ein|führen *ine·fōō·rèn*

laundromat n der Waschsalon *vash·za·long* Sn70

laundry n (*place*) die Wäscherei *ve·shè·rye*; (*clothes*) die schmutzige Wäsche *shmoo·tsi·gè ve·shè* A55, Sn71

lavatory n die Toilette *twa·le·tè* T156

law n das Gesetz *gè·zets*; **law and order** Recht und Ordnung *rekht oont ort·noong*

lawn n (*grass*) der Rasen *rah·zèn*

lawn mower n der Rasenmäher *rah·zèn·may·èr*

lawn tennis n das Rasentennis *rah·zèn·te·nis*

lawyer n der Rechtsanwalt *rekhts·an·valt* Sn84

laxative n das Abführmittel *ap·fōōr·mi·tèl*

lay vt legen *lay·gèn*; **to lay the table** den Tisch decken *dayn tish de·kèn*; **to lay the fire** das Feuer her|richten *dass foy·èr her·rikh·tèn*; **to lay down** hin|legen *hin·lay·gèn*; (*wine*) lagern *lah·gèrn*; **to lay off** (*workers*) Feierschichten machen lassen* *fye·èr·shikh·tèn ma·khèn la·sèn*

layer n die Schicht *shikht*

lazy adj faul *fowl*

lead[1] vt führen *fōō·rèn* □ vi (*in contest*) in Führung liegen* *in fōō·roong lee·gèn*; **this door leads into the garden** diese Tür führt in den Garten hinaus *dee·zè tōōr fōōrt in dayn gar·tèn hi·nows* □ n lead (*electrical*) das Kabel *kah·bèl*; (*dog's*) die Leine *lye·nè*

lead[2] n das Blei *blye*; (*in pencil*) der Graphit *gra·feet*

leaf n das Blatt *blat*

leak n (*water*) das Leck *lek*; (*gas*) die undichte Stelle *oon·dikh·tè shte·lè* □ vi lecken *le·kèn* T171, Sn49

lean adj (*meat*) mager *mah·gèr* □ vi sich neigen *zikh nye·gèn*; **to lean against something** sich gegen etwas lehnen *zikh gay·gèn et·vass lay·nèn*

learn vt lernen *ler·nèn*

lease n die Miete *mee·tè*

leash n die Leine *lye·nè*

least adj □ **the least money** das wenigste Geld *dass vay·nikh·stè gelt*; **the least amount** die geringste Menge *dee gè·ring·stè meng·è* □ adv **the least expensive** der/die/das billigste *der/dee/dass bi·likh·stè* □ n **he has the least** er hat am wenigsten *er hat am vay·nikh·stèn*; **at least** wenigstens *vay·nikh·stèns*; **not in the least** ganz und gar nicht *gants oont gar nikht*

leather n das Leder *lay·dèr*

leave n (*holiday*) der Urlaub *oor·lowp*; **on leave** auf Urlaub *owf oor·lowp* □ vi gehen* *gay·èn* □ vt (*room, club, school*) verlassen* *fer·la·sèn*; **I've left my umbrella** ich habe meinen Schirm vergessen *ikh hah·bè mine·èn shirm fer·ge·sèn*; **let's leave the dishes** lassen wir das Geschirr stehen *la·sèn veer dass gè·shir shtay·èn*; **leave it to me** lassen Sie mich nur machen *la·sèn zee mikh noor ma·khèn*; **leave your coat here** lassen Sie Ihren Mantel hier *la·sèn zee eer·èn man·tèl heer*; **to leave a message** eine Nachricht hinter|lassen* *ine·è nakh·rikht hin·tèr·la·sèn*; **to leave out** (*omit*) aus|lassen* *ows·la·sèn*

lecture n die Vorlesung *fōr·lay·zoong*

ledger n das Hauptbuch *howpt·bookh*

leek n der Poree *po·ray*

left adv □ **there's some cream left** es ist noch etwas Sahne übrig *es ist nokh et·vass zah·nè ōō·brikh*; **to turn left** links ab|biegen* *links ap·bee·gèn* □ adj **the left side** die linke Seite *dee ling·kè zye·tè* T100

left-handed adj linkshändig *links·hen·dikh*

leg n das Bein *bine*; **leg of lamb** die Lammkeule *lam·koy·lè*; **chicken leg** das Hühnerbein *hōō·nèr·bine* I24

legal adj legal *lay·gahl*

leisure n die Freizeit *frye·tsite*

leisure center n das Freizeitzentrum *frye·tsite·tsen·troom*

lemon n die Zitrone *tsi·trō·nè*

lemonade n die Limonade *lee·mō·nah·dè*

lemon juice n der Zitronensaft *tsi·trō·nèn·zaft*

lemon sole n die Seezunge *zay·tsoong·è*

lemon-squeezer n die Zitronenpresse *tsi·trō·nèn·pre·sè*

lend vt leihen* *lye·èn*

length n die Länge *leng·è*

lens n (*of glasses*) das Glas *glahs*; (*of camera*) die Linse *lin·zè*

lentils pl die Linsen (*pl*) *lin·zèn*

less adj □ **less meat** weniger Fleisch *vay·ni·gèr flyesh* □ adv **less quickly** nicht so schnell *nikht zō shnel* □ n **he has less** er hat weniger *er hat vay·ni·*

gèr; less than weniger als *vay·ni·gèr als*

lesson *n* die Stunde *shtoon·dè*

let *vt* (*allow*) lassen* *la·sèn*; (*rent out*) vermieten *fer·mee·tèn*; **to let someone do something** jemanden etwas tun lassen* *yay·man·dèn et·vass toon la·sèn*; **let me in** laß mich herein *lass mikh he·rine*; **let's go** gehen wir *gay·èn veer*; **they let him go** sie ließen ihn gehen *zee lee·sèn een gay·èn*; **to let (on stay)** zu vermieten *tsoo fer·mee·tèn*; **to let someone down** jemanden im Stich lassen* *yay·man·dèn im shtikh la·sèn*

letter *n* (*of alphabet*) der Buchstabe *bookh·shtah·bè*; (*message*) der Brief *breef* A25, Sn1

letter box *n* der Briefkasten *breef·kas·tèn*

lettuce *n* der Kopfsalat *kopf·za·laht*

level *n* die Ebene *ay·bè·nè* □ *adj* (*surface*) eben *ay·bèn*; (*horizontal*) waagerecht *vah·gè·rekht*

lever *n* der Hebel *hay·bèl*

Levis *pl* die Jeans (*pl*) *jeens*

liabilities *pl* (*on balance sheet*) die Passiva (*pl*) *pa·see·vah*

library *n* die Bibliothek *bib·lee·ō·tayk*

Libya *n* Libyen (*nt*) *leeb·yèn*

license *n* (*for driving*) der Führerschein *foo·rèr·shine*

license plate *n* das Nummernschild *noo·mèrn·shilt*

lick *vt* lecken *le·kèn*

licorice *n* die Lakritze *la·krits·è*

lid *n* der Deckel *de·kèl*

lie *n* (*untruth*) die Lüge *lōō·gè* □ *vi* liegen* *lee·gèn*; (*tell a lie*) lügen *lōō·gèn*; **to lie down** sich hin|legen *zikh hin·lay·gèn*

Liechtenstein *n* Liechtenstein (*nt*) *likh·tèn·shtine*

life *n* das Leben *lay·bèn*; **for life** auf Lebenszeit *owf lay·bèns·tsite*

lifebelt *n* der Rettungsgürtel *re·toongs·gōōr·tèl*

lifeboat *n* das Rettungsboot *re·toongs·bōt*

lifeguard *n* der Rettungsschwimmer *re·toongs·shvi·mèr*

life insurance *n* die Lebensversicherung *lay·bèns·fer·zikh·è·roong*

life jacket *n* die Schwimmweste *shvim·ve·stè*

life preserver *n* (*belt*) der Rettungsgürtel *re·toongs·gōōr·tèl*; (*jacket*) die Schwimmveste *shvim·ve·stè*

lift *vt* auf|heben* *owf·hay·bèn*

light *vt* (*fire, cigarette*) an|zünden *an·tsōōn·dèn* □ *n* das Licht *likht*; (*traffic light*) die Ampel *am·pèl*; **have you got a light?** haben Sie Feuer? *hah·bèn zee foy·èr* □ *adj* light (*bright, pale*) hell *hel*; (*not heavy*) leicht *lyekht*; **light music** die Unterhaltungsmusik *oon·tèr·hal·toongs·moo·zeek*; **as soon as it was light** sobald es hell war *zō·balt ess hel vahr*

light bulb *n* die Glühbirne *glōō·bir·nè*

lighter *n* das Feuerzeug *foy·èr·tsoyk*

lighthouse *n* der Leuchtturm *loykht·toorm*

light industry *n* die Leichtindustrie *lyekht·in·doo·stree*

lighting *n* (*on road*) die Beleuchtung *bè·loykh·toong*

light meter *n* der Belichtungsmesser *be·likh·toongs·me·sèr*

lightning *n* der Blitz *blits*

like *prep* wie *vee* □ *adj* ähnlich *ayn-*

likh; **what's it like?** wie ist es? *vee ist ess* □ *vt* like gern haben* *gern hah·bèn*; **I'd like to go** ich möchte gehen *ikh mur'kh·tè gay·èn*; **I'd like an ice cream** ich hätte gern ein Eis *ikh he·tè gern ine ise*; **what would you like?** was wollen Sie? *vass vo·lèn zee*

likely *adj* wahrscheinlich *vahr·shine·likh*; **he's likely to come** es ist wahrscheinlich, daß er kommt *ess ist vahr·shine·likh dass er komt*

lily *n* die Lilie *lee·lee·è*

lime *n* (*fruit*) die Limone *li·mō·nè*

lime juice *n* der Limonensaft *li·mō·nèn·zaft*

limit *n* die Begrenzung *bè·gren·tsoong*

limousine *n* die Limousine *li·moo·zee·nè*

limp *vi* hinken *hing·kèn*

line *n* die Linie *lee·nee·è*; (*railway*) die Bahnlinie *bahn·lee·nee·è*; (*telephone*) die Verbindung *fer·bin·doong*; (*people waiting*) die Schlange *shlang·è*; **to stand in line** Schlange stehen* *shlang·è shtay·èn*

linen *n* (*cloth*) das Leinen *lye·nèn*; (*for beds*) die Wäsche *ve·shè*; (*for table*) die Tischwäsche *tish·ve·shè*

liner *n* (*ship*) das Passagierschiff *pa·sa·zheer·shif*

lining *n* das Futter *foo·tèr*

linoleum *n* das Linoleum *lee·nō·le·oom*

lint *n* der Mull *mool*

lion *n* der Löwe *lur'·vè*

lip *n* die Lippe *li·pè*

lipstick *n* der Lippenstift *li·pèn·shtift*

liqueur *n* der Likör *lee·kur*

liquid *n* die Flüssigkeit *flōō·sikh·kite* □ *adj* flüssig *flōō·sikh*

liquid assets *pl* die verfügbaren Aktiva (*pl*) *fer·fōōk·ba·rèn ak·tee·va*

liquidation *n* die Liquidation *li·kvi·da·tsee·ōn*; **to go into liquidation** in Liquidation gehen* *in li·kvi·da·tsee·ōn gay·èn*

liquor *n* der Alkohol *al·kō·hol*

list *n* die Liste *li·stè* □ *vt* notieren *nō·tee·rèn*

listen *vi* zu|hören *tsoo·hur·èn*; **to listen to** zu|hören *tsoo·hur·èn*

list price *n* der Listenpreis *li·stèn·prise*

liter *n* das Liter *lee·tèr*

literature *n* die Literatur *li·te·ra·toor*

little *adj* klein *kline* □ *n* **a little** ein wenig *ine vay·nikh*

live[1] *adj* (*alive*) lebend *lay·bènt*

live[2] *vi* leben *lay·bèn*; (*reside*) wohnen *vō·nèn*

lively *adj* lebhaft *layp·haft*

liver *n* die Leber *lay·bèr*

living room *n* das Wohnzimmer *vōn·tsi·mèr*

load *n* die Last *last* □ *vt* (*gun, camera*) laden* *lah·dèn*; (*truck, ship*) beladen* *bè·lah·dèn*

loaf (*of bread*) *n* das Brot *brōt*

loan *n* das Darlehen *dar·lay·èn* □ *vt* leihen* *lye·èn*

lobby *n* (*entrance*) die Eingangshalle *ine·gangs·ha·lè*

lobster *n* der Hummer *hoo·mèr*

local *adj* hiesig *hee·zikh*; **a local call** (*on phone*) ein Ortsgespräch *ine orts·gè·shprekh*

lock *n* (*on door*) das Schloß *shloss*; (*in canal*) die Schleuse *shloy·zè* □ *vt* ab|schließen* *ap·shlee·sèn*; **the door's locked** die Tür ist abgeschlossen *dee tōōr ist ap·gè·shlō·sèn* A50

locker *n* das Schließfach *shlees·fakh*

lodger n der Untermieter *oon·tèr·mee·tèr*

lodgings pl die Pension *pen·zee·ōn*

loft n der Speicher *shpye·khèr*

log n (of wood) der Baumstamm *bowm·shtam*

logbook n (of car) der Kraftfahrzeugbrief *kraft·fahr·tsoyk·breef*

lollipop n der Lutscher *loot·shèr*

London n London (nt) *lon·don*

lonely adj (person) einsam *ine·zam*

long adj lang *lang*; how long is the river? wie lang ist der Fluß? *vee lang ist der floos*; 6 meters/months long 6 Meter/Monate lang *6 may·tèr/mō·na·tè lang*; how long is the program? wie lange dauert das Programm? *vee lang·è dow·èrt dass prō·gram* □ adv long lange *lang·è*; all day long den ganzen Tag *dayn gan·tsèn tahk*; I shan't be long ich bin gleich fertig *ikh bin glyekh fer·tikh*; as long as (provided that) so lange wie *zō lang·è vee*

long-distance adj Fern- *fern*; a long-distance call ein Ferngespräch *ine fern·gè·shprekh*

long drink n der Longdrink *long·drink*

long-term adj langfristig *lang·fri·stikh*

long wave n die Langwelle *lang·ve·lè*

look n der Blick *blik*; (appearance) das Aussehen *ows·zay·èn* □ vi blicken *bli·kèn*; (appear) aussehen* *ows·zay·èn*; to look at an|sehen* *an·zay·èn*; to look like aus|sehen* wie *ows·zay·èn vee*; to look after sich kümmern um *zikh kōō·mèrn oom*; to look for suchen *zoo·khèn*; to look forward to sich freuen auf *zikh froy·èn owf*; look out! Vorsicht! *fōr·zikht*; to look up (word) nach|schlagen* *nakh·shlah·gèn*

loop n die Schlinge *shling·è*

loose adj locker *lo·kèr*; (clothing) weit *vite*

lose vt verlieren* *fer·lee·rèn*; to lose one's way sich verlaufen* *zikh fer·low·fèn* □ vi lose (clock, watch) nach|gehen* *nakh·gay·èn* Sn82

loss n der Verlust *fer·loost* Sn78

lot n (at auction) das Los *lōs*; lots of or a lot of milk viel Milch *feel milkh*; lots of or a lot of people viele Leute *fee·lè loy·tè*; a lot better viel besser *feel be·sèr*

lotion n die Lotion *lō·tsee·ōn*

lottery n die Lotterie *lo·tè·ree*

loud adj laut *lowt*

loudly adv laut *lowt*

loudspeaker n der Lautsprecher *lowt·shpre·khèr*

lounge n (in house) das Wohnzimmer *vōn·tsi·mèr*; (in hotel) der Gesellschaftsraum *gè·zel·shafts·rowm*; (at airport) die Wartehalle *var·tè·ha·lè*

love vt lieben *lee·bèn*; to love doing something etwas gern tun* *et·vass gern toon*; I'd love to go ich würde sehr gerne gehen *ikh vōōr·dè zayr ger·nè gay·èn* □ n love die Liebe *lee·bè*; in love verliebt *fer·leept*; love from (on letter) viele liebe Grüße von *fee·lè lee·bè grōō·sè fon*

lovely adj schön *shur'n*; we had a lovely time es war sehr schön *ess vahr zayr shur'n*

low adj niedrig *need·rikh*; (in pitch) tief *teef*

Low Countries pl die Niederlande (pl) *nee·dèr·lan·dè*

lower adj niedriger *nee·dri·gèr*

low tide n das Niedrigwasser *nee·drikh·va·sèr*

LP n die LP *el·pay*

Ltd abbrev GmbH *gay·em·bay·hah*

luck n das Glück *glōōk*; good luck! viel Glück! *feel glōōk*; bad luck das Pech *pekh*

lucky adj □ to be lucky Glück haben* *glōōk hah·bèn*

luggage n das Gepäck *gè·pek* T23f, 97, A24

luggage cart n der Kofferkuli *ko·fèr·koo·lee*

luggage rack n (in train) das Gepäcknetz *gè·pek·nets*; (on car) der Gepäckträger *gè·pek·tray·gèr*

lump n (on skin) die Beule *boy·lè*; (in sauce) der Klumpen *kloom·pèn*; lump of sugar das Stück Zucker *shtook tsoo·kèr*

lunch n das Mittagessen *mi·tak·e·sèn* A26

lunch hour n die Mittagsstunde *mi·taks·shtoon·dè*

lung n die Lunge *loong·è*

Luxembourg n Luxemburg (nt) *look·sèm·boork*

luxurious adj luxuriös *look·soo·ree·ur's*

luxury n der Luxus *look·soos* □ adj (car, hotel) Luxus- *look·soos*

M

macaroni n die Makkaroni (pl) *ma·ka·rō·nee*

machine n die Maschine *ma·shee·nè* B74

machinery n die Maschinerie *ma·shee·nè·ree*

mackerel n die Makrele *ma·kray·lè*

mack(intosh) n der Regenmantel *ray·gèn·man·tèl*

mad adj (insane) verrückt *fe·rookt*; (angry) böse *bur'·zè*

madam n die gnädige Dame *mine·è dah·mè*

Madeira n (wine) der Madeira *ma·day·ra*

made-to-measure adj maßgeschneidert *mahss·gè·shnye·dèrt*

Madrid n Madrid (nt) *ma·drit*

magazine n (journal) die Zeitschrift *tsite·shrift*

magic n die Magie *ma·gee* □ adj magisch *mah·gish*

magnet n der Magnet *mag·nayt*

magnetic tape n das Magnetband *mag·nayt·bant*

magnificent adj großartig *grōs·ahr·tikh*

mahogany n das Mahagoni *ma·ha·gō·nee*

maid n das Dienstmädchen *deenst·mayt·khèn* A70

maiden name n der Mädchenname *mayt·khèn·nah·mè*

maid service n das Dienstmädchen *deenst·mayt·khèn*

mail n die Post *post* □ vt mit der Post schicken *mit der post shi·kèn*

mailbox n der Briefkasten *breef·kas·tèn*

mailing list n die Anschriftenliste *an·shrif·tèn·lis·tè*

mailman n der Briefträger *breef·tray·gèr*

mail order n □ to buy something by mail order etwas bei einem Versandhaus kaufen *et·vass bye ine·èm fer·zant·hows kow·fèn*

main adj Haupt- *howpt* □ n to turn the electricity/water off at the main den Hauptschalter/Haupthahn ab|schalten *dayn* howpt·shal·tèr/howpt·hahn ap·shal·tèn

mainland *n* das Festland *fest·lant*

mainly *adv* hauptsächlich *howpt·sekh· likh*

maintenance *n* die Wartung *var·toong*; (*of building*) die Unterhaltung *oon· tèr·hal·toong*

major *adj* Haupt- *howpt*

majority *n* die Mehrheit *mer·hite*; **elected by a majority of 5** mit einer Mehrheit von 5 Stimmen gewählt *mit ine·èr mer·hite fon 5 shti·mèn ge· vaylt*

make *n* (*of product*) die Marke *mar·kè* □ *vt* machen *ma·khèn*; **to make the beds** die Betten machen *dee be·tèn ma·khèn*; **to make someone sad** jemanden traurig machen *yay·man·dèn trow·rikh ma·khèn*; **to make someone do something** jemanden zwingen*, etwas zu tun *yay·man·den tsving·èn et·vass tsoo toon*; **to make do with something** mit etwas aus|kommen* *mit et·vass ows·ko·mèn*; **to make (oneself) up** sich schminken *zikh shming·kèn*

make-up *n* das Make-up *make·up*

male *adj* männlich *men·likh*

mallet *n* der Holzhammer *holts·ha·mèr*

malt *n* das Malz *malts*

Malta *n* Malta (*nt*) *mal·ta*

man *n* der Mann *man*; (*human race*) der Mensch *mensh*

manage *vt* (*business*) leiten *lye·tèn*; **can you manage?** geht es? *gayt ess*; **to manage to do something** es schaffen*, etwas zu tun *es sha·fèn et·vass tsoo toon*

management *n* (*of business*) die Leitung *lye·toong*; (*managers*) die Unternehmensleitung *oon·tèr·nay·mèns· lye·toong*

manager *n* der Geschäftsführer *ge· shefts·fŏŏ·rèr*

manageress *n* die Geschäftsführerin *gè·shefts·fŏŏ·rè·rin*

managing director, M.D. *n* der leitende Direktor *lye·tèn·dè dee·rek·tor*

manicure *n* die Maniküre *ma·nee·kŏŏ· rè*

manicure set *n* das Nagelnecessaire *nah·gèl·nay·se·sayr*

man-made *adj* künstlich *kŏŏnst·likh*

manner *n* die Art *art*

manners *pl* die Manieren (*pl*) *ma·neer· èn*

manpower *n* die Arbeitskräfte (*pl*) *ar· bites·kref·tè*

mansion *n* die Villa *vi·la*

mantelpiece *n* der Kaminsims *ka· meen·zims*

manual *adj* manuell *man·oo·el* □ *n* (*book*) das Handbuch *hant·bookh*

manufacture *vt* her|stellen *her·shte·lèn*

manufacturer *n* der Hersteller *her· shte·lèr*

manufacturing *n* die Herstellung *her· shte·loong*

many *pron* viele *fee·lè* □ *adj* many books viele Bücher *fee·lè bŏŏ·khèr*

map *n* (*of country*) die Landkarte *lant· kar·tè*; (*of town*) der Stadtplan *shtat· plahn* F8, L4, S101

marble *n* (*material*) der Marmor *mar· mor*; (*ball*) die Murmel *moor·mèl*

March *n* März (*m*) *merts*

march *vi* marschieren *mar·shee·rèn* □ *n* der Marsch *marsh*

margarine *n* die Margarine *mar·ga·ree· nè*

margin *n* (*on page*) der Rand *rant*

marina *n* der Yachthafen *yakht·hah· fèn*

marjoram *n* der Majoran *mah·yo·rahn*

mark *n* das Zeichen *tsye·khèn*; (*stain*) der Fleck *flek*; (*currency*) die Mark *mark*; (*in school*) die Note *nŏ·tè* □ *vt* markieren *mar·kee·rèn*; (*stain*) schmutzig machen *shmoot·sikh ma· khèn*

market *n* der Markt *markt*; **there is a good market for X** der Markt für X ist gut *der markt fŏŏr X ist goot* □ *vt* **market** (*product*) vertreiben* *fer· trye·bèn* Bm18

market-day *n* der Markttag *markt·tahk*

marketing *n* das Marketing *mar·kè· ting*

marketing manager *n* der Leiter des Marketing *der lye·tèr dess mar·kè· ting*

market-place *n* der Marktplatz *markt· plats*

market research *n* die Marktforschung *markt·for·shoong*

market value *n* der Marktwert *markt· vert*

marmalade *n* die Orangenmarmelade *o·rang·zhèn·mar·me·la·dè*

maroon *adj* kastanienbraun *kas·tahn· yen·brown*

marriage *n* die Ehe *ay·è*; (*wedding*) die Hochzeit *hokh·tsite*

married *adj* verheiratet *fer·hye·rah·tèt*; **they were married yesterday** sie haben gestern geheiratet *zee hah·bèn ge·stern ge·hye·rah·tèt* Mc51

marrow *n* (*vegetable*) der Gartenkürbis *gar·tèn·kŏŏr·bis*

marry *vt/i* heiraten *hye·rah·tèn*

martini *n* (*Brit*) der Martini *mar·tee· nee*; (*US*) der Martini-Cocktail *mar· tee·nee kok·tail*

marvelous *adj* wunderbar *voon·dèr· bahr*

marzipan *n* das Marzipan *mar·tsee· pahn*

mascara *n* die Wimperntusche *vim· pern·too·shè*

masculine *adj* männlich *men·likh*

mash *vt* zerstampfen *tser·shtam·pfèn*

mashed potatoes *pl* der Kartoffelbrei *kar·to·fèl·brye*

mask *n* die Maske *mas·kè* □ *vt* maskieren *mas·kee·rèn*

mass *n* (*church*) die Messe *me·sè*; **a mass of blossom** eine Meer von Blüten *ine mayr fon blŏŏ·tèn*

massage *n* die Massage *ma·sah·zhè* □ *vt* massieren *ma·see·rèn*

masseur *n* der Masseur *ma·sur*

masseuse *n* die Masseuse *ma·sur'·zè*

massive *adj* riesig *ree·zikh*

mass-produce *vt* serienweise her|stellen *zay·ree·èn·vye·zè her·shte·lèn*

mass production *n* die Massenproduktion *ma·sèn·prŏ·dook·tsee·ŏn*

mast *n* (*ship's*) der Mastbaum *mast· bowm*; (*radio*) der Sendeturm *zen· dè·toorm*

master *n* der Herr *her*

master key *n* der Hauptschlüssel *howpt·shlŏŏ·sèl*

masterpiece *n* das Meisterstück *mye· stèr·shtŏŏk*

mat *n* die Matte *ma·tè*; (*place mat*) das Set *set*; (*under a glass*) der Untersetzer *oon·tèr·zet·sèr*

match *n* das Streichholz *stryekh·holts*; (*sports*) der Wettkampf *vet·kampf* □ *vt* passen zu *pa·sèn tsoo* B43, S101

matchbox *n* die Streichholzschachtel *shtryekh·holts·shakh·tèl*

material *n* das Material *ma·tay·ree·ahl*; (*fabric*) der Stoff *shtof*

maternity dress *n* das Umstandskleid *oom·shtants·klite*

maternity hospital *n* das Entbindungsheim *ent·bin·doongs·hime*

mathematics *n* die Mathematik *ma·tay·mah·teek*

matter *n* □ **what's the matter?** was ist los? *vass ist lōs* □ **it doesn't matter** das macht nichts *dass makht nikhts*

mattress *n* die Matratze *ma·trats·è*

mature *adj* (*wine*) ausgereift *ows·gè·ryeft*; (*cheese*) reif *rife*

mauve *adj* mauve *mōv*

maximize *vt* maximieren *mak·see·mee·rèn*

maximum *n* das Maximum *mak·see·moom* □ *adj* Höchst- *hur·kst*

May *n* Mai (*m*) *mye*

may *vi* □ **may I come in?** darf ich eintreten? *darf ikh ine·tray·tèn*; **it may rain** es könnte regnen *ess kur·n·tè rayg·nèn*; **we may as well go** ich glaube, wir können gehen *ikh glow·bè veer kur·nèn gay·èn*

Mayday *n* das Sos-signal *ess·ō·ess·zig·nahl*

mayonnaise *n* die Mayonnaise *ma·yo·nay·zè*

mayor *n* der Bürgermeister *bōōr·gèr·mye·stèr*

me *pron* mich *mikh*; **give it to me** geben Sie es mir *gay·bèn zee ess meer*; **he gave it to me** er hat es mir gegeben *er hat es meer gè·gay·bèn*; **it's me** ich bin es *ikh bin ess*

meal *n* die Mahlzeit *mahl·tsite* E49

mean *adj* (*miserly*) geizig *gye·tsikh*; (*unkind*) gemein *ge·mine* □ *vt* (*signify*) bedeuten *bè·doy·tèn*; **to mean to do** beabsichtigen, zu tun *bè·ap·zikh·ti·gèn tsoo toon* B48

meaning *n* die Bedeutung *bè·doy·toong*

means *pl* das Mittel *mi·tèl*; **by means of** mittels *mi·tèls*

meanwhile *adv* inzwischen *in·tsvi·shèn*

measles *n* die Masern (*pl*) *mah·zèrn*

measure *vt/i* messen* *me·sèn*

measurements *pl* die Maße (*pl*) *mah·sè*; **bust measurements** der Brustumfang *broost·oom·fang*

meat *n* das Fleisch *flyesh*

mechanic *n* der Mechaniker *me·khah·ni·kèr* T160

media *pl* die Medien (*pl*) *may·dee·èn*

median strip *n* der Mittelstreifen *mi·tèl·shtrye·fèn*

medical *adj* medizinisch *may·di·tseen·ish*

medicine *n* (*pills etc*) das Medikament *may·dee·kah·ment*

Mediterranean *adj* Mittelmeer- *mit·èl·mayr*; **the Mediterranean (Sea)** das Mittelmeer *mit·èl·mayr*

medium *adj* mittlere *mit·lè·rè*; **medium wave** die Mittelwelle *mit·èl·ve·lè*

meet *vt* treffen* *tre·fèn*; (*make acquaintance of*) kennen|lernen *ken·èn·ler·nèn*; (*demand*)entsprechen* *ent·shpre·khèn*; **I'll meet you at the station** (*go to get*) ich werde Sie am Bahnhof ab|holen *ikh ver·dè zee am bahn·hôf ap·hō·lèn*

meeting *n* die Versammlung *fer·zam·loong*

melon *n* die Melone *me·lo·nè*

melt *vt/i* schmelzen* *shmel·tsèn*

member *n* das Mitglied *mit·gleet* L58

memo(randum) *n* die Notiz *nō·teetz*

memory *n* das Gedächtnis *gè·dekht·nis*; **one of my memories** eine von meinen Errinerungen *ine·è fon mine·èn er·in·è·roong·èn*

mend *vt* reparieren *ray·pa·ree·rèn*

menswear *n* die Herrenbekleidung *her·rèn·bè·klye·doong*

mental hospital *n* die psychiatrische Klinik *psō·khee·ah·tri·shè klee·nik*

mentholated *adj* Menthol- *men·tōl*

mention *vt* erwähnen *er·vay·nèn*; **don't mention it** das ist doch nicht der Rede wert *dass ist dokh nikht der ray·dè vert*

menu *n* die Speisekarte *shpye·zè·kar·tè* E9, 17f

merchant *n* der Kaufmann *kowf·man*; (*shopkeeper*) der Händler *hent·lèr*

merge *vi* fusionieren *foo·zee·ō·neer·èn*

merger *n* die Fusion *foo·zee·ōn*

meringue *n* die Meringe *me·ring·è*

merry *adj* lustig *loos·tikh*

merry-go-round *n* das Karussell *ka·roo·sel*

mess *n* die Unordnung *oon·ort·noong*; **to make a mess** Unordnung machen *oon·ort·noong ma·khèn*; **to make a mess of something** etwas in Unordnung bringen* *et·vass in oon·ort·noong bring·èn*

message *n* die Nachricht *nakh·rikht* A25, B79

messenger *n* der Bote *bō·tè*

metal *n* das Metall *may·tal*

meter *n* der Zähler *tsay·lèr*; (*measure*) der Meter *may·tèr*

method *n* die Methode *may·tō·dè*

Methodist *n* der Methodist *may·tō·dist*

methylated spirits *pl* der Brennspiritus *bren·shpee·ree·toos*

metric *adj* metrisch *may·trish*

Mexican *adj* mexikanisch *mek·si·kah·nish*

Mexico *n* Mexiko (*nt*) *mek·si·kō*

microchip *n* das Mikrochip *mee·krō·chip*

microcomputer *n* der Mikrocomputer *mee·krō·kom·pyoo·tèr*

microfiche *n* das Mikrofiche *mee·krō·feesh*

microfilm *n* der Mikrofilm *mee·krō·film*

microphone *n* das Mikrophon *mee·krō·fōn*

microprocessor *n* der Mikroprozessor *mee·krō·pro·tses·or*

microwave oven *n* der Mikrowellenofen *mee·krō·vel·èn·ō·fèn*

midday *n* der Mittag *mi·tahk*; **at midday** mittags *mi·tahks*

middle *n* die Mitte *mi·tè*; **right in the middle** genau in der Mitte *gè·now in der mi·tè*; **in the middle of the night** mitten in der Nacht *mi·tèn in der nakht*

middle-aged *adj* in den mittleren Jahren *in dayn mit·lè·rèn yah·rèn*

middle-class *adj* bürgerlich *bōōr·gèr·likh*

Middle East *n* der Nahe Osten *nah·è os·tèn*

middle management *pl* das mittlere Management *mit·lè·rè ma·nage·ment*

midnight *n* die Mitternacht *mi·tèr·nakht*; **at midnight** um Mitternacht *oom mi·tèr·nakht*

midwife *n* die Hebamme *hay·ba·mè*

might *vi* □ **it might rain** es könnte regnen *es kur·n·tè rayg·nèn*; **we**

might as well go ich glaube, wir können gehen *ikh glow·bè veer kur'·nèn gay·èn*

migraine *n* die Migräne *mi·gray·nè*

mild *adj* mild *milt*

mile *n* die Meile *mile·è*; **miles per hour, m.p.h.** ≈ Kilometer pro Stunde *ki·lö·may·tèr prö shtoon·dè*

mileage *n* die Meilenzahl *mile·èn·tsahl*

military *adj* militärisch *mi·li·tay·rish*

milk *n* die Milch *milkh* S37

milk chocolate *n* die Vollmilchschokolade *fol·milkh·sho·ko·lah·dè*

milkman *n* der Milchmann *milkh·man*

milkshake *n* das Milchmixgetränk *milkh·miks·gè·trenk*

mill *n* die Mühle *mōō·lè* □ *vt* mahlen* *mahl·èn*

milligram *n* das Milligramm *mi·li·gram*

milliliter *n* das Milliliter *mi·li·lee·tèr*

millimeter *n* der Millimeter *mi·li·may·tèr*

million *num* die Million *mi·lee·ōn*

millionaire *n* der Millionär *mi·lee·ō·nayr*

millionth *adj* millionstel *mi·lee·ōn·stèl*

mince *vt* hacken *ha·kèn*

mincer *n* der Fleischwolf *flyesh·volf*

mind *n* der Geist *gyest*; **to change one's mind** seine Meinung ändern *zine·è mine·oong en·dèrn*; **to make up one's mind** sich entschließen* *zikh ent·shlee·sèn* □ *vt* **I don't mind the heat** die Wärme macht mir nichts aus *dee ver·mè makht meer nikhts ows*; **I don't mind es** ist mir egal *es ist meer ay·gal*; **never mind** macht nichts *makht nikhts*; **do you mind if …?** haben Sie etwas dagegen, wenn …? *hah·bèn zee et·vass da·gay·gèn ven*; **mind the step** Vorsicht! Stufe! *för·zikht shtoo·fè*

mine *pron* meine(r/s) *mine·è(èr/·ès)*; *(plural)* meine *mine·è* □ *n* (for coal etc) das Bergwerk *berk·verk*

miner *n* der Bergarbeiter *berk·ar·bite·èr*

mineral water *n* das Mineralwasser *mi·nay·rahl·va·sèr*

minestrone (soup) *n* die Minestrone *mi·nes·trō·ne*

minibus *n* der Kleinbus *kline·boos*

minicomputer *n* der Minicomputer *mi·ni·kom·pyoo·tèr*

minimum *n* das Minimum *mi·ni·moom* □ *adj* Mindest- *min·dèst*

miniskirt *n* der Minirock *mi·ni·rok*

minister *n* (in government) der Minister *mi·nis·tèr*; (of religion) der Pfarrer *pfar·èr* Sn88

ministry *n* (government) das Ministerium *min·is·tayr·ee·oom*

mink *n* (fur) der Nerz *nerts*

mink coat *n* der Nerzmantel *nerts·man·tèl*

minor *adj* (road) Neben- *nay·bèn*; (injury, operation) leicht *lyekht*

minority *n* die Minderheit *min·dèr·hite*

mint *n* (herb) die Minze *min·tsè*; (confectionery) das Pfefferminz *pfef·èr·mints*

minus *prep* minus *mee·noos*; **at minus 2 degrees** bei 2 Grad minus *bye 2 grat mee·noos*

minute *n* die Minute *mi·noo·tè*; **just a minute** Moment mal *mo·ment mahl*

mirror *n* der Spiegel *shpee·gèl* S77

miscarriage *n* die Fehlgeburt *fayl·gè·boort*

miserable *adj* unglücklich *oon·glōōk·likh*

misprint *n* der Druckfehler *drook·fay·lèr*

Miss *n* Fräulein (*nt*) *froy·line*

miss *vt* (target) verfehlen *fer·fay·lèn*; (train) versäumen *fer·zoy·mèn*; **I miss my mother** meine Mutter fehlt mir *mine·è moo·tèr faylt meer*; **I miss London** ich vermisse London *ikh fer·mi·sè lon·don*; **to miss out** aus|lassen* *ows·la·sèn*

missing *adj* (object) verschwunden *fer·shvoon·dèn*; (person) vermißt *fer·mist*; **some pages are missing** es fehlen einige Seiten *es fay·lèn ine·i·gè zite·èn*; **my wallet is missing** meine Brieftasche ist verschwunden *mine·è breef·ta·shè ist fer·shvoon·dèn*

mist *n* der Nebel *nay·bèl*

mistake *n* der Fehler *fay·lèr*; **by mistake** aus Versehen *ows·fer·zay·èn*

mistress *n* (lover) die Geliebte *gè·leeb·tè*

mitt(en) *n* der Fausthandschuh *fowst·hant·shoo*

mix *vt* vermischen *fer·mi·shèn*; **to mix up** (confuse) durcheinander|bringen* *doorkh·ine·an·dèr·bring·èn* □ *vi* **mix** sich vermischen *zikh fer·mi·shèn*

mixed *adj* (co-ed) gemischt *gè·misht*; **mixed grill** der Grillteller *gril·te·lèr*

mixer *n* der Mixer *mik·sèr*

mixture *n* die Mischung *mi·shoong*

moan *n* das Stöhnen *shtur'n·èn* □ *vi* stöhnen *shtur'n·èn*

model *n* das Modell *mo·del*; (mannequin) das Mannequin *ma·nè·kan*; **a model railroad** eine Modelleisenbahn *ine·è mo·del·ize·èn·bahn*

modern *adj* modern *mo·dern* S91

modernize *vt* modernisieren *mo·dern·ee·zee·rèn*

modest *adj* bescheiden *bè·shide·èn*

modification *n* die Veränderung *fer·en·dè·roong*

modify *vt* verändern *fer·en·dèrn*

mohair *n* der Mohair *mo·hayr*

molasses *n* die Melasse *may·la·sè*

molecule *n* das Molekül *mo·lay·kōōl*

moment *n* der Augenblick *ow·gèn·blik*; **at the moment** augenblicklich *ow·gèn·blik·likh*

mom(my) *n* die Mutti *moo·tee*

Monaco *n* Monaco (*nt*) *mō·na·kō*

monastery *n* das Kloster *klōs·tèr*

Monday *n* Montag (*m*) *mōn·tahk*

monetary *adj* monetär *mo·nay·tayr*

money *n* das Geld *gelt*; **to make money** Geld verdienen *gelt fer·dee·nèn* M18, 19

money order *n* die Postanweisung *post·an·vye·zoong*

monitor *n* (TV) der Monitor *mo·ni·tor*

monk *n* der Mönch *mur'nkh*

monkey *n* der Affe *a·fè*

mono *adj* Mono- *mō·nō*; **in mono** in Mono *in mō·nō*

monopoly *n* das Monopol *mō·nō·pōl*

monorail *n* die Einschienenbahn *ine·sheen·èn·bahn*

monster *n* das Ungeheuer *oon·gè·hoy·èr*

month *n* der Monat *mō·nat*

monthly *adj* monatlich *mō·nat·likh* □ *n* die Monatszeitschrift *mō·nats·tsite·shrift*

monument *n* das Denkmal *denk·mahl*

mood *n* die Laune *low·nè*; **in a good mood** guter Laune *goo·tèr low·nè*

moon *n* der Mond *mōnt*

moor *vt* fest|machen *fest·ma·khèn*

mop *n* der Naßmop *nas·mop* □ *vt* auf|wischen *owf·vi·shèn*

moped *n* das Moped *mō·pet*

more *adj* mehr *mayr*; **more cheese/people** mehr Käse/Leute *mayr kay·zè/loy·tè* □ *pron* I'd like (some) more ich möchte noch etwas *ikh mur'kh·tè nokh et·vass* □ *adv* more dangerous than gefährlicher als *gè·fer·likh·èr als*; more or less mehr oder weniger *mayr ō·dèr vay·ni·gèr*

morning *n* der Morgen *mor·gèn*

Moroccan *adj* marokkanisch *ma·ro·kah·nish*

Morocco *n* Marokko (*nt*) *ma·ro·kō*

mortgage *n* die Hypothek *hōō·po·tayk* □ *vt* hypothekarisch belasten *hōō·po·tay·kah·rish be·las·tèn*

Moscow *n* Moskau (*nt*) *mos·kow*

moselle *n* (*wine*) der Moselwein *mō·zèl·vine*

mosque *n* die Moschee *mo·shay*

mosquito *n* die Stechmücke *shtekh·mōō·kè*

mosquito net *n* das Moskitonetz *mos·kee·tō·nets*

most *adv* □ the most beautiful der/die/das schönste *der/dee/dass shur'n·stè* □ *adj* most people die meisten Leute *dee mye·stèn loy·tè*; the most cars die meisten Wagen *dee mye·stèn vah·gèn* □ *pron* he has the most er hat das meiste *er hat dass mye·stè*; at the most höchstens *hur'kh·stèns*; to make the most of voll aus|nützen *fol ows·nōō·tsèn*

motel *n* das Motel *mō·tel*

moth *n* der Nachtfalter *nakht·fal·tèr*

mother *n* die Mutter *moo·tèr*

mother-in-law *n* die Schwiegermutter *shvee·gèr·moo·tèr*

motion *n* (*movement*) die Bewegung *bè·vay·goong*

motor *n* der Motor *mō·tor*

motorbike *n* das Motorrad *mō·tor·rat*

motorboat *n* das Motorboot *mō·tor·bōt*

motorcyclist *n* der Motorradfahrer *mō·tor·rat·fah·rèr*

motorist *n* der Autofahrer *ow·tō·fah·rèr*

mount *vt* steigen* auf *shtye·gèn owf*

mountain *n* der Berg *berk*

mountaineering *n* das Bergsteigen *berk·shtye·gèn*; to go mountaineering bergsteigen gehen* *berk·shtye·gèn gay·èn*

mouse *n* die Maus *mows*

mousse *n* die Cremespeise *kraym·shpye·zè*

mouth *n* der Mund *moont*; (*of animal*) das Maul *mowl*

move *vt* bewegen *bè·vay·gèn* □ *vi* sich bewegen *zikh bè·vay·gèn*; (*traffic*) voran|kommen* *fōr·an·ko·mèn*; (*change residence*) um|ziehen* *oom·tsee·èn*; to move in hinein|stellen *hin·ine·shtè·lèn*; to move out hinaus|räumen *hin·ows·roy·mèn*

movement *n* die Bewegung *bè·vay·goong*

movie *n* der Film *film*

movie camera *n* die Filmkamera *film·ka·mè·ra*

moving van *n* der Möbelwagen *mur'·bèl·vah·gèn*

moving walkway *n* der Rollsteg *rol·shtayk*

mow *vt* mähen *may·èn*

mower *n* die Mähmaschine *may·ma·shee·nè*

Mr *n* Herr (*m*) *her*

Mrs, Ms *n* Frau (*f*) *frow*

much *adv* □ much better/bigger viel besser/größer *feel be·sèr/grur's·èr* □ *adj* much milk viel Milch *feel milkh* □ *pron* have you got much? haben Sie viel? *hah·bèn zee feel*; not much nicht viel *nikht feel*

mud *n* der Schlamm *shlam*

muddle *n* das Durcheinander *doorkh·ine·an·dèr*; in a muddle völlig durcheinander *fur'·likh doorkh·ine·an·dèr*

muddy *adj* (*water*) schlammig *shla·mikh*; (*clothes*) schmutzig *shmoot·tsikh*

mud-flap *n* der Schmutzfänger *shmoots·feng·èr*

mudguard *n* der Kotflügel *kōt·flōō·gèl*

muffler *n* (*on car*) der Auspufftopf *ows·poof·topf*

mug *n* der Becher *be·khèr* □ *vt* überfallen* *ōō·bèr·fa·lèn*

multilevel *adj* mehrstöckig *mayr·shtur'·kikh*

multilingual *adj* mehrsprachig *mayr·shprah·khik*

multinational *adj* multinational *mool·ti·na·tsee·o·nahl*

multiple store *n* die Ladenkette *lah·dèn·ke·tè*

multiplication *n* die Multiplikation *mool·ti·pli·ka·tsee·ōn*

multiply *vt* multiplizieren *mool·ti·pli·tseer·èn*; to multiply 9 by 4 9 mit 4 multiplizieren 9 mit 4 *mool·ti·pli·tseer·èn*

mumps *n* der Mumps *moomps*

Munich *n* München (*nt*) *mōōn·khèn*

municipal *adj* städtisch *stet·ish*

murder *n* der Mord *mort* □ *vt* ermorden *er·mor·dèn*

muscle *n* der Muskel *moo·skèl* I28

museum *n* das Museum *moo·zay·oom* F11, L4

mushroom *n* der Pilz *pilts*

music *n* die Musik *moo·zeek*

musician *n* der Musiker *moo·zi·kèr*

Muslim *adj* mohammedanisch *mo·ham·e·dah·nish* □ *n* der Moslem *mos·lem*

mussel *n* die Miesmuschel *mees·moo·shèl*

must *vi* □ I must go ich muß gehen *ikh moos gay·èn*; you must come Sie müssen kommen *zee mōō·sèn ko·mèn*

mustard *n* der Senf *zenf*

mutton *n* das Hammelfleisch *ha·mèl·flyesh*

my *adj* mein(e) *mine(·è)*; my father mein Vater *mine fah·tèr*; my mother meine Mutter *mine·è moo·tèr*; my brothers/sisters meine Brüder/Schwestern *mine·è brōō·dèr/shve·stèrn*

myself *pron* selbst *zelpst*; I washed myself ich wusch mich *ikh voosh mikh*; I did it myself ich machte es selbst *ikh makh·tè es zelpst*

mystery *n* das Geheimnis *gè·hime·nis*

N

nail *n* der Nagel *nah·gèl* □ *vt* nageln *nah·gèln*

nailbrush *n* die Nagelbürste *nah·gèl·bōōr·stè*

nailfile *n* die Nagelfeile *nah·gèl·fye·lè*

nail polish *n* der Nagellack *nah·gèl·lack*

naked *adj* nackt *nakt*

name *n* der Name *nah·mĕ*; **what is your name?** wie heißen Sie? *vee hye·sĕn zee*; **my name is Paul** ich heiße Paul *ikh hye·sĕ Paul* T207

nap *n* (*sleep*) das Nickerchen *ni·kĕr·khĕn*

napkin *n* (*for table*) die Serviette *ser·vee·e·tĕ*

narrow *adj* eng *eng*

nasty *adj* ekelhaft *ay·kĕl·haft*

nation *n* die Nation *na·tsee·ōn*

national *adj* national *na·tsee·o·nahl*; **national anthem** die Nationalhymne *na·tsee·o·nahl·hōōm·nĕ*; **national dress** die Nationaltracht *na·tsee·o·nahl·trakht*

nationality *n* die Staatsangehörigkeit *shtahts·an·gĕ·hur·rikh·kite*

nationalize *vt* verstaatlichen *fer·shtaht·li·khĕn*

native *adj* einheimisch *ine·hye·mish*

natural *adj* natürlich *na·tōōr·likh*; (*connected with nature*) Natur- *na·toor*

naturalized *adj* eingebürgert *ine·gĕ·bōōr·gĕrt*

naturally *adv* (*of course*) natürlich *na·tōōr·likh*

nature *n* die Natur *na·toor*; (*type, sort*) die Art *art*

naughty *adj* ungezogen *oon·gĕ·tsō·gĕn*

nausea *n* die Übelkeit *ōō·bĕl·kite*

nave *n* das Kirchenschiff *kirkh·ĕn·shif*

navy *n* die Marine *ma·ree·nĕ*

navy blue *adj* marineblau *ma·ree·nĕ·blow*

near *adv* nah *nah* □ *prep* **near (to) the house** in der Nähe des Hauses *in der nay·ĕ des how·zĕs*; **near (to) Christmas** um Weihnachten herum *oom vye·nakh·tĕn he·room*

nearby *adv* in der Nähe *in der nay·ĕ*

nearly *adv* fast *fast*

nearsighted *adj* kurzsichtig *koorts·zikh·tikh*

neat *adj* ordentlich *or·dĕnt·likh*; (*liquor*) pur *poor*

necessary *adj* nötig *nur'·tikh*

neck *n* der Hals *hals*

necklace *n* die Halskette *hals·ke·tĕ*

necktie *n* die Krawatte *kra·va·tĕ*

need *vt* brauchen *brow·khĕn*; **I need to go** ich muß gehen *ikh moos gay·ĕn*; **you needn't come** Sie brauchen nicht (zu) kommen *zee brow·khĕn nikht (tsoo) ko·mĕn* S11

needle *n* die Nadel *nah·dĕl*

negative *n* (*of photo*) das Negativ *ne·ga·teef*

negotiable *adj* verkäuflich *fer·koyf·likh*

negotiate *vi* verhandeln *fer·han·dĕln*

negotiations *pl* die Verhandlungen (*pl*) *fer·hant·loong·ĕn*

neighbor *n* der Nachbar *nakh·bar*, die Nachbarin *nakh·ba·rin*

neighborhood *n* die Umgebung *oom·gay·boong*

neither *pron* keine(r/s) *kine·ĕ(·ĕr/·ĕs)* □ *adv* **neither ... nor** weder ... noch *vay·dĕr ... nokh* □ *conj* **I wasn't there and neither was he** ich war nicht da, und er auch nicht *ikh var nikht dah oont er owkh nikht*

nephew *n* der Neffe *ne·fĕ*

nerve *n* der Nerv *nerf*; (*courage*) der Mut *moot*

nervous *adj* (*person*) ängstlich *engst·likh*; **nervous breakdown** der Nervenzusammenbruch *ner·fĕn·tsoo·za·mĕn·brookh*

nest *n* das Nest *nest*

net *n* das Netz *nets* □ *adj* (*income, price*) Netto- *ne·tō*; **net weight** das Nettogewicht *ne·tō·gĕ·vikht*

neutral *adj* neutral *noy·trahl* □ *n* (*gear*) der Leerlauf *layr·lowf*

never *adv* nie *nee*; **he never comes** er kommt nie *er komt nee*

new *adj* neu *noy*

news *n* die Nachrichten (*pl*) *nakh·rikh·tĕn*

newsdealer *n* der Zeitungshändler *tsye·toongs·hent·lĕr*

newspaper *n* die Zeitung *tsye·toong* S98

newsstand *n* der Zeitungsstand *tsye·toongs·shtant*

New Year's Day *n* der Neujahrstag *noy·yahrs·tahk*

New Year's Eve *n* das Silvester *zil·ve·stĕr*

next *adj* (*stop, station, week*) nächste(r/s) *nekh·stĕ(·stĕr/·stĕs)*; **next of kin** der nächste Verwandte *nekh·stĕ fer·van·tĕ*

nice *adj* nett *net*

niece *n* die Nichte *nikh·tĕ*

night *n* die Nacht *nakht* A8

night club *n* das Nachtlokal *nakht·lō·kahl* L43

nightgown *n* das Nachthemd *nakht·hemt*

nightmare *n* der Alptraum *alp·trowm*

night porter *n* der Nachtportier *nakht·por·tyay*

night school *n* die Abendschule *ah·bĕnt·shoo·lĕ*

nil *n* Null (*f*) *nool*

nine *num* neun *noyn*

nineteen *num* neunzehn *noyn·tsayn*

ninety *num* neunzig *noyn·tsikh*

ninth *adj* neunte(r/s) *noyn·tĕ(·tĕr/·tĕs)*

nipple *n* (*on bottle*) der Sauger *zow·gĕr*

no *adv* (*as answer*) nein *nine*

nobody *pron* niemand *nee·mant*; **I can see nobody** ich sehe niemanden *ikh zay·ĕ nee·man·dĕn*

noise *n* das Geräusch *gĕ·roysh*; (*loud*) der Lärm *lerm*

noisy *adj* laut *lowt*

nominal *adj* (*fee*) nominell *no·mi·nel*

non- *pref* nicht- *nikht*

nonalcoholic *adj* alkoholfrei *al·kō·hol·frye*

none *pron* keine(r/s) *kine·ĕ(·ĕr/·ĕs)*

nonsense *n* der Unsinn *oon·zin*

nonsmoker *n* (*person*) der Nichtraucher *nikht·row·khĕr*; (*compartment*) das Nichtraucherabteil *nikht·row·khĕr·ap·tile*

noodles *pl* die Nudeln (*pl*) *noo·dĕln*

noon *n* Mittag (*m*) *mi·tahk*

no one *pron* niemand *nee·mant*; **I can see no one** ich sehe niemanden *ikh zay·ĕ nee·man·dĕn*

normal *adj* normal *nor·mahl*

normally *adv* (*usually*) normalerweise *nor·mah·lĕr·vye·zĕ*

north *n* der Norden *nor·dĕn* □ *adj* nördlich *nurt·likh* □ *n* **northeast** der Nordosten *nort·o·stĕn*; **northwest** Nordwesten (*m*) *nort·ve·stĕn*

North America *n* Nordamerika (*nt*) *nort·a·may·ri·ka*

northern *adj* nördlich *nurt·likh*

North Pole *n* der Nordpol *nort·pōl*

North Sea *n* die Nordsee *nort·zay*

nose *n* die Nase *nah·zĕ*

nosebleed *n* das Nasenbluten *nah·zĕn·bloo·tĕn*

not *adv* nicht *nikht*; **he did not or didn't do it** er hat es nicht getan *er* *hat es nikht gè·tahn*; **not at all** keineswegs *kine·ès·vaygs*; (*don't mention it*) gern geschehen *ger gè·shay·èn*

note *n* (*music*) die Note *nō·tè*; (*letter*) die Nachricht *nakh·rikht*; (*banknote*) der Schein *shine* M21

notepaper *n* das Briefpapier *breef·pa·peer* A43, S99

nothing *n* nichts *nikhts*

notice *n* (*poster*) die Anzeige *an·tsye·gè*; (*sign*) der Anschlag *an·shlak* □ *vt* bemerken *bè·mer·kèn*

notions *pl* die Kurzwaren (*pl*) *koorts·vah·rèn*

nougat *n* der Nougat *noo·gat*

nought *n* Null (*f*) *nool*

novel *n* (*book*) der Roman *rō·mahn*

November *n* November (*m*) *nō·vem·bèr*

now *adv* jetzt *yetst*; **now and then, now and again** ab und zu *ap oont tsoo*

nowadays *adv* heutzutage *hoyt·tsoo·tah·gè*

nowhere *adv* nirgends *nir·gènts*

nuclear *adj* (*energy, war*) Atom- *a·tōm*

nude *adj* nackt *nakt*

nuisance *n* der Ärgernis *er·gèr·nis*; **he's a nuisance** er ist lästig *er ist le·stikh*; **it's a nuisance** es ist ärgerlich *es ist er·gèr·likh*

null and void *adj* null und nichtig *nool oont nikh·tikh*

numb *adj* (*with cold*) gefühllos *gè·fool·lōs*

number *n* (*figure*) die Zahl *tsahl* Sn12

nun *n* die Nonne *no·nè*

nurse *n* die Krankenschwester *krang·kèn·shve·stèr* □ *vt* (*patient*) pflegen *pflay·gèn*

nursery *n* das Kinderzimmer *kin·dèr·tsi·mèr*

nursing home *n* die Privatklinik *pree·vaht·klee·nik*

nylon *n* das Nylon *nye·lon*

O

oak *n* die Eiche *eye·khè*

oar *n* das Ruder *roo·dèr*

oats *pl* der Hafer *hah·fèr*

obedient *adj* gehorsam *gè·hor·zahm*

obey *vi* gehorchen *gè·hor·khèn* □ *vt* **to obey someone** jemandem gehorchen *yay·man·dèm gè·hor·khèn*

object[1] *n* der Gegenstand *gay·gèn·shtant*

object[2] *vi* □ **to object to a remark** an einer Bemerkung Anstoß nehmen* *an ine·èr bè·mer·koong an·shtōs nay·mèn*

objective *n* das Ziel *tseel*

obligation *n* die Verpflichtung *fer·pflikh·toong*

oblong *adj* länglich *leng·likh*

obscure *adj* obskur *op·skoor*

obsession *n* die Besessenheit *bè·ze·sèn·hite*

obstacle *n* das Hindernis *hin·dèr·nis*

obtain *vt* bekommen* *bè·ko·mèn*

obvious *adj* offensichtlich *of·èn·zikht·likh*

obviously *adv* offensichtlich *of·èn·zikht·likh*

occasion *n* die Gelegenheit *gè·lay·gèn·hite*; (*special event*) das Ereignis *er·ige·nis*

occasional *adj* (*event*) gelegentlich *gè·lay·gènt·likh*

occasionally *adv* gelegentlich *gè·lay·gènt·likh*

occupation *n* (*job*) der Beruf *bè·roof*

occur *vi* (*happen*) geschehen* *gè·shay·èn*

ocean *n* der Ozean *ō·tsay·ahn*

o'clock *adv* □ **at 3 o'clock** um 3 Uhr *oom 3 oor*; **it's 4 o'clock** es ist 4 Uhr *ess ist 4 oor*

October *n* Oktober (*m*) *ok·tō·bèr*

odd *adj* (*number*) ungerade *oon·gè·rah·dè*; (*strange*) sonderbar *zon·dèr·bahr*

odds *pl* (*in betting*) die Gewinnchancen (*pl*) *gè·vin·shan·sèn*

odometer *n* ≈ der Kilometerzähler *ki·lō·may·tèr·tsay·lèr*

of *prep* von *fon*; **a friend of mine** ein Freund von mir *ine froynt fon meer*; **3 of them** 3 von ihnen *3 fon ee·nèn*; **14th of June** der vierzehnte Juni *der fir·zayn·tè yoo·nee*; **made of stone** aus Stein *ows shtine*

of course *adv* natürlich *na·tōōr·likh*

off *adj* (*machine, light*) aus *ows*; (*radio*) ausgeschaltet *ows·gè·shal·tèt*; (*water supply*) zu *tsoo* □ *adv* **a day off** ein Tag frei *ine tahk frye*; **3% off** 3% Nachlaß *3% nakh·las*; **6 kilometers off** 6 Kilometer entfernt *6 kee·lō·may·tèr ent·fernt* □ *prep* **to fall off a wall** von einer Wand fallen* *fon ine·èr vant fa·lèn*; **off the main road** abseits von der Hauptstraße *ap·zites fon der howpt·shtrah·sè*

offend *vt* beleidigen *bè·lye·di·gèn*

offer *vt* an|bieten* *an·bee·tèn*; **to offer to do something** sich an|bieten*, etwas zu tun *zikh an·bee·tèn et·vass tsoo toon* □ *n* der Angebot *an·gè·bōt*

office *n* das Büro *bōō·rō*; (*doctor's*) das Sprechzimmer *shprekh·tsi·mèr*

office-block *n* das Bürohochhaus *bōō·rō·hōkh·hows*

office hours *pl* die Dienstzeit *deenst·tsite*

officer *n* (*in army etc*) der Offizier *o·fee·tseer*; (*of police*) der Polizeibeamte *pō·lee·tsye·bè·am·tè*

office worker *n* der/die Büroangestellte *bōō·rō·an·gè·shtel·tè*

official *adj* offiziell *o·fee·tsee·el*

off-season *adj* in der Nebensaison *in der nay·bèn·zay·zōn*

offshore *adj* (*island*) küstennah *kōōs·tèn·nah*; **offshore sailing** das Segeln in Küstennähe *zay·gèln in kōōs·tèn·nay·è*

often *adv* oft *oft*

oil *n* das Öl *url*; (*for heating*) das Heizöl *hites·url*; (*petroleum*) das Erdöl *ayrt·url* T150

oil filter *n* das Ölfilter *url·fil·tèr*

oil pan *n* (*in car*) die Ölwanne *url·va·nè*

oil-rig *n* die Ölbohrinsel *url·bōr·in·zèl*

oil tanker *n* der Öltanker *url·tang·kèr*

ointment *n* die Salbe *zal·bè*

O.K., okay *adj* (*agreement*) okay *okay*; **it's OK** das ist in Ordnung *dass ist in ort·noong*

old *adj* alt *alt*; **how old are you?** wie alt sind Sie? *vee alt zint zee*

old-fashioned *adj* altmodisch *alt·mō·dish*

olive *n* die Olive *o·lee·vè*

olive oil *n* das Olivenöl *o·lee·vèn·url*

omelet *n* das Omlett *om·let*

on *adj* (*machine*) ein(geschaltet) *ine* (·gè·shal·tèt); (*light, radio*) an(geschaltet) *an*(·gè·shal·tèt); (*water supply*) auf *owf*; **when is the movie on?**

wann läuft der Film? *van loyft der film* □ *prep* on auf *owf*; **on the table** auf dem/den Tisch *owf daym/dayn tish*; **on the train** in dem Zug *in daym tsook*; **on the left/right** links/rechts *links/rekhts*; **come on Friday** kommen Sie am Freitag *ko·men zee am frye·tahk*; **on television** im Fernsehen *im fern·zay·en*

once *adv* einmal *ine·mahl*; (*formerly*) früher einmal *frōo·er ine·mahl*; **once more** noch einmal *nokh ine·mahl*

one *num* eins *ines*; **one day** eines Tages *ine·es tah·ges*; **which one** welche(r/s) *vel·khě(·khěr) khes*); **the one on the table** der/die/das auf dem Tisch *der/dee/dass owf daym tish*; **this one** diese(r/s) hier *dee·zě(·zěr·zěs) heer*; **one should...** man sollte... *man zol·tě*; **one another** einander *ine·an·děr*

one-armed bandit *n* der einarmige Bandit *ine·ar·mi·gě ban·deet*

one-day excursion *n* die Tagesrückfahrkarte *tah·ges·rōōk·fahr·kar·tě*

oneself *pron* sich selbst *zikh zelpst*; **to dress oneself** sich an|zieehn* *zikh an·tsee·en*

one-way street *n* die Einbahnstraße *ine·bahn·shtrah·sě*

one-way ticket *n* die einfache Fahrkarte *ine·fa·khě fahr·kar·tě* **T59**

onion *n* die Zwiebel *tsvee·běl*

only *adv* nur *noor*; **there are only 4** es sind nur 4 da *ess zint noor 4 dah* □ *adj* the only woman there die einzige anwesende Frau *dee ine·tsi·gě an·vay·zěn·dě frow*; **an only child** ein Einzelkind *ine ine·tsěl·kint*; **not only** nicht nur *nikht noor*

onto *prep* auf *owf*

OPEC *n* die OPEC-Staaten (*pl*) *ō·pek·shtah·těn*

open *adj* offen *o·fěn* □ *vt* (*window etc*) öffnen *urf·nen* □ *vi* (*store, bank*) auf|machen *owf·ma·khen*; (*play*) an|laufen* *an·low·fěn* **S1**

open-air *adj* im Freien *im frye·en*

open-plan *adj* Großraum- *grōs·rowm*

opera *n* die Oper *ō·pěr*

operate *vt* (*machine*) bedienen *be·dee·něn*

operation *n* die Operation *o·pay·ra·tsee·ōn*; (*enterprise*) das Unternehmen *oon·těr·nay·měn*

operator *n* die Vermittlung *fer·mit·loong*

opinion *n* die Meinung *mye·noong*; **in my opinion** meiner Meinung nach *mine·ěr mye·noong nakh*

opportunity *n* die Gelegenheit *gě·lay·gěn·hite*

opposite *adv* gegenüber *gay·gěn·ōō·běr*; **the house opposite** das Haus gegenüber *das hows gay·gěn·ōō·běr*; **the opposite sex** das andere Geschlecht *dass an·dě·rě gě·shlekht* □ *n* **opposite** das Gegenteil *gay·gěn·tile* □ *prep* gegenüber *gay·gěn·ōō·běr*

optician *n* der Optiker *op·ti·kěr*

optimistic *adj* optimistisch *op·tee·mis·tish*

option *n* die Wahl *vahl*

or *conj* oder *ō·děr*

orange *n* die Orange *ō·ran·zhě* □ *adj* orange *ō·ran·zhe*

orangeade *n* die Orangeade *ō·ran·zhah·dě*

orange juice *n* der Orangensaft *ō·ran·zhen·zaft*

orchard *n* der Obstgarten *ōpst·gar·těn*

orchestra *n* das Orchester *or·kes·těr*;

(*in theater*) die Orchestersitze (*pl*) *or·kes·těr·zit·sě*

order *n* (*in series*) die Reihenfolge *rye·ěn·fol·gě*; (*command*) der Befehl *bě·fayl*; (*for goods*) die Bestellung *bě·shte·loong*; **out of order** (*machine*) außer Betrieb *ow·sěr bě·treep*; **in order to do something** um etwas zu tun *oom et·vass tsoo toon* □ *vt* **order** (*goods, meal*) bestellen *bě·shte·lěn*

order-form *n* das Bestellformular *bě·shtel·for·moo·lahr*

ordinary *adj* gewöhnlich *gě·vur'n·likh*

organ *n* (*instrument*) die Orgel *or·gěl*

organization *n* die Organisation *or·ga·nee·za·tsee·ōn*

organize *vt* organisieren *or·ga·nee·zee·rěn*

oriental *adj* orientalisch *o·ree·en·tah·lish*

origin *n* der Ursprung *oor·shproong*

original *adj* (*earliest*) Original- *o·ree·gee·nahl*; (*creative*) originell *o·ree·gee·nel* □ *n* das Original *o·ree·gee·nahl*

originally *adv* (*at first*) ursprünglich *oor·shprüng·likh*

ornament *n* der Schmuck *shmook*

orphan *n* die Waise *vye·zě*

other *adj* andere *an·dě·rě*; **the other day** neulich *noy·likh* □ *pron* **the other** der/die/das andere *der/dee/das an·dě·rě* **S15**

otherwise *adv* anderweitig *an·děr·vye·tikh*; **otherwise engaged** anderweitig beschäftigt *an·děr·vye·tikh bě·shef·tikht*

ought *vi* □ **I ought to do it** ich sollte es tun *ikh zol·tě ess toon*; **he ought to win** er müßte gewinnen *er mōōs·tě gě·vi·něn*; **that ought to do** das müßte reichen *das mōōs·tě rye·khěn*

ounce *n* die Unze *oon·tsě*

our *adj* unser(e) *oon·zěr(·ě)*; **our father** unser Vater *oon·zěr fah·těr*; **our mother** unsere Mutter *oon·zě·rě moo·těr*; **our brothers/sisters** unsere Brüder/Schwester *oon·zě·rě brōō·děr/shve·stěr*

ours *pron* unsere(r/s) *oon·zě·rě (·rěr/·rěs)*; (*plural*) unsere *oon·zě·rě*

ourselves *pron* selbst *zelpst*; **we dressed ourselves** wir haben uns angezogen *veer hah·běn oons an·gě·tsō·gěn*

out *adv* (*not at home*) nicht da *nikht dah*; (*team, player*) ausgeschieden *ows·gě·shee·děn*; **the tide is out** es ist Ebbe *ess ist e·bě*; **the sun is out** die Sonne scheint *dee zo·ně shyent*; **the light is out** das Licht ist aus *das likht ist ows* □ *prep* **out of** (*outside*) außerhalb von *ow·sěr·halp fon*; **to be out of gasoline** kein Benzin mehr haben* *kine ben·tseen mayr hah·běn*; **made out of wood** aus Holz *ows holts*; **he ran out of the house** er lief aus dem Haus *er leef ows daym hows*

outboard *adj* Außenbord- *ow·sěn·bort*

outdoor *adj* im Freien *im frye·en*

outdoors *adv* draußen *drow·sěn*

outfit *n* (*clothes*) die Kleidung *klye·doong*

outing *n* der Ausflug *ows·flook*

outlet *n* (*electric*) die Steckdose *shtek·dō·zě*

outline *n* (*summary*) der Umriß *oom·riss*

outlook *n* die Aussicht *ows·zikht*

out-of-date *adj* (*passport, ticket*) abgelaufen *ap·gě·low·fěn*

output n die Produktion *prŏ·dook· tsee·ŏn*

outside n die Außenseite *ow·sèn·zye·tè* □ *adj* the outside wall die Außenwand *ow·sèn·vant*; the outside lane (in road) die Überholspur *ōō·bèr· hŏl·shpoor* □ *prep* outside the house außerhalb des Hauses *ow·sèr·halp des how·zès* □ *adv* to be outside draußen sein* *drow·sèn zine*; to go outside nach draußen gehen* *nakh drow·sèn gay·èn*

outsize *adj* (clothes) in Übergröße *in ōō·bèr·grur'·sè*

outskirts *pl* der Stadtrand *shtat·rant*

oval *adj* oval *o·val*

oven n der Backofen *bak·ō·fèn*

over *adv* □ to fall over hin|fallen* *hin· fa·lèn*; to knock over um|werfen* *oom·ver·fèn*; to turn something over etwas um|drehen *et·vass oom·dray· èn*; come over here kommen Sie hierher *ko·mèn zee heer·her*; he's over here on holiday er ist im Urlaub hier *er ist im oor·lowp heer*; the match is over das Spiel ist aus *dass shpeel ist ows* □ *prep* to jump over something über etwas springen* *ōō·bèr et·vass shpring·èn*; it weighs over a kilo es wiegt über ein Kilo *es veekt ōō·bèr ine kee·lō*

overall n die Kittelschürze *ki·tèl· shŏŏr·tsè*

overalls *pl* der Overall *ō·ver·ahl*

overcoat n der Mantel *man·tèl*

overdose n die Überdosis *ōō·bèr·dō·zis*

overdraft n die Kontoüberziehung *kon·tō·ōō·bèr·tsee·oong*

overdrive n der Schnellgang *shnel· gang*

overexposed *adj* (photo) überbelichtet *ōō·bèr·bè·likh·tèt*

overhead *adj* (railway) Hoch– *hōkh* □ *adv* oben *ō·bèn* □ n allgemeine Unkosten *pl al·gè·mye·nè oon·kos· tèn*

overheat *vi* (engine) heiß|laufen* *hise· low·fèn*

overnight *adj* (a stay) von einer Nacht *fon ine·èr nakht* □ *adv* (happen) über Nacht *ōō·bèr nakht*

overpass n die Überführung *ōō·bèr· fōō·roong*

overseas *adv* in Übersee *in ōō·bèr·zay* □ *adj* (market) in Übersee *in ōō·bèr· zay*; (visitor) aus dem Ausland *ows daym ows·lant*

overtime n die Überstunden (pl) *ōō· bèr·shtoon·dèn*; to work overtime Überstunden machen *ōō·bèr·shtoon· dèn ma·khèn*

overture n die Ouvertüre *ō·ver·tōō·rè*

overweight *adj* zu schwer *tsoo shvayr*

owe *vt* (money) schulden *shool·dèn*; he owes me $5 er schuldet mir $5 *er shool·dèt meer $5*

own *adj* eigen *ige·èn* □ n he did it on his own er hat es allein gemacht *er hat ess a·line gè·makht* □ *vt* own (possess) besitzen* *be·zit·sèn*

owner n der Eigentümer *eye·gèn·tōō· mèr*, die Eigentümerin *eye·gèn·tōō· mè·rin*

ownership n der Besitz *be·zits*

oxygen n der Sauerstoff *zow·èr·shtof*

oyster n die Auster *ows·tèr*

P

pace n der Schritt *shrit*; (speed) das Tempo *tem·pō*; to keep pace with Schritt halten* mit *shrit hal·tèn mit*

Pacific Ocean n der Pazifik *pa·tsee·fik*

pacifier n der Schnuller *shnoo·lèr*

pack *vt* (goods) ein|packen *ine·pa·kèn*; to pack one's suitcase seinen Koffer packen *zine·èn ko·fèr pa·kèn* □ n pack die Schachtel *shakh·tèl*; (of cards) das Spiel *shpeel*

package n das Paket *pa·kayt*

package deal n das Pauschalangebot *pow·shahl·an·gè·bōt*

package holiday n die Pauschalreise *pow·shahl·rye·zè*

packet n das Paket *pa·kayt* S103

packing n (material) die Verpackung *fer·pa·koong*

packing case n die Kiste *kis·tè*

pad n (notepaper) der Schreibblock *shripe·blok*

paddle n der Schläger *shlay·gèr*; (oar) das Paddel *pa·dèl* □ *vi* waten *vah·tèn*

padlock n das Vorhängeschloß *fŏr· heng·è·shlos*

page n die Seite *zye·tè* □ *vt* ausrufen lassen* *ows·roo·fèn la·sèn*

pageboy n der Page *pah·zhè*

paid *adj* (vacation) bezahlt *bè·tsahlt*

pail n der Eimer *ime·èr*

pain n der Schmerz *shmerts* I17

painful *adj* schmerzhaft *shmerts·haft*

painkiller n das schmerzstillende Mittel *shmerts·shtil·èn·dè mi·tèl*

paint n die Farbe *far·bè* □ *vt* malen *mah·lèn*

painter n der Maler *mah·lèr*; (decorator) der Anstreicher *an·shtrye·khèr*

painting n (picture) das Gemälde *gè· mel·dè*

pair n das Paar *pahr*; pair of shoes Paar Schuhe *pahr shoo·è*; pair of scissors die Schere *shay·rè*; pair of trousers die Hose *hō·zè*

pajamas *pl* der Pyjama *pü·zha·ma*

Pakistan n Pakistan (nt) *pah·kis·tahn*

Pakistani *adj* pakistanisch *pa·kis·tah· nish*

palace n der Palast *pa·last*

pale *adj* blaß *blass*

Palestine n Palästina (nt) *pa·les·tee·na*

Palestinian *adj* palästinensisch *pa·les· ti·nen·zish*

palm n (of hand) die Handfläche *hant· fle·khè*

palm-tree n die Palme *pal·mè*

pan n (saucepan) der Topf *topf*; (frying pan) die Bratpfanne *braht·pfa·nè*

pancake n der Pfannkuchen *pfan·koo· khèn*

pane n die Scheibe *shye·bè*

panic n die Panik *pah·nik*; in a panic in Panik *in pah·nik* □ *vi* panic in Panik geraten* *in pah·nik gè·rah·tèn*

pant *vi* keuchen *koy·khèn*

panties *pl* der Slip *slip*

pantomime n das Weihnachtsmärchen *vye·nakhts·mer·khèn*

pants *pl* die Hose *hō·zè*; (undergarment) der Slip *slip*

pant(s) suit n der Hosenanzug *hō·zèn· an·tsook*

panty hose n die Strumpfhose *shtroompf·hō·zè*

paper n das Papier *pa·peer*; (newspaper) die Zeitung *tsye·toong*; papers (passport etc) die Papiere *pa· pee·rè* □ *vt* paper (wall) tapezieren *ta·pay·tsee·rèn*

paperback n das Taschenbuch *ta·shèn· bookh* S101

paper clip n die Büroklammer *bōō·rō· kla·mèr*

paprika n der Paprika *pa·pree·ka*

par n *(golf)* der Par *par*; *(business)* der Nennwert *nen·vert*; **above par** über dem Nennwert *ōō·bèr bayn·nen·vert*

parachute n der Fallschirm *fal·shirm*

parade n der Umzug *oom·tsook*

paragraph n der Absatz *ap·zats*

parallel adj parallel *pa·ra·lel*

paralyzed adj gelähmt *gè·laymt*

parasol n der Sonnenschirm *zo·nèn· shirm*

parcel n das Paket *pa·kayt* Sn4

pardon excl Entschuldigung *ent·shool· di·goong*; **pardon me?**, **(I beg your) pardon?** bitte? *bi·tè*

parents pl die Eltern *(pl) el·tèrn*

Paris n Paris *(nt) pa·rees*

park n der Park *park* □ vt parken *par· kèn* □ vi **can I park here?** kann man hier parken? *kan man heer par·kèn* T118f

parka n der Parka *par·ka*

parking disk n die Parkscheibe *park· shye·bè*

parking lights pl das Parklicht *park· likht*

parking lot n der Parkplatz *park·plats* T121

parking meter n die Parkuhr *park·oo· èr*

parking-ticket n der Strafzettel *shtraf· tse·tel*

parliament n das Parlament *par·la· ment*

Parmesan n der Parmesan *par·may· zahn*

parsley n die Petersilie *pay·tèr·zeel·yè*

parsnip n der Pastinak *pas·tee·nak*

part n der Teil *tile*; *(of machine)* das Teil *tile*; *(in hair)* der Scheitel *shye· tèl*; *(in play)* die Rolle *ro·lè* □ vt *(separate)* trennen *tre·nèn* T179, Sn37

participate vi teil|nehmen* *tile·nay· mèn*

participation n die Teilnahme *tile·nah· mè*

particular adj besondere(r/s) *bè·zon· dè·rè(·rèr/·rès)* □ n **in particular** besonders *bè·zon·dèrs*

particularly adv besonders *bè·zon·dèrs*

partition n *(wall)* die Trennwand *tren· vant*

partly adv teilweise *tile·vye·zè*

partner n der Partner *part·nèr*, die Partnerin *part·nèr·in*

partridge n das Rebhuhn *rep·hoon*

part-time adj Halbtags- *halp·tahks*

party n *(celebration)* die Party *pahr· tee*; *(group)* die Gruppe *groo·pè*; *(political)* die Partei *par·tye*

pass n *(permit)* der Ausweis *ows·vice*; *(in mountains)* der Paß *pas* □ vt *(place)* vorbei|gehen* an *fōr·bye·gay· èn an*; *(car)* überholen *ōō·bèr·hō· lèn*; *(exam)* bestehen* *bè·shtay·èn*; *(time)* verbringen* *fer·bring·èn*; *(hand on: object)* reichen *rye·khèn*; **please pass the sugar** reichen Sie mir bitte den Zucker *rye·khèn zee meer bi·tè dayn tsoo·kèr*

passage n der Gang *gang*

passenger n der Fahrgast *fahr·gast*

passenger seat n der Beifahrersitz *bye· fah·rèr·zits*

passion n die Leidenschaft *lye·dèn· shaft*

passport n der Reisepaß *rye·zè·pas* T11f, Sn82

past adj vergangene(r/s) *fer·gang·è·nè (·nèr/·nès)* □ n die Vergangenheit *fer·gang·èn·hite* □ adv to run past vorbei|laufen* an *fōr·bye·low·fèn an* □ prep **he ran past me** er ist an mir vorbeigelaufen *er ist an meer fōr·bye· gè·low·fèn*; **he's past forty** er ist über vierzig *er ist ōō·bèr fir·tsikh*

pasta n die Nudeln *(pl) noo·dèln*

paste n *(glue)* der Kleister *klye·stèr*; **meat paste** die Pastete *pas·tay·tè*

pasteurized adj pasteurisiert *pas·tur· ee·zeert*

pastille n die Pastille *pa·sti·lè*

pastry n der Teig *tike*; *(cake)* das Gebäck *gè·bek*

pat vt tätscheln *tet·shèln*

patch n *(of material)* der Flicken *fli· kèn*; *(for eye)* die Augenklappe *ow· gèn·kla·pè*; *(spot)* der Fleck *flek*

pâté n die Pastete *pas·tay·tè*

patent n das Patent *pa·tent*

patent leather n das Lackleder *lak·lay· dèr*

path n der Weg *vayk*

patience n die Geduld *gè·doolt*

patient adj geduldig *gè·dool·dikh* □ n der Patient *pa·tsee·ent*, die Patientin *pa·tsee·en·tin*

patio n die Terrasse *te·ra·sè*

pattern n der Muster *moos·tèr*; *(dress-making)* das Schnittmuster *shnit· moos·tèr*; *(knitting)* die Strickanleitung *shtrik·an·lye·toong*

pause n die Pause *pow·zè* □ vi eine Pause machen *ine·è pow·zè ma·khèn*

pavement n *(sidewalk)* der Bürgersteig *bōō·gèr·shtike*; *(roadway)* die Straße *shtrah·sè*

paw n die Pfote *pfō·tè*

pay n das Gehalt *gè·halt* □ vt bezahlen *bè·tsah·lèn*; **to pay back** *(money)* zurück|zahlen *tsoo·rōōk·tsah·lèn*; **to pay for** bezahlen *bè·tsah·lèn*; **to pay off** *(workers)* aus|zahlen *ows·tsah·lèn*

payable adj zahlbar *tsahl·bahr*

payee n der Zahlungsempfänger *tsah· loongs·emp·feng·èr*

paying guest n der zahlende Gast *tsah· lèn·dè gast*

payment n die Bezahlung *bè·tsah· loong*

payroll n die Belegschaft *bè·layk·shaft*

peace n der Frieden *free·dèn*; *(calm)* die Ruhe *roo·è*

peaceful adj ruhig *roo·ikh*

peach n der Pfirsich *pfir·zikh*

peak n *(of cap)* der Schirm *shirm*; *(of mountain)* der Gipfel *gip·fèl*

peak hours pl die Hauptverkehrszeit *howpt·fer·kayrs·tsite*

peanut n die Erdnuß *ert·noos*

pear n die Birne *bir·nè*

pearl n die Perle *per·lè*

peas pl die Erbsen *(pl) erp·sèn*

pebble n der Kiesel *kee·zèl*

peck vt picken *pi·kèn*

peculiar adj *(strange)* seltsam *zelt·zam*

pedal n die Pedal *pay·dahl*

pedalo n das Tretboot *trayt·bōt*

pedestrian n der Fußgänger *foos·geng· èr*

pedestrian crossing n der Fußgängerüberweg *foos·geng·èr·ōō·bèr·vayk*

pedestrian precinct n die Fußgängerzone *foos·geng·èr·tsō·nè*

pediatrician n der Kinderarzt *kin·dèr· artst*, die Kinderärztin *kin·dèr·erts· tin*

peel vt schälen *shay·lèn* □ vi (person) sich pellen *zikh pe·lèn* □ n die Schale *shah·lè*

peg n der Hering *hay·ring*; (for coat) der Haken *hah·kèn*

pen n der Kugelschreiber *koo·gèl·shrye·bèr* S99

pencil n der Bleistift *blye·shtift*

penetrate vt durch|dringen* *doorkh·dring·èn*

penicillin n das Penizillin *pe·nee·tsi·leen*

penis n der Penis *pay·nis*

penknife n das Taschenmesser *ta·shèn·me·sèr*

pen pal n der Brieffreund *breef·froynt*, die Brieffreundin *breef·froyn·din*

pension n (from State) die Rente *ren·tè*; (from company) die Pension *pen·zee·ôn*

pensioner n der Rentner *rent·nèr*, die Rentnerin *rent·nèr·in*

pension fund n der Rentenfonds *ren·tèn·fong*

penthouse n das Penthouse *pent·hows*

people pl die Leute (pl) *loy·tè* Mc18, 25, 50

pepper n der Pfeffer *pfe·fèr*; (capsicum) die Paprikaschote *pa·pree·ka·shô·tè*; green/red pepper die grüne/rote Paprikaschote *grö·nè/rô·tè pa·pree·ka·shô·tè*

peppermint n (confectionery) das Pfefferminz *pfe·fèr·mints*; (plant) die Pfefferminze *pfe·fèr·min·tsè*

pepper pot n der Pfefferstreuer *pfe·fèr·shtroy·èr*

peppery adj gepfeffert *gè·pfe·fèrt*

per prep pro *prô*; **per hour** pro Stunde *prô shtoon·dè*; **$3 per kilo** $3 das Kilo *$3 dass kee·lô*; **per person** pro Kopf *prô kopf*; **per day** pro Tag *prô tahk*; **per annum** pro Jahr *prô yahr*; **20 per cent** 20 Prozent *20 prô·tsent* Bm26

percentage n der Prozentsatz *prô·tsent·zats* Bm26

percolate vt (coffee) zu|bereiten *tsoo·bè·rye·tèn*

percolator n die Kaffeemaschine *ka·fay·ma·shee·nè*

perfect adj vollkommen *fol·ko·mèn*

perform vi (business) etwas leisten *et·vass lye·stèn*

performance n die Leistung *lye·stoong*; (of play) die Vorstellung *fôr·shte·loong* L49, 52

perfume n das Parfüm *par·füm* S47

perhaps adv vielleicht *fee·lyekht*; **perhaps he'll come** er wird vielleicht kommen *er virt fee·lyekht ko·mèn*

period n (of time) der Zeitraum *tsite·rowm*; (punctuation) der Punkt *poonkt*; (menstruation) die Periode *pay·ree·ô·dè* □ adj (furniture) antik *an·teek*

perm n die Dauerwelle *dow·èr·ve·lè*

permanent adj ständig *shten·dikh*

permanently adv ständig *shten·dikh*

permanent wave n die Dauerwelle *dow·èr·ve·lè* Sn39

permission n die Erlaubnis *er·lowp·nis*

permit vt (something) erlauben *er·low·bèn*; **to permit someone to do something** jemandem erlauben, etwas zu tun *yay·man·dèm er·low·bèn et·vass tsoo toon* □ n permit die Genehmigung *gè·nay·mi·goong*

Persian adj persisch *per·zish*

person n der Mensch *mensh*; **in person** persönlich *per·zur'n·likh*

personal adj persönlich *per·zur'n·likh*; (private) privat *pree·vaht*

personal assistant, P.A. n der Privatsekretär *pree·vaht·zay·kray·ter*

personality n (character) der Charakter *ka·rak·tèr*; (celebrity) die berühmte Persönlichkeit *bè·rööm·tè per·zur'n·likh·kite*

personally adv persönlich *per·zur'n·likh*

personnel n das Personal *per·zô·nahl*

personnel department n die Personalabteilung *per·zô·nahl·ap·tile·oong*

personnel manager n der Personalchef *per·zô·nahl·shef*

perspire vi schwitzen *shvit·sèn*

persuade vt überreden *öö·bèr·ray·dèn*; **to persuade someone to do something** jemanden überreden, etwas zu tun *yay·man·dèn öö·bèr·ray·dèn et·vass tsoo toon*

peseta n die Pesete *pay·zay·tè*

pessimistic adj pessimistisch *pe·see·mis·tish*

pet n das Haustier *hows·teer*

petroleum jelly n die Vaseline *va·zay·lee·nè*

petticoat n der Unterrock *oon·tèr·rok*

pharmacist n der Apotheker *a·pô·tay·kèr*

pharmacy n die Apotheke *a·pô·tay·kè*

pheasant n der Fasan *fa·zahn*

phone n das Telefon *tay·lay·fôn*; **he's on the phone** er ist am Telefon *er ist am tay·lay·fôn* □ vt phone an|rufen* *an·roo·fèn* A35, Sn11f

phone-call n das Telefongespräch *tay·lay·fôn·gè·shprekh*

photo n das Foto *fô·tô*

photocopy n die Fotokopie *fô·tô·kô·pee* □ vt fotokopieren *fô·tô·kô·pee·rèn* Bm15

photograph n die Fotografie *fô·tô·gra·fee* □ vt fotografieren *fô·tô·gra·fee·rèn* S54

photographer n der Fotograf *fô·tô·grahf*

photography n die Fotografie *fô·tô·gra·fee*

phrase n die Phrase *frah·zè*

phrase book n der Sprachführer *shprakh·föö·rèr*

physical adj körperlich *kur·pèr·likh*

physics n die Physik *föö·zik*

piano n das Klavier *kla·veer*

pick n (pickaxe) die Picke *pi·kè* □ vt (flower) pflücken *pflöö·kèn*; (choose) aus|wählen *ows·vay·lèn*; **to pick up** (object) auf|heben* *owf·hay·bèn*; **to pick up a friend** einen Freund ab|holen *ine·èn froynt ap·hô·lèn*

pickaxe n die Picke *pi·kè*

picket n der Streikposten *shtrike·pos·tèn*

pickles pl die Pickles (pl) *pi·kèls*

picnic n das Picknick *pik·nik*; **to go on a picnic** ein Picknick machen *ine pik·nik ma·khèn* L38

picture n das Bild *bilt*; (drawing) die Zeichnung *tsyekh·noong*; (photo) das Foto *fô·tô*; (movie) der Film *film*

pie n die Tortelett *tor·tè·let*; (meat) die Pastete *pas·tay·tè*

piece n das Stück *shtöök*; **piece of furniture** das Möbelstück *mur'·bèl·shtöök*; **a good piece of work** gute Arbeit *goo·tè ar·bite*

piecework n die Akkordarbeit *a·kort·ar·bite*

pier n der Pier *peer*

pierce *vt* durchstechen* *doorkh·shte·khèn*

pig *n* das Schwein *shvine*

pigeon *n* die Taube *tow·bè*

pigskin *n* das Schweinsleder *shvines·lay·dèr*

pilchard *n* die Sardine *zar·dee·nè*

pile *n* der Stapel *shtah·pèl* □ *vt* to pile up auf|stapeln *owf·shtah·pèln*

pill *n* die Tablette *ta·ble·tè*; *(contraceptive)* die Pille *pi·lè*; to be on the pill die Pille nehmen* *dee pi·lè nay·mèn*

pillar *n* die Säule *zoy·lè*

pillow *n* das Kopfkissen *kopf·ki·sèn* A44

pillowcase, pillowslip *n* der Kopfkissenbezug *kopf·ki·sèn·bè·tsook*

pilot *n* der Pilot *pee·lõt*

pilot light *n (gas)* die Zündflamme *tsöönt·fla·mè*

pimple *n* der Pickel *pi·kèl*

pin *n* die Stecknadel *shtek·nah·dèl*; *(safety pin)* die Sicherheitsnadel *zikh·èr·hites·nah·dèl* □ *vt* heften *hef·tèn*

pinball *n* der Flipper *fli·pèr*

pinch *vt* kneifen* *knye·fèn* □ *n (of salt etc)* die Prise *pree·zè*

pine *n* das Kiefernholz *kee·fèrn·holts*; *(tree)* die Kiefer *kee·fèr*

pineapple *n* die Ananas *a·na·nas*

ping-pong *n* das Pingpong *ping·pong*

pink *adj* rosa *rõ·za*

pint *n* das Pint *pyent*; a pint of beer ein Glas Bier *ine glahs beer*

pipe *n (tube)* das Rohr *rõr*; *(for smoking)* die Pfeife *pfye·fè*; *(musical)* die Flöte *flur·tè*; *(bag)*pipes der Dudelsack *doo·dèl·zak*

pipeline *n* die Pipeline *pipe·line*

piston *n* der Kolben *kol·bèn*

pit *n* die Grube *groo·bè*

pitch *vt (tent)* auf|stellen *owf·shte·lèn*

pitcher *n* der Krug *krook*

pity *n* das Mitleid *mit·lite*; what a pity! wie schade! *vee shah·dè*

pizza *n* die Pizza *pit·sa*

place *n* der Ort *ort*; *(seat)* der Platz *plats*; in place an der richtigen Stelle *an der rikh·ti·gèn shte·lè*; out of place *(object)* nicht an der richtigen Stelle *nikht an der rikh·ti·gèn shte·lè*; come back to our place kommen Sie noch zu uns mit *ko·mèn zee nokh tsoo oons mit* □ *vt* place *(put)* stellen *shte·lèn*; *(a bet)* setzen *zet·sèn*; to place an order with someone jemandem einen Auftrag erteilen *yay·man·dèm ine·èn owf·trahk er·tile·èn*

place mat *n* das Set *set*

place setting *n* das Gedeck *gè·dek*

plaice *n* die Scholle *sho·lè*

plaid *n* das Plaid *playt*

plain *n* die Ebene *ay·bè·nè* □ *adj (clear)* klar *klahr*; *(simple: cooking etc)* einfach *ine·fakh*; *(not patterned)* einheitlich *ine·hite·likh*; plain chocolate die bittere Schokolade *bi·tè·rè shõ·kõ·lah·dè*; plain yogurt das Naturjoghurt *na·toor·yõ·goort*

plait *n (of hair etc)* der Zopf *tsopf*

plan *n* der Plan *plahn* □ *vt* planen *plah·nèn*; *(make a design)* einen Entwurf an|fertigen von *ine·èn ent·voorf an·fer·ti·gèn fon*

plane *n (in air)* das Flugzeug *flook·tsoyk*; *(tree)* die Platane *pla·tah·nè*; *(tool)* der Hobel *hõ·bèl*; by plane mit dem Flugzeug *mit daym flook·tsoyk* B78

planet *n* der Planet *pla·nayt*

planetarium *n* das Planetarium *pla·nay·tah·ree·oom*

plank *n* das Brett *bret*

planning *n (economic)* die Planung *plah·noong*

plant *n* die Pflanze *pflant·sè*; *(factory)* das Werk *verk*; *(equipment)* die Anlagen *(pl)* an·lah·gèn* □ *vt* pflanzen *pflant·sèn*

plaster *n (for wall)* der Putz *poots*; plaster cast *(for limb)* der Gipsverband *gips·fer·bant*; plaster of Paris der Gips *gips*

plastic *n* das Plastik *pla·stik* □ *adj* Plastik- *pla·stik*; plastic surgery die plastische Chirurgie *pla·sti·shè khee·roor·gee*

plastic bag *n* die Plastiktüte *pla·stik·tõõ·tè* S28

plate *n* der Teller *te·lèr*; *(of glass, metal)* die Scheibe *shye·bè*

plated *adj* □ gold plated vergoldet *fer·gol·dèt*

platform *n (in station)* der Bahnsteig *bahn·shtike*; *(in hall)* das Podium *põ·dee·oom*; *(of oil-rig)* die Plattform *plat·form* T65

platinum *n* das Platin *plah·teen*

play *vt/i* spielen *shpee·lèn*; to play football Fußball spielen *foos·bal shpee·lèn*; to play the violin Geige spielen *gye·gè shpee·lèn*; to play with spielen mit *shpee·lèn mit* □ *n* play *(theatrical)* das Theaterstück *tay·ah·tèr·shtöök*

player *n (in sport)* der Spieler *shpee·lèr*, die Spielerin *shpee·lè·rin*

playground *n* der Spielplatz *shpeel·plats* C9

play-group *n* die Spielgruppe *shpeel·groo·pè*

playing card *n* die Spielkarte *shpeel·kar·tè*

playing field *n* der Sportplatz *shport·plats*

playpen *n* das Laufgitter *lowf·gi·tèr*

pleasant *adj* angenehm *an·gè·naym*; *(person)* freundlich *froynt·likh*

please *adv* bitte *bi·tè*

pleased *adj* zufrieden *tsoo·free·dèn*

pleasure *n* das Vergnügen *fer·gnõõ·gèn* Bm32

pleasure boat *n* der Vergnügungsdampfer *fer·gnõõ·goongs·damp·fèr*

pleated *adj* gefältelt *gè·fel·tèlt*

plenty *n* □ plenty of milk viel Milch *feel milkh*; thank you, that's plenty danke, das ist reichlich *dang·kè dass ist ryekh·likh*

plexiglas *n* das Plexiglas *plek·see·glahs*

pliers *pl* die Zange *tsang·è*

plimsolls *pl* die Turnschuhe *(pl)* toorn·shoo·è*

plot *n (of land)* das Stück *shtöök*; *(in play)* die Handlung *hant·loong*

plow *n* der Pflug *Pflook*

plug *n (for basin etc)* der Stöpsel *shtur·p·sèl*; *(electric)* der Stecker *shte·kèr*; *(in car)* die Zündkerze *tsöönt·ker·tsè* □ *vt* verstopfen *fer·shtop·fèn*; to plug something in etwas hinein|stecken *et·vass hin·ine·shte·kèn*

plum *n* die Pflaume *pflow·mè*

plumber *n* der Klempner *klemp·nèr*

plump *adj* rundlich *roont·likh*

plus *prep* plus *ploos*

plywood *n* das Sperrholz *shper·holts*

p.m. *adv* nachmittags *nakh·mi·tahks*

pneumonia *n* die Lungenentzündung *loong·èn·ent·sõõn·doong*

poached *adj* pochiert *po·sheert*

P.O. Box *n* das Postfach *post·fakh*

pocket *n* die Tasche *ta·shè*

pocketbook *n* die Brieftasche *breef·ta·shè*

pocketknife *n* das Taschenmesser *ta·shèn·me·sèr*

pocket money *n* das Taschengeld *ta·shèn·gelt*

podiatrist *n* der Fußpfleger *foos·pflay·gèr*, die Fußpflegerin *foos·pflay·gè·rin*

poem *n* das Gedicht *gè·dikht*

poetry *n* die Lyrik *lōō·rik*

point *vt* (*gun*) richten *rikh·tèn* □ *vi* to point at *or* to something auf etwas zeigen *owf et·vass tsye·gèn*; to point something out (*show*) auf etwas zeigen *owf et·vass tsye·gèn* □ *n* (*tip*) die Spitze *shpit·sè*; (*in time*) der Augenblick *ow·gèn·blik*; (*in space*) die Stelle *shte·lè*; (*dot, sport: in score, subject*) der Punkt *poonkt*; (*electric outlet*) die Steckdose *shtek·dō·zè*; **decimal point** das Komma *ko·ma*; **3 point 4 3** Komma 4 3 *ko·ma 4*; **he answered him point by point** er antwortete ihm Punkt für Punkt *er ant·vor·tè·tè eem poonkt fōōr poonkt*; **what's the point?** was soll's? *vass zols*

point of view *n* der Gesichtspunkt *gè·zikhts·poonkt*

poison *n* das Gift *gift*

poisonous *adj* giftig *gif·tikh*

poker *n* (*card game*) das Poker *pō·kèr*

Poland *n* Polen (*nt*) *pō·lèn*

Polaroid *adj* Polaroid- *pō·la·rō·eet*

pole *n* (*wooden*) die Stange *shtang·è*

Pole *n* der Pole *pō·lè*, die Polin *pō·lin*

police *n* die Polizei *po·li·tsye* T209, Sn75f, Ea8

police car *n* das Polizeiauto *po·li·tsye·ow·tō*

policeman *n* der Polizist *po·li·tsist*

police station *n* die Polizeiwache *po·li·tsye·va·khè*

policewoman *n* die Polizistin *po·li·tsis·tin*

policy *n* die Politik *po·li·teek*; (*insurance*) die Police *po·lee·sè*

polio *n* die Polio *pō·lee·ō*

polish *n* (*for shoes*) die Schuhcreme *shoo·kraym*; (*for floor*) das Bohnerwachs *bō·nèr·vaks* □ *vt* (*shoes, metal*) putzen *poot·sèn*; (*wood*) polieren *po·lee·rèn*

Polish *adj* polnisch *pol·nish*; **he's Polish** er ist Pole *er ist pō·lè*; **she's Polish** sie ist Polin *zee ist pō·lin* □ *n* Polish Polnisch (*nt*) *pol·nish*

polite *adj* höflich *hurf·likh*

political *adj* politisch *po·li·tish*

politician *n* der Politiker *po·li·ti·kèr*, die Politikerin *po·li·ti·kè·rin*

politics *n* die Politik *po·li·teek*

pollution *n* die Umweltverschmutzung *oom·velt·fer·shmoot·soong*

polo *n* das Polo *pō·lō*

polo neck *n* der Rollkragen *rol·krah·gèn*

polyester *n* der Polyester *po·lō·es·tèr*

polyethylene *n* das Polyäthylen *pō·lee·e·tee·layn*

polyethylene bag *n* die Plastiktüte *pla·stik·tōō·tè*

pomegranate *n* der Granatapfel *gra·naht·ap·fèl*

pond *n* (*natural*) der Teich *tyekh*; (*artificial*) das Becken *be·kèn*

pony *n* das Pony *pō·nee*

pool *n* (*of rain*) die Pfütze *pfōōt·sè*; (*swimming*) das Schwimmbecken *shvim·be·kèn*; (*game*) das Poolbillard *pool·bil·yart*

poor *adj* arm *am*; (*mediocre*) mittelmäßig *mi·tèl·may·sikh*

pop *adj* (*music, art*) Pop *pop*

pop concert *n* das Popkonzert *pop·kon·tsert*

popcorn *n* das Popcorn *pop·korn*

pope *n* der Papst *pahpst*

pop group *n* die Popgruppe *pop·groo·pè*

poplar *n* die Pappel *pa·pèl*

poplin *n* der Popelin *po·pè·leen*

popsicle *n* das Eis am Stiel *ice am shteel*

popular *adj* beliebt *bè·leept*; (*fashionable*) modisch *mō·dish*

population *n* die Bevölkerung *bè·furl·kè·roong*

porcelain *n* das Porzellan *por·tse·lahn*

porch *n* der Vorbau *fōr·bow*

pork *n* das Schweinefleisch *shvine·è·flyesh*

porridge *n* der Haferbrei *hah·fèr·brye*

port *n* (*for ships*) der Hafen *hah·fèn*; (*wine*) der Portwein *port·vine*

portable *adj* tragbar *trahk·bahr*

porter *n* (*for luggage*) der Gepäckträger *gè·pek·tray·gèr*; (*doorkeeper*) der Pförtner *pfurt·nèr* T26

portfolio *n* die Aktenmappe *ak·tèn·ma·pè*

porthole *n* das Bullauge *bool·ow·gè*

portion *n* die Portion *por·tsee·ōn*

Portugal *n* Portugal (*nt*) *por·too·gal*

Portuguese *adj* portugiesisch *por·too·gee·zish*; **he's Portuguese** er ist Portugiese *er ist por·too·gee·zè*; **she's Portuguese** sie ist Portugiesin *zee ist por·too·gee·zin* □ *n* Portuguese Portugiesisch (*nt*) *por·too·gee·zish*

position *n* (*of body*) die Lage *lah·gè*; (*place, job*) die Stelle *shte·lè*

positive *adj* positiv *pō·zi·teef*; (*definite*) streng *shtreng*

possibility *n* die Möglichkeit *murg·likh·kite*

possible *adj* möglich *mur·g·likh*

possibly *adv* vielleicht *fee·lyekht*; **to do all one possibly can** alles Mögliche tun* *a·lès mur·g·li·khè toon*

post *n* (*pole*) der Pfosten *pfos·tèn*; (*mail*) die Post *post*; **by post** mit der Post *mit der post* □ *vt* post mit der Post schicken *mit der post shi·kèn*

postage *n* das Porto *por·tō*

postal *adj* Post- *post*

postal district *n* der Postort *post·ort*

postal order *n* die Postanweisung *post·an·vye·zoong*

post-box *n* der Briefkasten *breef·kas·tèn*

postcard *n* die Postkarte *post·kar·tè* L17, S102, Sn2

post-code *n* die Postleitzahl *post·lite·tsahl*

postdate *vt* vor|datieren *fōr·da·tee·rèn*

poster *n* das Plakat *pla·kaht*

postman *n* der Briefträger *breef·tray·gèr*

post office *n* das Postamt *post·amt*; **the Post Office** die Post *post*; **I must go to the post office** ich muß zur Post gehen *ikh moos tsoor post gay·èn* F9

post-office box *n* das Postfach *post·fakh*

postpone *vt* verschieben* *fer·shee·bèn*

pot *n* der Topf *topf*

potato *n* die Kartoffel *kar·to·fèl*

pottery *n* die Keramik *kay·rah·mik*; (*workshop*) die Töpferei *tur'p·fè·rye*

pot(ty) *n* das Töpfchen *tur'pf·khèn*

poultry *n* das Geflügel *gè·flōō·gèl*

pound *n* das Pfund *pfoont*

pour *vt* (*tea, milk*) ein|schenken *ine·sheng·kèn* ◻ *vi* strömen *shtrur'·mèn*

powder *n* das Pulver *pool·vèr*; (*cosmetic*) der Puder *poo·dèr*

powder room *n* die Damentoilette *dah·mèn·tŏ·a·le·tè*

power *n* (*of machine*) die Leistung *lye·stoong*; (*authority*) die Autorität *ow·tŏ·ree·tet*; (*electricity*) der Strom *shtröm*

powerful *adj* kräftig *kref·tikh*; (*person*) mächtig *mekh·tikh*

P.R. *n* die Public Relations

practical *adj* praktisch *prak·tish*

practice *vt/i* ◻ to practice running das Laufen üben *dass low·fèn ōō·bèn*; to practice the piano Klavier üben *kla·veer ōō·bèn*

Prague *n* Prag (*nt*) *prahk*

pram *n* der Kinderwagen *kin·dèr·vah·gèn*

prawn *n* die Garnele *gar·nay·lè*

pray *vi* beten *bay·tèn*

prayer *n* das Gebet *gè·bayt*

precinct *n* (*administrative area*) der Bezirk *bè·tsirk*

precious *adj* (*jewel etc*) wertvoll *vert·fol*

precise *adj* genau *gè·now*

precision *n* die Genauigkeit *gè·now·ikh·kite*

predict *vt* voraus|sagen *fŏr·ows·zah·gèn*

prediction *n* die Voraussage *fŏr·ows·zah·gè*

prefer *vt* vor|ziehen* *fŏr·tsee·èn*

preferred stock *n* die Vorzugsaktien (*pl*) *fŏr·tsooks·ak·tsee·èn*

pregnant *adj* schwanger *shvang·èr*

prejudice *n* das Vorurteil *fŏr·oor·tile*

preliminary *adj* einleitend *ine·lye·tènt*

première *n* die Premiere *prè·mee·ay·rè*

premises *pl* die Räumlichkeiten (*pl*) *roym·likh·kite·èn*

premium *n* die Prämie *pray·mee·è*

prepaid *adj* vorausbezahlt *fŏr·ows·bè·tsahlt*

preparation *n* die Vorbereitung *fŏr·bè·rye·toong*

prepare *vt* vor|bereiten *fŏr·bè·rye·tèn*; (*meal*) zu|bereiten *tsoo·bè·rye·tèn* ◻ *vi* he's preparing to leave er macht Anstalten abzufahren *er makht an·shtal·tèn ap·tsoo·fah·rèn*

Presbyterian *adj* presbyterianisch *pres·bōō·tay·ree·ah·nish*

prescription *n* das Rezept *ray·tsept* I47

present *adj* anwesend *an·vay·zènt*; the present king der jetzige König *der yet·si·gè kur'·nikh* ◻ *n* present (*gift*) das Geschenk *gè·shenk*; at present im Augenblick *im ow·gèn·blik* ◻ *vt* present (*give*) übergeben* *ōō·bèr·gay·bèn* S7, 111

presentation *n* die Vorlage *fŏr·lah·gè*

preserve(s) *n* die Marmelade *mar·mè·lah·dè*

president *n* (*of country*) der Präsident *pre·zi·dènt*; (*of company*) der Aufsichtsratsvorsitzende *owf·zikhts·rahts·fŏr·zit·sèn·dè*

press *n* die Presse *pre·sè* ◻ *vt* drücken *drōō·kèn*; (*iron*) bügeln *bōō·gèln*; press the button drücken Sie den Knopf *drōō·kèn zee dayn knopf*

press-campaign *n* die Pressekampagne *pre·sè·kam·pan·yè*

pressure *n* der Druck *drook*; the pressures of modern life die Belastungen des modernen Lebens *dee bè·las·toong·èn des mŏ·dèr·nèn lay·bèns*; he was under great pressure er war großen Belastungen ausgesetzt *er vahr grŏ·sèn bè·las·toong·èn ows·gè·zetst*

pressure cooker *n* der Dampfkochtopf *dampf·kokh·topf*

pressure group *n* die Pressure-Group

prestige *n* das Prestige *pres·tee·zhè*

pretax *adj* (*profit*) brutto *broo·tŏ*

pretend *vi* so tun*, als ob *zŏ toon als op*; to pretend to do something vor|geben*, etwas zu tun *fŏr·gay·bèn et·vass tsoo toon*

pretty *adj* (*woman, child*) hübsch *hōōpsh*; (*dress*) schön *shur'n*

preview *n* die Vorschau *fŏr·show*

previous *adj* frühere(r/s) *frōō·è·rè(·rèr/·rès*); on the previous day am Tag vorher *am tahk fŏr·her*

price *n* der Preis *price* ◻ *vt* (*goods*) den Preis fest|setzen *dayn price fest·zet·sèn*

price list *n* die Preisliste *price·lis·tè*

price range *n* die Preisklasse *price·kla·sè*

prick *vt* stechen* *shte·khèn*

pride *n* der Stolz *shtolts*

priest *n* der Priester *prees·tèr* Sn88

primary *adj* (*education*) Grundschul- *groont·shool*

prime minister, P.M. *n* der Premierminister *prè·mee·ay·mee·nis·tèr*, die Premierministerin *prè·mee·ay·mee·nis·tè·rin*

prince *n* der Prinz *prints*

princess *n* die Prinzessin *print·ses·in*

principal *n* (*of school etc*) der Rektor *rek·tor*, die Rektorin *rek·tŏ·rin*

print *vt* (*book, newspaper*) drucken *droo·kèn*; (*write in block letters*) in Druckschrift schreiben* *in drook·shrift shrye·bèn* ◻ *n* die Schrift *shrift*; (*photographic*) der Abzug *ap·tsook*; out of print vergriffen *fer·gri·fèn* S53

printer *n* der Drucker *droo·kèr*

printout *n* der Ausdruck *ows·drook*

prison *n* das Gefängnis *gè·feng·nis*; in prison im Gefängnis *im gè·feng·nis*

prisoner *n* der/die Gefangene *gè·fang·è·nè*

private *adj* privat *pre·vaht*; (*secluded*) abgelegen *ap·gè·lay·gèn*; (*confidential*) vertraulich *fer·trow·likh*; private lesson der Privatunterricht *pree·vaht·oon·tèr·rikht*; in private privat *pree·vaht*

private enterprise *n* das Privatunternehmen *pree·vaht·oon·tèr·nay·mèn*

private sector *n* der Privatbereich *pree·vaht·bè·ryekh*

prize *n* der Preis *price*

probable *adj* wahrscheinlich *vahr·shine·likh*

probably *adv* wahrscheinlich *vahr·shine·likh*

problem *n* das Problem *prŏ·blaym* A72

procedure *n* das Verfahren *fer·fah·rèn*

process *n* das Verfahren *fer·fah·rèn*; (*method*) der Prozeß *prŏ·tses* ◻ *vt* verarbeiten *fer·ar·bye·tèn*; (*application, order*) bearbeiten *bè·ar·bye·tèn*

produce *vt* (*manufacture*) her|stellen *her·shte·lèn*; (*play*) die Regie führen bei *dee ray·zhee foo·rèn bye*; (*movie*) produzieren *pró·doot·see·rèn* □ *n* (*products*) das Erzeugnis *er·tsoyk·nis*

producer *n* (*manufacturer*) der Hersteller *her·shte·lèr*; (*agricultural*) der Erzeuger *er·tsoy·gèr*; (*of play*) der Regisseur *ray·zhee·sur*; (*of movie*) der Produzent *pró·doot·sent*

product *n* das Produkt *pro·dookt* Bm23

production *n* die Produktion *pro·dook·tsee·ôn*; (*of play*) die Inszenierung *ins·tsay·nee·roong*

productivity *n* die Produktivität *pro·dook·tee·vee·tet*

profession *n* der Beruf *bè·roof*

professional *adj* beruflich *bè·roof·likh*; (*not amateur*) Berufs- *bè·roofs*

professor *n* der Dozent *dô·tsent*

profit *n* der Gewinn *gè·vin*

profitability *n* die Rentabilität *ren·ta·bi·lee·tet*

profitable *adj* rentabel *ren·tah·bèl*

profiterole *n* die Profiterole *pro·fee·tè·rôl*

profit-making *adj* rentabel *ren·tah·bèl*

profit margin *n* die Gewinnspanne *gè·vin·shpa·nè*

profit-sharing *n* die Gewinnbeteiligung *gè·vin·bè·tile·i·goong*

program *n* (*radio, TV*) die Sendung *zen·doong*; (*brochure, computer*) das Programm *prô·gram* □ *vt* programmieren *prô·gra·mee·rèn* L50

programmer *n* (*person*) der Programmierer *prô·gra·mee·rèr*, die Programmiererin *prô·gra·mee·rèr·in*

programming *n* (*computer*) das Programmieren *prô·gra·mee·rèn*

progress *n* die Fortschritte (*pl*) *fort·shri·tè*; to make progress Fortschritte machen *fort·shri·tè ma·khèn*

prohibit *vt* verbieten* *fer·bee·tèn*

project *n* (*plan*) das Projekt *prô·yekt*; (*venture*) das Unternehmen *oon·tèr·nay·mèn*

projector *n* der Projektor *prô·yek·tor*

promenade *n* (*by sea*) die Promenade *pro·mè·nah·dè*

promise *n* das Versprechen *fer·shpre·khèn* □ *vt* versprechen* *fer·shpre·khèn*

promote *vt* (*person*) befördern *bè·fur·dèrn*; (*product*) werben* für *ver·bèn foor*

promotion *n* (*of person*) die Beförderung *bè·fur·dè·roong*; (*of product*) die Werbung *ver·boong*

pronounce *vt* aus|sprechen* *ows·shpre·khèn*

pronunciation *n* die Aussprache *ows·shpra·khè*

proof *n* der Beweis *bè·vice*; (*of photo*) der Probeabzug *prô·bè·ap·tsook*; a 70° proof whiskey Whisky mit 70 Volumenprozent Alkohol *vis·kee mit 70 vo·loo·mèn·prô·tsent al·kô·hôl*

proper *adj* (*appropriate*) passend *pa·sènt*; (*correct*) richtig *rikh·tikh*; (*respectable*) anständig *an·shten·dikh*

properly *adv* richtig *rikh·tikh*

property *n* das Eigentum *eye·gèn·toom*; (*estate*) der Besitz *bè·zits*

prophylactic *n* (*contraceptive*) das Kondom *kon·dôm*

proposal *n* (*suggestion*) der Vorschlag *fôr·shlahk*

propose *vt* (*suggest*) vor|schlagen* *fôr·shlah·gèn*; to propose a toast to someone einen Toast auf jemanden

aus|bringen* *ine·èn tôst owf yay·man·dèn ows·bring·èn*

proposition *n* (*proposal*) der Vorschlag *fôr·shlahk*

prospect *n* die Aussicht *ows·zikht*

prospectus *n* der Prospekt *prô·spekt*

prosperous *adj* wohlhabend *vôl·hah·bènt*

protect *vt* beschützen *bè·shóòt·sèn*

protein *n* das Protein *prô·tay·een*

protest *n* der Protest *prô·test* □ *vi* protestieren *prô·tes·tee·rèn*

Protestant *adj* protestantisch *prô·tes·tan·tish*

prototype *n* der Prototyp *prô·tô·toop*

proud *adj* stolz *shtolts*; proud of stolz auf *shtolts owf*

prove *vt* beweisen* *bè·vye·zèn*

provide *vt* zur Verfügung stellen *tsoor fer·foo·goong shte·lèn*; to provide someone with something jemanden mit etwas versorgen *yay·man·dèn mit et·vass fer·zor·gèn* □ *vi* to provide for someone für jemanden sorgen *foor yay·man·dèn zor·gèn*

provided, providing *conj* vorausgesetzt, daß *fôr·ows·gè·zetst dass*; provided (that) he comes vorausgesetzt, daß er kommt *fôr·ows·gè·zetst dass er komt*

province *n* (*region*) die Provinz *prô·vints*

provincial *adj* ländlich *lent·likh*

proviso *n* der Vorbehalt *fôr·bè·halt*

prune *n* die Backpflaume *bak·pflow·mè*

P.S. *abbrev* PS *pay·ess*

psychiatric *adj* psychiatrisch *psoo·khee·ah·trish*

psychiatrist *n* der Psychiater *psoo·khee·ah·tèr*, die Psychiaterin *psoo·khee·ah·tè·rin*

psychological *adj* psychologisch *psoo·khô·lô·gish*

psychologist *n* der Psychologe *psoo·khô·lô·gè*, die Psychologin *psoo·khô·lô·gin*

psychology *n* die Psychologie *psoo·khô·lô·gee*

P.T.O. *abbrev* b.w.

pub *n* die Kneipe *knye·pè*

public *adj* öffentlich *urf·fènt·likh* □ *n* das Publikum *poob·li·koom*; in public in der Öffentlichkeit *in der urf·fènt·likh·kite*

public conveniences *pl* die Toiletten (*pl*) *tô·a·le·tèn*

publicity *n* die Werbung *ver·boong*

publicity campaign *n* die Werbekampagne *ver·bè·kam·pan·yè*

public relations *n* die Public Relations (*pl*)

public relations officer *n* der Pressesprecher *pre·sè·shpre·khèr*

public school *n* die staatliche Schule *shtaht·li·khè shoo·lè*

public sector *n* die öffentliche Hand *urf·fènt·li·khè hant*

publish *vt* veröffentlichen *fer·urf·fènt·li·khèn*

publisher *n* der Verleger *fer·lay·gèr*, die Verlegerin *fer·lay·gè·rin*

pudding *n* der Nachtisch *nakh·tish*

puddle *n* die Pfütze *pfoot·sè*

pull *vt/i* ziehen* *tsee·èn*; to pull something out etwas heraus|ziehen* *et·vass her·ows·tsee·èn*; to pull out of a deal aus einem Geschäft aus|steigen* *ows ine·èm gè·sheft ows·shtye·gèn*; the car pulled in der Wagen hielt an *der vah·gèn heelt an*; he pulled out to pass the car er scherte aus, um den

Wagen zu überholen *er shayr·tè ows,*
oom dayn vah·gèn tsoo ōō·bèr·hō·
lèn; **to pull something off** etwas ab|-
ziehen* *et·vass ap·tsee·èn*

pullover *n* der Pullover *poo·lō·vèr*

pump *n* die Pumpe *poom·pè* □ *vt* pumpen *poom·pèn*

pumpkin *n* der Kürbis *kōōr·bis*

punch *n (blow)* der Schlag *shlahk;*
(drink) die Bowle *bō·lè* □ *vt (with
fist)* mit der Faust schlagen* *mit der
fowst shlah·gèn; (ticket etc)* lochen
lo·khèn

punctual *adj* pünktlich *pōōnkt·likh*

puncture *n* die Reifenpanne *rye·fèn·*
pa·nè

punish *vt* bestrafen *bè·shtrah·fèn*

punishment *n* die Strafe *shtrah·fè*

pupil *n* der Schüler *shōō·lèr,* die Schülerin *shōō·lèr·in*

purchase *n* der Einkauf *ine·kowf* □ *vt*
kaufen *kow·fèn*

pure *adj* rein *rine*

purée *n* das Püree *pōō·ray*

purple *adj* violett *vee·ō·let*

purpose *n* der Zweck *tsvek;* on purpose absichtlich *ap·zikht·likh*

purse *n (for money)* das Portemonnaie
port·mo·nay; (lady's bag) die Handtasche *hant·ta·shè*

push *vt* schieben* *shee·bèn; (button)*
drücken *drōō·kèn; (product)* propagieren *prō·pa·gee·rèn;* push it in
drücken Sie es hinein *drōō·kèn zee
ess hin·ine*

put *vt* stellen *shte·lèn;* **to put one's
things away** seine Sachen auf|räu-
men *zine·è za·khèn owf·roy·mèn;* **to
put back** *(replace)* zurück|stellen
tsoo·rōōk·shte·lèn; **to put down a
parcel** ein Paket nieder|setzen *ine
pa·kayt nee·dèr·zet·sèn;* **to put on a
dress** ein Kleid an|ziehen* *ine klite
an·tsee·èn;* **to put on the light** das
Licht an|machen *dass likht an·ma·*
khèn; **to put on the brakes** bremsen
brem·zèn; **to put out the light** das
Licht aus|machen *dass likht ows·ma·*
khèn; **he put out his hand** er streckte
seine Hand aus *er shtrek·tè zine·è
hant ows;* **to put someone through**
(on phone) jemanden verbinden*
yay·man·dèn fer·bin·dèn; **to put up a
notice** ein Plakat auf|hängen *ine pla·*
kaht owf·heng·èn; **to put up capital**
Kapital bereit|stellen *ka·pee·tahl bè·*
rite·shte·lèn

puzzle *n* das Rätsel *ret·sèl; (jigsaw)*
das Puzzle *poo·zèl*

pyramid *n* die Pyramide *pōō·ra·mee·dè*

Q

quail *n* die Wachtel *vakh·tèl*

quaint *adj* malerisch *mah·lèr·ish*

qualification *n (diploma etc)* die Qualifikation *kva·li·fi·ka·tsee·ōn; (restriction)* die Einschränkung *ine·shreng·*
koong

qualified *adj* ausgebildet *ows·gè·bil·dèt*

qualify for *vt (grant etc)* in Frage kommen* für *in frah·gè kom·èn fōōr; (in
sports)* sich qualifizieren für *zikh
kva·li·fi·tsee·rèn fōōr*

quality *n* die Qualität *kva·li·tayt;
(characteristic)* die Eigenschaft *eye·
gèn·shaft;* **quality goods** die Qualitätswaren (pl) *kva·li·tayts·vah·rèn*

quantity *n* die Menge *meng·è*

quarantine *n* die Quarantäne *kva·ran·
tay·nè;* **to put a dog in quarantine** ei-

nen Hund unter Quarantäne stellen
*ine·èn hoont oon·tèr kva·ran·tay·nè
shtel·èn*

quarrel *n* der Streit *shtrite* □ *vi* sich
streiten* *zikh shtrye·tèn;* **to quarrel
with somebody** sich mit jemandem
streiten* *zikh mit yay·man·dèm
shtrye·tèn*

quarry *n* der Steinbruch *shtine·brookh*

quart *n ≈* das Liter *lee·tèr*

quarter *n* das Viertel *fir·tèl;* **a quarter
of an hour** eine Viertelstunde *ine·è
fir·tèl·shtoon·dè;* **(a) quarter to 4**
(ein) Viertel vor 4 *(ine) fir·tèl fōr 4;*
(a) quarter past 4 (ein) Viertel nach
4 *(ine) fir·tèl nakh 4*

quartz *n* der Quarz *kvarts*

quayside *n* der Kai *kye*

queen *n* die Königin *kur'n·i·gin*

queer *adj (strange)* eigenartig *eye·gèn·
ar·tikh*

question *n* die Frage *frah·gè;* **to ask a
question** eine Frage stellen *ine·è
frah·gè shtel·èn;* **it's a question of** es
handelt sich um *ess han·dèlt zikh
oom;* **out of the question** nicht in
Frage *nikht in frah·gè*

question mark *n* das Fragezeichen
frah·gè·tsye·khèn

questionnaire *n* der Fragebogen *frah·
gè·bō·gèn*

quiche *n* die Quiche *keesh*

quick *adj* schnell *shnel;* **be quick!** mach
schnell! *makh shnel*

quickly *adv* schnell *shnel* Sn57

quiet *adj (place)* ruhig *roo·ikh; (person)* still *shtil; (holiday)* geruhsam
gè·roo·zam; **be quiet!** Ruhe! *roo·è*

quietly *adv (speak)* leise *lye·zè; (walk,
work)* ruhig *roo·ikh*

quilt *n* das Federbett *fay·dèr·bet*

quit *vt (leave)* verlassen* *fer·las·èn* □ *vi
(give up)* auf|geben* *owf·gay·bèn*

quite *adv (fairly)* ziemlich *tseem·likh;
(absolutely)* ganz *gants;* **quite a few**
ziemlich viele *tseem·likh fee·lè*

quiz *n* das Quiz *kvis*

quota *n (of goods)* das Kontingent
kon·ting·gent

quotation *n (passage)* das Zitat *tsi·
taht; (price)* die Preisangebot *price·
an·gè·bōt*

quote *vt (passage)* zitieren *tsi·teer·èn;
(price)* nennen* *nen·èn*

R

rabbi *n* der Rabbiner *rah·bee·nèr*

rabbit *n* das Kaninchen *ka·neen·khèn*

rabies *n* die Tollwut *tol·voot*

race *n* die Rasse *ra·sè; (sport)* das
Rennen *re·nèn;* **the races** das Pferderennen *pfer·dè·re·nèn*

racecourse *n* die Rennbahn *ren·bahn*

racehorse *n* das Rennpferd *ren·pfert*

race relations *pl* die Beziehungen zwischen den Rassen *bè·tsee·oong·èn
tsvi·shèn dayn ra·sèn*

race track *n* die Rennstrecke *ren·shtre·
kè*

racial *adj* Rassen- *ra·sèn*

rack *n (for luggage)* das Gepäcknetz
gè·pek·nets; (for wine) das Gestell
gè·shtel; (for dishes) der Ständer
shten·dèr

racket *n (tennis)* der Schläger *shlay·gèr*

radar *n* das Radar *ra·dahr*

radar trap *n* die Radarfalle *ra·dahr·fa·
lè*

radial ply *adj* Gürtel- *gōōr·tèl*

radiator n der Heizkörper *hites·kur· pèr;* (of car) der Kühler *kōō·lèr*

radio n der Rundfunk *roont·foonk;* (radio set) das Radio *rah·dee·ō;* on the radio im Radio *im rah·dee·ō* A5

radish n das Radieschen *ra·dees·khèn*

rag n der Lappen *la·pèn*

ragged adj (clothes) zerlumpt *tser· loompt*

raid n (military) der Angriff *an·grif;* (by police) die Razzia *ra·tsee·a;* (by criminals) der Überfall *ōō·bèr·fal*

rail n das Geländer *gè·len·dèr;* rails (for train) die Schienen (pl) *shee· nèn;* by rail per Bahn *per bahn*

railings pl das Geländer *gè·len·dèr*

railroad n die Eisenbahn *eye·zèn·bahn*

railroad station n der Bahnhof *bahn· hōf*

rain n der Regen *ray·gèn* □ vi regnen *rayg·nèn;* it's raining es regnet *ess rayg·nèt*

rainbow n der Regenbogen *ray·gèn·bō· gèn*

raincoat n der Regenmantel *ray·gèn· man·tèl*

rainy adj regnerisch *rayg·nè·rish*

raise vt heben* *hay·bèn;* (price) erhöhen *er·hur·èn;* (family) groß|ziehen* *grōs·tsee·èn* □ n die Erhöhung *er· hur·oong*

raisin n die Rosine *ro·zee·nè*

rake n der Rechen *re·khèn*

rally n (political) die Kundgebung *koont·gay·boong;* (sporting) die Rallye *ra·lee*

ramp n die Rampe *ram·pè;* entrance ramp die Auffahrt *owf·fahrt;* exit ramp die Autobahnausfahrt *ow·tō· bahn·ows·fahrt*

ranch n die Ranch *ranch*

random adj willkürlich *vil·kōōr·likh;* at random aufs Geratewohl *owfs gè· rah·tè·vōl*

range n (variety) das Sortiment *zor· tee·ment;* (of mountains) die Kette *ke·tè;* (of missile) die Reichweite *ryekh·vye·tè* □ vi to range from X to Y von X bis Y gehen* *fon X bis Y gay·èn*

range finder n (on camera) der Entfernungsmesser *ent·fer·noongs·me·sèr*

rank n (status) der Rang *rang*

rare adj selten *zel·tèn;* (steak) nicht durchgebraten *nikht doorkh·gè·brah· tèn*

rash n der Hautausschlag *howt·ows· shlahk*

raspberry n die Himbeere *him·bay·rè*

rat n die Ratte *ra·tè*

rate n (price) der Tarif *ta·reef;* at the rate of in einem Tempo von *in ine· èm tem·pō fon;* rate of inflation die Inflationsrate *in·fla·see·ōnz·rah·tè;* rate of exchange der Wechselkurs *vek·sèl·koors* Sn18

rates pl (local tax) die Grundsteuer *groont·shtoy·èr*

rather adv (quite) ziemlich *tseem·likh;* I'd rather go to the movies ich würde lieber ins Kino gehen *ikh vōōr·dè lee·bèr ins kee·nō gay·èn*

ratio n das Verhältnis *fer·helt·nis*

rationalization n die Rationalisierung *ra·tsee·ō·na·lee·zee·roong*

rationalize vt rationalisieren *ra·tsee·ō· na·lee·zee·rèn*

ravioli n die Ravioli (pl) *ra·vee·ō·lee*

raw adj roh *rō*

raw material n die Rohstoffe (pl) *rō· shto·fè*

ray n der Strahl *shtrahl*

razor n der Rasierapparat *ra·zeer·a· pa·raht* A45

razor blade n die Rasierklinge *ra·zeer· kling·è*

reach vt (arrive at) an|kommen* an/in *an·ko·mèn an/in;* (with hand, contact) erreichen *er·rye·khèn* □ n out of reach außer Reichweite *ow·sèr ryekh·vye·tè;* within easy reach of the sea in unmittelbarer Nähe des Meeres *in oon·mi·tèl·bah·rèr nay·è dess me·rès*

reaction n die Reaktion *ray·ak·tsee·ōn*

reactor n der Reaktor *ray·ak·tor*

read vt/i lesen* *lay·zèn*

readdress vt um|adressieren *oom·a· dre·see·rèn*

reading n das Lesen *lay·zèn*

ready adj bereit *bè·rite;* ready to do something bereit, etwas zu tun *bè· rite et·vass tsoo toon*

ready-cooked adj vorgekocht *fōr·gè· kokht*

ready-made adj (clothes) Konfektions- *kon·fek·tsee·ōns*

ready-to-wear adj Konfektions- *kon· fek·tsee·ōns*

real adj wirklich *virk·likh;* (genuine) echt *ekht;* it's a real problem das ist wirklich ein Problem *dass ist virk· likh ine pro·blaym;* in real terms effektiv *e·fek·teef*

real estate n die Immobilien (pl) *i·mō· bee·lee·èn*

realize vt begreifen* *bè·grye·fèn;* (assets) realisieren *ray·a·lee·zee·rèn*

really adv wirklich *virk·likh*

realtor n der Grundstücksmakler *groont·shtōōks·mah·klèr*

rear adj (seat) Rück- *rōōk;* (wheel) Hinter- *hin·tèr* □ vt (children, cattle) auf|ziehen* *owf·tsee·èn*

rear view mirror n der Rückspiegel *rōōk·shpee·gèl*

reason n der Grund *groont*

reasonable adj vernünftig *fer·nōōnf· tikh*

receipt n die Quittung *kvi·toong;* (for parcel) der Empfangsschein *emp· fangs·shine;* receipts (income) die Einnahmen (pl) *ine·nah·mèn* M15

receive vt (letter) erhalten* *er·hal·tèn;* (guest) empfangen* *emp·fang·èn*

receiver n (phone) der Hörer *hur·èr*

recent adj neueste(r/s) *noy·è·stè(·stèr/ ·stès)*

recently adv kürzlich *kōōrts·likh*

reception n (gathering) der Empfang *emp·fang;* (in hotel etc) die Rezeption *re·tsep·tsee·ōn*

reception desk n die Rezeption *re· tsep·tsee·ōn*

receptionist n (in hotel) der Empfangschef *emp·fangs·shef,* die Empfangsdame *emp·fangs·dah·mè*

recession n die Rezession *ray·tse·see· ōn*

recipe n das Rezept *ray·tsept*

recognize vt erkennen* *er·ke·nèn*

recommend vt empfehlen* *emp·fay·lèn* . E11, 19

record n (register) die Unterlagen (pl) *oon·tèr·lah·gèn;* (file) die Akte *ak·tè;* (disk) die Schallplatte *shal·pla·tè;* (in sports) der Rekord *ray·kort* □ adj (production, crop etc) Rekord- *ray· kort* □ vt (sound) auf|nehmen* *owf· nay·mèn;* (write down) auf|zeichnen *owf·tsyekh·nèn*

record-player n der Plattenspieler *pla‧tèn‧shpee‧lèr*

recover vi *(from illness)* sich erholen *zikh er‧hö‧lèn*

recruit vt *(personnel)* ein|stellen *ine‧shte‧lèn* □ n der/die Neue *noy‧è*

recruitment n die Einstellung *ine‧shte‧loong*

red adj rot *röt*

red currant n die rote Johannisbeere *rö‧tè yö‧ha‧nis‧bay‧rè*

red-haired adj rothaarig *röt‧hah‧rikh*

redirect vt *(letter)* nach|senden* *nakh‧zen‧dèn*

redistribute vt um|verteilen *oom‧fer‧tye‧lèn*

redistribution n die Umverteilung *oom‧fer‧tye‧loong*

red light n *(traffic light)* das Rotlicht *röt‧likht*; to go through a red light eine Ampel überfahren* *ine‧è am‧pèl ōō‧bèr‧fah‧rèn*

red light district n die Strichgegend *shtrikh‧gay‧gènt*

red tape n der Papierkrieg *pa‧peer‧kreek*

reduce vt reduzieren *ray‧doo‧tsee‧rèn*; *(price)* herab|setzen *her‧ap‧ze‧tsèn* □ vi *(lose weight)* ab|nehmen* *ap‧nay‧mèn*

reduction n die Reduktion *ray‧dook‧tsee‧ōn*; *(in price)* der Nachlaß *nakh‧las*; to buy something at a reduction etwas verbilligt kaufen *et‧vass fer‧bi‧likht kow‧fèn*

redundant adj *(worker)* arbeitslos *ar‧bites‧lös*

referee n *(football)* der Schiedsrichter *sheets‧rikh‧tèr*; *(boxing)* der Ringrichter *ring‧rikh‧tèr*; *(judo)* der Kampfrichter *kampf‧rikh‧tèr*

reference n *(mention)* die Erwähnung *er‧vay‧noong*; *(testimonial)* die Referenz *ray‧fay‧rents*; his reference to this matter seine Bemerkungen zu dieser Sache *zine‧è bè‧mer‧koong‧èn tsoo dee‧zèr za‧khè*; with reference to your letter mit Bezug auf Ihren Brief *mit bè‧tsook owf ee‧rèn breef*

refer to vt *(allude to)* sich beziehen* auf *zikh bè‧tsee‧èn owf*; *(consult)* nach|schlagen* in *nakh‧shlah‧gèn in*

refine vt raffinieren *ra‧fi‧nee‧rèn*

refinery n die Raffinerie *ra‧fee‧ne‧ree*

reflect vt reflektieren *ray‧flek‧tee‧rèn*; *(in mirror)* spiegeln *shpee‧gèln*

reflector n *(on cycle, car)* der Rückstrahler *rōōk‧shtrah‧lèr*

refreshments pl die Erfrischungen *(pl)* *er‧fri‧shoong‧èn*

refrigerator n der Kühlschrank *kōōl‧shrank*

refund vt rück|vergüten *rōōk‧fer‧gōō‧tèn* □ n die Vergütung *fer‧gōō‧toong*

refusal n die Ablehnung *ap‧lay‧noong*

refuse vt ab|lehnen *ap‧lay‧nèn*; to refuse to do something sich weigern, etwas zu tun *zikh vye‧gèrn et‧vass tsoo toon*

regarding prep in bezug auf *in bè‧tsook owf*

regardless of prep ohne Rücksicht auf *ö‧nè rōōk‧zikht owf*

regatta n die Regatta *ray‧ga‧ta*

region n die Gegend *gay‧gènt*; *(administrative)* das Gebiet *gè‧beet* Mc23

register n das Register *ray‧gi‧ster*

registered letter n der eingeschriebene Brief *ine‧gè‧shree‧bè‧nè breef* Sn7

registered mail n □ by registered mail per Einschreiben *per ine‧shrye‧bèn*

registered trademark n das eingetragene Warenzeichen *ine‧gè‧trah‧gè‧nè vah‧rèn‧tsye‧khèn*

regret vt bedauern *bè‧dow‧èrn*

regular adj regelmäßig *ray‧gèl‧may‧sikh*; *(usual, size)* normal *nor‧mahl*; *(ordinary)* gewöhnlich *gè‧vur'n‧likh*

regulation n *(rule)* die Vorschrift *för‧shrift*

rehearsal n die Probe *prö‧bè*

rein n der Zügel *tsōō‧gèl*

reject vt ab|lehnen *ap‧lay‧nèn* □ n die Ausschußware *ows‧shoos‧vah‧rè*

relation n der/die Verwandte *fer‧van‧tè*

relative n der/die Verwandte *fer‧van‧tè* □ adj relativ *ray‧la‧teef*

relax vi sich entspannen *zikh ent‧shpa‧nèn*

release vt *(prisoner)* frei|lassen* *frye‧la‧sèn*; *(book, film)* heraus|bringen* *her‧ows‧bring‧èn*

relevant adj relevant *ray‧lay‧vant*; relevant to relevant für *ray‧lay‧vant fōōr*

reliability n *(of person)* die Zuverlässigkeit *tsoo‧fer‧le‧sikh‧kite*

reliable adj zuverlässig *tsoo‧fer‧le‧sikh*

relief n *(from pain, anxiety)* die Erleichterung *er‧lyekh‧tè‧roong*

religion n die Religion *ray‧lee‧gee‧ōn*

religious adj *(person)* gläubig *gloy‧bikh*

rely on vt *(person)* sich verlassen* auf *zikh fer‧la‧sèn owf*

remain vi bleiben* *blye‧bèn*; *(be left over)* übrig|bleiben* *ōō‧brikh‧blye‧bèn*

remark n die Bemerkung *bè‧mer‧koong*

remarkable adj außergewöhnlich *ows‧èr‧gè‧vur'n‧likh*

remedy n das Heilmittel *hile‧mi‧tèl*; a remedy for ein Mittel gegen *ine mi‧tèl gay‧gèn*

remember vt sich erinnern an *zikh er‧in‧èrn an*

remind vt erinnern *er‧in‧èrn*; to remind someone of something jemanden an etwas erinnern *yay‧man‧dèn an et‧vass er‧in‧èrn*

remittance n die Überweisung *ōō‧bèr‧vye‧zoong*

remote control n die Fernsteuerung *fern‧shtoy‧èr‧oong*

remove vt entfernen *ent‧fer‧nèn*; *(stain)* beseitigen *bè‧zye‧ti‧gèn*

renew vt *(subscription, passport)* verlängern *fer‧leng‧èrn*

rent n die Miete *mee‧tè* □ vt *(house etc)* mieten *mee‧tèn*; *(car)* leihen* *lye‧èn* T106, A59

rental n die Leihgebühr *lye‧gè‧bōōr* A64

rental car n der Mietwagen *meet‧vah‧gèn*

reorder vt *(goods)* neu bestellen *noy bè‧shte‧lèn*

reorganization n die Umorganisation *oom‧or‧ga‧ni‧za‧tsee‧ōn*

reorganize vt um|organisieren *oom‧or‧ga‧ni‧zee‧rèn*

repair vt reparieren *ray‧pa‧ree‧rèn* T178, S97, Sn44

repay vt *(sum)* zurück|zahlen *tsoo‧rōōk‧tsah‧lèn*; *(person)* vergelten* *fer‧gel‧tèn*

repeat vt wiederholen *vee‧dèr‧hö‧lèn*

repeat order n die Nachbestellung *nakh‧bè‧shte‧loong*

repetition n die Wiederholung *vee‧dèr‧hö‧loong*

replace vt *(put back)* zurück|legen

tsoo·rōōk·lay·gèn; (*substitute*) ersetzen *er·zet·sèn*

replacement *n* der Ersatz *er·zats* Sn55

reply *vi* erwidern *er·vee·dèrn*; **to reply
to a question** auf eine Frage antworten *owf ine·è frah·gè ant·vor·tèn* □ *n*
reply die Antwort *ant·vort*

report *vt* (*tell about*) melden *mel·dèn*;
(*in press*) berichten *bè·rikh·tèn* □ *n*
der Bericht *bè·rikht*; (*in press*) die
Reportage *ray·por·tah·zhè*

reporter *n* (*press*) der Reporter *ray·
por·tèr*

represent *vt* (*symbolize*) symbolisieren
zōōm·bō·li·zee·rèn; (*act as deputy
for*) vertreten* *fer·tray·tèn*

representative *n* der Vertreter *fer·tray·
tèr* T19

republic *n* die Republik *ray·poo·bleek*

republican *adj* republikanisch *ray·poo·
bli·kah·nish*

reputation *n* der Ruf *roof*

request *n* die Bitte *bi·tè*

require *vt* (*need*) brauchen *brow·khèn*

requirement *n* das Bedürfnis *bè·dōōrf·
nis*

reroute *vt* um|leiten *oom·lye·tèn*

resale *n* □ not for resale nicht zum
Weiterverkauf bestimmt *nikht tsoom
vye·tèr·fer·kowf bè·shtimt*

rescue *vt* retten *re·tèn* □ *n* die Rettung
re·toong

research *n* die Forschung *for·shoong*

resell *vt* weiter|verkaufen *vye·tèr·fer·
kow·fèn*

resemble *vt* ähneln *ay·nèln*; **he resembles his father** er ähnelt seinem
Vater *er ay·nèlt zine·èm fah·tèr*

reservation *n* (*of seats, rooms etc*) die
Vorbestellung *fōr·bè·shte·loong*;
(*doubt*) der Vorbehalt *fōr·bè·halt*

reserve *vt* (*seat, room*) vor|bestellen
fōr·bè·shte·lèn; (*tickets*) bestellen *bè·
shte·lèn* E3f

reserves *pl* die Reserven (*pl*) *ray·zer·
vèn*

residence *n* die Wohnung *vō·noong*

residence permit *n* die Aufenthaltsgenehmigung *owf·ent·halts·gè·nay·mi·
goong*

residential *adj* (*area*) Wohn- *vōn*

resign *vi* kündigen *kōōn·di·gèn*

resignation *n* die Kündigung *kōōn·di·
goong*

resist *vt* widerstehen* *vee·dèr·shtay·èn*

resistance *n* (*to illness*) die Widerstandsfähigkeit *vee·dèr·shtants·fay·
ikh·kite*

resort *n* der Urlaubsort *oor·lowps·ort*;
in the last resort im schlimmsten Fall
im shlim·stèn fal □ *vi* **to resort to**
greifen* zu *grye·fèn tsoo*

resources *pl* die Mittel (*pl*) *mi·tèl*

respect *n* die Achtung *akh·toong* □ *vt*
achten *akh·tèn*

respectable *adj* anständig *an·shten·
dikh*

responsibility *n* die Verantwortung *fer·
ant·vor·toong*; **this is your responsibility** dafür sind Sie verantwortlich
da·fōōr zint zee fer·ant·vort·likh

responsible *adj* verantwortungsbewußt
fer·ant·vor·toongs·bè·voost; **responsible for** (*to blame*) verantwortlich
für *fer·ant·vort·likh fōōr*; **he's responsible for the department** er ist
für die Abteilung zuständig *er ist
fōōr dee ap·tye·loong tsoo·shten·dikh*

rest *vi* sich aus|ruhen *zikh ows·roo·èn*
□ *n* (*repose*) die Ruhe *roo·è*; **all the
rest** der ganze Rest *der gan·tsè rest*

restaurant *n* das Restaurant *res·tō·rant*
E1f

restrict *vt* beschränken *bè·shreng·kèn*;
(*speed*) begrenzen *bè·gren·tsèn*

restriction *n* die Beschränkung *bè·
shreng·koong*

restroom *n* die Toilette *tō·a·le·tè*

result *n* das Resultat *ray·zool·taht*

retail *n* der Einzelhandel *ine·tsèl·han·
dèl* □ *vt* im Einzelhandel verkaufen
im ine·tsèl·han·dèl fer·kow·fèn

retailer *n* der Einzelhändler *ine·tsèl·
hent·lèr*

retail price *n* der Einzelhandelspreis
ine·tsèl·han·dèls·prise Bm28

retire *vi* auf|hören zu arbeiten *owf·hur·
èn tsoo ar·bye·tèn*

retired *adj* im Ruhestand *im roo·è·
shtant*

retiree *n* der Rentner *rent·nèr*, die
Rentnerin *rent·nè·rin*

retirement *n* der Ruhestand *roo·è·
shtant*

retrain *vt* um|schulen *oom·shoo·lèn*
□ *vi* um|lernen *oom·ler·nèn*

retraining *n* die Umschulung *oom·
shoo·loong*

retread *n* der lauffflächenerneuerte
Reifen *lowf·fle·khèn·er·noy·èr·tè rye·
fèn*

retrieve *vt* (*data*) ab|fragen *ap·frah·gèn*

retrospect *n* □ **in retrospect** im Rückblick *im rōōk·blik*

return *vi* (*come back*) zurück|kehren
tsoo·rōōk·kay·rèn; (*go back*) zu-
rück|gehen* *tsoo·rōōk·gay·èn* □ *vt*
(*give back*) zurück|geben* *tsoo·rōōk·
gay·bèn*; (*send back*) zurück|senden*
tsoo·rōōk·zen·dèn □ *n* (*going/coming
back*) die Rückkehr *rōōk·kayr*;
(*profit*) der Gewinn *gè·vin*

rev *n* (*in engine*) die Umdrehung *oom·
dray·oong* □ *vt* auf Touren bringen*
owf too·rèn bring·èn

revenue *n* die Einnahmen (*pl*) *ine·nah·
mèn*

reverse *n* (*gear*) der Rückwärtsgang
rōōk·verts·gang; **in reverse** (**gear**) im
Rückwärtsgang *im rōōk·verts·gang*

review *n* der Überblick *ōō·bèr·blik*; (*of
book etc*) die Kritik *kri·teek* □ *vt*
überprüfen *ōō·bèr·prōō·fèn*

revise *vt* (*estimate etc*) revidieren *ray·
vi·dee·rèn*; (*schoolwork*) wiederho-
len *vee·dèr·hō·lèn*

revive *vt* (*person*) beleben *bè·lay·bèn*
□ *vi* wieder zu sich kommen* *vee·dèr
tsoo zikh ko·mèn*

revolution *n* (*political*) die Revolution
ray·vo·loo·tsee·ōn

revue *n* die Revue *rè·vōō*

reward *n* die Belohnung *bè·lō·noong*

rheumatism *n* der Rheumatismus *roy·
ma·tis·moos*

Rhine (*wine*) der Rhein *rine*

Rhine (*wine*) der weiße Rheinwein
vye·sè rine·vine

Rhone *n* die Rhone *rō·nè*

rhubarb *n* der Rhabarber *ra·bar·bèr*

rhythm *n* der Rhythmus *rōōt·moos*

rib *n* die Rippe *ri·pè*

ribbon *n* das Band *bant*

rice *n* der Reis *rise*

rich *adj* reich *ryekh*; (*food*) schwer
shvayr

ride *n* (*in vehicle*) die Fahrt *fahrt*; (*on
horse*) der Ritt *rit*; **to go for a ride**
(*by car*) eine Fahrt mit dem Auto
machen *ine·è fahrt mit daym ow·tō
ma·khèn*; **to give someone a ride into
town** jemanden in die Stadt fahren*

yay·man·dèn in dee shtat fah·rèn □ vt
to ride a horse reiten* rye·tèn; to ride
a bicycle Rad fahren* raht fah·rèn
L31

ridge n der Kamm kam
ridiculous adj lächerlich le·khèr·likh
riding n das Reiten rye·tèn; to go riding reiten gehen* rye·tèn gay·èn
rifle n das Gewehr gè·vayr
right adj (correct) richtig rikh·tikh;
(morally good) recht rekht; (not left)
rechte(r/s) rekh·tè(·tèr·tès); yes,
that's right ja, das ist richtig ya dass
ist rikh·tikh □ adv to turn right rechts
ab|biegen* rekhts ap·bee·gèn; right
in the middle genau in der Mitte gè·
now in der mi·tè □ n right (right-
hand side) die Rechte rekh·tè; (enti-
tlement) das Recht rekht; on the
right rechts rekhts; to the right nach
rechts nakh rekhts T100
right-handed adj rechtshändig rekhts·
hèn·dikh
right of way n (on road) die Vorfahrt
fór·fahrt
ring n der Ring ring □ vt to ring the
(door)bell läuten loy·tèn □ vi ring
klingeln kling·èln S93
rink n die Bahn bahn
rinse vt spülen shpōō·lèn □ n (hair conditioner) die Spülung shpōō·loong
riot n der Aufruhr owf·roor
rip vt zerreißen* tser·rye·sèn □ vi
reißen* rye·sèn
ripe adj reif rife
rise vi (go up) nach oben fahren* nakh
ō·bèn fah·rèn; (prices) steigen*
shtye·gèn; (person) auf|stehen* owf·
shtay·èn; (sun) auf|gehen* owf·gay·
èn □ n (in prices, wages) die Steigerung shtye·gè·roong
risk n das Risiko ree·zi·kō □ vt riskieren ris·kee·rèn
risotto n der Risotto ri·zo·tō
rival n der Rivale ri·vah·lè, die Rivalin
ri·vah·lin; a rival firm eine Konkurrenzfirma ine·è kon·koo·rents·fir·ma
river n der Fluß floos
road n die Straße shtrah·sè T133, F17
road block n die Straßensperre shtrah·
sèn·shpe·rè
road map n die Straßenkarte shtrah·
sèn·kar·tè
road sign n das Verkehrszeichen fer·
kayrs·tsye·khèn
road test n der Straßentest shtrah·sèn·
test
road works pl die Straßenbauarbeiten
(pl) shtrah·sèn·bow·ar·bye·tèn
roar vi brüllen brōō·lèn; (engine) heulen hoy·lèn □ n das Gebrüll gè·brōōl;
(of engine) das Heulen hoy·lèn
roast vt braten* brah·tèn; roast meat
der Braten brah·tèn
rob vt (person) berauben bè·row·bèn;
(bank) aus|rauben ows·row·bèn
robbery n der Raub rowp
robe n (after bath) der Bademantel
bah·dè·man·tèl
robot n der Roboter ro·bo·tèr
rock n (boulder) der Felsblock fels·
blok; (substance) der Fels fels; on
the rocks (with ice) mit Eis mit ise
□ vt rock wiegen vee·gèn
rocket n die Rakete ra·kay·tè
rock ('n' roll) n der Rock 'n' Roll rok
èn rōl
rod n (metallic) die Stange shtang·è;
(fishing) die Angelrute ang·èl·roo·tè
roll n die Rolle ro·lè; (bread) das Brötchen brur't·khèn □ vt/i rollen ro·lèn;

to roll up (newspaper etc) auf|rollen
owf·ro·lèn
roller skates pl die Rollschuhe (pl) rol·
shoo·è
rolling pin n das Nudelholz noo·dèl·
holts
Roman adj römisch rur'·mish; **Roman
Catholic** römisch-katholisch rur'·
mish·ka·tō·lish
Romania n Rumänien (nt) roo·may·
nee·èn
Romanian adj rumänisch roo·may·nish
□ n (language) Rumänisch (nt) roo·
may·nish
romantic adj romantisch ro·man·tish
Rome n Rom (nt) rōm
roof n das Dach dakh
roof rack n der Dachträger dakh·tray·
gèr
room n das Zimmer tsi·mèr; (space)
der Platz plats A4f, A13f
room service n der Zimmerservice tsi·
mèr·sur·vees
root n die Wurzel voor·tsèl
rope n das Seil zile
rose n die Rose rō·ze
rosé n der Rosé ro·zay
rot vi faulen fow·lèn
rotten adj (wood etc) faul fowl
rough n (golf) das Rauh row □ adj
rauh row; (sea) stürmisch shtōōr·
mish; (not gentle) hart hart; a rough
estimate eine grobe Schätzung ine·è
grō·bè shet·soong
roughly adv grob grōp; (approxi-
mately) ungefähr oon·gè·fayr
roulette n das Roulett roo·let
round adj rund roont □ n (circle) der
Kreis krise; (in sport, of talks) die
Runde roon·dè □ prep to go round a
field um ein Feld herum|gehen* oom
ine felt he·room·gay·èn; we sat round
the table wir saßen um den Tisch herum veer zah·sèn oom dayn tish he·
room; to go round the shops ein|kau-
fen gehen* ine·kow·fèn gay·èn; it's
round the corner es ist um die Ecke
ess ist oom dee e·kè □ adv to turn
something round etwas herum|dre-
hen et·vass her·oom·dray·èn
round figure/number n die runde Zahl
roon·dè tsahl
round trip n die Rundreise roont·rye·
zè
round trip (ticket) n die Rückfahrkarte rōōk·fahr·kar·tè
route n die Strecke shtre·kè F19f
routine n die Routine roo·tee·nè □ adj
routinemäßig roo·tee·nè·may·sikh
row[1] n die Reihe rye·è □ vi (sport) rudern roo·dèrn
row[2] n (noise) der Krach krakh
rowing n (sport) das Rudern roo·dèrn
royal adj königlich kur'·nik·likh
R.S.V.P. abbrev u.A.w.g.
rub vt reiben* rye·bèn; to rub out aus|-
radieren ows·ra·dee·rèn
rubber n (material) der Gummi goo·mi
rubber band n das Gummiband goo·
mi·bant
rubbish n die Abfälle (pl) ap·fe·lè;
(nonsense) der Quatsch kvatch
ruby n der Rubin roo·been
rucksack n der Rucksack rook·zak
rudder n das Ruder roo·dèr
rude adj unhöflich oon·hur'f·likh
rug n der Vorleger fōr·lay·gèr
rugby n das Rugby rug·bee
ruin n die Ruine roo·ee·nè □ vt zerstören tser·shtur'·rèn
ruins pl die Ruinen (pl) roo·ee·nèn

rule *n* (*regulation*) die Regel *ray·gèl*; (*for measuring*) das Lineal *li·nay·ahl* □ *vt* regieren *ray·gee·rèn*

ruler *n* (*leader*) der Herrscher *her·shèr*; (*for measuring*) das Lineal *li·nay·ahl*

rum *n* der Rum *room*

rumble *vi* grollen *gro·lèn* □ *n* das Grollen *gro·lèn*

rump steak *n* das Rumpsteak *roomp·stayk*

run *n* (*outing*) die Fahrt *fahrt*; (*in stocking*) die Laufmasche *lowf·ma·shè* □ *vi* laufen* *low·fèn*; the trains run every hour die Züge fahren stündlich *dee tsöö·gè fah·rèn shtöönt·likh*; the road runs past the house die Straße führt am Haus vorbei *dee shtrah·sè föört am hows för·bye*; this car runs on diesel dieses Auto fährt mit Diesel *dee·zès ow·tö fert mit dee·zèl*; to run after someone jemandem nach|laufen* *yay·man·dèm nakh·low·fèn*; to run away weg|laufen* *vek·low·fèn*; to run down or over (*car etc*) überfahren* *öö·bèr·fah·rèn*; we've run out of milk wir haben keine Milch mehr *veer hah·bèn kine·è milkh mayr* □ *vt* run (*a business, country*) führen *föö·rèn*

runner beans *pl* die Stangenbohnen (*pl*) *shtang·èn·bö·nèn*

running costs *pl* die Betriebskosten (*pl*) *bè·treeps·kos·tèn*

runway *n* die Piste *pis·tè*

rural *adj* ländlich *lent·likh*

rush *vi* eilen *eye·lèn* □ *vt* (*goods*) eilends senden* *eye·lènts zen·dèn* □ *n* die Eile *eye·lè*; we had a rush of orders wir hatten eine Flut von Aufträgen *veer ha·tèn ine·è floot fon owf·tre·gèn*

rush hour *n* die Stoßzeit *shtös·tsite*

Russia *n* Rußland (*nt*) *roos·lant*

Russian *adj* russisch *roo·sish*; he's Russian er ist Russe *er ist roo·sè*; she's Russian sie ist Russin *zee ist roo·sin* □ *n* Russian (*language*) Russisch (*nt*) *roo·sish*

rust *n* der Rost *rost* □ *vi* rosten *ros·tèn*

rustproof *adj* nicht rostend *nikht ros·tènt*

rusty *adj* rostig *ros·tikh*

rutabaga *n* die Rübe *röö·bè*

rye *n* der Roggen *ro·gèn*; rye (whiskey) der Roggenwhisky *ro·gèn·vis·kee*

rye bread *n* das Roggenbrot *ro·gèn·bröt*

S

saccharin *n* das Saccharin *zakh·a·reen*

sachet *n* das Briefchen *breef·khèn*

sack *n* der Sack *zak* □ *vt* (*dismiss*) entlassen* *ent·la·sèn*

sad *adj* traurig *trow·rikh*

saddle *n* der Sattel *za·tèl*

safe *adj* (*out of danger*) sicher *zi·khèr*; (*not dangerous*) ungefährlich *oon·gè·fayr·likh* □ *n* der Tresor *tray·zor*

safeguard *n* der Schutz *shoots*

safety *n* die Sicherheit *zi·khèr·hite*

safety belt *n* der Sicherheitsgurt *zi·khèr·hites·goort*

safety pin *n* die Sicherheitsnadel *zi·khèr·hites·nah·dèl*

sage *n* (*herb*) der Salbei *zal·bye*

sail *n* das Segel *zay·gèl* □ *vi* segeln *zay·gèln* L26

sailboat *n* das Segelboot *zay·gèl·böt* L24

sailor *n* der Matrose *ma·trö·zè*

saint *n* der/die Heilige *hye·li·gè*

sake *n* □ for my sake meinetwegen *mine·èt·vay·gèn*

salad *n* der Salat *za·laht* E42

salad dressing *n* die Salatsoße *za·laht·zö·sè*

salary *n* das Gehalt *gè·halt*

sale *n* der Verkauf *fer·kowf*; (*cheap prices*) der Ausverkauf *ows·fer·kowf*; on sale or return auf Kommission *owf ko·mi·see·ön*

sales *pl* (*cheap prices*) der Ausverkauf *ows·fer·kowf*

sales assistant *n* der Verkäufer *fer·koy·fèr*, die Verkäuferin *fer·koy·fè·rin*

salesman *n* (*rep*) der Vertreter *fer·tray·tèr* Bm21

sales manager *n* der Verkaufsleiter *fer·kowfs·lye·tèr*

saliva *n* der Speichel *shpye·khèl*

salmon *n* der Lachs *laks*

saloon *n* (*bar*) die Bar *bar*

salt *n* das Salz *zalts* S35

salt cellar *n* der Salzstreuer *zalts·shtroy·èr*

salty *adj* salzig *zal·tsikh* E34

same *adj* selbe(r/s) *zel·bè(·bèr/·bès)*; the same book as (*similar*) das gleiche Buch wie *dass glye·khè bookh vee* □ *pron* all the same trotzdem *trots·daym*; (the) same again please! dasselbe nochmal, bitte *das·zel·bè nokh·mahl bi·tè*

sample *n* (*of goods*) das Muster *moo·stèr* □ *vt* (*wine*) probieren *prö·bee·rèn* Bm23

sanctions *pl* die Sanktionen (*pl*) *zank·tsee·ö·nèn*

sand *n* der Sand *zant*

sandal *n* die Sandale *zan·dah·lè*

sandbank *n* die Sandbank *zant·bank*

sandwich *n* die Doppelschnitte *do·pèl·shni·tè*; a ham sandwich ein Schinkenbrot (*nt*) *ine shing·kèn·bröt*

sandy *adj* (*beach*) Sand- *zant*-

sanitarium *n* das Sanatorium *za·na·tö·ree·oom*

sanitary napkin *n* die Damenbinde *dah·mèn·bin·dè*

sarcastic *adj* sarkastisch *zar·ka·stish*

sardine *n* die Sardine *zar·dee·nè*

Sardinia *n* Sardinien (*nt*) *zar·dee·nee·èn*

satellite *n* der Satellit *za·tè·leet*

satin *n* der Satin *za·tañ*

satire *n* (*play*) die Satire *za·tee·rè*

satisfactory *adj* zufriedenstellend *tsoo·free·dèn·shte·lènt*

satisfy *vt* zufrieden|stellen *tsoo·free·dèn·shte·lèn*

saturate *vt* (*market*) sättigen *ze·ti·gèn*

Saturday *n* Sonnabend (*m*) *zon·ah·bènt*

sauce *n* die Soße *zö·sè*

saucepan *n* der Kochtopf *kokh·topf*

saucer *n* die Untertasse *oon·tèr·ta·sè*

sauna *n* die Sauna *zow·na* A11

sausage *n* die Wurst *voorst*

sausage roll *n* die Bratwurst im Schlafrock *braht·voorst im shlahf·rok*

sauté *adj* geröstet *gè·rur·stèt*

save *vt* (*person*) retten *re·tèn*; (*money*) sparen *shpah·rèn*

savings account *n* das Sparkonto *shpahr·kon·tö*

savings and loan association *n* die Bausparkasse *bow·shpahr·ka·sè*

savings bank *n* die Sparkasse *shpahr·ka·sè*

savory *adj* (*not sweet*) pikant *pi·kant*

say vt sagen zah·gèn; could you say that again? könnten Sie das wiederholen? kur'n·tèn zee dass vee·dèr·hō·lèn

scab n der Schorf shorf

scald vt verbrühen fer·brōō·èn

scale n (of fish) die Schuppe shoo·pè; (of map) der Maßstab mahs·shtahp; (on thermometer) die Skala skah·la; (music) die Tonleiter tōn·ly·tèr; scale of charges die Gebührenordnung gè·bōō·rèn·ort·noong

scales pl (for weighing) die Waage vah·gè

scallion n die Schalotte sha·lo·tè

scallop n die Jakobsmuschel yah·kops·moo·shèl

scalp n der Kopfhaut kopf·howt

scampi n die Scampi (pl) skam·pi

Scandinavia n Skandinavien (nt) skan·dee·nah·vee·èn

Scandinavian adj skandinavisch skan·dee·nah·vish

scar n die Narbe nar·bè

scarce adj rar rahr

scarcely adv kaum kowm

scared adj □ to be scared Angst haben* angst hah·bèn

scarf n der Schal shahl

scarlet adj scharlachrot shar·lakh·rōt

scene n die Szene stsay·nè; (sight) der Anblick an·blik

scenery n die Landschaft lant·shaft

scenic route n die landschaftlich schöne Strecke lant·shaft·likh shur'·nè shtre·kè

scent n (smell) der Duft dooft; (perfume) das Parfüm par·fōōm

schedule n das Programm prō·gram; (of trains etc) der Fahrplan fahr·plahn; on schedule (train) pünktlich pōōnkt·likh

scheduled flight n der Linienflug lee·nee·èn·flook

scheme n (plan) der Plan plahn

school n die Schule shoo·lè

science n die Wissenschaft vi·sèn·shaft

science fiction n die Science-Fiction

scientific adj wissenschaftlich vi·sèn·shaft·likh

scientist n der Wissenschaftler vi·sèn·shaft·lèr, die Wissenschaftlerin vi·sèn·shaft·lè·rin

scissors pl die Schere shay·rè

scooter n der Motorroller mo·tōr·ro·lèr

scope n □ within the scope of im Bereich von im bè·ryekh fon

score n der Spielstand shpeel·shtant □ vt (goal) schießen* shee·sèn

Scot n der Schotte sho·tè, die Schottin sho·tin

Scotch n (liquor) der Scotch skotsh

Scotch tape n der Tesafilm tay·za·film

Scotland n Schottland (nt) shot·lant

Scottish adj schottisch sho·tish; he's Scottish er ist Schotte er ist sho·tè; she's Scottish sie ist Schottin zee ist sho·tin

scourer n der Topfkratzer topf·kra·tsèr

scrap n (bit) das Stückchen shtōōk·khèn

scrape vt schrammen shra·mèn

scratch vt kratzen kra·tsèn

scream vi schreien* shrye·èn

screen n (partition) der Schirm shirm; (TV) der Bildschirm bilt·shirm; (movie) die Leinwand line·vant

screw n die Schraube shrow·bè

screwdriver n der Schraubenzieher shrow·bèn·tsee·èr

sculpture n die Skulptur skoolp·toor

sea n das Meer mayr; to go by sea mit dem Schiff fahren* mit dem shif fah·rèn

seafood n die Meeresfrüchte (pl) may·rès·frōōkh·tè

sea level n der Meeresspiegel may·rès·shpee·gèl

seam n der Saum zowm

search vt durchsuchen doorkh·zoo·khèn; to search for suchen zoo·khèn

seasick adj seekrank zee·krank

seaside n die Küste kōō·stè; seaside resort die Küstenbadestadt kōōs·tèn·bah·dè·shtat

season n die Jahreszeit yah·rès·tsite; the vacation season die Feriensaison fay·ree·èn·zay·zōn; strawberries are in season es ist die richtige Zeit für Erdbeeren ess ist dee rikh·ti·gè tsite fōōr ert·bay·rèn

seasoning n das Gewürz gè·vōorts

season ticket n die Zeitkarte tsite·kar·tè

seat n der Sitzplatz zits·plats; please take a seat setzen Sie sich bitte zet·sèn zee zikh bi·tè T10, 45, 73

seat belt n der Sicherheitsgurt zi·khèr·hites·goort

seaweed n die Alge al·gè

second n (time) die Sekunde ze·koon·dè □ adj zweite(r/s) tsvye·tè(·tèr/·tès)

secondary adj (importance) sekundär zay·koon·dayr

secondary school n die höhere Schule hur'·è·re shoo·lè

second-class adj zweiter Klasse tsvye·tèr kla·sè

second floor n der erste Stock er·stè shtok

secondhand adj (car etc) gebraucht gè·browkht S17

secret adj geheim gè·hime □ n das Geheimnis gè·hime·nis

secretary n der Sekretär zay·kray·tayr, die Sekretärin zay·kray·tay·rin Bm7, 13

secretary of state n der Außenminister ow·sen·mee·nis·tèr

sector n (economy) der Sektor zek·tōr; private sector der Privatsektor pree·vaht·zek·tōr; public sector der öffentliche Sector ur'·fènt·li·khè zek·tōr

security n (at airport) der Sicherheitsdienst zi·khèr·hites·deenst; (for loan) die Sicherheit zi·khèr·hite

sedan n (car) die Limousine lee·moo·zee·nè

sedative n das Beruhigungsmittel bè·roo·i·goongs·mi·tèl

see vt/i sehen* zay·èn; I want to see a doctor ich möchte zu einem Arzt ikh mur'kh·tè tsoo ine·èm artst; to see someone off at the station zum Bahnhof bringen* yay·man·dèn tsoom bahn·hōf bring·èn; to see someone home jemanden nach Hause bringen* yay·man·dèn nakh how·zè bring·èn; to see to something sich um etwas kümmern zikh oom et·vass kōō·mèrn

seed n der Samen zah·mèn

seem vi scheinen* shye·nèn

seersucker n der Krepp krep

seesaw n die Wippe vi·pè

seldom adv selten zel·tèn

selection n die Auswahl ows·vahl S47, 93, Bm23

self-contained adj (apartment) separat zay·pa·raht

self-employed *adj* selbständig *zelp·shten·dikh*

selfish *adj* egoistisch *ay·gó·is·tish*

self-service *adj* mit Selbstbedienung *mit zelpst·bè·dee·noong*

sell *vt* verkaufen *fer·kow·fèn* S8f

semifinal *n* das Halbfinale *halp·fee·nah·lè*

semiskilled *adj* angelernt *an·gè·lernt*

senate *n* (*political*) der Senat *zay·naht*

senator *n* der Senator *zay·nah·tor*

send *vt* schicken *shi·kèn*

sender *n* der Absender *ap·zen·dèr*

senior *adj* (*in rank*) vorgesetzt *fõr·gè·zetst*; (*in age*) älter *el·tèr*

sense *n* (*feeling*) das Gefühl *gè·fool*; (*common sense*) der Verstand *fer·shtant*; *sense of humor* der Sinn für Humor *zin fõõr hoo·mõr*, *to make sense* (*expression*) Sinn ergeben* *zin er·gay·bèn*

sensible *adj* vernünftig *fer·nõõnf·tikh*

sentence *n* der Satz *zats*

separate *adj* separat *zay·pa·raht*

September *n* September (*m*) *zep·tem·bèr*

serious *adj* ernst *ernst*

serve *vt* (*customer*) bedienen *bè·dee·nèn*; (*food*) servieren *zer·vee·rèn*

service *n* (*in restaurant*) die Bedienung *bè·dee·noong*; (*bus etc*) die Verbindung *fer·bin·doong*; (*for car*) die Inspektion *in·shpèk·tsee·õn*; (*in church*) der Gottesdienst *go·tès·deenst*

service area *n* die Tankstelle und Raststätte *tank·shte·lè oont rast·shte·tè*

service charge *n* die Bedienung *bè·dee·noong*

service industry *n* die Dienstleistungsbranche *deenst·lye·stoongs·brañ·shè*

service station *n* die Großtankstelle *grõs·tank·shte·lè* F10

serviette *n* die Serviette *zer·vee·e·tè*

set *n* (*collection*) der Satz *zats* □ *vt* (*alarm*) stellen *shte·lèn*; *to set the table* den Tisch decken *dayn tish de·kèn*; *to have one's hair set* sich die Haare legen lassen* *zikh dee hah·rè lay·gèn la·sèn*; *to set off* or *out* sich auf|machen *zikh owf·ma·khèn*

settle *vt* (*argument*) bei|legen* *bye·lay·gèn*; (*bill*) bezahlen *bè·tsah·lèn* □ *vi* (*wine*) sich beruhigen *zikh bè·roo·i·gèn*; *to settle out of court* sich vergleichen* *zikh fer·glye·khèn*; *to settle in* sich ein|leben *zikh ine·lay·bèn*

settled *adj* (*weather*) beständig *bè·shten·dikh*

seven *num* sieben *zee·bèn*

seventeen *num* siebzehn *zeep·tsayn*

seventeenth *adj* siebzehnte(r/s) *zeep·tsayn·tè(·tèr/·tès)*

seventh *adj* siebte(r/s) *zeep·tè(·tèr/·tès)*

seventy *num* siebzig *zeep·tsikh*

several *adj* mehrere *may·rè·rè* □ *pron* *several of us* einige von uns *ine·i·gè fon oons*

sew *vi* nähen *nay·èn*

sewing machine *n* die Nähmaschine *nay·ma·shee·nè*

sex *n* das Geschlecht *gè·shlekht*

sexual intercourse *n* der Geschlechtsverkehr *gè·shlekhts·fer·kayr*

sexy *adj* sexy *sek·see*

shade *n* der Schatten *sha·tèn*; (*for lamp*) der Lampenschirm *lam·pèn·shirm*

shades *pl* (*sunglasses*) die Sonnenbrille *zo·nèn·bri·lè*

shadow *n* der Schatten *sha·tèn*

shake *vt* schütteln *shõõ·tèln*; *to shake hands with someone* jemandem die Hand geben* *yay·man·dèm dee hant gay·bèn* □ *vi* shake zittern *tsi·tèrn*

shall *vi* □ I shall do it ich werde es tun *ikh ver·dè ess toon*; shall I do it? soll ich es tun? *zol ikh ess toon*; **shall we come tomorrow?** sollen wir morgen kommen? *zo·lèn veer mor·gèn ko·mèn*

shallow *adj* flach *flakh*

shame *n* die Schande *shan·dè*; *what a shame!* wie schade! *vee shah·dè*

shampoo *n* das Shampoo *sham·poo* Sn39

shandygaff *n* das Bier mit Limonade *beer mit lee·mõ·nah·dè*

shape *n* die Form *form*

share *n* (*part*) der Anteil *an·tile*; (*finance*) die Aktie *ak·tsee·è* □ *vt* (*money, room*) teilen *tye·lèn*

shark *n* der Hai *hye*

sharp *adj* scharf *sharf*

sharp practice *n* die Gaunereien (*pl*) *gow·nè·rye·èn*

shave *vi* sich rasieren *zikh ra·zee·rèn*

shaver *n* der Rasierapparat *ra·zeer·a·pa·raht*

shaving brush *n* der Rasierpinsel *ra·zeer·pin·zèl*

shaving cream *n* die Rasiercreme *ra·zeer·kraym*

shaving soap *n* die Rasierseife *ra·zeer·zye·fè*

shawl *n* das Tuch *tookh*

she *pron* sie *zee*

shed *n* der Schuppen *shoo·pèn*

sheep *n* das Schaf *shahf*

sheepskin *n* das Schaffell *shahf·fel*

sheer *adj* (*stockings*) sehr dünn *zayr dõõn*

sheet *n* das Bettlaken *bet·lah·kèn*; (*of paper*) das Blatt *blat*

shelf *n* das Regal *ray·gahl*

shell *n* die Schale *shah·lè*

shellfish *n* (*on menu*) Schaltiere (*pl*) *shahl·tee·rè*

shelter *n* (*for waiting under*) der Unterstand *oon·tèr·shtant* □ *vi* (*from rain etc*) sich unter|stellen *zikh oon·tèr·shte·lèn*

shelve *vi* (*beach*) ab|fallen* *ap·fa·lèn* □ *vt* (*project*) ad acta legen *at ak·ta lay·gèn*

sherbet *n* das Fruchteis *frookht·ice*

sheriff *n* der Sheriff

sherry *n* der Sherry

shift *n* (*change*) die Änderung *en·dè·roong*; (*of workmen*) die Schicht *shikht* □ *vt* *to shift gear* schalten *shal·tèn*

shin *n* das Schienbein *sheen·bine*

shine *vi* (*sun etc*) scheinen* *shye·nèn*; (*metal*) glänzen *glen·tsèn*

shingles *n* (*illness*) Gürtelrose (*f*) *gõõr·tèl·rõ·zè*

shiny *adj* glänzend *glen·tsent*

ship *n* das Schiff *shif* □ *vt* (*goods*) verschiffen *fer·shi·fèn*

shipbuilding *n* der Schiffsbau *shifs·bow*

shipment *n* die Sendung *zen·doong*

shipping agent *n* der Reedereivertreter *ray·dè·rye·fer·tray·tèr*

shipping company *n* die Schiffahrtsgesellschaft *shif·fahrts·gè·zel·shaft*

shipyard *n* die Werft *verft*

shirt *n* das Hemd *hemt* S65, Sn64

shiver *vi* zittern *tsi·tèrn*

shock n der Schock *shok*; *(electric)* der Elektroschock *e·lek·trō·shok*

shock absorber n der Stoßdämpfer *shtōs·demp·fèr*

shoe n der Schuh *shoo*; *(of brake)* der Bremsschuh **brems·shoo** S66

shoelace n der Schnürsenkel *shnōōr·seng·kèl*

shoeshop n das Schuhgeschäft *shoo·gè·sheft*

shoot vt *(injure)* an|schießen* *an·shee·sèn*; *(kill)* erschießen* *er·shee·sèn* □ vi schießen* *shee·sèn*

shop n das Geschäft *gè·sheft*

shoplifting n der Ladendiebstahl *lah·dèn·deep·shtahl*

shopping n die Einkäufe *(pl)* ine·koy·fè*; to go shopping ein|kaufen gehen* *ine·kow·fèn gay·èn*

shopping bag n die Einkaufstasche *ine·kowfs·ta·shè*

shopping center n das Einkaufszentrum *ine·kowfs·tsen·troom*

shop steward n der gewerkschaftliche Vertrauensmann *gè·verk·shaft·li·khè fer·trow·èns·man*

shop window n das Schaufenster *show·fen·stèr*

shopworn adj angestaubt *an·gè·shtowpt*

shore n *(of sea)* der Strand *shtrant*; *(of lake)* das Ufer *oo·fèr*

short adj kurz *koorts*; *(person)* klein *kline*; **to be short of something** etwas zu wenig haben* *et·vass tsoo vay·nikh hah·bèn*; **he gave me short change** er hat mir zuwenig herausgegeben *er hat meer tsoo·vay·nikh he·rows·gè·gay·bèn*

shortage n der Mangel *mang·èl*

shortbread n das Shortbread

shortcut n die Abkürzung *ap·kōōr·tsoong* T130

short drink n der Kurze *koort·sè*

shorten vt verkürzen *fer·kōōr·tsèn*

shortfall n das Defizit *day·fee·tsit*

shorthand n die Kurzschrift *koorts·shrift*

shorthand typist n die Stenotypistin *shtay·nō·tōō·pist·in*

short list n die engere Wahl *eng·è·rè vahl*

shortly adv *(soon)* in Kürze *in kōōr·tsè*

shorts pl die Shorts *(pl)* shorts*; *(underwear)* die Unterhose *oon·tèr·hō·zè*

short-staffed adj □ **to be short-staffed** zuwenig Personal haben* *tsoo·vay·nikh per·zō·nahl hah·bèn*

short term adj kurzfristig *koorts·fris·tikh*

short wave n die Kurzwelle *koorts·ve·lè*

shot n *(from gun)* der Schuß *shoos*

should vi □ **we should buy it** wir sollten es kaufen *veer zol·tèn ess kow·fèn*; **I should like a…** ich hätte gern ein… *ikh he·tè gern ine*

shoulder n die Schulter *shool·tèr*

shout n der Ruf *roof* □ vi rufen* *roo·fèn*

shovel n die Schaufel *show·fèl*

show n *(exhibition)* die Ausstellung *ows·shte·loong*; *(in theatre)* die Show *shō* □ vt zeigen *tsye·gèn*; **to show someone out** jemanden hinaus|begleiten *yay·man·dèn hi·nows·bè·glye·tèn* □ vi *(show (be visible)* zu sehen sein* *tsoo zay·èn zine*

show business n das Showgeschäft *shō·gè·sheft*

shower n *(rain)* der Schauer *show·èr*; *(bath)* die Dusche *doo·shè* A4, 91

showroom n der Ausstellungsraum *ows·shte·loongs·rowm*

shrewd adj gewitzt *gè·vitst*

shrimp n die Garnele *gar·nay·lè*

shrink vi ein|laufen* *ine·low·fèn*

shrinkage n die Einbußen *(pl)* ine·boo·sèn*

Shrove Tuesday n Fastnachtsdienstag *(m)* fast·nakhts·deens·tahk*

shrub n der Busch *boosh*

shrug vi die Achseln zucken *dee ak·sèln tsoo·kèn*

shut vt schließen* *shlee·sèn*; **to be shut** *(door)* zu sein* *tsoo zine* □ vi shut *(door, window)* zu|gehen* *tsoo·gay·èn*

shutter n *(on window)* der Fensterladen *fen·stèr·lah·dèn*; *(in camera)* der Verschluß *fer·shloos*

shuttle (service) n *(airline)* der Pendelverkehr *pen·dèl·fer·kayr*

shy adj schüchtern *shōōkh·tèrn*

Sicily n Sizilien *(nt)* zee·tsee·lee·èn*

sick adj *(ill)* krank *krank*; **to be sick** *(vomit)* brechen* *bre·khèn*; **I feel sick** mir ist schlecht *meer ist shlekht*

sickly adj krank *krank*

sickness n *(illness)* die Krankheit *krank·hite*; *(nausea)* die Übelkeit *ōō·bèl·kite*

side n die Seite *zye·tè*; **the right side** *(of cloth etc)* die rechte Seite *dee rekh·tè zye·tè*; **the wrong side** die Rückseite *rōōk·zye·tè*; **this side up** oben *ō·bèn*

sideboard n die Anrichte *an·rikh·tè*

sidelights pl *(on car)* die Parklichter *(pl)* park·likht·èr*

side-street n die Seitenstraße *zye·tèn·shtrah·sè*

sidewalk n der Bürgersteig *bōōr·gèr·shtike*

siesta n die Siesta *zee·es·ta*

sieve n das Sieb *zeep* □ vt sieben *zee·bèn*

sigh vi seufzen *zoyf·tsèn*

sight n *(spectacle)* der Anblick *an·blik*; **to have poor sight** schlecht sehen* *shlekht zay·èn*; **to see the sights** eine Stadt besichtigen *ine·è shtat bè·zikh·ti·gèn*

sightseeing n Besichtigungen *(pl)* bè·zikh·ti·goong·èn*

sign n *(mark)* das Zeichen *tsye·khèn*; *(notice)* das Schild *shilt* □ vt *(document)* unterzeichnen *oon·tèr·tsyekh·nèn* T186

signal n das Signal *zig·nahl* T184

signature n die Unterschrift *oon·tèr·shrift*

signpost n der Wegweiser *vayk·vye·zèr*

silence n die Stille *shti·lè*

silent adj still *shtil*

silk n die Seide *zye·dè*; **a silk dress** ein Seidenkleid *(nt)* ine zye·dèn·klite* S65

silly adj albern *al·bèrn*

silver n das Silber *zil·bèr*; *(money)* das Silbergeld *zil·bèr·gelt*; **a silver bracelet** ein silbernes Armband *ine zil·bèr·nès arm·bant* S92, 96

similar adj ähnlich *ayn·likh*; **to be similar to** ähneln *ay·nèln*

simmer vi sieden* *zee·dèn*

simple adj einfach *ine·fakh*

since prep seit *zite*; **I've been here since 4 o'clock** ich bin schon seit 4 Uhr hier *ikh bin shōn zite 4 oor heer*

□ *conj* since we arrived seit wir anka- men *zite veer an·kah·mèn*; since he's ill da er krank ist *dah er krank ist*
sincere *adj* aufrichtig *owf·rikh·tikh*
sincerely *adv* □ yours sincerely mit freundlichen Grüßen *mit froynt·likh·èn grŏŏ·sèn*
sing *vt/i* singen* *zing·èn*
single *adj* (not double) einzeln *ine· tsèln*; (not married) ledig *lay·dikh*; a single bed ein Einzelbett (nt) *ine· tsèl·bet*; a single room ein Einzelzim- mer (nt) *ine·tsèl·tsi·mèr*; a single ticket eine einfache Fahrkarte *ine·è ine·fakh·è fahr·kar·tè*
sink *n* (basin) der Spülstein *shpool· shtine* □ *vi* sinken* *zing·kèn*
sir *n* mein Herr *mine her*
siren *n* die Sirene *zee·ray·nè*
sirloin *n* das Filet *fee·lay*
sister *n* die Schwester *shve·stèr*
sister-in-law *n* die Schwägerin *shvay· gè·rin*
sit *vi* sitzen* *zi·tsèn*; to sit down sich setzen *zikh zet·sèn*
site *n* (of building) das Gelände *gè·len· dè*
sitting room *n* das Wohnzimmer *vōn· tsi·mèr*
situation *n* (place) die Lage *lah·gè*; (circumstances) die Situation *zi·too· a·tsee·ōn*
six *num* sechs *zeks*
sixteen *num* sechzehn *zekh·tsayn*
sixteenth *adj* sechzehnte(r/s) *zekh· tsayn·tè(·tèr/·tès)*
sixth *adj* sechste(r/s) *zeks·tè(·tèr/·tès)*
sixty *num* sechzig *zekh·tsikh*
size *n* die Größe *grur·sè*
skate *n* (for ice) der Schlittschuh *shlit· shoo*; (fish) der Rochen *ro·khèn* □ *vi* Schlittschuh laufen* *shlit·shoo low· fèn*
skateboard *n* das Rollbrett *roll·bret*
skating rink *n* die Eisbahn *ice·bahn*
sketch *n* (drawing) die Skizze *ski·tsè* □ *vt* skizzieren *ski·tsee·rèn*
skewer *n* der Spieß *shpees*
ski *n* der Ski *shee* □ *vi* Ski fahren* *shee· fah·rèn* L37
ski boot *n* der Skistiefel *shee·shtee·fèl*
skid *n* das Schleudern *shloy·dèrn* □ *vi* schleudern *shloy·dèrn*
skier *n* der Skiläufer *shee·loy·fèr*, die Skiläuferin *shee·loy·fè·rin*
skiing *n* Skifahren (nt) *shee·fah·rèn*; to go skiing Skifahren gehen* *shee·fah· rèn gay·èn*
ski lift *n* der Skilift *shee·lift*
skill *n* das Geschick *gè·shik*
skilled *adj* (workers) ausgebildet *ows· gè·bil·dèt*
skillet *n* die Bratpfanne *braht·pfa·nè*
skim milk *n* die entrahmte Milch *ent· rahm·tè milkh*
skin *n* die Haut *howt* S43
ski pants *pl* die Skihose *shee·hō·zè*
skirt *n* der Rock *rock* Sn64
ski run *n* die Skipiste *shee·pis·tè*
skull *n* der Schädel *shay·dèl*
sky *n* der Himmel *hi·mèl*
skyscraper *n* der Wolkenkratzer *vol· kèn·krat·sèr*
slack *adj* (loose) locker *lo·kèr*; (busi- ness) flau *flow*
slacks *pl* die Hose *hō·zè*
slam *vt* zu|schlagen* *tsoo·shlah·gèn*
slang *n* der Slang *sleng*
slap *vt* schlagen* *shlah·gèn*
slate *n* die Schieferplatte *shee·fèr·pla· tè*

slave *n* der Sklave *sklah·vè*, die Skla- vin *sklah·vin*
sled(ge) *n* (toboggan) der Schlitten *shli·tèn*
sleep *n* der Schlaf *shlahf* □ *vi* schlafen* *shlah·fèn* □ *vt* the apartment sleeps three in der Wohnung können 3 Per- sonen schlafen *in der vō·noong kur· nèn 3 per·zō·nèn shlah·fèn*
sleeping bag *n* der Schlafsack *shlahf· zak*
sleeping car *n* der Schlafwagen *shlahf· vah·gèn*
sleeping pill *n* die Schlaftablette *shlahf·ta·ble·tè*
sleet *n* der Schneeregen *shnay·ray·gèn*
sleeve *n* der Ärmel *er·mèl*
sleigh *n* der Schlitten *shli·tèn*
slice *n* die Scheibe *shye·bè* □ *vt* in Scheiben schneiden* *in shye·bèn shnye·dèn* S34
slide *vi* rutschen *root·shèn* □ *n* (chute) die Rutschbahn *rootsh·bahn*; (photo) das Dia *dee·a*
slide rule *n* der Rechenschieber *rekh· èn·shee·bèr*
slight *adj* (small) gering *gè·ring*
slim *adj* schlank *shlank*
sling *n* (for arm) die Schlinge *shling·è*
slip *vi* (slide) gleiten* *glye·tèn*; (trip) aus|rutschen *ows·root·shèn* □ *n* (underskirt) der Unterrock *oon·tèr· rok*; (of paper) der Zettel *tse·tèl*
slipper *n* der Hausschuh *hows·shoo*
slippery *adj* rutschig *root·shikh*
slogan *n* der Werbespruch *ver·bè· shprookh*
slope *n* (angle) die Neigung *nye· goong*; (sloping ground) der Hang *hang*
slot *n* der Schlitz *shlits*
slot machine *n* der Automat *ow·tō· maht*
slow *adj* langsam *lang·zam*; my watch is slow meine Uhr geht nach *mine·è oor gayt nakh* □ *vi* to slow down or up langsamer fahren* *lang·zam·èr fah·rèn* B27
slowdown *n* der Bummelstreik *boo· mèl·shtrike*
slump *n* der Rückgang *rook·gang* □ *vi* stürzen *shtoor·tsèn*
smack *vt* einen Klaps geben* *ine·èn klaps gay·bèn* □ *n* der Klaps *klaps*
small *adj* klein *kline*
smallpox *n* die Pocken (pl) *po·kèn*
smart *adj* (elegant) elegant *e·lay·gant*; (clever) schlau *shlow*
smash *vt* zerschmettern *tser·shme·tèrn*
smell *n* der Geruch *gè·rookh* □ *vt* rie- chen* *ree·khèn* □ *vi* to smell of garlic nach Knoblauch riechen* *nakh knop·lowkh ree·khèn*
smile *n* das Lächeln *lekh·èln* □ *vi* lä- cheln *lekh·èln*
smock *n* der Kittel *ki·tèl*
smoke *n* der Rauch *rowkh* □ *vt/i* rau- chen *row·khèn*; do you smoke? rau- chen Sie? *row·khèn zee* Mc33
smoked *adj* (salmon etc) geräuchert *gè·roy·khèrt*
smoker *n* (person) der Raucher *row· khèr*; (compartment) das Raucherab- teil *row·khèr·ap·tile*
smooth *adj* glatt *glat*
smuggle *vt* schmuggeln *shmoo·gèln*
snack *n* der Imbiß *im·biss*
snack bar *n* die Imbißstube *im·biss· shtoo·bè* T42
snail *n* die Schnecke *shne·kè*
snake *n* die Schlange *shlang·è*

snap *vi* (*break*) brechen* *bre·khèn*

snap fastener *n* der Druckknopf *drook·knopf*

snatch *vt* schnappen *shna·pèn*

sneakers *pl* die Freizeitschuhe (*pl*) *frye·tsite·shoo·è*

sneeze *n* das Niesen *nee·zèn* □ *vi* niesen *nee·zèn*

snob *n* der Snob *snop*

snobbish *adj* versnobt *fer·snopt*

snooker *n* Snooker (*nt*) *snoo·kèr*

snore *vi* schnarchen *shnar·khèn*

snorkel *n* der Schnorchel *shnor·khèl*

snow *n* die Schnee *shnay* □ *vi* schneien *shnye·èn*; it's snowing es schneit *ess shnite*

snowball *n* der Schneeball *shnay·bal*

snowdrift *n* die Schneewehe *shnay·vay·è*

snowman *n* der Schneemann *shnay·man*

snowplow *n* der Schneepflug *shnay·pflook*

snuff *n* der Schnupftabak *shnoopf·ta·bak*

so *adv* □ so pleased that... so froh, daß... *zō frō dass*; I hope so hoffentlich *ho·fènt·likh*; so many so viele *zō fee·lè*; so much so viel *zō feel* □ *conj* and so we left und daher sind wir gegangen *oont dah·her zint veer gè·gang·èn*; so do I ich auch *ikh owkh*; so is he er auch *er owkh*; he did it so that I would go er tat es, damit ich gehen würde *er taht ess da·mit ikh gay·èn vōōr·dè*

soak *vt* (*washing*) ein|weichen *ine·vye·khèn*

soap *n* die Seife *zye·fè* A42

soap-flakes *pl* die Seifenflocken (*pl*) *zye·fèn·flo·kèn*

soap powder *n* das Seifenpulver *zye·fèn·pool·vèr*

sober *adj* (*not drunk*) nüchtern *nōōkh·tèrn*

soccer *n* Fußball (*m*) *foos·bal*

social *adj* sozial *zo·tsee·al*

socialism *n* der Sozialismus *zō·tsee·a·lis·moos*

socialist *n* der Sozialist *zō·tsee·a·list* □ *adj* sozialistisch *zō·tsee·a·li·stish*

social security *n* die Sozialversicherung *zō·tsee·al·fer·zi·khè·roong*

social services *pl* die Sozialversorgung *zo·tsee·al·fer·zor·goong*

social worker *n* der Sozialarbeiter *zō·tsee·al·ar·bye·tèr*, die Sozialarbeiterin *zō·tsee·al·ar·bye·tè·rin*

society *n* die Gesellschaft *gè·zel·shaft*

sock *n* die Socke *zo·kè*

socket *n* (*electrical*) die Steckdose *shtek·dō·zè*

soda *n* (*chemical*) das Soda *zō·da*; a whiskey and soda ein Whisky Soda *ine vi·skee zō·da*

soda water *n* das Sodawasser *zō·da·va·sèr*

sofa *n* das Sofa *zō·fa*

soft *adj* (*not hard*) weich *vyekh*; (*not loud*) leise *lye·zè*; (*drink*) alkoholfrei *al·kō·hol·frye*

soft-boiled *adj* □ a soft-boiled egg ein weiches Ei *ine vye·khès eye*

software *n* die Software

soil *n* die Erde *er·dè*

solar *adj* Sonnen- *zo·nèn*

soldier *n* der Soldat *zol·daht*

sold out *adj* ausverkauft *ows·fer·kowft*

sole *n* die Sohle *zō·lè*; (*fish*) die Seezunge *zay·tsoong·è*

solid *adj* (*not hollow*) massiv *ma·seef*;

(*strong, not liquid*) fest *fest*; in solid gold in massivem Gold *in ma·see·vèm golt*

solution *n* die Lösung *lur·zoong*

solve *vt* (*problem*) lösen *lur·zèn*

some *adj* □ some apples ein paar Äpfel *ine pahr ep·fèl*; some bread etwas Brot *et·vass brōt*; some people einige Leute *i·ni·gè loy·tè* □ *pron* some (of it) was left es war etwas übrig *ess vahr et·vass ōō·brikh*; some (of them) were... einige waren... *i·ni·gè vah·rèn*

somebody, someone *pron* jemand *yay·mant*

someplace *adv* irgendwo *ir·gènt·vō*

something *pron* etwas *et·vass*; something bigger etwas Größeres *et·vass grur·sè·rès*

sometimes *adv* manchmal *mankh·mal*

somewhere *adv* irgendwo *ir·gènt·vō*

son *n* der Sohn *zōn* Sn83, C10, 13, 16

son et lumière *n* das Son et Lumière *soñ ay lōō·myehr*

song *n* das Lied *leet*

son-in-law *n* der Schwiegersohn *shvee·gèr·zōn*

soon *adv* bald *balt*; he came too soon er ist zu früh gekommen *er ist tsoo frōō gè·ko·mèn* B9

sophisticated *adj* (*machine*) hochentwickelt *hōkh·ent·vi·kèlt*; (*person*) kultiviert *kool·ti·veert*

sore *adj* (*painful*) schmerzend *shmer·tsènt*

sorry *adj* traurig *trow·rikh*; (I'm) sorry es tut mir leid *ess toot meer lite*

sort *n* (*kind*) die Art *art*

SOS *n* SOS (*nt*) *ess·ō·ess*

soufflé *n* der Auflauf *owf·lowf*

soul *n* die Seele *zay·lè*

sound *n* das Geräusch *gè·roysh* □ *vi* it sounds like a car es hört sich wie ein Auto an *ess hurt zikh vee ine ow·tō an* □ *vt* to sound one's horn hupen *hoo·pèn*

sound track *n* die Tonspur *tōn·shpoor*

soup *n* die Suppe *zoo·pè* E36

sour *adj* sauer *zow·èr*

source *n* die Quelle *kve·lè*

south *n* der Süden *zōō·dèn* □ *adv* nach Süden *nakh zōō·dèn* □ *n* southeast der Südosten *zōōt·o·stèn*; southwest der Südwesten *zōōt·we·stèn*

South Africa *n* Südafrika (*nt*) *zōōt·a·fri·ka*

South African *adj* südafrikanisch *zōōt·a·fri·kah·nish*

South America *n* Südamerika (*nt*) *zōōt·a·may·ri·ka*

South American *adj* südamerikanisch *zōōt·a·may·ri·kah·nish*

southern *adj* südlich *zōōt·likh*

South Pole *n* der Südpol *zōōt·pōl*

souvenir *n* das Andenken *an·deng·kèn*

Soviet *adj* sowjetisch *sov·ye·tish*

Soviet Union *n* die Sowjetunion *sov·yet·oo·nyōn*

soy beans *pl* die Sojabohnen (*pl*) *zō·ya·bō·nèn*

soy sauce *n* die Sojasoße *zō·ya·zō·sè*

spa *n* der Kurort *koor·ort*

space *n* (*gap*) die Lücke *lōō·kè*; (*room*) der Raum *rowm*; (*universe*) der Weltraum *velt·rowm*

spacecraft *n* das Raumschiff *rowm·shif*

spade *n* der Spaten *shpah·tèn*; spades (*cards*) Pik (*nt*) *peek*

spaghetti *n* die Spaghetti (*pl*) *shpa·ge·tee*

Spain *n* Spanien (*nt*) *shpah·nee·èn*

Spanish adj spanisch shpah·nish; he's Spanish er ist Spanier er ist shpah·nee·èr; she's Spanish sie ist Spanierin zee ist shpah·nee·è·rin □ n Spanish Spanisch (nt) shpah·nish

spare adj □ spare wheel das Reserverad ray·zer·vè·raht; spare time die Freizeit frye·tsite □ n spare (part) das Ersatzteil er·zats·tile

spare rib n das Rippchen rip·khèn

spark n der Funke foong·kè

sparkle vi funkeln foong·kèln

sparkling adj (wine) Schaum- showm

spark plug n die Zündkerze tsöönt·kert·sè

sparrow n der Spatz shpats

spatula n der Spatel shpah·tèl

speak vt/i sprechen* shpre·khèn; do you speak English? sprechen Sie Englisch? shpre·khèn zee eng·lish; to speak to someone about something mit jemandem über etwas sprechen* mit yay·man·dèm öö·bèr et·vass shpre·khèn B24

speaker n (electrical) der Lautsprecher lowt·shprekh·èr

special adj besondere(r/s) bè·zon·dè·rè(·rèr/·rès)

specialize vi sich spezialisieren zikh shpe·tsee·a·lee·zee·rèn; to specialize in sich spezialisieren auf zikh shpe·tsee·a·lee·zee·rèn owf

specific adj spezifisch shpe·tsee·fish

specifications pl die technischen Angaben tekh·ni·shèn an·gah·bèn

specify vt genau an|geben* gè·now an·gay·bèn

specimen n die Probe prö·bè

speech n die Sprache shprah·khè; (oration) die Rede ray·dè

speed n die Geschwindigkeit gè·shvin·dikh·kite □ vi to speed up beschleunigen bè·shloy·ni·gèn

speedboat n das Schnellboot shnel·böt

speeding n (in car) das zu schnelle Fahren tsoo shne·lè fah·rèn

speed limit n die Geschwindigkeitsbegrenzung gè·shvin·dikh·kites·bè·gren·tsoong

speedometer n der Tachometer takh·o·may·tèr

spell vt (in writing) buchstabieren bookh·shta·bee·rèn □ n (period) die Weile vye·lè

spend vt (money) aus|geben* ows·gay·bèn; (time) verbringen* fer·bring·èn

spice n das Gewürz gè·vöörts

spicy adj würzig vöört·sikh

spider n die Spinne shpi·nè

spill vt verschütten fer·shöö·tèn □ vi sich ergießen* zikh er·gee·sèn

spin vi (rotate) sich drehen zikh dray·èn □ vt (wool) spinnen* shpi·nèn

spinach n der Spinat shpi·naht

spin-dry vt trocken|schleudern tro·kèn·shloy·dèrn

spine n (backbone) das Rückgrat röök·graht

spirit n (soul) der Geist gyest; spirits (alcohol) die Spirituosen (pl) shpi·ri·too·ö·zèn; in good spirits gut aufgelegt goot owf·gè·laykt

spit vi spucken shpoo·kèn □ n (for roasting) der Bratspieß braht·shpees

spite n die Gehässigkeit gè·he·sikh·kite; in spite of trotz trots

splash n der Spritzer shprit·sèr □ vt bespritzen bè·shprit·sèn □ vi spritzen shprit·sèn

splint n die Schiene shee·nè

splinter n (wood) der Splitter shpli·tèr

split vt (tear) spalten shpal·tèn; (divide, share) teilen tye·lèn □ vi (tear) zerreißen* tser·rye·sèn □ n der Riß riss

spoil vt (damage) verderben* fer·der·bèn; (child) verwöhnen fer·vur·nèn

spoiled adj (milk) sauer zow·èr

spokesman n der Sprecher shpre·khèr

sponge n der Schwamm shvam; (cake) der Rührkuchen rüör·koo·khèn

spoon n der Löffel lur·fèl

spoonful n der Löffelvoll lur·fèl·fol

sport coat, sport jacket n das Sportjackett shport·ya·ket

sport(s) n der Sport shport L28, Mc20

sport(s) car n der Sportwagen shport·vah·gèn

sportswear n die Sportkleidung shport·klye·doong

spot n (patch) der Fleck flek; (dot) der Punkt poonkt; (pimple) der Pickel pi·kèl; (locality) die Stelle shte·lè; on the spot an Ort und Stelle an ort oont shte·lè

spot check n die Stichprobe shtikh·prö·bè

spotlight n der Scheinwerfer shine·ver·fèr

sprain n die Verrenkung fer·reng·koong □ vt to sprain one's ankle sich den Fuß verstauchen zikh dayn foos fer·shtow·khèn

spray n (of liquid) der Spray shpray; (container) die Sprühdose shpröö·dö·zè □ vt (liquid) spritzen shprit·sèn

spread vt (butter) verstreichen* fer·shtrye·khèn; (news) verbreiten fer·brye·tèn; (payments) verteilen fer·tye·lèn; to spread something out etwas aus|breiten et·vass ows·brye·tèn

spring n (season) der Frühling fröö·ling; (coil) die Feder fay·dèr; (of water) die Quelle kve·lè

spring onion n die Schalotte sha·lo·tè

sprinkle vt □ to sprinkle with water mit Wasser besprengen mit va·sèr bè·shpreng·èn; to sprinkle with sugar mit Zucker bestreuen mit tsoo·kèr bè·shtroy·èn

sprouts pl der Rosenkohl rö·zèn·köl

spy n der Spion shpee·ön, die Spionin shpee·ö·nin

squall n die Bö bur'

square n das Quadrat kva·draht; (in town) der Platz plats □ adj quadratisch kva·drah·tish; a square meter ein Quadratmeter (nt) kva·draht·may·tèr; 3 meters square 3 Meter im Quadrat 3 may·tèr im kva·draht

squash vt (crush) zerquetschen tser·kvet·shèn □ n (sport) Squash (m) skvosh; (gourd) der Kürbis köör·bis

squeeze vt (lemon) aus|pressen ows·pre·sèn; (hand) drücken dröö·kèn □ n (financial) die Geldknappheit gelt·knap·hite

squirrel n das Eichhörnchen eyekh·hurn·khèn

stab vt erstechen* er·shte·khèn

stable n der Stall shtal □ adj stabil shta·beel

stadium n das Stadion shtah·dee·on

staff n das Personal per·zö·nahl

stage n (in theatre) die Bühne böö·nè; (period) das Stadium shtah·dee·oom; in stages in Etappen in ay·tap·èn

stain n der Fleck flek □ vt beflecken bè·fle·kèn Sn65

stained glass window n das bunte Glasfenster boon·tè glahs·fen·stèr

stainless adj (steel) rostfrei rost·frye

stair n die Stufe shtoo·fè

staircase n das Treppenhaus *tre·pèn· hows*

stairs pl die Treppe *tre·pè* I4

stake n (in gambling) der Einsatz *ine· zats*; **to be at stake** auf dem Spiel stehen* *owf daym shpeel shtay·èn*

stale adj (bread) altbacken *alt·ba·kèn*; **the room smells stale** dieses Zimmer riecht muffig *dee·zès tsi·mèr reekht moo·fikh*

stall n (stand) der Stand *shtant* □ vi (car engine) ab|würgen *ap·vöör·gèn*

stalls pl (in theatre) das Parkett *par·ket*

stamp n (postage) die Briefmarke *breef·mar·kè*; (rubber) der Stempel *shtem·pèl* □ vt (letter) frankieren *frang·kee·rèn*; (visa) stempeln *shtem· pèln* Sn2, 3

stand n (stall) der Stand *shtant* □ vi stehen* *shtay·èn*; **to stand up** auf|stehen* *owf·shtay·èn* □ vt (put) stellen *shte·lèn*; (bear) ertragen* *er· trah·gèn*; **to stand for** (signify) bedeuten *bè·doy·tèn*; **to stand out** auf| fallen* *owf·fa·lèn*

standard n die Norm *norm* □ adj (size) Normal- *nor·mahl*; (model) Standard- *shtan·dart*

standard of living n der Lebensstandard *lay·bèns·shtan·dart*

staple n die Heftklammer *heft·kla·mèr*

stapler n die Heftmaschine *heft·ma· shee·nè*

star n der Stern *shtern*; (celebrity) der Star *star*

starch n die Stärke *shter·kè*

stare vi starren *shtar·rèn*; **to stare at somebody** auf jemanden starren *owf yay·man·dèn shtar·rèn*

start vt beginnen* *bè·gi·nèn* □ vi an| fangen* *an·fang·èn* □ n (beginning) der Anfang *an·fang*

starter n (in car) der Anlasser *an·la·sèr*

starve vi verhungern *fer·hoong·èrn*

state vt erklären *er·kleh·rèn* □ n (condition) der Zustand *tsoo·shtant*; **the State** der Staat *shtaht*; **the States** die Vereinigten Staaten (pl) *fer·ine·ikh· tèn shtah·tèn*

statement n die Aussage *ows·zah·gè*

station n der Bahnhof *bahn·hóf*; (radio) der Sender *zen·dèr* F3

stationer's (shop) n das Schreibwarengeschäft *shripe·vah·rèn·gè·sheft*

stationery n die Schreibwaren (pl) *shripe·vah·rèn*

station wagon n der Kombiwagen *kom·bee·vah·gèn*

statistic n die Statistik *shta·ti·stik*

statistical adj statistisch *shta·ti·stish*

statistics n die Statistik *shta·ti·stik*

statue n die Statue *shtah·too·è*

stay n (period) der Aufenthalt *owf·ènt· halt* □ vi bleiben* *blye·bèn*; (reside) wohnen *vö·nèn*; **to stay the night** übernachten *öö·bèr·nakh·tèn*; **to stay with friends** bei Freunden untergebracht sein* *bye froyn·dèn oon·tèr· gè·brakht zine*; **to stay in** zu Hause bleiben* *tsoo how·zè blye·bèn*; **to stay up** (at night) auf|bleiben* *owf· blye·bèn* A3

steady adj fest *fest*; (pace) gleichmäßig *glyekh·may·sikh*

steak n das Steak *stayk*

steal vt stehlen* *shtay·lèn*; **to steal something from someone** jemandem etwas stehlen* *yay·man·dèm et·vass shtay·lèn*

steam n der Dampf *dampf* □ vt (food) dämpfen *demp·fèn*

steamer n (ship) der Dampfer *damp· fèr*

steep adj steil *shtile*

steel n der Stahl *shtahl*

steer vt (car) lenken *leng·kèn*; (boat) steuern *shtoy·èrn*

steering n (in car) die Lenkung *leng· koong*

steering column n die Lenksäule *lenk· zoy·lè*

steering-wheel n das Lenkrad *lenk· raht*

stem n der Stengel *shteng·èl*

stenographer n die Stenotypistin *shtay· nō·tōō·pist·in*

step n (pace) der Schritt *shrit*; (stair) die Stufe *shtoo·fè*; **to take steps to do something** Schritte unternehmen*, etwas zu tun *shri·tè oon·tèr·nay·mèn et·vass tsoo toon*

stepbrother n der Stiefbruder *shteef· broo·dèr*

stepdaughter n die Stieftochter *shteef· tokh·tèr*

stepfather n der Stiefvater *shteef·fah· tèr*

stepladder n die Trittleiter *trit·lye·tèr*

stepmother n die Stiefmutter *shteef· moo·tèr*

stepsister n die Stiefschwester *shteef· shve·stèr*

stepson n der Stiefsohn *shteef·zōn*

stereo(phonic) adj stereo(phonisch) *ste·ray·ō(·fō·nish)* □ n Stereo (nt) *ste·ray·ō*; **in stereo** in Stereo *in ste· ray·ō*

sterile adj steril *shte·reel*

sterilize vt (disinfect) sterilisieren *shte· ri·li·zee·rèn*

sterling n das Pfund Sterling *pfoont ster·ling*

stew n der Eintopf *ine·topf*

steward n der Steward *styoo·art*; (at club) der Kellner *kel·nèr*

stewardess n die Stewardeß *styoo·ar· des*

stick n der Stock *shtok* □ vt (with glue etc) kleben *klay·bèn*

sticking-plaster n das Heftpflaster *heft· pfla·stèr*

sticky adj klebrig *klay·brikh*

stiff adj steif *shtife*

stiletto heels pl die Bleistiftabsätze (pl) *blye·shtift·ap·zet·sè*

still adj (motionless) bewegungslos *bè· vay·goongs·lōs*; (wine etc) ohne Kohlensäure *ō·nè kō·lèn·zoy·rè* □ adv (up to this time) noch *nokh*; (nevertheless) trotzdem *trots·daym*

sting vt/i stechen* *shte·khèn* □ n der Stich *shtikh*

stipulate vt fest|setzen *fest·zet·sèn*

stipulation n die Bedingung *bè·ding· oong*

stir vt rühren *rōō·rèn*

stitch n (sewing) der Stich *shtikh*; (pain) die Stiche (pl) *shti·khè*

stock n (have in shop) führen *fōō·rèn* □ n (supply) der Vorrat *fōr·raht*; (in shop) das Warenlager *vah·rèn·lah· gèr*; (for soup etc) die Brühe *brōō·è*; **stocks** (financial) Aktien und Wertpapiere (pl) *ak·tsee·èn oont vert·pa· pee·rè*; **in stock** vorrätig *fōr·ray·tikh*

stockbroker n der Börsenmakler *bur· sèn·mah·klèr*

stock exchange n die Börse *bur·sè*

stockholder n der Aktionär *ak·tsee·o· nayr*

stocking n der Strumpf *shtroompf*

stock market n der Börsenmarkt bur·
sèn·markt
stole n (wrap) die Stola shtō·la
stomach n der Magen mah·gèn I36
stomach ache n die Magenschmerzen
(pl) mah·gèn·shmert·sèn; **I have (a)
stomach ache** ich habe Magen·
schmerzen ikh hah·bè mah·gèn·
shmert·sèn S43
stone n der Stein shtine
stony adj steinig shtye·nikh
stool n der Hocker ho·kèr
stop n (bus stop) die Haltestelle hal·tè·
shte·lè □ vi an|halten* an·hal·tèn;
(person) stehen|bleiben* shtay·èn·
blye·bèn; **to stop doing something**
auf|hören, etwas zu tun owf·hur·rèn
et·vass tsoo toon □ vt stop (car etc)
stoppen shto·pèn; (person) an|hal·
ten* an·hal·tèn; **to stop someone doing
something** jemanden davon ab|
halten*, etwas zu tun yay·man·dèn
da·fon ap·hal·tèn et·vass tsoo toon; **to
stop a check** einen Scheck sperren
ine·èn shek shpe·rèn T85
stopcock n der Absperrhahn ap·shper·
hahn
stoplights pl die Bremslichter (pl)
bremz·likh·tèr
stopover n (air travel) die Zwischen·
landung tsvi·shèn·lan·doong
stopper n der Propfen prop·fèn
stop watch n die Stoppuhr shtop·oo·èr
store vt lagern lah·gèrn □ n (stock) der
Vorrat fòr raht; (shop) das Geschäft
gè·sheft; (big shop) das Kaufhaus
kowf·hows; (warehouse) das Lager
lah·gèr
store room n der Lagerraum lah·gèr·
rowm
storm n der Sturm shtoorm
stormy adj stürmisch shtöör·mish
story n die Geschichte gè·shikh·tè; (in
building) das Stockwerk shtok·verk
stove n der Kochherd kokh·hert A73
straight adj gerade gè·rah·dè; (drink)
pur poor □ adv (shoot, write etc) ge·
rade gè·rah·dè; **to go straight home**
direkt nach Hause gehen* dee·rekt
nakh how·zè gay·èn; **straight away**
sofort zō·fort
strain vt (tea etc) sieben zee·bèn;
(muscle) zerren tse·rèn
strainer n das Sieb zeep
strange adj (unknown) fremd fremt;
(unusual) seltsam zelt·zam
stranger n der/die Fremde frem·dè
strangle vt erwürgen er·vöör·gèn
strap n der Riemen ree·mèn
strapless adj trägerlos tre·gèr·lòs
straw n das Stroh shtrō
strawberry n die Erdbeere ayrt·bay·rè
streak n der Streifen shtrye·fèn
stream n der Bach bakh
streamlined adj (car) stromlinienför·
mig shtröm·leen·yèn·fur·mikh
street n die Straße shtrah·sè
streetcar n die Straßenbahn shtrah·
sèn·bahn
streetlamp n die Straßenlaterne
shtrah·sèn·la·ter·nè
strength n die Kraft kraft; (of girder,
rope etc) die Stärke shter·kè
strengthen vt verstärken fer·shter·kèn
stress n (emphasis) die Betonung bè·
tō·noong; (tension) der Streß shtress
stretch vt (fabric etc) dehnen day·nèn
□ vi sich dehnen zikh day·nèn
stretcher n die Tragbahre trahk·bah·rè
strict adj streng shtreng
strike vt (hit) schlagen* shlah·gèn; **to**

strike a match ein Streichholz an|
reißen* ine shtrike·hults an·rye·sèn;
the clock struck three die Uhr schlug
drei dee oo·èr shlook drye □ vi strike
(workers) streiken shtrye·kèn □ n
(industrial) der Streik shtrike; **on
strike** im Ausstand im ows·shtant
strikebound adj vom Streik betroffen
fom shtrike bè·tro·fèn
strike-breaker n der Streikbrecher
shtrike·bre·khèr
striker n der/die Streikende shtrye·
kèn·dè
string n die Schnur shnoor; (of instru·
ment) die Saite zye·tè
string bag n das Einkaufsnetz ine·
kowfs·nets
strip n (stripe, length) der Streifen
shtrye·fèn
stripe n der Streifen shtrye·fèn
strip-lighting n die Neonbeleuchtung
nay·on·bè·loykh·toong
stripper n die Stripperin shtri·pè·rin
striptease n Striptease (nt) shtrip·teez
stroke vt streicheln shtrye·khèln □ n
(swimming) der Zug tsook; (golf)
der Schlag shlahk; (illness) der
Schlaganfall shlahk·an·fal
stroll n der Spaziergang shpa·tseer·
gang; **to go for a stroll** einen Spazier·
gang machen ine·èn shpa·tseer·gang
ma·khèn
stroller n der Sportwagen shport·vah·
gèn
strong adj (person) kräftig kref·tikh;
(structure, material) stark shtark; **it
has a strong smell** es riecht stark ess
reekht shtark
strongbox n die Geldkassette gelt·ka·
se·tè
strongroom n die Stahlkammer shtahl·
ka·mèr
structure n die Struktur shtrook·toor;
(building) das Gebäude gè·boy·dè
struggle n der Kampf kampf □ vi
(physically) kämpfen kemp·fèn; **to
struggle to do something** sich an|
strengen, etwas zu tun zikh an·
shtreng·èn et·vass tsoo toon
stub n (of check) der Abschnitt ap·
shnit
stubborn adj stur shtoor
stuck adj □ **it's stuck!** es klemmt! ess
klemt; **I'm stuck** ich komme nicht
weiter ikh ko·mè nikht vye·tèr
stud n der Nagel nah·gèl; (for collar)
der Kragenknopf krah·gèn·knopf
student n der Student shtoo·dent, die
Studentin shtoo·den·tin M5
student driver n der Fahrschüler fahr·
shöö·lèr
studio n das Studio shtoo·dee·ō
study vt/i studieren shtoo·dee·rèn □ n
(room) das Arbeitszimmer ar·bites·
tsi·mèr; **to enjoy one's studies** sein
Studium genießen* zine shtoo·dee·
oom gè·nee·sèn
stuff n (things) die Sachen (pl) za·
khèn; (substance) das Zeug tsoyk
stuffed adj gefüllt gè·föölt
stuffing n (in chicken etc) die Füllung
föö·loong
stuffy adj stickig shti·kikh
stun vt betäuben bè·toy·bèn
stupid adj dumm doom
style n der Stil shteel
stylish adj elegant ay·lay·gant
subcommittee n der Unterausschuß
oon·tèr·ows·shoos
subcontract n der Untervertrag oon·
tèr·fer·trahk

subcontractor n der Unterkontrahent *oon·tèr·kon·tra·hent*

subject n (*topic*) das Thema *tay·ma*; (*person*) der Staatsbürger *shtahts·bōōr·ger*, die Staatsbürgerin *shtahts·bōōr·ge·rin*; (*in school*) das Fach *fakh* □ *adj* **subject to** abhängig von *ap·heng·ikh fon*

submarine n das Unterseeboot *oon·tèr·zay·bōt*

submit vt (*proposal*) vor||legen *fōr·lay·gèn*

subordinate adj untergeordnet *oon·tèr·gè·ort·nèt* □ n der/die Untergebene *oon·tèr·gay·bè·nè*

subscriber n der Abonnent *a·bo·nent*

subscribe to vt (*periodical*) abonnieren *a·bo·nee·rèn*

subscription n (*to periodical*) das Abonnement *a·bo·ne·mong*; (*to club*) der Beitrag *bye·trahk*

subsidiary adj Tochter- *tokh·tèr* □ n (*company*) die Tochtergesellschaft *tokh·tèr·gè·zel·shaft*

subsidize vt subventionieren *zoop·ven·tsee·ō·nee·rèn*

subsidy n die Subvention *zoop·ven·tsee·ōn*

substance n die Substanz *zoop·stants*

substandard adj minderwertig *min·dèr·ver·tikh*

substitute n der Ersatz *er·zats* □ vt to **substitute something for something else** etwas durch etwas anderes ersetzen *et·vass doorkh et·vass an·dè·rès er·zet·sèn*

subtitle n (*of movie*) der Untertitel *oon·tèr·tee·tèl*

subtle adj fein *fine*

subtotal n die Zwischensumme *tsvi·shèn·zoo·mè*

subtract vt ab||ziehen* *ap·tsee·èn*

suburb n der Vorort *fōr·ort*; **the suburbs** der Stadtrand *shtat·rant*

suburban adj vorstädtisch *fōr·shte·tish*

subway n (*underground passage*) die Unterführung *oon·tèr·fōō·roong*; (*railway*) die U-Bahn *oo·bahn*

succeed vi erfolgreich sein* *er·folk·ryekh zine*; **he succeeded in doing it** es ist ihm gelungen, es zu tun *ess ist eem gè·loong·èn ess tsoo toon*

success n der Erfolg *er·folk*

successful adj erfolgreich *er·folk·ryekh*

such adj solche(r/s) *zolkh·è(·èr/·ès)*; **such a lot of** so viele *zō fee·lè*; **such a book** ein solches Buch *ine zol·khès bookh*; **such books** solche Bücher *zol·khè bōō·khèr*

suck vt saugen *zow·gèn*

sudden adj plötzlich *plur'ts·likh*

suddenly adv plötzlich *plur'ts·likh* T195

sue vt verklagen *fer·klah·gèn*

suede n das Wildleder *vilt·lay·dèr*

suet n das Nierenfett *nee·rèn·fet*

suffer vi leiden* *lye·dèn* □ vt (*pain, grief*) erleiden* *er·lye·dèn*

sugar n der Zucker *tsoo·kèr* S34

sugar bowl n die Zuckerdose *tsoo·kèr·dō·zè*

suggest vt vor||schlagen* *fōr·shlah·gèn*

suggestion n der Vorschlag *fōr·shlahk*

suicide n der Selbstmord *zelpst·mort*

suit n (*men's*) der Anzug *an·tsook*; (*women's*) das Kostüm *kos·tōōm*; (*cards*) die Farbe *far·bè*; (*astronaut, diver*) der Anzug *an·tsook* □ vt **that hat suits you** dieser Hut steht Ihnen gut *dee·zèr hoot shtayt ee·nèn goot*; **does Thursday suit you?** paßt Ihnen

Donnerstag? *past ee·nèn do·nèrs·tahk* S66, S81

suitable adj geeignet *gè·ike·nèt*; (*fitting*) angemessen *an·gè·me·sèn*

suitcase n der Koffer *ko·fèr* T31, Sn52

sultana n die Sultanine *zool·ta·nee·nè*

sum n (*total amount*) die Summe *zoo·mè*; (*problem*) die Rechenaufgabe *re·khèn·owf·gah·bè*

summary n die Zusammenfassung *tsoo·za·mèn·fa·soong*

summer n der Sommer *zo·mèr*

summons n die Vorladung *fōr·lah·doong*

sum total n die Endsumme *ent·zoo·mè*

sun n die Sonne *zo·nè*

sunbathe vi in der Sonne liegen* *in der zo·nè lee·gèn*

sunburn n (*painful*) der Sonnenbrand *zo·nèn·brant* S43

sunburned adj sonnengebräunt *zo·nèn·gè·broynt*; (*painfully*) sonnenverbrannt *zo·nèn·fer·brant*

Sunday n Sonntag (m) *zon·tahk*

sun dress n das Sonnenkleid *zo·nèn·klite*

sunglasses pl die Sonnenbrille *zo·nèn·bri·lè*

sun-hat n der Sonnenhut *zo·nèn·hoot*

sunlamp n die Höhensonne *hur'·en·zo·nè*

sunny adj sonnig *zo·nikh*

sunrise n der Sonnenaufgang *zo·nèn·owf·gang*

sunroof n das Schiebedach *shee·bè·dakh*

sunset n der Sonnenuntergang *zo·nèn·oon·tèr·gang*

sunshade n (*over table*) der Sonnenschirm *zo·nèn·shirm* L23

sunshine n der Sonnenschein *zo·nèn·shine*

sunstroke n der Sonnenstich *zo·nèn·shtikh* I35

suntan n die Sonnenbräune *zo·nèn·broy·nè*

sun-tanned adj sonnengebräunt *zo·nèn·gè·broynt*

suntan oil n das Sonnenöl *zo·nèn·ur'l*

sun visor n (*in car*) die Sonnenblende *zo·nèn·blen·dè*

superannuation n die Rente *ren·tè*

superior adj (*quality*) großartig *grōs·ar·tikh* □ n der/die Vorgesetzte *fōr·gè·zet·stè*

supermarket n der Supermarkt *zoo·pèr·markt*

superstition n der Aberglaube *ah·bèr·glow·bè*

superstore n der große Supermarkt *grō·sè zoo·pèr·markt*

supertanker n der Supertanker *zoo·pèr·tang·kèr*

supervise vt beaufsichtigen *bè·owf·zikh·ti·gèn*

supervisor n der Aufseher *owf·zay·èr*, die Aufseherin *owf·zay·èr·in*

supper n (*main meal*) das Abendessen *ah·bènt·e·sèn*; (*snack*) der späte Imbiß *shpay·tè im·bis*

supply vt (*goods*) liefern *lee·fèrn*; **to supply someone with something** jemanden mit etwas versorgen *yay·man·dèn mit et·vass fer·zor·gèn* □ n **supply** (*stock*) der Vorrat *fōr·raht*; **supply and demand** Angebot und Nachfrage *an·gè·bōt oont nakh·frah·gè*

support vt unterstützen *oon·tèr·shtōōt·sèn* □ n (*moral, financial*) die Unterstützung *oon·tèr·shtōōt·soong*

suppose *vt* an|nehmen* *an·nay·mèn*;
he's supposed to be an engineer er
soll angeblich Ingenieur sein *er zol
an·gayp·likh in·zhe·nee·ur zine*;
you're supposed to do it today Sie
sollen es heute machen *zee zo·lèn ess
hoy·tè ma·khèn*

suppository *n* das Zäpfchen *tsepf·khèn*

surcharge *n* der Zuschlag *tsoo·shlahk*

sure *adj* sicher *zi·khèr*; it's sure to work
das geht sicher *das gayt zi·khèr*

surely *adv* bestimmt *bè·shtimt*

surface *n* die Oberfläche *ō·bèr·fle·khè*

surface mail *n* □ to send something
surface mail etwas auf dem Landweg
schicken *et·vass owf daym lant·vayk
shi·kèn*

surf board *n* das Surfboard *zurf·bort*

surfing *n* Surfen (*nt*) *zur·fèn*; to go
surfing surfen gehen* *zur·fèn gay·èn*

surgeon *n* der Chirurg *khee·roork*

surgery *n* (*operation*) die Chirurgie
khee·roor·gee

surname *n* der Nachname *nakh·nah·
mè*

surplus *n* der Überschuß *ōō·bèr·shoos*

surprise *vt* überraschen *ōō·bèr·ra·shèn*
□ *n* die Überraschung *ōō·bèr·ra·
shoong*

surprised *adj* überrascht *ōō·bèr·rasht*;
surprised at überrascht über *ōō·bèr·
rasht ōō·bèr*

surround *vt* umgeben* *oom·gay·bèn*

surroundings *pl* die Umgebung *oom·
gay·boong*

survey *n* (*of land*) die Vermessung *fer·
me·soong*; (*of building*) die Begut·
achtung *bè·goot·akh·toong*

surveyor *n* (*of land*) der Landvermes·
ser *lant·fer·me·sèr*; (*of building*) der
Baugutachter *bow·goot·akh·tèr*

survive *vi* überleben *ōō·bèr·lay·bèn*;
(*custom*) fort|bestehen* *fort·bè·
shtay·èn*

suspend *vt* (*worker*) suspendieren
zoos·pen·dee·rèn

suspenders *pl* die Hosenträger (*pl*) *hō·
zèn·tray·gèr*

suspension *n* (*on car*) die Aufhängung
owf·heng·oong

swallow *vt/i* schlucken *shloo·kèn*

swamp *n* der Sumpf *zoompf*

swan *n* der Schwan *shvahn*

sway *vi* schwanken *shvang·kèn*

swear *vi* (*curse*) fluchen *floo·khèn*; he
swears that... er schwört, daß... *er
shvurt dass*

sweat *n* der Schweiß *shvice* □ *vi*
schwitzen *shvit·sèn*

sweater *n* der Pullover *poo·lō·vèr* S62

sweatshirt *n* das Sweatshirt *swet·shurt*

Swede *n* der Schwede *shvay·dè*, die
Schwedin *shvay·din*

swede *n* die Kohlrübe *kōl·rōō·bè*

Sweden *n* Schweden (*nt*) *shvay·dèn*

Swedish *adj* schwedisch *shvay·dish* □ *n*
Schwedisch (*nt*) *shvay·dish*

sweep *vt* (*floor*) fegen *fay·gèn*

sweet *n* (*candy*) das Bonbon *bon·bon*
□ *adj* süß *zōōs*; (*music*) wohlklin·
gend *vōl·kling·èn*; (*cute, pretty*)
niedlich *neet·lich*; (*kind*) lieb *leep*

sweet corn *n* der Mais *mice*

sweet potato *n* die Batate *ba·tah·tè*

swell (up) *vi* (*limb etc*) an|schwellen*
an·shve·lèn

swelling *n* (*lump*) die Schwellung *shve·
loong*

swerve *vi* aus|schwenken *ows·shveng·
kèn*

swim *vi* schwimmen* *shvi·mèn* □ *vt* to

swim the Channel den Ärmelkanal
durchschwimmen* *dayn er·mèl·ka·
nahl doorkh·shvi·mèn*

swimming *n* Schwimmen (*nt*) *shvi·
mèn*; to go swimming schwimmen
gehen* *shvi·mèn gay·èn*

swimming pool *n* das Schwimmbad
shvim·baht A11

swimming trunks *pl* die Badehose *bah·
dè·hō·zè*

swimsuit *n* der Badeanzug *bah·dè·an·
tsook*

swing *n* die Schaukel *show·kèl* □ *vi*
schwingen* *shving·èn* □ *vt* schaukeln
show·kèln

Swiss *adj* schweizerisch *shvye·tsè·rish*;
he's Swiss er ist Schweizer *er ist
shvye·tsèr*; she's Swiss sie ist Schwei·
zerin *zee ist shvye·tsè·rin*

switch *n* der Schalter *shal·tèr* □ *vt* to
switch on (*light, TV*) ein|schalten
ine·shal·tèn; (*engine*) an|lassen* *an·
la·sèn*; to switch off aus|schalten *ows·
shal·tèn*; (*engine*) ab|schalten *ap·
shal·tèn*

switchboard *n* die Zentrale *tsen·trah·lè*

switchboard operator *n* der Telepho·
nist *tay·lay·fon·ist*, die Telephonistin
tay·lay·fon·is·tin

Switzerland *n* die Schweiz *shvites*; to
Switzerland in die Schweiz *in dee
schvites*; in Switzerland in der
Schweiz *in der schvites*

swollen *adj* angeschwollen *an·gè·shvo·
lèn*

sword *n* das Schwert *shvert*

syllable *n* die Silbe *zil·bè*

syllabus *n* der Lehrplan *layr·plan*

symbol *n* das Symbol *zōōm·bōl*

symmetrical *adj* symmetrisch *zōō·may·
trish*

sympathetic *adj* mitfühlend *mit·fōō·
lènt*

sympathy *n* das Mitgefühl *mit·gè·fōōl*

symphony *n* die Symphonie *zōōm·fō·
nee*

symposium *n* das Symposium *zōōm·
pō·zee·oom*

symptom *n* das Symptom *zōōmp·tōm*

synagogue *n* die Synagoge *zōō·na·gō·
gè*

synchromesh *n* das Synchrongetriebe
zōōn·krōn·gè·tree·bè

syndicate *n* der Verband *fer·bant*

synthetic *adj* Kunst- *koonst*

Syria *n* Syrien (*nt*) *zōō·ree·èn*

Syrian *adj* syrisch *zōō·rish*

syrup *n* der Sirup *zee·roop*; (*golden*)
syrup der gelbe Sirup *gel·bè zee·roop*

system *n* das System *zōōs·taym*

systematic *adj* systematisch *zōōs·tay·
mah·tish*

systems analyst *n* der Systemanalytiker
zōōs·taym·a·na·lōō·ti·kèr

T

tab *n* das Etikett *ay·ti·ket*

table *n* der Tisch *tish*; (*list*) die Tabelle
ta·be·lè E3f

tablecloth *n* die Tischdecke *tish·de·kè*

table-mat *n* der Untersetzer *oon·tèr·
zet·sèr*

tablespoon *n* der Eßlöffel *ess·lur·fèl*

tablet *n* (*medicine*) die Tablette *ta·ble·
tè*

table tennis *n* das Tischtennis *tish·te·
nis*

tack *n* (*nail*) der kleine Nagel *kline·è
nah·gèl* □ *vi* (*sailing*) auf|kreuzen
owf·kroy·tsèn

tackle vt (problem) an|gehen* an·gay·
èn; (in sports) an|greifen* an·grye·
fèn □ n (gear) die Ausrüstung ows·
rōō·stoong
tactics pl die Taktik tak·tik
tag n das Etikett ay·ti·ket
tail n der Schwanz shvants
tailcoat n der Frack frak
tailgate n (of car) die Hecktür hek·
tōōr
tailor n der Schneider shnye·dèr
take vt (remove, acquire) nehmen*
nay·mèn; (win: prize) bekommen*
bè·ko·mèn; he took it from me er hat
es mir weggenommen er hat ess meer
vek·ge·no·mèn; to take someone to
the station jemanden zum Bahnhof
bringen* yay·man·dèn tsoom bahn·
hōf bring·èn; take this to the post office bringen Sie dies zur Post bring·
èn zee dees tsoor post; to take a
photo ein Foto machen ine fō·tō ma·
khèn; we took the train wir sind mit
dem Zug gefahren veer zint mit
daym tsook gè·fah·rèn; do you take
sugar? nehmen Sie Zucker? nay·mèn
zee tsoo·kèr; I'm taking French at
school ich lerne in der Schule Französisch ikh ler·nè in der shoo·lè fra·
tsur·zish; to take a decision eine
Entscheidung treffen* ine·è ent·shye·
doong tre·fèn; to take an exam eine
Prüfung machen ine·è prōō·foong
ma·khèn; it takes a lot of effort es
macht viel Mühe ess makht feel mōō·
è; it takes an hour es dauert eine
Stunde ess dow·èrt ine·è shtoon·dè; to
take something away etwas weg|neh-
men* et·vass vek·nay·mèn; to take
something back (return) etwas zu-
rück|bringen* et·vass tsoo·rōōk·
bring·èn; to take off (clothes) aus|zie-
hen* ows·tsee·èn; (plane) ab|fliegen*
ap·flee·gèn; to take someone out to
the theatre jemanden ins Theater
aus|führen yay·man·dèn ins tay·ah·
tèr ows·fōō·rèn; to have a tooth taken
out sich einen Zahn ziehen lassen*
zikh ine·èn tsahn tsee·èn la·sèn; to
take over a firm eine Firma übernehmen* ine·è fir·ma ōō·bèr·nay·mèn; to
take up a sport an|fangen* einen
Sport auszüben an·fang·èn ine·èn
shport ows·tsoo·ōō·bèn
take-away n (of food) zum Mitnehmen
tsoom mit·nay·mèn
take-home pay n der Nettolohn ne·tō·
lōn
takeoff n (of plane) der Abflug ap·
flook
takeover n die Übernahme ōō·bèr·
nah·mè
take-over bid n das Übernahmeangebot ōō·bèr·nah·mè·an·ge·bōt
talc(um powder) n der Talkumpuder
talk·oom·poo·dèr
talent n die Begabung bè·gah·boong
talk vi sprechen* shpre·khèn; to talk to
someone about something mit jemandem über etwas sprechen* mit yay·
man·dèm ōō·bèr et·vass shpre·khèn;
to talk something over etwas besprechen* et·vass bè·shpre·khèn □ vt to
talk nonsense Unsinn reden oon·zin
ray·dèn □ n talk (conversation) das
Gespräch gè·shprekh; (lecture) der
Vortrag for·trahk; talks (negotiations) die Gespräche (pl) gè·
shprekh·è
tall adj groß grōs; how tall are you?
wie groß sind Sie? vee grōs zint zee

tame adj (animal) zahm tsahm
tan adj hellbraun hel·brown □ n (on
skin) die Bräune broy·nè □ vi (in
sun) braun werden* brown ver·dèn
tangerine n die Mandarine man·da·
ree·nè
tangle vt verwirren fer·vi·rèn
tango n der Tango tan·gō
tank n (of car) der Tank tank; (military) der Panzer pan·tsèr
tanker n (ship) das Tankschiff tank·
shif; (truck) der Tankwagen tank·
vah·gèn
tap n (for water) der Hahn hahn □ vt
klopfen an klop·fèn an
tape n das Band bant; (magnetic) das
Tonband tōn·bant □ vt (record) auf|-
nehmen* owf·nay·mèn
tape measure n das Maßband mahs·
bant
tape record vt auf|nehmen* owf·nay·
mèn
tape recorder n das Tonbandgerät tōn·
bant·gè·ret
tap-water n das Leitungswasser lye·
toongs·va·sèr A31
tar n der Teer tayr
target n die Zielscheibe tseel·shye·bè;
(sales etc) das Ziel tseel
tariff n (list of charges) der Tarif ta·
reef; (tax) der Zoll tsol
tarmac n der Makadam ma·ka·dam
tart n die Torte tor·tè
tartan n der Schottenstoff sho·tèn·
shtof; a tartan skirt ein Rock im
Schottenkaro ine rok im sho·tèn·ka·
rō
tartar sauce n die Remouladensoße
ray·moo·lah·den·zō·sè
task n die Aufgabe owf·gah·bè
taste n der Geschmack gè·shmak; in
poor taste geschmacklos gè·shmak·
lōs; in good taste geschmackvoll gè·
shmak·fol □ vt taste schmecken
shme·kèn; (try) probieren prō·bee·
rèn
tax n die Steuer shtoy·èr □ vt besteuern bè·shtoy·èrn A9
taxable adj steuerpflichtig shtoy·èr·
pflikh·tikh
taxation n die Besteuerung bè·shtoy·è·
roong
tax-free adj steuerfrei shtoy·èr·frye
taxi n das Taxi tak·see; to go by taxi
mit dem Taxi fahren* mit daym tak·
see fah·rèn
taxi stand n der Taxistand tak·see·
shtant
T-bone steak n das T-bone-Steak tee·
bōn·shtayk
tea n der Tee tay; (meal) das Abendbrot ah·bènt·brōt; mint tea der Pfefferminztee pfe·fèr·mints·tay E63
tea bag n der Teebeutel tay·boy·tèl
tea break n die Pause pow·zè
teach vt unterrichten oon·tèr·rikh·tèn;
to teach someone something jemanden in etwas unterrichten yay·man·
dèn in et·vass oon·tèr·rikh·tèn
teacher n (secondary school) der Lehrer lay·rèr, die Lehrerin lay·rè·rin;
(primary school) der Grundschullehrer groont·shool·lay·rèr, die Grundschullehrerin groont·shool·lay·lè·rin
teacup n die Teetasse tay·ta·sè
team n das Team teem
teapot n die Teekanne tay·ka·nè
tear¹ vt (rip) zerreißen* tser·rye·sèn
□ n der Riß ris Sn48, 74
tear² n die Träne tray·nè; in tears in

Tränen aufgelöst *in tray·nèn owf·gè·lur'st*

tearoom *n* die Teestube *tay·shtoo·bè*

teaspoon *n* der Teelöffel *tay·lur'·fèl*

tea strainer *n* das Teesieb *tay·zeep*

teat *n* (*for bottle*) der Gummisauger *goo·mee·zow·gèr*

technical *adj* technisch *tekh·nish*

technician *n* der Techniker *tekh·ni·kèr*, die Technikerin *tekh·ni·kè·rin*

technique *n* die Technik *tekh·nik*

technological *adj* technologisch *tekh·no·lō·gish*

technology *n* die Technik *tekh·nik*

tee *n* (*in golf*) das Tee *tee*

teenager *n* die (der) Jugendliche(r) *yoo·gènt·li·khè(r)*

tee shirt *n* das T-shirt *tee·shirt*

telecommunications *pl* das Fernmeldewesen *fern·mel·dè·vay·zèn*

telegram *n* das Telegramm *tay·lay·gram* Sn4

telegraph *vt* telegraphieren *tay·lay·gra·fee·rèn*

telephone *n* das Telefon *tay·lay·fōn*; to be on the telephone gerade telefonieren *gè·rah·dè tay·lay·fō·nee·rèn*; by telephone telefonisch *tay·lay·fō·nish* □ *vt* telephone (*person*) an|rufen* *an·roo·fèn* T156, Ea7

telephone booth *n* die Telefonzelle *tay·lay·fōn·tse·lè*

telephone call *n* der Telefonanruf *tay·lay·fōn·an·roof* Bm4

telephone directory *n* das Telefonbuch *tay·lay·fōn·bookh* Sn22

telephone exchange *n* das Fernsprechamt *fern·shprekh·amt*

telephone number *n* die Telefonnummer *tay·lay·fōn·noo·mèr* Sn21

telephone operator *n* der Telefonist *tay·lay·fō·nist*, die Telefonistin *tay·lay·fō·nis·tin*

telephoto lens *n* das Teleobjektiv *tay·lay·op·yek·teef*

telescope *n* das Teleskop *tay·lay·sköp*

televise *vt* im Fernsehen senden* *im fern·zay·èn zen·dèn*

television *n* das Fernsehen *fern·zay·èn*; (*set*) der Fernseher *fern·zay·èr*; on television im Fernsehen *im fern·zay·èn* A5

telex *n* das Fernschreiben *fern·shrye·bèn*; by telex fernschriftlich *fern·shrift·likh* □ *vt* telex fernschriftlich mit|teilen *fern·shrift·likh mit·tile·èn* A35, Bm16

tell *vt* (*fact, news*) sagen *zah·gèn*; (*story*) erzählen *er·tsay·lèn*; to tell someone something jemandem von etwas erzählen *yay·man·dèm fon et·vass er·tsay·lèn*; to tell someone to do something jemandem sagen, er solle etwas tun *yay·man·dèm zah·gèn er zo·lè et·vass toon*; I can't tell the difference between them ich sehe keinen Unterschied zwischen ihnen *ikh zay·è kye·nèn oon·tèr·sheed tsvi·shèn ee·nèn*

teller *n* der Kassierer *ka·see·rèr*, die Kassiererin *ka·see·rè·rin*

temper *n* □ in a bad temper schlechter Laune *shlekh·tèr low·nè*; to lose one's temper die Beherrschung verlieren* *dee bè·her·shoong fer·lee·rèn*

temperature *n* die Temperatur *tem·pay·ra·toor*; to have a temperature (*fever*) Fieber haben* *fee·bèr hah·bèn*; to take someone's temperature jemandes Temperatur messen* *yay·man·dès tem·pay·ra·toor me·sèn*

temple *n* (*building*) der Tempel *tem·pèl*

temporary *adj* provisorisch *pro·vi·zō·rish*

tempt *vt* in Versuchung führen *in fer·zoo·khoong fōō·rèn*

ten *num* zehn *tsayn*

tenant *n* der Mieter *mee·tèr*, die Mieterin *mee·tè·rin*

tend *vi* □ to tend to do something die Tendenz haben*, etwas zu tun *dee ten·dents hah·bèn et·vass tsoo toon*

tender *adj* (*meat, vegetables*) zart *tsart* □ *vi* to tender for something ein Angebot für etwas machen *ine an·gè·bōt fōōr et·vass ma·khèn*

tennis *n* das Tennis *te·niss* L30

tennis court *n* der Tennisplatz *te·niss·plats*

tennis racket *n* der Tennisschläger *te·niss·shlay·gèr*

tense *adj* (*muscles*) gespannt *gè·shpant*; (*person*) angespannt *an·gè·shpant*

tent *n* das Zelt *tselt* A85

tenth *adj* zehnte(r/s) *tsayn·tè(·tèr/·tès)*

tent pole *n* die Zeltstange *tselt·shtang·è*

tent stake *n* der Zeltpflock *tselt·pflok*

term *n* (*of school etc*) das Trimester *tri·mes·tèr*; (*word*) der Ausdruck *ows·drook*; during his term of office während seiner Amtsdauer *vay·rènt zine·èr amts·dow·èr*; terms (*of contract*) die Bedingungen (*pl*) *dee bè·ding·oong·èn*

terminal *n* (*air terminal*) das Terminal *ter·mi·nahl*; (*buses*) die Endstation *end·shta·tsee·ōn*; (*electricity*) der Pol *pōl*; (*computer*) das Terminal *ter·mee·nal*

terrace *n* (*of café*) die Terrasse *te·ra·sè*

terrible *adj* furchtbar *foorkht·bahr*; (*weather*) schrecklich *shrek·likh*

territory *n* das Gebiet *gè·beet*

terrorism *n* der Terrorismus *te·ro·ris·moos*

terrorist *n* der Terrorist *te·ro·rist*, die Terroristin *te·ro·ris·tin*

terylene *n* das Terylene *te·rōō·layn*

test *n* (*trial, check*) die Probe *prō·bè*; (*medical*) die Untersuchung *oon·tèr·zoo·khoong*; (*in school etc*) der Test *test*; (*driving test*) die Fahrprüfung *fahr·prōō·foong* □ *vt* testen *tes·tèn*; (*ability*) auf die Probe stellen *owf dee prō·bè shte·lèn*

test-drive *n* die Probefahrt *prō·bè·fahrt* □ *vt* to test-drive a car ein Auto probefahren* *ine ow·tō prō·bè·fah·rèn*

text *n* der Text *tekst*

textbook *n* das Lehrbuch *lay·bookh*

textiles *pl* die Textilien (*pl*) *teks·tee·lee·èn*

texture *n* die Textur *teks·toor*

than *conj* als *als*

thank *vt* danken *dang·kèn*; to thank someone jemandem danken *yay·man·dèm dang·kèn*; thank you danke *dang·kè*; thanks to dank *dank*

that *adj* diese(r/s) *dee·zè(·zèr'·zès)*; (*remote*) jene(r/s) *yay·nè(·nèr'·nès)*; that boy der Junge da *der yoong·è dah*; that woman diese Frau (da) *dee·zè frow (dah)*; that one diese(r/s) *dee·zè(·zèr'·zès)*; (*remote*) jene(r/s) *yay·nè(·nèr'·nès)* □ *pron* that das *dass*; give me that geben Sie mir das *gay·bèn zee meer dass*; that is (*to say*)... das heißt... *dass hyest*; the photo that I gave you das Foto, das ich Ihnen gab *dass fŏ·tŏ dass ikh ee·nèn gap* ◻ *conj* I hope that… ich hoffe, daß… *ikh ho·fè dass*

thaw *vi (ice)* tauen *tow·èn*; *(frozen food)* auf|tauen *owf·tow·èn* ◻ *vt (food)* auf|tauen *owf·tow·èn*

the *art* ◻ the boy der Junge *der yoong·è*; the woman die Frau *dee frow*; the book das Buch *das bookh*; the boys die Jungen *dee yoong·èn*

theater *n* das Theater *tay·ah·tèr*; to go to the theater ins Theater gehen* *ins tay·ah·tèr gay·èn*

their *adj* ihr(e) *eer·(è)*

theirs *pron* ihre(r/s) *ee·rè(·rèr/·rès)*

them *pron* sie *zee*; buy them kaufen Sie sie *kow·fèn zee zee*; show them the books zeigen Sie ihnen die Bücher *tsye·gèn zee ee·nèn dee bōō·khèr*; he spoke to them er sprach mit ihnen *er shprakh mit ee·nèn*; it's them! sie sind es *zee zint ess*

themselves *pron* ◻ they wash themselves sie waschen sich *zee va·shèn zikh*; they did it themselves sie taten es selbst *zee tah·tèn ess zelpst*

then *adv* dann *dan*; from then on von da an *fon da an*

theory *n* die Theorie *tay·ŏ·ree*

there *adv* da *dah*; there is/are es gibt *ess gipt*; is there anyone there? ist da jemand? *ist dah yay·mant*; he went there er ist hingegangen *er ist hin·gè·gang·èn*; there he/she is! da ist er/sie! *dah ist er/zee*

thermometer *n* das Thermometer *ter·mŏ·may·tèr*

Thermos *n* die Thermosflasche *ter·mos·fla·shè*

these *adj, pron* diese *dee·zè*

they *pron* sie *zee*; they say that… *(people in general)* man sagt, daß… *man zahkt dass*

thick *adj* dick *dik*; 3 meters thick 3 Meter dick *3 may·tèr dik*

thief *n* der Dieb *deep* Ea3

thin *adj* dünn *dōōn*; *(material)* leicht *lyekht*

thing *n* die Sache *za·khè*; the best thing would be… das beste wäre… *dass bes·tè vé·rè*

think *vi* denken* *deng·kèn*; to think of something an etwas denken* *an et·vass deng·kèn*; to think about someone an jemanden denken* *an yay·man·dèn deng·kèn*; I think so ich glaube schon *ikh glow·bè shōn*; to think something over über etwas nach|denken* *ōō·bèr et·vass nahkh·deng·kèn*

third *adj* dritte(r/s) *dri·tè(·tèr/·tès)* ◻ *n* third (gear) der dritte Gang *dri·tè gang*

third party insurance *n* die Haftpflichtversicherung *haft·pflikht·fer·zee·kher·oong*

Third World *n* die Dritte Welt *dri·tè velt*

thirsty *adj* durstig *door·stikh*; to be thirsty Durst haben* *doorst hah·bèn*

thirteen *num* dreizehn *drye·tsayn*

thirteenth *adj* dreizehnte(r/s) *drye·tsayn·tè(·tèr/·tès)*

thirtieth *adj* dreißigste(r/s) *drye·sikh·stè(·stèr/·stès)*

thirty *num* dreißig *drye·sikh*

this *adj* diese(r/s) *dee·zè(·zèr/·zès)*; this boy dieser Junge *dee·zèr yoong·è*; this woman diese Frau *dee·zè frow*; this one diese(r/s) *dee·zè(·zèr/·zès)* ◻ *pron* this das *dass*

thorough *adj (work)* gründlich *grōōnt·likh*

those *adj, pron* diese *dee·zè*

though *conj, adv* ◻ though you may think… obwohl Sie denken könnten… *op·vohl zee deng·kèn kur'n·tèn*; he's happy, though er ist jedoch glücklich *er ist yay·dokh glōōk·likh*

thought *n* der Gedanke *gè·dang·kè*

thousand *num* tausend *tow·zènt*

thousandth *adj* tausendste(r/s) *tow·zènt·stè(·stèr/·stès)*

thread *n* die Faden *fah·dèn*

threat *n* die Drohung *drŏ·oong*

threaten *vt* bedrohen *bè·drŏ·èn*

three *num* drei *drye*

thriller *n* der Reißer *rye·sèr*

throat *n* der Hals *hals* S43, I33

throttle *n (in car)* der Gashebel *gahs·hay·bèl*

through *prep* durch *doorkh*; through the wood durch den Wald *doorkh dayn valt*; (all) through the year das ganze Jahr hindurch *dass gan·tsè yahr hin·doorkh*; Monday through Friday von Montag bis Freitag *fon mŏn·tahk bis frye·tahk*; I couldn't get through *(on phone)* ich bin nicht durchgekommen *ikh bin nikht doorkh·gè·ko·mèn*; put me through to Mr X verbinden Sie mich bitte mit Herrn X *fer·bin·dèn zee mikh bi·tè mit hern X*; when I'm through with my work wenn ich mit meiner Arbeit fertig bin *ven ikh mit mine·èr ar·bite fer·tikh bin*

through train *n* der durchgehende Zug *doorkh·gay·èn·dè tsook*

throw *vt* werfen* *ver·fèn*; *(rider)* ab|werfen* *ap·ver·fèn*; to throw a 6 *(dice)* eine Sechs würfeln *ine·è zeks vōōr·fèln*; to throw away weg|werfen* *vek·ver·fèn*

thumb *n* der Daumen *dow·mèn* ◻ *vt* to thumb a ride per Anhalter fahren* *per an·hal·tèr fah·rèn*

thumbtack *n* der Reißnagel *rice·nah·gèl*

thump *n (noise)* das dumpfe Krachen *doom·pfè kra·khèn*

thunder *n* der Donner *do·nèr*

thunderstorm *n* das Gewitter *gè·vi·tèr*

Thursday *n* Donnerstag *(m) do·ners·tahk*

thus *adv (in this way)* so *zŏ*

thyme *n* der Thymian *tōō·mi·ahn*

tick *n (mark)* der Haken *hah·kèn* ◻ *vt* ab|haken *ap·hah·kèn* ◻ *vi (clock)* ticken *ti·kèn*

ticket *n (for train, plane, boat)* die Karte *kar·tè*; *(for bus, metro)* der Fahrschein *fahr·shine*; *(for theatre)* die Eintrittskarte *ine·trits·kar·tè*; *(label)* das Etikett *ay·ti·ket*; *(parking)* der Strafzettel *shtrahf·tse·tèl* T59

ticket office *n* der Fahrkartenschalter *fahr·kar·tèn·shal·tèr* T1

tickle *vt* kitzeln *kit·tsèln*

tide *n* die Gezeiten *(pl) gè·tsye·tèn*; the tide is in/out es ist Flut/Ebbe *ess ist floot/e·bè* Mc11

tidy *adj (person)* ordentlich *or·dènt·likh*; *(room, papers)* aufgeräumt *owf·gè·roymt*

tie *n* die Krawatte *kra·va·tè* ◻ *vt* binden* *bin·dèn*; to tie up a parcel ein Paket verschnüren *ine pa·kayt fer·shnōō·rèn*; to tie up capital Kapital festlegen *ka·pi·tahl fest·lay·gèn*

tie-up *n (traffic)* die Stockung *shto·koong*

tiger n der Tiger *tee·gèr*

tight adj (rope) straff *shtraf*; (clothes) eng *eng*; (schedule) sehr knapp *zayr knap*

tights pl die Strumpfhose *shtroompf·hö·zè*

tile n (on floor, wall) die Fliese *flee·zè*; (on roof) der Ziegel *tsee·gèl*

till prep, conj bis *biss* □ n (cash register) die Kasse *ka·sè*

time n die Zeit *tsite*; what's the time? wie spät ist es? *vee shpayt ist ess*; the time is 5 o'clock es ist 5 Uhr *ess ist 5 oor*; the first time das erste Mal *das er·stè mahl*; how many times? wie oft? *vee oft*; a short time eine kurze Zeit *ine·è koor·tsè tsite*; a long time lange *lang·è*; to have a good time sich gut amüsieren *zikh goot a·mü·zee·rèn*; for the time being vorübergehend *fōr·ōō·bèr·gay·ènt*; from time to time von Zeit zu Zeit *fon tsite tsoo tsite*; just in time gerade noch rechtzeitig *gè·rah·dè nokh rekht·tsye·tikh*; on time rechtzeitig *rekht·tsye·tikh* T5

timetable n (for trains etc) der Fahrplan *fahr·plan* T55

time zone n die Zeitzone *tsite·tsō·nè*

tin n (substance) das Zinn *tsin*

tin foil n die Alufolie *a·loo·fō·lee·è*

tip n (end) die Spitze *shpi·tsè*; (money given) das Trinkgeld *trink·gelt* □ vt (tilt) kippen *ki·pèn* E46

tire n der Reifen *rye·fèn* T168

tired adj müde *mōō·dè*; I'm tired of it ich habe es satt *ikh hah·bè ess zat*

tissue n (handkerchief) das Papiertaschentuch *pa·peer·ta·shèn·tookh*

tissue paper n das Seidenpapier *zye·dèn·pa·peer*

title n der Titel *tee·tèl*

T-junction n (on road) die T-Kreuzung *tay·kroy·tsoong*

to prep zu *tsoo*; to the station zum Bahnhof *tsoom bahn·hōf*; to go to London nach London gehen* *nahkh lon·don gay·èn*; to France nach Frankreich *nahkh frank·ryekh*; to Switzerland in die Schweiz *in dee shvites*; to school/town in die Schule/Stadt *in dee shoo·lè/shtat*; give it to me geben Sie es mir *gay·bèn zee ess meer*; he wants to leave er will weggehen *er vil vek·gay·èn*; I forgot to do... ich habe vergessen, ... zu tun *ikh hah·bè fer·ge·sèn ... tsoo toon*

toast n der Toast *tōst*; to propose a toast to someone einen Trinkspruch auf jemanden aus|bringen* *ine·èn trink·shprookh owf yay·man·dèn ows·bring·èn*

toaster n der Toaster *tōs·tèr*

tobacco n der Tabak *ta·bak* S105

tobacconist n der Tabakhändler *ta·bak·hent·lèr*

tobacconist's (shop) n der Tabakladen *ta·bak·lah·dèn*

today adv heute *hoy·tè*

toe n die Zehe *tsay·è*

toffee n das Karamelbonbon *ka·ra·mel·bon·bon*

together adv zusammen *tsoo·za·mèn*

toilet n die Toilette *tō·a·le·tè* T1

toilet paper n das Toilettenpapier *tō·a·le·tèn·pa·peer* A54

toiletries pl die Toilettenartikel (pl) *tō·a·le·tèn·ar·tee·kèl*

toilet water n das Toilettenwasser *tō·a·le·tèn·va·sèr*

token n (voucher) der Gutschein *goot·*

shine; (for machine) die Marke *mar·kè*

toll n (on road etc) der Zoll *tsol*

toll bridge n die gebührenpflichtige Brücke *gè·bōō·rèn·pflikh·ti·gè brōō·kè*

tomato n die Tomate *tō·mah·tè* S34

tomorrow adv morgen *mor·gèn* T1, I53

ton n die Tonne *to·nè*

tone n der Ton *tōn*

tongue n die Zunge *tsoong·è*

tonic n (medicine) das Tonikum *tō·ni·koom*

tonic water n das Tonic *to·nik*

tonight adv heute abend *hoy·tè ah·bènt*

tonne n die Tonne *to·nè*

tonsillitis n die Mandelentzündung *man·dèl·ent·tsōōn·doong*

too adv (also) auch *owkh*; he's too big er ist zu groß *er ist tsoo grōs*; too much zuviel *tsoo·feel*; too many books zu viele Bücher *tsoo fee·lè bōō·khèr*

tool n das Werkzeug *verk·tsoyk*

tooth n der Zahn *tsahn* I60

toothache n die Zahnschmerzen (pl) *tsahn·shmer·tsèn*; to have a toothache Zahnschmerzen haben* *tsahn·shmer·tsèn hah·bèn* S43, I58

toothbrush n die Zahnbürste *tsahn·bōōr·stè*

toothpaste n die Zahnpasta *tsahn·pa·sta*

top n (of mountain) der Gipfel *gip·fèl*; (of ladder) das obere Teil *ō·be·rè tile*; (of table) die Oberfläche *ō·bèr·fle·khè*; (lid) der Deckel *de·kèl*; (of bottle) der Verschluß *fer·shlooss*; on top of auf *owf* □ adj top obere(r/s) *ō·be·rè(·rèr/·rès)*; (in rank) erste(r/s) *er·stè(·stèr/·stès)*; (best) beste(r/s) *bes·tè(·tèr/·tès)*

top hat n der Zylinder *tsōō·lin·dèr*

topic n das Thema *tay·ma*

toss vt (salad) anmachen *an·ma·khèn*; to toss a coin eine Münze hoch|werfen* *ine·è mōōn·tsè hōkh·ver·fèn*

total n die Gesamtmenge *gè·zamt·meng·è* □ adj völlig *fur·likh*

touch vt berühren *bè·rōō·rèn* □ n in touch with in Verbindung mit *in fer·bin·doong mit*

tough adj (meat etc) zäh *tsay*; (material) strapazierfähig *shtra·pa·tseer·fay·ikh*

tour n die Rundfahrt *roont·fahrt* □ vt (town) eine Rundfahrt machen durch *ine·è roont·fahrt ma·khèn doorkh*

tourism n der Tourismus *too·ris·moos*

tourist n der Tourist *too·rist*, die Touristin *too·ris·tin*

tourist class n die Touristenklasse *too·ris·tèn·kla·sè*

tourist office n das Fremdenverkehrsamt *frem·dèn·fer·kayrs·amt*

tourist trade n das Fremdenverkehrsgewerbe *frem·dèn·fer·kayrs·gè·ver·bè*

tow vt (trailer) ziehen* *tsee·èn*; in tow Fahrzeug wird abgeschleppt *fahr·tsoyk virt ap·gè·shlept*

toward(s) prep gegen *gay·gèn*; to look towards something auf etwas hin|sehen* *owf et·vass hin·zay·èn*; to come towards someone auf jemanden zu|kommen* *owf yay·man·dèn tsoo·ko·mèn*; his attitude towards others seine Haltung anderen gegenüber *zine·è hal·toong an·de·rèn gay·gèn·ōō·bèr*

tow-bar n (on car) die Schleppstange shlep·shtang·è
towel n das Handtuch hant·tookh
tower n der Turm toorm
town n die Stadt shtat T96
town hall n das Rathaus raht·hows
tow truck n der Abschleppwagen ap·shlep·vah·gèn
toy n das Spielzeug shpeel·tsoyk
toyshop n der Spielwarenladen shpeel·vah·rèn·lah·dèn
trace n (mark) die Spur shpoor
track n (of animal) die Spur shpoor; (pathway) der Pfad pfaht; (on record) das Stück shtōōk; (for trains) das Gleis glise; (sports) die Rennbahn ren·bahn
track suit n der Trainingsanzug tray·nings·an·tsook
tractor n der Traktor trak·tor
trade n der Handel han·dèl
trade-in n □ as a trade-in in Zahlung in tsah·loong
trade mark n das Warenzeichen vah·rèn·tsye·khèn
trade name n der Handelsname han·dèls·nah·mè
trader n der Händler hent·lèr
trade union n die Gewerkschaft gè·verk·shaft
trading stamp n die Rabattmarke ra·bat·mar·kè
tradition n die Tradition tra·di·tsee·ōn
traffic n (cars) der Verkehr fer·kayr
traffic circle n der Kreisverkehr krise·fer·kayr
traffic jam n der Verkehrsstau fer·kayrs·shtow
traffic lights pl die Verkehrsampel fer·kayrs·am·pèl
trailer n (for goods) der Anhänger an·heng·èr; (home on wheels) der Wohnwagen vōn·vah·gèn
train n der Zug tsook; (on dress) die Schleppe shle·pè; by train mit dem Zug mit daym tsook □ vt train (apprentice) aus|bilden ows·bil·dèn; (dog) dressieren dre·see·rèn □ vi (athlete) trainieren tray·nee·rèn; to train as a teacher eine Lehrerausbildung machen ine·è lay·rèr·ows·bil·doong ma·khèn T2f, 53f, 65f
trainee n der/die Auszubildende ows·tsoo·bil·dèn·dè
training n (for job) die Ausbildung ows·bil·doong; (for sports) das Training tray·ning
tram(car) n die Straßenbahn shtrah·sèn·bahn T81
tramp n der Landstreicher lant·strye·khèr
tranquilizer n das Beruhigungsmittel bè·roo·i·goongs·mi·tèl
transaction n das Geschäft gè·sheft
transatlantic adj transatlantisch tranz·at·lan·tish
transfer vt (money) überweisen* ōō·bèr·vye·zèn
transistor n der Transistor tran·zis·tor
transit n □ in transit im Transit im tran·zit
transit visa n das Transitvisum tran·zit·vee·zoom
translate vt übersetzen ōō·bèr·zet·sèn
translation n die Übersetzung ōō·bèr·zet·soong
transmission n (of car) das Getriebe gè·tree·bè
transmitter n der Sender zen·dèr
transparent adj durchsichtig doorkh·zikh·tikh

transport n der Transport trans·port □ vt transportieren trans·por·tee·rèn
trap n die Falle fa·lè
trash n der Abfall ap·fal
trash can n der Abfalleimer ap·fal·ime·èr
travel n das Reisen rye·zèn □ vi reisen rye·zèn □ vt (a distance) zurück|legen tsoo·rōōk·lay·gèn
travel agency n das Reisebüro rye·zè·bōō·rō
travel agent n der Reiseveranstalter rye·zè·fer·an·shtal·tèr
traveler n der/die Reisende rye·zèn·dè
traveler's check n der Reisescheck rye·zè·shek M12, 24
tray n das Tablett ta·blet
treacle n der Sirup zee·roop
treasure n der Schatz shats
Treasury n das Finanzministerium fi·nants·mi·ni·stay·ree·oom
treat vt behandeln bè·han·dèln; I'll treat you to an ice cream cone ich gebe Ihnen ein Eis aus ikh gay·bè ee·nèn ine ise ows □ n a little treat eine kleine Freude ine·è kline·è froy·dè
treatment n die Behandlung bè·hant·loong
tree n der Baum bowm
trend n (tendency) die Tendenz ten·dents
trial n (test) die Probe prō·bè; (in law) der Prozeß prō·tses
triangle n das Dreieck drye·ek
tribe n der Stamm shtam
trick n (clever act) das Kunststück koonst·shtōōk; (malicious) der Trick trik; (in cards) der Stich shtikh □ vt mit einem Trick betrügen* mit ine·èm trik bè·trōō·gèn
trifle n (dessert) der Trifle trye·fèl
trim vt (hedge) stutzen shtoot·sèn; (hair) nach|schneiden* nahkh·shnye·dèn; (decorate) besetzen bè·zet·sèn
trip n (journey) die Reise rye·zè; (excursion) der Ausflug ows·flook; to go on a trip to the beach einen Ausflug ans Meer machen ine·èn ows·flook ans mayr ma·khèn □ vi trip (stumble) stolpern shtol·pèrn
tripe n die Kaldaunen (pl) kal·dow·nèn
tripod n das Stativ shta·teef
trivial adj geringfügig gè·ring·fōō·gikh
trolley n (for purchases) der Einkaufswagen ine·kowfs·vah·gèn; (for luggage) der Kofferkuli ko·fèr·koo·lee
troop n der Trupp troop
tropical adj tropisch trō·pish
tropics pl die Tropen (pl) trō·pèn
trot vi (horse) traben trah·bèn
trouble n (problems) die Schwierigkeiten (pl) shwee·rikh·kite·èn; the troubles in this country die Unruhen in diesem Land dee oon·roo·èn in dee·zèm lant; to take trouble over something sich mit etwas viel Mühe geben* zikh mit et·vass feel mōō·è gay·bèn; stomach trouble die Magenbeschwerden (pl) mah·gèn·bè·shver·dèn; engine trouble der Motorschaden mō·tor·shah·dèn; to be in trouble in Schwierigkeiten sein* in shwee·rikh·kite·èn sine Sn45
trouble-shooter n (political) der Vermittler fer·mit·lèr; (technical) der Störungssucher shtur·oongs·zoo·khèr
trousers pl die Hose hō·zè Sn64
trouser-suit n der Hosenanzug hō·zèn·an·tsook
trout n die Forelle fo·re·lè

truck n (vehicle) der Lastwagen last·vah·gèn

truckstop n das Fernfahrerlokal fern·fah·rèr·lo·kahl

true adj wahr vahr

truffle n (fungus) die Trüffel trōō·fèl

truly adv □ yours truly hochachtungsvoll hōkh·akh·toongs·fol

trump n (cards) der Trumpf troompf □ vt übertrumpfen ōō·bèr·troomp·fèn

trumpet n die Trompete trom·pay·tè

trunk n (of tree) der Stamm shtam; (for clothes etc) der Überseekoffer ōō·bèr·zay·ko·fèr; (in car) der Kofferraum ko·fèr·rowm

trust vt (person) vertrauen fer·trow·èn; **to trust someone** jemandem vertrauen yay·man·dèm fer·trow·èn □ n **trust** (company) der Trust trust

truth n die Wahrheit vahr·hite

try vt versuchen fer·zoo·khèn; (in law) vor Gericht stellen fōr gè·rikht shte·lèn; **to try to do something** versuchen, etwas zu tun fer·zoo·khèn, et·vass tsoo toon; **to try on a dress** ein Kleid an|probieren ine klite an·prō·bee·rèn

T-shirt n das T-Shirt tee·shirt

tube n die Tube too·bè

Tuesday n Dienstag (m) deens·tahk

tulip n die Tulpe tool·pè

tuna fish n der Thunfisch toon·fish

tune n die Melodie may·lo·dee □ vt (engine) ein|stellen ine·shte·lèn; (instrument) stimmen shti·mèn

tunic n (of uniform) der Uniformrock oo·ni·form·rok

Tunisia n Tunesien (nt) too·nay·zyen

Tunisian adj tunesisch too·nay·zish

tunnel n der Tunnel too·nèl

turbot n der Steinbutt shtine·boot

turkey n der Truthahn troot·hahn

Turkey n die Türkei tōōr·kye

Turkish adj türkisch tōōr·kish

Turkish delight n das Lokum lo·koom

turn n (bend in road) die Kurve koor·vè; **it's your turn** Sie sind an der Reihe zee zint an der rye·è; **in turn** abwechselnd ap·vek·sèlnt □ vi turn (person, car) ab|biegen ap·bee·gèn; **he turned (around)** er drehte sich um er dray·tè zikh oom; **to turn back** um|kehren oom·kay·rèn; **to turn professional** Profi werden* prō·fi ver·dèn □ vt turn drehen dray·èn; **to turn on** (light) ein|schalten ine·shal·tèn; (water) an|stellen an·shte·lèn; **to turn off** (light) aus|drehen ows·dray·èn; (water) ab|stellen ap·shte·lèn; **to turn down** (heat) herunter|stellen he·roon·tèr·shte·lèn; (volume) leiser stellen lye·zèr shte·lèn; **to turn up** (heat, volume) höher stellen hur·èr shte·lèn; **to turn something over** et·was um|drehen et·vass oom·dray·èn

turnover n (money) der Umsatz oom·zats; (in goods) der Warenumschlag vah·rèn·oom·shlahk

turnpike n die gebührenpflichtige Autobahn gè·bōō·rèn·pflikh·ti·gè ow·tō·bahn

turn signal n der Blinker bling·kèr

turquoise adj türkis tōōr·kees

turtle soup n die Schildkrötensuppe shilt·krur·tèn·zoo·pè

tutor n der Privatlehrer pri·vaht·lay·rèr, die Privatlehrerin pri·vaht·lay·rè·rin

tuxedo n der Smoking smō·king

TV n der Fernseher fern·zay·èr A5

tweed n der Tweed tweed

tweezers pl die Pinzette pin·tse·tè

twelfth adj zwölfte(r/s) tsvur'lf·tè(·tèr/·tès)

twelve num zwölf tsvur'lf

twenty num zwanzig tsvan·tsikh

twice adv zweimal tsvye·mahl

twig n der Zweig tsvike

twill n der Köper kur·pèr

twin beds pl zwei Einzelbetten tsvye ine·tsèl·be·tèn

twins pl die Zwillinge (pl) tsvi·ling·è

twist vt drehen dray·èn □ vi (road) sich schlängeln zikh shleng·èln

two num zwei tsvye

two-piece n der Zweiteiler tsvye·tile·èr

tycoon n der Magnat mag·naht

type n (sort) die Art art □ vt (letter) tippen ti·pèn

typewriter n die Schreibmaschine shripe·ma·shee·nè

typewritten adj maschinegeschrieben ma·shee·nè·gè·shree·bèn

typical adj typisch tōō·pish

typist n die Stenotypistin shtay·nō·tōō·pist·in Bm13

U

ugly adj (object, person) häßlich hes·likh

ulcer n das Geschwür gè·shvōōr

ultimatum n das Ultimatum ool·ti·mah·toom

umbrella n der Schirm shirm; (on table) der Sonnenschirm zo·nèn·shirm

umbrella stand n der Schirmständer shirm·shten·dèr

umpire n der Schiedsrichter sheets·rikh·tèr

unable adj □ **to be unable to do something** etwas nicht tun können* et·vass nikht toon kur·nèn

unanimous adj (decision) einmütig ine·mōō·tikh

unarmed adj (person) unbewaffnet oon·bè·vaf·nèt

unavoidable adj unvermeidlich oon·fer·mite·likh

unbearable adj (pain) unerträglich oon·er·trayk·likh

unbeatable adj (offer) unschlagbar oon·shlahk·bar

unbiased adj unparteiisch oon·par·tye·ish

unbreakable adj unzerbrechlich oon·tser·brekh·likh

uncertain adj (fact) unsicher oon·sikh·èr

unchanged adj unverändert oon·fer·en·dèrt

uncle n der Onkel ong·kèl

uncomfortable adj unbequem oon·bè·kvaym

unconditional adj (offer) bedingungslos bè·ding·oongs·lōs

unconscious adj bewußtlos bè·voost·lōs I16

uncover vt auf|decken owf·de·kèn

under prep unter oon·tèr; **under the table** unter dem/den Tisch oon·tèr daym/dayn tish; **under a kilometer** unter einem Kilometer oon·tèr ine·èm ki·lō·may·tèr; **under repair** in Reparatur in ray·pa·ra·toor

undercooked adj nicht gar nikht gar

underdeveloped adj (country) unterentwickelt oon·tèr·ent·vi·kèlt

underdone adj (steak) nicht durchge-

braten *nikht doorkh·gè·brah·tèn*;
(*food in general*) nicht gar *nikht gar*
underexposed *adj* unterbelichtet *oon·
tèr·bè·likh·tèt*
undergraduate *n* der Student *shtoo·
dent*, die Studentin *shtoo·den·tin*
underground *adj* (*pipe etc*) unterir·
disch *oon·tèr·ir·dish*; **underground
railway** die U-bahn *oo·bahn*
underline *vt* unterstreichen* *oon·tèr·
shtrye·khèn*
underneath *prep* unter *oon·tèr*; **under·
neath the book** unter dem/den Buch
oon·tèr daym/dayn bookh □ *adv* **it's
underneath** es ist darunter *ess ist da·
roon·tèr*
underpaid *adj* unterbezahlt *oon·tèr·bè·
tsahlt*
underpants *pl* die Unterhose *oon·tèr·
hô·zè*
underpass *n* die Unterführung *oon·tèr·
fōō·roong*
undershirt *n* das Unterhemd *oon·tèr·
hemt*
understand *vt/i* verstehen* *fer·shtay·
èn*; **we understand that…** wir gehen
davon aus, daß… *veer gay·èn da·fon
ows das*
understanding *n* das Verständnis *fer·
shtent·nis*; (*agreement*) die Abma·
chung *ap·makh·oong*
undertake *vt* unternehmen* *oon·tèr·
nay·mèn*; **to undertake to do** sich
verpflichten, zu tun *zikh fer·pflikh·
tèn tsoo toon*
undertaking *n* (*enterprise*) die Unter·
nehmung *oon·tèr·nay·moong*;
(*promise*) die Verpflichtung *fer·
pflikh·toong*
undervalue *vt* unterbewerten *oon·tèr·
bè·ver·tèn*
underwear *n* die Unterwäsche *oon·tèr·
ve·shè*
underwrite *vt* (*insurance*) versichern
fer·zi·khèrn; (*finance*) garantieren
ga·ran·tee·rèn
underwriter *n* der Versicherer *fer·zi·
khè·rèr*
undo *vt* öffnen *ur'f·nèn*
undress *vt* aus|ziehen* *ows·tsee·èn* □ *vi*
sich aus|ziehen* *zikh ows·tsee·èn*
unearned income *n* das Kapitalein·
kommen *ka·pi·tahl·ine·ko·mèn*
uneconomic *adj* unwirtschaftlich *oon·
virt·shaft·likh*
uneconomical *adj* unökonomisch *oon·
ur'·ko·nō·mish*
unemployed *adj* arbeitslos *ar·bites·lôs*;
the unemployed die Arbeitslosen (*pl*)
ar·bites·lô·zèn
unemployment *n* die Arbeitslosigkeit
ar·bites·lō·zikh·kite
UNESCO *n* die Unesco *oo·ne·skô*
unfair *adj* unfair *oon·fehr*; (*competi·
tion*) unlauter *oon·low·tèr*
unfasten *vt* auf|machen *owf·ma·khèn*
unfold *vt* entfalten *ent·fal·tèn*
unfortunate *adj* (*event*) unglücklich
oon·glöök·likh
unfortunately *adv* leider *lye·dèr*
unhappy *adj* unglücklich *oon·glöök·
likh*
uniform *n* die Uniform *oo·ni·form*
unilateral *adj* einseitig *ine·zye·tikh*
union *n* die Vereinigung *fer·ine·i·
goong*; (*trade union*) die Gewerk·
schaft *gè·verk·shaft*
unique *adj* einzigartig *ine·tsikh·ar·tikh*
unisex *adj* Unisex- *oo·ni·seks*
unit *n* die Einheit *ine·hite*; (*of machin·
ery, furniture*) das Element *e·le·ment*

unite *vt* vereinigen *fer·ine·i·gèn*
United Kingdom, U.K. *n* das Verei·
nigte Königreich *fer·ine·ikh·tè kur'·
nikh·ryekh*
**United Nations Organization, UN,
UNO** *n* die Vereinigten Nationen
(*pl*) *fer·ine·ikh·tèn na·tsee·ô·nèn*
United States (of America), US(A) *n*
die Vereinigten Staaten (von Ame·
rika) (*pl*) *fer·ine·ikh·tèn shtah·tèn*
(*fon a·me·ri·ka*)
unit price *n* der Preis pro Einheit *prise
prô ine·hite*
universal *adj* allgemein *al·gè·mine*
universe *n* das Weltall *velt·al*
university *n* die Universität *oo·ni·ver·
si·tayt*
unkind *adj* unfreundlich *oon·froynt·
likh*
unknown *adj* unbekannt *oon·bè·kant*
unless *conj* □ **unless we come** wenn
wir nicht kommen *ven veer nikht ko·
mèn*
unlikely *adj* unwahrscheinlich *oon·
vahr·shine·likh*
unlimited *adj* unbegrenzt *oon·bè·
grentst*
unlined *adj* (*clothes*) ungefüttert *oon·
gè·fōō·tert*
unlisted *adj* die nicht im Telefonbuch
steht *dee nikht im tay·lay·fōn·bookh
shtayt*
unload *vt* (*vehicle*) entladen* *ent·lah·
dèn*; (*goods*) ab|laden* *ap·lah·dèn*
unlock *vt* auf|schließen* *owf·shlee·sèn*
unlucky *adj* unglückselig *oon·glöök·
zay·likh*
unnatural *adj* unnatürlich *oon·na·tōōr·
likh*
unnecessary *adj* unnötig *oon·nur'·tikh*
unofficial *adj* inoffiziell *in·o·fi·tsee·el*;
unofficial strike der wilde Streik *vil·
dè shtrike*
unpack *vt* aus|packen *ows·pa·kèn*
unpaid *adj* (*debt*) unbezahlt *oon·bè·
tsahlt*
unpleasant *adj* unangenehm *oon·an·gè·
naym*
unprofitable *adj* wenig einträglich *vay·
nikh ine·trayk·likh*
unreasonable *adj* (*demand, price*)
übertrieben *ōō·bèr·tree·bèn*
unripe *adj* unreif *oon·rife*
unsalted *adj* (*butter*) ungesalzen *oon·
gè·sal·tsèn*
unscrew *vt* auf|schrauben *owf·shrow·
bèn*
unskilled labor *n* die ungelernten Ar·
beiter *oon·gè·lern·tèn ar·bye·tèr*
unsuitable *adj* unpassend *oon·pa·sènt*
untidy *adj* unordentlich *oon·or·dènt·
likh*
untie *vt* (*parcel*) auf|schnüren *owf·
shnōō·rèn*; (*animal*) los|binden* *lôs·
bin·dèn*
until *prep, conj* bis *biss*
unusual *adj* ungewöhnlich *oon·gè·
vur'n·likh* S117
unwrap *vt* aus|packen *ows·pa·kèn*
up *prep* □ **to go up a hill** einen Berg
hinauf|gehen* *ine·èn berk hin·owf·
gay·èn*; **up till now** bis jetzt *biss yetst*;
up to 6 bis zu 6 *biss tsoo 6* □ *adv* **up
there** dort oben *dort ô·bèn*; **he isn't
up yet** (*out of bed*) er ist noch nicht
auf *er ist nokh nikht owf*
update *vt* auf den neuesten Stand brin·
gen* *owf dayn noy·èst·èn shtant
bring·èn*
uphill *adv* bergauf *berk·owf*; **to go up·
hill** steigen* *shtye·gèn*

upkeep *n* der Unterhalt *oon·tèr·halt*
upon *prep* auf *owf*
upper *adj* obere(r/s) *ō·bèr·è(·èrl·ès)*
upset price *n* der Mindestpreis *min·dèst·prise*
upside down *adv* verkehrt herum *fer·kehrt he·room*; **to turn something upside down** etwas um\|drehen *et·vass oom·dray·èn*
upstairs *adv* oben *ō·bèn*
upturn *n* (*in business*) der Aufschwung *owf·shvoong*
upward(s) *adv* aufwärts *owf·verts*
urban *adj* städtisch *shte·tish*
urgent *adj* dringend *dring·ènt*; (*letter*) Eil- *ile*
urgently *adv* dringend *dring·ènt*
us *pron* uns *oons*; **it's us** wir sind's *veer zints*
use *n* die Verwendung *fer·ven·doong*; **in use** in Gebrauch *in gè·browkh*; **it's no use** es hat keinen Zweck *ess hat kine·èn tsvek* □ *vt* use benutzen *bè·noo·tsèn*
used *adj* (*car etc*) Gebraucht- *gè·browkht*; **to get used to** sich gewöhnen an *zikh gè·vur'·nèn an* □ *vi* **we used to go** früher gingen wir *frōō·èr ging·èn veer*
useful *adj* nützlich *nōōts·likh*
useless *adj* nutzlos *noots·lōs*
U.S.S.R. *n* die UdSSR *oo·day·ess·ess·ehr*
usual *adj* gewöhnlich *gè·vur'n·likh*
usually *adv* gewöhnlich *gè·vur'n·likh*
U-turn *n* (*in car*) die Wende *ven·dè*

V

vacancy *n* (*job*) die freie Stelle *frye·è shte·lè*; (*in hotel etc*) das freie Zimmer *frye·è tsi·mèr*; **no vacancies** belegt *bè·laygt* A12
vacant *adj* (*seat, toilet*) frei *frye*
vacation *n* die Ferien (*pl*) *fay·ree·èn*; **on vacation** im Urlaub *im oor·lowp* Mc21
vacationer *n* der Urlauber *oor·low·bèr*, die Urlauberin *oor·low·bè·rin*
vaccination *n* die Schutzimpfung *shoots·imp·foong*
vacuum cleaner *n* der Staubsauger *shtowp·zow·gèr*
vague *adj* vage *vah·gè*
vain *adj* eitel *eye·tèl*; **in vain** vergebens *fer·gay·bèns*
valet *n* (*in hotel*) der Hausdiener *hows·dee·nèr*
valid *adj* gültig *gōōl·tikh*
valley *n* das Tal *tahl*
valuable *adj* wertvoll *vert·fol*
valuables *pl* die Wertgegenstände (*pl*) *vert·gay·gèn·shten·dè*
value *n* der Wert *vert* □ *vt* schätzen *she·tsèn*
value-added tax *n* die Mehrwertsteuer *mehr·vert·shtoy·èr*
valve *n* das Ventil *ven·teel*
van *n* der Lieferwagen *lee·fèr·vah·gèn*
vandal *n* der Rowdy *row·dee*
vanilla *n* die Vanille *va·nil·lè*; **vanilla ice cream** das Vanilleeis *va·nil·lè·ise*
variable *adj* variabel *va·ree·ah·bèl* □ *n* die Variable *va·ree·ah·blè*
variation *n* die Veränderung *fer·en·dè·roong*
variety *n* die Auswahl *ows·vahl*
variety show *n* die Varietévorführung *va·ree·ay·tay·for·fōō·roong*
various *adj* verschieden *fer·shee·dèn*
varnish *n* der Lack *lak*

vary *vi* unterschiedlich sein* *oon·tèr·sheet·likh zine*
vase *n* die Vase *va·zè*
vaseline *n* die Vaseline *va·zè·lee·nè*
Vatican *n* der Vatikan *va·ti·kahn*
veal *n* das Kalbfleisch *kalp·flyesh*
vegetables *pl* das Gemüse *gè·mōō·zè* E26
vegetarian *adj* vegetarisch *ve·gay·tah·rish*
vehicle *n* das Fahrzeug *fahr·tsoyk*
veil *n* der Schleier *shlye·èr*
vein *n* die Vene *vay·nè*
velvet *n* der Samt *zamt*
vending machine *n* der Verkaufsautomat *fer·kowfs·ow·tō·maht*
vendor *n* der Verkäufer *fer·koy·fèr*
Venice *n* Venedig (*nt*) *ve·nay·dikh*
venison *n* das Rehfleisch *ray·flyesh*
ventilator *n* der Ventilator *ven·ti·la·tor*
venture *n* die Unternehmung *oon·tèr·nay·moong*
veranda *n* die Veranda *ve·ran·da*
verbal *adj* (*agreement*) mündlich *mōōnt·likh*
verdict *n* das Urteil *oor·tile*
verge *n* der Rand *rant*
vermouth *n* der Wermut *ver·moot*
version *n* die Darstellung *dar·shte·loong*
versus *prep* gegen *gay·gèn*
vertical *adj* senkrecht *zenk·rekht*
very *adv* sehr *zehr*; **the very last** der allerletzte *der al·lèr·lets·tè*; **I like it very much** ich habe es sehr gerne *ikh hah·bè es zehr ger·nè*
vest *n* die Weste *ve·stè*
vet(erinary surgeon) *n* der Tierarzt *teer·artst*
veto *vt* sein Veto ein\|legen gegen *zine vay·tō ine·lay·gèn gay·gèn* □ *n* das Veto *vay·tō*
V.H.F. *abbrev* UKW *oo·ka·vay*
via *prep* via *vee·a*
viaduct *n* der Viadukt *vee·a·dookt*
vicar *n* der Pfarrer *pfa·rèr*
vice chairman *n* der stellvertretende Vorsitzende *shtel·fer·tray·tèn·dè for·zit·sèn·dè*
vice president *n* der Vizepräsident *vee·tsè·pray·zee·dent*
vice versa *adv* umgekehrt *oom·gè·kayrt*
victim *n* (*of accident etc*) das Opfer *op·fèr*
victory *n* der Sieg *zeek*
video *n* das Fernsehen *fern·zay·èn*; **on video** im Fernsehen *im fern·zay·èn*
videocassette *n* die Videokassette *vee·day·ō·ka·set·tè*
videocassette recorder *n* der Videorekorder *vee·day·ō·re·kor·dèr*
videotape *n* das Videoband *vi·day·ō·bant*
Vienna *n* Wien (*nt*) *veen*
view *n* (*the outside*) *vōs·zikht*; (*opinion*) die Ansicht *an·zikht* A5
villa *n* die Villa *vi·la*
village *n* das Dorf *dorf*
vinaigrette (sauce) *n* die Salatsoße *za·laht·zō·sè*
vine *n* die Rebe *ray·bè*
vinegar *n* der Essig *e·sikh*
vineyard *n* der Weinberg *vine·berk*
vintage *n* der Jahrgang *yahr·gang*; **a vintage wine** ein edler Wein *ine ayt·lèr vine*
vinyl *n* das Vinyl *vee·nōōl*
violence *n* die Gewalttätigkeit *gè·valt·tay·tikh·kite*
violin *n* die Geige *gye·gè*
V.I.P. *n* der VIP *vee·eye·pee*

visa, visé 234

visa, visé n das Visum vee·zoom
visible adj sichtbar zikht·bar
visit vt besuchen bè·zoo·khèn □ n der
Besuch bè·zookh; (stay) der Aufenthalt owf·ènt·halt Mc40
visitor n der Besucher bè·zoo·khèr, die
Besucherin bè·zoo·khè·rin
visual aids pl das Anschauungsmaterial
an·show·oongs·ma·tay·ree·ahl
vital adj (essential) unerläßlich oon·èr·
les·likh
vitamin n das Vitamin vi·ta·meen
V-neck n der V-Ausschnitt fow·ows·
shnit
vocabulary n der Wortschatz vort·
shats; (list of words) das Wörterverzeichnis vur·tèr·fer·tsyekh·nis
vodka n der Wodka vod·ka
voice n die Stimme shti·mè
void adj (contract) ungültig oon·gööl·
tikh
vol-au-vent n das Pastetchen pas·tayt·
khèn
volcano n der Vulkan vool·kahn
volleyball n der Volleyball vo·li·bal
voltage n die Spannung shpa·noong
volume n (sound) die Lautstärke lowt·
shter·kè; (capacity) das Volumen vo·
loo·mèn; (book) der Band bant;
volume of sales der Umsatz oom·zats
vomit vi sich erbrechen* sikh er·bre·
khèn
vote n die Stimme shti·mè □ vi wählen
vay·lèn; to vote for stimmen für shti·
mèn föör
voucher n der Gutschein goot·shine

W

wading pool n das Planschbecken
plansh·be·kèn
wafer n die Waffel va·fèl
waffle n die Waffel va·fèl
wag vt (tail) wedeln mit vay·dèln mit
wage, wages n der Lohn lôn
wage earner n der Lohnempfänger
lôn·emp·feng·èr
wage freeze n der Lohnstopp lôn·shtop
wagon n der Karren ka·rèn
wagon-lit n der Schlafwagen shlaf·vah·
gèn
waist n die Taille tal·yè
wait vi warten var·tèn; to wait for
someone auf jemanden warten owf
yay·man·dèn var·tèn; to keep
someone waiting jemanden warten
lassen* yay·man·dèn var·tèn la·sèn
waiter n der Kellner kel·nèr E44
waiting list n die Warteliste var·tè·lis·tè
waiting room n (at station) der Wartesaal var·tè·zahl
waitress n die Kellnerin kel·nè·rin
wake vt wecken ve·kèn □ vi to wake up
auf|wachen owf·va·khèn
Wales n Wales (nt) waylz
walk vi gehen* gay·èn; (for pleasure,
exercise) zu Fuß gehen* tsoo foos
gay·èn □ n der Spaziergang shpa·
tseer·gang; to go for a walk spazie-
ren|gehen* shpa·tsee·rèn·gay·èn L35
walking n das Spazierengehen shpa·
tsee·rèn·gay·èn
walking stick n der Spazierstock shpa·
tseer·shtok
walkout n der Streik shtrike
wall n (inside) die Wand vant; (outside) die Mauer mow·èr
wallet n die Brieftasche breef·ta·shè
Sn80
wallpaper n die Tapete ta·pay·tè

wall-to-wall carpet(ing) n der Teppichboden te·pikh·bô·dèn
walnut n die Walnuß val·noos
waltz n der Walzer val·tsèr
wander vi schlendern shlen·dèrn
want vt (wish for) wollen* vo·lèn;
(need) brauchen brow·khèn; to want
to do something etwas tun wollen*
et·vass toon vo·lèn
war n der Krieg kreek
ward n (in hospital) die Station shta·
tsee·ôn
wardrobe n (furniture) der Kleiderschrank klye·dèr·shrank
warehouse n das Lagerhaus lah·gèr·
hows
warm adj warm varm; I'm warm mir
ist warm meer ist varm □ vt warm
wärmen ver·mèn
warn vt warnen var·nèn; to warn
someone of something jemanden vor
etwas warnen yay·man·dèn fôr et·
vass var·nèn
warrant(y) n die Garantie ga·ran·tee
Warsaw n Warschau (nt) var·show
wart n die Warze var·tsè
was vi □ I/he was ich/er war ikh/er
vahr
wash vt waschen* va·shèn □ vi to wash
(oneself), to wash up sich waschen*
zikh va·shèn A95
washable adj waschbar vash·bar S88
washbasin, washbowl n das Waschbecken vash·be·kèn A52
washcloth n der Waschlappen vash·la·
pèn
washing n (clothes) die Wäsche ve·shè;
to do the washing die Wäsche waschen* dee ve·shè va·shèn
washing machine n die Waschmaschine vash·ma·shee·nè
washroom n der Waschraum vash·
rowm A93
waste n die Verschwendung fer·shven·
doong; (rubbish) der Abfall ap·fal
□ vt verschwenden fer·shven·dèn
waste paper basket n der Papierkorb
pa·peer·korp
watch n die Armbanduhr arm·bant·oo·
èr □ vt beobachten bè·ô·bakh·tèn;
(TV, play) an|sehen* an·zay·èn; to
watch a match bei einem Wettkampf
zu|sehen* bye ine·èm vet·kampf tsoo·
zay·èn
water n das Wasser va·sèr A78, L20,
Mc10
watercress n die Kresse kre·sè
waterfall n der Wasserfall va·sèr·fal
water heater n das Heißwassergerät
hise·va·sèr·gè·ret
watermelon n die Wassermelone va·
sèr·may·lô·nè
waterproof adj wasserundurchlässig
va·sèr·oon·doorkh·le·sikh
water-skiing n das Wasserskilaufen va·
sèr·shee·low·fèn; to go water-skiing
Wasserski laufen* va·sèr·shee·low·fèn
L27
watt n das Watt vat
wave vi winken ving·kèn □ n die Welle
ve·lè
wavy adj (hair) wellig ve·likh
wax n das Wachs vaks; (in ear) das
Ohrenschmalz ô·rèn·shmalts
way n (manner) die Weise vye·zè; (in)
a different way auf eine andere
Weise owf ine·è an·dè·rè vye·zè;
which is the way to London? wie
kommt man nach London? vee komt
man nakh lon·don; to ask the way to
Paris nach dem Weg nach Paris fra-

gen *nakh daym vayk nakh pa·rees
frah·gèn*; it's a long way this way
dass ist vite; to be in the way im Weg
stehen* *im vayk shtay·èn*; on the way
unterwegs *oon·tèr·vayks*; this way
please hierher bitte *heer·hayr bi·tè*;
by the way übrigens *ōō·bri·gèns* F1f

we *pron* wir *veer*

weak *adj* (person) schwach *shvakh*;
(tea) dünn *dōōn*

wealth *n* der Reichtum *ryekh·toom*

wealthy *adj* reich *ryekh*

weapon *n* die Waffe *va·fè*

wear *vt* (clothes) tragen* *trah·gèn* □ *vi*
(fabric) sich ab|nutzen *zikh ap·noot·
sèn*; to wear something out etwas ab|
nutzen *et·vass ap·noot·sèn* □ *n* wear
and tear die Abnutzung *ap·noot·
soong*

weather *n* das Wetter *ve·tèr*

weather forecast *n* die Wettervorhersage *ve·tèr·fór·her·zah·gè*

weave *vt* weben *vay·bèn*

wedding *n* die Hochzeit *hokh·tsite*

wedding dress *n* das Brautkleid *browt·
klite*

wedding present *n* das Hochzeitsgeschenk *hokh·tsites·gè·shenk*

wedding ring *n* der Ehering *ay·è·ring*

Wednesday *n* Mittwoch (m) *mit·vokh*

weed *n* das Unkraut *oon·krowt*

week *n* die Woche *vo·khè* T108, Mc44

weekday *n* der Wochentag *vo·khèn·
tahk*

weekend *n* das Wochenende *vo·khèn·
en·dè*

weekly *adj, adv* wöchentlich *vur·
khènt·likh* □ *n* (periodical) die Wochenzeitschrift *vo·khèn·tsite·shrift*

weigh *vt* wiegen* *vee·gèn*

weight *n* (mass) das Gewicht *gè·vikht*

welcome *adj* willkommen *vil·ko·mèn*
□ *n* der Empfang *emp·fang* □ *vt* begrüßen *bè·grōō·sèn*

weld *vt* schweißen *shvye·sèn*

well *n* (for water) der Brunnen *broo·
nèn* □ *adv* gut *goot*; to be well wohl
sein* *vōl zine*; get well soon gute Besserung *goo·tè be·sè·roong*; well! also!
al·zō

wellington boot *n* der Gummistiefel
goo·mi·shtee·fèl

Welsh *adj* walisisch *va·lee·zish* □ *n*
Walisisch (nt) *va·lee·zish*

were *vi* □ you were Sie waren *zee vah·
rèn*; we were wir waren *veer vah·rèn*;
they were sie waren *zee vah·rèn*

west *n* der Westen *ve·stèn*; the West
der Westen *ve·stèn* □ *adv* west nach
Westen *nakh ve·stèn*

western *adj* westlich *vest·likh* □ *n*
(movie) der Western *ves·tèrn*

West Germany *n* die Bundesrepublik
boon·dès·ray·poo·bleek

wet *adj* (clothes) naß *nass*; (weather,
day) regnerisch *rayg·nè·risch*; (paint)
frisch *frish*; (climate) feucht *foykht*

whale *n* der Wal *vahl*

wharf *n* der Kai *kye*

what *adj* welche(r/s) *vel·khè(·khèr/
·khès)*; what book? welches Buch?
vel·khès bookh; what languages?
welche Sprachen? *vel·khè shprah·
khèn* □ *pron* what was *vass*; what do
you want? was wollen Sie? *vass vo·
lèn zee*; I saw what happened ich
sah, was passiert ist *ikh zah vass pa·
seert ist*; what's it called? wie heißt
es? *vee hyest ess*; what a mess! (in
room) was für eine Unordnung! *vass
fōōr ine·è oon·ort·noong*

wheat *n* der Weizen *vye·tsèn*

wheel *n* das Rad *raht*; (steering wheel)
das Lenkrad *lenk·raht*

wheelbarrow *n* die Schubkarre *shoop·
ka·rè*

wheelchair *n* der Rollstuhl *rol·shtool*
I6

when *conj* (with present tense) wenn
ven; (with past tense) als *als*; (in
questions) wann *van*; the day when
we... am Tag, als wir... *am tahk als
veer*

where *conj* wo *vō*; where are you from?
woher kommen Sie? *vō·her ko·mèn
zee*; where are you going? wohin gehen Sie? *vō·hin gay·èn zee*

whether *conj* ob *op*

which *adj* welche(r/s) *vel·khè(·khèr/
·khès)*; which book? welches Buch?
vel·khès bookh; which languages?
welche Sprachen? *vel·khè shprah·
khèn*; which one of you? wer von Ihnen? *vehr fon ee·nèn* □ *pron* the
book, which is long das Buch, das
lang ist *dass bookh dass lang ist*; the
apple which you ate der Apfel, den
Sie gegessen haben *der ap·fèl dayn
zee gè·gè·sèn hah·bèn*; I don't know
which to take ich weiß nicht, welches
ich nehmen soll *ikh vice nikht vel·
khès ikh nay·mèn zol*; after which
wonach *vō·nakh*; the chair on which
der Stuhl, worauf der *der shtool vō·rowf*

while *n* die Weile *vye·lè* □ *conj* während *vay·rènt*

whip *n* die Peitsche *pye·tshè* □ *vt*
(cream, eggs) schlagen* *shlah·gèn*

whipped cream *n* die Schlagsahne
shlahk·zah·nè

whirlpool *n* der Strudel *shtroo·dèl*

whirlwind *n* der Wirbelwind *vir·bèl·
vint*

whisk *n* der Schneebesen *shnay·bay·
zèn*

whiskey *n* der Whisky *vis·kee*

whisper *vi* flüstern *flōō·stèrn*

whistle *n* (sound) der Pfiff *pfif*; (object) die Pfeife *pfye·fè* □ *vi* pfeifen*
pfye·fèn

white *adj* weiß *vice*

whitebait *n* der Breitling *brite·ling*

White House *n* das Weiße Haus *vye·sè
hows*

whiting *n* der Weißling *vice·ling*

Whitsun *n* Pfingsten (nt) *pfing·stèn*

Whitsunday *n* Pfingstsonntag (m)
pfingst·zon·tahk

who *pron* wer *vehr*

whole *adj* (complete) ganz *gants*

wholesale *n* der Großhandel *grōs·han·
dèl* □ *adj* (price) Großhandels- *grōs·
han·dèls* □ *adv* (sell) im Großhandel
im grōs·han·dèl Bm28

wholesaler *n* der Großhändler *grōs·
hend·lèr*

wholewheat bread *n* das Vollkornbrot
fol·korn·brōt

whom *pron* den *dayn*, die *dee*, das
dass; the man whom you see der
Mann, den Sie sehen *der man dayn
zee zay·èn*; the boy with whom... der
Junge, mit dem... *der yoong·è mit
daym*

whooping cough *n* der Keuchhusten
koykh·hoo·stèn

whose *adj* □ whose book is this? wem
gehört dieses Buch? *vaym gè·hurt
dee·zès bookh*; the man, whose son
der Mann, dessen Sohn *der man de·
sèn zōn*; I know whose it is ich weiß,

wem das gehört *ikh vice vaym dass gĕ·hurt*

why *adv* warum *va·room*

wick *n* (*of cigarette lighter*) der Docht *dokht*

wicked *adj* böse *bur'·zĕ*

wicker *n* das Korbgeflecht *korp·gĕ·flekht*

wide *adj* (*broad*) breit *brite*; (*range*) groß *grös*; **4 cm. wide** 4 cm. breit *4 cm. brite*

wide-angle lens *n* das Weitwinkelobjectiv *vite·ving·kĕl·op·yek·teef*

widow *n* die Witwe *vit·vĕ*

widower *n* der Witwer *vit·vĕr*

width *n* die Breite *brite·ĕ*

wife *n* die Frau *frow* T12, 111, S111

wig *n* die Perücke *pay·rŏŏ·kĕ*

wild *adj* (*animal*) wild *vilt*; (*flower*) wildwachsend *vilt·vak·sĕnt*; (*tribe*) unzivilisiert *oon·tsi·vi·li·zeert*

wildlife *n* die Tierwelt *teer·velt*

will *n* (*testament*) das Testament *tes·ta·ment* □ **vi he will do it** er wird es tun *er virt ess toon*

willing *adj* □ **willing to do something** bereit, etwas zu tun *bĕ·rite et·vass tsoo toon*

win *vt/i* gewinnen* *gĕ·vi·nĕn*; (*contract*) bekommen* *bĕ·ko·mĕn*

wind¹ *n* (*breeze*) der Wind *vint*; (*in stomach*) die Blähung *blay·oong*

wind² *vt* wickeln *vi·kĕln*; **to wind up a clock** eine Uhr auf|ziehen *ine·ĕ zoo owf·tsee·ĕn*

windmill *n* die Windmühle *vint·mŏŏ·lĕ*

window *n* das Fenster *fen·stĕr*; (*of shop*) das Schaufenster *show·fen·stĕr* B66, S73

window shade *n* das Springrollo *shpring·ro·lö*

window shopping *n* der Schaufensterbummel *show·fen·stĕr·boo·mĕl*

windshield *n* die Windschutzscheibe *vint·shoots·shye·bĕ* T153

windshield washer *n* die Scheibenwaschanlage *shye·bĕn·vash·an·lah·gĕ* T154

windshield wiper *n* der Scheibenwischer *shye·bĕn·vi·shĕr* T166

windsurfing *n* das Windsurfing *vint·sur·fing*; **to go windsurfing** windsurfen *vint·sur·fĕn*

windy *adj* (*place*) windig *vin·dikh*

wine *n* der Wein *vine* B64, E10f, 57f

wine cellar *n* der Weinkeller *vine·ke·lĕr*

wineglass *n* das Weinglas *vine·glas*

wine list *n* die Weinkarte *vine·kar·tĕ*

wine waiter *n* der Weinkellner *vine·kel·nĕr*

wing *n* der Flügel *flŏŏ·gĕl*

wink *vi* zwinkern *tsving·kĕrn*

winner *n* der Sieger *zee·gĕr*, die Siegerin *zee·gĕ·rin*

winter *n* der Winter *vin·tĕr*

winter sports *pl* der Wintersport *vin·tĕr·shport*

wipe (off) *vt* ab|wischen *ap·vi·shĕn*

wire *n* der Draht *draht*; (*electrical*) die Schnur *shnoor*; (*telegram*) das Telegramm *tay·lay·gram*

wise *adj* (*person*) weise *vye·zĕ*; (*decision*) vernünftig *fer·nŏŏnf·tikh*

wish *n* der Wunsch *voonsh*; **with best wishes** (*on gift*) mit besten Grüßen *mit bes·tĕn grŏŏ·sĕn*; (*on letter*) alles Gute *a·lĕs goo·tĕ* □ *vt/i* **I wish I could...** ich wünschte, ich könnte... *ikh vŏŏnsh·tĕ ikh kur'n·tĕ*; **to wish for**

something sich etwas wünschen *zikh et·vass vŏŏn·shĕn*

witch *n* die Hexe *hek·sĕ*

with *prep* mit *mit*; **red with anger** rot vor Wut *röt för voot*

withdraw *vt* (*money*) ab|heben* *ap·hay·bĕn*

without *prep* ohne *ö·nĕ*

witness *n* der Zeuge *tsoy·gĕ*, die Zeugin *tsoy·gin* □ *vt* (*signature*) bestätigen *bĕ·shtay·ti·gĕn* T210

wobble *vi* (*chair etc*) wackeln *va·kĕln*

wolf *n* der Wolf *volf*

woman *n* die Frau *frow*

womb *n* der Mutterleib *moo·tĕr·lipe*

wonder *vi* □ **to wonder whether...** sich fragen, ob... *zikh frah·gĕn op*

wonderful *adj* wunderbar *voon·dĕr·bahr*

wood *n* (*material*) das Holz *holts*; (*forest*) der Wald *valt*

wooden *adj* hölzern *hur'l·tsĕrn*

wool *n* die Wolle *vo·lĕ*

woolen *adj* Woll- *vol*

word *n* das Wort *vort*; **word for word** Wort für Wort *vort för vort*

work *n* die Arbeit *ar·bite*; (*art, literature*) das Werk *verk*; **to go to work** arbeiten gehen* *ar·bye·tĕn gay·ĕn* □ *vi* **work** arbeiten *ar·bye·tĕn*; (*clock, mechanism*) funktionieren *foonk·tsee·ön·eer·ĕn*; (*medicine*) wirken *vir·kĕn*; **to work out** (*problem*) lösen *lur'·zĕn* Sn47

workday *n* der Arbeitstag *ar·bites·tak*

worker *n* der Arbeiter *ar·bye·tĕr*, die Arbeiterin *ar·bye·tĕ·rin*

work force *n* die Arbeiterschaft *ar·bye·tĕr·shaft*

working capital *n* das Betriebskapital *bĕ·treeps·ka·pi·tahl*

working-class *adj* der Arbeiterklasse *der ar·bye·tĕr·kla·sĕ*

working hours *pl* die Arbeitsstunden (*pl*) *ar·bites·shtoon·dĕn*

working order *n* □ **to be in working order** gut funktionieren *goot foonk·tsee·ön·eer·ĕn*

workman *n* der Arbeiter *ar·bye·tĕr*

work of art *n* das Kunstwerk *koonst·verk*

works *pl* (*mechanism*) das Getriebe *gĕ·tree·bĕ*

workshop *n* die Werkstatt *verk·shtat*

world *n* die Welt *velt*

world power *n* die Weltmacht *velt·makht*

world war *n* der Weltkrieg *velt·kreek*

worm *n* der Wurm *voorm*

worn *adj* abgetragen *ap·gĕ·trah·gĕn*

worn-out *adj* (*object*) abgetragen *ap·gĕ·trah·gĕn*; (*person*) erschöpft *er·shur'pft*

worried *adj* besorgt *bĕ·zorkt*

worry *n* die Sorge *zor·gĕ*

worse *adj, adv* schlechter *shlekh·tĕr*

worst *adj* □ **the worst book** das schlechteste Buch *dass shlekh·tĕs·tĕ bookh* □ *adv* **he did it worst** er machte es am schlechtesten *er makh·tĕ ess am shlekh·tĕs·tĕn*

worth *adj* □ **to be worth $5** $5 wert sein* *$5 vert zine*; **DM50 worth of gas** Benzin für DM50 *ben·tseen för DM50*; **it's worth it** es ist der Mühe wert *ess ist der mŏŏ·ĕ vert*

worthwhile *adj* (*activity*) lohnend *lö·nĕnt*

would *vi* □ **she would come if...** sie würde kommen, wenn... *zee vŏŏr·de ko·mĕn ven*; **would you like a cup of**

coffee? möchten Sie eine Tasse Kaffee? *mur'kh·tèn zee ine·è ta·sè ka·fay*

wound *n* (*injury*) die Wunde *voon·dè*

wrap *vt* ein|wickeln *ine·vi·kèln*; **to wrap up a parcel** ein Paket ein|packen *ine pa·kayt ine·pa·kèn* □ *n* wrap (*shawl*) das Umhangtuch *oom·hang·tookh* S26

wrapper *n* (*paper*) die Verpackung *fer·pa·koong*

wrapping paper *n* das Packpapier *pak·pa·peer*

wreck *n* (*ship*) das Wrack *vrak* □ *vt* zum Wrack machen *tsoom vrak ma·khèn*; (*plans*) zunichte machen *tsoo·nikh·tè ma·khèn*

wrench *n* der Schraubenschlüssel *shrow·bèn·shlüs·sèl*

wrestling *n* das Ringen *ring·èn*

wring *vt* (*clothes*) aus|wringen* *ows·vring·èn*

wrinkle *n* die Runzel *roon·tsèl*

wrist *n* das Handgelenk *hant·gè·lenk*

write *vt/i* schreiben* *shrye·bèn*; **to write down** auf|schreiben* *owf·shrye·bèn*; **to write off a debt** eine Schuld ab|schreiben* *ine·è shoolt ap·shrye·bèn*

writer *n* der Autor *ow·tör*

writing *n* die Handschrift *hant·shrift*; **in writing** schriftlich *shrift·likh*

writing paper *n* das Schreibpapier *shripe·pa·peer*

wrong *adj* falsch *falsh*; **you're wrong** Sie haben unrecht *zee hah·bèn oon·rekht*; **what's wrong?** was ist los? *vass ist lōs*; **to go wrong** (*machine*) nicht in Ordnung sein* *nikht in ort·noong zine*

X

Xerox *n* die Xerokopie *kse·ro·ko·pee* □ *vt* xerokopieren *kse·ro·ko·pee·rèn*

X-ray *n* (*photo*) die Röntgenaufnahme *rur'nt·gèn·owf·nah·mè* □ *vt* röntgen *rur'nt·gèn*

Y

yacht *n* die Jacht *yakht*

yachting *n* das Segeln *zay·gèln*; **to go yachting** segeln gehen* *zay·gèln gay·èn*

yard *n* (*of building*) der Hof *hôf*; (*measure*) das Yard *yart*

yawn *vi* gähnen *gay·nèn*

year *n* das Jahr *yahr*

yearly *adj, adv* jährlich *yehr·likh*

yeast *n* die Hefe *hay·fè*

yellow *adj* gelb *gelp*

yes *adv* ja *ya*; (*in answer to negative question*) doch *dokh*

yesterday *adv* gestern *ge·stèrn*

yet *adv* noch *nokh*; **not yet** noch nicht *nokh nikht*

yield *n* der Ertrag *er·trahk*; (*financial*) der Gewinn *gè·vin* □ *vt* (*investment*) ein|bringen* *ine·bring·èn* □ *vi* (*to traffic*) Vorfahrt gewähren *för·fahrt gè·vay·rèn*

yoga *n* der Joga *yō·ga*

yogurt *n* der Joghurt *yog·oort*

you *pron* (*familiar form*) du *doo*; (*polite form*) Sie *zee*; (*plural form*) ihr *eer*; **he's watching you** er sieht dich/Sie/euch an *er zeet dikh/zee/oykh an*; **milk is good for you** Milch ist gesund *milkh ist gè·zoont*

young *adj* jung *yoong*

your *adj* (*familiar form*) dein(e) *dine (·è)*; (*polite form*) Ihr(e) *eer(·è)*; (*plural form*) euer(e) *oy·èr(·è)*; **your father** dein/Ihr/euer Vater *dine/eer/oy·èr fah·tèr*; **your sisters** deine/Ihre/eure Schwestern *dine·è/eer·è/oy·rè shve·stèrn*

yours *pron* (*familiar form*) deine(r/s) *dine·è(·èr/·ès*); (*polite form*) Ihre(r/s) *eer·è(·èr/·ès)*; (*plural form*) eure(r/s) *oy·rè(·rèr/·rès)*

yourself, yourselves *pron* selbst *zelpst*; **you've hurt yourself/yourselves** Sie haben sich weh getan *zee hah·bèn zikh vay ge·tahn*; **you did it yourself/yourselves** Sie haben es selbst gemacht *zee hah·bèn ess zelpst gè·makht*

youth *n* (*period*) die Jugend *yoo·gènt*

youth club *n* der Jugendklub *yoo·gènt·kloop*

youth hostel *n* die Jugendherberge *yoo·gènt·her·ber·gè*

Yugoslavia *n* Jugoslawien (*nt*) *yoo·go·sla·vee·èn*

Yugoslav(ian) *adj* jugoslawisch *yoo·go·sla·vish*

Z

zebra *n* das Zebra *tse·bra*

zero *n* die Null *nool*; (*in roulette*) die Zero *zay·rō*

zinc *n* das Zink *tsink*

zip code *n* die Postleitzahl *post·lite·tsahl*

zipper *n* der Reißverschluß *rise·fer·shloos* Sn74

zone *n* die Zone *tsō·nè*; (*postal*) der Postbezirk *post·bè·tsirk*

zoo *n* der Zoo *tsō* C9

zoom lens *n* das Zoom *zoom*

zucchini *pl* die Zucchini (*pl*) *tsoo·kee·nee*

238
Notes